BEFORE WE DISAPPEAR INTO OBLIVION

McGill-Queen's Studies in Ethnic History
Series Two: John Zucchi, Editor

39 No Free Man
*Canada, the Great War, and
the Enemy Alien Experience*
Bohdan S. Kordan

40 Between Dispersion
and Belonging
*Global Approaches to
Diaspora in Practice*
Edited by Amitava Chowdhury
and Donald Harman Akenson

41 Running on Empty
*Canada and the Indochinese
Refugees, 1975–1980*
Michael J. Molloy, Peter
Duschinsky, Kurt F. Jensen,
and Robert J. Shalka

42 Twenty-First-Century
Immigration to North America
Newcomers in Turbulent Times
Edited by Victoria M. Esses
and Donald E. Abelson

43 Gaelic Cape Breton Step-Dancing
*An Historical and Ethnographic
Perspective*
John G. Gibson

44 Witness to Loss
*Race, Culpability, and Memory
in the Dispossession of Japanese
Canadians*
Edited by Jordan Stanger-Ross
and Pamela Sugiman

45 Mad Flight?
*The Quebec Emigration to the
Coffee Plantations of Brazil*
John Zucchi

46 A Land of Dreams
Ethnicity, Nationalism, and the
Irish in Newfoundland, Nova
Scotia, and Maine, 1880–1923
Patrick Mannion

47 Strategic Friends
*Canada-Ukraine Relations from
Independence to the Euromaidan*
Bohdan S. Kordan

48 From Righteousness to Far Right
*An Anthropological Rethinking
of Critical Security Studies*
Emma Mc Cluskey

49 North American Gaels
*Speech, Story, and Song
in the Diaspora*
Edited by Natasha Sumner
and Aidan Doyle

50 The Invisible Community
Being South Asian in Quebec
Edited by Mahsa Bakhshaei,
Marie Mc Andrew, Ratna Ghosh,
and Priti Singh

51 With Your Words in My Hands
*The Letters of Antonietta Petris
and Loris Palma*
Edited and translated by
Sonia Cancian

52 The Least Possible Fuss and Publicity
*The Politics of Immigration in
Postwar Canada, 1945–1967*
Paul A. Evans

53 Peronism as a Big Tent
*The Political Inclusion of
Arab Immigrants in Argentina*
Raanan Rein and Ariel Noyjovich
Translated by Isis Sadek

54 The Boundaries of Ethnicity
*German Immigration and the
Language of Belonging in Ontario*
Benjamin Bryce

55 Before We Disappear into Oblivion
*San Francisco's Russian Diaspora
from Revolution to Cold War*
Nina Bogdan

BEFORE WE DISAPPEAR INTO OBLIVION

SAN FRANCISCO'S RUSSIAN DIASPORA

FROM REVOLUTION TO COLD WAR

NINA BOGDAN

McGill-Queen's University Press

Montreal & Kingston · London · Chicago

© McGill-Queen's University Press 2025

ISBN 978-0-2280-2473-6 (paper)
ISBN 978-0-2280-2489-7 (ePDF)
ISBN 978-0-2280-2490-3 (ePUB)

Legal deposit second quarter 2025
Bibliothèque et Archives nationales du Québec

Printed in Canada on acid-free paper that is 100% ancient-forest-free, containing 100% sustainable, recycled fibre, and processed chlorine-free.

McGill-Queen's University Press in Montreal is on land which long served as a site of meeting and exchange amongst Indigenous Peoples, including the Haudenosaunee and Anishinabeg nations. In Kingston it is situated on the territory of the Haudenosaunee and Anishinaabek. We acknowledge and thank the diverse Indigenous Peoples whose footsteps have marked these territories on which peoples of the world now gather.

LIBRARY AND ARCHIVES CANADA CATALOGUING IN PUBLICATION

Title: Before we disappear into oblivion : San Francisco's Russian diaspora from revolution to Cold War / Nina Bogdan.
Other titles: San Francisco's Russian diaspora from revolution to Cold War
Names: Bogdan, Nina, author
Series: McGill-Queen's studies in ethnic history. Series two ; 55.
Description: Series statement: McGill-Queen's studies in ethnic history. Series two ; 55 | Includes bibliographical references and index.
Identifiers: Canadiana (print) 20240524403 | Canadiana (ebook) 20240524438 | ISBN 9780228024736 (paper) | ISBN 9780228024897 (ePDF) | ISBN 9780228024903 (ePUB)
Subjects: LCSH: Russians—California—San Francisco—History—20th century. | LCSH: Russians—California—San Francisco—Ethnic identity—History—20th century. | LCSH: Russians—California—San Francisco—Social conditions—20th century. | LCSH: Russians—California—San Francisco—Economic conditions—20th century.
Classification: LCC F869.S39 R93 2025 | DDC 979.4/0049171—dc23

This book was designed and typeset by Lara Minja in Warnock Pro 10.5/13.5pt. Copyediting by Jared Toney.

McGill-Queen's University Press
Suite 1720, 1010 Sherbrooke St West, Montreal, QC, H3A 2R7

Authorized safety representative in the EU: Mare Nostrum Group BV, Mauritskade 21D, 1091 GC Amsterdam, the Netherlands, gpsr@mare-nostrum.co.uk

The entire expanse of San Francisco Bay was revealed, in a marvelous
shade of violet blue, and the massive towers of the Golden Gate
Bridge under construction across the strait ... quite suddenly,
the masts of the far-off ships below, and the tram creeping along
towards the Fillmore presented another city before me ... the old
tree-lined boulevard materialized, and the monument at the top of
the marble staircase, also leading to a port; a breath of wind blowing
from the Black Sea and the distant Anatolian shores enveloped me.
I hurriedly looked around to assure myself that the buildings, their
outlines etched into my memory, were really there. But, behind me,
the Fillmore arches stretched in a dark ribbon against the azure
sky ... and I came down to earth, recalling with the clarity – and
melancholy one experiences in such moments – that this was
San Francisco.

PETER BALAKSHIN, momentarily transported to the city of Odessa.
"Spring over the Fillmore," 237–8.
January 1936, San Francisco.

CONTENTS

Figures and Tables ix
Acknowledgments xiii

Introduction 3

1
Russians in San Francisco Prior to 1917
Pan-Ethnic Orthodoxy and Emerging Communities 27

2
The Mysterious Russian Arrives
Ethnic and Class Ambiguities 44

3
Between Dreams and Reality
Culture, Conflict, Identity, and Byt 70

4
"Even the Teetotalers Drank"
Surviving On and Off the Job in America 101 .

5
Imagined Russia
Homeland Hearths and Dreamlike Landscapes 140

6
Family Matters
Nostalgic Homelessness and Dual Lives 175

7

"White Russians in the 'New World'"

Marketing and Monitoring Identity   212

8

Constructed Mirages

Authentic and Imagined Russian Enclaves   238

9

Pawns on a Chessboard

The New Exodus and the Post-War Russian Community   266

Conclusion   324

Notes   331

Selected Bibliography   377

Index   393

FIGURES and TABLES

Figures

1.1 Depiction of Bishop Vladimir. *San Francisco Chronicle*, 7 February 1890. 32

1.2 St. Basil's Russian Orthodox Cathedral, 1713–1715 Powell Street, 1889. Shapiro Papers, Box 11:57, Hoover Institution Archives (HIA). 36

2.1 "From Royal Robes to Rags." *San Francisco Chronicle*, 16 May 1920. 53

2.2 Nadia Shapiro and group of arriving students. *San Francisco Daily News*, 30 August 1922. 57

3.1 Diamond Jubilee night parade float under construction. Photographer unknown. Courtesy of Museum of Russian Culture in San Francisco (MRC), Events and Arts (E/A) File. 78

3.2 Russian float in night parade, 12 September 1925. Photographer Vasily(?) Arefieff (1896–1982), identified by surname only, *Russkaia zhizn'*, 25 September 1925. Courtesy of MRC, E/A File. 78

3.3 Alexander Ignatieff in costume prior to night parade, 12 September 1925. Photographer unknown (possibly Arefieff). Courtesy of MRC, E/A File. 79

3.4 Bank of Italy, corner of Post and Fillmore, 1926, AAC 4291. Courtesy of San Francisco History Center (SFHC), San Francisco Public Library (SFPL). 87

4.1 Russian women workers at sugar refinery in San Francisco, 10 June 1926. Photographer unknown. Polosuhin/Polon Family Collection, courtesy of Deirdre Visser. 129

5.1 Chapel at Fort Ross, 1901, possibly from series by *Oakland Tribune* photographer, 1900–1906. Courtesy of Fort Ross Library Archives (FRLA) Photo Collection, vol. VI, "Chapel to 1920." 142

5.2 Holy Trinity Cathedral at Van Ness and Green Streets, ca. 1920s. Photographer unknown. Courtesy of MRC, Holy Trinity Cathedral (HTC) File. 152

5.3 Harry Koblick at 1010 Fillmore Street store, 1919, SFP78-001-070. Courtesy of San Francisco History Center (SFHC), San Francisco Public Library (SFPL). 157

5.4 O'Farrell Street looking east to Fillmore Street, 1930, AAB 4831. Courtesy of SFHC, SFPL. 158

5.5 Group visiting Fort Ross, ca. 1920s. Photographer unknown. Courtesy of Fort Ross Library Archives (FRLA), Photo Collection, vol. VIII, "Chapel and Orthodox Services." 166

5.6 Holy Trinity congregation visit to Fort Ross, 4 July 1933. Photographer unknown. Photo belonged to Mercedes Stafford. Courtesy of FRLA, Photo Collection, vol. VII, "Chapel 1920s–90s." 168

5.7 Chapel at Fort Ross, ca. 1939–41. Photographer unknown. Courtesy of FRLA, Photo Collection, vol. VII, "Chapel 1920s–90s." 168

6.1 Children's Day Home, 1929, 2174 Post Street. Photographer P. Afanasieff. Children's Home File album, 1925–50. Courtesy of MRC, Children's Home (CH) File. 183

6.2 Children's Day Home, ca.1933, 2174 Post Street. Photographer unknown. Courtesy of MRC, CH File. 183

6.3 Dr Antonina Maximova-Kulaev at exposition of Community Chest agencies in San Francisco, 16 June 1934. Photographer unknown. Courtesy of MRC, CH File. 185

6.4 Oleg Vassiliyevsky/Vassil and Olga Afanasieff wedding photo, 3 March 1940, at Holy Virgin Cathedral on Fulton Street. Poss. photographer P. Afanasieff. Courtesy of Christy Gerhart. 191

6.5 Matinee performance at Russian Center, 2450 Sutter Street, 12 April 1959. Author's personal collection. 209

7.1 William Westerfeld House, 1198 Fulton Street, undated, AAC 5855. Courtesy of SFHC, SFPL. 215

Figures and Tables

7.2 Excerpt from a Marysville Sheriff's Office wanted poster, ca. January 1928. Arthur C. Landesen Papers, Box 2.2, HIA. 223

7.3 Folsom Prison photo of Andrew Rogojin/Kraft aka Rogozinski, 18 February 1937. Folsom State Prison Records, 1879–1949, ID #R136. Department of Corrections, California State Archives (CSA), Office of the Secretary of State, Sacramento, California. 225

7.4 Dina Valenko and two friends ca. late 1920s in San Francisco. Photographer unknown. Courtesy of Red Shuttleworth. 226

8.1 26 April 1936 Fair at Stern Grove. Photographer unknown. Courtesy of MRC, E/A File. 242

8.2 Boris Kramarenko and his orchestra, 26 April 1936 Fair. Afanasieff Photo Studio, 1812 Divisadero Street. Courtesy of MRC, E/A File. 243

8.3 Tatiana Popow, Paul Shulgin, and two unidentified people, 26 April 1936, Stern Grove. Photographer unknown. Courtesy of MRC, E/A File. 243

8.4 Group of attendees at 1937 *Yarmarka* at Stern Grove. Photographer unknown. Courtesy of Eugenia Bailey. 245

8.5 Turn Verein Center, 2450 Sutter Street, 1911 (the Russian Center from 1940), AAC 5467. Courtesy of SFHC, SFPL. 255

Tables

I.1 US Census. Russian foreign-born in San Francisco/Bay Area, 1910–50. 20

4.1 Russian male student death by suicide. 110

4.2 Incidents of Russian male early death (prior to age fifty) among inter-war arrivals. 111

9.1 Transports carrying Russian displaced persons from Philippine Islands, 1950–52. 283

9.2 Displaced persons arriving from Tubabao detained prior to US entry. 293

9.3 Russian Center board presidents to 1964. 306

9.4 Organizations formed after World War II. 310

ACKNOWLEDGMENTS

When I initially envisioned this book, my primary focus was on what I came to call Imagined Russia – an exploration of how people find ways to cope with the enormous stresses of migration, particularly under forced circumstances. In the case of Russians in California, such coping was facilitated by the rediscovered relics marking a historic Russian presence: Fort Ross. As my research advanced, however, Russian-American identity formation in San Francisco and the multiplicity of forms of "Russian" identity, both in terms of self-perception and the perceptions of others, began to take precedence.

Many thanks to everyone at the Department of History at the University of Arizona for their support in all stages of this book project and to Laurie Manchester at Arizona State University, who referred me to McGill-Queen's University Press. Thank you to everyone at the press for all their efforts and special thanks to editors Richard Ratzlaff and Michaela Jacques for their guidance, assistance, and support throughout the process.

I would also like to express my gratitude to the staff at all of the archives and libraries I visited, without which this book would not have been written: the Hoover Institution Library and Archives, the Museum of Russian Culture, the Alaska State Museum Archives, the California State Archives, the Immigration History Research Center, the Kennan Institute, the Fort Ross Conservancy Center, the San Francisco History Center, the Western Diocese Archive of ROCOR, the Library of Congress, and NARA.

And a very special thank you as well to those who took the time to discuss with me their experiences as members of the Russian diaspora in San Francisco: Natalie Sabelnik, Eugenia Bailey, and the late Nikolai Massenkoff.

BEFORE WE DISAPPEAR INTO OBLIVION

══ INTRODUCTION ══

San Francisco today is still the greatest and the only Russian city abroad.

IVAN STENBOCK-FERMOR, 1976[1]

Urban legends surrounding the William Westerfeld House in San Francisco, built in 1889 and located southwest of the Fillmore District, began in the inter-war era, and continue to circulate in the contemporary period. One of the most persistent of such legends is that the building housed either a Russian embassy or consulate in the 1930s.[2] However, the Westerfeld building, a gothic Victorian construction, never housed any official Russian government representation, either prior to 1917 (the year of the Bolshevik Revolution) or afterwards. Russian émigrés, who arrived in San Francisco after 1917, founded a "Russian Club," moving into the building in 1928, where they ran a campaign to pass legislation intended to provide an avenue for undocumented Russians to remain in the United States. The "Club," however, was generally a social center and, for some, a residence, with émigrés renting rooms in the house from the 1930s to the 1950s.[3]

The Westerfeld House was the first built structure that émigré Russians acquired for long-term community, cultural, and social purposes in San Francisco. The building's importance as a center of Russian activities informed a later decision, in 1939, to purchase another architecturally impressive building in one of the city's two Russian neighborhoods, at 2450 Sutter Street. The Russian Center building became a place of sanctuary, not so much for people, but for culture. Fearing denationalization for the generation of youth growing up in America severed from the Russian homeland, as well as loss of material culture – artifacts, relics, documents, and photographs, which many émigrés had brought with them – Russian groups rallied the community, raised funds, and purchased the former Turn Verein Center. Émigré Alexander Varguin (1884–1953), the driving force behind the effort, as well as first and twice re-elected board president, stated that the founding of the center was the "happiest moment" in his life.[4] It remains the Russian Center of San Francisco to the present day and has housed the Museum of Russian Culture, a repository of an invaluable archive, since 1948. The solidity of a physical structure provided a sense of security for Russian arrivals, traumatized by years of upheaval and warfare in their homeland, flight, homelessness, exile, and, uniquely, statelessness: their ancestral home literally disappeared from maps of the world after December of 1922, incorporated into the Union of Soviet Socialist Republics (USSR).

As the Russian émigré community coalesced, its members faced ongoing challenges and choices with respect to identity formation in an alien land. Over time, as they began to accept that the way home was closed, they realized that their culture might well "disappear into oblivion" without concrete efforts to maintain it for posterity.[5] References to "disappearing" arose in part because of the unique situation of émigrés: the homeland they had left no longer existed as a political entity as of 1923. Even more salient, however, was the recognition of, and reaction to, the coercive nature of the American assimilation process, more so in the nativist and politically fraught post-Red Scare (1918–20) environment into which they arrived. Initially confident that Americans would come to understand and accept them, émigrés soon realized that to be welcome in America they not only had to adapt, but to change who they were to suit American sensibilities. As long as they remained identifiably Russian, they also remained exotic and alien in American eyes.

The circumstances of émigré arrival in the United States, as "exiles" fleeing the 1917 Bolshevik Revolution or the ensuing Russian Civil War (1918–22), contributed to popular, and often inaccurate, characterizations about them.[6] A 1940 San Francisco Works Progress Administration (WPA) city guide described inter-war émigrés as "defiantly monarchist in politics and orthodox [sic] in religion." That assessment promoted an image of an out-of-touch and fanatic group "defiantly" resisting assimilation. Most (though certainly not all) émigrés were indeed Russian Orthodox, but the failure to capitalize the word also indicated reluctance on the part of the writer to identify Eastern Orthodoxy as a bona fide religion. The characterization went on to describe former imperial military officers "appearing in faded regimentals" in "courtly ceremonials of their former life."[7] Such narratives implied a disconnection

Introduction | 5

from reality among émigrés, supposedly focusing on reliving moments of past glory, mourning not only their lost elite status but the monarchy under which they had lived. As V.M. Selunskaia notes, however, Russia Abroad as a whole was "tarred ... with the brush of its most conservative faction, the militant monarchists," who constituted no more than one quarter of all inter-war émigrés.[8] Moreover, the public discourse about San Francisco's Russian diaspora erased the heterogenous and multi-generational community that inhabited the Fillmore District in the inter-war period – a community with schools; social, drama, literary, and athletic clubs; restaurants and cafés; a multitude of businesses; a *banya* (public bathhouse); and, of course, churches.

Selunksaia goes on to discuss the heterogeneity of the dialogue within Russia Abroad per se, a factor that characterized the Russian community in San Francisco, particularly due to the diverse nature of the émigrés with respect to social class and geographic origin.[9] Moreover, the fact that the Russian professional and middle classes were well-represented in San Francisco also spoke to the diverse nature of the community on that basis alone, particularly given the argument of William G. Wagner, for example, that the nascent middle class in Russia was both "ideologically and politically divided" in the early twentieth century (i.e., even prior to departure from Russia).[10]

The prevalent characterizations of émigrés, rampant in public discourse in the 1920s (discussed in chapter 2), and carrying over by inertia into later discussions about the diaspora, reinforced the characterization of Russians outside of Russia as both "czarists" and performers, with the two intertwined. As czarists, a term implying fanaticism and an inordinate attachment to the monarchy, Russians were both out of touch with the reality of modern America and objects of curiosity. In tandem, Americans recognized individuals as "Russian" only when they displayed or performed their culture: dance, song, and elaborate raiment represented "Russianness." In "everyday" contexts, émigrés remained invisible and therefore often unrecognized residents of San Francisco. Russian train car cleaners or sewing machine operators, jobs émigrés often held in the inter-war period, garnered attention in public discourse only to point out how far the mighty had fallen.

Racial vs Social Hierarchical Paradigms

Arriving in San Francisco in the inter-war period, Russians became "inbetween" people, as James Barrett and David Roediger coined and utilized the term: Eastern European immigrants whose cultural markers differed significantly from the Anglo-Protestant norm.[11] Roediger's subsequent explorations of whiteness, and how incoming European peasants or urban poor attained it, focused on the working class, particularly in the eastern United States.[12] Russian inter-war arrivals to San Francisco, however, were mostly literate and often well-educated.[13] Nevertheless, their poverty placed most of them firmly among the working class. Elena Dubinets refers to what is commonly known as the "first wave" of Russian émigrés (post-1917) as the "cream of creative and intellectual society," but the San Francisco community included a significant contingent of "ordinary" people, neither artists nor intellectuals, but those with at least a secondary school education who had been caught up in the Civil War in Siberia either as combatants or civilians in the crossfire.[14] Arrival in steerage from the "Orient" to the ports of San Francisco and Seattle placed them under scrutiny and commensurate official action, including detention as possible undesirables.

The racial hierarchy that existed in the United States from the colonial era forward came to include, by the early twentieth century, various European "types" as inferior to Anglo-Protestants. Gradations of acceptability of specific Europeans were fluid depending on a variety of factors: time period, rates of immigration, class considerations, location, and degree of cultural difference to the preferred WASP standard.[15] That hierarchical racial paradigm, which informed American ethnic history, persisted in the early twentieth century in large part due to the "imperatives of capitalism": the importance of access to cheap labor, particularly industrial, beginning in the late nineteenth century, to maximize profits, thus fueling growth, a factor which, ironically, encouraged the importation of "undesirables" as large-scale industrialization commenced. Moreover, millions of immigrants who began arriving in the 1880s to labor in America's coal mines, steel mills, and industrial concerns were Slavs, often characterized in anti-immigration literature as "invaders."[16]

The adhesion to a hierarchal racial paradigm was just as, if not more, prevalent in the western United States. Frank Van Nuys points out that the West had a critical role in reinforcing the notion of American identity as a WASP identity. In the West, immigration "restriction or exclusion" of undesirables was both official policy and a methodology, focusing particularly on excluding "non-whites" but extending to any immigrant unfortunate to have arrived in steerage.[17] Entry into the United States was a grueling and often humiliating process for penniless immigrants of the "laboring" class. US immigration authorities at Angel Island Immigration Station (AIIS) in San Francisco, for example, labeled prospective Russian university students as members of that class largely due to their impoverished status but also in view of their "foreignness" and, critically, their point of departure from the "Orient" (chapters 2 and 4). The few Russian émigrés who arrived in first or second class, particularly if able to show a substantial amount of money at entry, generally escaped both scrutiny and detention: wealth paved the way for acceptance.

This book examines the processes that led to Russian émigrés "incorporating into whiteness," particularly with respect to why, how, and when they began to identify as "white" once in America.[18] Claudia Sadowski-Smith notes that this process was complete for all turn-of-the-twentieth-century European immigrants by the 1940s. The identification of Europeans as "white" in America, however (i.e., categorizing Slavs, for example, and therefore Russians, as "Caucasians" in the inter-war period), was a dominant culture effort to maintain the established hierarchal racial paradigm by devaluing cultural self-identification among previously undesirable European immigrant groups.[19] Russian émigrés were certainly strongly attached to their cultural heritage, but whether more so than other immigrants is certainly arguable. The combined factors of general literacy and commensurate educated status, and the fact of being reluctant immigrants, however, problematized the top-down process of erasing their heritage in favor of a general concept of "whiteness." How and when, or even if, Russians arriving in the inter-war period began to self-identify as white was a complex process that did not necessarily fall in line with dominant culture pressures to maintain the racial hierarchy, and was linked to their strong identification with "Russianness," that intangible factor that was all the more critical because of the recognition over time that the Russia they had known no longer existed as a physical entity. Indeed, the factor of "statelessness," resulting from the disappearance of their homeland and, commensurately, the place of birth of Russian culture, made their immigration experience distinctive in two fundamental ways: return, even for a visit, was generally not an option, thus severing family ties in a way that other immigrants did not experience. Moreover, the desire to preserve Russian culture was not based simply on nostalgic longing for home but on the conviction that their culture would disappear unless they made efforts to preserve it.

The multi-ethnic nature of the Russian diaspora also complicated the immigration process, particularly for the post-World War II incoming wave (chapter 9), reinforcing to that group, even more so than for the inter-war wave, the absolute imperative of being perceived as "white" in America. The dynamics played out in San Francisco against the backdrop of not only the Cold War, but the Civil Rights movement, a time when being both "white" and middle class was an identity to attain and maintain, a marker of economic success for previously impoverished immigrants, by default accepting the now entrenched hierarchy of race as a norm of American life.[20]

Ethnicity and Race in Imperial Russia

The inter-war émigrés came from a Russan imperial society that revolved around an alternate paradigm, focusing on social status without consideration of race or ethnicity as such. In the Russian Empire, the concept of being "Russian" as an identity related to a number of factors, but race was rarely, if ever, invoked. One critical factor in Paul Bushkovitch's discussion was a perceived loyalty to the state, specifically the czar, as the manifestation of that state, but, after 1905, the year of the failed revolution, an identification with cultural markers, social ranking, or location (Russia proper versus Siberia or borderlands) as well.[21] The latter identification was particularly prevalent among San Francisco arrivals as many were from Siberia, some using "Siberian" in lieu of, or, depending on the circumstance, as a synonym for, "Russian." Émigré Nadia Shapiro, in fact, who wrote extensively about the experience of being Russian in America, pointedly described the post-1917 arrivals in San Francisco as "Siberians."[22]

A social hierarchy existed in pre-revolutionary Russian society dividing all Russian subjects into estates (i.e., nobility, clergy, merchants, townsmen, peasants) but, from the Muscovite period (1500s) forward, rulers utilized practical and flexible policies to minimize conflict. Although Russians are Slavs per se, non-Slavs inhabited all areas of the Russian Empire (founded by Peter the Great in the 1700s) and were members of every estate. In other words, no racial or ethnic estate existed in Russia. Those at the bottom of the class pyramid, the peasantry, were also the ethnic majority as Slavs. Racialist paradigms did not prevail in terms of either official or unofficial policy in Russian proper, its borderlands, or its sole non-contiguous imperial colonial project in Alaska and northern California.[23]

Social and Racial Categories in Alaska

The Russian imperial project in Alaska (circa 1732–1867) also showcased the differing emphasis on establishing societal hierarchy in the Russian Empire versus the United States. Russian imperial officials had addressed intermarriage between Russians and Native Alaskans by creating a new social estate for their children and "borrowed" the term "Creole" in the early nineteenth century to identify people of Native Alaskan and Russian heritage, born in Alaska.[24] Sonia Luehermann, citing Lydia Black, considers extraterritorial birth as the root factor of identification, rather than race.[25] The term "Creole" is prevalent in ethnic self-identification in the continental United States in differing but related contexts, specifically in the American South, but all are rooted in race.[26]

The specific application of the appellation "Creole" remains arguable in the historic Russian-Alaskan context. Michael Oleksa has made the case that being Creole in the Russian period indicated social class rather than ethnic background, with Native Alaskans also identifying as Creole in relation to their occupation/position in the Russian America Company.[27] Upon the purchase of Alaska in 1867, Americans, in census and other documents, began to interpret Creole as a strictly racial, rather than a socio-cultural, category, and eliminated the term in efforts to categorize Alaskan residents as either "white" or "non-white" in line with the racial paradigm in the continental United States, replacing Creole with "mixed race" in such documents.[28]

As Mae Ngai points out, US census officials in the late nineteenth century began to utilize census information to attempt to restrict the immigration of undesirable (i.e., non-Western European) peoples, but, in the case of Alaska, the census played a role in reinforcing the racial dichotomy of white/non-white people in territories where the majority of the population was Indigenous, thus contributing as well to the "amalgamation" of descendants of Europeans in the United States into a "single white American race."[29] The Orthodox Church played an important role in the history of ethnic relations both in Alaska and in San Francisco as, despite Russian dominance, church members consistently referenced the church's pan-ethnic nature, discussed in chapter 1 as a preface to the arrival of the post-1917 diaspora to San Francisco.

Pan-Ethnic Orthodoxy in San Francisco

The 1849 Gold Rush in California transformed San Francisco from a settlement to an "urban center," and the region's first Orthodox immigrants – Serbs, Greeks, and Syrians – arrived in the 1850s.[30] Without a place of worship to attend, the various ethnic groups of Orthodox faith in San Francisco attended services held by Russian priests on visiting Imperial Navy warships from 1859 to 1864, thus setting the stage for Russian domination. Nevertheless, the charter of the Greek-Russian-Slavonian Orthodox Eastern Church and Benevolent Society and Parish, formed and registered in 1867, specifically stated that the society was "pan-ethnic" and "its common language was English." In 1870, the parish began publication of *The Slavonian*, a multilingual newspaper, "a testimony to its missionary and *pan-ethnic* spirit."[31]

The issue of "pan-ethnicity" was a critical one with respect to how dominant culture representatives viewed, and public discourse characterized, the Russian Orthodox Church in San Francisco going forward. Syrians, for example, were not considered "white."[32] Native Alaskans and Creoles who relocated to San Francisco after the American takeover may have been identified as Russian due to their Russian surnames, whether or not they happened to have Russian ancestors, thus contributing to the mytho-poetic notion that a substantial Russian community had existed in San Francisco since the city's founding. From the 1870s to 1890s, no more than a few hundred people identified as permanent Orthodox residents in the city, and most were not ethnic Russians from Russia. In contrast, by the early twentieth century, those who identified as Orthodox in Alaska numbered more than 11,000.[33] Despite the fact that the high clergy were generally ethnically Russian going forward in San Francisco, the Orthodox Church was and remained a multi-ethnic church even after Greeks and Serbs formed their own parishes in the early 1900s, in a time period characterized by growing nativism, xenophobia, and racial animus, with a commensurate exponential increase in eugenics movements and theories. In fact, in the early twentieth century, "white supremacy remained as San Franciscan as the city's fog."[34]

Is San Francisco a "Russian" City?

The perception of San Francisco as a "Russian" city, as stated by émigré Stenbock-Fermor in the epigraph, is one that developed much later in the timeline for Americans of Russian heritage, after World War II, and had its roots in the mytho-poetic ideations about the nineteenth-century

Russian presence in California. Following that presence, which left behind relics for later rediscovery, a "wave" of Russian "exiles," in this narrative, arrived in San Francisco after 1917 and lived out their lives mourning lost empire. Because little physical evidence survived to attest to a Russian presence in the Fillmore, and due to the noted repetition of tropes in American public discourse, the inter-war community took its place in the narrative as a group of monarchist expatriates, languishing in exile, surviving from the sale of gold and jewels they fortuitously brought with them, while taking part in their nostalgic "ceremonials."

Moreover, San Francisco was not a part of global inter-war émigré discourse with respect to its status as a Russian diasporic center, as were the capital cities of Europe. Paris, for example, was not only the recognized political center of the Russian emigration, it rivaled Moscow as a center for Russian literature at the time, as did Berlin, which saw an influx of up to a "quarter million" Russian expatriates in the 1920s (as opposed to the estimated 6,000–15,000 émigrés in San Francisco at any given time in the inter-war period), and was also a center of Russian émigré publishing.[35]

The lengthier history of a Russian "community" in San Francisco speaks much more to diversity of "Russian" identity (i.e., few Russian Orthodox lived in the city prior to the post-1917 wave, while non-Russian Orthodox populations, particularly Serbs, were a constant from the 1850s forward).[36] Native Alaskan and Creole Orthodox had a role in the creation of Orthodox societies in San Francisco and, as noted, due to their surnames, may have been identified as Russian by outsiders, reinforcing the notion of the pan-ethnicity of Orthodoxy and the uncertainty among Euro-Americans about Russian whiteness in nineteenth-century San Francisco.

That uncertainty about Russian ethnic identity remained a factor in public discourse given the increasingly stringent legal restrictions on Eastern European immigration (discussed below) in the inter-war period, influencing the process of Russian immigrant and émigré acculturation to American society going forward. The primary focus of this book is on the internal dynamics of the inter-war San Francisco Russian community and the negotiation of their identity within a distinctive American urban environment that included a diverse Russian population. That diversity, though leading to occasional conflict in the inter-war period, did not preclude efforts to cooperate in recognition of common goals. The most "Russian" aspect of San Francisco in the inter-war period, in fact, was that it had two very distinct Russian neighborhoods, neither of which was dominated by "czarists."

Selected Historiography

Although this is an "American" immigration and ethnic history, the tendency to distinguish the history of "Russia Abroad" as Russian history complicates the categorization. As such, this book draws from several historiographies with common threads: immigration and diaspora studies, the ethnic history of San Francisco as part of the spatial American West as well as the Pacific Rim, and the history of the global Russian diaspora, particularly after 1917. The geography of the migration experiences centers on San Francisco and northern California as the point of settlement, but necessarily touches on the journey from Russia, usually via China, and the Pacific Rim, particularly the west coast of North America, from Alaska to Mexico. Such a journey differed from what Alexandre Vassiliev refers to as the "classic route" out of Russia heading south to Kiev (from Moscow and St Petersburg), "then Odessa or Yalta."[37]

The factor of an increasing number of Russian arrivals at the port of San Francisco in the 1920s, a port that also saw the greatest influx of Asian immigrants to the United States, had a role in how immigration officials perceived Russians, who arrived there from what officials referred to as the "Orient" in the inter-war period. The work of Erika Lee and Judy Yung, exploring the experiences of Chinese, Japanese, Korean, Jewish, and Russian immigrants entering San Francisco, provides a foundation for further inquiry in this book as to how Russians incorporated what they witnessed in that process into their own path to becoming American and attaining a commensurate "state of whiteness."[38]

The experiences of Russians in the inter-war period, when the consciousness of American nationalism provided further impetus to "make San Francisco American," a process that began earlier on, spoke as well to the distinctive nature of San Francisco space: a city on the far periphery of the American nation-state, in the American "West" and therefore on the "frontier," which was distinctive both spatially and culturally.[39] Elliot Robert Barkan quotes Frank Norris in his observations about "little Russias" scattered up and down the coast "from Mexico to Oregon" in the context of unassimilated groups as early as 1900, likely referring to Spiritual Christian (non-Orthodox) communities. But by 1920, when the number of new immigrants doubled in Arizona, California, New Mexico, Texas, and Washington, Russians were in the top ten of "foreign" arrivals, and that number only increased in the 1920s and 1930s.[40]

Introduction | 13

San Francisco is also a port city and door to the Pacific, through which people from a vast array of places, often from the "Orient," entered. The term "Orient" in that period identified people from exotic and non-European places, therefore unlikely candidates for Americanization.[41] Moreover, the definition of "American" in the early-twentieth-century American West not only implied "Euro-American," but specific European groups. Public discourse in Bisbee, Arizona, for example, a mining boomtown with a population of close to 50,000 at the turn of the twentieth century, identified English, Welsh, and Scottish workers as acceptable candidates to join Bisbee's "American camp," while Italian, Spanish, Slavonian (i.e., Slavs from the Balkans), Swedish, or Portuguese were not. The alteration from a "white man's camp" to an "American camp" began when significant numbers of arriving Slavs began to compete for mining jobs.[42] Ingrained prejudices about the foreignness of Eastern Europeans in the American West led to observations that "Bohunks" were not "our kind of white."[43]

A central discussion in this book concerns the issue of "race" in America, a term that eugenicists utilized in the 1920s to distinguish non-Western Europeans from the American "norm" of desirable groups (e.g., the "Slavic race"). Contemporary discussion generally utilizes the term "ethnicity" in place of "race" as the term "race" has come to focus on physical attributes, particularly skin color, over cultural difference. Thomas Guglielmo and Arnold R. Hirsch explored the history of Italians (Southern Europeans) and Poles (Eastern Europeans) respectively, attaining a "state of whiteness" in inter-war Chicago in the context of the racial hierarchy, with African Americans and Mexican Americans occupying those same urban spaces. Both scholars found that racial prejudices among Eastern and Southern European immigrants developed only over time as they began to identify more as "white" rather than as members of a particular ethnic group or, subsequently, as hyphenated Americans (e.g., Italian-American).[44] The experiences of Russians in San Francisco in the inter-war period speak to dominant culture prevalent discriminatory practices directed against Asian people, in particular, practices which incoming Russians observed firsthand, and which also affected some Russians whom officials did not perceive as "white." Such practices created a perceived necessity for Russians to distinguish themselves as white upon arrival, immediately initiating the submergence of Russian identity.[45]

In terms of "Russia Abroad," scholars use the term to describe diasporic Russian émigré communities in the post-Russian Revolution/inter-war era largely as a characterization of the intellectual and cultural activities in urban environments, particularly in Europe and especially Paris, Berlin, and Prague.[46] As there was no Russia to which they could return, émigrés set out to create a "real Russia temporarily located spatially" abroad in urban spaces where émigrés congregated.[47] That "real Russia" spoke to intellectual achievement and contribution, particularly in the literary sphere, as explored by Greta Slobin, and to the fact that these inter-war communities, desiring to maintain a Russian "national identity," did not integrate into the host country dynamic.[48] Marc Raeff's *Russia Abroad* is the seminal work on the diaspora as a whole, asserting that "Russia Abroad" as a manifestation of Russia outside of Russia disappeared when World War II began.

The rise of Nazi Germany and war in Europe disrupted processes of integration that may have begun for some émigrés, setting into motion new mass migrations both out of the Soviet Union during World War II and out of Europe following the war. These post-war migrations included both inter-war émigrés and Soviet Displaced Persons, who relocated throughout the world. The inter-war émigré community in China, with the largest such populations in the cities of Harbin and Shanghai, also migrated out post-war, including through both forced and voluntary repatriation to the Soviet Union, and to the United States, Australia, and South America. Thousands arrived in San Francisco, many via Tubabao in the Philippine Islands, to where they had fled in 1949, living in a refugee camp for up to three years (chapter 9).

Apart from Susan Hardwick's overview of Russian immigration to the "North American Pacific Rim" throughout the nineteenth and twentieth centuries, in-depth discussions of the Russian Orthodox community that formed in San Francisco in the 1920s are limited to a series of masters' theses. The first was written in 1972 by Alexandra Glazunova (1914–2015), herself an émigré who arrived in the later inter-war period in 1937. Glazunova highlighted Russian "self-imposed isolation," a theme taken up by subsequent chroniclers of San Francisco's inter-war Russian community and one this book directly challenges. Public discourse, both Russian and American in San Francisco, indicated a high level of Russian social interaction with non-Russians, and an expeditious rate of acculturation, particularly among the younger generation, which, combined with other factors, led to an equally expeditious dispersal of the community out of the Fillmore.

Glazunova also pointed out, referencing San Francisco's Russian community of the 1970s, that "a high percentage of Russian-Americans TODAY are well-educated, resourceful people with strong family and religious ties," concluding that the "Russian-American community will not tolerate any longer disrespect or abuse."[49] Such assertions spoke to the ongoing defensiveness and insecurity of ethnic Russians in the United States, a critical factor in the development of Russian-American identity that this book also addresses.[50] Hardwick alludes to lingering fears of governmental authority among Russian Americans in her discussion of methodology and attempts at documenting interviews (in the 1980s and 1990s), ascribing that fear to persecution in the Soviet Union.[51] Though certainly relevant among groups arriving after World War II, such a conclusion does not take into account the experiences of Russians with American culture and authorities, both inter-war and post-war, a factor very relevant to the defensiveness indicated by Glazunova.

The global inter-war Russian diaspora is generally omitted from discussion of diasporic groups despite the fact that Robin Cohen's definition of a diaspora, for example, includes all aspects of their experience: traumatic dispersal, with trauma a particular critical factor relevant to the discussion in this book; mytho-poetic collective memories about the ancestral home; dreams of return; and solidarity with co-ethnic members in other countries.[52] As Slobin points out, the Russian diaspora has been "largely overlooked" in diasporic studies, while existing studies of urban inter-war Russian émigré communities outside the United States, in contrast, point to the persistence of diasporic identity among émigrés as they deliberately remained distinct from, and unassimilated in, societies where they settled.[53]

In San Francisco, however, most Russian émigrés initially lived in the Fillmore neighborhood, which included significant contingents of Eastern European Jewish, Japanese, Filipino, and African-American residents. The dynamics differed from those of European cities where Russians stood out as newcomers, with most Fillmore residents relatively new to San Francisco and, in many cases, to the United States. Fillmore and Western Addition neighborhood 1930 census records indicate a diverse population, with home countries of residents listed as, among others, Mexico, El Salvador, Nicaragua, Panama, Chile, the Dominican Republic, Jamaica, Japan, the Philippine Islands, most countries of Europe, and transplants from numerous American states, living side by side.

Russian émigrés also interacted with Russian Spiritual Christians (referred to as "Sectarians" in Russia), who had established a community in San Francisco, prior to World War I, on Potrero Hill, south of Market Street, the city's main thoroughfare. The term Spiritual Christians encompasses a number of non-Orthodox groups originally from the Russian Empire who had split from the Orthodox Church. A colloquial appellation for one of the groups was "Molokane" (plural).[54] Though this book focuses on the Russian émigré experience, the importance of the Spiritual Christian community in the context of Russian émigré adjustment and acculturation necessitates discussion of the interactions between the two groups.

Russian émigrés were admittedly reluctant immigrants. Moreover, the homeland they had left, torn apart by civil war, soon ceased to exist. Nevertheless, despite difficulties with language acquisition, émigrés generally had more options to improve their long-term economic situation than did their compatriots in Europe and China. Citizenship was a viable option in America, and despite a concerted effort to maintain cultural heritage, many in San Francisco chose to naturalize early on. Although émigrés continued to identify as "White Russian," and the term entered the lexicon in American public discourse with references (often erroneous) to the Russian community (discussed further below), those who arrived in the early 1920s often naturalized by 1930. Almost all émigrés who arrived in the 1920s and 1930s (a continuing flow via various ports of entry) had naturalized by 1941.[55] As such, even if they continued to interact with their compatriots with respect to maintaining Russian cultural heritage abroad, they took an early critical step in altering their Russian diasporic identity, as part of the naturalization process included renouncing "all allegiance and fidelity" to any "foreign" entity. Moreover, in an effort to avoid nativist prejudice, many de-Russified their surnames in that process, officially altering them upon naturalization, either by abbreviating them or changing them completely.[56]

Svetlana Boym's work on nostalgia as well as her discussion about the Russian concept of *byt* (everyday life) informs much of my discussion on life choices and diasporic identity, particularly relevant with respect to how Russians viewed adjustment to life in America both for themselves and their children in an "Imagined Russia," a conceptualized notion of "Russia outside of Russia," integrated into the built environment of San Francisco and the landscapes of northern California (chapter 5).[57]

Intertwined with nostalgia for the homeland and remembrance of Russia was the on-going trauma stemming from the violence of the

Introduction | **17**

Civil War, forced migration, nativist hostility, and the coercive nature of the assimilation process. The role of trauma with respect to the process of acculturation to American society remained an underlying factor informing Russian émigré, and later Russian-American, life. The triad of the "emigratory experience" described by Zofia Rosińska certainly informed Russian diasporic life in exile: "identity, memory, and melancholy."[58] The violence, chaos, and displacement of the Civil War, however, which most émigrés in San Francisco had experienced either in combat as members of the military, as support staff (e.g., medical personnel), or as civilians in Siberia, left an indelible mark on émigré consciousness, taking an enormous toll on individuals and therefore on the community as a whole, in a time when trauma as an injury to the mind and body was little understood.[59] Moreover, forced migration and the circumstances of arrival in America in an atmosphere that was both politically hostile and nativist added yet another layer of trauma both for the inter-war group and displaced persons arriving in the post-World War II era. Creating the comfort of an "Imagined Russia" in San Francisco mitigated the trauma of loss but was subject to dominant culture pressure to assimilate. The inter-war and post-war Russian communities dealt with such pressure in different ways, leading to both the ultimate "disappearance" of the inter-war community, and the post-World War II formation of a Russian-American identity that was rigidly circumscribed in response to continuing negative characterizations of Russians as possible spies or, as one US senator opposing the acceptance of displaced persons after World War II declared, "the refuse of Europe."[60]

Imagined Russia

The "Imagined Russia" émigrés created in northern California differed from "Russia Abroad" in a number of key ways. The fact of an already existing cohesive Russophone community in San Francisco (the Spiritual Christians) contributed to how the inter-war émigré community developed. Though arriving émigrés were somewhat defensive in the face of the pro-Soviet views of many Spiritual Christians, the experience of encountering a Russian community whose memories of the Russian Empire were ones of persecution informed a perspective of recognizing authentic Russian culture outside their own group. Moreover, the émigrés settled in a neighborhood with a significant Eastern European Jewish population (some of whom spoke Russian as their first language), the majority of whom had also left the Russian Empire prior to World War I, fleeing pogroms.[61]

In spatial terms, Imagined Russia was a mental territory that integrated both San Francisco's urban environment and the landscapes in northern California where Russians lived, worked, built community, and maintained cultural heritage. Katherine Morrissey explores the "regional bonds" inhabitants of the American West created in the formulation of mental territories in the spaces they settled, bonds which informed their perceptions of their identity in a new environment.[62] Russians settling in San Francisco were linked through common culture prior to arrival, but circumstances of their settlement in an unfamiliar place forged new bonds among them as they sought to make sense of their lives, their roots violently torn from the Russian earth. In this space where they settled, they found an avenue to link them to the homeland through extant relics of a Russia now vanished, particularly Fort Ross, contributing to a sense of purpose and belonging while also facilitating the formation of community in the difficult period of initial adjustment.

Despite the significance of imperial project relics in providing that link, however, Imperial Russia as a political entity was not the focus of Imagined Russia in exile. The journey across the Pacific left émigrés with a perception of the fluidity and connected nature of space, which they referenced when exploring emotions and sensations about the landscapes of northern California and the objects they discovered that were familiar to them. Though far from the center of the European émigré milieu then, where polemics and debates raged about Russian identity abroad, and where the threat of Soviet anti-émigré activity was palpable and ever-threatening, émigrés in San Francisco felt linked to the Russian homeland of their memories as a place that existed outside the realm of war, violence, or even politics to some degree, where they would someday return, crossing back over the ocean which had brought them to America. [63] The reality was, however, almost no one returned, except those who chose, ironically, to accept the Soviet regime: a few individuals from the San Francisco community did repatriate after World War II.

The fact of taking US citizenship, forcing renunciation of loyalty to Russia as a political entity in any form, made Imagined Russia particularly salient as both a mental territory and a refuge. The vast majority of the San Francisco Russian émigré community, sustained by their dreams of Russia "out of time and space" (i.e., a Russia untouched by the violence

Introduction | 19

that had rent their homeland asunder, pitting Russians against one another and leading to the deaths of millions) eventually assimilated.[64] This was in direct contrast to the observations of Dubinets, for example, of first-wave composers in Europe who "refused to assimilate" in anticipation of return.[65]

The fact that Russians in San Francisco, and in the US in general, were especially vulnerable to targeting as politically suspect, in view of steadily increasing US government agency fears of "Red" infiltration of American society from 1917 forward, led to the expeditious naturalizations and efforts to "blend" in among the inter-war group, thus beginning the process of assimilation, whether inadvertent or deliberate. Cognizant of the fact that dominant American culture had a limited tolerance for self-determination of "foreign" groups, particularly with respect to nationalist-oriented organizations, the community made an effort to introduce Russian culture to American to mitigate suspicion (chapter 3). In the post-World War II group, on the other hand, the focus on maintaining Russian heritage was combined with a concerted and ultimately successful effort to join the American white middle class (chapter 9).

Estimated Russian Population in San Francisco

In terms of numbers, the inter-war Russian émigré diaspora in San Francisco was a comparatively small group. Census information, as shown in table I.1, indicates that between 6,000 and 10,000 Russians lived in the city or the immediate Bay Area at any given time in the inter-war period. That data, however, likely undercounts total numbers of incoming Russians, some of whom, deliberately or not, missed the counts. Census number totals are also unreliable with respect to the count of Russian émigrés because the Russian population in San Francisco included the Potrero Hill Spiritual Christian community and the Russian Jewish population centered in the Fillmore District, both groups preceding the émigrés in arrival.

The Russian Jewish population was generally amalgamated into the "Eastern European Jewish" population and very often into the overall Jewish population in San Francisco, which, according to Fred Rosenbaum, was majority German speaking from Central Europe with a "sprinkling" of Jews from czarist Russia, at least until 1917. The Fillmore neighborhood, where most émigrés settled after 1917, was one of three "traditional Jewish areas" in San Francisco with higher numbers of Eastern European Jews, including those who had departed from the Austro-Hungarian

Table I.1 US Census. Russian foreign-born in San Francisco/East Bay, 1910–50

Year	San Francisco	Oakland/Berkeley/Alameda	Total SF and East Bay
1910	4,640	799	5,439
1920	5,752	2,340	8,092
1930	7,455	1,611	9,066
1940	7,380	2,404	9,784
1950	7,830	3,331	11,161

Empire prior to World War I and therefore did not speak Russian. The 1920 census listed 5,800 Jews born in the Russian Empire living in all of San Francisco, with presumably a quarter to a third of the total in the Fillmore neighborhood.[66] John Glad notes an "estimate" of 10,000–15,000 Russians settling in San Francisco in the 1920s, and is probably correct, but provides no source for this number.[67]

Geography played a major role in the make-up of the inter-war (and to a great degree, post-World War II) Russian community in San Francisco. Most émigrés who settled in San Francisco arrived on the west coast of the United States, Canada, and Mexico from China between 1918 and 1941, the year the United States entered World War II and immigration was halted. Many had sojourned in Harbin, a city in northern China situated on the Songhua River, prior to re-emigrating to San Francisco. Harbin had come under Russian "influence" in 1898 as part of the Russian government's colonial expansion in support of the Russian Chinese Eastern Railway (CER).[68] That Russian influence permeated both the built environment and culture of the city. Stone and Glenny use the term "peculiar" to describe Harbin's role in Russian emigration out of Russia because such emigration began prior to the post-revolution exodus.[69]

In 1922, largely as a consequence of the Civil War, the Russian population in Harbin increased to 120,000 from 34,200 in 1916 (the Chinese population was 94,000 in 1918).[70] The city was unable to sustain such an influx of refugees, most of whom, fleeing the violence, had little or no resources. These Russians, who re-emigrated out of China often to San Francisco or Seattle, included former military who had served in Admiral Alexander Kolchak's forces, some high-ranking generals and officials, but mostly middle-ranking officers and soldiers who had retreated through Siberia, crossing into China in 1920–21.[71] Both the military men and civilians arriving in Harbin were often Siberians by birth, but also included

Introduction | 21

natives of southwestern Russia and the Volga River region, such as the towns of Saratov, Samara, Simbirsk (now Ulyanovsk), and Kazan, who were forced to retreat eastward as the White Armies lost ground in the Civil War. As such, civilians included members of the urban professional or middle classes: bankers, doctors, teachers, merchants, and industrialists, as well as artists or writers. Some were farmers, both from Siberia and areas in southwest Russia, and factory workers from those regions.[72]

Russians emigrating out of China in the inter-war period, however, also included those born there after 1900 to Russian subjects who had relocated to work for the CER or to take advantage of economic opportunities the railway brought to the area, in towns along the railway zone in China: Manzhouli, Hailar, Tsitsikar (now Qiqihar), Imianpo (now Yimianpo), Handaohedze and Pogranichnaya (now Suifinhe), and particularly Harbin.[73] By one count, twenty-eight different ethnic groups from the Russian Empire settled in Harbin beginning in 1899.[74]

A smaller contingent of émigrés arriving in San Francisco via China were from "European" Russia and the territories that made up the Russian Empire – the present-day Baltic countries of Latvia, Estonia, and Lithuania, and present-day Belarus, Ukraine, Moldova, and Romania. Others came from urban settlements of what are now the countries of Kazakhstan and Turkmenistan. Some had been displaced from their homes during World War I or had fled east during the Civil War, eventually reaching China or Japan from where they continued on to San Francisco.[75]

Wherever their origins, the incoming groups to San Francisco were multi-generational. Though many men and women in all age groups arrived without family, entire families entered as well, including grandparents, parents, and children. Others were able to find family members through the extensive networks of communication that existed, including ads in émigré newspapers seeking family members that had been separated in the chaos. The multi-generational aspect of the community greatly influenced the drive to immediately establish educational and other institutions intended to maintain cultural heritage in exile (chapter 6).

Upon seeking entry into the United States, Russians faced the results of nativist and xenophobic legislation. In response to increased Eastern and Southern European migration in the late nineteenth and early twentieth centuries, Congress passed restrictive laws, beginning with the Immigration Act of 1917, which also further restricted immigration of peoples from most of Asia.[76] To preclude the entry of "undesirables," the act stipulated a literacy test and an $8 immigration tax, also barring disabled people, paupers, anarchists, and prostitutes. Subsequently, the Immigration Restriction Act of 1921 included a quota system to impose numerical limits on immigration, favoring Northern and Western European immigrants as the quota was based on three percent of the number of residents from particular countries per the 1910 US census. Finally, the Johnson-Reed Act of 1924 restricted the total number of immigrants to 155,000 per year with quotas reduced to two percent of populations based on the 1890 census, "assigning" Slavs to a category of "inferior nations" and "races."[77] It also "reaffirmed" restrictions against various undesirables.[78] As Ngai states in her analysis of the history of the act, along with reinforcing the by-then accepted racial hierarchy, serving the desires of WASP Americans to "maintain social and political dominance," the 1924 act instituted American "nationalism based on race."[79] Tightening the quotas for Southern and Eastern Europeans promoted what Ali Behdad terms the fiction of a "homogenized imagined community" in the United States, supposedly existing since the founding of the nation by Western Europeans.[80] In practical terms, the act severely disrupted the migration of Russians as the annual Russian quota dropped from 34,247 (6,849 monthly) in 1921/22 to 2,248 as of 1 July 1924.[81] The Soviet Union was still identified as "Russia, European and Asiatic" in the 1929 quota specification, reinforcing, in a sense, the "inbetween" nature of Russian arrivals.[82]

White Russian Identity

The term "émigré," as opposed to "immigrant," harked back to the aristocrats and nobility who fled the French Revolution in the eighteenth century, but did not reflect the reality of the social and class identity of San Francisco's inter-war Russian diaspora. Nevertheless, it has entered the lexicon to describe Russians with certain characteristics who left Russia after the Bolshevik Revolution.[83] As self-identified political and religious refugees at a time when refugees had no special status under US immigration law, émigrés also identified as "White Russians," a term that emphasized their political opposition to the "Red" Bolshevik regime in a simplification of the generally chaotic period of the Civil War. The appellation "White" in this context was a purely political term, adopted by the military factions (the White Guard) opposing the "Red" (Communist) Guard. In the interests of clarity, in this book "White" Russian is capitalized while "white" and "whiteness" as a social construct of race is not. I use these terms, émigré and White Russian, relatively interchangeably throughout this book.

Introduction | **23**

Émigré ideation of the Russian Empire as an amalgamation of nationalities and cultures was evident in how émigrés arriving in San Francisco identified as "Russian" irrespective of ethnicity in, for example, Russian National Student Association applications, or in celebrations of culture under the umbrella word of "Russian" (events described in chapter 8). Such ideations assumed an overarching binary of oppressed people, regardless of ethnicity, versus an imposed communist dictatorship. Émigré use of the term "Russian" in this period implied all peoples of the former Russian Empire and/or Russophone subjects of that empire (including those born in China in the early twentieth century), while recognizing the multi-ethnic nature of that empire: "rabid nationalism" and "weaponizing" of ethnic and cultural identity evident today, as discussed by Dubinets, was not part of émigré self-identification of Russianness in inter-war San Francisco. Moreover, none of the versions of Russian "self" as Dubinets lists (Imperial Russian, Soviet, and post-Soviet) applied in the San Francisco community context.[84] Broadly, the Russian self of most émigrés was a "post-Imperial" one, with recognition of the critical importance of February/March 1917 events (the first revolution). The evolution to "Russian American" took place under a hostile host nativist and political gaze. Even those who identified as monarchists nevertheless often naturalized quickly, not necessarily because of a wish to become Americans but more because of nativist suspicions of their disloyalty if they did not.[85]

The trope of the White Russian émigré as the exiled monarchist aristocrat persisted at times with the active participation of émigrés themselves who recognized early on that both race and class played critical roles in the opportunities available to newcomers and in the processes of acceptance into American society. Becoming that aristocrat was not difficult due to the unshakeable interest of Americans in royalty and aristocracy. The pressure to be something more than an impoverished refugee may certainly have had an influence on how some portrayed themselves: "captains became generals," and people of ordinary origins became princes and princesses. According to émigré Alexander Voloshin, a journalist and sometime actor who lived in Los Angeles, such "self-promotions" happened regularly in Hollywood, where a "lively and close-knit community" of Russian émigrés existed by the late 1920s.[86] These self-promotions occurred in other contexts and were indicative of a mutual need: Americans wanted to think they were hob-nobbing with Russian aristocracy while Russians hoped to bring attention to possible business endeavors, jump-start film or stage careers, or create entry into certain social circles.

When the Katenka Café opened in downtown San Francisco in 1926, the promotional advertisement leaned heavily on its "royal" nature to attract patrons, proclaiming that "the atmosphere of Imperial Russia is harmoniously blended with the magnificence of the Russian Court" at the restaurant.[87] By 1927, American reporters had grown jaded, placing "nobility" in quotes when referencing Russians and noting, for example, that, "No one questions authenticity of titles any more. They are entirely too numerous," indicating skepticism of claimed noble origins. "A few are genuine," opined one writer, "but the majority are spurious. Every social aspirant has a pet prince or duke to tote around."[88] Natalie Zelensky describes the American interest in Russian exiles as part of a process to reify a pleasing and entertaining Russian past (e.g., "samovars and troikas, balalaikas and palaces"), all exotic (to Americans) symbols of Russian culture.[89] The depiction of such objects, however, took place in the context of performance or entertainment by people who were, or claimed to be, aristocrats. Indeed, the very title of Zelensky's book speaks to that notion: *Performing Tsarist Russia in New York* – "Tsarist Russia" conceptually privileges the notion of exiled nobility. The relentless focus on exiled elites in Europe and New York, playing out as it did in San Francisco's (English-language) public discourse, obfuscated the actual nature of the Russian community in that city (chapter 2).

Methodology

The literacy of the émigrés contributed to a surfeit of written materials in the archives. Generated writings and collected materials by and about Russian émigrés in both American and émigré publications make up much of my source base. It is, perhaps, indicative that ruminations about the "Russian self" that spoke to the evolution of identity came from women (e.g., Nadia Shapiro, Antonina Von Arnold, and Eugenia Isaenko). As important, however, were the lives of those who did not set down their thoughts: tracing the life histories of Russians through documents (immigration, census, directory) provided critical information about the paths of individuals as they dealt with the "everyday" (*bytovye*) issues of adjustment to American life. An almost complete run of the Russian-language *Russkaia zhizn'* (Russian life) newspaper (1922–27) provided invaluable insights into the daily life and interactions of the Russian communities.

Introduction | 25

Transcripts of oral histories of Russian émigrés who had arrived in the inter-war period, a project conducted under the auspices of the University of California, Berkeley, also provided insights into the dynamics of that community, as well as a glimpse into the stages of Russians "becoming American" through their own eyes, looking back into time. As those latter interviews took place much later (the earliest in 1961), interrogating the recollections was a critical part of integrating them into the narrative.

Indicative of continuing dominant culture perceptions, in 1961 an interviewer described San Francisco's Russian Americans as a "conspicuous and picturesque element" when he spoke with inter-war arrival Elizabeth Malozemoff (1882–1974), foregrounding the community as visible in terms of performative aspects of their culture, also erroneously implying that the inter-war group had not assimilated. The interviewer's description actually concerned the post-World War II arrivals who had, by then, established themselves primarily in the Richmond District, west of the Fillmore.[90]

Of the five interviews I personally conducted, four were for earlier but related projects. My father, Gregory Bogdan, and godfather, Igor Prohoda, were both born in Soviet Ukraine and were both displaced persons in Germany after World War II. My mother was born in Harbin and was patrilineally descended from the Ukhtomsky and Nazariev families in Simbirsk. My parents and godfather all came to San Francisco after World War II, by various routes, and I grew up in San Francisco during the height of the "hippie" and "flower power" era, which many Russian Americans, including my parents, viewed with a jaundiced eye.

Other interviews originally for my dissertation were with Natalie Sabelnik and Nikolai Massenkoff, who arrived in San Francisco from Tubabao (the Philippines) after World War II. In preparing this book manuscript, I was also very fortunate to speak with Eugenia Bailey, who was born in San Francisco, a few months after her parents arrived on US Army Transport (USAT) *Merritt* in July of 1923; her accounts are a first-hand look at the Russian Fillmore in the 1930s.

Chapter Organization

The book follows a general chronological timeline with chapters 2 through 8 exploring the Russian diaspora's arrival, settlement, and acculturation in San Francisco during the inter-war period (1918–41), focusing on internal group dynamics, interactions with other Russophone groups and non-Russians, and the foundational creation of institutions (churches, schools, artistic and literary groups) that survived the physical dispersal of the inter-war community. As the 1917 Bolshevik Revolution was at the root of a mass Russian exodus out of Russia and a simultaneously increasing US government focus on the dangers that "Moscow," capital of the new Soviet state, posed to America, I utilize that year as a boundary indicating change in the nature of the Russian community in San Francisco.

As a preface to inter-war Russian arrival, chapter 1 outlines the formation of the nineteenth-century multi-ethnic Orthodox community and relevant perceptions of race/ethnicity prevalent at the time, as well as the settlement of groups from the Russian Empire in San Francisco prior to 1917. Chapter 9 examines the arrival and settlement of the post-World War II Russian diaspora in San Francisco, the challenges they faced in the McCarthy era, and the commensurate formulation of a particular Russian-American identity that dovetailed neatly with the development of America's post-war white middle class.

The concept for this book arose long before 24 February 2022, the date of the Russian invasion of Ukraine. Although this book does not cover the history of the Ukrainian diaspora, it is important to note that a Ukrainian cultural organization, Prosvita (Enlightenment), existed in San Francisco in the inter-war period, and advertised in *Russkaia zhizn'*, a pan-Slavic publication at the time.[91] The Ukrainian diaspora, like the Russian diaspora, was both diverse and culturally cohesive, with celebrations of Ukrainian history and discussions about self-determination taking place in San Francisco's multi-cultural environment. In an eerie and sorrowful repetition of forced exodus a century later, the 2022 war has created new Ukrainian and Russian diasporas. The circumstances of conflict may differ, but one of the consequences of violence perpetrated on civilian populations always remain the same: trauma with repercussions extending to future generations.

Unless otherwise noted, all translations of Russian into English are mine. Given the broad range of English-language versions of Russian names, I generally use those versions that individuals selected as they became American citizens, but, in certain cases, utilize alternate versions (e.g., "Barskii" rather than "Barsky" as the former is the spelling the Hoover Institution Archive utilizes for the individual's papers). For transliterated Russian text (e.g., book titles), I utilize the Library of Congress transliteration system including the soft sign but omitting other diacritics.

— 1 —

RUSSIANS IN SAN FRANCISCO PRIOR TO 1917
Pan-Ethnic Orthodoxy and Emerging Communities

The idea of teaching, in our common schools, a language which according to the ablest scholars of Western Europe who have studied it, is little better than barbarous in sound, construction and general development, and almost totally devoid of literature worthy of the name, is almost too irrational to be ridiculous. We suppose that the prosperity of our Alaskan ice and fur trade and whale fishing would be wonderfully increased by teaching our youth the Russian language. Wouldn't it be better, however, to teach them to talk Esquimaux [sic], and live on sperm candles and fish oil?

GOLDEN ERA newspaper in San Francisco, 1869[1]

In a few days a religious festival somewhat novel on this coast will be celebrated in the little Russian Church on Greenwich Street.

SAN FRANCISCO CHRONICLE, 1880[2]

Dark Mysteries Connected with the Greek Church ... It is openly charged that murder and arson have been committed by church officials, and yet no one has been brought to justice. For eighteen years past the church has been torn by dissension and held up to the world as a perfect sink of iniquity.

EXAMINER, C. 1891[3]

San Francisco's nineteenth-century public discourse periodically referenced the "dark" nature of the Orthodox Church to reinforce the notion that, notwithstanding its established presence in the city, it was not an "American" institution. The Orthodox Church was, after all, "Eastern" in the sense of "Oriental" rather than Occidental." Moreover, the language of Russia was "barbarous," equivalent to or perhaps less prestigious than "Esquimaux," purportedly spoken in Alaska, while Russian culture was "devoid of literature." Public discourse about the likely murder of a priest in 1878 and a fire in the Russian cathedral in 1889 characterized the incidents as indicative of the "dark" and "mysterious" nature of the church.

Orthodox institutions, however, pre-dated the advent of "Western" Christianity in Alaska, and Orthodox immigrants of varying ethnic backgrounds had arrived in San Francisco with the 1849 Gold Rush. Bishop John Mitropolsky (1836–1914) transferred the cathedra from Sitka, Alaska to San Francisco in 1872 (thus the reference in the epigraph to its "eighteen-year history"), due in part to the increasing numbers of Orthodox faithful, particularly Creoles and Native Alaskans, relocating to San Francisco after the "sale" of Alaska to the United States in 1867. Public discourse referenced these arrivals, likely because they had Russian surnames, as "Russian immigrants from Alaska," labeling them as foreigners in "American" space.[4] Most Russian-born Russians in Alaska, however, had returned home in 1867.[5]

The multi-ethnic nature of the Orthodox Church in San Francisco in the nineteenth century contributed to San Francisco public discourse defining it as foreign, with occasional forays into racialist commentary about its members. Prior to 1917, the bishops and some of the priests serving at the church were subjects of the Russian Empire. Therefore, they were, as public discourse portrayed them, foreigners in America, but the parishioners, whatever their ethnic background, were generally not. Public discourse also focused on scandal and conflicts within the church, with clergy and parishioners targeted by the press. The exotic spectacle of church rituals and church-related activities, in contrast, engendered curiosity, and a consequent interest in the church as a "peculiar" institution in San Francisco's cosmopolitan milieu, balancing the rhetoric of purported unsavory practices by Orthodox Church members. The exotic nature of the church, then, was both attractive and problematic, depending on the context.

The experiences of Russian Orthodox clergy and congregants in San Francisco in this period highlighted the otherness of Russians in terms of culture and religion under the American gaze, touching as well on issues of race, because Orthodoxy encompassed a number of ethnic groups not considered "white" (e.g., Syrians and Native Alaskans).[6] Notwithstanding the occasional vituperative commentary, Orthodox clergy and parishioners nonetheless established the church in San Francisco as an institution serving an ethnically diverse community.

Non-Orthodox Russian communities included Spiritual Christians, who immigrated in substantial numbers to San Francisco between 1904 and 1914 when World War I began in Europe, and opponents of the Russian Imperial regime, some fleeing from Siberian exile. Jewish subjects of the empire, some of whom identified as Russian and/or spoke Russian as their native language, depending on point of origin, also settled in San Francisco prior to 1917. The nature of San Francisco as a "frontier" city on the periphery of the expanding American nation-state allowed for an eclectic collection of groups to settle there with a variety of Russians among them. American public discourse of the period, however, tended to focus on the Orthodox Church and its members as a visibly "foreign" group in San Francisco as the city evolved from a nineteenth-century "frontier" town to a twentieth-century urban "cosmopolitan" center.

A Church Scandal

An 1891 case brought to trial in San Francisco involving the alleged abuse of boys studying at the Russian Orthodox Church school highlighted both the discomfort of dominant culture representatives with the concept of a multi-ethnic church as well as the notion that San Franciscans viewed the Orthodox Church as culturally exotic and a source of spectacle. Authorities charged two church employees, Deacon Evfimiy Alexine and Paul Ligda, with physical abuse and neglect of the boys, all of whom were Native Alaskan or Creole. In the ensuing coverage of the trial, however, newspaper reporters made a point of denigrating the boys, who ranged in age from nine to fifteen years. For no apparent reason except to provide public spectacle, authorities took fourteen boys to the "city prison to be held as witnesses" and reporters described the procession to the jail as "an Indian kindergarten out for an airing."[7]

The logic of incarcerating young boys, who were victims, prior to their court testimony, spoke to the nature of dominant culture attitudes. A reporter described the face of Andrew Kaveutk, "an Indian [sic] from Sitka," as "broad as a full moon and as round as a doughnut," adding that his "small, squint eyes are as black as jet"; the mother of James Corocoran, thirteen years old, of "very fair complexion" and "blue eyes and flaxen hair," was a "now dead half-breed Russian woman." Elias Nalk, also thirteen, was an "Esquimau [sic] whose features do not indicate a high order of intellect."

Further, the report continued, "And so they run, Esquimaux [*sic*], Russians, half-breeds, and nondescripts. Many of their names end with the Russian 'off' and Peter, Paul, and Nicholas seem to be the favored given names."[8] The focus on "half-breed" or mixed-race children indicated anxiety about miscegenation, though being Russian, in and of itself, was also problematic in this narrative. Commentary regarding the boys' surnames referenced the assumption that Russian men fathered children with Native Alaskan women as Russian surnames often ended with "off," but Orthodox Native Alaskans and Creoles may have had names ending with "off," whether due to intermarriage or because they had adopted Orthodoxy.[9] Reporters also scoffed at the idea that the boys, particularly because of their heritage, were in a place of learning, referring to them as "Little Alaskans," and "so-called scholars," while the school was a "purported" seminary. The boys were "ostensibly to be educated as missionaries or preachers," implying that such was unlikely, given their Indigenous background.[10]

The incident of alleged abuse reinforced the notion that the church and those who practiced the religion were barbaric, despite the fact that no one was convicted. Alexine and Ligda did admit to striking some of the boys, but the case ended in a hung jury. The "scandalous" aspects of the case dominated any investigative work, likely confusing the jury with its focus on Russian foreigners who practiced a "dark" religion in a "sink of iniquity," mistreating children, while the boys became fodder for racist public commentary.[11]

A Peculiar Institution

The history of the Russian Orthodox Church in San Francisco in the latter half of the nineteenth century did seem to include an inordinate litany of tragic death and scandal. The impression of exaggerated drama, however, was conveyed by public discourse of the time – newspaper editors, competing for readership, relished any hint of the sensational and the Russian Orthodox Church, its clergy, and parishioners, situated on the edge of the cultural order, which provided ample fodder. Barbara Berglund explains the nature of this cultural ordering in San Francisco as part of the process of establishing a "distinctly American society built on nationally dominant hierarchies of race, class, and gender."[12] Russians deviated from the standard conception of "Americanism" in terms of language, culture, and faith, while the multi-ethnic nature of the Orthodox Church reinforced that deviation. The relatively small numbers of

Orthodox parishioners, however, though engendering inordinate scrutiny, was a factor shielding the community from violent attack in a city with a history of violence against groups perceived as foreign or not "American," the latter term a synonym for "white" in that context.

The clergy, as representatives of the church, attracted attention as foreigners with strange customs, which led to commensurate suspicion and, on occasion, maltreatment. When Russian Orthodox priest Father Pavel Kedrolivansky died of an untreated head injury at San Francisco City Prison Hospital in June of 1878, the jury in the inquest did censure police agencies for lax procedures, but there was no resolution to the case. Someone had attacked Kedrolivansky and left him unconscious in the street, after which police incarcerated him without medical care. Evidence disappeared and the perpetrator was never found. Kedrolivansky left behind a wife, Alexandra, and six children, who remained in San Francisco's Orthodox community.[13] Bishop Nestor (Zakkis), who subsequently arrived in 1879 to head the diocese, died in 1882 while visiting Alaska, falling overboard from a ship on which he was traveling. The circumstances of his death remained unclear but public discourse noted in discussing the two incidents that "a fatality seems to attach itself to the Greco-Russian clergy of this diocese," absolving the city of responsibility in the case of Kedrolivansky's death and ascribing mystical causes to the death of Bishop Nestor.[14]

The subsequent head of the San Francisco Russian Orthodox Church, Bishop Vladimir (Sokolovsky-Antonov, 1852–1931), arrived in 1888 but remained only three years, enduring commentary both about his physical appearance and the nature of his congregation. Public discourse about the bishop noted his long "intensely" black beard, the "locks" of his long hair, his attire (a "cap of purple velvet" and purple silk robe), as well as his stature: reports consistently described him as being "seven feet tall"[15] (figure 1.1). An observer at one of the bishop's first services at the cathedral made note of the ethnically diverse congregation:

> The people present were types of many nationalities. There were several Alaskan Indians in the congregation, who had been sent hither to study the Russian language by missionaries of the Russo-Greek Church. Dr Arbeely, the Syrian, was present. He is a member of the church. There were a number of colored people there who had been converted in the South. Spaniards, British, Greeks, Russians, Poles and Tartars made up the greater part of the congregation.[16]

Figure 1.1 Bishop Vladimir as depicted in a San Francisco newspaper, in church regalia including the *klobuk*, a tall head covering, which may have led to the claim that he was "seven feet tall."

Native Alaskans likely already spoke Russian, as it continued to be the *lingua franca* in several regions of Alaska long after the US purchase in 1867.[17] Selecting one individual as "the Syrian" implied (erroneously) that he was the only person of that ethnic background in San Francisco, thus turning him into a curiosity. The observer's comments about the "colored people" and other "nationalities," particularly the mention of "Tartars," indicated incomprehension and curiosity, as well as uneasiness with the ethnic make-up of the congregation.[18] That curiosity morphed sharply into contempt towards both the Russian clergy and Native Alaskan seminary students in the later public discourse.

Notwithstanding San Francisco's pride in its "cosmopolitanism" as a developing urban center, the presence of a multi-ethnic congregation was a cause of uneasiness that would periodically manifest itself in derogatory public discourse. A larger context for this public discourse was the environment of unmitigated violence in northern California in the post-Gold Rush period, which included the genocide of Indigenous peoples throughout the state, and anti-immigrant gangs targeting non-Europeans in San Francisco to make the city "safe for white Americans."[19]

By the late nineteenth century such overt violence had receded within the urban space of San Francisco, but narratives about problematic "foreign" practices and institutions remained a constant in public discourse, highlighting as well non-European manifestations of Orthodoxy. When Syrians participated in a Christmas service, chanting a psalm in Arabic, a non-Orthodox observer noted that "their chant was even less musical than that of the other participants in the service" and "its discord struck the congregation."[20] Orthodox Church services are chanted or sung and the derisive comment indicated the practice of outsiders observing religious ritual without comprehension, leading here as well to biased observations about perceived "foreignness" based on the non-European nature of the congregants.

Bishop Vladimir also had to deal with manifestations of political suspicions, a harbinger of what was to come in the twentieth century when he clashed with Russian expatriate, eye and ear doctor Nicholas Sudzilovsky/Russel (1850–1930). Russel took advantage of his own westernized appearance and self-described expertise on the "peculiar" Russian Orthodox Church to accuse its representatives of espionage. The bishop declared in response that the "Russian Church has no spies in its employ in San Francisco" and hastened to assure San Franciscans that "Russia and the United States are the best of friends."[21] The accusations and exchange about espionage led to further discourse comparing the repressive Russian regime in negative terms to "free America."[22] Perhaps to redirect the hostility, the bishop "discontinued the commemoration of the Russian Imperial Family" as part of his church service, instead including the name of the US president.[23]

How Native Alaskan and Creole students had to endure attacks in public discourse, how the authorities addressed violence against the church, how public discourse characterized Bishop Vladimir, and how the press covered the stories all pointed to a particular narrative about Russians that focused on their cultural otherness, with names and surnames an "easy" indicator of "Russianness." Boys studying at the Russian Church school since 1872, however, were of varied backgrounds. In 1880 the group included Andrew Kashevaroff, Vasily Kashevaroff, Nikolai Netsvetoff, and Ivan Dabovich, all, except for Dabovich, Creoles from Alaska. Dabovich, later Father Sebastian, was the founder of the Serbian Orthodox Church in America.[24]

The Orthodox community then, remained on the edge of the cultural spectrum of familiarity in San Francisco society. As one reporter noted,

"There is enough in the mass of the Greek Catholic Church to suggest its relationship to religious observances of other denominations but there is also a great deal of dissimilarity."[25] In other words, the relatively few Orthodox residents provided an interesting counterpoint of exoticism without threat to the dominant Anglo Protestant culture, established in the post-1849 frenzy and California's subsequent American statehood. As such, public discourse and the nation-making process as it took place in San Francisco, an urban center on the far periphery of the state, placed the small Orthodox community at a particular level in the cultural order. The church, which public discourse invariably labeled as "exotic" and "oriental," was nevertheless a recognized part of the San Francisco religious community, albeit a "peculiar" member: "San Francisco has a Greek church among other things of a cosmopolitan character. Its *peculiar* worship is carried on with appropriate ceremonies at the residence of the Russian Bishop, Johannes [John Mitropolsky], at the corner of Pierce and Green streets."[26] Language referencing the church, Russians, Slavs, or Greeks focused on the ornateness of that church and the curious, "unusual," or even "spectacular" nature of Orthodox ritual (e.g., "Spectacular Ceremonial Attends the Ordination of a Priest at the Greek Cathedral").[27] The Orthodox, a small group, provided interesting spectacle without danger of overwhelming the existing and dominant cultural structure.

Depending on the situation, however, undercurrents of racial animus rose to the surface to emphasize the un-American nature of the church because of its failure to maintain racial divisions. Given that factor, people who had identified as Creole or Native Alaskan in Alaska prior to the US takeover likely made efforts to "blend" in as Russians, avoiding clarifying their ethnicity when in San Francisco, therefore erasing their identities and their presence in the history of San Francisco's Russian Orthodox Church. Seminary student Andrew Kashevaroff (1863–1940), for example, who later served as a clergyman in Alaska, identified as an American of Russian heritage in his adult years, effectively erasing his Native Alaskan roots (further discussed in chapter 2). The erasure of Native Alaskan identity may have played out as well among Orthodox families with Native Alaskan roots in San Francisco. Descriptions of events organized by Orthodox ladies' societies, particularly in the 1890s to 1910s, focused on their picturesque eastern European flavor, for example, indicating the acceptable limits of exoticism.[28]

The Russian Church in the Built Environment

The notion that Orthodoxy was "exotic," unlike Western Christian denominations, was reinforced in the early 1880s when Bishop Nestor directed the reconstruction of a building at 1713–1715 Powell Street into a Russian Orthodox cathedral with its distinctive cupolas (figure 1.2). As an architectural object in the heart of the San Francisco urban landscape, the cathedral publicly expressed Russian Orthodox identity.[29] Prior to that, Orthodox places of worship in the city had not stood out prominently; subsequent public discourse labeled the structure "oriental style," noting that the church "shone with oriental splendor" and that "the music was entirely Eastern."[30] Moreover, such discourse described "Russian" or "Greek" church practices as unusual or even, as noted in the epigraph, "novel," to reinforce the notion that Russians, unlike Americans, were new arrivals, thus erasing the Russian presence from California history.[31]

In 1900, newly appointed Bishop Tikhon announced plans to build a new "handsome Oriental cathedral" (the newspaper's terminology) closer to the "city center," as Russians and Slavs resided in "all" sections of the city by that time.[32] The Orthodox Ladies' Society spearheaded activities to raise money with $1,000 subscribed by 1903. Funds from the Russian government factored into this project, which had shifted to build, in a reporter's words, a "heavy stone structure of mosque design" in the "north end of the city, with picturesque surroundings."[33] A "mosque" design was unequivocally "oriental" in the parlance of the period, indicating an amalgamation of non-occidental architectural forms in the minds of observers.

In the end, however, the church leadership, in view of the increase in the Orthodox population on the east coast following almost two decades of Eastern European immigration, decided to move the See from San Francisco to New York in 1905 and began negotiations to sell the cathedral (dedicated in 1897 to the Holy Trinity). Plans were in place by early 1906 for the Washington Square Theater Company to purchase the land, tear down the cathedral, and build a "playhouse."[34] The church leadership declared intentions to build a small church to replace the cathedral, noting a "strong feeling among [San Francisco's Orthodox] clergy and congregation in favor of erecting the new house of worship at the top of Russian hill [sic]."[35] Despite the relocation of the See, then, the perception of San Francisco as a place with its own Russian history, spiritually linked to Russia through Orthodoxy in particular, had begun to inform intra-Russian discourse.

Figure 1.2 St Basil's (later Holy Trinity) Russian Orthodox Cathedral at 1713–1715 Powell Street, 1889.

The aim of building a Russian church on Russian Hill spoke to its significance to the Orthodox congregation by that time. One of legends about the hill, its crest at the intersection on Vallejo Street between Jones and Taylor Streets, was that a Russian cemetery had been located there in the period of Russian Imperial exploration of northern California in the early nineteenth century. As early as 1824, a visiting Russian sloop captain noted a pyramid-shaped grave marker surrounded by a trellis erected by a countryman to mark the grave of a sailor who had died in port, on the top of what came to be known as Russian Hill.[36] By 1906, the perception that Russian Hill was sacred ground because Orthodox faithful had been laid to rest in that space was prevalent enough to influence the high clergy's decision about church location.[37] Andrew Kashevaroff, who played there with his schoolmates in the late 1870s, and subsequently investigated the history of the hill, concluded however that only individual graves had been located there, not a Russian Orthodox cemetery per se.[38] In fact, the soil on "the crest of Vallejo Street" was "hard clay," while other San Francisco hilltops were sand-covered, thus indicating a practical reason for selecting the site as a burial ground.[39] Nevertheless, several decades later, the semi-legendary history of the space had begun to inform church decisions with plans to maintain an Orthodox Church presence in that space in perpetuity.

Those plans fell through when the Holy Trinity Cathedral burned to the ground after the Great Earthquake in April of 1906. The sale of the land had been completed but, perhaps due to cost, the diocese chose to rebuild on the corner of Van Ness and Green Streets instead, just west of Russian Hill, and construction of the new Holy Trinity Cathedral was completed in 1909.[40] Despite the disaster that destroyed most of the city, and the existence of a relatively small Orthodox community in San Francisco, the historic Russian presence was nevertheless significant enough to Orthodox Church leadership to maintain a presence in that urban space, a factor which played a critical role in the post-1917 arrival of thousands of Russian émigrés.

Pre-1917 Russian Expatriates

That long-standing Russian presence in northern California, ironically, drew subjects of the empire to San Francisco despite their opposition to that selfsame empire and to the Russian Orthodox Church as an institution under control of the czar. Though the dissidents opposed the regime, they settled near to the only space in the continental United States where the remnants of a Russian imperial colonial project existed: Fort Ross in Sonoma County, north of San Francisco, a relic of that period, standing in ruins, yet retaining a significance to pre-1917 Russian clergy and subsequently to Russian émigrés (see chapter 5). Moreover, San Francisco was the only city in the American West, outside of Alaska, where a Russian Orthodox cathedral had been located since the late nineteenth century.

Members of all twelve Russian expatriate groups categorized by John Glad in his 1999 study were represented in San Francisco, boasting both a distinctive continuity and diversity of Russian presence. In Glad's discussion, the inter-war émigrés were the seventh group chronologically. Members of the first six are noted selectively below to illustrate that diversity (e.g., political dissidents and exiles, Jews fleeing pogroms, economic émigrés, and expatriates departing after the failed 1905 revolution). San Francisco, then, a relatively small urban space and population (49 square miles and 400,000 people in 1910) in comparison to, for example, New York (468 square miles and four million people in 1910), also a destination point for expatriates from the Russian Empire, played a significant role in Russian diasporic history.[41]

An 1867 arrival who opposed both the Russian Empire and the Orthodox Church hierarchy was Agapius Honcharenko (1832–1916), "a Ukrainian nationalist and missionary" who "established a Russian printing press, with the aim of uniting Siberia and America."[42] Honcharenko was born in Kiev and ran afoul of both the Russian monarchy and church bureaucracy, ending an extensive travel history in California. He was a driving force behind the semi-monthly newspaper (published in English and Russian) titled both *Alaska Herald* and *Svoboda* (Freedom), established in 1868, which staunchly opposed czarism and for which he initially received a subsidy of $50 per issue from the US State Department.[43] Formally, he published the paper under the auspices of the Russian and Pan-Slavic Benevolent Society, a group that consisted of what he called "former Alaskan and Russian immigrants" in San Francisco who opposed the czar, but who were actually mostly people of Native Alaskan heritage, given his own reference to members as "Aleutian sailors."[44] The society's founder, in fact, was Creole seaman Ilarion Arkhimandritoff (1819–1872), educated both in Alaska and in Russia at the Kronstadt Naval Academy.[45] The purpose of the newspaper was to inform "the Russians of the Pacific coast" and Alaska about American laws and customs.[46] Honcharenko spoke "for the interests of the native citizens of Alaska" as well as "Russians" who lived in California. He characterized Americans as occupiers of Alaska, and claimed that American soldiers were murdering "the people they were sent to protect" in Alaska, under US Army military administration until 1877.[47] His vituperative attacks caused him to lose his US subsidy.[48] His perspective, however, also encapsulated a pan-ethnic view of social equality and justice that ran counter to the dominant culture pattern: identifying as Ukrainian at a time when Ukraine was not an independent state, he nevertheless spoke of Russian-American cooperation but, more importantly, championed peoples, namely Native Alaskans, subjected to the power politics and economic exploitation (and, on the American side, racialist policies) of hegemonic entities, both the US government and the Russian Empire.

Other Russian expatriates, who also made their home in San Francisco and its environs prior to 1917, later interacted with the Russian émigré community despite having very differing political perspectives, giving indication of the eclectic nature of that community in the inter-war period. Olga Gordenker (1852–1932) and her husband, Vladimir, felt compelled to leave Russia with their children after the *Okhrana* (czarist secret police) took an interest in their activities, arriving in the United States in the 1883. Olga was descended from a noble Russian family, the Palitzines, but developed a socialist political outlook upon leaving "home and fortune to work with the common people." The Gordenkers settled in Glen Ellen in Sonoma County, purchasing and working a farm.[49] Vladimir feuded with Bishop Vladimir, but Olga, on her part, later associated with the inter-war Russian Orthodox community.[50]

Another member of the nobility with socialist inclinations was Feodor Postnikov (1872–1952), an engineer who settled in the Bay Area in 1906. An officer in the Russian Imperial Army, and a graduate of the Imperial Military Engineering Academy in St Petersburg, he first visited San Francisco in 1903, meeting Father Pashkovsky (later Bishop and Metropolitan Theophilus) at the Holy Trinity Cathedral. Postnikov decided to immigrate as he feared further violence after the failed revolution of 1905.[51] He immigrated with his wife and seven children and by 1907 had earned a civil engineering degree at the University of California at Berkeley, going on to a rather incredible career. He ran a farm and a ranch, enlisted in the US Army during World War I, reaching the rank of captain, built and flew balloons, sold real estate, taught engineering courses, and did all manner of engineering work.[52]

Jewish subjects of the Russian Empire and residents from western areas (now Belarus and Ukraine) who arrived in New York prior to 1917 migrated west, drawn perhaps by San Francisco's reputation as a "frontier" city of opportunity. Nathan Merenbach (1895–1983), for example, born in Feodosia, Ukraine, arrived in 1913 and continued to San Francisco, attending the University of California at Berkeley. He served in the US Army during World War I and was admitted to the California State Bar, running a successful legal practice for several decades.[53] Pamphil Tesluck (1888–1965) arrived from western Ukraine in 1908, subsequently settling in San Francisco where he ran a very successful real estate and insurance business.[54] These expatriates, who had left the Russian Empire either to escape persecution or for economic reasons, later interacted with the post-1917 wave of émigrés (chapter 3).

The Spiritual Christian Community

Russian Spiritual Christians arrived in a steady stream to San Francisco beginning about 1904 with subsequent groups arriving for a decade via various routes: across the Atlantic to American ports on the east coast or the Gulf of Texas; across the Pacific from China to Hawaii and then to San Francisco; and later via the Panama Canal, which opened in 1914.[55]

The Molokane, a Spiritual Christian group, were forcibly displaced from Russia proper by Czar Nicholas I in the 1840s, due in part to their open antipathy to the Russian Orthodox Church. Many settled in Transcaucasia, including Kars (now in Turkey).[56] Subsequent migrations out of Russia began in the 1890s. In October of 1906, a group of twenty Molokan families arrived in San Francisco from Hawaii, where they had initially attempted to settle.[57] Unhappy with conditions in Hawaii, to where they had been recruited by plantation agents with (unmet) promises of good pay, the group migrated to San Francisco, where a few Molokan families already lived. Thenceforth, the community grew steadily, and the population reached approximately 1,000 by 1911.[58] Close-knit, generally endogamous, and holding to traditions that differ significantly from Orthodox practices, the Molokane viewed the world outside their communities as separate from their way of life. Those within the community were *svoi* (ours) and those outside were *ne nashi* (not ours).[59]

The settlement of Potrero Hill, south of Market Street, San Francisco's main thoroughfare, began upon their arrival. Vasily Fetesoff (1882–1968), a member of the 1906 group, recalled their trek down Market Street, covered by debris after the earthquake and fires, south to the foot of Potrero Hill, where they initially built their own shelters. As more Molokane arrived, the area became known as "Russian Hill," leading to the unique situation of two "Russian hills" in a relatively small urban space by 1917, one actually populated by Russians, while the other, a site with spiritual and historic significance to the Orthodox faithful, became a wealthy neighborhood economically out of reach for incoming Russian émigrés.[60]

Radical Russians

San Francisco and the west coast were destinations for individuals fleeing Siberian exile. A reporter interviewed Demetrius Konoplitzky, on his way to a friend in San Francisco, in Vancouver in 1891. Arrested by the Russian *Okhrana* for his work on a radical democratic newspaper in the city of Kazan, he arrived as a stowaway from Vladivostok after escaping his prison chain gang. The reporter editorialized about the Russian penal system with a comment sympathetic to Konoplitzky's suffering: "knowing what we do of Russian methods," without explaining what these methods were, but implying that "we" (Americans) know they are horrific.[61]

The contradictions in how American authorities and the media thought about Russia and Russians were evident here: the czar was an oppressor of freedom and so Russians were right to oppose him, engendering sympathy among Americans particularly during the regime of the last czar, Nicholas II. US authorities began to adopt a completely opposing view, however, as radical activity increased in the United States in the period leading up to and after World War I, with Russian males acquiring an image as violent and dangerous anarchists, thus reinforcing the necessity to actively exclude them from entry into the United States.

By the early 1900s, in fact, Russians appeared to have already developed a reputation as dangerous radicals in the American West, perhaps stemming from that flow of Siberian escapees arriving on the west coast. In 1906, authorities found "two infernal machines" at Union Station in Denver, which contained "gun cotton" that exploded when removed. The reporter writing the story made the vague assertion that "some Russian refugee from San Francisco" carried the bombs to Denver before deciding to discard them as too volatile to transport. He did not provide an explanation as to why the individual involved was Russian or a "refugee," nor what it was that they planned to blow up.[62]

Radical activities in the West leading up to US entry into World War I led to clashes between authorities and labor rights proponents. The Union of Workers of the United States and Canada/Union of Russian Workers (UORW), a radical labor organization, had a branch in San Francisco. "Russian immigrants" killed two San Francisco policemen in 1916 with subsequent encounters between the police and Russian anarchists ending with the deaths of the latter.[63] The violence characterizing these encounters spilled over into the post-World War I environment with authorities viewing Russians with suspicion (chapter 2).

Concurrently, Czar Nicholas II, particularly after the 1905 Revolution, appeared as a cruel and barbaric despot in American public discourse, in line with the narratives of Russian expatriate opponents of the regime. President Woodrow Wilson saw no basis for "ties of amity" between America and Russia and his administration saw the removal of the czar as a positive step. The October 1917 Revolution, however, when the Bolsheviks seized power, created alarm, as the new government represented a possible threat to US economic interests, which Imperial Russia had not.[64] Moreover, romantic ideations of oppressed Russians fighting for freedom disappeared in the face of social and political unrest at home, which only increased after World War I when returning American soldiers, who found themselves unemployed and even homeless, clashed with police authorities.[65]

The small pre-1917 San Francisco Orthodox community attracted sufficient attention in public discourse to create an image of an exotic and foreign group. That identification of Orthodoxy with foreignness was complicated by the fact that the Orthodox Church was multi-ethnic in an environment where non-Europeans faced challenges with respect to acceptance. Anxiety about Russian culture and ethnicity, based in large part on that multi-ethnic nature of the Russian Orthodox Church congregation, continued into the inter-war period, a microcosm of the broader eugenics movement nationwide, led by people such as Madison Grant, who categorized Russians as Asiatic and therefore inferior.[66] It was indicative that a leading figure in the crafting of the Johnson-Reed Act of 1924, which severely restricted Eastern European immigration, was New York lawyer John Trevor, a "leading restrictionist" and "associate of Madison Grant."[67]

Moreover, after 1917, US officials added political suspicion to their perspective about categorizing Russian people as problematic immigrants. Many of those who had left Imperial Russia prior to 1917, whether due to persecution or disenchantment with the regime, may have supported the ideals of the Russian revolutions, but did not take part in violence, while others remained apolitical in the United States. Workers identifying as ethnically "Russian," however, often learned that "free America" suddenly became markedly less free for certain groups of people targeted as anarchists or revolutionaries. Playwright and social commentator Edward Hale Bierstadt noted in his 1921 treatise about Americanization that "America has never seemed ... especially free" for pre-World War I immigrants from the Russian Empire.[68] Anarchist groups in the US early on adopted the phrase "Free Country" as a strictly ironic term when referencing the routine violence against "immigrants, workers, and African Americans" in particular.[69]

Despite the complexity of its position in San Francisco and its perceived foreignness, the Russian Orthodox Church, embodied in the Holy Trinity Cathedral, now reconstructed at the base of Russian Hill, became a bridge in an alien environment for the incoming Russians after 1917. The history of the Russian Orthodox Church, an institution of paramount importance to many émigrés in exile, had a role in developing nostalgic ideations of their homeland and perceptions of the meaning of their experience of exodus and settlement in northern California. As a familiar institution and literal place of refuge, it mitigated dominant culture hostility stemming, in part, from the very event that caused their exodus from the Russian homeland: the Bolshevik Revolution. That event, in turn, was at the root of the first Red Scare in the United States, which, though short-lived, had a critical role in both politicizing and criminalizing Russian immigrants in American eyes, prefacing a period when the US government actively began to restrict immigration of all Eastern (and Southern) Europeans as undesirable on overtly cultural and ethnic, then referred to as "racial," grounds. That focus on ethnocultural inferiority also obscured dominant culture fears of political upheaval, particularly given the labor conditions new immigrants faced in industrializing America, and arriving émigrés, notwithstanding their level of education, often joined the ranks of the working class, given their lack of proficiency in English.

As Russian émigrés seeking refuge began their journeys across oceans and continents, this new America, altered by the very revolution that the émigrés were fleeing, somewhat reluctantly cracked open its doors to them. Most émigrés knew little about the American way of life and had never, prior to the devastation of the Civil War, given a thought to leaving Russia, much less immigrating to America. These were not the immigrants to whom Americans were accustomed and who bore the brunt of eugenicists' xenophobic diatribes; the "tired" and "poor"[70] who, in the narrative of American elites, were fortunate to gain entry and have the chance to become American in the "land of opportunity," taking on the difficult and dangerous jobs that "real Americans" did not want. Impoverished and in need of opportunity, the Russian émigrés certainly were but most of them, at least in the 1920s, had no interest in becoming American.

— 2 —

THE MYSTERIOUS RUSSIAN ARRIVES
Ethnic and Class Ambiguities

The Russia of the Czars, with its serfs and its imperial rulers, its dungeons and its Siberia, its anarchists and its secret police, has been regarded by the outside world, particularly America, as a land of mystery and murder, scarcely touched by the softening hand of civilization. The war has drawn aside a corner of this curtain of mystery, but only to reveal a country in strife, of revolution, and counterrevolution, pogroms, and riots, until one pictures a land as wild and as lacking in the ordinary elements of law and humanity as primeval America when the red savage ruled the forests.

LITERARY DIGEST, 1918[1]

But the greatest mystery is the Russian émigré himself.

NEW YORK TIMES, 1923[2]

Nadia Shapiro arrived in San Francisco from Harbin in August of 1922, one of approximately 500 Russian students sponsored by the Harbin Student Aid Committee and YMCA. The students came to obtain a university education for the purposes of helping to rebuild their Russian homeland, destroyed by years of war and revolution. In any case, that was the common narrative. Whether communicating with Americans or amongst themselves, students consistently referenced a return to Russia at some nebulous point in time. Shapiro, at the age of twenty-four, was a likely student candidate and, unlike the majority of Russians arriving in this period, had studied English.[3] Nevertheless, at the behest of a US Bureau of Investigation agent, immigration officers detained Shapiro's entire group upon entry at AIIS for examination due to suspicions about the "so-called" students attempting to enter the United States. Both a subject of the interrogation and the interpreter, given the lack of Russian-speaking US officials, Shapiro focused on the scholarly nature of the group's intentions. The agent, however, described the arrivals in his report as "not of a particularly intelligent type or kind."[4]

Nevertheless, authorities did not detain Shapiro at AIIS for long, and she, taking on the role of spokeswoman for her group, declared to reporters curious about the arriving Russians that she hoped to study journalism in the United States, after which she and other students would "go back to Russia with our knowledge: there we shall teach our people how America does it."[5] Shapiro spent little time as a student, however, taking a few journalism courses while getting her bearings. Down to her last five dollars, she pitched the editor of the *San Francisco Examiner* in March of 1923, and he hired her as one of only two female reporters at that newspaper. Shapiro utilized her position as an American journalist to advocate for her countrymen and women, immediately grasping the complex nature of being Russian in America, given that her own first encounter with authorities involved interrogation of her identity. In one of her early columns she related the story of her friend "Tatiana" who, after fruitlessly searching for a job, finally acquired a position because the hiring company's personnel manager noticed her application out of hundreds of others: Tatiana's name was the same as one of the murdered daughters of the last Russian czar, Nicholas II.[6] During the job interview, Tatiana neither confirmed nor denied her identity and, apparently leaving her interviewer with the impression that she was hiring royalty, Tatiana was offered a $100 per month clerical job. Shapiro, alluding to the American affinity for blonde women, titled the article: "Mystery is better than peroxide when you're looking for a job."[7]

The "mysteriousness" of Russia as a country in American public discourse extended to its people, who began to appear in ever larger numbers on the west coast of the United States, generally migrating from China, after 1918. "Mysteriousness," similar to exoticism, picturesqueness, or strangeness, was a code word for the otherness of Russians and the country they came from, "primeval" as the America of "the red savages," and "lacking in the ordinary elements of law and humanity" in the words of the *Literary Digest* contributor cited in the epigraph. As such, despite a frank American fascination with Russian aristocracy, the suitability of most Russians, denizens of this land of "mystery and murder," for entry, remained in question.[8] The concept of "mystery" encompassed uncertainty, discomfiture, and anxiety, expressed in nativist rhetoric about the increasing number of non-Western European foreigners arriving from the "East" (i.e., the "Orient").

Not only mysterious, Russian aristocrats, depicted in San Francisco newspaper illustrations in the early 1920s in fanciful and elaborate garb, also earned the label of "exotic," particularly since the depictions almost uniformly portrayed women. The term "exotic" in San Francisco's public discourse in the 1920s often referred to women from the "East," and, as such, carried racial overtones given that immigrants from the "Far East" to the American West were usually Asian.[9] That being said, Russian identity in the post-revolution period, with its complicated ethnic, class, and historical permutations, had a certain fluidity in America, and even more so in the American West, giving Russians options that other "exotic" immigrants generally did not have. Russians were nominally European, escaping the periodic manifestations of endemic racism against Chinese and Japanese people in the American West.[10] Russian émigrés, however, as Eastern Europeans, and arriving in San Francisco from the "Orient," still confronted official and unofficial attitudes, rhetoric, and public discourse identifying them as culturally and "racially" inferior.

The notion of the Russian as "Oriental" was one that émigrés could exploit in different contexts, such as in European capitals, particularly Paris, where Russians worked rather successfully in the fashion industry in the inter-war period, and/or in terms of entertainment, blending exotic, purportedly Oriental, costuming and accoutrements with an existing "interest in exotic Slavic beauty."[11] The circumstances of arrival at a west coast port city, however, of groups dominated by males (instead of exotic beautiful women), usually in steerage, amongst equally impoverished travelers from Asian countries, were, in the eyes of AIIS officials, more reminiscent of an "invasion," given the hostility to Asian immigration. As such, once gaining entry, acculturating to American society during the inter-war period included embarking on the process of attaining a "state of whiteness," which involved distinguishing Russian culture and ethnicity as strictly European while simultaneously downplaying or even erasing cultural markers Americans found excessively "foreign," including names.

Americans, influenced by US government official rhetoric in the post-World War I Red Scare environment, on the one hand, and media sources on the other, developed certain gendered images of Russians, one of which spoke directly to the stereotypes of the *Literary Digest* excerpt:

the Russian anarchist and/or "Bolshevist" communist was a dangerous, "savage," and murderous male. In contrast, the "émigré" was an aristocratic, exotic, and romantic sojourner, often pictured as female, seeking shelter in civilized America. The first was a candidate for exclusion or deportation, the second an object of fascination, pity, and salacious interest.

Complicating the reception and perception of Russians as well was the political fallout of the Bolshevik Revolution. Immediately prior to the first arrival of Russians from the Far East on the west coast, the US government had taken steps to monitor and control entry and activities of anarchists and radicals, leading to large-scale programs that set the stage for the creation of the American surveillance state, largely focusing on foreigners, and Russians in particular. US officials, generally uninformed about the complex political situation in Russia, did not distinguish between "Red" (later "Soviet") and "White" Russians. Because post-World War I social and labor violence created a war zone mentality in American urban spaces, perceptions of Russians as radicals reinforced hostility specific to their ethnic identification.

The focus on émigrés in public discourse as feminine representations of the "exotic," on the other hand, at once elite and ornamental, but also powerless, created an image for the public encouraging acceptance, as opposed to the negative perceptions of Russian males. Émigrés seemed to recognize this dichotomy, with women often in the forefront of incoming groups for photographic purposes, and in subsequent performative displays of Russian culture in public events (discussed below and in chapter 3). Complicating the situation further for male arrivals, the acting Imperial Russian consul in San Francisco, George Romanovsky (1886–1933), had cooperated enthusiastically with local authorities to find purported anarchists or Bolsheviks, focusing on the activities of Spiritual Christians on Potrero Hill, even while acknowledging that the hunt for foreign invaders identified as dangerous was a promulgation of stereotypes that potentially harmed all Russian arrivals. Conscious of nativist and official hostility on both ethnic/cultural and political grounds, émigrés contributed to a narrative that they were sojourners in the United States, soothing fears of another immigrant invasion by non-Western Europeans, perceived as uncivilized, likely communists or anarchists, rivals in the labor market, and carriers of disease.[12]

Aliens of the Anarchistic and Kindred Classes

Events in Russia after the Bolshevik seizure of power in October of 1917, particularly the bloody and protracted Civil War, contributed to an increasing sense of unease on the part of President Woodrow Wilson and administration officials. Upon the Red Army victory, the fear of communism became a pillar in the foundation of US policy as evidenced by military and governmental preparations for domestic insurrection. US government concerns about communist infiltrators contributed to the creation of a threatening image of the mysterious Russian and, after the Bolshevik seizure of power, anyone identified as "Russian" in the immigration process was automatically labeled a "Bolshevik agent" by immigration authorities, regardless of political affiliation, social status, or background.[13]

The growing fear of communism culminated in the detention and deportation of mostly working-class Russian immigrants nationwide during the "Red Scare" of 1918–20, when émigrés were just beginning to arrive at US ports.[14] Attorney General A. Mitchell Palmer approved raids of "subversive organizations" by federal agents and local police in 1919, netting self-identified anarchists such as Emma Goldman and Alex Berkman; the majority of Russians or Slavs deported, however, were simply members of labor organizations gathering to learn English or life skills such as driving.[15]

Federal officials had established new country-wide security systems and measures during World War I, which continued after the war's end. In the western United States, Army military intelligence, partnering with local law enforcement and "local patriotic groups," ran surveillance operations, covertly entering workplaces and residences. The western faction of the Industrial Workers of the World (IWW) was very active in San Francisco, as was the UORW. In response, Army intelligence housed its west coast headquarters in the Flood Building in San Francisco (where Romanovsky also had an office) in 1918, pooling intelligence with the Office of Naval Intelligence and the Bureau of Investigation, also based in the building. The US Post Office assisted in censorship during the war, and the military examined "one hundred thousand pieces of mail" in San Francisco in the summer of 1918 every week, indicating an already well-established surveillance state.[16]

The "war spirit" fomented paranoia, often directed against Russians in particular.[17] Elena Varneck (1890–1976), an employee of the Russian Embassy in Washington, DC, in 1917, who remained in America, shared her recollections with émigrés in San Francisco upon relocating to the

Bay Area: "Those of us who were here ... [from 1918 to 1921] ... of course remember the insane Red Scare of [A. Mitchell] Palmer and [Clayton R.] Lusk and the *hysterical* demands ... to be one nation with one language."[18] Cognizant of dominant culture xenophobia aimed at non-Western Europeans, Russians understood early on that maintaining cultural heritage in a nativist environment required delicate negotiation.

A post-World War I Army War College committee report, drafted in response to increased racial unrest and labor strikes, identified the United States as an "Anglo-Saxon" nation under threat from "Russians and Austro-Hungarians" as the "most dangerous element" and "Eastern and Southern Europeans" as "fomenters of revolution." The War Plans Division subsequently "developed War Plans White," a blueprint to combat a possible domestic insurrection.[19] Dominant culture fear of steady large-scale non-Western European immigration led, as noted, to the increasingly restrictive laws over the course of the early 1920s. In correspondence, officials regularly referred to arrests and deportations of "aliens of the anarchistic and kindred classes" as the individuals and groups of greatest concern, with the majority Slavic.[20] AIIS, where arriving immigrants were detained, was also a hub of deportation activity under a Department of Labor deportation program that began in 1914, lasting through 1931: a regular "deportation train," which began in Seattle, stopped in San Francisco, and headed east, collecting "deports" on its way to New York. The westbound line took a southern route, terminating at AIIS.[21] Simply being identified as a radical was enough to get a Russian immigrant deported: Paul Melnicoff, an associate of Alexander Gavriloff, who had admittedly attempted to assassinate a police informant in San Francisco, was arrested, confined at AIIS, and deported in 1920.[22]

As overt actions and raids wound down due to public discomfort, covert monitoring programs developed into institutionalized intelligence and counterintelligence systems in the United States. The Red Scare "established patterns of thought that would become revitalized in later times of crisis," during labor unrest in the 1930s and the McCarthyist period in the 1950s in particular.[23] The "first Cold War," in fact, lasted until 1933, when President Franklin D. Roosevelt normalized relations with the Soviet Union.[24] Even with that normalization of relations, however, rhetoric pointed to the "Kremlin" and "Moscow" as directing activities bent on undermining American institutions. Foreigners and Russians were consistently identified as such no matter how long they had been in the United States, constituted an internal threat, as long as they manifested markers of "Russianness."

Consul Romanovsky in San Francisco

In San Francisco, George Romanovsky, the acting Russian consul, maintained a close relationship with local law enforcement in their efforts to monitor radical groups. After the fall of the Imperial Russian government in February/March of 1917, the Russian Imperial consul in San Francisco, Artemy Wywodtseff (1853–1946), had continued operations with the financial support of the US government, stepping down in December of 1917. Romanovsky took on the role of acting consul.[25] He noted in 1919 that both federal and local law enforcement put quite a lot of effort into "catching Bolsheviks" as directed by government agency officials in Washington, DC. Further, the consul wrote, "I would not be surprised if there was an attack [by American Legion members] on so-called Russian Hill where Russian immigrants live in San Francisco. According to my information and [according] to the Department of Justice, there is a warehouse where underground literature is stored and a small-scale printing press."[26] "So-called Russian Hill" was, in fact, Potrero Hill.[27] In an earlier report, Romanovsky made a point to specify that the "Russian Bolsheviks" in San Francisco were all "Sectarians": "Holy Jumpers, Baptists, Subbotniks and those who referred to themselves as Molokane," deliberately distancing Orthodox Russians from Potrero Hill population.[28]

Romanovsky continued San Francisco Imperial Russian consulate practices of keeping tabs on Russian expatriates and developed a close relationship with the San Francisco Police Department. Consular files included information on groups such as the Workers' Red Cross and the San Francisco Society for the Co-operation with the Russian Revolution.[29] He not only translated a circular of the UORW, seized under a search warrant for a federal agency, but also provided an eleven-page list of names of Russian "Bolsheviki and Radicals" from his own files to that agency.[30]

Despite his cooperation with US authorities, Romanovsky was cognizant of the fact that those authorities preferred to focus their efforts on "foreign" threats, particularly Russians, rather than on homegrown leftists. In his opinion, American leftists with extremist views fomented most of the unrest in the United States and supported the Bolsheviks in Russia: "the Americans are loathe to admit that the leaders of the Bolshevik movement (as I cannot call it anything else) in the States are not Russians or foreigners but one hundred percent born and bred Americans."[31] Nevertheless, Romanovsky's attitude towards working-class

Russians was "haughty" and those who approached him for assistance as an official representative of the (anti-Bolshevik) Russian government, faced an "icy reception."[32]

Romanovsky's efforts to assist law enforcement clearly distinguished between opponents or supporters of the Bolshevik regime. In his report, he related that the Department of Justice was preparing to arrest several Russian agitators in San Francisco whose names had been on the aforementioned list of "Bolsheviki and Radicals." One of these radicals slated for arrest was Molokan Fred Sysoeff (1881–1968), a leading figure in his community who had arrived in 1906 and who later clashed with the émigré community about their representations of Russian culture in public events (see chapter 3).[33] When the authorities did not take action against radicals quickly enough, "patriotic" groups like the American Legion stepped in, "storming the headquarters of the Communist Labor Party and the office of the *World*, a radical newspaper in Oakland" in November of 1919. They "dismantled both places and made a bonfire outside of red flags, pamphlets, and revolutionary leaflets."[34] Despite the recognition that homegrown radicals led most of the unrest, the image of the dangerous Russian, promulgated by US government authorities, taken up by groups such as the American Legion and helped along by Romanovsky, informed the actions of immigration authorities when processing the increasing number of Russian arrivals at AIIS from 1918 forward.[35]

As early as 1918, Romanovsky had recognized the significance of the post-revolution Russian refugee phenomenon, and its differing nature in comparison with pre-1917 arrivals, noting that the Russians fleeing the situation in their homeland belonged, in large part, to the "educated class."[36] Romanovsky's zealous assistance to US authorities and enthusiastic condemnation of one group of Russians, however, contributed to reinforcing a certain image of all Russians to American officials. Russian students, hundreds of whom arrived between 1920 and 1925 from Harbin, complained in 1923 in the Berkeley-based Russian National Student Association (RNSA) bulletin that Americans considered "all Russian students Bolsheviks" questioned the students' right to come to America, and were of the opinion that "the majority of Russian students are morphine addicts and smoke opium."[37] The labeling of Russians as exotic (in addition to being radical), combined with the fact that they came from the Far East, therefore included the stigma of exotic and/or illicit behavior. Russians became identified with drug use, an undesirable "foreign" habit which stemmed from and/or contributed to an ambiguity in perception about Russian ethnicity. According to Berglund, opium dens in San Francisco were "tourist destinations" that "differentiated Chinese from white Americans."[38] Since Russians coming to San Francisco were arriving from China and were culturally different from Western Europeans, Americans ascribed "exotic" unwholesome habits to them.

Aristocrats, Femme Fatales, and Red Agents

Given the lack of knowledge about Russia, Americans generally did not understand why the émigrés were coming to the United States. While public discourse did identify Russia as a violent and "primeval" place, Nadia Shapiro noted that Americans often asked her why the Russians had not fought the Bolsheviks, indicating a complete unawareness of the Civil War and its consequences in terms of massive casualties and destruction.[39]

Coverage in San Francisco newspapers in the early 1920s skewed towards romanticized accounts focusing on arriving exiled Russian nobility to attract readership, which often provided an impression of refugees who either did not need assistance or who well-deserved their now straitened circumstances after years of living in luxury at the expense of the oppressed Russian people. An article detailing the escape of Grand Duchess Olga, sister of the murdered czar, in "From Royal Robes to Rags," included a subheading declaring that the "beautiful Grand Duchess Olga" was "rescued from a life of abject poverty in a broken-down box car"[40] (figure 2.1).

Another writer cautioned readers to "be kind to your cook and your chauffeur because they may be Russian nobles and noblewomen in disguise."[41] Exiled Russians in Paris, in the meantime, were "cling[ing] pathetically to ... the old embassy building ... where their aristocratic tottering heeltreads echo through the empty halls," while the Russians in Montmartre enjoyed their "certain flare of mystery – especially women ... as has always the Russian in the Western world."[42] Prevailing notions, then, continued to characterize "exiled" Russians as pathetic but also enigmatic and mysterious in their new situations of poverty. One article title asked readers, "Does a General Wait on Your Table or a Countess Mend Your Clothes?" gleefully focusing on the comeuppance former elites now experienced.[43] That these articles appeared in the *San Francisco Chronicle*, despite the fact that the vast majority of refugee nobility either remained in Europe or settled in the eastern United States, misrepresented the nature of the growing Russian community in San Francisco and reinforced the idea that all Russians who opposed the Bolshevik

Ethnic and Class Ambiguities | 53

Figure 2.1 The *San Francisco Chronicle* published this illustrated article depicting Grand Duchess Olga Alexandrovna (1882–1960), sister of Czar Nicholas II, in "royal robes" in background and scrubbing floors in the foreground. The caption under her portrait noted that it was taken "while she was at the height of her popularity at the Imperial Court of Russia," underscoring the changed circumstances in which she lived. She did flee Russia in February of 1920 after spending some months in the Crimea, though she likely never scrubbed floors.

regime were elites. Even popular American fiction of the period utilized "bedraggled expatriate" and "somewhat ridiculous" Romanoff cousins or "ex-Dukes" to characterize the diaspora.[44]

The reference to women "especially" in the above-noted article on Paris, on the other hand, was indicative of depictions of Russian émigré women, with San Francisco newspapers including elaborate illustrations of Russian women in traditional dress, either emphasizing their physical appearance (i.e., their "beauty," exoticism, and consequent ornamental value), the "unspeakable" conditions they endured, and/or dramatically focusing on the pathos or "romance" of aristocrats reduced to poverty.[45]

Reporters inevitably focused on young attractive "aristocratic" women among arrivals, thus effectively erasing the identities of other arrivals. USAT *Merritt*, a ship carrying 526 Russian naval officers, seamen, military men, and their families from the Philippines, where they had landed after leaving Vladivostok, docked in San Francisco on 1 July 1923. A full-page spread with photographs covering the event focused on Mrs Lydia Klymontovich (1901–1964), describing her as a "pretty Russ [sic] noblewoman" in the title, and noting that she and her young daughter were "two charming members of the party of pilgrims." Klymontovich, "driven by revolutionists from her feudal estate in Russia" and looking "every inch an aristocrat," was "universally pronounced the prettiest woman among all the Russian pilgrims."[46] Her class status and physical appearance within the group garnered attention, obscuring the fact that the group consisted mostly of military and naval men, as well as seventeen members of the group who were illiterate, easing her way for entry, but providing an inaccurate impression of the group.

The insistence on characterizing Russian refugees in ways that emphasized elite origins was not limited to adults. In August of 1920, the city of San Francisco had welcomed what the American press called a "Kiddie Ship," a transport carrying approximately 800 Russian children bound for their home in Petrograd after being stranded in Siberia for more than two years while the Civil War raged. San Francisco city fathers were enthusiastic about the event and met the children with festivities when it docked at Pier 29. The newspapers described the children as "little Olgas and little Ivans" and, with no basis, identified them as "little scions of the old Russian aristocracy." In reality, the children's parents' occupations ran the gamut from engineers and surgeons to shop managers, mechanics, clerks, factory workers, and washerwomen – with perhaps a few out of the 800 belonging to the upper classes.[47]

Individual stories involving dramatic flight and triumphant escape fed the public's appetite. Eighteen-year-old Tamara Laub (1901–1983), with her "pathetic, piquant little face ... lighted with the great flashing dark eyes of the Slavic beauty" caused a stir by performing in "Cossack" costume in San Francisco after arrival in 1920, with two daggers "dangling from her waist and a belt of cartridges encircling her throat." She told a

Ethnic and Class Ambiguities | 55

"thrilling tale" of "capture by revolutionists in Odessa ... escape on an English transport, her arrival here and reception by the Russian consul, George Romano[v]sky." Laub utilized the attention to further a stage career, a useful tactic for Russian women who needed to make a living, parlaying their talent into income. Laub contributed to her romantic image by telling the press that her father was a nobleman who lost his estates and to whom she sent food and assistance.[48] Her father Alexander Lawb, however, had arrived at Blaine, Washington, in 1919 and was residing in San Francisco in 1920.[49] Émigrés learned early on to manipulate tropes to their benefit.

With the continuing influx of refugees streaming in from the Far East, San Francisco publications had plenty of fodder, albeit selectively chosen, to continue presenting an exotic, picturesque, and feminized aspect of the Russian diaspora to the public. Russian males entering through AIIS, however, were a potential threat and detention was an automatic response. In February of 1918, officials detained Nathan S. Kaplan, president of the Russian Art Film Corporation, who had in his possession a motion picture film of the actual Bolshevik seizure of power, as "customs regulations prohibit[ed] the importation of prize-fight pictures" and the customs censor considered the footage of the fighting to be more of a "free-for-all fight" rather than "a sure enough war." Reducing the October Revolution to the level of a street brawl, officials held the filmmaker on charges of attempting to import contraband. Kaplan fruitlessly claimed to be French and based in Yokohama, evidently recognizing that Russianness was a liability and attempting to distance himself from that identity.[50]

News coverage of immigration authorities in San Francisco detaining men from Russia after 1917 focused on possible "Bolshevist" affiliations of the subjects involved. Four Provisional All-Russian Government officials, headquartered in Omsk, Siberia, forced out when Admiral Alexander Kolchak's supporters seized power in November of 1918, set off for Paris via San Francisco, and were summarily detained by US authorities at AIIS in February of 1919. A reporter referred to one of the group, Nicolai Avksentyev, as a "visitor" to San Francisco, obfuscating the fact that he had been forcibly detained. Why authorities decided to investigate the group was unclear (though all four were, in fact, Socialist-Revolutionaries, they likely did not share this information with officials).[51] All were released and continued their travels, ending their lives in exile either in Europe or the United States.

Two other officials, this time of the Kolchak government, which had fallen by the end of 1919, Vladimir Vichmitroff and Denepro [sic] Salavieff, "were removed with great secrecy by the immigration officials to Angel Island" upon arrival that same year. A headline screamed that port officials had seized "Russians as 'Red' Agents" and authorities convened a special board of inquiry to investigate their right to remain in country despite acknowledging that the men had been "in favor with the [anti-Bolshevik] Kolchak government prior to its collapse" in November.[52] The following day a new headline declared, "US Releases Russians Held as Bolsheviki," and the two men were allowed to depart as "no reason for their detention was found."[53]

The policy of US immigration agents at AIIS, with respect to Russian males, was to detain first and ask questions later; detention of all third-class passengers soon became *de rigueur*.[54] The fear of radicalism also trumped notions of non-threatening femininity. Lubov Shulgovsky (1880–1970), who had arrived on USAT *Merritt* with her husband and two children, was "ordered deported" as immigration officials decided she had "radical views." Her grief-stricken husband and children were admitted, protesting that Lubov was no radical but "a mild, loving helpmate and mother."[55] Newspapers added fuel to the fire, titling an article "*Red* Refugees Denied Entry," despite the fact that the group had departed Vladivostok as the Red Army entered the city, and were therefore clearly "White" Russians.[56] Shulgovsky was slated for exclusion. At that point, the circumstances of the case become murky. Contrary to the accusation of her "radical views," the board of inquiry roster listed the entire family as Liable to be Public Charges (LPCs), which focused on economic, rather than political, concerns. Authorities subsequently reprieved the detainees due to more pressing issues, and by December of 1923 Lubov was out of custody and living in a San Francisco hotel.[57] The arbitrary justifications for detention and commensurate lack of transparency served to further traumatize people who had already experienced years of violence and displacement, the consequences playing out over time.

Sojourners, not Immigrants

Similar to Nadia Shapiro, arrivals claiming student status in the early 1920s, consciously responding to American nativist feeling and rhetoric, stressed their intentions to return to their homeland when speaking with the press or officials. Prospective student Nadejda Hayeff (1901–1996) told a reporter that the Bolsheviks had confiscated her family home in

Ethnic and Class Ambiguities | 57

Figure 2.2 An enlarged photo of Nadia Shapiro upon arrival at AIIS in August of 1922, representing the group of students with whom she arrived. Below, she is in a group of male students. The caption noted that the students were "held for US quiz," which was, in reality, an intensive interrogation of the group by both US Labor and Justice Department officials.

Blagoveshchensk on the Amur River in 1919 and "expressed herself as eager to learn about America and American ways of doing things in the hope that someday she may return to her native country and aid in its reconstruction."[58] Hayeff studied at the University of California for two years and ultimately returned to Harbin, albeit after naturalizing in 1931. She and her second husband relocated to the east coast in 1935 when the situation in Harbin deteriorated further.[59]

Reporters interviewed a group of prospective women students who arrived in April of 1922, all of whom made clear they did not intend to settle in America permanently. Vera Buria (1902–1990), and incorrectly identified sisters Haipias (Ruzanna) (1906–1995) and Olga (Natalia) (1901–1997) Grdzelowa, who were Armenian, stated intentions to study nursing at the University of California at Berkeley, noting they were "looking forward to returning to their native land when the followers of Lenine [sic] and Trotsky have been driven from power." All three settled in the United States.[60]

Nadia Shapiro, a photo of her smiling face appearing in a local paper, took on the mission of explaining Russian identity to Americans upon arrival, stressing, for example, her family's "middle-class" status[61] (figure 2.2). A significant number of those arriving in San Francisco, like Shapiro, represented the professional and middle classes, the latter a stratum of society emerging during the late imperial period.[62]

Nadia Shapiro: Reporter and Spokeswoman

Shapiro, in her roles as a reporter and unofficial spokeswoman of the forming Russian community, was instrumental in raising certain questions about the meaning of ethnicity, culture, and "being" Russian in San Francisco in her reporting and writing in the 1920s and 1930s.

She stressed her family's "middle-class" rather than "bourgeois" or "intelligentsia" status when discussing her history, using a term Americans might understand, particularly given the American penchant for labeling Russians either aristocrats or peasants. As it happened, though Shapiro's family background was similar to that of many émigrés in San Francisco, it did include some anomalous aspects. Her father, Lazar Shapiro, whose own father had converted to Lutheranism from Judaism, had raised Shapiro and her sister Maria as Lutherans. Shapiro, however, was intimately familiar with the rituals, customs, and history of Russian Orthodoxy, which facilitated her relationships with all Russian émigré groups in San Francisco. Born in what is now the country of Ukraine, Shapiro spent her childhood and teenage years in the Siberian cities of Irkutsk and Blagoveshchensk-on-the-Amur. As such, for the rest of her life, Shapiro considered Siberia her home, wrote nostalgically about growing up there, and explored Siberian-Alaskan-Californian connections in her writings.[63]

Shapiro, particularly through her work at the *San Francisco Examiner* until 1932 (using the pen surname Lavrova), became somewhat of a bridge between San Francisco society and the Russian community. She cultivated an enormous coterie of friends, acquaintances, and professional contacts among Americans and Russians. Her narrative about Russia in her professional writing and correspondence with Americans paralleled the general Russian émigré narrative – the Bolshevik seizure of power was a disaster for Russia and the Reds showed their true brutal colors in the Civil War. Her recollections included Red Guard troops "butchering" thousands of people "in the streets" of Blagoveshchensk when her family fled in 1918 under machine gun fire across the frozen Amur River into China. Such were the violent and horrific experiences of many Russian refugees, though Shapiro also wrote of her feelings of excitement amidst the horror, perhaps indicative of her own risk-taking nature.[64]

Working at a San Francisco newspaper, Shapiro utilized her knowledge of the situation in Russia to further her journalistic career, actively highlighting the problems of Russian refugees in China in the 1920s. Although she was able to bring her mother to live with her in 1929, she never saw her father or sister again. Her family circumstances, then, paralleled those of many émigrés, who were often separated from family during the war or the process of migration and, in many cases, never reunited. Antonina von Arnold (1896–1988), for example, a student who came to San Francisco in 1923, recalled her father's face as he watched her train depart from the station in Harbin, looking "intent and slightly dreamy as if he knew we shall never see each other again. Never see each other again. Never, never."[65]

Shapiro considered her family as Russian middle class and members of the intelligentsia, equating the latter to the American concept of liberalism. In her description of the San Francisco émigré community, she later wrote to a Library of Congress librarian: "we are all '[W]hites' – that goes without saying, but we are liberals."[66] In a response to an American would-be author, inquiring about the particulars of Russian profanity, she wrote, "yes, I'm a thoroughgoing Liberal but I draw the line [at] Marxism and abhor communism: I have seen enough of them … during the first years of the revolution in Russia."[67] That identification with liberalism was not hers alone. Antonina Von Arnold used the term to describe her brother Boris's outlook, for example, tracing it to her family's elite and therefore educated background rather than his lived experience in the United States.[68] Shapiro's identification of her family as "middle class" was not entirely successful. An acquaintance, American writer Barrett Willoughby (1901–1959), effusively wrote in a recommendation about Shapiro's writing talents that "she is an aristocrat to the tips of her little fingers," insisting with a kind of intransigence that even those Russians who denied being aristocrats nevertheless had to be to conform to American-generated stereotypes.[69]

By 1924, Shapiro was an established reporter and, as much as she was able given the constraints on her by her editors, she focused her writing on human interest stories about Russians, the growing community in San Francisco, and the history of the Russian presence in San Francisco, northern California, and Alaska. In November of 1924 she spotlighted the life of the "Fighting Priest," Father Andrew Kashevaroff, once a student at the seminary in San Francisco, when he returned to the city from his home in Alaska in connection with "the biggest fight of his life ... defying the Moscow government that is trying to get possession of the Russian churches on American soil."[70] The battle concerned Russian Orthodox Church property worth many thousands of dollars with the Soviet government sending "Red" Archbishop Ivan Kedrovsky to New York to seize that property. The initial efforts proved unsuccessful and Kedrovsky filed lawsuits to gain title, including to properties in Alaska.[71]

Shapiro's prose about Alaska evoked the romanticized view of the Russian imperial project in Alaska and Northern California that became an integral part of the San Francisco Russian Orthodox community's narrative about their Russian-American identity. This narrative encompassed the spatial and spiritual foundation of an Imagined Russia that intersected with their Russian Orthodox faith, linking them spiritually to a space where that faith had become intertwined with Indigenous and pre-Euro-American history:

> Alaska ... the land of ... distant [C]reole villages, that in every tradition perpetuate eighteenth century Russia ... Alaska that has received gifts from [C]atherine the Great; Alaska, where eighty years ago the Russian Governor used to give balls for officers of visiting Russian warships; Alaska, where Russian church bells were cast over a hundred years ago at Sitka, one of which hangs in an orange grove at Ramona, California; Alaska, where early in the nineteenth century Russian mills ground flour and Russian workmen built ships for Spaniards of California.[72]

The language of Shapiro's description was evocative of what came to be the nostalgic narrative of Russian émigrés in San Francisco as they sought to make connections between their ancestral home, the Russian cultural legacy both in Alaska and northern California, and extant relics of empire, a mental territory that provided a spiritual foundation for their evolving Russian-American identity. Over time, the narrative informed the evolution of Russian émigré identity into Russian Americans, facilitated by the historic, but more importantly spiritual, links to the physical spaces they now inhabited. Shapiro effectively touched on every aspect of what would soon be a mytho-poetic collective memory informing Russian-American identity – the "[C]reole villages" supposedly perpetuating eighteenth-century Russia, the gifts of the Russian empress Catherine the Great providing a connection to the Romanoff dynasty (the martyrdom of the last czar and his family playing a critical part in the émigré narrative of traumatic loss); the church bells, essential to Orthodox worship, and a concrete artifact critical to Russian religious ritual, which were (arguably) cast in Sitka and sent to California.

The history of Alaska was important in another way with respect to defining Russian identity in America: the American view after the purchase of Alaska by the United States was that Russians were foreigners, which made their descendants, who in Alaska were almost all of Russian and Native Alaskan heritage, "foreign" as well. Shapiro's portrayal of Kashevaroff was the basis for how Barrett Willoughby, who billed herself as an "Alaskan" novelist, portrayed him in her 1930 "nonfiction" book about Alaska and its Russian history, *Sitka: Portal to Romance*.[73] Shapiro was a reliable source for Willoughby about Russian Orthodox practices, and Russian customs, history and societal structure, subjects about which Willoughby was uninformed.[74] Shapiro also wrote a full-page article about Willoughby's "romantic" novel about Alaska, *Rocking Moon*, providing free publicity.[75]

A critical difference in how the two writers portrayed Kashevaroff, however, was that Shapiro focused on his identity as an American of Russian heritage while Willoughby highlighted his foreignness – it is indicative that Willoughby described Sitka as "the quaint old Russian capital" and the first Russian American Company manager, Alexander Baranoff (1747–1819), as a "dare-devil little Iron Governor," just as she insisted on addressing Shapiro in virtually all of her letters to her as "little Nadia."[76] Infantilizing Shapiro under the guise of praise or affection established a dominant/subordinate relationship, something Willoughby consciously promulgated in her correspondence with her, as part of a generally patronizing attitude towards Russians as people with "quaint" customs and traditions, which placed them at a disadvantage to "modern" Americans. Willoughby's ideations of America as a modernizing nation in the inter-war period spoke to the perception of the United States as the emerging leader in terms of progress, both industrial and social, in the world. Russians in America, coming from a "backward" or even "primeval" country, to which they were, moreover, nostalgically attached, in the view of Euro-American social elites such as Willoughby, remained on a subordinate level if they failed to Americanize, or, in other words, completely assimilate.[77]

Shapiro actively contradicted Willoughby's impulse to place Russians in a subordinate category in comparison with (white) Americans but, in the process, erased Kashevaroff's Indigenous heritage. In her article about

Kashevaroff, Shapiro described him as trilingual, "preaching in slow solemn Russian, or precise English, or guttural Aleut," and as a Russian Orthodox priest who was conscious of the importance of maintaining Indigenous culture and Native Alaskan identity, insisting that native youths not "neglect their ceremonies and tribal traditions."[78] Kashevaroff was descended from the son of a Russian serf, Filipp Artamonovich, who came to Alaska in 1793 and married an Alutiiq woman, Alexandra Ryseva. Their descendants made up an "enormous" and very prominent family in Alaska, which was designated Creole by the Russian government due to Ryseva's Indigenous heritage.[79] After the American purchase of Alaska, however, Father Kashevaroff (as did other people of mixed Russian and Native Alaskan heritage) consciously downplayed that heritage, insisting that his family was "of pure Russian blood" even though his grandmother (and mother) were of Native Alaskan ancestry.[80] That effort to highlight Russian background over Indigenous ancestry spoke directly to American legal and social racial discrimination when Alaska became a US territory in 1867.[81] The subterfuge was so complete however, that Shapiro wrote in her article that Kashevaroff was "one of only ten full-blooded Russians in Alaska, the great majority of Russian Orthodox parishioners being Creoles, some with only a tinge of Aleut blood." Notwithstanding this privileging of Russian heritage, she also pointed out that "with *Russian freedom from race prejudice* he tries to bridge for … [his parishioners] … the gap between their own secluded villages and modern America." Shapiro attributed Kashevaroff's lack of "race prejudice" to his "Russianness," while the reality was that Kashevaroff himself was of Native Alaskan origins but chose to obscure that fact, perhaps to protect his children, five daughters and a son, some of whom attended school and lived in the continental United States.[82]

Willoughby, in her later book about Sitka, devoted an entire chapter to Kashevaroff and repeatedly emphasized his foreignness, labeling him a "connecting link between the Russian past and the American present," reinforcing the notion that Russianness was a curiosity in modern America: when meeting, Kashevaroff bowed over her hand in "his charming foreign manner"; Kashevaroff's "English was delivered with Russian vividness and a faint accent that made interesting his most commonplace utterances"; he used American slang in a "naïve and delightful" manner.[83] Kashevaroff, however, had been born in Kodiak in 1863, attended school in San Francisco, and was an American citizen, as he related later in their discussion when describing how white Americans accused him of

Ethnic and Class Ambiguities | 63

preaching "allegiance to the Czar" when he foiled their attempts to take advantage of the "Indians." Just as in his conversation with Shapiro, he focused on his family's Russianness, distancing himself culturally from his Native Alaskan congregants.[84]

The triad of Nadia Shapiro/Lavrova, Father Andrew Kashevaroff, and Barrett Willoughby illustrated aspects of the complicated nature of being Russian in America. Willoughby insisted on characterizing Shapiro as a Russian aristocrat, despite Shapiro's own explanation of her background, and Russian people and culture as "quaint." "Little" Nadia was Willoughby's own personal Russian, giving Willoughby an air of legitimacy when writing about Russians, but, in their correspondence, Willoughby pointed to Shapiro's foreignness and therefore inability to understand America without Willoughby's guidance. As a descendant of Russian colonizers, Kashevaroff was also a curiosity to Willoughby, who framed him as such in her writing about the "romantic" period of Russian colonization of Alaska.[85] Shapiro, who had to have some understanding of the social and sexual history of Alaska (i.e., Russian and/or Siberian men arriving without families cohabited with or married Native Alaskan women), nevertheless chose to follow along with Kashevaroff's insistence of his "pure" Russianness, but felt the need to stress Russian "lack of race prejudice." A factor in this subterfuge was the erasure of the heritage of women in the Kashevaroff family, all of whom, including Kashevaroff's wife, were descendants of both Russians and Native Alaskans. The purpose of Kashevaroff's subterfuge, however, was not to emphasize his "pure" Russianness to Russians but to Americans who, as much as they considered Russians "exotic," "mysterious," and "foreign," nevertheless did selectively grant them "whiteness," something a Native Alaskan's heritage would complicate given the racism Americans brought with them when they occupied Alaska.

Shapiro was aware of Willoughby's patronizing attitude, noting how the latter depicted Alaskan Creoles "in a condescending manner" in her writing, and considered Russian characters that Shapiro created authentic only if they were "vulgar" and "picturesque" with no "redeeming" features. Shapiro chided Willoughby for her "subconscious objections" to Shapiro's "Russian viewpoint," which in Willoughby's eyes did not understand or sufficiently respect American culture, accusing Willoughby of living in "your little ivory tower" on Hillcrest (in the community of San Carlos south of San Francisco). Shapiro's earnings, until she acquired a steady US government job after World War II, were very modest, unlike

Willoughby, whose books were quite successful. Shapiro explored all aspects of San Francisco life in line with her adventurous and curious nature. Thus, Shapiro noted that her social milieu included people that Willoughby never encountered: Shapiro ate lunch in cafeterias on the waterfront, "even" speaking to longshoremen she met "without being introduced"; she and Constance Dixon, daughter of artist Maynard Dixon, patronized speakeasies in San Francisco without male escorts, places that Willoughby considered beneath her. Shapiro noted in 1941 that the situation, in which Willoughby was "consciously or unconsciously ... attempting to create an inferiority complex" in Shapiro's mind, had gone on for many years and she felt it necessary finally to "stop and clarify it."[86]

Willoughby commensurately objected to Shapiro's mention of the "Amos and Andy Show" in a novel Shapiro was writing. To Willoughby, the show (on the radio in the 1920s and voiced by white actors) was an embarrassment and an "insult to Americans," and her objection was that Shapiro, a foreigner, selected a show that depicted African-American rather than Euro-American culture (her objection was not about the inherent racism of white actors profiting from their racialized depiction of African-American culture; it was that the show was "low" culture). Shapiro, bowing to Willoughby's authoritative knowledge of what was or was not proper, acquiesced to changing the reference.[87]

The prevalence of racism in America towards African Americans may well have gone over Shapiro's head – Russian émigrés' knowledge of US history encompassed the view, at least initially, that the enslavement of African people had been a negative phenomenon in US history, similar to serfdom in Russia, and was ended by President Abraham Lincoln during the American Civil War, leading to equality for all peoples.[88] *Russkaia zhizn'*, for example, the local Russian-language newspaper which began circulating in 1922, ran a full-page tribute to Abraham Lincoln in 1926 in honor of his birthday.[89] Jim Crow laws, oppression and persecution of African Americans, extra-legal actions against them with no consequence for the perpetrators, and continued economic and social discrimination perpetrated against African Americans in the post-Reconstruction era US South were subjects far removed from Russian émigrés' lives in San Francisco.

That being said, the reality of racism in America appeared clear to those who chose to see that reality, particularly émigrés who envisioned their future lives in America as an endless succession of menial jobs – in factories, on farms, as servants, or industrial workers. An émigré doctor, who could not find work in a medical facility due to his poor English, for example, and therefore working in a tannery "horrific in its unsanitary conditions," described himself as a "white negro" [sic] in American eyes, noting that difficult laborious work in America was considered "fit for a Negro or a Russian."[90] In making such a characterization, the émigré clearly understood the hierarchy of race that existed in the United States as well as dismissive attitudes towards Russians, whom Americans deemed inferior and suited only for industrial or menial jobs. Poet and writer Taisiia Bazhenova (1900–1978), asking the question as to whether Russians could be happy in America, noted that, in her experience, though "all kinds of people" applied for jobs at factories in San Francisco, including "Italians, Russians, Germans, French, Hawaiians, Negroes and Poles," most factories hired "only whites, no people of color." Bazhenova worked at garment factories and noted that only once did she see an African-American woman working at such a factory, at Levi Strauss.[91]

An émigré who openly criticized American racism was Victor Arnautoff (1896–1979), an Imperial Russian Army officer who, ironically, became a committed communist in the United States. An artist in San Francisco, he joined the American Communist Party in 1938 and worked as a muralist and professor at Stanford University. His art challenged dominant culture interpretations of US history: murals he painted in 1936, under the WPA program, at George Washington High School in San Francisco (a high school which many children of Russian émigrés attended over the years), depicted Washington as a slaveholder and Manifest Destiny as a genocidal policy.[92] In his autobiography, written after he repatriated to the Soviet Union in the 1960s, Arnautoff wrote of structural racism in the United States and condemned Stanford colleagues who feared to sign petitions advocating for civil rights, accusing them of moral cowardice in the fight against racism.[93] Arnautoff was undoubtedly a significant anomaly in terms of his extreme swing in ideology from White Army officer to devoted communist, but that factor also gave him the freedom to openly criticize American society as, beginning in 1936, he began to petition for entry to the Soviet Union.[94] Most émigrés, however, were not secure enough in their status, particularly given the recent history of identifying Russian immigrants with anarchism or Bolshevism, to express criticism of the country that was sheltering them, particularly since they had no intention of going to the Soviet Union. Though discussion about the difficulties of adjusting to American life took place in Russian-language public discourse in the 1920s (see chapter 3), acculturation over time negated the impulse, for most, to critique the society in which they lived, particularly if their identification as "white" Americans became, in the post-World War II period, just as, or more important than, identifying as "Russian Americans." Nevertheless, protests against American norms with respect to racist policies certainly did occur. Artist Michael Chepourkoff (1899–1955), who earned an art degree from UC Berkeley in 1929, witnessing the internment of Japanese Americans during World War II, tried to arrange for two of his interned friends to hold an art show. Both his art and his recollections indicated a disillusionment with the mythologies of American equality and freedom from oppression.[95]

Shapiro, on her part, was quick to pick up the American language of race, using the word "white" in a way that was not common to Russian expression at the time. In her autobiographical writings, she first quoted "a friend" and then simply began to write in her (English-language) recollections that she was "the first and only white girl who ever worked on a Japanese paper" when she lived for a year in Japan with her sister in 1919–1920.[96] In an article she wrote describing the desperate situation of Russian refugees and residents of Harbin in 1923, who were stateless, she wrote of the "200,000 white people ... placed in a position practically unknown until now to international law," as the identification documents they legally had to carry were issued in the Chinese language, which Shapiro described as "a string of incomprehensible hieroglyphs." She concluded that the situation was likely "the first and only case when white men and women have Chinese passports for all purposes of international relations."[97]

Her deliberate use of the term "white" to describe Russians in China played directly to American sympathies and fears of "yellow peril," focusing on race as opposed to culture.[98] In a 1925 article, Shapiro described how 300 Russian refugees replaced the Chinese crew of a steamer, who had walked off as part of a general strike, in Hong Kong. "The Orient is not a comfortable place for a stranded white man, who cannot possibly compete with coolie labor," Shapiro wrote.[99] Once again, Shapiro was attempting to distance Russians and Chinese as whites and non-whites. And here she referred to Chinese laborers as "coolies," taking another step in the direction of denigrating non-white laborers as "cheap" labor, with which "white men" could not compete. Focusing on Russians as white people in Asia played into the existing racial hierarchy in San Francisco that had developed by the late nineteenth century. Chinese people were at the bottom of this hierarchy in a racial divide configured between

"Chinese" and "white" rather than "black" and "white" as existed in the eastern and southeastern United States in particular.[100]

Russians were confronted with the issue of race immediately upon arrival in San Francisco. Attorneys handling the case of a group of Russian students detained by immigration officials at AIIS on 15 July 1923, because the monthly quota was full, planned to argue for their release based on their whiteness, according to the RNSA Bulletin. The law that officials had cited to hold the students, according to their attorney's opinion, "should apply only to members of the colored races, not whites." Authorities had made an "indefensible error," which he hoped the court would correct.[101] The importance of whiteness became clear to incoming Russians immediately upon or even prior to entry into the United States. They also recognized the dangers facing immigrants whom authorities did not perceive as white.

The effort to distance Russian from Chinese people in the eyes of Americans was just that: an effort under the American gaze. Amongst themselves, perspectives differed, depending on an individual's lived experience and, critically, how long they had lived in the United States. A writer in the 1920s noted that the reason Russians who served as soldiers in the Chinese emperor's armies did not feel like foreigners in the East, unlike in the West, was because of this "great history" of Chinese-Russian interaction.[102] Acknowledging feeling "foreign" in America spoke to the difficulties of the acculturation process. Nevertheless, an inevitable shift in perspective to identify as racially white was a response to experiences during the immigration process and recognition of the existing racial hierarchy. Given the economic difficulties that most émigrés experienced, the shift in their world view was accompanied by an acknowledgment that "whiteness" and therefore identifying as "white," which spoke to absorption of the hierarchical racial paradigm as "normal," led to acceptance and opportunity for economic betterment in the United States.[103]

The uncertainty about Russian ethnicity among Americans, in its turn, surfaced time and again in various circumstances, underscoring the necessity to appear white. In the mid-1930s, for example, the California State Emergency Relief Administration (SERA) funded a survey conducted by anthropologist Paul Radin (1883–1951), a nineteenth-century immigrant from the Russian Empire. Interviewers working under his guidelines were amateurs and did not utilize questionnaires. An interviewer wrote in a summary of information about a Russian émigré identified only as "Gleb" born in (likely) Orenburg, a city in southwest Russia, in 1901: "From his facial characteristics, it is impossible to tell his racial origin, for the traces of oriental influences are entirely absent. Therefore, we must assume his ancestors lived in this vicinity for centuries unmolested by the hordes of Genghis Khan."[104] Presumably, the American interviewer had spoken to a number of Russians, perhaps born in Siberia, given that these interviews took place in San Francisco, who appeared to him to have "traces of oriental influences" with respect to ethnic background – the only logical reason he chose to expound on "racial origin."[105]

The émigrés' relationship with American dominant culture began and remained on uneasy ground: existing American tropes about Russians and the commensurate American gaze that viewed the Russian as colorfully exotic (female) or inferior and dangerous (male) foreigners served to contribute to the development of a community ethos among émigrés that was often defensive. Referencing Russians as "mysterious" spoke to cultural difference, but, in San Francisco, the issue of ethnicity, referred to as "race" in the period in question, hovered persistently in discussion of acceptance of Russians into America. Questions that both American eugenicists and dominant culture representatives of the period raised about "race" necessitated a reframing of Russian identity in America, a reframing which began early on with Shapiro's discussions about the "whiteness" of Russians in Asia. As will become evident, the specificities of their culture – literature, music, art, language, religion, and history – informed émigré identity as Russian people. Culturally, "whiteness" as an identity held no meaning for Russian newcomers to America, something that began to change almost immediately as they encountered American immigration and legal policies as well as societal norms.

Russians identified as European upon arrival on American shores (although Russians from Siberia often initially identified as "Siberian"), but were faced with notions of Eastern European or Slavic inferiority incorporated into American immigration laws in the 1920s. Those ideas forced reflection on prejudices directed against Russian people. Changing conceptions of race in the inter-war era and the development of the notion of "Caucasian" vs "Oriental" also played a role in the development of what would later become a Russian-American identity. As Matthew Jacobson discusses, the process of identifying previously undesirable groups as white in America began in the inter-war period, thus maintaining lines of division based on race, with "Celts, Teutons, and Slavs" placed into the "Caucasian" category, thus providing Russians in America, as Slavs, official entry into whiteness.[106]

An additional complicating factor for Russians, however, generally absent from the experiences of other ethnic groups, was that simply identifying as "Russian" in America gave a political connotation to everything émigrés said or did from the moment of arrival, given the installation of the Bolshevik regime in Russia. Combined with the existing hostility and paranoia among US officials stemming from the anarchistic nature of pre-World War I Russian immigrants and their involvement in labor unrest, arriving Russians were faced immediately with the question of how to safely express their cultural identity, or whether to express it at all.

Acculturating under conditions of economic difficulty, socio-political complexity, negative public discourse, and contradiction contributed to an existing need among émigrés to, at times, detach from everyday American life. Their ability to do so spoke to their emotional and spiritual link to their homeland culture, a culture which they brought with them to America, and which became a bastion of moral support through the tumultuous period of the inter-war era.

—3—

BETWEEN DREAMS AND REALITY
Culture, Conflict, Identity, and *Byt*

Involuntarily, you are transported to dear faraway snow-covered
Russia or sunlit Ukraine with its towering poplars, trilling of
countless nightingales, and quiet magical moonlit nights.

CONCERT REVIEW, 1926[1]

Sameness in life and in work kills spontaneity in a person and
destroys his individuality, turning them into a soulless automaton
... People need a way to escape into a fairytale world, but to escape
without destroying themselves.

ANONYMOUS, 1927[2]

Among the few joys of Russian existence abroad, we should note a
great one in San Francisco: Italian opera director Gaetano Merola ...
[has established] a permanent opera and ballet.

RUBEZH CORRESPONDENT, circa 1933[3]

As early as 1923, San Franciscans took notice of a visibly developing
Russian artistic community in the city and its environs, with reporters
highlighting several venues: a Russian "artists' club" on O'Farrell Street;
a "dramatic studio" where "young amateurs stage plays" by Alexander
Ostrovsky and Anton Chekhov; and weekly Sunday post-church service
meetings in Holy Trinity Cathedral's basement, "where the only Russian
library of the city has been founded by the Rev. [Vladimir] Sakovich."
Even the town of Berkeley, across the bay and home to the University of
California, boasted a Russian art "cooperative" studio.[4] The creative efforts
of Russian artists, actors, and musicians, both amateur and professional,

may have provided San Franciscans with the sense that their city, on the periphery of the American nation-state and as such, perhaps, "provincial," was becoming increasingly sophisticated due to such an inflow of talent. The welcome of Russian artists seemed disconnected from the actual experiences of most Russian émigrés upon arrival at AIIS, where US officials were questioning the logic of accepting so many penniless refugees who might also harbor secret "Red" sympathies. Nevertheless, the focus on art and culture in the growing Russian community, though it did obscure the realities of the hardships of immigration, did speak to an important facet of life and identity formation for the Russian diaspora in San Francisco.

Despite the interest in and admiration directed towards Russian talent, drama critic Buford Gordon Bennett (1900–1984) pointedly focused on the "foreign" nature of Russians who had "braved the perils of their own *volcanic* Russia and traversed the *dangerous wastes* of Siberia," crossing "the wide Pacific" and landing in San Francisco to bring their art to the "Western World." Her language reinforced the prevailing notion of Russia as an uncivilized place, particularly when juxtaposed against the "West." In the theater, she felt she was in a "foreign land ... 'hurled' among strangers who speak a foreign tongue, think in a foreign way, and act according to foreign standards" when she attended a rehearsal of Russian director Joseph Dalgeim's Chat Noir cabaret at the Curran Theater on Geary Street in November of 1923. Seated between Russian consul George Romanovsky, whose pedantic commentary she found annoying, and *Russkaia zhizn'* reporter Nicholas Berger (1885–1939), she felt as if she were in "Petrograd or Moscow," likely the only Russian cities known to her. Romanovsky was eager to clarify aspects of Russian culture to Bennett, but his enthusiastic explanations fell on deaf ears as "everything ... was strangely foreign" in her view, excepting Austrian composer Johann Strauss's waltz, "The Pearl." Bennett's commentary was parochial given her credentials as a drama critic: though she acknowledged that the language of music was universal, she nevertheless concluded her review with the observation that the Russian performers had turned the theater into "a strange world, full of strange peoples," reinforcing their alienness.[5]

Identity formation in exile was part of a balancing act that émigrés, like all immigrants, had to negotiate. Life in America had its express demands for all immigrants, but émigrés, as reluctant immigrants and self-professed sojourners, had additional obstacles to overcome. The process of immigration, even if a voluntary and desirable choice of an individual, is nevertheless stressful, requiring enormous life changes and adjustments even in the best of circumstances.[6] Anxiety is a "constant feature of any migratory process."[7] The process for émigrés was abrupt, traumatic, fear-driven, and not voluntary. Moreover, few left for the United States with the conscious notion that they would immediately reinvent themselves as something other than people of Russian heritage. Even if they came to recognize early on that return to Russia was likely an impossibility, the decision to alter identity by changing surnames, for example, was not made lightly. In their interactions with Americans over time, Russians made conscious efforts to persuade Americans to accept them as they were, but culture clashes and misunderstandings often precluded achieving such goals except in very limited circumstances, such as in the development of interpersonal relationships (including marriages).

A further complication was the fact that members of the existing Russian community on Potrero Hill had no fond nostalgic recollections of the Russian Empire, often holding pro-Soviet beliefs. Many Spiritual Christians identified with the working class and had for years experienced the challenging conditions of both urban and rural laborers in California. Their perceptions of émigrés as elitists contributed to conflict, with spokesmen for Spiritual Christians assailing émigré groups as reactionary monarchists in the Russian press, despite the fact that the vast majority of émigrés in San Francisco dreamed of return to a democratic Russia.[8] Moreover, the reality of life for émigrés in the United States was that many of them worked as laborers, at menial working-class jobs, often for the rest of their lives. Class affiliations, then, were not clearly defined and became even more ambiguous over time, depending on perceptions of lived experience.

Neither did the émigrés have a unifying ideology. Being "White Russian" meant being anti-Bolshevik, not monarchist, in terms of political affiliation. Shapiro noted that the term "White Russians" was not sufficiently "inclusive" as the community included socialists, for example, and proposed that a more appropriate appellation was "anti-Bolsheviks."[9] Veterans who had fought in the Civil War and civilians who had experienced the horrors of that war were unified chiefly and sometimes only by their belief in the illegitimacy and criminality of the Bolshevik regime. Their feelings about the Romanoffs, for example, may have been linked to their nostalgic ideations of their Russian ancestral home, but that nostalgia spoke to cultural identity, rarely to their political beliefs. In the inter-war era, amid Russia Abroad in the larger context, many Russian émigrés were, in the words of Raeff, "monarchist in a vague sentimental

Culture, Conflict, Identity, and *Byt* | **73**

way" that had little to do with political affiliation or outlook.[10] Such a perspective remained prevalent among the inter-war Russian community in San Francisco.

The divide between the émigrés and the Spiritual Christians was not necessarily as definitive as it appeared in public discourse, however. Because an Orthodox community had existed in San Francisco prior to 1917, small though it was, some long-time Russian residents played a role in assisting in both émigré acculturation and interaction with the Potrero Hill community. These individuals associated with both communities and created links, which facilitated the process, along with evolving political convictions on both sides, of decreasing animosities over time. Moreover, the experiences of a group of Spiritual Christians who returned from an attempt to repatriate to the Soviet Union as part of a commune in the 1920s had a role in modifying their beliefs with respect to the Bolshevik-led government.

Another divide that formed, however, was one based on age, with younger Russians, who did not have their own memories of Russia, holding to the notion that maintenance of Russian language and traditions interfered with acculturation to American society. To the younger generation, whether it was the group that bridged the connection between Russian and American identity because they received their higher education in the United States, or those who arrived as children, adopting English as their first language, life in the United States often initially entailed living a dual life (discussed further in chapter 6). If these young people remained involved in Russian community activities, events, and cultural life, it was certainly so. One life, within the intimacy of family and Russian community events and traditions, encompassed the imagined Russian homeland in California with a spiritual connection to the Russia of their nostalgic ideations, and the other, the everyday interactions with Americans on the job or otherwise. Creative or artistic activities were a means of dealing with the difficulties of everyday life. Nonetheless, the practice of many adult émigrés, who held menial jobs but lived what they considered their "real" lives through Russian community activities, was generally not a viable option for younger people.

In this sense, the Russian concept of *"byt"* or "everyday life" played a significant role in how adult Russians coming to America in the inter-war period viewed possibilities of maintaining a fulfilling life. Boym's discussion of *byt*, translated in the context she explores as "everyday routine and stagnation," traces the intellectual history of the term in a discussion of "the opposition between … [*byt*] … and 'real' life" – the latter providing spiritual sustenance, purpose, and meaning.[11] As Catriona Kelly explains, the term *byt* "means something extremely basic," yet there is no one equivalent word or phrase for it in translation.[12] The concept was foundational in the struggle of émigrés to find a way to survive mentally in an alien environment as the conflict between "stagnation" and meaningful activity became magnified in the United States, where the bluntly materialistic culture brought material rewards and a chance of economic stability in return for "hard work," demanding both time and dedication, but little spiritual fulfillment. James Hassell quotes émigré Tatiana Metternich, who recalled how Russian refugee men in Paris, many of whom worked as taxi drivers, "joked about their work as it if had nothing at all to do with their real life," and Jean Delage, who distinguished between a Cossack colonel's "former life," which he lived in the evenings, donning his uniform and associating with compatriots, as opposed to his "real life," working as a porter.[13] These interpretations lacked the context of *byt*, an inevitable circumstance, particularly for people living in straitened economic conditions, as most émigrés did in San Francisco. Slobin discusses *byt* in the context of the struggle of Russian writers abroad "to preserve the language and culture of the diaspora," but that struggle among émigrés in San Francisco involved preserving cultural identity on a personal level as well, in a nativist environment that viewed Russian language and culture as obstacles to Americanization.[14] Many chose to live their "real" lives in what was, ironically, an "Imagined Russia," where they could connect emotionally, artistically, and spiritually with their homeland through creative expression and community events. Younger people, however, were not necessarily willing to privilege Russian culture over American, particularly if such privileging meant living in poverty.

The conflicts between "real" life and *byt* were also between Russian and American values, particularly in view of growing émigré acknowledgment that the Russia they had known now existed only within them, thus reinforcing the sense of responsibility to preserve it. Alexandra Serebrennikova corresponded from China with poet Boris Volkov (1894–1954), who worked as a stevedore in San Francisco. She responded to his closing comment in his letter, "Time to go to bed – I have to go to work tomorrow":

> A kind of sadness wafted over me when I read these lines. Is life in America only physical labor, work without end, mechanical ... without a glimmer of ingenuity or creativity?[15]

Serebrennikova's perspective indicated that she was able, despite the difficulties of life in China, to retain a sense of ingenuity, visualizing life in America, based on Volkov's description, as lacking in the type of creative stimulation she (and he) needed. In 1946, San Francisco Russian community leader Nikolay Borzov (1871–1955), in discussion with writer George Grebenstchikoff (1883–1964) about American values, wrote: "Americans know how to suck the lifeblood out of people, with a sweet pleasant smile, mayhap, on their faces all the while."[16] In her reminiscences, Antonina Von Arnold matter-of-factly noted that harmful competitive practices to "get ahead," were an "easy virtue of Americans," as was their "enslavement with things material."[17] These observations spoke to a recognition that maintaining the type of spiritual life émigrés yearned for, in the context of both a vanished homeland and the specificities of life in America, was not a given, particularly for the many who struggled to simply make ends meet. The generational divide, though not strictly defined, was particularly evident in that context of American life. Settling for a rich spiritual and cultural life at the expense of material comforts was not an option for those young Russians who rejected the notion that their real lives should take place in a dreamland that had nothing to do with the realities of American life, which emphasized the criticality of economic success. The recognition of this constant struggle perhaps played out in the making of a film by Russian Club members in 1933, titled "Dreams and Reality." Although the central theme of the film is unknown, the title is evocative of the experiences of San Francisco's Russian diaspora, whose dreams, hopes, and memories crashed against the inevitable realities of life as immigrants in America.[18]

The 1920s were largely a period of adjustment and cultural adaptation for émigrés, who learned about Americans and their way of life but did not, despite some concerted effort, succeed in teaching Americans much about Russian culture. Many émigrés completed the naturalization process by 1930 (despite the continuing narrative of return) but often remained closely linked to the Russian community they helped establish. Despite intra-Russian conflicts, disappointments, and failures in cross-cultural ventures, the foundation they established played a critical role in the continuity of Russian community in San Francisco going forward.

Performance of Identity and Intra-Russian Conflict

As the incoming émigrés in San Francisco began to organize into various groups including church-related organizations around the Holy Trinity Cathedral, charitable mutual aid associations, and literary/artistic circles, they, understanding the tenuous position of Russians in America, made efforts to control the perception of the émigré community's public profile. More often than not, those émigrés who initially attempted to cultivate relationships with Americans encountered incomprehension, or what was to the Russians open insults. Elena Grot (1891–1968), a poet and leading figure in the organization of émigré cultural events in San Francisco, related how, for example, "well-educated Americans asked me with amazement if there really were universities in my country."[19] Grot, from the city of Tobolsk, had immigrated with husband Alexander (1891–1980) in 1921.[20] She remained a leading force in the cultural life of the community, writing for both Russian language newspapers in the 1920s, *Russkaia gazeta* and *Russkaia zhizn'*, and taking part in a range of cultural activities and events, with groups initially meeting in a "modest" apartment.[21]

Because Russian professional artists sought opportunities in Los Angeles (due to the growing film industry) or New York (America's largest cultural center), San Francisco Russian cultural organizations were often amateur in nature, including "ordinary" people interested in the arts.[22] Artist Ivan Kalmykov (1866–1925), for example, spent only a few months in the Bay Area after starting the cooperative art studio in Berkeley in 1923, working with New York-born Grigory W. Golubeff (1891–1958), organizer of the Russian Artists' Club in San Francisco. Kalmykov departed almost immediately for Los Angeles. Nevertheless, Russians in San Francisco needed creative outlets, holding "day jobs" and combining creative activities with efforts to convey information about Russian culture to the American public through performance in various venues, with mixed results. Observers noted that "quietly and unobtrusively San Francisco had become an art center for a large number of talented Russians, who find in the California city a second home where to live and create."[23] Many of these "talented" Russians, however, had few options given lack of English-language knowledge and struggled to make a living.

A major event in September of 1925 was the California Jubilee in San Francisco, a massive week-long celebration of California's seventy-fifth anniversary of admission to the Union. Former California senator James Duval Phelan contacted Russian artist Avenir Le Heart/Liebhart (1885–1951), who

Culture, Conflict, Identity, and *Byt* | 77

was based in Los Angeles, about organizing the Russian community to participate in the parade of nations, an event showcasing the different ethnic groups in California. Phelan's request to Le Heart indicated a desire for picturesque tableaux, in keeping with the image of Russians as exotic and quaint. A complication arose, however, when Russian Spiritual Christian groups, whom Le Heart had invited to participate, insisted on marching under the Soviet flag. A proclamation of leftist political affiliations, particularly to the new communist state, was certainly not what Phelan had in mind. The pro-Soviet groups were subsequently "uninvited," and the émigrés marched under the tricolor Russian flag, with marchers surrounding a huge horse-drawn float topped with a representation of the czarist double-headed eagle (figure 3.1).[24] Russia in the parade was personified by Natalia Ilyina (1902–1996), wife of artist Gleb Ilyin (1889–1968). Dressed in elaborate pre-Petrine *boyar* costume and seated on a throne placed on the main float, Ilyina literally performed the feminized image of Russia, while also playing into the trope of the exotic and ornamental Russian émigré, a message that may have somewhat overwhelmed the intent of the Russians to showcase both their cultural autonomy and the richness of that culture (figure 3.2).[25] The lone and insipid mention in the *San Francisco Examiner* of Russian participation in the event was "a pretty girl, beseated on a throne represent[ing] … unified Russia."[26] Ilyina was surrounded on the float by women in costume, reinforcing the focus on the feminine (men in *boyar* costumes walked alongside the float and received little notice). Placing the women in a prominent central position in the contingent may have been a conscious tactic on the part of the Russian creative department in their organization of the parade.

Such a tactic spoke to how the Americans continued to perceive Russian men at the time: media coverage of Russian participation indicated some discomfort with overtly masculine imagery. The post-parade review in *Russkaia zhizn'* newspaper noted parade participant Alexander Ignatieff (1902–1984) representing Ilya Muromets, a legendary *bogatyr* (knight) who led the Russian procession in the parade symbolizing the "great power" of (Imperial) Russia.[27] Ignatieff was certainly an appropriate choice: arriving in 1923 as a student from Harbin, he stood over six feet tall and initially earned his living as a prize-fighter (figure 3.3).[28] His costume included a helmet, armor, a shield, and a spear, and he was mounted on a horse. In other words, it would have been impossible to miss him. An American reporter did note the "noble knight on a black charger" in the Russian contingent.[29] The official English-language program, which included a

Figure 3.1 The float for the Diamond Jubilee parade under construction at a lot on Van Ness Street (now Avenue) near the intersection of Green Street, circa early September 1925. Holy Trinity Cathedral is just south of the lot. Note the double-headed eagle atop the float, which earned umbrage from the Potrero Hill Russian community. Avenir Le Heart/Liebhart (1885–1951) stands in foreground at right in hat and suit. The other men and boys are unidentified, but all were likely members of the "Green Street" Russian community.

Figure 3.2 The Russian float in the night parade (one of the Diamond Jubilee events) on 12 September 1925 in San Francisco. Natalia Ilyin is seated atop, representing Russia, flanked by two guards. The women in her "court" are unidentified. All were dressed in elaborate pre-Petrine *boyar* costume including *kokoshniks*, traditional headdresses.

Culture, Conflict, Identity, and *Byt*

Figure 3.3 Alexander Ignatieff as the *bogatyr* (knight) who likely led the night parade Russian contingent in full costume, with weaponry, and his black horse. This photo was taken just prior to the event on 12 September 1925. Ignatieff is standing in front of the float on which Natalia Ilyin was later seated.

detailed order of procession for each parade group, however, made no mention of a knight riding a horse, indicating that the Russian side may have omitted him from a roster submitted to the parade officials.[30]

Not only did parade officials place great emphasis on the submission of "foreign" groups to the authority of the state (thus the disinvited pro-Soviet contingent), public discourse labeled the Russian and Chinese parade groups, unlike other "ethnic" group participants, as both "foreign" and "alien": the subheading of one article pointedly noted "Chinese lead aliens" (the other "aliens" were Russians).[31] For immigrants in general, and particularly those identified as perennially "alien," patriotism and loyalty, in the eyes of dominant culture representatives such as Phelan, "consisted essentially of willing submissiveness."[32] As such, the Russian creative committee may have omitted the figure of a knight in armor, carrying weaponry, leading to the erroneous description in the program.

The fallout from excluding San Francisco's pro-Soviet Russian groups included an enraged response against the "monarchists from Green Street," instead of against Phelan, who likely had a say in their exclusion.[33] Soon after the event, in a letter to the editor of *Russkaia zhizn'* newspaper, signed by Fred Sysoeff among others, the Russians who took part in the parade were accused of "presumptuousness" for taking part in the parade "in the name of the entire Russian colony." The latter characterization, interestingly, though castigating the "Green Street" contingent, combined the two communities into one, indicating that even in 1925 when conflicts between the two groups arose regularly, Sysoeff acknowledged their "Russianness" in common against the backdrop of American society. The writers accused all the parade participants of not only being "adherents of the czarist regime," with their "cardboard two-headed eagles," but also members of the Black Hundred, a Russian ultra-nationalist anti-Semitic extremist group in pre-revolutionary Russia.[34]

In point of fact, the émigrés arriving in San Francisco in the 1920s settled primarily in the Fillmore District, populated since the early 1900s by Jewish immigrants, some from the Russian Empire, who had either settled in the neighborhood upon arrival or moved there after the fire in 1906 destroyed the area south of Market Street.[35] The neighborhood was both residential and commercial with businesses frequently located on the ground floor of multi-unit apartment buildings. The interaction between the Jewish Russians and the incoming émigrés was based on common language and culture. Valentina Vernon (1899–1981), an émigré who owned the Russian Tea Room from 1924 to 1941, first on Russian Hill and later in the downtown business district, recalled that Russian Jewish storekeepers were "very very nice" and "helped the [arriving] Russians to settle in the Fillmore District." A pharmacist she recalled as "Mr Bachman," realizing the economic difficulties of the émigrés, arranged with Russian-speaking doctors to "make a special mark on the prescriptions," and charged Russian patients half price.[36] Joseph Cykman (1883–1965), another druggist who arrived with his family in 1922, owned "two wonderfully stocked" pharmacies in the Fillmore.[37] As such, the beginnings of San Francisco's "little Russian world," as described in later years by émigré social worker Antonina Von Arnold, encompassed members of the Jewish community.[38] The Fillmore was the central focal point of what was an urban enclave encompassing a number of ethnic groups, but which developed an unmistakable Russian atmosphere (chapter 5).

The diversity of the incoming Russians played a part in how the community developed, with people of varied geographic origins, social classes, and religious affiliations mingling. Many of the émigrés, as noted previously, were from the eastern and Siberian parts of Russia, as opposed to the western areas of the Russian Empire where the Jewish Pale was located (present-day Poland, Belarus, Ukraine, and Moldova), and

Culture, Conflict, Identity, and *Byt*

where pogroms targeting the Jewish population of the late czarist period took place.[39] Although the San Francisco émigré community was predominantly Russian Orthodox, post-1917 arrivals included Lutherans, Roman Catholics, Sectarians, Old Believers, Jewish Russians, and a few Muslims.[40] If they had been members of the intelligentsia in Russia, they had generally supported the February Revolution and accepted the abdication of the czar in favor of a more democratic form of government. If they were townsmen, merchants, farmers from Siberia, or other classes, support of the monarchy was certainly not a given. Ignatieff, for example, who portrayed the medieval knight, worked as a floor-layer in San Francisco for the rest of his life, and came from a somewhat petit bourgeois background in Harbin, not an "adherent of the czarist regime." His father, like thousands of Russians, had sought economic opportunity in Harbin, unavailable to them in Russia, in the early 1900s.[41]

Others in the Russian community held to the view that the February (not October) Revolution was "natural and historically inevitable in the process of the cultural development of the Russian people." Boris Volkov and George Kirov/Kirillov (1896–1992), a journalist who also plied a variety of trades, founded a "progressive" Russian group in 1930 to educate Americans about Russia. They labeled their group "non-partisan" and specifically excluded both communists and monarchists as groups with philosophies incompatible with democratic beliefs. Volkov considered Siberia his home and noted in correspondence to fellow Siberian Grebenstchikoff, that the "Siberian question" (i.e., Siberia's role in a post-Soviet Russia) was important to the group as well, nodding perhaps to the possibility of Siberian autonomy.[42]

A few months later, following the first outburst, another group claiming to represent Russian laborers and workers in San Francisco published a statement in the Russian newspaper accusing the "existing Russian organizations ... [of] ... regurgitating long obsolete slogans of the old landowners of Russia" and labeled those organizations as "undemocratic," "anti-democratic," and "counter-revolutionary."[43] Émigrés certainly would have agreed that they were "counter-revolutionary," but the implication here was that all Russians who did not support the Soviet regime were reactionary, former landowning nobility, and supporters of the monarchy. The nobility was greatly under-represented in San Francisco, although, admittedly, brothers Gleb and Peter (1887–1950) Ilyin, who were of a noble family, took leading roles in organizing events such as the parade. Nevertheless, for Spiritual Christians to claim that they were sole representatives of Russian workers and laborers was somewhat disingenuous since most émigré men were, in fact, working as laborers (see chapter 4).

Members of yet another group, the Society of Russian Culture in San Francisco, founded in 1927, declared that they, as Russians, did not accept Bolshevism, but neither did they wish a restoration of what had been, now "vanished into oblivion."[44] Arthur Landesen (1874–1935), a Bank of Italy employee who handled consular duties to assist the Russian "colony" in San Francisco from 1926, also specified to those who inquired that he considered himself to be the "official Representative of the First Russian Provisional Government, which was established after the revolution in March 1917."[45] His public identification as a representative of the short-lived provisional government, rather than the monarchy, indicated that the general outlook of the Russian community was in agreement with his position.

Undue attention to elite status or commensurate rhetoric in public discourse was rare and earned umbrage when it did occur in the 1920s. When an unnamed member of the newly founded Russian Club gave an interview to an American newspaper in 1927 and informed the reporter that club members were all "peers" (titled persons), princes, or courtiers of the last czar's Russian court, naming as such Ilyin and others, a facetious "letter to my auntie" appeared in the Russian newspaper. Editor Pavel Karelin (1884–1939) expressed surprise and poked fun at the pretensions of those who "would provide such information to American reporters."[46] Karelin noted that he knew most of the people named and certainly had a high opinion of them as fine people, but was so "amazed" to discover their elite status that his "pen fell out of ... [his] ... hand" from the shock, noting that even Fred M. Clarke, the Russian paper's publisher, was included in the group, and Clarke, as Karelin pointed out, "was an American."[47] The inclusion of Clarke as a "peer" was an example of the frequent miscommunications with American press representatives, who tenaciously sought aristocrats in the Russian "colony."

The focus on elaborate raiment and symbols of the czarist regime by the community in the parade, however, which exacerbated the antagonistic outbursts of the Spiritual Christians community, had been a conscious concerted effort to distance that community from radical elements, particularly since the dispute regarding flags had threatened general Russian participation in the event. Assuaging fears of a fifth column played a role in how émigrés portrayed their culture to the public. Moreover, given that the inter-war period in the United States was one of reinforcement and consolidation of national feeling, émigrés certainly understood that the popularized concept of "one hundred percent Americanism" specifically eschewed the idea of hyphenated Americans, much less manifestations of any "foreignness."[48] By focusing on previous iterations of Russian culture (pre-Petrine costumes and the medieval *bogatyr*), émigrés attempted to draw American attention to factors that posed no threat to American national consciousness or nation-building.[49] Several of the Russian groups walking in the parade, in fact, focused instead on the historic, albeit romanticized, Russian presence in California in an attempt to show the Russians' link to American soil, but that message was obscured behind the focal point of the Russian procession: the float with the double-headed eagle carrying Natalia Ilyin and her "court."[50]

Avoiding the label of "foreigner" was undoubtedly a factor in the decision for many to become US citizens early on. Whether or not they hoped to return to Russia, citizenship guaranteed a security they did not have as non-citizens, particularly because the documents they may have held connecting them to Russia had become invalid in 1921.[51] To maintain a status as a temporary resident in the United States contributed to a sense of insecurity more tenuous and uncertain than for other immigrants in view of the circumstance that Russians no longer had a home country. Vladimir F. Peshehonov (1887–1939), who arrived as a "student" in 1923, reflected on the meaning of Russian participation in the parade in the context of the "right to citizenship," combining it with references to émigré loyalty to their Russian homeland:

> Our participation in the parade was, in its own way, an examination for the right to citizenship. For Russian émigrés explicitly, and for Russian identity in the broader sense, our participation and our success have a two-fold significance. On the one hand, it is purely practical. Upon evoking the sympathy of Americans ... [our participation and success] ... will make it easier for Russians to gain ... [American] ... trust and, with that, will help émigrés secure their well-being. On the other hand, it is political. The whole world will now know that in faraway San Francisco, the love of the Russian people for their tormented motherland has not died nor has their loyalty to their historic national flag.[52]

Peshehonov's usage of the word "trust" was indicative of his acknowledgment of the tenuous position of Russian émigrés, relating directly to suspicion of Russia, now part of the Soviet Union, on political grounds.

Reference to the necessity of establishing Russian well-being and practical acceptance spoke also to that sense of unease and insecurity relating to negative characterizations of Russian ethnicity, culture, and customs in nativist America. And his reference to "their tormented motherland" had by now become a *leitmotif* in émigré discourse to reinforce the brutal nature of Bolshevik occupation.

The parade had, in effect, been a balancing act for émigrés to show enthusiasm for American political and cultural institutions while showcasing the richness of their own history and culture. Deliberately referencing certain symbols and events of Russia that clearly spoke to its past in such a public display identified them as non-threatening: the monarchy as a historical aspect of Russian culture with all of the accompanying regalia, imagery and emblems, such as the double-headed eagle (condemned by the Spiritual Christians); period clothing, which was also in direct contrast to the representations of Soviet "proletarian" garb and representations; and the tricolor Russian flag instead of the red Soviet hammer and sickle. Émigrés who saw the abdication of Czar Nicholas II as a necessary step on the path to a democratic modern state nevertheless considered associations with that aspect of Russian history and its symbols as a "safe" option in United States – one that clearly distanced them from any connection to the current Soviet regime.

Fred Sysoeff, however, not only castigated the émigrés as a homogenous elitist (and anti-Semitic) group in the Russian-language press, but likely promulgated those views outside the community to emphasize the stark difference between working-class Russian immigrants and the supposed monarchist "elites." The divide, though real, was not as sharply defined as public discourse indicated, with social interaction continuing between the two groups throughout the inter-war period, belying the hostile rhetoric in public discourse. In the early to mid-1920s, members of the Spiritual Christian community were also involved in a movement to repatriate, which explained, at least in part, their fearless and open support of the Bolshevik Revolution. As a result of that attempted repatriation, however, the divide between the two communities narrowed by the 1930s, likely because the vision of an egalitarian and socially just Soviet society Spiritual Christians anticipated altered when they encountered the regime firsthand.

Re-emigration to Russia

In 1922, Russian groups in California and other regions of the United States and Canada formed agricultural "communes," upon petitioning the Bolshevik government for permission to return and work the land.[53] That spring, a New York attorney and Russian government representative had announced that "a Russian colony in California is anxious to sell its farms and possessions and return to Russia."[54] "California Commune" members, who were generally American Communist Party members, established more than two dozen separate communes in the southern regions of the Soviet Union. Molokan families in San Francisco simultaneously formed a separate agricultural commune group. Promised land allotments by the Soviet government, several families sold all their belongings, purchased required farm equipment and other supplies, and departed for the Don region of Russia, convinced that the new government would provide supportive conditions for farmers. In their perception, "every consideration was subordinate to the interests of the laborer" in this new Russia, unlike what they had experienced in the United States for the past decade.[55]

Almost immediately upon arrival, however, the Molokane bore the brunt of attacks and robberies from "former Cossacks" purportedly displaced by the commune.[56] The San Francisco group began to petition for return. Unfortunately, they had never become US citizens, nor had they applied for travel permits that would have allowed them to return as resident aliens, as they assumed they would settle in the Soviet Union permanently. The quota for Russian immigrants to the United States was full for the "next 8 years" according to Kiprian Shanovsky (1884–1965), a former Russian Imperial official in San Francisco who had arrived in 1909. Shanovsky associated with both the émigré and Potrero Hill Russian communities and became a point of contact for the group that wished to return due to his official position at San Francisco's Bank of Italy's Russian Department. He shared the content of letters he received from those who had not followed his advice about taking US citizenship prior to departure. The children who had accompanied their parents to the Soviet Union, however, had been born in America, and were therefore US citizens, so they could return if they had their birth certificates.[57]

One of the children, Mary Bataiff (1905–1981), whom Nadia Shapiro described in her coverage of the ensuing events as a "determined San Francisco flapper," began a letter-writing campaign to US officials, engaging them in the effort to bring home the group (her parents and siblings among them). Mary wrote to Shanovsky in December of 1925 on behalf of the adults, focusing on the fact that the children wanted to return to America.[58] That focus on the children disguised the actual problems the Molokane faced: ongoing attacks and increasing Soviet government hostility. Losing all their investments, five San Francisco families returned in 1928, their perspective of the Soviet Union as a haven for workers and farmers shifting. Most subsequently naturalized.[59] Vasily Fetesoff, a member of the commune, spoke about their experiences in a public meeting upon his return.[60]

Intra- and Inter-Group Dynamics

The shift in thinking about the reality of Soviet governmental actions and policy may have contributed to a softening in perspective toward the "Green Street" contingent's hostility toward the Bolsheviks. Inter-group communication and activities between the two communities increased over time as well, in part thanks to the efforts of Russians such as Shanovsky, who was, for example, a congregant of Holy Trinity and treasurer of the Russian Club, as well as conductor of the Molokan Choir in the 1920s.[61] He had developed networks of business associates, both Russian and American, by that time, and his position at the Bank of Italy gave him some authority with respect to advising newcomers. As head of the Russian Department, opened in 1921 at the Bank of Italy (founded by Amadeo P. Giannini, in 1904), Shanovsky drew in Russian customers.[62] The bank's Russian-language information booklet included lists of Russian Orthodox, Jewish religious, and American secular holidays, indicating the bank served all the Russian communities in the city.[63] As the Russian community expanded, Giannini, harkening to his roots of serving the working man or woman, opened a Russian department aimed at integrating Russians into the larger community and hired Russians as employees (figure 3.4).[64]

Other pre-1917 Russians immigrants in San Francisco (noted in chapter 1) also developed relationships with the émigré community. Feodor Postnikov, long settled in America by 1920, wrote articles and essays about Russian immigration issues for the Russian newspapers. Postnikov met one of the first student groups arriving in San Francisco from Harbin in 1921, writing, "They need our advice in this first period, our sympathy and help in finding a 'job.'"[65] Despite his socialist leanings, Postnikov was sympathetic to fellow Russians, whatever their political viewpoints, arriving penniless and with few prospects. His leadership

Culture, Conflict, Identity, and *Byt* | 87

Figure 3.4 The Bank of Italy, Post and Fillmore branch, 1926. The Russian Department at this branch opened on 1 January 1926, and the assistant manager in charge was Gabdulla aka George Gafaroff (1903–?). A.M. Wywodtseff was manager of this branch in November 1927. Kiprian Shanovsky oversaw all the Russian departments for the bank. Émigrés worked as Russian department heads at other branches as well: in 1926, Pavel Orloff (1903–1990) and Sergei Samorukoff (1884–1970) at the main branch on the corner of Market, Powell, and Eddy Streets; George Nikolashin (1897–1966) at the branch on 24th and Bryant Streets.

role was relevant enough that when he stopped participating in community activities, people inquired about his absence.[66]

Long-time Sonoma County Russian resident and fellow socialist Olga Gordenker was vice president of the Russian émigré drama circle in 1926, and wrote for *Russkaia zhizn'*, reviewing, for example, a production of Chekhov's "The Cherry Orchard" by younger members of the group, chiding those who articulated "'silly' criticism" of the amateur endeavor. She asked: "Would it not be more appropriate to take off one's hat and bow from the waist to the Drama Society" for their efforts and for providing a "healthy outlet for youth, and shelter in the evenings to those without shelter – refugees who have lost their families?"[67] Gordenker also empathized with the new arrivals and the difficulties they faced, notwithstanding her political views. Significantly, Bishop Theophilus of Holy Trinity (formerly Father Pashkovsky) led the service at her funeral in 1932, eulogizing her as a person whose "tolerant, sympathetic outlook caused her to make friends among widely varied people, from staid conservatives to radicals ... And this trait we admired in her."[68] It was indicative that the bishop made a point to stress the importance of sympathy for people notwithstanding their political beliefs, an indication of tolerance emanating from an Orthodox spiritual leader of the community (who had also been a pre-1917 member of the clergy in San Francisco).

Jewish Russian attorney Nathan Merenbach's legal advice column appeared regularly in *Russkaia zhizn'* in the 1920s and he continued to advertise his services in Russian newspapers and event programs into the post-war period, practicing law into the 1970s. At Nathan's persuasion, his brother Simon relocated to San Francisco in 1926 from Los Angeles to run a housing construction and real estate sales business aimed at providing homes to the Russian "colony." According to Nathan, he frequently had to save his Russian clients from deals made with unscrupulous realtors and developers and hoped that with Simon's assistance the cases of Russians being defrauded would decrease.[69]

Real estate sales, in fact, became a common occupation for émigrés as they followed in the footsteps of several early arrivals such as realtor Pamphil Tesluck. Tesluck remained actively involved in the Holy Trinity Cathedral Parish and in the later founding of the Russian Center in 1939, continuing his association with the Russian émigré community into the post-World War II era. He also "married into" the community as his second wife was émigré Evdokia Georgesco, who arrived in San Francisco in 1925.[70]

The motivations for the pre-1917 Russian migrants with respect to leaving the Russian Empire certainly differed from those of the émigrés. In Postnikov's case, for example, he preferred the American representative form of government over a monarchy as a place to raise his children. Postnikov's enthusiasm for America and American culture, however, underwent adjustments over time. He initially changed his name to Fred A. Post when he became an American citizen, but petitioned the court in 1918 to change it back officially to Feodor Alexis Postnikov, indicating, perhaps, some dissatisfaction with subsuming his identity under an Americanized name. His daughter Valeria was dismayed at his decision to change back his name, indicating the differing perspective of youth: "I was so anxious to be an 'American' like the other kids that it was quite a blow to me when Dad insisted that we change our name back to Postnikov ... we loved feeling 'Americanized,'" indicating a different generational perspective about that process.[71]

An experience with US police authorities may have also shaken Postnikov's confidence in the American system. In 1919, he visited the offices of *The World* newspaper in Oakland, which also housed the Socialist Party's office, to buy literature about current events in Russia. There, he found plainclothes Oakland Police officers clearing out the office after a raid. In response to Postnikov's suggestion that "they prosecute ... [the organization] ... in a legal way," the policemen attacked and beat him. Postinkov was hospitalized and then jailed, even going to trial, but was ultimately acquitted. Despite his experience and lengthy career, he began to have trouble supporting his family in the 1920s, in part due to his political views. He later moved to Arkansas where he lived until his death in 1952.[72]

Failed Rapprochement

San Francisco provided a distinctive environment for the Russians to settle because of the varied representations of Russian identity they encountered in that urban space, but also because of the city's history and character: a port city on the Pacific coast, a first stop for travelers and immigrants from "the Orient," in effect sharing an ocean with the homeland the Russia émigrés had reluctantly left, and an urban center in the American West with a historic Russian and Orthodox presence. Despite a diverse multi-ethnic population and a significant number of Roman Catholics, however, Anglo-Protestant culture dominated in San Francisco because the economic, and commensurately social, elites were Anglo-Protestant: "Some of the wealthiest and most powerful families in the West" (e.g., the Crockers, Huntingtons, Floods, Hopkins's and Stanfords) built mansions on Nob Hill, to the north of the Fillmore.[73]

The commitment to maintain a Russian cultural presence dovetailed with recognition that to survive in the United States, Russian émigrés had to adapt to American cultural norms. In these efforts, they received encouragement from Merenbach, Shanovsky, and Postnikov, who urged émigrés to network with Americans through social events, considering such a natural way for them to commingle and form social relationships that could lead to employment opportunities. In late 1925 and early 1926, a series of articles appeared in *Russkaia zhizn'* supporting efforts to organize a "Russian-American Club." USAT *Merritt* arrival Boris Zonn (1889–1944), and editor of *Russkaia mysl* ("Russian thought") in 1927–28, noted that such previous attempts had failed, blaming the fact that most Russians did not yet know English and that the meeting topics selected were "dull," particularly for Russians tired after working all day. Zonn quoted an opinion of an American acquaintance that while Americans liked to talk about sports and money, Russians conversed about topics boring and sometimes incomprehensible to average Americans, indicating that both sides recognized the mutual bewilderment. Two American engineers initiated this latest effort after "studying the mistakes" of previous Russian American rapprochement attempts, acknowledging that Americans did not understand Russian "attitudes," but wishing to end the Russians' "isolation." Émigré Michael A. Bodisco (1887–1961) noted, in turn, that the impression of many that "the dollar" ruled American society was a biased one and stated his convictions that Americans simply needed an opportunity to understand that Russians were not only at the same "cultural level" as Americans but were even, in some ways, superior. He went on to say that in comparison with its technological advancements, American culture was "quite insipid," but conceded that it nevertheless had much that was interesting, particularly with respect to literature and theater.[74] Much as the Russians needed the Americans (as opposed to the Americans not needing them at all), they, in the content of these articles published in the Russian newspaper, which Americans thankfully could not read, nevertheless indicated that they would not tolerate condescension or superior attitudes from the "insipidly cultured" Americans, something that likely played a part in the failure of these attempts at rapprochement.

The first "informational" event, a concert and ball, held on 6 February 1926 at the Old Elks Club on Powell Street, failed completely with respect to any of the aims of the organizing members, which included both Americans and Russians. Few Americans attended the event; the concert program began a half hour late due to a streetcar accident; the program, in which Russian émigré performers Emma B. Mirovich and Tamara Laub sang and danced respectively, did not end until 11 p.m., at which time most of the Americans present promptly departed. Apart from the lateness of the hour, which tired the Americans, several of them stated that "they felt like outsiders amidst Russian speech they could not understand."[75] Watching Russian performers was something to which Americans were amenable, but socializing with large numbers of for-

Culture, Conflict, Identity, and *Byt* | 91

eigners who made no effort to speak English was not. Networking may have worked in more personalized situations: émigré and social worker Antonina Von Arnold noted that a small number of émigré engineers, architects, and physicians had the good fortune to come in contact with Americans who were "intrigued or entertained" by them in the early years of emigration and thus extended them opportunities that they otherwise may not have had. By the 1930s, however, according to Von Arnold, "there was nothing novel ... [about] ... a Russian émigré in San Francisco."[76] As a novelty or a curiosity, Russians garnered attention and some learned to utilize that attention to improve their economic situation, particularly if they were engaged in a profession they could parlay into an American career. In most cases, however, all Russians had to interest Americans was their "Russianness," and the interest therefore lasted only as long as such Americans were entertained.

N. Zelensky points out the "surprising" popularity of Russian shows and performances, namely Nikita Balieff's vaudeville *Chauve-Souris*, which was wildly successful on New York's Broadway and elsewhere in the United States in the 1920s (Joseph Dalgeim's version playing in San Francisco as well, as noted earlier), in view of nativist and political suspicion of Russians at the time. Further, "Russian émigrés were able to bypass the xenophobic trend" in a period when a "more inclusive understanding of whiteness" was taking place, providing Slavs an entrée into the ranks of white people in America. Notwithstanding the entry into whiteness through the medium of entertaining audiences, émigrés, according to Zelensky, capitalized on the phenomenon by engaging in "deliberate and marketable auto-Orientalism," given the existing perception of Russians as Asiatic, or, at the very least, "exotic."[77] The contradictions in play here are manifold but the crux of the argument, apart from the noted hostility towards Asian immigrants in San Francisco, hinged on the notion of performance. The nature of such performance necessitated subordination to the American gaze given the language in descriptions of that performance: "barbaric," "half-barbaric," "quaint," and "exotic" were terms to draw in American audiences in line with the notion of spectacle depicting uncivilized, even savage (as noted in the epigraph to chapter 2), people. In other words, the "eager consumption" of the "colorful Other" was not, in and of itself, a pathway to acceptance of Russian people as equals, at least as long as they remained identifiably Russian.[78]

For Russian elites, however, who appeared to dominate the émigré community in New York, according to Zelensky, gaining entrée into whiteness was less problematic by virtue of their class. Moreover, becoming white in the United States entailed acceptance of the American racial paradigm – once one perceives oneself as white (i.e., once one accepts the "'public and psychological wage' of whiteness"), one acknowledges that the racial hierarchy is valid.[79] In other words, a "state of whiteness" is achieved not only when dominant culture representatives perceive a group as white but when that group perceives *itself* as white. If Russians facilitated that process by catering to popular conceptions of Russian identity to outsiders, including "projection of the exotic self" through auto-Orientalism, they opened the door to collaboration on cultural appropriation and, commensurately, caricature, which, as illustrated by Harlow Robinson throughout his book and descriptions of Russians in American films, began in the inter-war period and continued onward through the Cold War era.[80] The American interest in aristocracy was a boon in social terms for those who could play that card, unlike in France, for example, where "Frenchmen generally, care[d] nothing for the Russian refugee's antecedents."[81] Marrying Russian aristocrats had cachet among Americans (chapter 6): Prince Serge Belosselsky-Belozersky (1895–1978), the "scion of an ancient and noble princely family" and oft-cited leader of the Russian community in New York, the "bearer and preserver of all the rich traditions of Imperial Russia," married an American heiress, Florence Crane (1909–1969), in 1943. Without his title, he would not have had entry into that society (Crane's grandfather was a member of the Millionaires Club).[82] The "social collateral" may have benefitted a contingent within the emigration, but was an impetus to others to distance themselves from the reinforced stereotypes of exotic Russian identity, the more so when realizations set in that émigrés were not sojourners but would likely spend the rest of their lives in America.[83] Being "intriguing" or "entertaining" to Americans, as Von Arnold noted, similar to Barrett Willoughby's relationship with Shapiro, placed Russians into subordinate, and therefore demeaning, roles which, by their very nature, were also of limited utility in the long road of building lives in America.

Émigrés in San Francisco persevered in attempting to find common ground, however, outside the paradigm of Russian performers in spectacles for American audiences, forming the Russian-American Society, which held lectures and involved the Rotary Club so that leading American industrialists and businessmen would take interest. The society invited Stanley Powell of California Packing Corporation to talk about his business and opportunities for individuals in American industry, for example, advertising in the newspaper and assuring Russians that they would be able to ask questions in both Russian and English.[84] In promoting another event in February of 1927, the organizers inadvertently underlined the lack of mutual interest, stating that they would attempt to make the evening interesting "for both Russians and Americans."[85] The failure to find common ground was cultural but also based on economic circumstances – the Americans whom Russian organizers were attempting to woo were wealthy, the elite of San Francisco society and, as such, considered themselves, if anything, as benefactors in the attempted rapprochement. To them, the Russians remained exotic, therefore interesting, but not their social equals. The Russians, likely sensing this bias, given the above-noted commentary about American culture, refused to make an effort to socialize on American terms, for example speaking English with an accent that might lead to condescension or humiliation. Nodding to that existing condescension in an article about the aims of the Russian-American Society, Nadia Shapiro utilized the word "romantic" in an ironic sense when describing American reactions to Russian admirals working as janitors and high-placed ladies as dishwashers, her point being the lack of "romance" in the situation for the selfsame Russians.[86] The commentary fell on deaf ears and these initial attempts at rapprochement faded.

Nevertheless, feeling the need for a centralized meeting place, a group with an alternate outlook about how to coordinate social events with Americans founded the "Russian Club" in July of 1927, with no pretenses that non-Russians would be members. However, when the club held its opening event, Gleb Ilyin's speech was in both Russian and English, and of the more than 500 people who attended the event, there were 150 "Americans" (meaning non-Russians) representing various organizations and clubs in San Francisco. They were, in effect, guests, and the Russians were their hosts. That group touted the event as a success as a good time was had by all. The club's stated purpose was to be a "purely social and cultural institution" and, significantly, "entirely apolitical in nature," but one that could "create the best conditions for rapprochement with American society."[87] Despite the stated optimism, organizers recognized that Russians were in a country that was "completely alien in spirit and lifestyle," but had adapted, as "each person could" and "with varying success." Further, the club, in the view of one supporter of the idea, gave Russians the "opportunity to tear themselves away from unappealing American everyday life," referencing, once more, the dreariness of *byt*.[88] If Americans came to the event, so be it, but the new Russian Club, finding its permanent home at the Westerfeld House at 1198 Fulton Street, remained centered on Russian interests and it was up to the Americans to make an effort to get involved and thus subordinate their interests to Russian ones.[89]

In concert with these efforts and general community growth and development, émigrés took part in cultural activities, including celebrations and commemorations, which spoke not only to the interest in the Russian historical presence in northern California space but to faith and belief, as measures to find meaning in their exodus and assist in combatting denationalization, stereotypes, or erroneous narratives about Russia (chapter 5). Theatrical and musical productions encompassing a broader cultural focus were also critical to intra-community engagement, and allowed some interaction with Americans, both through utilizing available spaces and American attendance at events. These events included both well-known visiting émigré artists such as Sergey Rachmaninoff and productions by local Russian talent.[90] As such, the intellectual and cultural activities were not limited to a select group of elites who dominated intellectual discourse within the diasporic group, as was the case in urban centers such as Paris. Though some émigré artists and writers in San Francisco did attain broad renown in their fields, the local community atmosphere was, by and large, more egalitarian and inclusive in nature because so many of those involved were not professional actors, artists, or writers.[91] Cultural activities, encompassing both "high" culture (literary, artistic, and intellectual pursuits), folk or popular culture (festivals and fairs), and events aimed at the younger generation, such as cabarets, were, by and large, inclusive manifestations of Russian identity both with respect to intention and tone throughout the inter-war period. The fairly broad array of activities available encouraged members of the Russian community to take part, whether through participation or attendance at lectures, musical and theatrical performances, dances, festivals, or trips to Fort Ross, for example, for commemorative events, which began in 1925.[92] Many events taking place within the urban space of San Francisco required venues rented from Americans, who thus became cognizant of the Russian community. Nevertheless, such interactions reinforced the notion that Russians were performers or entertainers under the American gaze and, apart from such events, Russians may indeed have remained invisible in San Francisco society, largely because so many of them worked at the types of jobs where they were remained "unseen" as laborers and domestics.

Pursuit of Art

Both teaching and pursuit of art, whether music, performance, or creating artwork, played a significant role in community activity throughout the inter-war era. Vocal, piano, and ballet studios played multiple roles: as ways to earn money through lessons; as a method to broaden the horizons of children, as well as adults, through music, singing, and dance; and as a vehicle for heritage maintenance. Dance teachers such as Tamara Laub and Nadejda Ermoloff (1904–1988) opened studios in separate spaces, given the need for a dance area, but those who gave vocal, recital, or piano lessons likely often worked out of their apartments or rented rooms.[93] Some instructors who were performers in their own right, such as pianist Elizabeth Boris (1888–1956), may have advertised in other venues apart from Russian newspapers as her students included Japanese children and "other foreigners" (i.e., non-Russians) as described in a Russian newspaper article about a student performance at Sorosis Hall in 1938.[94]

The impetus to maintain a creative life drew in émigrés with various backgrounds. Yefim Beliaeff/Paul White (1887–1949), an attorney in Russia, made a living variously teaching music, the Russian language, and oratory, repairing and tuning musical instruments, and giving lessons in the balalaika, mandolin, and guitar. The variety of activities to make money in his case centered on his artistic talents and knowledge. He also took part in literary-art and drama groups upon arrival and directed theater productions under the auspices of several theater groups in the 1920s and 1930s. His new profession as an educator in the humanities and arts, then, as with most émigrés who formed a core group that persisted in intellectual or artistic activity, was intertwined with his desire to maintain a "real" life outside of *byt*.[95]

Though not a professional actor or director, Beliaeff's reminiscences indicated that he felt himself proficient enough to critique everyone else, perhaps epitomizing the problematics of unifying people who came from varied social backgrounds to attain a common goal, even if it was simply to stage a play. The sniping spoke to the divided nature of the emigration and indirectly, perhaps, to the complexities of Russian society in terms of political change and modernization in the time period leading up to World War I. As a society in flux, with increasing mobility between classes, some Russians likely had trouble adjusting to societal change and carried their biases with them into exile.[96] Émigrés were conscious of the excessive in-fighting: M. Shevchenko wrote in 1926 that "perhaps, we émigrés ... do not think of ourselves as socially one unit," indicating the circumstance of chance or luck that brought them to the United States, combined with class differences and their varied points of origin.[97] The developing narrative around the relics of empire in California and the historic Russian Orthodox presence (chapter 5) began to countermand that narrative of chance and assisted in the development of a community ethos.

Beliaeff had a hand in organizing the Artists of Russian Theater (ART) group in the early 1930s, which proved long-lasting, continuing into the post-World War II era, engaging many émigrés in theater productions.[98] Simultaneously, cabaret and dance establishment proprietors provided lighter entertainment to help people cast off the daily grind and forget "their melancholy and the monotony" of *byt*.[99] Under the direction of professional cabaret actor George/Yuriy Bratoff (1891–1956) (whom Beliaeff typically characterized as obnoxious and contentious), and with financial help from Russian Jewish émigré Jacob Boxer (1886–1955), the "more bohemian" Kolobok Theater opened, staging skits and sketches to attract the younger crowd, who liked to dance the foxtrot or play pool, thus successfully engaging Russian youth who may have drifted away from the community otherwise, a process already in motion by the 1930s.[100] Focusing on culture rather than politics, the Russian Drama Society staged Maxim Gorky's play "The Lower Depths" at Turn Verein Hall in September of 1924. Gorky, after all, was now a "Soviet" writer, but that did not seem to have any bearing on émigrés' decision to engage with his work. Admittedly, the distinction between "Soviet" and émigré writers remained blurred even in Europe through the mid-twenties. Beliaeff made a point to say that he hated the play, indicating his personal feelings for Gorky, but that it "went well."[101]

The generally amateur nature of San Francisco's émigré arts groups combined with the contentious atmosphere may have been an impetus for some with professional-level talent to leave the enclave to practice their craft, in that process honing a different talent: that of self-promotion in the American marketplace. Some, such as dancers Sergei Utemoff (1901–1995) and Nadejda Ermoloff, for example, eventually headed to New York or Los Angeles where opportunities were available for actors, dancers, musicians, and entertainers, while others took less traveled routes.[102]

Prospective student and singer Serafim Strelkoff (1904–?) married Galina Sakovich (1909–?), Father Vladimir's daughter, and migrated to Gary, Indiana, in the late 1920s where he worked at a steel mill, simultaneously pursuing a singing career after winning first prize in a singing contest. He later worked in Los Angeles, singing in "several films which had a Russian setting."[103] Strelkoff billed himself as the "singing globetrotter," providing accounts of his "adventures" as part of his performance in venues in the midwest. A 1939 blurb about his life noted that he "wandered into China as a consequence of the Russian revolution and from there stevedored his way to America."[104] Strelkoff admittedly utilized his migration experiences to publicize his "brand" and attract audiences, but the result was a commensurate trivialization in American public discourse of both the Russian Civil War and the traumatic experience of forced Russian exodus.

"To Live Some Other Fantastic Life"[105]

The divide between those who sought to keep Russian culture as a central focal point of their "real" lives (generally émigrés who had arrived as adults) and those who were more inclined to Americanize and pursue material success (generally younger émigrés) formed quickly. Elena Grot described this rift as a "hopelessly deep abyss" of only ten years (not a "generation gap" per se), believing that younger Russians in the San Francisco community never experienced the literary and artistic treasure house that was Russia because they grew up in the period of World War I, the revolutions, and civil war, when they were "poisoned by gas" and "torn up by bombs"; when, instead of hearing renowned orchestras, listening to the best professors, or reading literature, they experienced "cannon fire, hunger, and endless terror," and, critically, in emigration, "the dust of machinery, clanging of dirty dishes," and "weariness from dull oppressive work," once again acknowledging the role of *byt*. Grot concluded that they "learned to fear thought, not having tasted the joy it gives." In her perspective, these experiences were why some of the youthful members of the community were at odds with her generation's interest in lengthy lectures on all manner of literary, artistic, scientific, or historical topics, preferring to go dancing or listening to jazz. Grot wrote the article after hearing a young audience member comment at a scholarly lecture, "my God, what a bore."[106]

That cultural divide emerged and broadened as the younger generation grew up – those who were born in the United States or were young enough when they arrived to attend American schools – sharply dividing the community as time passed into the generation that had known Russia prior to World War I and those who knew it only from the memories of their parents. Whether that younger group maintained a sense of Russianness was complicated by numerous other factors related to family, social life, and connection to the Russian community. One observer mused that on holidays such as those celebrating St Tatyana, even people who had become accustomed to the demands of "systematic American labor" were at least able to forget those demands briefly: "Tomorrow they will again have to ... become useful members of society."[107] Fundamental, however, was the understanding, in the experience of growing up in America, that one's "use" to society was measured by often hard unremitting labor and success was measured in terms of material wealth. A creative life was a luxury some felt they could not afford.

The San Francisco Russian community nevertheless recognized that Russians in other countries were generally even worse off financially, particularly the disabled, and began holding events such as the annual "Invalid Ball," which raised substantial amounts of money for impoverished and disabled veterans in Europe. Of critical significance to émigrés was the fact that these veterans had sacrificed their health and well-being for Russia and were now destitute. In 1939, the chairman of the Invalid Committee, Veterans' Society member Colonel Vasily M. Korjenko (1891–1961), at a meeting commemorating the "Day of the Russian Invalid," expressed his chagrin at the lack of participation of Russian youth in activities to raise money, indicating a clear generational divide that existed by that time:

> I must note with great regret the absence of young people in the cause to assist the disabled. I made an attempt to get in touch with [Russian] young people ... But here it turns out they have no idea who the disabled are, where they came from, and why they are disabled. An attempt to arrange a discussion ... about this matter also ended in failure as none of them have the time or the desire to talk about it.[108]

Korjenko specified that he was referring to people twenty-two to twenty-five years old (i.e., young adults who had been born between 1914–17), had no memories of Russia prior to the World War I, and who had experienced their formative years through a prism of violence and chaos. By 1939, they likely held jobs and perhaps had started families, and felt no connection to those who had sacrificed and suffered for a cause that had become unreal to them, perhaps in part because those formative years held so many painful memories of loss and dislocation. This particular aspect of

Culture, Conflict, Identity, and *Byt*

the cause was also depressing on its own – the struggle to find economic stability in America, particularly during the Depression era, was hard enough without being reminded of all those who were much worse off, with no hope of any real improvement apart from the few dollars they might receive from the United States. In that sense, if being Russian meant having to be constantly reminded of loss and suffering, some of the younger generation decided to leave their Russianness behind.

The Russian émigrés arriving in San Francisco, several thousand by 1925, the year of the Diamond Jubilee, changed the face of the existing small Russian Orthodox community centered on the Holy Trinity Cathedral. By virtue of their refugee status as well as lived experience in the Russian Civil War, émigrés also pushed back against the pro-Soviet convictions of the mostly working-class Spiritual Christian communities, who initially saw nothing but benefits from the Bolshevik Revolution and whose collective memories of Russian imperial power were overwhelmingly negative. The circumstance of two Russian communities, both considering themselves representatives of authentic Russian culture, with often directly opposing political viewpoints, existing in the same relatively small urban space, shaped the dynamic of both those communities in ways that continued to play out over the inter-war period. Both groups, however, continued efforts to maintain Russian culture and their respective customs and traditions, leading in the 1930s to significant rapprochement (chapter 8). The urban center of New York, which experienced its own influx of Russian émigrés in the inter-war period, and approximately the same number overall (6,000), included a much larger contingent of non-émigré Russian populations (60,000) in a city with a much larger population overall (over five million in 1920), which likely led to a different dynamic.[109]

That initial disparity in viewpoints among the two groups in San Francisco, however, as much as the location of the Holy Trinity Cathedral to the northeast of the Fillmore District, may have had something to do with the impetus for many of the émigrés to cluster in that neighborhood, establishing a "little Russian world of their own," rather than settling in the existing Russian neighborhood on Potrero Hill.[110] In some instances, as with the group who arrived on USAT *Merritt*, Russians received housing assistance and were directed to apartments in the area of Divisadero and Sutter and what is now the Western Addition, an affordable neighborhood west and southwest of the Fillmore.[111] The Jewish Russians in the Fillmore often had just as negative recollections of pre-revolutionary Russia as the Spiritual Christians, but that factor seemed less problematic to the Russian Orthodox-Russian Jewish relationship. By 1923, in any case, the need to create that Russian world became apparent as the Russia that had been their homeland no longer existed: the Soviet Union came into being in December of 1922. From 1922, Russian refugees in Europe were able to obtain Nansen passports, travel documents that attested to their previous status as subjects of the now vanished Russian Empire.[112] In essence, however, Russians abroad became stateless, motivating decisions to apply for US citizenship early on. The psychological pressures of acknowledging the futility of hope in return placed additional pressure on the psyche of Russian men, particularly veterans, some of whom had fought for Russia in two back-to-back wars. The moral support of their peers assisted in mitigating the weight of that burden as they began to acculturate to American society, the subject of the following chapter.

4

"EVEN THE TEETOTALERS DRANK"
Surviving On and Off the Job in America

We had always thought of the Russians as people who wrote merry
little tales about insanity and suicide, drank vodka, and scorned razors.

JOURNALIST WALTER VOGDES, 1923[1]

How dreadful, terrified, and cold one feels at the sound of this siren:
may it be thrice damned.

RUSSIAN STUDENT on lumber mill shift change, 1924[2]

In these difficult and joyless days of our émigré existence,
pitiless fate has dealt us the cruelest of blows.

BARON ALEXIS P. BOODBERG on the death
of Colonel Vladimir I. Konevega, 1934[3]

George Valter (1909–1970) arrived in San Francisco from Harbin in 1928
and took jobs with C&H Sugar and Western Sugar Companies, subsequently working as a longshoreman at Hills Brothers Coffee for
twenty-five years. He was also a charter member of the International
Longshore and Warehouse Union (ILWU), founded after San Francisco's 1934 General Strike and the base of the California Popular Front.[4]
George was secretary-treasurer of ILWU Local 6 at the time of his death.
A member of the Russian Orthodox Holy Virgin Church Parish, he and
Olga Salamaha (1909–1992) married at the church in 1931, and they
baptized their only son there in 1947. George voted the Democratic
ticket from the time of his naturalization in 1933 and enlisted in the US
military during World War II.[5] In short, George's life choices spoke to divergent aspects of Russian identity in the United States. Most émigrés, for

example, eschewed labor activism, given the leadership of leftist groups in advocacy for labor rights in the 1930s, notwithstanding the fact that émigrés employed as laborers would have benefited from improved safety standards. George's eldest brother, Konstantin (1903–1924), had enrolled at Whittier College in southern California and died in a work-related accident, perhaps spurring George to advocate for labor rights and safety through the ILWU.[6]

Konstantin arrived with a student group in San Francisco in 1921 and headed to Los Angeles. Like most Russian students, he needed to earn money to live while going to school. His employer, the California Cyanide Company, provided its product as a pesticide to citrus growers. In July 1924, while lifting a tank of cyanide gas out of a truck, Konstantin inhaled gas that had escaped through the tank's safety valve. The crew foreman later told authorities that he had attempted first aid and eventually managed to "flag down a car" to take the young man to the hospital, but Konstantin died shortly after arrival as his lungs were paralyzed and he could not take in any air. On that same day, Aurelio Aponte, a Huntington Beach plant worker, also died from cyanide poisoning. The deaths of both young men were ruled "unavoidable" and "accidental" by a coroner's jury in the inquest that officials completed less than a week later.[7]

Work-related accidents took their toll on the Russian community: working conditions were often problematic regardless of location, rural or urban. The death of naval pilot Peter Golovinsky (1897–1925), for example, occurred in the heart of San Francisco in October of 1925. Golovinsky had arrived with his wife Tatyana (1904–1970) on USAT *Merritt*. He lost his footing and fell while washing windows on the fourth floor level of the St Francis Hotel in downtown San Francisco. Like many other Russian military veterans, Golovinsky initially obtained janitorial work, but switched to window washing, up to sixteen hours a day.[8]

The available jobs for non-English speaking Russian veterans like Golovinsky, just as jobs for students in straitened economic circumstances like Valter, were such that the risk of injury or even death were distinct possibilities. A split second of inattention could well be fatal. The expendability of laborers was evident in the quick resolution of the inquest regarding Valter's and Aponte's deaths and in the circumstances of Golovinsky's accident – why was he not strapped in? Was it his choice or a lack of safety standards? Golovinsky may have chosen a job with an element of danger (dangling unsecured from a great height), which helped to maintain his identity in an alien society, in which Russian men often felt marginalized. That circumstance, and their status as often penniless refugees, in an environment of actual or perceived societal indifference, contributed to undermining the mental health of individuals already traumatized by years of warfare, displacement, and loss.

Russian émigré men struggled with establishing an identity in exile that provided them with a sense of purpose and meaning, a battle that continued even after gaining a measure of economic stability. Émigré organizations played an important role by helping to provide that purpose and meaning. Trauma was endemic to the experience of forced exodus and migration, but veterans also typically suffered from physical injuries, disabilities, and PTSD (then called "shellshock").[9] Dubinets discusses the "prolonged trauma" resulting from emigration with the possibility of no return among those who departed the Soviet Union in a later period, but the trauma for inter-war émigrés was compounded over and over: the extended and horrific violence of the Civil War, the protracted journeys out of Russia into China, unable to absorb the tens of thousands of refugees, and subsequent efforts to go to America, thus further physically distancing themselves from the homeland. Once reaching the "safety" of San Francisco, arrivals endured the entry process, experiencing detention and, finally, the recognition that return was unlikely.[10]

Two important émigré groups formed to assist émigrés with some of the practical issues of adjustment to life in America, and to provide moral support, were the Society of Russian Veterans of the Great War (World War I) and the RNSA, the latter including veterans as well. Many of the Russian military and naval personnel who arrived on USAT *Merritt* became members of these and other émigré organizations.[11] To some extent, the two groups, both male-dominated, complemented one another: one of the goals of the Veterans' Society was to maintain a link to the Russian past, to the history, traditions, and culture that formed their ideations of Russian identity. The Russian students grappled with planning for and creating a future, not just for veterans but Russian men (and, to some extent, women), who came to realize that they would live out their lives on foreign soil.

The issue of struggles with mental health among émigrés remained a real concern throughout the inter-war period even as they set out to find a place in American society. The very process of forced displacement brought on "anxiety, unconscious ambivalence, and psychological instability," but émigrés also experienced extended periods in transit, loss of family, and a problematic arrival process. Taisiia Bazhenova, who was detained on arrival at AIIS in 1925, recalled that they were treated like "prisoners under escort."[12] Economic circumstances made finding jobs an immediate priority. While willing, Russian men faced both physical and intangible obstacles in their search for and successful retention of jobs, the 1920s job market taking them all over California.

Striving to attain an education so as to work at a profession provided meaning and purpose, particularly in view of the oft-articulated dream, among both veterans and students, of returning to rebuild Russia as an impetus; material and economic success in the United States, in other words, were secondary factors. In fact, many of those who did later embark on successful careers in San Francisco as engineers, bank employees, or businessmen, upon realizing that they would not be returning to Russia, centered their personal and social lives around San Francisco's multiplying Russian émigré institutions as they found that their employment did not meet that criterion of a higher purpose.

Why Do the Russians Not Dance?

The US acceptance of 526 members of the Stark flotilla, who arrived in San Francisco on USAT *Merritt*, provided them with a safe haven, but that acceptance came with the realization that Russians as refugees were objects of often derisive public discourse, which focused on the "colorfulness" of Russians as people (i.e., as caricatures). Reporters covering the months-long journey of the flotilla as it had made its way from Russia to Korea, China, and finally the Philippines noted that the "tattered remnants" of the Russian Navy were accustomed to the "comforts" and "luxuries" of life, implying quite wrongly that most of the group belonged to the elite classes. The voyage was "one of the strangest cruises" in history, according to another reporter, minimizing the desperation of those who had embarked on the journey and the tragic nature of the journey itself – between 9,000 and 11,000 people originally left Vladivostok on a flotilla of ships, and fewer than 900 arrived in the Philippines months later: some left behind at various ports when ships were deemed unseaworthy, others victims of disease, some washed overboard in storms.[13]

In April of 1923, President Warren G. Harding had made the decision to allow a limited number of flotilla refugees in the Philippines to come to the United States based on the opinion of Secretary of War John W. Weeks that the Russians would make "desirable citizens," as most of them, in his view, were "skilled workers or professional or technical men."[14] Given that the refugees were literally penniless, Admiral Yuriy Stark sold off scrap iron and copper from the ships to pay the $8 per person charge for US visas. General George W. Reed, in command of US forces in the Philippines, offered the use of USAT *Merritt* to transport the group to San Francisco. More than 200 men remained behind, some already working on plantations on Mindanao. US officials urged Admiral Stark to accompany the group to San Francisco, as they routinely privileged elite status, but he refused, and eventually left for France.[15]

Acting Consul Romanovsky in San Francisco, learning that permission had been granted for these Russian refugees to depart for the United States in May of 1923, wrote to financial attaché Sergei Ughet in New York, asking him to clarify US government plans for assistance with food and shelter.[16] Ughet explained that the responsibility of the American government and the Red Cross ended once the refugees arrived in San Francisco.[17] Fortuitously, Russian émigrés had founded the Russian Refugee Relief Society of America, based in New York, and formed to assist refugees arriving there from Constantinople. The society members took part in the creation of a sub-committee to assist the refugees on USAT *Merritt* and proposed that a YMCA representative, Charles W. Riley, who had accompanied "a bunch of Czecho-Slovak legionnaires to Vladivostok" after the Bolshevik seizure of power, take charge of the effort.[18]

Ughet cautioned Romanovsky about possible protests regarding the acceptance of the refugees by "radical agencies" since, as far as Ughet knew, the Russian immigration quota for the fiscal year was full. He advised minimizing statements to newspapers.[19] As it turned out, US authorities deliberately planned the arrival of the ship for 1 July, the beginning of a new fiscal year, which allowed entry of the large group, as, crucially, the passengers had no special status and were processed as regular immigrants. Consequently, their arrival disrupted entry for other Russian entrants with visas in hand, many of them students, also arriving in July, resulting in extraordinarily lengthy detention periods at AIIS. As noted in chapter 2, more than two dozen passengers from USAT *Merritt* were also detained, some for months, for various reasons (illiteracy, mental health issues, as LPCs, and as supposed "radicals"). Immigration law allowed only 20 per cent of the annual allowed total of entrants with immigrant visas to enter per month, and that total would decrease to 10 per cent in 1924.[20] In contrast to the experience of the group, Russian Rear Admiral Boris Doudoroff (1882–1965), who had coordinated with American officials from Japan with respect to allowing the Stark flotilla to dock in the Philippines, traveled second class to San Francisco in November of 1923 with his family and two servants, and showed $30,000 to immigration authorities, thus avoiding scrutiny or detention.[21]

Upon arrival in San Francisco, reporters covering the arrival of this "little bit of Russia," seeing the group on the deck "gay with the colors of their garb," expected "at any moment to see them begin a Russian dance." The refugees did not comply, however, a reporter commenting that "it seemed as if the refugees had forgotten how to laugh."[22] The arrivals were wearing donated clothing from the Red Cross and from Honolulu residents, where the transport had stopped, as their own clothing had disintegrated during the months at sea. The condescending references by reporters to their "gay" garb indicated they were wearing a hodgepodge of items, not ethnic costumes. The reporter went on to describe the group as "members of the nobility, with their wives and children, teachers, agricultural experts, scientists, and officials," which differed substantially from the description of the appointed leader of the group, Lt General Peter Heiskanen (1860–1927), who listed "doctors, butchers, bakers, mechanics, engineers, even a priest." Many of the younger men self-identified as sailors, mechanics, or farmers.[23] The American correspondents nonetheless avidly searched for "the big men" on board, finding only the general himself, his son Boris (1897–1970), Father Sergei Denisoff (1886–1963), and "Prince Kangalov," actually Georgian noble Erakle Hounhaloff (1895–1970).[24] The characteristic search for elites effectively erased the remaining Russians from the narrative. Most of them were "ordinary" people, some with family (seventy married couples and thirty-three of those with children), who had boarded ships in Vladivostok as the Red Army neared the city. A *Russkaia zhizn'* reporter noted the evident disappointment of the American correspondents when they found out that the majority of the people in the group were mostly "ordinary" folk, adding to their chagrin that the arrivals declined to dance upon arrival.[25]

Upon entry, arrivals went to work immediately – by 12 July, Lt Colonel Andrei Kolosoff (1870–1939) was working nights laying streetcar tracks and sailor Ivan Chursin (1892–1980) found work on a chicken farm.[26] Many others left San Francisco to work in the lumber industry, box factories, and fruit picking.[27] Those who remained in San Francisco received housing assistance from charitable organizations, occupying apartments in groups. The Nikonenkos, Paul (1899–1997) and Maria (1903–1990), whose daughter Eugenia was born in San Francisco in November, lived with another family upon arrival, and for the next ten years, in her recollections, until they were able to save enough money to rent their own flat, where they nevertheless rented rooms to lodgers to make ends meet. In 1930, the Nikonenkos were living with Peter (1896–1986) and Anna Fedorkin (1901–1996) and two roomers (seven people total) in one apartment on Broderick Street.[28]

Mental Health in Exile

Inter-war "Russia Abroad" was largely skewed male with some émigré enclaves, such as in Belgrade, Yugoslavia, up to 70 per cent male, but most approximately 60 per cent.[29] As the White Armies had disintegrated, military men fled abroad, some with families, but many without. The struggle for survival among Russian war veterans in immigration, many of them permanently disabled, continued abroad. In San Francisco, veterans organized early on and, despite limited job prospects, generally did not suffer the dire circumstance of their compatriots in other countries. The lack of resources to deal with mental health among impoverished immigrants became critical over time, however. Eugenia Bailey, who grew up in the Fillmore, recalled that Russian male suicide was an ever-present issue in the inter-war period.[30]

The Russian émigré press reported widely on the incidence of suicide. In Harbin, suicide reached epic proportions in the mid-1920s, and reports of suicide among disabled Russian veterans in Europe indicated their desperation: "thousands" were buried in unmarked graves.[31] "Mr A," a military veteran and Stark fleet member who had remained in the Philippines in 1923, noted that suicides were "especially common" among "white" (i.e., Russian, as opposed to Filipino) laborers on the banana plantation where he worked. That mounting suicide rate amongst his friends was one of the reasons he left for San Francisco.[32] "Mr A" was likely Andre Antonoff (1899–1982), who arrived in 1932 from Manila. He appeared to acculturate well to American life, balancing it with ties to the Russian community, marrying an American widow in 1936, and helping her raise her two children. He and his wife were godparents to Vsevolod/ George (1903–1967) and Zinaida (1918–2004) Mitrofanoff/Pierce's son, born in 1946, and christened at the Holy Virgin Cathedral. Andre was also a member of the Former Russian Officers' Naval Club and owned Andy's Grocery on Ninth Street in San Francisco.[33]

San Francisco's émigré community did not escape its share of painful instances when despair overcame hope or faith, however. Apart from workplace or other accidents and disease, suicide was a significant cause of early deaths among Russian men. Out of approximately 460 males who identified as "students," most of whom arrived in San Francisco or Seattle between 1920 and 1925, fourteen were confirmed suicides with nine dying prior to 1943 and five later in life (table 4.1). More than 120 émigré men with ties to the San Francisco community, most of whom arrived in the 1920s, died by their mid-forties (table 4.2), which, even in the period in question, was relatively young and indicated "unnatural" death. Apart from suicide, known causes of death included workplace and other accidents, or illness. For a significant number of the total, including three who died in mental institutions, however, a cause of death was not available from existing documents, and given that apart from the patients at the institutions they did not die in hospital (which would have indicated illness), the cause of death may have been accident or suicide. Relatives may have preferred to keep cause of death confidential in the case of suicide as well. The types of workplace accidents highlighted the unsafe working conditions of the period while health issues often stemmed from untreated conditions. Though when G. Brajnikoff, a "talented" and "athletic" student, died of pneumonia, his friends believed that his death was due to the "carelessness" of his doctor.[34] The sheer number of early deaths of relatively young men affected the community as a whole: arriving in the United States, after all, despite the forced nature of their immigration, was nevertheless a positive step for displaced persons who knew that the alternatives to life in America were uniformly worse. Gaining "safety," however, is also a factor in survivors of trauma committing suicide years after experiencing violent or horrific events.[35] In the case of Russians veterans, specifically, though they had reached a "safe" environment after surviving the trauma of war, that environment was nevertheless alien to them. They were not home, nor could they go home.

For the community, losing men to suicide or even to accidental death or illness in the "land of opportunity" reinforced the already grim outlook for the future of Russian culture abroad. Suicide is a sin in the Orthodox faith and the church forbids prayer for those who take their own lives.[36] Given the strong religious faith of many Russian émigrés, perhaps made even stronger in exile as they sought comfort in the church and its institutions, the stigma of suicide was enormous, but the pain of those who nevertheless chose to take their own lives was such that it overcame that stigma.

Surviving On and Off the Job in America | 109

The specific reasons for suicide were often unknown as victims either did not leave notes or referenced a generally distraught state of mind. Prospective student and veteran Alexander Fedoroff (1900–1923) hung himself in his room. Detained upon arrival for three months at AIIS in July 1923 because of the full Russian quota, Fedoroff could not find work once released and "lost mental equilibrium." Stricken at the tragedy of Fedoroff's suicide, fellow student Nicholas Masloff (1900–1938), who also died young of liver cirrhosis, wrote a poem in his memory, asking the community not to judge him as "life ... does not provide the wine of forgetfulness to everyone."[37] Another veteran, Nikolai Ostankoff (1895–1926), jumped off the veranda of the Cliff House at Land's End in San Francisco, a popular restaurant and tourist destination just south of the mouth of the Golden Gate, leaving his neatly folded coat with naturalization papers behind.[38]

Sergei Trinko (1904–1941), a native of Harbin who arrived in San Francisco in 1922, hung himself in his apartment, leaving a note stating that no one was to blame for his death, the reporter of *Russian Life-News* noting that "loneliness and disappointment in life" likely played a part in Trinko's decisions.[39] Victor Vinogradoff (1901–1937), who blew himself up with dynamite near the mining town of Isaiah in Butte County, California, also left a note, signing it "Funny Guy," but writing that "nobody could understand" him. The sheriff was able to connect Vinogradoff to a money order he had sent earlier and thus identify him. Vinogradoff, who arrived on USAT *Merritt* with his mother and siblings, nevertheless felt isolated and alienated in America.[40] George Volojaninoff (1902–1938), who had worked as a cooper since arrival in 1923, climbed to the roof of an apparently randomly selected apartment house "shortly after dawn," removing "all identifying marks from his clothes" before jumping. The American newspaper reporter noted that Volojaninoff "chose the house of strangers ... for a place of death," sympathizing with the building residents forced to witness the act.[41]

Attaining the goal of higher education and a good job in the difficult years of the Depression did not preclude acts of desperation. "Brilliant student" Nicholas Denisoff (1900–1934) graduated with a master's degree in engineering from the University of California at Berkeley in 1932. He hung himself in his room in that city two years later. "A victim of ill health," Denisoff had recently been hired as a mining engineer.[42]

The economic difficulties during the Depression certainly may have led to an increased rate of suicide, but a direct correlation is difficult

Table 4.1 Russian male student death by suicide (of approximately 460 1921–1925 arrivals)

Name	Year/ place of birth	Veteran (self-identified)	Month/year arrived	Enrolled or degree/ occupation	Year/ place of death
N.I. Denisoff	1900/Kaluga	N	October 1923	Engineering degree/mining engineer	1934/ Berkeley, CA
A.A. Fedoroff	1900/Orenburg	Y	July 1923	Unemployed	1923/ Berkeley, CA
G.V. Fescoff	1904/Chita	N	October 1923	Enrolled/ chemist	1942/ Berkeley, CA
V.A. Kalishevsky	1895/Tbilisi	Y	July 1921	Engineering degree/ engineer	1958/ Beaumont, TX
P.R. Karpooshko	1892/Kiev	Unknown	December 1922	Worked as electrician	1960/Paris, France
V.A. Laskaviy	1897/Kiev	Y	January 1923	Dishwasher	1938/Seattle
N.P. Ostankoff	1895/Kazan	Y	September 1923	Unknown if enrolled/ Ernest J. Sultan Manufacturing employee	1926/ San Francisco
A.A. Rastrepin	1889/ Krasnoyarsk	Y	January 1923	Cook/chef (retired)	1975/ San Francisco
L.A. Sharaeff	1901/Kharkov	Y	July 1923	Salesman, photographer	1961/ San Mateo County, CA
A.I. Sidoroff	1890/1893/ Moscow	Y	September 1923	Printer	1934/ San Francisco
S.A. Trinko	1904/Hailar Station	N	August 1922	Laborer	1941/ San Francisco
V.V. Vladykin	1899/1900/ Moscow	Y	July 1923	Enrolled Department store manager	1962/ San Francisco
G.V. Volojaninoff (Volsh/Walsh)	1902/Chita or Ust-Kara (now Ust-Karsk), Zabaikal *obl.*	Y	September 1923	Machine Cooper, Western Cooperage Co.	1938/ San Francisco
Y.G. Yagodnikoff (James Berry)	1903/Harbin	Y	July 1923	Janitor, Alameda County Title Insurance Co.	1935/ Oakland, CA

Sources: California, US, County Death Records; Texas, *US, Death Certificates.*

Table 4.2 Incidents of Russian male early death (prior to age fifty) among inter-war arrivals

Name	Year of birth/ place of birth	Month/ year of arrival	Occupation	Year of death/cause/ (location, if not SF)
V.I. Argunoff	1900/ Blagoveshchensk	August 1922	Laborer	1924/ Workplace accident (?) (funeral costs charged to Great Western Power)
N.V. Artukhoff	1903/Kishinev	July 1923	Sailor/painter/ carpenter	1928/Lymphosarcoma of small intestines
A.S. Babaiantz	1899/?	July 1923	Seaman/ Laborer	1925/illness
I.V. Babin	1900/1906/ Blagoveshchensk	October 1923	Laborer	1932/Suicide
L.N. Bambulevich	1914/Harbin	August 1940	Laborer, lumber company	1942/Suicide (Humboldt County)
S.S. Bardin	1889/1892/ Urupino (Urupinsk?), Don Region	December 1922	Painter	1935/Poisoning by insecticide- contaminated baking soda
L.E. Baturin	1894/Votkinsk	September 1922	Mechanic/ machinist	1934/Tuberculosis
M.M. Bazileff	1905/Vladivostok	July 1923	Fireman/Miner	1941/Tuberculosis, Weimar TB Sanitorium, Placer County
V.K. Belokriloff (Beloff)	1901/Cherepanova	July 1923	Laborer	1943/Unknown (San Joaquin Co)
A.V. Berejkoff	1884/1885/ Vladivostok	July 1923	Engineer/ Mechanic	1931/Suicide
A.H. Birich	1901/Hakodate, Japan	July 1923	Waiter	1937/Unknown (Los Angeles)
G.A. Birukoff	1903/Odessa	July 1923	Laborer	1926/Unknown (Sacramento)
S.V. Bojanoff/ Bajanoff	1903/Kharkov	July 1923	Sailor/ mechanic	1927/Motorcycle accident/ fractured skull (Sacramento)
G. Bondarenko/ Bandarenko	1899/Rostov	October 1923	Cook	1933/Unknown
K.A. Bondarenko	1884 or 1898/ Krolevets	July 1923	Farmer	1924/Unknown (Sonora CA)
I.S. Borisoff	1900/Khabarovsk	July 1923	Artist	1941/Unknown (New York)
G.W. Brajnikoff	1901/Russia	Prior to 1921	Student	1921/Pneumonia (Alameda County)

Table 4.2 (continued)

Name	Year of birth/ place of birth	Month/ year of arrival	Occupation	Year of death/cause/ (location, if not SF)
I.G. Buharoff	1903/Harbin	September 1928	Mechanic	1942/Unknown
A.I. Chebotareff	1901/Kharkov	July 1923	Laborer	1946/Unknown
V.V. Checkovich	1899/Moscow	September 1923	Longshoreman	1945/Brain hemorrhage
N.S. Chernyh	1895/Tomsk	August 1922/1923	Mechanical engineer	1924/Unknown
N.N. Daniloff	1895/Chita	October 1923	Laborer	1937/Hemorrhage/ apoplexy
V.A. Davidoff	1904/Handaohedze	July 1923	Motor mechanic	1924/Unknown (Placer County)
A.E. Dedenko	1908/Ufa	July 1923	Assistant bookkeeper/ WWII: U.S. Navy	1942/ Killed in action, USS. Calhoun
N.V. Demicheff	1904/Verhneudinsk	July 1923	Jeweler	1949/Gunshot wound to the chest during store robbery
N.I. Demin/ De Min	1895/Vladivostok	July 1923	Pool room/ restaurant proprietor	1931/Illness
O.E. Dorojensky	1905/Petrograd	June 1924	Factory worker	1928/Suicide
A.A. Drosdoff	1915/China	June 1929	Student	1932/Chronic pulmonary tuberculosis
V.P. Dubovetsky (Basil Duvost)	1903/Moscow	December 1922	Student/Hotel employee	1935/Poisoned by gas in war? (patient, SF Hospital, 1930-1932)
V.V. Elvitsky/ Ilvitsky	1914/Harbin	November 1926	Teamster/ Fireman	1946/Fighting fire— Hotel Herbert
E. P. Emelianoff	1890//Russia	July 1923	Laborer	1935/ Pneumonia
A.L. Farinsky	1909/Harbin	1923	Hatter	1943/Pneumonia
V.P. Fedoolov	1909/Barnaul	September 1927	Student	1949/ Unknown (patient, Mendocino State Hospital for Insane)
M.S. Fedorkin	1902/Harbin	September 1926	Janitor	1937/Suicide
C.F. Forofontoff/ Farafontoff	1887/Astrakhan	July 1923	Pot washer	1928/Chronic pulmonary tuberculosis

Table 4.2 (continued)

Name	Year of birth/ place of birth	Month/ year of arrival	Occupation	Year of death/cause/ (location, if not SF)
A.A. Gavriloff	1898/Ufa	November 1926	Laborer, Bonneville Power Project, Portland, OR	1940/Coronary occlusion, Portland, Oregon
N.V.Georgesco	1892/Bucharest, Romania/Kharkov	March 1925	Musician	1927/Illness
J.F. Gerak	1903/Chita	July 1923	Shoemaker	1946/Unknown
V.G. Girgilevich (Gil/Gill)	1896/Volyn obl.	March 1923	Student	1934/Unknown (Patient at SF Hospital, 1930)
L.K. Globa	1901/Poltava	July 1923	Laborer/ Fisherman	1942/Unknown (In hospital, San Pedro, CA)
P.A. Golovinsky	1896/Moscow	July 1923	Window washer	1925/Fall from window cleaning platform, St Francis Hotel
F.V. Grigorieff	1895/Amur region	September 1923	Oil worker, Shell Refinery	1929/Two-week illness (Contra Costa County)
V.L. Grigorieff	1911/1912/Chita	February 1929	Jeweler	1931/Heart failure after tonsillectomy
L I. Ignatoff (Ignoff)	1908/Harbin	September 1928	Auto painter	1940/Suicide (murder-suicide)
A.M. Ivakin	1894/Rostov-on-the-Don	July 1923	Mechanic	1938/Hodgkin's disease (?) (Oakland)
A.Ivanoff	1885/Vladimir	July 1923	Miner/Laborer	1927/ Suicide (Rio Dell, CA)
A.T. Ivanoff	1893/ Blagoveshchensk	September 1923	Del Monte Factory employee	1927/Unknown
K.L. Ivanoff	1900/Skuliany, Bessarabian gub.	August 1922	Engineering degree/ engineer	1929/Workplace accident, oil well, (Carpentaria, CA)
M.F. Ivanoff	1897/Tambov	July 1923	Accountant	1931/Acute dilatation of the heart
N.I. Ivanoff	1903/1904/1905/ Kharkov	September 1923	Shipping clerk, W&J Sloan Home Furnishings	1946/Coronary occlusion
P.M. Ivleff/Ivaeff	1893/Petrograd	February 1923	Miner/Laborer	1933/Unknown

Table 4.2 (continued)

Name	Year of birth/ place of birth	Month/ year of arrival	Occupation	Year of death/cause/ (location, if not SF)
J.J. Kilovsky	1901/Riga	July 1923	Seaman	1939/Unknown
N.G. Kirichenko	1896/Kiev	July 1923	Laborer	1926/Unknown
B.D. Kongue	1899/Russia	September 1924	Russian Naval officer/ unknown	1926/Unknown
G.A Korotenko	1903/Nikolayev	July 1923	Laborer	1943/Unknown
V.N. Kositsin (Nefed)	1895/1897/ Blagoveshchensk	April 1922	Printer/Janitor	1942/Unknown
F.I. Kotoff	1901/1903/Petrograd	February 1923	House painter	1929/Unknown (Seattle)
K.R. Kotovsky	1884/Kargopol	Oct 1923	SPCo yardman	1932/Gunshot wound to chest (self-inflicted?)
A. S. Koudrin	1888/Verny	September 1923	Watchman/ Laborer, Pacific Lumber Company	1932/Bilateral pulmonary tuberculosis
A.M. Kourlin	1899/Samara	July 1923	Laborer	1929/Unknown
V.L. Krakaw	1899/ Blagoveshchensk	June 1939	Furniture company employee	1942/Suicide
B.A. Kravchenko	1908/Harbin	January 1931	Laborer	June 1931/ Drowned, Russian River
G.K. Kuguenko	1902/Koryukivka (?), Chernihiv *obl.*	1923	Stevedore	1940/Pneumonia
Father T.I. Lavrischeff	1896/Karaliak, Samara gub.	July 1923	Priest	1937/Pneumonia (Washington, DC)
G.K./C. Lebedeff (Swan)	1909/Harbin	July 1925	Ship rigger, Western Pipe & Steel; grocery store clerk	1942/Drowned between Piers 27 and 29, San Francisco Bay
M.P. Lebedeff (Lebee)	1898/Orenburg	July 1923	House painter	1935/Fall from scaffolding/ work accident
N.G. Malleck	1904/Poltava	Before 1932 or 1937	YMCA masseur	1938/Kidney disease
A.S. Maslenikoff	1898/Malaya Vishera	January 1921	Actor	1931/Cancer (Los Angeles)
N.N. Masloff	1900/Moscow	July 1923	Painter	1938/Cirrhosis of liver

Table 4.2 (continued)

Name	Year of birth/ place of birth	Month/ year of arrival	Occupation	Year of death/cause/ (location, if not SF)
B.V. Melikov	1897/Saratov	March 1923	Hospital orderly/ pharmacist	1935/Heart attack
M.S. Miagkoff	1910/Russia	1938 (?)	Singer (?)	1940/Unknown
M.I. Mihailoff	1910/Narva	August/ November 1938	Painter	1947/Tuberculosis
N.A. Mihailoff/ Mihaloff	1900/1901/Ufa	June 1921	Salesman, bakery	1934/Suicide
N. N. Miroluboff	1909/Harbin	August 1929	Cook	1953/Suicide
G.V. Mizhevich	1904 (?)/Unknown	Unknown	Unknown	1940/Drowned in river; buried in potter's field, Sacramento
B.A. Nazaroff	1904/1907/Harbin	August 1923	Watchmaker/ Painter/Waiter	1932/Suspected suicide (fall from overpass/bridge)
G.A. Nazaroff	1911/Batumi	August 1923	Laborer	1955/Coronary insufficiency (in Stockton State Hospital for the Insane, CA, 1940)
G.E. Nikitin	1902/Karalat, Astrakhan obl.	July 1923	Stevedore	1937/Suicide
V. Novombergsky	1900/Tomsk	July 1923	Laborer/Artist	1938/Brief illness (Humboldt County resident; working in Petaluma on Redwood Empire display for 1939 SF exposition)
I.P. Pankratoff	1900/Orenburg	September 1923	Janitor	1942/Unknown (at Mendocino State Hospital for Insane)
I.I. Pashenko	1882/Ekaterinoslav (Dnipro)	March 1921	Engineer/auto mechanic (?)	1925/Unknown
V.N. Pirovsky	1900/Spassk	July 1923	Laborer	1933/Pneumonia
D.E. Polajenko	1901/1903/Perm	October 1923	Janitor	1931/Unknown
V.P. Petroff	1887/Menzelinsk, Ufa gub.	August 1922	Laborer	1923/Workplace accident, quarry cliff cave-in
E.P. Pogrebniakoff (Pogre)	1906/Harbin	June 1940	Engineer/ plumber	1948/Heart failure
N.N. Popoff (Ross)	1895/Chita	December 1922	Deck hand, Southern Pacific	1932/Suicide (initially considered accidental drowning or foul play)

Table 4.2 (continued)

Name	Year of birth/ place of birth	Month/ year of arrival	Occupation	Year of death/cause/ (location, if not SF)
F.A. Pykhaloff	1894/ Verkhneudinsk(?)	July 1923	Tinsmith	1932/Tuberculosis (patient, SF Hospital, 1930)
G.S. Reabinin (Rayburn)	1900/Rybinsk	March 1923 (New York)	Window dresser	1933/Pulmonary tuberculosis
S.S. Reabinin (Rayburn)	1920/Rybinsk	October 1923 (New York)	High school student	1935/Car accident
J.J. Rojnovsky	1900/Akhaltskihe (?)	July 1923	Paper hanger	1935/Unknown; interred Juneau, AK
V.I. Saenko	1890/Odessa	July 1923	Laborer	1927/Carcinoma of esophagus
N.P. Sartory/ Sartori	1898/Saratov	July 1923	Worker at Sonoma State Home	1934/Tuberculosis
S.A. Savin	1901/Russia	Prior to 1925	Floor layer	1939/ Unknown
V.P. Schelkunoff/ Shelton	1900/Moscow	September 1920	Engineer	1947/ Unknown
A.N. Schneider	1896/Nikolayevsk-on-Amur (?)	March 1923	Architectural draftsman/ presser	1934/Cavernous sinus thrombosis
I.F. Sergeeff	1902/Orenburg	January 1923	US Army engineers	1930/Pulmonary tuberculosis in home for disabled veterans (Southern California)
V. Sergeeff	1899/Karalat	July 1923	Fisherman	1927/ Unknown Alameda CA
F. Shander	1903/?	By December 1923	Busboy/painter	1933/Alcohol poisoning
G.V. Shaposhnikoff	1904/Novonezhino	January 1923	Hatter	1946/Aneurism
V.V. Shimonaeff,	1901/Samarkand	July 1919	Driver	1925-1927?/No information; not listed in parents' 1927 naturalization application
A. Smirnoff	1907/Russia	Unknown	Unknown	1927/Unknown
F.I. Smirnoff	1904/1905/Merv	July 1923	Cosmetologist/ members Ships' Clerks Assoc., Local 34 ILWU	1949/Unknown
V.I. Smoliakoff	1907/Petrograd	March 1922 (in New York)	Translator/ clerk	1943/Pneumonia
S.V. Solovieff	1895/Tientsin	Aug 1927	Clothing presser	1940/Cardiac failure
M.M. Stashuk	1907/Khabarovsk	September 1923	Upholsterer	1945/Heart disease, Sonoma County Hospital

Table 4.2 (continued)

Name	Year of birth/ place of birth	Month/ year of arrival	Occupation	Year of death/cause/ (location, if not SF)
V.I. Stashuk	1888/Kiev (?)	1923 (?)	Laborer, Southern Pacific RR Co.	1930/Carcinoma/ pulmonary tuberculosis
V.Y. Stepanoff (Stevens)	1893/1896/ Kharkov	March 1923	Millwright	1941/Acute coronary artery occlusion
S.A. Sukhikh	1896/Perm	July 1923	Farmer	1933/Pulmonary tuberculosis
A.A. Sushkoff	1909/Harbin	September 1926	Hat finisher	1940/Heart attack (Guerneville)
I.V. Tarakanoff	1904/Vladivostok	July 1923	Laborer	1931/Suicide
P.M. Tatarintseff	1886/?	January 1923	House painter	1926/Accidental? poisoning/ ingested overdose of opiate
A.P. Tsvetkoff	1896/Kostroma	September 1923	Draftsman/ mechanical engineer	1941/Unknown (New York)
M.I. Tueff	1896/Nolinsk	July 1923	Oiler, PG&E	1931/Drowned in Amador County river
D.D. Ushakoff	1897/Orel or Vilnius	September 1921	Salesman	1941/Unknown (Los Angeles)
K.I. Valter	1902/1903/Harbin	September 1921	Student, Whittier College	1924/Workplace accident; cyanide poisoning (Los Angeles)
V.L. Venikoff	1886/1887/Yelabuga	August 1923	Laborer	1929/Unknown
V.S. Vesnin	1912/Moscow	February 1929	Shipping clerk	1935/Car accident (Guerneville)
V.V. Vinogradoff	1901/Vladivostok	July 1923	Miner/laborer	1937/Suicide (Butte County, CA)
M.S. Volokin	1888/Herson	October 1923	House painter	1933/Heart failure
V.A. Vstovsky (Stovsky)	1897/Vladivostok	January 1923	Real estate agent	1940/Unknown
F.A. Yagotin	1884/Dmitrovka	July 1923	Stevedore	1929/ Ludwig's angina
M.T. Yaytsky	1895/Pavlovsk	December 1925	Car cleaner	1938/Workplace accident (hit by train?)
A.P. Yermakoff	1911/Ochakov (Ukraine)	August 1929	Machine operator, metal shop	1941/Unknown
J.I. Zebzieff	1894/	July 1923	Grocer, Zeber's Market	1939/Coronary occlusion

Sources: California, US, County Death Records; "Passenger Lists of Vessels Arriving at San Francisco, California," NAI 4498993; "Petitions for Naturalization, 8/6/1903–12/29/1911," NAI 605504.

to establish. In two cases of suicide at the height of the Depression, for example, both men were employed. Michael Fedorkin (1902–1937), a thirty-five-year-old motorman for the Market Street railway and brother of student Peter, shot himself in the heart after an argument with his wife.[43] Gregory Nikitin (1902–1937), who was employed as a dock worker, hung himself in the attic of his home.[44] Family circumstances in these cases may have exacerbated mental health issues.

Many of the incidents of suicide occurred years after arrival in San Francisco, indicating that these men attempted to adjust to their new life but that the past trauma "contaminated" the present – affecting the capability of "spontaneous involvement" in life because of ever-present "inner chaos" they were attempting to suppress – thus the often extreme circumstances of jumping off cliffs or buildings or even blowing themselves up.[45] The experience of the war in which many of them fought or the violence they encountered continued to be "their sole source of meaning," which provided no way forward for them.[46]

The issue of access to mental health care, particularly among people who already felt insecure about their status in an alien environment, was a sensitive topic, and many of those who suffered either did so in silence or, as is evident from the incidents of suicide, took drastic steps to find relief. Some were institutionalized. Students Ivan Pankratoff (1900–1942), Vasily Ermakoff (1896–1969), and Vadim Fedoolov (1909–1949) were all committed to the Mendocino State Hospital for the Insane in Ukiah, California in the inter-war period. Pankratoff worked as a janitor, Ermakoff on the railroad, and Fedoolov had been a student at the Georgia Institute of Technology in Atlanta before returning to San Francisco.[47] Several Russian émigré men were also patients at the Stockton State Hospital for the Insane as of 1940.[48]

The difficulties and pressures of life in immigration affected all émigrés, of course, not only veterans. People unable to mentally cope with continuing challenges they faced, in combination with the issue of unaddressed traumatic experiences, may have suffered nervous breakdowns. Eugene Chernigovsky/Chern (1894–1950) worked as a musician and teacher until the early 1930s. His wife Nina (1894–1983) had a successful career as a bacteriologist. As the Depression worsened, however, Eugene could not find employment in his field and worked as a janitor. By 1940, he and Nina were divorced, and he was institutionalized at Mendocino State Hospital. He died alone in his apartment in San Francisco under unclear circumstances.[49]

Physical disability or illness were aspects of émigrés' lives that complicated already tenuous situations, but these were factors for which organizations were often able to provide either material or moral aid. Dealing with mental health issues was beyond the capabilities of peers, Russian émigré doctors (even though they communicated with patients in their native language), or even clergy, particularly if individuals were estranged from the church. Trauma, as Dr Van Der Kolk found in his study of the topic, not only reorganizes how people's minds and brains "manage perceptions," but the "very capacity to think," altering the body's responses to stimuli and causing physical symptoms and illnesses. Moreover, formulating a "coherent account" of traumatic events is, on its own, a struggle. Therefore, when veterans gathered and talked about the past, many nevertheless likely avoided discussing the painful events or provided a "cover story" for "public consumption," none of which was sufficient to heal such deep wounds.[50] Combined with the discomfort émigrés felt in an alien milieu and the subsequent realization of the reality of permanent exile, as the cases noted above indicate, many young men, unable to cope with either aspects of their lives in emigration or their mental health situations overall, were left, as a Russian expression fittingly describes, "to the vagaries of fate" (*na proizvol sudby*) in a foreign land. The high "unnatural" death-rate also spoke directly to what Sadowski-Smith refers to in her study of post-Soviet immigrant whiteness, as the "exceptionalist mythology of the United States as an immigrant nation": those who felt that they had not or could not "achieve the American Dream" disappeared from narratives about the immigration experience as they complicated efforts to periodically resurrect that mythologized history of immigration, which stressed the narrative that hard work and determination were all the ingredients necessary for a fulfilled and happy life.[51]

Nadia Shapiro, in her review of Dalgeim's 1923 Chat Noir Cabaret (chapter 3), highlighting its "broad Russian humor," opined that "jaded Russian nerves produced the artistic cabaret." The "funniest number," she noted, revolved around the Civil War experience, a war in which "two millions of [*sic*] Russian soldiers were killed in the prime of their lives during the bloodiest eight years Russia has ever known." The number was a "burlesque" in the spirit of "The Parade of Wooden Soldiers," first presented by *La Chauve-Souris* (The Bat) touring revue, originating in Moscow in the early 1900s, and satirizing Czar Paul I's mania for marching soldiers: not receiving an order to halt, they marched on to Siberia. Shapiro concluded that the cabaret was "a true artistic expression of a neurotic age." The response to the tragedy of the Civil War using humor, particularly given expectations of grim performances by "morbid Russians" (a phrase she used to describe how Americans perceived them), spoke to the acknowledgment that émigrés were traumatized as a group with their Civil War experiences being a root cause of that trauma.[52] Her observations, however, indicated that some people found ways to process their experiences through artistic expression. Some shared their thoughts and recollections of the war in public discourse, attempting to expunge the "morbid" scenes in their minds. A contributor to *Russkaia zhizn'* wrote that the "nightmarish" scenes she witnessed during the Civil War continued to haunt her. She recalled corpses of soldiers lying outside the hospital where she worked. They had fallen through river ice and were still encased in the recovered ice blocks, their facial expressions of final agony clearly visible. She expressed amazement that she was still able to "appreciate what was good and beautiful in life."[53] Notwithstanding these communal coping mechanisms, a significant number of men retreated from the realities of American life; unable to engage with others to mitigate pain or sorrow, they committed desperate acts to relieve their suffering.

In a fictional story about an émigré considering the implications of the Nazi German invasion of Poland on 1 September 1939, writer Peter Balakshin (1898–1990) included a vignette of a Russian priest (unnamed but likely based on Father Vladimir Sakovich) meeting an arriving Russian woman at the dock and telling her of the "tragic death" of her husband at his workplace. This vignette, inserted as one in a series of observations and recollection of the narrator as he strolls the Fillmore, acknowledged the reality of life in emigration.[54]

Society of Veterans of the Great War

In light of the pressures of life in immigration, a group of veterans formed the Society of Russian Veterans to aid in maintaining morale. The impetus initially came from the board of the Artillery Group at the Officers' Employment and Mutual Aid Union in Harbin in November of 1923, who asked for support from the San Francisco group to form a fund of assistance to immigrate to America.[55] A subsequent discussion of the matter over a "cup of tea" amongst a group of eleven military officers in San Francisco led to the formation of the Veterans' Society.[56]

Differences in class and social status may have played out in the intra-group dynamic of the Veterans' Society in San Francisco, given the significant proportion of former military men who were from Siberia and the Far East of Russia. Career military officer Theodore Olferieff noted that the attitudes of Siberian troops he encountered in the World War I were much more egalitarian than those of military men from European Russia, with few Siberian officers from the nobility.[57] Adherence to "egalitarian" principles may have precluded membership for men who considered the society's leadership elitist: in other words, veterans who felt the leadership did not represent them may not have joined at all or may have left the organization, further exacerbating the loneliness many of them felt. An articulated goal of the society, after all, was to unite Russian veterans of the World War I in order to answer the "call of Grand Duke Nikolay Nikolayevich [Romanoff] to save the Motherland."[58] Moreover, the career military officer who accepted the group's invitation to head the society, Lt General Alexis P. Boodberg (1869–1945), was also titled nobility, a baron, and he remained president until his death. Universally respected, Boodberg stood above any infighting amongst different factions but, in his role as president of the society and chief contributor/editor to the society newsletter, leaned firmly in the direction of monarchy, idealizing the last czar, Nicholas II, despite publishing alternate perspectives regarding the efficacy of autocratic monarchy as a system of government. His writings, much like those of émigrés who tended to dominate public discourse, particularly with respect to defining émigré identity, developed an indelible sanctity around the czar's and Empress Alexandra's image and person, particularly in view of their family's martyrdom.[59] Boodberg was also the head of the North American chapter of the Russian All-Military Union (ROVS), which contributed to his standing as a leading voice in the Russian community.[60] That being said, the Veterans' Society exited ROVS in late 1938 due to members' objections to the organization's closeness to the "monarchist cause" in Europe, indicating an alternate outlook (i.e., even if Boodberg, as president, leaned in the direction of monarchy, members' views with respect to amenable (or not) political associations prevailed).[61]

Nevertheless, Boodberg was generally the voice of the society as he wrote and/or edited much of the material in its newsletter, first published in May of 1926, and lectured often on a variety of subjects under the auspices of the society.[62] Boodberg's ruminations on various historical subjects clearly favored empire. In discussing the Philippines' struggle for independence in 1932, for example, he favored American hegemony, at the same time frowning on aspects of capitalism.[63] Boodberg's assessment did not take into account the dynamics of the American exploitation of labor in the Philippines, which, given his position, would likely have been known to him, particularly since Russians who were unable to enter the United States with the Stark group in 1923 remained as laborers on plantations owned by expatriate Americans. An account by K. Liubarsky described endless back-breaking work weeding hemp fields for 1.5 pesos a day, with workers forced to buy provisions from the American owner's company store at inflated prices. Liubarsky noted ironically that the labor system in this "colony" of the "most civilized and freest republic" in the world (i.e., the United States) exceeded by far in terms of exploitation any such by a Russian village "*kulak*," recognizing American exploitation of laborers abroad.[64]

Notwithstanding his own perspectives, Boodberg conceded to publishing the call articulated at the Russia Abroad Congress in Europe in the first society newsletter, which, among other statements of appeal to the "Russian people" (both in the Soviet Union and abroad), noted that the ideology of autocratic monarchism, described as "what had been," had "run its course."[65] Boodberg actually came from a family that an acquaintance described as "liberal nobility and intelligentsia" who spoke "a different language every day of the week" in order to keep "seven languages going." His professional military career, therefore, was "very much frowned at by his sister and her liberal friends," many of whom did not emigrate and subsequently perished in the Stalinist purges of the 1930s.[66] Leaving behind family in Russia, and then witnessing the liquidation of that family from a position of helplessness abroad reinforced existing political and ideological perspectives, confirming impressions about the brutality of the Soviet regime.

Among its achievements in its first two years, the Veterans' Society established a loan fund, a jobs bureau, a library, and the tradition of holding what came to be called the annual "Invalid Ball," noted earlier, to benefit disabled Russian veterans around the world. The society also initiated a plan to organize the Consolidated Commission of Russian Organizations in 1925 under the leadership of former Russian Consul General Artemy Wywodtsev.[67] The commission included eleven Russian "national organizations" as member groups for the purpose of centralizing planning of participation in the Diamond Jubilee parade that year (chapter 3).[68]

Taking advantage of the Russian contingent's success in the parade (winning the second prize cup, which remains in the Veterans' Society holdings), organization leaders created a permanent Consolidated Committee of Russian National Organizations, which consisted of the Society of Veterans, the Holy Trinity Cathedral Committee, the Russian Mutual Aid Society, the Society for the Protection and Education of Children (chapter 6), the Association of Former Russian Naval Officers and Sailors, the Society of Engineers and Technicians, and the RNSA. The main goal of the committee was to present a unified front of the San Francisco "Russian Colony" in "relations with official (US) agencies," indicating recognition that the fractured nature of Russia Abroad disempowered it and contributed to the marginalization of Russians. Proposed projects included: founding a Russian Center, which would house a library, hall, and stage, a medical clinic, and a school; developing a member insurance policy, including life, health, and workman's compensation in recognition of the precarious situation workers in America endured; establishing a credit union; and establishing ties to national Russian organizations in other countries. The committee did not achieve these goals but laid the foundation for cooperative community effort going forward. True to émigré form, however, the Veterans' Society left the committee after only one year due to "complete disagreement with the current committee members in the understanding, interpretation, and application" of the committee's powers.[69]

The Russian National Students Association

Many of the students who came to San Francisco from Harbin in the 1920s were also veterans who had fought with Admiral Kolchak's Army in Siberia, sojourning in Harbin after crossing the border in 1919–1920.[70] In the fall of 1923, the RNSA board in Berkeley, California received a letter from the president of the Mutual Aid Society in Harbin warning that more than 200 destitute Russian young people there, who had fled the "political hurricane" that had swept over Russia, faced a coming winter with no food, shelter, or warm clothing. Local charities were overwhelmed, reinforcing the urgent need to get Russian young people to the United States.[71]

The combined and persistent efforts of several organizations culminated in successfully bringing approximately 550 students to San

Francisco from 1920 through 1925, as discussed in reference to Nadia Shapiro's experiences as a prospective student in chapter 2. Despite the focus of reporters on arriving women students, the majority (approximately 85 per cent) were men. Organizations and individuals involved were the Harbin Committee Rendering Aid to Students of Higher Educational Institutions, the International Committee of the YMCA, and the last Russian Ambassador in Washington, DC, Boris Bakhmeteff, who was also instrumental in providing financial assistance, establishing and directing the Russian Humanitarian Fund and the Fund for Aid to Russian Students.[72] Secondary school graduates in Harbin, many of them children of Russians employed by the CER, applied to the Mutual Aid Society, which assisted in obtaining US visas.[73] The student groups, however, included more recent arrivals to Harbin, such as the Civil War veterans, than local residents, leading to a board of inquiry at AIIS on 10 August 1922 in which two arriving students were interrogated about their intentions, and a subsequent investigation by the US Departments of Labor and Justice in view of the "advanced age" (late twenties and older) of the majority of Russian "students."[74]

In fact, according to Vasiliy Ushanoff (1904–1989), who arrived as a student in Seattle in 1922, the initial idea to send Russian young people to America focused on men who had fought the Bolsheviks rather than the secondary school graduates. Out of approximately 460 males who filled out RNSA applications and/or self-identified as students upon entry into the United States, more than 260 noted military or naval service in the "German War" (World War I) and/or the Civil War as *junkers* (cadets), regular soldiers or sailors, officers, medics, or railroad engineers.[75]

The prospective students, the first of whom arrived in the late summer and fall of 1920, therefore avoiding the intensive scrutiny that began in August of 1922, quickly learned the realities of life in the United States — the $50 that many brought with them did not last long. In San Francisco (and Berkeley, across the bay), however, a network of people assisted in acclimation, notably George Martin Day, the foreign student secretary of the YMCA at the University of California, and Charles Riley, noted previously. Students developed their own information and communication network to assist in day-to-day life and to find a way to subsist, including communicating about available jobs, until they could enroll. Their early efforts culminated in the founding of the RNSA, headquartered in Berkeley, near the university, in February of 1921, an organization with a charter, by-laws, and dues-paying members.[76]

Cognizant of anti-immigration feeling in the United States, the Harbin organizers of the student groups deliberately limited the numbers to approximately twenty-five to thirty-five members at a time, generally ranging in age from eighteen to thirty-five, in order to avoid the appearance of mass emigration. The terms of the students' entry into to the US were somewhat nebulous as, from 1921, they were immigrants who came under the quota for Russians instituted by the Emergency Immigration Act of 1921, but they *and* their sponsors, including George Day, reiterated their goal to acquire an education and thenceforth return to Russia to rebuild the country. In other words, students did not openly identify as economic or political immigrants per se, stating intent to remain four to five years. The Harbin YMCA assisted with obtaining the visas initially but, from mid-1923, due to pressure from both the US Bureau of Investigation (later the Federal Bureau of Investigation/FBI) and US immigration authorities, the YMCA retreated from participation, and the students had to obtain individual visas based on actual enrollment in a specific university.[77]

The US Bureau of Investigation, in fact, sent Agent H.W. Hess in August of 1922 to follow up on complaints from AIIS Commissioner Edward White, who warned that if the flow of Russians was not stopped, the country would soon "be filled with a cheap class of labor."[78] As noted, Hess interrogated Nadia Shapiro and her group. In subsequent interviews with George Day and student Sergei Kovaleff (1899–1949), Harbin Committee representative and group leader, he inquired as to students' political views, implying in his report on the matter that the groups might not only be sympathetic to but have a link to the Soviet government, as a group of Soviet students had also just arrived at Berkeley for training in engineering and technical fields. Hess, as was typical, did not distinguish between émigré and Soviet Russians. Hess also concluded that Russian students were mostly working as laborers but that "unfortunately under immigration regulations it would be impossible to disbar these men unless they did become public charges at a later date." Indicating his complete misinterpretation of the facts, he wrote that "under the guise of 'students,'" groups "are being recruited in the various parts of Russia and will be sent out from Harbin," leaving open as to whether the issue was simply one of importing cheap labor or an attempt to infiltrate the United States with communists, his wording implying the latter possibility.[79]

Though officials continued to cast about for a way to legally preclude entry of more "students" from, in their characterization, the "Orient," US

Consul George Hanson in Harbin, sympathetic to the plight of Russian émigrés, declared to officials that the consulate "makes no distinction between an applicant who claims he is a student and an ordinary emigrant" (at least through mid-1923) with respect to issuing visas, indicating that he would continue to issue visas as he saw fit.[80]

A visa, however, did not guarantee entry into the United States. The possibility of being turned away even with visa in hand because the quota was full took a mental toll on people already suffering from the trauma of war and displacement, such as in the case of veteran Fedoroff, who took his own life after being detained for more than three months. Incidents of exclusion due to a full quota occurred, exacerbating an already tension-filled situation. As Sakovich points out, "inconsistent enforcement" of regulations spoke to the arbitrary nature of "legal" immigration.[81] When the quota was full, would-be entrants had the choice of either returning to their port of departure and making another attempt or remaining in detention at AIIS, depending on space availability. Most detentions were short-term, days or weeks, but in that summer and fall of 1923, for example, Fedoroff's group was detained for months.[82] Moreover, authorities split up families to remain within quota limits. Nikolai Yakubovsky (1886–1933) and daughter Tamara (1905–1994) were excluded upon arrival in mid-July of 1923, even though officials admitted his wife Sophie (1884–1987) and son Vadim (1921–2003). Although a reporter covering the case claimed the family's attorney managed to forestall the exclusion at the last moment, Nikolai and Tamara were, in fact, debarred (refused entry), returning in October.[83] Émigré reporters described the chaotic nature of immigrating to the United States in the summer of 1923, noting that "Angel Island is overflowing" and citing the reason as ships "hurrying" to take on passengers, doing so strictly depending on ability to pay.[84]

The arriving Russian students were also victims of both Consul Romanovsky's campaign against radicals in San Francisco and of well-meaning Americans like Day, who tended to mischaracterize the situation that awaited Russians in the United States. The disparaging comments of US officials about the students' lack of intelligence, candidacy for cheap labor, and the suspicion about their political beliefs had their roots, at least in part, in the efforts of Romanovsky to assist law enforcement, characterizing Russians in San Francisco as not only illiterate, but worse: radical. He thus added to the suspicions about all Russian immigrants' political reliability notwithstanding his own efforts to distinguish émigrés from "Sectarians."

Day, on his part, who corresponded with Russian aid committee officials in Harbin, persisted in presenting a rosy interpretation of realities of arrival in the United States. Day insisted that students arriving in August of 1922 "made an excellent impression upon both the Immigration authorities at San Francisco and Angel Island and in University circles here at Berkeley."[85] The initial board of inquiry, however, which led to the investigation and attempts to exclude Russians, was directed at the students in Kovaleff's group, which arrived 9 August. The hostility students encountered from official quarters contributed to uncertainty, confusion, and fear about their future in America. It was also indicative that at the hearing, Day, testifying as a witness, deliberately minimized his own role in the process of bringing students to San Francisco, indicating his own apprehension of US government scrutiny.[86]

The automatic detention of most Russians was also a consequence of their arrival in steerage. In contrast, the Olferieff family, who arrived in first class in 1920 from Japan, "had no immigration papers, only a 'Declaration of Alien About to Depart for the United States' issued by the American Consulate General in Yokohama." They were, however, able to debark in San Francisco "without much scrutiny."[87] Consul Romanovsky, who distinguished "elite" arrivals, wrote a letter to the immigration commissioner at AIIS in August of 1923 urging him to release Nicholas Sartory (1898–1934), a student who had arrived in July but was detained due to the full quota. Sartory was Gleb Ilyin's cousin and Romanovsky vouched for him, assuring the commissioner that the Ilyin family were "so situated that they can ensure that Mr. Sartor[y] will be satisfactorily provided for during his student days and will be in no danger of becoming a public charge."[88] Authorities released Sartory, an officer and veteran, though several in the same group were excluded. Sartory, however, never enrolled in university. He held various jobs but was hospitalized by 1930 and died of tuberculosis.[89]

Official scrutiny of those arriving in steerage continued throughout the inter-war period. Bazhenova, as noted, arriving in 1925, described how steerage passengers were not allowed to speak to relatives who came to meet them and were led, under guard, to immediate detention. Detained men and women were separated.[90] Both Nadia Shapiro and Alexandra Tolstoy (arriving in 1922 and 1931 respectively) experienced not only intrusive and humiliating medical examinations and procedures but also unsanitary practices by medical personnel on AIIS, indicating a disregard for the safety of arriving immigrants. As Behdad notes, eugenicist narratives about defective Southern and Eastern European immigrants were promulgated by medical doctors and public health officials determining entry processes at Ellis Island and AIIS.[91]

Employment Options

Once allowed entry, prospective students had to find work immediately as, by and large, their English language abilities were non-existent and therefore even if they had funding (which most did not), they could not enroll in universities.[92] In the 1920s, available jobs for non-English speakers included those on farms and at lumber mills, in mines, on pipe- and track-laying crews, in restaurants, and in certain types of factories such as tanneries, paper mills, soap-making and sugar-producing plants, where pay was low, the work often physically difficult and dangerous.[93]

The older the student, the more difficult it was to work at physically demanding jobs, particularly if they were veterans with injuries; older students also had more trouble learning English sufficiently well to enroll. Veterans' Society member Vladimir Nechorosheff (1885–1963), for example, who arrived on USAT *Merritt*, had lost an eye, and suffered hearing damage as a result of his service in the wars. His age and injuries contributed to his inability to acquire sufficient English-language proficiency. He stated the intention to enroll at the University of California in an RNSA application, but never did, working as a laborer for the rest of his life.[94]

George Day acted as a cheerleader, writing that the "period of mental and spiritual testing" the students were undergoing would be worth it in the end as they would save money from their labors in the "lumber mills, mines, other factories or ... [jobs in] ... Berkeley or San Francisco" sufficient to enroll for at least two semesters at the university. He urged them to stay strong and keep in mind that many had succeeded due to "persistence, patience, and hard work."[95] Saving money, however, had its difficulties as most lumber mill or mining jobs were in remote company towns with high-priced goods in company stores. Peter Reshetnikoff/ Resh (1899–1966) wrote that everything was "so expensive" in Westwood, the small town in Lassen County where many students worked at the lumber mill or box factory.[96] Reshetnikoff enrolled at a university in 1924 but dropped out and became a house painter.[97]

Figure 4.1 Three women laborers, standing by a sugar refinery, likely Western Sugar at Potrero Point, dated 10 June 1926. At left is Alexandra/Alice ("Shura") Gavriloff, later Polosuhin/Polon (1901–1960). The other two women are identified as "Nina" and possibly "Kira." Alexandra arrived in San Francisco with husband Gabriel Gavriloff/Goff (1893–1957), and son Gabriel in 1923. The Gavriloffs divorced and Alexandra married Dmitry Polosuhin/Polon (1897–1990) in 1939.

In California, jobs were available in Siskiyou County and Humboldt Counties (lumber mills, box factories), Yuba County (fruit-picking), Amador and Plumas Counties (mining), and Stockton in San Joaquin County (paper factory).[98] Jobs locally included work at Southern Pacific Railroad yards in San Francisco, Oakland, and Richmond washing train cars, sugar refining and oil companies in Crockett, and the shipyards in Oakland and Alameda. Wages ranged from $3.00 to $4.00 a day with six ten-hour days a week. *Russkaia zhizn'* regularly published company ads and listings seeking workers, the RNSA provided job information in bulletins, and students corresponded both with RNSA officials and each other about available jobs.[99] One newspaper listing included janitorial jobs at Stanford University, openings at Red River Lumber Company in Westwood, copper and gold mines in Colorado and California, dam construction in Keddie and Shasta, California, and the California and Hawaiian Sugar Refinery Corporation in Crockett.[100] Western Sugar Refinery also had a large plant in San Francisco at Potrero Point, employing both men and women (figure 4.1). The wages students or émigrés earned, though low, were standard; in other words, the complaints made by Department of Labor and Justice officials with respect to Russians undermining wages for Americans were baseless.

Prospective students expected to learn English while working and hoped to save enough money to get them through the academic year with promises from Day of scholarships, but Day initially misrepresented the availability of scholarships, warning in August of 1922 that "future groups [should] not ... count on them at all."[101] Even learning English was problematic: Nikanor Uteeff (1890–1961) could not afford to pay for an English teacher in Scotia, and thus wrote that he was "learning English very slowly." Uteeff had to wait until the early 1930s to enroll and study engineering.[102] Long hours precluded language lessons as well. Konstantin Shishkin (1891–1963) wrote to his younger brother, Boris (1896–?), who worked as a laborer in Alameda, that he worked ten hours a day, six days a week at the Red River Lumber Company in Westwood, and hoped to begin learning English in a month's time as he was "tired at the end of the day."[103] When working in the fields picking fruits or almonds, students often lived in barns or tents where it was also difficult to engage in serious study. Mikhail Gollandskoff (1899–1952) wrote to the RNSA secretary about working conditions and the "hellish" heat.[104]

When students found work outside the Bay Area, they wrote to friends or directly to the RNSA to inform others about available jobs, pay, and conditions, even the clothing required. A prospective student wrote that there were jobs where he was located laying pipe and railroad track, ditch-digging, or lumberjacking, but all required "substantial physical strength." He added that those who wished to come should bring, among other things, "two changes of warm underwear ... sturdy work shoes, dark blue workpants and good leather gloves" as mornings and nights were cold, all significant expenditures.[105]

At places of employment to which prospective students and other Russians gravitated through word of mouth, the environment had the potential to become "Russian." By 1924, "all train car washers" at the Southern Pacific Railroad station in San Francisco were Russian and "everyone" spoke Russian – supposedly, "even the Italian foremen" were

Surviving On and Off the Job in America

learning Russian. In other circumstances, having many Russians together led to different sorts of problems: in Westwood, a conflict between the "White" Russians and "Reds" erupted to the point that "many Russians were fired," with mill management refusing to hire Russians afterward.[106]

RNSA Membership

By 1926, approximately one hundred Russians had enrolled at the University of California at Berkeley, that number including student group members as well as young people who had arrived on their own or with parents. Émigré reporter Nikolai Dvorgitsky/All (1893–1977) noted how most Russian students' statuses differed from those of Americans: the Americans visited their "comfortable club" after class to smoke cigars by the fireplace, listen to concerts on the radio, read, or play chess. Russian students, on the other hand, raced to their restaurant jobs to wash dishes or to an apartment house to sweep floors.[107] In the Bay Area, students also attended Stanford University in Palo Alto, Healds College in San Francisco, San Francisco State Teachers College, California School of Fine Arts, College of the Pacific, and Mills College in Oakland.[108]

Although RNSA members pledged to "uphold the national (Russian) platform," which actually meant that members could not be communists/Bolsheviks, the charter of the society, as in most Russian social groups in the inter-war period, mandated its strictly "apolitical" nature.[109] In a lengthy initial debate about proposed unification of the Russian Students Club (RSC) and the RNSA at the University of California in October of 1921 (which did not happen), the issue of adopting the Russian tricolor flag as the official emblem of the unified group became a cause for dissension between the groups. The RSC representative, Solomon P. Milovich (1890–1975), opposed flying the flag as he felt outsiders would then identify students as monarchists. RNSA members Victor Borzov (1899–1975) and Boris Von Arnold (1897–1965), among those who supported having a national flag, felt that it would provide a better image of Russians to Americans as firmly anti-Bolshevik. In other words, those who supported flying a national flag were most concerned about American perceptions of Russians as possible communists.[110]

The RSC included both members whose families had arrived in the earlier migration waves, prior to 1917, and some who arrived after 1918. Of the twenty-one members in 1923, all of whom identified as "Russian," given their membership in the club, twelve were Jewish, one Georgian, two

Serbs, and several from western regions of the Russian Empire, present-day Ukraine, Belarus, and Poland. Milovich was born in Verkhnodniprovsk, now in Ukraine, arriving in 1918. As the RSC spokesman, he represented the views of members, who wished to avoid any link to Imperial Russia. That being said, none of the RSC members were students sponsored by the Soviet government. In other words, there were three separate "Russian" student groups at Berkeley in the early 1920s – the RNSA, the RSC, and the Soviet student group, noted earlier, with US officials unable or unwilling to distinguish between their differing circumstances.[111]

Students who, for one reason or another, distanced themselves from the RNSA, dropping out and/or failing the pay dues, found that a higher education was either unattainable or undesirable, indicating both a varied range of perspectives as well as social class differences. The commensurate differing perspectives also indicated that some students saw their future in the United States upon arrival. Alexander Ignatieff (chapter 3), who was "enthusiastic" about life in America, dropped out of university after one semester and worked as a floor layer and contractor.[112]

Student Michael Bricksin (1903–1982), born in China, maintained RNSA membership while attending the university in Berkeley and completing a mining engineering degree, but also focused on a future in the United States. Upon graduation in 1934, he moved to Selby in Contra Costa County to work for American Smelting and Refining, about thirty miles northeast of San Francisco. Bricksin married an American woman in 1931 and they raised their children outside of the émigré milieu, relocating to the Sacramento area after his retirement, where Bricksin played both tennis and ice hockey into his seventies, earning the nickname "Iron Mike."[113] The combination of marrying a non-Russian, completing an American higher education, and obtaining commensurate employment in his field that required immediate and permanent residence outside the Russian community were all factors that contributed to Bricksin's Americanization and the likely circumstance that his children did not speak Russian. Both of Bricksin's sisters resided in the Bay Area and, like Bricksin, also married Americans, likely contributing to a reduced focus on maintaining Russian cultural heritage.[114]

Those who enrolled in universities, completed degrees, maintained RNSA membership, and remained in the community had key roles in the development of Russian cultural life. By 1926, the RNSA had 500 members. Its headquarters were initially on Center Street in Berkeley, moving to a larger space on Durant Avenue in 1923 where homeless students could

Surviving On and Off the Job in America | 133

live temporarily.[115] The organization also maintained an office in the basement of Holy Trinity Cathedral in San Francisco, and the interrelationships between the RNSA, the church, and the charitable, drama, literary, art, sports, and other associations and clubs that formed in the early 1920s were critical in establishing foundations for the growing and interconnected community.[116]

Even if students initially thought that the possibility of return to Russia existed after completion of their studies, that end goal of a degree served to ground them – in other words, as they planned to stay in San Francisco for four or five years, they felt it important to create a network for moral support, organizing, for example, cultural events such as the St Tatyana's Day Ball every January beginning in 1923. St Tatyana is the patron saint of students; the tradition to honor higher education had begun in Russian with the founding of the first university in Moscow in 1755.[117]

RNSA organizers made a conscious effort to appeal to students' sense of Russianness, noting in a form letter to members that the slogan of "nationally-minded students" was "in unification there is strength." By completing their education students would be instrumental "in the matter of resurrecting ... [Russia's] ... national power." The references to Russia's "rebirth," "resurrection," and "rebuilding" appeared repeatedly in RNSA literature to encourage students to persevere and maintain a spirit of unified Russianness.[118] When student Anna Perova died of pneumonia in Whittier, California in September of 1923, her obituary in the Russian Student Bulletin extolled her "faith in the rebirth of Russia."[119] As the years passed and students successfully completed degrees, found jobs, and purchased homes in San Francisco, the sense of unity engendered initially reinforced the importance of maintaining cultural heritage even if or specifically *because* return to the homeland was no longer a consideration for the current generation.

Surviving on the Job

Certain incidents relating to employment spoke to possible interethnic strife with Russians typically typecast as unwelcome "Reds." Ivan Gruzdeff (1899–1976), who initially worked as a train car washer and deck-hand, claimed that the "Italian-looking young man" at the counter of the employment bureau in San Francisco refused to take his documents after finding out he was Russian, telling him "Russians are bad.

I have never met a good Russian in my entire life," and accusing him of being a "Bolshevik."[120] Veteran and student Boris Shebeko (1900–1975), who worked both at Southern Pacific and Key System Train companies, noted that he had a poor relationship with his Italian boss, "Rossi," who, among other things, delayed issuing gloves to Shebeko to clean train cars with sulfuric acid, which dissolved even the gloves. Shebeko's reference to the ethnicity of his boss indicated interethnic strife, although, by Shebeko's own account, he was often at odds with his bosses.[121]

Shebeko may have done his part to contribute to a negative impression of Russians as well. He worked no fewer than seven different jobs before he was accepted to the University of California to study engineering. His supervisor at his first job at the Del Monte Packing Plant in Berkeley fired him after only seven hours because he caught Shebeko deliberately stalling the assembly line so he could rest. At a subsequent job spray-painting automobile fenders, Shebeko became sleepy from the monotony and accidently sprayed his African-American co-worker with green paint, the latter retaliating in kind. They were both fired. Other jobs he quit from boredom or fatigue.[122] Younger men like Shebeko likely felt resentment, and acted upon it, in response to the realization that the climb up the employment ladder for non-English speakers was either slow or impossible despite the standard narrative of opportunity and material success for those who sacrificed and worked hard. Student Ivan Elovsky (1896–1967) noted that students learned quickly that "those who do not work, do not eat," and the necessity of eating sent many to jobs where a "human being was no longer a human being but simply a unit of labor," indicating recognition of their expendability.[123]

To those who found comfort among their own, living in poverty while serving a higher calling was preferable to mindless or meaningless work. It was indicative that Colonel Vladimir Konevega (1885–1934), a Veterans' Society member from the day of his arrival from Harbin in 1926, initiated the idea of providing meals for unemployed veterans at the society during the Depression in 1932, taught himself to cook and bake, and, when twice offered employment outside of the society, refused, as he felt duty-bound to help his fellow veterans, despite his poverty (veterans who worked in the kitchen received free meals but no pay).[124] That thinking also underlined the cultural divide between generations, with older émigré males finding solace in maintaining relationships with their compatriots within nonstandard employment contexts in the United States as well as in émigré cultural activities.

The trope about Russian generals working at menial jobs in emigration did have a basis in reality. Given the age of higher-ranking military men, lack of English-language ability, and poverty, their choices were limited. General Viktorin Moltchanoff (1886–1975), who had fought the Bolsheviks up and down the Volga and in Siberia, arrived in Seattle in August of 1923 with his family. Even upon arrival in the United States, he "thought we might return." Soon, however, he "broke with ... [his] ... past" as he "had to earn a living." Moltchanoff worked in building maintenance and later supervised a group of "former White Russian officers as maintenance men whom he continued to command using Russian as if they were still on the battlefield in Siberia."[125] He sponsored others to come to the United States including Shebeko, Colonel Avenir Efimoff (1888–1972), Colonel Boris Von Vakh (1882–1958) and his wife Zoe (1893–1987), all of whom arrived in Seattle in September of 1923.[126] All of the men, along with General Nikolai Saharov (1893–1951) and Prince Alexis Kropotkin (1859–1949), initially worked with Moltchanoff at the California Steel Corporation in Berkeley, loading steel sheets.[127]

Some émigrés of the privileged classes had a harder time adjusting to the social milieu where they worked. General Saharov went to work in his striped uniform pants and emphasized his rank to his American co-workers. They subsequently "gifted" him with a toilet seat to use as frame for his "official portrait." Saharov did not take this lightly and quit his job, returning to Shanghai after the incident, where he successfully ran a beekeeping business until forced to re-emigrate to the United States in 1949. Prince Alexei Kropotkin, however, a relative of the famous anarchist Peter Kropotkin, did not focus on his origins, conducted himself with "dignity and good humor," and therefore had no issues with the workers at the plant.[128]

Moltchanoff, as did other veterans and émigrés, had alternate means to maintain a sense of pride and dignity because of the forming Russian community, even if the job to which he was relegated was one he never conceived of doing in the past. The Veterans' Society and the Association of Former Russian Naval Officers provided venues for veterans' social and intellectual lives. The Holy Trinity Cathedral (and later the Holy Virgin Cathedral) provided spiritual sustenance. For male camaraderie and activity, the younger men formed the Mercury Soccer Club and the Russian Athletic Society in 1923, practicing regularly and playing other soccer teams in San Francisco and the Bay Area.[129] Something as seemingly minor as checking out Russian-language books made a significant difference in émigrés lives – the Veterans' Society had a 2,900-volume library by 1934.[130]

Jobs and Identity

The accounts of Russian student experiences in the workplace indicated that those experiences were not uniform, but a theme running throughout the narrative spoke to the dissimilar outlooks of Americans and Russians with respect to "jobs." By March of 1921, there were approximately 40,000 people who identified as Russians living in California overall, and the problem of finding jobs dominated Russian-language discourse.[131] A 1921 article directing Russians to the Russian Department of the American Red Cross's Information Bureau stated the problem outright: "Difficult is the lot of the Russian immigrant" if they did not speak English.[132]

The importance of having a "job" was such that Russian-language newspapers wrote the word transliterated into Cyrillic, rather than translating it into Russian, and placed it in quotation marks.[133] A "job" was an American concept – in the United States, a "job," to a great extent, defined a man's place in society and the choices open to Russian men – no matter their previous occupation, rank, or education – were limited to laborers' jobs. That particular struggle affected men much more than women in terms of their sense of self-worth, despite the fact that the majority of Russian women held "jobs" as well.[134]

In tandem, males were the focus of depictions of job-seeking Russians in the Russian press. *Russkaia gazeta* ("Russian newspaper"), a newspaper that began circulating in 1921 in California, dealt with the issue using ironic humor, publishing anecdotes, acknowledging the large number of veterans with its depiction of a poor "Russian refugee general" who wandered around Union Square (in downtown San Francisco), "scratched the bridge of his nose" and wondered "where can I get a job?"[135] Hassel, focusing on the Russian émigré male experience in France, makes the case that "the typical émigré defined *himself* in terms of what he had been before the revolution" and "*his* subsequent occupations mattered little regarding *his* sense of status."[136] Such a characterization applied generally to the older generation of émigré men in San Francisco, but also had to do with individual attitudes. General Moltchanoff, for example, accepted having to work as a laborer and janitor but maintained his dignity because of a personal sense of self-worth. He maintained a circle of compatriots around him who continued to regard him as a leader, experiencing that group support. General Saharov, on the other hand, by stressing his previous status to Americans, perhaps due to a sense of frustration or insecurity at perceived disrespect, elicited mockery and subsequently withdrew, not only from his "job" but from America itself.

Parisian émigré Tatiana Metternich noted that "the revolution had been more devastating to men than women," in part because women's identity was intertwined primarily with family relationships and friends while "a man's work has been primary to his self-definition."[137] The term "work," however, needs further definition as men of certain social status did not have "jobs" in Russia in the sense understood in industrial societies. Their identity was therefore intertwined with social status, military rank, and occupation, if any. Because material success was important both to the American ethos in general, however, and to the American definition of masculinity specifically (unlike, perhaps, in France), Russian men in the United States who had been members of the elite, military, or professional classes had to struggle to come to terms with the fact that in their American lives, their occupations might never be commensurate with their former status. Moreover, as Gail Bederman notes, working hard and gaining economic independence were included in "codes of manliness" in the United States, as an underlying tenet in American culture identified economic independence, in particular, as "strength," and dependence on family or society, therefore, as "weakness."[138] Such concepts of manliness were at odds with émigré perspectives about membership in groups, for example, which supported individuals both morally, and, to some extent, materially. In the process of Americanization, the idea of "independence" as "strength" influenced how younger men may have dealt with integration into American society versus the extent of their continued interaction with the émigré community. A lack of material success, over time, particularly for younger arrivals, may have indeed been a contributor to despair and subsequent self-destructive acts then, as they came to perceive the circumstance of material poverty as a "weakness" they were unable to overcome.

In the initial period, group associations were a critical factor in easing the effects of cultural shock. The trauma of the émigré experience contributed to group cohesion and facilitated at least the initial efforts to seek and find comfort among their own.[139] Those émigrés who remained in the San Francisco Bay Area, associating with other émigrés, joining organizations, attending church, and reading Russian newspapers began to feel a sense of community as they shared experiences and began to formulate and share the collective nostalgic memories of their homeland, a way as well to escape the dreariness of *byt*. Utilizing nostalgia to find meaning in life in exile was a means to forestall despair. Those who left the community and/or the Bay Area lost that connection. Away from the nucleus that was the Russian Orthodox Church and the expanding circles of community (both religious and secular) that surrounded it, many shed cultural markers, and particularly if they Americanized their name, expeditiously blended into American society, taking an alternate route to find a way to survive in America.

Boris Von Arnold (who kept his Swedish family surname) married outside the Russian community, moved to New York in 1930, and had a successful career as a teacher and psychologist living on Park Avenue. But apart from providing current addresses, he did not communicate with sister Antonina in San Francisco for over twenty years, "disassociating" himself completely. Their mother thought he had died. He finally visited Antonina when their mother was able to immigrate to the United States in 1954 from China.[140] Such estrangement may have stemmed from a desire to obscure "Russianness" or, at the very least, to control how others perceived that individual's Russian background. Elite heritage was a benefit. In Antonina's view, Boris maintained what she called his "Russian ego" largely because his wife's family put a "premium" on his "unquestionable gentle birth," an avenue of acceptance for Russians in American society of which he was able to take advantage.[141]

As the Russian community in San Francisco coalesced, members sought to bolster one another through organizations and social groups that fed cultural hunger and provided solace in exile. Migrating to San Francisco from China (i.e., distancing themselves geographically from the Russian "earth") reinforced the possibility that going home would not happen in their lifetime, but that realization did not lessen the need to maintain a connection to Russia through a kind of collective consciousness – the "real life" of veterans, students, émigrés, and their families rather than the everyday life of toil and hardship. The struggle to gain entry to the United States took a mental toll, however, as did the difficult adjustments to life once arrived, on people who had experienced almost a decade of upheaval and violence. Upon attaining the immediate goal of successful entry, the reality of life in American sank in and, for some, that reality was unbearable.

The Veterans' Society, led by older men in the community attempting to retain a link to the Russia they had "lost" and the RNSA, (generally) younger men looking to the future, whether in a new Russia or the United States, provided a foundation for the community going forward, despite an inevitable generational divide with respect to the extent of acculturation or assimilation to American society. Both groups made efforts to maintain Russian traditions, to organize and participate in commemorative and celebratory events that developed and reinforced a sense of community and belonging to people traumatized by years of war and forced migration. Both the veterans and the students, as well, made a concerted effort in this period to avoid politicization of the groups, while often referencing the importance of democracy and democratic ideals. Nevertheless, they uniformly stated that pro-communist/Bolshevik supporters need not apply for membership.

Survival of individuals in a place where some felt unwelcome and others trapped was critical, but no less important was the survival of Russian culture. In fact, to some extent culture took precedence by virtue of the status of most Russians in American society in the inter-war period. Lacking the resources to assist individuals in crisis, or to substantively alter poor living or job conditions, groups could nevertheless mobilize to organize cultural events and institutions. The diversity of the community contributed to rifts but also brought balance. No one group dominated but all groups contributed something to the effort.

Moreover, given the history of the space where émigrés had arrived and settled, the roots they began to sink in San Francisco found familiar soil. Despite the difficulties of acculturating to an unfamiliar society, the history émigrés began to rediscover with respect to Russian California, provided some sense of connection to the homeland, due in great part to the surviving relics of the nineteenth-century Russian imperial project. The history of a Russian presence had left its mark on the space, contributing to a sense of a mental territory, integrated with Orthodoxy, whose followers had raised structures, particularly temples, thus creating sacred spaces, familiar and welcoming to new arrivals. The comfort of an Imagined Russia became increasingly salient to émigrés, and this mental territory, intertwined with the built environment of San Francisco's urban space, reinforced efforts to retain cultural autonomy, the subject of the following chapter.

—5—

IMAGINED RUSSIA
Homeland Hearths and Dreamlike Landscapes

I keep running into … a Russia out of time and space, a Russia that
has ceased to exist in its geographical situation, but [which] lingers
on in the minds of the men and women who had known it.

NADIA SHAPIRO[1]

What are Orthodox churches, especially in far-off lands, but schools
of Russian history for a Russian person?

FATHER SERGEI LEPORSKY[2]

Situated on a bluff overlooking the Pacific Ocean, Fort Ross, a nineteenth-
century Russian American Company outpost and currently a state park,
is about ninety miles north of San Francisco. The final leg of the journey
to this historic site necessitates travel on a narrow, winding, often fog-
shrouded coastal highway that borders a steep cliff, sharply dropping
down to the ocean rocks below. Approaching Ross, the road turns inland
and is flanked by gently rolling grass-covered hills, lush green in winter,
brittle yellow in summer. Prior to 1937, the year the Golden Gate Bridge
was completed, travel to Fort Ross/Mettini from San Francisco involved
ferry crossings, train rides, and stagecoaches.[3] As automobile ownership
increased in the 1920s, driving to Ross, after crossing the bay by ferry,
was a possibility, but the roads were rough and there were no guarantees
of arriving on the same day of departure, given possible breakdowns
or obstacles.

Poet and writer Boris Volkov recounted his 1937 visit to Fort Ross, the
first summer after the opening of the Golden Gate Bridge. In his description
of the visit, he wrote of his feelings of "[Russian] national pride" and the

sense that visiting the space was a "return to my motherland." At Ross, Volkov wrote, *he* was the host and the Americans accompanying him were *his* guests. The ground they walked under the "remarkable California sky and its streaming clouds" was Russia in his eyes. The perception of the landscape and relics of an abandoned settlement as "Russia" was, in Nadia Shapiro's words, "out of time and space." Volkov's yearning to experience both a spiritual and physical representation of his motherland facilitated a link to the Russia of his memories at Ross.[4]

Volkov, self-admittedly not particularly religious, nevertheless focused on the rebuilt but somewhat decrepit Russian Orthodox chapel within the "Fort" enclosure, and exhorted his own countrymen to donate authentic Russian Orthodox icons for the chapel, replacing the "cheap multicolored Catholic pictures" someone had placed there. The chapel, in its rustic beauty amidst a serene landscape, "involuntarily melted [his]... heart," spurring nostalgic recollections of Russian built environments. The fact that Volkov, who alluded to his estrangement from the church, nevertheless viewed the space as something other than a paean to Russian imperial colonization, spoke to the inherent power of that landscape to spiritually unify a community that was often fractured by disagreements: a Fort Ross Initiative Group announcement about the 1937 gathering invited everyone "who valued the Russian past" to the celebration, church service, and tour of Ross on that day, an annual event since 1925.[5]

The spatial aspect of Imagined Russia as a mental territory for the San Francisco diasporic community encompassed both urban built environments and natural landscapes. Such a mental territory was distinctive when placed against the background and context of the larger Russia Abroad, generally concentrated in urban centers. Russian émigrés created a remarkably multi-faceted community in the 1920s, with a commercial "Russian center" in the Fillmore District of San Francisco developing by 1926, southwest of the religio-cultural focal point, the Holy Trinity Cathedral. The community included a broad range of commercial establishments, which played an important role in the continuance of artistic, intellectual, and educational activities as émigrés gained some economic stability. In turn, they made concerted efforts to establish societies and institutions as a means to preserve their culture in the face of pressure to assimilate. Scholars have noted the "invisibility" of the San Francisco Russian inter-war community, but that perceived "invisibility" was based on outsiders' perceptions of Russian identity.[6]

Figure 5.1 The chapel at Fort Ross, 1901. This is the original chapel, built in 1824. The description on the verso refers to it as the "Greek" chapel.

Absorbing the nineteenth-century Russian imperial/colonial project into their collective identity as Russians in America, émigrés focused on Fort Ross as an object of nostalgia, a site of memory (*lieu de mémoire*) linked to their ideation of an imperial, holy, and now tormented Russia.[7] As a surviving relic of the Russian imperial project, Ross was a site of memory linked to Russian native soil, a space representing the Russia of their nostalgic dreams in physical form (figure 5.1). Russian émigrés' absorption of the historical Russian presence in northern California to define their identity and place in that space was no less significant, both in developing a spiritual connection to the landscapes and the earth the diaspora now inhabited, and in claiming a place for themselves and their descendants in a society that often looked at Russians in askance.

The San Francisco Community in the Context of "Russia Abroad"

As Russian émigrés settled in northern California, their perceptions of what was a distinct mental territory developed into an "Imagined Russia" that encompassed urban "third space," a buffer, both mental and physical, for immigrant groups providing relief from dominant culture pressures to assimilate. For Russian émigrés, historic relics, commensurate sacred spaces, and the landscapes on which they stood provided a connection to the earth, expanding Imagined Russia outside the urban environment.[8] San Francisco was at the center of this network of geographic spaces, connected in the mind's eye, stretching as far north as Alaska, where historic and cultural sites, particularly Orthodox churches, dotted the northern landscape.

San Francisco also differed from European centers of émigré life in that it was a very recently constructed built environment, both a "frontier" and port city, evolving in the dynamic period of the 1920s to an even more populated urban center. Émigrés settled in areas west of the newly constructed "downtown" area, which had been destroyed by the fires after the 1906 earthquake, based largely on affordability, in neighborhoods of older buildings where rents were cheaper.[9] They expanded on the existing commercial and business establishments in and around the Fillmore and Western Addition neighborhoods, owned by earlier arriving Russian and other Jewish immigrants, creating an identifiable Russian neighborhood with its own center. Utilizing the built environment and urban space in which they settled, the community created a self-sustaining business enclave that served its members in both a practical everyday sense (such as grocery stores) and in an artistic/educational sense (e.g., arts groups, schools, dance studios, and music lessons). Moreover, American culture, which valued entrepreneurship, provided economic options, particularly for those able and willing to take risks, less available to émigrés in European countries.[10]

In exploring those options, newly arrived Russians took up various trades and engaged in business opportunities in the inter-war era, such as opening shops, selling real estate, or managing gas stations. Émigrés with medical backgrounds and sufficient language skills opened medical and dental offices, first serving the Russian community, and later expanding practices to the community at large. "T," a practicing physician in Russia who came to San Francisco in 1923 at the age of thirty-five, worked as a janitor and studied English for years to pass exams to become a doctor in the US. His first office was in the émigré community at his home address. By the mid-1930s, he had an office downtown and though Russians were the "backbone" of his "American career as a doctor," they also recommended him to Americans, thereby growing his practice.[11]

Imagined Russia in California, then, consisted of artistic and intellectual circles, religious and educational institutions, a commercial and service sector (which did, however, suffer severe reverses during the Depression), and, crucially, a cultural and historic link to the geographic space where the diaspora had settled. Though émigré rhetoric focused on eventual return to Russia, assuming a collapse of the USSR, reinforcing a sojourner mentality initially, a substantial number had become US citizens by the early 1930s. In the USSR, de facto dictator Joseph Stalin's consolidation of power in that period reinforced the belief that return for "White Russians" was unrealistic. Rather than leading to a concerted effort to assimilate, however, the understanding that return was not a viable option led, instead, to the conviction among a core group of committed community members that preservation of Russian heritage and culture was of paramount concern.

The mental territory encompassing non-urban spaces and natural landscapes inspired Russian intellectual creativity, including the production of literature, poetry and art about Russian California and Alaska, which émigrés often intertwined with critical aspects of the American historical experience, particularly "Independence Day," as a concept in their understanding of self-determination. Émigré narratives focused on the spiritual significance of Ross, despite the original purpose of the outpost as a commercial and agricultural outpost, through pilgrimages to the space and annual events beginning in 1925, documenting the process of remembrance for posterity to preclude "disappearance into oblivion." The process of discovery also reinforced the necessity of challenging American perspectives of Russian history and culture.

Foundation of "Imagined Russia"

Upon their arrival in the United States, Russian émigrés were not only a traumatized, but also a "deterritorialized," group, disconnected by violence both from their physical homeland and, initially, from the place they finally landed.[12] The process of establishing a connection, both tangible and intangible, to that territory, was facilitated by the journey to the American continent. The Pacific Ocean, which brought Russians to San Francisco, stretched back to the shores of the Russian Far East, and, by extension, Siberia and Russia, linking them to their homeland.

The nostalgia for Siberia was at times prevalent in reminiscences and writings of émigrés in San Francisco given their origins. Nadia Shapiro's musings about home, for example, focused on a magical Eden-like land. She recalled the "glorious butterflies [that] danced among yellow poppies, blue bells and orange lilies" and "the masses of ... fragrant white flowers I used to pick on Siberian meadows," her heart suffering "a little secret twinge" of melancholic nostalgia for her home.[13] That nostalgia for landscapes and natural settings, memories of spaces of tranquility and calm brought comfort in the face of more recent memories of home of war and violence. Such ideations encompassed the physical Russia that was lost to émigrés, fueling nostalgia for Russian native soil, the Russian "earth," underlying a mourning for a "great" Russia (in the imperial sense), a "holy" Russia (in the religio-spiritual sense), and the *leitmotif* of a "tormented" Russia, all of which had their own place in the narrative of mytho-poetic Russia as a foundation of diasporic identity, and the self-imposed task to carry on Russian culture outside the homeland as both an homage to ancestors and a foundation for the future generation.

The remnants of the nineteenth-century Russian presence in California provided a medium to connect the diaspora spiritually to the "Russian earth." It is indicative that when Baron Alexis Boodberg passed away in 1945, members of the Veterans' Society gave the priest a handful of "native [Russian] soil," to place in his coffin.[14] The importance of native soil and native land to displaced Russians underlay their efforts to come to terms with exile and the growing possibility of no return for their generation: "Though torn from our native soil, the roots that sustain us with the life-giving sap of Russian culture from within have not withered."[15] The metaphorical "tearing" of those roots for Russians had caused both mental and physical pain at the time of departure.[16] Their native land, a land that Russian émigrés, considered, in a mytho-poetic sense, the "terrestrial image of heaven," had been torn apart by civil war, and their last memories of homeland, quite opposite from any Eden, were those of destruction, violence, and carnage.[17] As such, given forced departure, the foundation of Russian diasporic identity was also rooted in historical trauma, which as Greta Slobin noted, informed the creativity of Russian writers even prior to emigration (i.e., in response to the violence of World War I).[18] Survivors of that war and the ensuing years of even greater violence and subsequent forced migration gathered in a distinctive place, both alien and familiar to them, bound chiefly by the consequent collective trauma of their experiences. The familiar were concrete objects linked to the Russia of their memories, embodied in San Francisco by the Holy Trinity Cathedral, with its seven bells, the largest of which had been gifted by Czar Alexander III to the first cathedral in 1888, as well as by the ruins of Ross, where one of the only standing (albeit rebuilt) structures at the time was an Orthodox chapel. The comfort of such objects meant that all was not lost: a pathway to maintain Russian culture abroad appeared, providing a framework for mytho-poetic nostalgic ideations of the homeland, an avenue to mitigate memories of chaos and commensurate despair, "the poetic prevail[ing] over the memories of violence."[19] Hope for the future, particularly for the future generation, encompassed a vision of an Imagined Russia existing side by side with the American reality in the space they now inhabited, which would facilitate retention of critical cultural values and traditions even as émigrés evolved into Russian Americans.

Imagined Russia in California brought solace and a dream of healing and restoration. To Russian people, as discussed by Valerie Kivelson, "location was a marker of identity," and by imagining Russia in California as an extension of the Russia that "had been," the diaspora came to terms with the idea that the Russia they had "lost" was not lost *forever*.[20] They represented Russia in waiting – return, though delayed, was nevertheless inevitable. Why else would they have been brought here by fate to this place where the remnants and relics of the Russian Empire had endured? If not they, then their children would return some day, reinforcing the importance of retaining cultural values. The landscapes of northern California – Muir Woods, the Russian River Valley, and the magnificent coastline of the Pacific Ocean stretching north from San Francisco to Bodega Bay, Point Reyes, and Fort Ross – gained a significance in Russian eyes beyond the natural splendor. Russians in California, in Bazhenova's musings, felt

> a pull to the north, to the windy and cold ocean shore, to the damp environs of Russian River, which flows through the hills and the gigantic trees of the Redwood Empire. All four counties – Mendocino, Sonoma, Napa, and Lake – are situated on the same plane, and are steeped in the memories of Russian people who live here, working, and dreaming, as we all do, about Russia. Perhaps that is why we are pulled here to these places, which were sanctified by the presence of our ancestors dear to us in spirit and blood ... Russians are firmly attached to the land on which the first Russians walked in California. This unites us with the country that gave us shelter, which became our second homeland; this brings us closer, in our mind's eye, to faraway Russia; this heals the bitterness of that loss.[21]

The natural landscape – the river, the forests, and the ocean shore – pulled at them as a place of refuge to sink their roots. The attachment to the land was largely spiritual in nature. That spiritual link to natural settings was foundational in Orthodox religious practice and tradition: for clerical families, an accepted form of recreation was to spend "time amidst nature," which they also associated with "family bonding, spiritual communion, and love of *rodina* (homeland)."[22] In Bazhenova's interpretation of the pull to these spaces, she also sought to define their relationship to their "second homeland," the United States, linking their gratitude for the shelter they found to the process of healing and restoration of hope in the future. The Russia of their memories lay beyond the Pacific Ocean, a medium that provided an organic connection to that homeland. Not only had their ancestors, crossing that ocean, brought both Russian culture and the Orthodox faith with them to Alaska and California, but that very ocean, which had also brought the diaspora to the American continent, had also washed the shores of the Russian landscape, creating a spatial link to the Motherland. Volkov, who described himself as a "Siberian American," wrote: "I truly came to love the Pacific Ocean. It linked me to my old Motherland, splashing at my feet here in California, and also washing up on the opposite shore, at Vladivostok."[23] He was not the first to make this observation: a member of a group of

Orthodox clergy who had visited Ross in 1905 noted that he had bathed in the waters (of the Pacific Ocean) that had "once washed upon some Russian shore."[24] The perception of space as interconnected through land and waterscapes rather than delineated by national borders facilitated development of a sense of belonging in their new environment for émigrés, despite ongoing nativist and political suspicions.

The relics and sacred spaces in Alaska and in northern California, particularly Fort Ross, facilitated the convergence of Orthodoxy and Russian national identity in exile. The forming community absorbed the singularity of the historical Russian imperial presence in California and Alaska as part of their developing identity as Russian Americans. The reference to the Russian historical presence on American shores, in concert with a focus on the role of the Russian Orthodox faith in that experience, appeared often in émigré writings.[25] They could stand on the "cold ocean shore" of the Pacific, a link joining the place they now inhabited with tormented Russia, the center of Russian Orthodoxy; the motherland was just over the horizon, visible in the mind's eye, waiting for her children to return home to her.

The diasporic longing for the homeland, combined with the growing awareness of the possibility of permanent separation from that homeland, created a particular collective identity and formation of bonds among Russian émigrés in San Francisco, many of whom had been in transit for extended periods of time. Suffering from identity discontinuity upon arrival and feeling an urgent need to establish that identity once regrouped in San Francisco, their activities included founding organizations that provided a sense of security but also transforming the urban landscape in which they settled.[26] Their sense of dislocation prompted a concerted effort to change "the physical and cultural environment" they now inhabited in order to create community but also to form spiritual connections to the spaces where fate, rather than chance, in this narrative, had brought them.[27] As such, both the urban environment of San Francisco and the landscapes to the north provided opportunities to create what Lefebvre called "special preserves" of "religio-political space," providing both spiritual comfort and a sense of belonging to a group that had a shared history of exodus, but also feelings of alienation and persecution exacerbated by continuing dominant culture suspicion.[28]

The political aspect of exile for White Russians remained ever-present. Confusion about White Russian identity contributed to their sense of alienation as, no matter which way the political winds blew, Americans misinterpreted that identity. Some Americans assumed that whatever conflicts had existed amongst Russians had been resolved by the early 1930s. In 1933, Consular Agent Arthur Landesen received inquiries from local organizations inquiring about establishing friendly ties with Soviet groups. He pointed out that he did not represent the Soviet government and directed them to contact San Francisco's Soviet trade representative.[29] The perceived economic successes of the Soviet Union during the global depression spurred an "admiration for communism" which, in the eyes of Boris Shebeko, "lasted for a long time."[30] The fact that the 1930s were also a period of artificially-created famine and renewed oppression of the peasantry in the Soviet Union, expansion of labor and concentration camps (later known as the GULAG), and mass arrests and political purges was dismissed as propaganda by proponents of Soviet social and economic policies. Credible figures, such as journalists Walter Duranty and Anna Louise Strong, wrote positive assessments of the USSR under Stalin throughout the 1930s, Duranty winning a Pulitzer Prize for his coverage in 1932.[31] Émigrés who spoke out to those outside their own circles about Soviet repressions were either ignored or shouted down as reactionaries. Inter-war anti-Communist writings by Russian émigré writers "sounded like voices in the wilderness," according to émigré literary historian and UC Berkeley professor (1946–1967) Gleb Struve (1898–1985).[32] Peter Balakshin related his experience of listening to "Miss D … chiding Russian émigrés" for their stance opposing the government of Soviet Russia "simply" because their money had been taken from them and family members executed.[33] Elizabeth Malozemoff, a descendant of serfs who had been a Social Democrat in Russia, recalled Americans discounting her arguments about the "dangers of communism."[34] In response, émigrés retreated from discourse about their history with outsiders. The lack of discourse on a topic critical to Russian identity outside the Soviet Union did create somewhat of an insular environment, reinforcing and solidifying the idea that Americans were incapable of understanding the émigré perspective. Russian émigrés, as individuals, tended therefore to show a certain face to the outside world outside the "territory" they had created. As such, they may have rarely exposed their inner selves, or perhaps their "real" selves, outside their own intimate circles, in this way perpetrating the stereotypes of Russian "mysteriousness."

Interpretations of San Francisco's Russian Diaspora

The assertions of the few scholars who have examined San Francisco's Russian inter-war community that the Russians, as a group, "remained one of the least obvious, least influential, and least visible ethnic groups" in San Francisco is, to some extent, understandable, as is the assessment that members of that community deliberately "disguised their Russian origin" leading to "a pattern of ethnic enclosure and isolation from the surrounding population."[35] These assessments are in line with available descriptions about Russians in San Francisco in inter-war American public discourse. In 1923, Robert H. Willson wrote a descriptive article about the Russian "colony" in San Francisco and concluded that "the colony is almost void" of Russian "shops, restaurants and places of entertainment," describing émigrés as people with "cosmopolitan ... inclinations." He concluded that émigrés were incapable of establishing a "distinctive colony of their own" because they had no common culture or history. In contrast, observers in this period noted the beginnings of an "artistic" Russian community (chapter 3), reinforcing the notion that Russians became "visible" to non-Russians only as performers. Moreover, contributing to the tropes of the day, Willson began his article with an anecdote about a Russian "duke" he encountered whose job was washing cars, claiming, with absolutely no evidentiary basis, that the thousands of Russians in America who had fled the Bolshevik Revolution were accustomed to wealth, power, and intellectual and artistic pursuits in that order.[36] The 1940 WPA San Francisco city guide (noted in the Introduction) repeated Willson's language verbatim, declaring that Russians had never "created a distinctive colony of their own," effectively erasing them from San Francisco's inter-war history.[37]

Russians did "disguise" their origins, altering names, and those "disguises" were meant to facilitate life in a nativist environment. Nevertheless, given that Russians continued to hold events throughout the inter-war period in public venues, interacted with Americans at events they hosted, and established businesses aimed at a Russian clientele, they were "visible" to those who wished to see. Developing a "dual identity" (chapter 6), was, in its own way, a "disguise" for interacting with the outside world. Russian émigré realtors, for example, may have marketed their services to Russians on the basis of common heritage while downplaying that heritage when dealing with non-Russians. The mental territory émigrés created, which provided a sense of security in a nativist and politically hostile climate, was a buffer, and, as such, perhaps, an "ethnic enclosure," but the neighborhood in which they lived was multi-ethnic, indicating that any "enclosure" was also fluid, allowing for interaction. Tangible physical manifestations of a Russian presence began to emerge over time in the neighborhood, such as signage, but the intangible aspects of that territory, the feelings of comfort of a "Russian hearth" were aimed at and evident to Russians. Their "invisibility" outside of public performance was an aspect of both the tropes that surrounded Russian identity and their economic marginalization.

San Francisco's Historical and Physical Environment

The fact that the geographic space of San Francisco figured in the history of Russian exploration and settlement of Alaska and the coastline of what came to be California provided a sense of connection, facilitating the sinking of metaphorical "roots."[38] Most important, however, was the historic Orthodox presence, which was small, but permanent, from the 1860s forward, as noted in chapter 1.

The Holy Trinity Cathedral, since 1909 located on the corner of Van Ness and Green Streets, was the only Russian Orthodox Church constructed in the Byzantine style in San Francisco in the inter-war period, thus a singular familiar structure to émigrés in an otherwise alien environment (figure 5.2). In the Russian language, as Vera Shevzov points out, a church building is "often referred to as a temple (*khram*)" and had a historically critical role "in fostering Orthodox identity," perhaps even more so in exile. Shevzov discusses the temple as a "distinctive feature of Russian Orthodoxy," as well as its importance to all Orthodox Russians, regardless of educational level, salient in terms of the variety of Russian social class representation in the San Francisco community.[39] The resident rector of Holy Trinity, Father Vladimir Sakovich (1883–1931), who had arrived with his family in 1918, played a seminal role in actively welcoming incoming Russians to his congregation, assisting newcomers. A congregant wrote of the feelings of "trepidation" they all felt when arriving in an "unknown country" hoping to find something that would "give us heart." Father Sakovich, by meeting "each and every ship with [Russian] immigrants," did just that, cheering them, giving them "useful advice," and assisting with practical yet critical issues of finding work and places to live.[40] His role as a representative of the Orthodox Church and clergyman at Holy Trinity reinforced the idea that the cathedral was both a physical and spiritual place of refuge.

Figure 5.2 The Holy Trinity Cathedral on Van Ness Avenue and Green Streets, completed in 1909; n.d., circa 1920s. The Church's bell tower and domed roof are aspects identifying it as an Orthodox temple to arriving émigrés. The crowd standing outside indicates it might be a Sunday, after services.

The cathedral became a physical and spiritual focal point around which émigrés built their community, although admittedly their influx changed the nature of the existing congregation, many of whom were not ethnically Russian (chapter 6). The church was a "source of consolation and a link with the past ... [embodying] ... the millennial history of Russia," a history specifically centered on the emigres' identity as members of that church.[41] Moreover, the cathedral's architectural form, like the relics at Ross (particularly the chapel), reinforced the concept of Russia existing "out of time and space." That familiarity of form, both exterior and interior, and sensation within the sacred space (smell of incense, sound of bells ringing, chanting) for émigrés, almost all of whom had likely attended church in childhood, whatever their religious feeling in adulthood, eased the process of transition to the unfamiliar environment outside the sacred space in which they now had to live out their lives.

As an institution, the Russian Orthodox Church was persecuted in the officially atheistic Soviet Union, which was a factor leading to an increased sense of loyalty to the church among Russians abroad, even among those, like Volkov, who may not have been particularly religious prior to exodus. That sense of persecution entered into the diaspora's collective memories as a critical factor leading to flight from a regime hostile to their identity. Moreover, the history of Holy Trinity was directly linked to imperial, holy, and tormented Russia: Russian Orthodox clergymen had founded the church in San Francisco and rebuilt it after its destruction in the 1906 fire. The violent Bolshevik targeting of clergy of the Orthodox Church, as well as the destruction of temples in Russia, commensurately reinforced the conviction, over time, of the impossibility of either reconciliation with the regime, and therefore of return while the Bolsheviks were in power.[42] Violent action toward the church and its representatives in Soviet Russia provided confirmation of the Soviet regime as a "satanic" power, legitimating émigrés' choices to oppose it.[43] Maintaining the Russian Orthodox faith and remembrance of "holy" Russia in the grip of that "satanic" enemy became part of the Orthodox émigré narrative about the meaning of their exodus and therefore their identity formation in exile, particularly in terms of retaining cultural autonomy. Moreover, in San Francisco, the link to holy and tormented Russia through the figure of Patriarch Tikhon (Bellavin), bishop of the Aleutian Islands and North America (based in San Francisco 1898–1905), who had played a critical role in the history of the church outside Russian borders, imbued significance to Holy Trinity Cathedral, given its symbolic importance in the history of the church in San Francisco. Patriarch Tikhon subsequently headed and led the Russian Orthodox Church in Moscow until 1925, the first clergyman to hold that position in 200 years, ultimately sacrificing his life while in a position of confrontation with the Bolshevik regime, becoming a martyr. The patriarch's condemnation of the Bolsheviks after their seizure of power, his persecution, even torture, by the Bolshevik government, and his death in 1925 under suspicious circumstances, reported in *Russkaia zhizn'*, underscored that significance.[44] In 1926, a year after the patriarch's death, a member of the community called for the construction of a monument to him either in New York or San Francisco, noting that Bishop Tikhon's vestments, remaining at Holy Trinity, were sacred relics.[45]

The significance of Holy Trinity remained evident even after the schism which led to the founding of the Holy Virgin Parish in 1927 (chapter 6). Admiral Boris Doudoroff, who was instrumental in the organization of the new Holy Virgin Parish and purchase of a building to house the new church, returned to worship at Holy Trinity, causing a stir in the congregation, and newspaper commentary questioning his motives, referring to him scornfully as a "wandering Pharisee."[46] The implication of the commentary was that whatever Dooudoroff's stated reasons to found a second church, such reasons were ultimately political, not religious, as evidenced by the pull to worship at Holy Trinity.

The very aspects of the physical structure of Holy Trinity drawing American comment were those that provided a sense of Russia "out of time and space" for émigrés seeking the comfort of home. The church diocese had raised $25,000 to build the cathedral at the western foot of Russian Hill after the first cathedral burned to the ground. The American reporter covering the new cathedral's consecration in July of 1909 commented on the "purely Russian" style of architecture of the "striking little edifice," labeling the church "one of the most unique houses of worship in the city."[47] The building was actually constructed in an "eclectic" style, integrating Russian "elements" into the American Revival-era design: ornamental gables and gilded crosses and finials atop the bell tower and dome.[48] Though the structure lacked the cupolas of the Powell Street cathedral, the bell tower and the domed roof identified the construction as "eastern" (i.e., "oriental") to Americans, while to Orthodox the rounded dome represented the "celestial realm stretching out over ... [the faithful's] ... earthly existence," the form providing an "Orthodox sky" under which they met in prayer.[49]

The church commensurately became a social center for new arrivals: a 1925 editorial in *Russkaia zhizn'* noted that all Russians "who have come to San Francisco during the past three years ... [know that] ... the Russian church at 1520 Green Street"... [is the place to go] ... from 10 a.m. to 1 p.m. on Sundays" to learn the latest news and information.[50] Parishioners emphasized the role of Father Sakovich and his wife Maria, *Matushka*, in providing the warmth and heartfelt simplicity that helped new arrivals take comfort from the church, indicating the critical importance of local clergy to maintaining faith amongst the congregation, particularly in the face of the later disputes in the Russian Orthodox Church abroad, which likely had an effect in some émigrés severing or limiting connections with the church.[51] A manifestation of Imagined Russia in San Francisco in the inter-war period, the cathedral was not just a place of worship but a sanctuary, a meeting place, a cultural reference point, and a center of both enlightenment and education for children.[52]

Spatially, the symbolic importance of Russian Hill just east of the cathedral remained centered on the sacredness of the space as a burial ground (chapter 1). By 1925, contributors to *Russkaia zhizn'* began to

Homeland Hearths and Dreamlike Landscapes | 155

elaborate on the generally accepted version of the history of the hill with stories about "Cossacks looking for adventure" who were buried there. Russians interred there, however, as noted earlier, were likely sailors who had arrived as part of Russian scientific expeditions in the early nineteenth century, or trappers who had died while in port, since no Russian settlement had existed in San Francisco (then Yerba Buena) in the first half of the nineteenth century.[53]

The sacredness of burial grounds where Orthodox believers were laid to rest, however (crucially, outside of their Russian homeland), was an integral cornerstone of Russian diasporic collective memories delineating Russian Orthodox space. In the absence of built churches or houses of worship, Orthodox faithful often pray and worship in cemeteries. Orthodox cemeteries were often located adjacent to churches or included chapels on their grounds, but even without structures built specifically for gathering and prayer, cemeteries, as consecrated ground where Orthodox faithful are buried, are sacred ceremonial spaces.[54] For example, on *Radonitsa* (the "Day of Rejoicing") on the ninth day after Easter, Orthodox visit family members' graves and bring food, blessed by a priest, to feast in company with the departed, traditions they maintained wherever they resided.[55] The ritual and tradition of *Radonitsa* were dependent on communities being able to establish sacred burial grounds or having access to burial grounds where Orthodox were laid to rest.[56]

The Russian Neighborhood in the Fillmore/Western Addition

In direct contradiction to Willson's dismissal of a Russian community, such a community in the Fillmore was quite evident by 1926. Along with the Jewish residents in the Fillmore and the adjacent Western Addition, the neighborhoods included Filipino, Japanese, and African-American enclaves.[57] Peter Balakshin commented on the diverse atmosphere in his "tales" of the inter-war Fillmore, describing how Euro-American, Asian-American, and African-American mothers showed off their "spring" babies during their neighborhood walks.[58] S.R. Martin Jr, an African American who as a young boy lived briefly in the Fillmore in 1942, recalled San Francisco as "Oz," a magical or fantastical place. He and his family lived in a flat on O'Farrell Street. The "racial and ethnic variety of people" in the neighborhood affected Martin "powerfully." Among his recollections were visits to Zimmet's Toy Store (Jewish-owned) on the same block where they lived, eating tempura prawns at a Japanese restaurant (though he noted that the flat his family lived in had been "taken over" from the Japanese owners, who had been interned in camps by that time), and observing with interest Filipino "hep cats" wearing "zoot suits," who congregated on Fillmore Street.[59]

Boris Shebeko, who lived in the East Bay, acknowledged that "most" of the Russian émigrés settled "close to the Fillmore" because of the Russian Jewish community. Shebeko went on to say "we made all our purchases in the Jewish stores on Fillmore Street," but followed up with the observation that "the Jews, at that time, were quite pro-Soviet, and when we came to their stores they called us White bandits."[60] Shebeko specifically said "we" and "us" typically amalgamating all Russian émigrés into his own perspective, although, by his own admission, he never lived in the Fillmore and therefore did not do his daily shopping there. Perhaps the negative commentary was directed towards him personally. Harry Koblick (1877–1930), for example, who owned Fillmore Bookstore, emigrated to America from Kishinev, Bessarabia (now Chișinău, Moldova), then in the Russian Empire, in 1904 (figure 5.3). A likely reason for his departure was the 1903 Kishinev pogrom, a rampage in which dozens of Jewish people (including children) were killed, hundreds injured, and Jewish women raped.[61] Koblick registered as a socialist upon US naturalization and advocated for workers' rights. He may certainly have clashed with Shebeko, given Koblick's lived experience and political leanings, juxtaposed against Shebeko's categorization of those who viewed the Russian Empire in a negative light as "pro-Soviet" by default.[62] In the contrasting recollections of Jewish Russian resident Raye Rich (1909–2002), whose father Isaak Wall owned Wall's Grocery and Delicatessen on Fillmore Street in the 1920s and 1930s, "even the Russian priest that used to be on Green Street" (likely Rev. Sakovich) came in to purchase "her mother's homemade pickles, potato salad, and coleslaw," lingering "for Russian conversation." Moreover, Isaak Wall closed his store for Jewish holidays but also for "three hours on Good Friday 'out of respect for the Russian Church.'"[63] The hostility that Shebeko recalled then was derived from his own biases, reinforced over time by narratives that overshadowed the reality on the ground in the inter-war period.

By 1926, *Russkaia zhizn'* newspaper ads for businesses referred to a specific area of the Fillmore District as a "Russian center," and editor Pavel Karelin claimed facetiously that Americans who ventured there brought their own Russian interpreters.[64] The core area encompassed a segment

Figure 5.3 Harry Koblick (Koblik), a pre-World War I arrival, in front of his store at 1010 Fillmore Street in 1919. According to Jerry Flamm, who grew up in the neighborhood, Mr Koblik sold comic books, stationery, books, and tobacco.

of several city blocks with O'Farrell, Ellis, and Eddy Streets running east and west, intersecting with Fillmore and Webster Streets running north and south (figure 5.4). Karelin wrote that "O'Farrell is ever more turning into a Russian street. Russian speech, Russian stores, Russian goods." *Kilka* and sprats (canned fish), Russian candy and other goods available at Vladimir Anichkoff's (1871–1939) Russian bookstore on O'Farrell Street made it seem to customers, Karelin averred, that they were in a store in the Russian provincial cities of Voronezh or Tambov rather than in faraway America.[65] This "Russian center" included, among other businesses, the aforementioned bookstore and café, a women's fashions store, a jeweler, a dairy and grocery store, a Singer Sewing Machine outlet, a heating system installer, another Russian café, a pharmacist, a barbershop, and a Russian *banya* (public bathhouse). The owners of all the establishments were either Russian émigrés or Russians (Jewish or Christian) who had come to San Francisco prior to the Russian Revolution.[66] The large number of businesses at the same addresses indicated, however, that turnover was high even before the Depression took its toll.

Figure 5.4 O'Farrell Street looking east to Fillmore Street, 1930. The Swedenborgian Church (conical tower), at left in background, was at 1640/1650 O'Farrell Street, between Fillmore and Webster Streets, an area of the "Russian center" of the 1920s.

Shebeko provided his alternative perspective that émigrés "lived in clusters close to Jewish stores," but that they moved away when they learned English and therefore, in his view, there was no Russian "colony" in San Francisco similar to the "Italian colony … centered on Columbus Avenue or the Chinese colony in Chinatown." Shebeko dismissed the idea that a Russian émigré community existed at all, effectively erasing them in his desire not to acknowledge the diversity of the enclave, also ignoring the Potrero Hill community in his musing about "Russian" neighborhoods. With this commentary, Shebeko was dancing around the nationalist and post-World War II neo-monarchist perspectives that defined "real" Russian identity in ethno-religious, rather than cultural, terms. His recollections (related in 1961) contradicted the contemporaneous descriptions of Russians who actually lived and worked in the Fillmore.[67] Shebeko's commentary promoted the idea that no Russian community existed in 1920s San Francisco, contributing to the same narrative by outside observers who did not recognize Russians outside of venues where they performed as Russians, in costume and surrounded

Homeland Hearths and Dreamlike Landscapes | 159

by symbols of the monarchy, as was the case, for example, in the 1925 Diamond Jubilee parade, or as performers on stage. The diversity of the neighborhood and the heterogeneity of the Russians living and work- ing in that neighborhood clashed with Shebeko's post-war perception of White Russian/émigré identity, which was manifested as not only racially white but middle-class, politically and socially conservative (generally Republican), and Russian Orthodox (chapter 9).

In direct contradiction to Shebeko's recollections, Russians owned or ran well over one hundred commercial establishments or services in the Fillmore/Western into the 1940s that specifically catered to the Rus- sian community (advertising in the Russian newspaper). Food culture was inarguably fundamentally important both as a conduit to nostalgic reminiscences of home and as a medium of bringing people together in an environment where they felt less alone. Approximately 40 per cent were restaurants, other types of food and drink establishments, or food stores, including bakeries. The Waxman family, who arrived from Russia prior to 1917 "without a kopek," first sold bread from a bakery wagon; by the mid-1920s, they owned several bakeries both in the Fillmore and other neighborhoods, selling their baked goods "all over San Francisco." Valentina Vernon recalled that they turned out excellent Russian bread.[68] Ukraine Bakery was also a long-standing business in the neighborhood, "famous for its bagels, pumpernickel bread, and apple strudel."[69] On Po- trero Hill, meanwhile, Samaduroff Bakery at 960 Rhode Island Street also sold "Russian" black bread and white "milk" bread, making deliveries all over the city in their van.[70]

A new arrival described his search for a recommended Russian restau- rant in 1926, providing a narrative about negotiating the physical and social space of San Francisco as he sought the comfort of a Russian hearth. Instructed to take the number 4 streetcar to Buchanan Street, he waited in vain one evening on Market Street. Deciding to set off on foot towards his destination, he negotiated through crowds of "cocky" Americans, and jumped onto a packed streetcar, disembarking on Bu- chanan Street, and spotting a storefront with "large dimly lit windows" advertising a "Russian Restaurant" in gold lettering: inside, "a small room, twelve tables covered by white tablecloths, a Victrola, two gold cages with canaries, and a white cat sprawled on the floor." First course soup choices were "Malorussian (Ukrainian) *borsch*" or *shchi*, (cabbage soup) with sau- erkraut; second course options were *pelmeni* (dumplings) or beef tongue. He described the patrons he saw upon entering:

In the corner, a gentleman with the mustache of a "Zaporozhian," swallowing his last spoonful of borsch, likely dreaming of a bottle of Russian beer from Kiev. Next to him, a fellow in eyeglasses, carefully sorting through some papers ... And here are two young lady university students in modest hats ... then four young men, students, laughing merrily... and the memory came to me of my rosy, bright, enchanted youth, and I recalled the pleasant student life I once lived. Suddenly I heard the singing and weeping of ancient bells, while from the open windows of a church, amid the scent of birch and incense, I heard the harmonious singing of a choir. And I imagined how at any moment a bearded Moscow cab driver would roll up to me and say: "Where to, sir?" Thank you "Russian Restaurant," for the Russian hearth, thank you for the *borsch* and *pelmeni*.[71]

Judging by the description, the restaurant in the above account was at 1698 O'Farrell Street, in the heart of the Russian "center."[72] It is indicative that almost all the people in the restaurant, including the writer, were single males, apart from the two university students. Couples were less likely to eat out, indicating that the act of eating out was a way to combat loneliness. Writer Eugenia Isaenko (1899–1969) emphasized that many couples eked out a living and thus had no money for such luxuries, with women, despite working outside the home, maintaining traditional roles as cooks for the family, reinforcing the daily grind aspect of émigré life for women who may have had aspirations for higher education or careers in the arts.[73] Eugenia Bailey recalled that on very rare occasions her parents did have a night out at a Russian restaurant owned by Nickolas (1895–1931) and Katherine Demin (1896–1979) in the 1920s. Nickolas also ran the Mercury Sports Club (which included a billiard parlor) at the same address at 1695 O'Farrell Street. Bailey noted, however, that the establishment was simply a "house," with no signage that would indicate to anyone outside the community that a restaurant or club was located there.[74] Valentina Nazaroff's (1881–1960) restaurant, located at 1850 Geary Street in the 1930s, was in her apartment and earned a mention in the 1940 WPA city guide as a generic "Russian" restaurant, clearly well-known even to non-Russians, despite the lack of name.[75] The storefronts and exteriors on these streets, if they advertised "Russian" cuisine in the Latin alphabet, contributed to an atmosphere of welcome to Russians and exoticism to Americans. As noted by Bailey, however, Russian shops did not necessarily "stand out": Russians, after all, "knew where the stores" or restaurants and gathering places were without advertising, contributing to the sense of an Imagined Russian space existing parallel to the "American" world.[76]

The description of the Russian restaurant within the enclave focused on the ambience as reminiscent of a familial "hearth": a physical space that evoked comforting memories and nostalgic thoughts of the homeland, in part because Americans were conspicuously absent from that space so that a patron could forget for a moment where he was. Peter Balakshin wrote of such a mental transposition in a different context when he was momentarily transported to Odessa as he gazed at San Francisco's Bay.[77] It was Balakshin as well who wrote of alternate impressions of the Fillmore, which residents encountered in their everyday lives (*bytovaya zhizn'*). He described the "larcenous visage" of the neighborhood in the evening, and youths with "depraved gray faces prowling in the crowd"; an amputee with haunted eyes selling prohibited lottery tickets; and gum-chewing prostitutes on the "dirty sidewalks" beckoning to prospective clients.[78] The ambience of the Russian restaurant, however, with the Russian patrons and their conversations, even their appearance, prompted a happy memory for the customer, involving church bells, choral singing, scents of birch and incense – all of these represented the Russia of his fond memories where he spent his happy youth, which, in his idealized recollections, included no thieves, impoverished disabled persons, or prostitutes.

Russians who arrived with some means or who were able to save money started businesses that offered a chance for a steady income. Vladimir Anichkoff, noted earlier, who worked as a bank manager in Russia, arrived in the US with 200,000 prewar Russian rubles, which he opined were worth about $1 in 1924, but little US currency, and, like most émigrés, first worked in a factory, while his wife, Maria, worked in a cannery. He opened his bookstore and café, Russkaia Kniga, in 1923 on Sutter Street, later relocating to the "Russian center" on O'Farrell Street where it remained from 1926 to the 1940s. In an interview in the mid-1930s, he said that his family lived tolerably well, although the Depression had greatly affected business.[79]

Other businesses that had staying power were hair and beauty salons as well as clothing stores, speaking to the changing appearance of Russian women as they adapted to American society. Bazhenova noted in a short story significantly titled "Alien Shore" that women who curled their hair, powdered their faces, and painted their lips were hired over those who did not, even for factory jobs. A character in her story explained that old age in America "revolts everyone" because it "reminds people of death," indicating a further obstacle for older women in the employment market.[80] Approximately eight Russian-owned beauty shops were open at various times in the Russian center area. Some émigrés opened such shops further east downtown catering to American clientele: Vassily (Val) Klensky (1898–1974) co-owned the Benedict Salon at 150 Powell Street and bought out his American partner in 1941; he was also in business with Jewish Russian hairdresser/shop owner Boris Boxer (1893–1951).[81] Jacob Boxer and his family, from Irkutsk in Siberia, arrived in San Francisco in 1931 from Shanghai. Four of his siblings (including Boris) had arrived earlier and were all in the same business. Jacob ran two successful beauty and hair salons in the Fillmore. When he passed away in 1955, obituaries in two San Francisco Russian émigré newspapers referenced his professional theater-related (hair and make-up) and charitable contributions to the San Francisco Russian community, including raising funds to purchase the Russian Center building.[82] Beauty and fashion likely enticed customers from outside the Russian enclave and were spheres in which exoticism or sophistication likely attracted women seeking beauty "secrets" or "exotic" (i.e., unusual) accessories, and perceived exoticism in such contexts was an advantage.

The most successful of such entrepreneurs in the clothing industry, however, left the enclave, carrying on her business into the post-World War II period. Nathalie Nikolayevsky/Nicoli (1900–1980), the Anichkoffs' daughter, initially worked in a factory, but started a fashion clothing firm with husband Lev/Leon (1892–1974), which by 1950 had attained a sales volume of $2 million a year. By that time, they owned two buildings in downtown San Francisco and lived in a mansion in Hillsborough, one of the wealthiest suburbs in the San Francisco Bay Area, south of the city. They did not abandon the "White Russian exiles," however, providing employment to émigrés, many of whom worked as clothing "pressers," and starting the "Anichkoff Fund" in 1950 to assist displaced persons with payment for passage to America. Despite altering their surname, Nathalie did not obscure her Russian origins: society columns in the 1950s all focused on her elite Russian background as a "descendant of one of Russia's oldest families." Newspaper columnists also consistently mentioned the fact that she and her husband moved in the same circles as the "leaders of the White Russian colony of San Francisco," Prince Vasiliy (1907–1989) and Princess Natalia Romanoff née Galitzine (1906–1989).

Nathalie, then, epitomized the Russian aristocrat that Americans envisioned as typical and desirable representatives of the émigré wave that had arrived in the 1920s: sophisticated, charming, artistic, with ties to exiled royalty, but one who was even more worthy of notice because she was a successful businesswoman in a glamorous industry.[83]

The Hero-Knight Ross

The phrase "leaders of the White Russian colony" was strictly an American interpretation of the role of the Romanoffs in San Francisco's Russian community. Prince Vasiliy Romanoff's rank distinguished him, but even that rank had no bearing on his position as an individual in the community. The nostalgic longing that encompassed memories of Imperial Russia was for a place, not a person. As such, the relics of empire, such as the remaining structures of Ross, largely in ruins in 1925, and the landscape on which the ruins stood, took on a powerful role as a site of memory, connecting the diaspora to the Russia of their nostalgic memories. Memories of the homeland and its history "took root" in these objects, providing content for narratives relevant to their identity.[84] Ross became a "symbolic site of identity" to émigrés seeking a connection to the homeland, as it provided a medium through which they could look nostalgically to the past, commemorating ancestors, with visitations and pilgrimages. Ross became a religio-political as well as a religio-spiritual space. Apart from the religious and sacred aspects of the chapel as a place of worship and therefore sacred ground, the political aspect developed in concert with developing émigré interpretations of the history of that space.[85]

The standard American dominant culture narrative either depicted the Russian "advance" into California as a rapacious military invasion involving battles with Indigenous people and the Spanish and Mexican governments or, alternatively, erased the Russian presence completely when celebrating Euro-American pioneers who flooded the region beginning in 1849 (the start of the Gold Rush and several decades after the Russians had founded the Ross settlement), thus populating the space to enable statehood. Dependent on Euro-American accounts, émigrés developed a narrative of that history, consequently focusing on the militarized aspect of Ross. When recommending daytrips to Ross, for example, in the inter-war period, American writers described it as an "almost impregnable fortress" of "Russian occupation."[86]

Prior to 1917, three of the Russian Orthodox bishops based in San Francisco had made pilgrimages to Ross, even inquiring as to the possibility of purchasing the property for the church in the late nineteenth century, but not because they perceived it as a "fortress."[87] Bishop Tikhon led a group of clergy to the site in February of 1905, spending the night within the walls of what remained of the enclosure amidst, according to then Father Pashkovsky's description, a "dreamlike landscape" of "magical" beauty, where "on a green field, as if on a soft velvet carpet, it seemed as if the Russian hero-knight, the old man Ross, slept and dreamed his heroic dreams."[88] The reference to Ross as a medieval "hero-knight" (*bogatyr*) spoke to mytho-poetic ideations about the purposes of Ross rather than imperial conquest (interestingly, a perspective articulated while the Empire still existed), which had focused on efforts by Ross's founders to create (albeit unsuccessfully) a food supply for perennially starving Russian America Company employees in Alaska. The chapel, built on the initiative of the Orthodox settlers (as there was no priest assigned to Ross), indicated their dedication to the faith in holding prayer meetings even with no spiritual leader and informed the clergy's ideations about the space.[89]

"Fort" Ross was therefore indeed a misnomer. As noted in a 1992 Department of Parks and Recreation report, "the defensive aspects of Colony Ross have been over-emphasized in both the priority of reconstruction and reinterpretation," with the settlement made to look like a "US cavalry fort depicted in a Hollywood Western movie." Discourse about the Ross settlement in the late nineteenth and early twentieth centuries undoubtedly contributed to the incorrect characterization and later Cold War-era literature re-emphasized the trend of portraying Russians, always and ever, as aggressors and would-be conquerors. The people who did inhabit the Ross space in the nineteenth century did not necessarily refer to the settlement as a "fort," despite the stockade and the cannon which occasionally fired in salute to incoming ships. Most of the people who lived in the settlement (Native Alaskans and Creoles as well as Native Californians) lived outside the walls, and those settlements were never recreated.[90]

The main purpose of the settlement was to function as an agricultural colony and, if possible, to trade with the Spanish, despite Spanish hostility to the Russian presence, small though it was. Hunting for sea otter was also a primary purpose, but the Russians very quickly exterminated the local sea otter population to the point that even today sightings are rare north of Monterey.[91] Even the appellation of "Commandant" and the subsequent use of "Commandant's House" to describe the structure where the Russian American Company manager (not "commandant") lived, was adopted by Americans from the Spanish.[92]

In 1925, *Russkaia zhizn'* ran an article commemorating the first organized pilgrimage of Russians to Fort Ross in July of that year, and the words "Fort Ross," the title of the article, were in the Latin alphabet rather than Cyrillic, indicating a reluctance to label the relic a military installation in Russian, given the spiritual purposes of the planned visit. The history of the site in this first article included inaccuracies, noting that the chapel was built by "Russians from Alaska and Siberia": those "Russians" were likely Native Alaskans or Creoles, given that few Russians actually lived at Ross, apart from the "manager" and his cohort.[93] The writer also used the term "pioneer spirit" to explain the reasoning behind the settlement's founding, equating it to the "the restless spirit of [the Cossack] Yermak" and his "thirst for new places and adventures" – rhetoric that echoed the popular versions of Euro-American incursions into the American West by "pioneers," but not accurate given the practical needs of the Russian American Company to establish a steady food supply. The decision to build the settlement had been based on practical and commercial considerations, a detail that had little significance in the role of Ross with respect to émigré ideations of its meaning in the context of the Russian historical presence.[94]

That first group visit to Ross took place at invitation of the Sebastopol chapter of the Native Sons of the Golden West to members of the Holy Trinity Cathedral congregation to attend a traditional July 4 celebration.[95] A church service preceded the early morning departure from the Holy Trinity Cathedral with another church service at the Fort Ross chapel planned upon arrival, setting the tone of the journey as a pilgrimage, despite the fact that many members of the congregation did not actually reach Ross in that first endeavor. The trek was a long and arduous one after the ferry crossing, with a several-hour journey northward to the Sonoma County coast, emphasizing the character of that journey as a test of endurance and persistence rather than a recreational and relaxing day trip. Some people had bought seats in a rented truck or bus while others drove their own vehicles, several of which broke down on the way, stranding members of the congregation.[96] The religious focus and demanding nature of the trek, however, reinforced the tone of the visit as a pilgrimage, and that the Russians, brought by fate, had a role

Figure 5.5 An undated photo of a group visiting Fort Ross. The photo is in the collection marked "Chapel & Orthodox Services," so the people in this photo might be members of the Holy Trinity congregation visiting Fort Ross in 1925 or a subsequent year. The chapel in this photo is the reconstructed version, built with four windows instead of the original three, altered cupola roof, and a Roman cross on the bell tower. The original chapel collapsed in the 1906 earthquake and the California state legislature funded the reconstruction, completed in 1916.

(and therefore a purpose) as stewards of that space. In essence, by commemorating the site, the community included it into their own collective memories, "sanctifying" the space as not simply a historic site, but as a place that linked them spiritually to their homeland.[97]

That first visit set into motion efforts to learn about the history of Ross and to continue interaction as much as community members were able, given the distance and the difficult traveling conditions (figure 5.5). In writing about a 1927 trip, the author noted that "access to [Ross] in past years [has been] … terribly difficult due to bad road."[98] Annual pilgrimages on July 4 nevertheless continued, as well as special trips for religious ceremonies, such as baptisms at the chapel, and individual excursions: Nadia Shapiro visited in 1926 with a group of friends.[99]

At times, however, émigrés who claimed to be celebrating heritage veered towards self-caricature rather than authenticity. In April of 1934, Valentina Vernon's ex-husband, Captain Igor Waripaeff-Vernon (1894–1974), married Vera Gray née Sprink (1894–1978) in the chapel.

Waripaeff-Vernon, "an aviator in the imperial Russian Guard during the World War," stated somewhat incongruously that he and his bride "wanted the kind of wedding we used to know in the land of the czars." The bell of the chapel rang "happily" for these "Russians of the old order" who "sought to recall ... [the days of vanished empire] ... with a ceremony in the imperial tradition."[100] Given the rustic simplicity of the chapel, the effusive description about imperial tradition might have made the two Russian Orthodox cathedrals in San Francisco more appropriate choices for their wedding. The couple purportedly chose the chapel due to "memories of the native land and the belief that some of their ancestors had once been at Fort Ross." The vagueness of the latter statement indicated that it might have been a fanciful notion articulated to impress American guests. Waripaeff-Vernon also noted that prior to the "downfall of the Russian Empire," he had been a "Count," once again playing to the notion of the prevalence of Russian nobility among émigrés.[101]

Vera Gray, born in Moscow, had earlier caused an uproar in San Francisco society by leaving her first husband to openly cohabitate with émigré Nicholas Prassinos. Vera had married Indis Alfred Gray in Vladivostok in 1915 and they came to San Francisco in 1919.[102] She met Prassinos at a San Francisco "Russian club" in 1921. Her declarations of love for him were published in the local paper as she had insisted on being jailed with her lover upon their arrest at the Golden Gate Hotel at the behest of Prassinos's abandoned wife. The publicly dramatic and even theatrical nature of Vera's love affair (she and Prassinos later parted ways), like her 1934 marriage in the so-called "imperial tradition," contributed to the prevailing notions of Russian exoticism and public performance of certain aspects of identity. The reporter covering the story in 1921, interestingly, noted that Vera was, despite the scandal, "a well-bred Russian woman," bowing to the tropes of the period that depicted Russian elite "well-bred" women as seductresses.[103]

Photos commemorating Russian community visits in the 1930s show congregants standing in front of the chapel, usually with Father Alexander Viacheslavoff (1884–1938), indicating its significance (figure 5.6). When reconstructed in 1916, however, the chapel differed from the original structure as the builders had had no input from architects knowledgeable about Orthodox church architecture. Moreover, the cross on the bell tower was Roman Catholic, not Russian Orthodox, "a serious error with theological implications" that was not corrected for more than twenty years, almost the entire inter-war period.[104] The continuing focus on the chapel as both

Figure 5.6 Holy Trinity congregation visit to Fort Ross, 4 July 1933. Father Alexander Viacheslavoff is in the center of the group.

Figure 5.7 Undated photo, taken between 1939 and 1941, showing the Orthodox cross on the chapel placed upside down.

Homeland Hearths and Dreamlike Landscapes | **169**

a historic artifact and a sacred space for Russian Orthodox did play a part in the replacement of the cross in 1939, albeit an Orthodox cross placed upside down, which then required a letter to the governor of California "signed by several hundred people" and two years for a correction of that egregious error (figure 5.7).[105] Émigré involvement in the Ross "project," then, was an almost continual effort to correct errors resulting from dominant culture insistence to reconstruct "authentic" and historic Russian architectural forms without context or input from Russian, Orthodox, and/or Indigenous people, similar to the reconstruction of the "fort."

Creative Work

The mytho-poetic aspect of Ross fueled creative efforts of émigré writers and poets, both professional and amateur, using for inspiration the relics of empire, the land, and the seascapes surrounding San Francisco. Selected encounters of Russian "adventurers" in California, such as the romanticized and oft-recounted saga of Imperial Chamberlin Nikolay Rezanov and the daughter of the Spanish commandant of the San Francisco Presidio, Concepción Argüello, in 1806, also garnered attention. In the early 1930s, Vladimir Anichkoff wrote an entire series of poems about Russian Alaska, Fort Ross, Russian River (initially named "Slavyanka"), and the Rezanov-Argüello romance. In his poem about Fort Ross, he made a point of mentioning "gray-eyed Indians," acknowledging marriages between Kashaya-Pomo women and Russian men. The epilogue to the series was a poem about the loss of the holy motherland, the Russian blood spilled, the destruction of churches in Russia, and a condemnation of the celebration of the murderers who killed the Russian imperial family, linking Imagined Russia with the triad of imperial, lost, and tormented Russia. He began writing that last poem on 4 July 1930, at Russian River, and read it to an audience at Fort Ross on 4 July 1932, reinforcing the importance of these two spaces to his creative effort and the significance of American Independence Day, albeit in a mytho-poetic sense, as a concept Russians in exile appreciated in view of its celebration of liberation from oppression.[106]

Bazhenova also delved into Russian California history against the background of the northern California landscape. Her poems were titled "Russian River," "Overlooking the Bay" (in honor of the restoration of Fort Ross in the early 1930s), and "California." The Rezanov-Argüello romance was also a subject of a poem, following the lead of the American authors who had earlier utilized it as an inroad to the "romantic" history of

California.[107] Bazhenova referenced the California landscape and a destroyed ruin in the context of disappeared Russian imperial glory: "In May the grasses turn yellow / Long gone are Rezanov and Conchita / No imperial Russian glory / In the forgotten charred remains."[108] A note of melancholy permeated her writing here, often present in the contemplation of Russian life abroad.

Other works about the history of Russian America appeared in newspapers for the Russian reading public or journals published by émigrés. In 1933–34, for example, Peter Balakshin, Nadia Shapiro, Elizabeth Malozemoff, and several others collaborated on publishing a *California Almanac* showcasing Russian émigré writers. Shapiro noted that the first issue was not very good but that the second focused on "Russian America" and was more successful, the term, according to Shapiro, "reflecting the life and art of Russians living in the United States," including articles and essays exploring the history of nineteenth-century Russian America. Her focus on "life and art" acknowledged the criticality of the role of art in émigré life.[109]

Because émigrés initially intermixed information they gleaned from American sources and the limited Russian sources to which they had access, they repeated erroneous information of adversarial and conquest narratives. Members of the executive committee of the Fort Ross Initiative Group, formed by émigrés in San Francisco, traveled to Ross to take photographs for an album in August of 1936. By that time, the state of California had reconstructed some of the collapsed and missing stockade walls and the southeast blockhouse, as well as the officer's barracks.[110] The authors dedicated the album to the "Russian pioneering heroes" who "landed on the shore of the New Continent" in the eighteenth century and, in a description of a photo of the rebuilt main gate, noted that both "Indians and the Spanish" made constant but fruitless attempts to break into the fort, failing due to the bravery of the beleaguered Russians.[111]

The dependence on American sources in the inter-war period led to a tendency to imitate the rhetoric of American expansionism and conquest, which both obfuscated the nature of the Russian settlement and produced contradictory accounts. Church historians had utilized the phrase "men of valor and initiative," along with references to heroism when recounting Russian imperial-sponsored visits to the Americas and the Russian American Company employees who built Ross. That phrase, and the term "Russian pioneers," appeared in émigré inter-war accounts about the settlement, but "valor and initiative" in the original context of narratives by members of the clergy certainly did not refer to military action against Indigenous inhabitants.[112] The erroneous implications of the language affected historical accuracy in other ways. In a review of the Fort Ross Album in a Shanghai Russian émigré newspaper, *Slovo*, the author wrote that Ivan Kuskov, the Russian American Company employee who founded Ross in 1812, was killed by Native Americans in one of their "frequent" attacks at Bodega Bay and that his grave had been preserved there.[113] Kuskov had actually returned to Russia, where he died, and had been buried in his hometown of Totma. As late as 1951, San Francisco Russian Historical Society president Alexander Farafontoff (1889–1958) repeated the erroneous information about Kuskov dying at the hands of "hostile Indian tribes," though he did acknowledge in that article that there were conflicting accounts about Kuskov's fate. In that same article, Farafontoff, in contrast to earlier writings, stressed the "very friendly and business-like relationship" between the Russians and the Indigenous people in California, "unlike" with the Spanish. He also made clear his perspective that "the land belonged" to the Native Americans.[114] In her own 1940 article, Bazhenova first stated that the Russians hid behind the tall wooden stockade of Ross when Indians attacked but immediately contradicted the statement: "However, the Indians rarely attacked as they had a quite friendly relationship with the Russians," indicating both discomfort with and uncertainty about American narratives.[115]

The Euro-American characterizations of Ross, however, went so far as to describe it as part of a military mission to colonize the American West, or at least the Pacific coast, a plot foiled by Euro-Americans who arrived just in time to seize the land for the United States, aided by the Mexican government, who did not want the Russians in California either. The Mexican government facilitated "the creation of new ... [Euro-American] communities north of San Francisco to block Russian expansion south." The Russians, "unable to expand to more favorable land," abandoned the settlement soon after, leaving by 1841.[116]

The annual July 4 visits that began in 1925 continued during World War II. In 1942, the Holy Trinity congregation made the pilgrimage despite a wartime shortage of automobile tires: "According to established tradition of paying our respects to our ancestors on Independence Day ... a service was held last Saturday [at Fort Ross]." Further, Father Gregory Shutak "passionately called for all to prayerfully honor the memory of our ancestors, the founders of this historic church, and called Fort Ross a rock of faith, which now strengthens our faith in the holy victory of our motherland." The reference to the Russian motherland in the context of the Soviet-American alliance during the war indicated a renewed expectation of change in the Soviet Union (chapter 8).[117]

Many of the people who continued to travel to the Independence Day services every year became members or supporters of the Fort Ross Initiative Group, and in 1937 they formed the Russian Historical Society, whose goals were not only to study the history of the Russian presence in America but to organize efforts to preserve Russian émigré history and Russian heritage.[118] The society reiterated its task of learning "what Russians did here in America," indicating the continuation of the process of rediscovery that had begun more than a decade earlier.[119] The creation of the society was also a link in the process of founding the Museum of Russian Culture and Archive in San Francisco after World War II (chapter 8).

Farafontoff, the society's president, described himself as a Siberian from the Yenisei River region, which in part spurred his interest in the history of Ross. But his efforts to create a historical monument there to commemorate Russian contributions were also fueled by a desire "to help Americans both understand Russians as well as like them."[120] In an interview with Shapiro, Farafontoff stressed his "blood ties" to Siberia and Irkutsk: "Perhaps the blood of my ancestors has an effect as to why I always felt a pull to go east."[121] The focus on "blood ties" in the "east" was indubitably a euphemistic way to acknowledge Indigenous (Siberian) roots. Farafontoff also recognized the ongoing cultural divide given that he admitted here that (in his perspective) Americans neither understood Russians nor liked them.

As part of its mission, the Russian Historical Society had begun to explore the idea of creating an archive in light of the realization that much of the cultural and historic material brought by émigrés to America was being lost. Seeing Ross in its initial decrepit and decayed condition reinforced the understanding of the threat to the émigrés' cultural heritage, at risk of disappearing once they were gone. In rediscovering the history of Russian America, émigrés realized how a dominant culture narrative, which considered them alien, might quickly erase their presence (or mischaracterize it) if left alone to do so. Moreover, the younger generation did not necessarily value that culture sufficiently to preserve it. Farafontoff articulated the problem in a 1940 general meeting:

> Treasures are being lost, disappearing: some, such as books, manuscripts, and letters are simply being thrown into the garbage or burned while that which is "more valuable" in the eyes of our youth: silver and gold items – artifacts of a remarkable past – are sold for their weight to the jeweler.

Farafontoff's focus on the commodification of Russian artifacts indicated a concern about American values adopted by the younger generation as well as the loss of interest in both Russian heritage and family history by that generation. By the time of the meeting in 1940, his initial goal of drawing in Americans had also faded. Though commentary about facilitating convergence between America and a non-Soviet Russia of the future remained in discussions about the purposes of the Russian Historical society, Farafontoff stated bluntly that the effort to preserve Russian émigré or Russian-American history was the duty of Russians as Russian history was "commonly falsified" by non-Russians, and "non-Russians" in this context meant Americans.[122]

The Russian imperial presence, with its colonization process, had left behind material culture in California to be rediscovered, restored, and reimagined as a spiritual progenitor of exiled Russian refugees, bereft of their homeland but creating a link with those remnants of empire and thus a foundation for an Imagined Russia. Unlike groups who had left the empire prior to 1917, whose collective memories of Imperial Russia and consequent exodus often spoke of oppression and intolerance, the émigrés formed a nostalgic vision of their native land as a politically and economically burgeoning, culturally rich Orthodox homeland. On the brink of modernization, their homeland was destroyed by the Bolshevik regime, a vision which provided a unifying ideology, particularly given common experiences fighting in the Civil War. For all its possible faults (and these faded in relevance over time), Russia remained their ancestral, spiritual, and intellectual home, the natural landscape and built environment of which played an integral part in collective memory recollection and visualization. The rediscovery of the Russian imperial presence in the space émigrés now inhabited in California helped to form a link to their native land, now existing "out of time and space." Such a link allowed them to remain Russian both within the mental territory of Imagined Russia and amidst the processes of acculturation. In the spaces they appropriated, the Russian corners populating that mental territory – the church, Fort Ross, their enclave in San Francisco and, later the built structure of a new Russian Center, founded in 1939 – they were the "hosts" and those who entered Russian spaces did so as guests, an empowering process for previously stateless refugees who were adjusting to a new reality.

The individuals who pursued creative and artistic endeavors, historical research, and pragmatic steps to establish a solid foundation that would outlast their lives succeeded in doing so. By writing their own history they provided a record for future generations and began the process to ensure a measure of stability for the community: acquiring a physical space that would be their Russian corner and that would hold their history (chapter 8). By the mid-1930s, many had crossed a Rubicon of shedding émigré identity and becoming Russian Americans, but the benefits of citizenship did not necessarily include an automatic sense of belonging, particularly against the background of continuing negative perceptions of Russians in various, often contradictory, contexts: as reactionaries on the one hand and communist spies on the other; as thwarted invaders of America or hopelessly backward foreigners. As is evident, some émigrés found ways to utilize tropes for their own purposes, but by and large the sense of alienation Russians felt informed much of their activity.

By creating organizations independent of American dominant culture, Russians were able to take first steps to ensure their culture and history did not "disappear into oblivion." Recognizing also that dominant culture institutions directed historical narratives, Russians did not embrace overtures by Americans to become involved in Russian efforts at heritage preservation, largely forging their own way, perhaps given the missteps with respect to the chapel reconstruction and cross placement. Economic realities tended to modify grand visions, however, as a desire to be independent of American patronage or control did not take into account the expense of maintaining cultural heritage sites, an endeavor which requires deep pockets and is therefore out of reach for smaller groups existing within larger dominant cultural environments.

Those who focused their efforts on this cultural preservation were also generally of the older generation: people who recognized that they would likely die outside the homeland and who recognized that younger Russians, even those born in Russia (or China) who had immigrated with their parents, were in the process of becoming Americanized and therefore would not necessarily value that heritage and culture, particularly in the face of dominant culture pressure. The struggle to preserve some connection to Russian culture among youth in an alien society that was in the throes of its own modernization drive began upon arrival. Many émigrés took part in that effort, with women shouldering much of the burden, the subject of the following chapter.

FAMILY MATTERS
Nostalgic Homelessness and Dual Lives

No American with deep roots in the American soil can understand the nostalgic homelessness of immigrant children, the pathos of second-generation aliens.

EUGENE LYONS, 1937[1]

Perhaps I recall this impression of gloom because of our gray shabby figures: all of us newly arrived refugees; but perhaps the gloom simply pervaded my own mind.

OLGA ILYIN[2]

The Kourlin family – Alexander, Olga, and baby George – arrived in San Francisco on USAT *Merritt* in 1923. George was not yet four months old, born in Fort Olongapo in the Philippines. The following year Olga gave birth to a daughter, whom they named Vera (Faith). The Kourlins did not live in the Fillmore but in the Potrero Hill neighborhood, perhaps seeking more space for their growing family. But Alexander, who worked as a laborer, died of unknown causes in 1929. Olga stayed on in the neighborhood, on De Haro Street, taking in lodgers. By 1934, however, both Olga and daughter Vera were very ill; Vera died of a brain tumor in May and Olga of chronic pulmonary tuberculosis in September. Eleven-year-old George was left an orphan.[3]

Fellow USAT *Merritt* arrival Alex Sozonoff (1895–1973) and his wife Maria (1894–1955) took George in. In 1940, they resided together with Daniel Pavlenko (1901–1953), another *Merritt* passenger who lived with the Sozonoffs until his death in 1953, indicating long-lasting kin relationships formed in migration. George thereafter forged his own path in life, worked a variety of jobs, enlisted in the Navy in 1943 and fought in World War II, then attended the University of Colorado, joined the Air Force, and served in Korea and Vietnam. Despite the losses George incurred in childhood, the promise of the American dream seemed to hold true for him: he obtained a higher education, joined the military, earning the rank of captain in the Air Force, raised a family, and lived out his life in Arizona. Whether deliberately or resulting from his life choices (none of his three spouses were of Russian heritage), once he left the Russian community in San Francisco, he never returned.[4]

George's loss of family happened after arrival in the United States, but the Kourlins' experiences as refugees, displaced by war, and the commensurate struggles to reach a safe haven, had to have informed the development of his identity in America to some degree. Joining the American military was often a factor in the complete assimilation of young men of Russian heritage, but other factors may have been in play. Both his parents died young, perhaps in consequence of circumstances of that displacement (i.e., no access to medical care), and he also lost his only sibling, leaving him with no family in America, despite his kinship ties to the Sozonoffs. The trauma of loss may have been related, in his mind, to his Russian heritage, spurring him to move on to an "American life," instead of leading a "dual" life. Poet Elena Grot had noted that the circumstances in which young people lived their lives in Russia, beginning in August of 1914 when their country entered World War I, added to the mental and emotional burdens caused by forced migration (chapter 3). The burdens imposed on parents were often borne by their children as well, even if they grew up in America, and remaining in the community necessitated engagement with those burdens.

Grot had pointed to the fact of instability, conditions in their war-torn homeland, and the dangerously violent circumstances in which many émigrés had spent their youth.[5] The reconfigurations of "traditional" family norms with respect to marriage, divorce, and decisions on whether to have children likely resulted at least in part from those experiences. Once in the United States, interpersonal relationships did not stabilize. American life and culture were unfamiliar to Russian émigrés in terms of the differences in language, religion, and customs. Moreover, the 1920s were years of political and social upheaval in the United States as well as years of modernization, industrialization, expansion of the consumer-oriented economy, and continuing shifts in social norms. These nationwide trends were evident to one degree or another in San

Francisco, a growing city with a population of over 500,000 people in 1920. In other words, though émigrés were arriving to a society that promised a certain socio-economic and political stability, societal norms in America, already unfamiliar, were in great flux, which contributed to the stresses of forced migration while allowing, simultaneously, for a greater range of life choices.

Finding a balance between maintaining Russian language, customs, cultural and religious traditions, and "fitting in" to American society was a complex process and one that did not necessarily follow a pattern. In fact, many émigrés (the first generation) and their children (both first and second generation) often lived various manifestations of dual lives. Such a dual life could either be a comfort or a burden, and as the younger generation reached adulthood, they made individual life choices about who they were going to be in America. The "dual lives/identity" experience is an integral part of the historic immigration process in America for Eastern Europeans, where "old country" customs in the early twentieth century period of mass emigration to the United States were derided by Americanization proponents as backward and out of place in modern America. Eastern Europeans were targets of Americanization proponents due to the significant differences in language and culture.[6] Immigrants and their children lived one life in the intimate circles of family and social networks and a second life, their "American life," in the outside world. Émigré social worker Antonina Von Arnold, in fact, in her voluminous writings often referenced "my American Story," "my American history," and "my American life," consciously distinguishing it from her "Russian" life.[7] Moreover, as reluctant immigrants, the desire of émigrés to maintain cultural heritage and Russian identity was perhaps more acute than of economic immigrants who acted immediately on intentions to "become American" and shed cultural markers as quickly as possible. Identifying as Russian, and particularly as "White Russian," however, necessitated constant explanations involving personal identity, Russian culture and history, a process both daunting and exhausting in view of the tropes and stereotypes prevalent in American society.

The Russian Family in Emigration

Persistent tropes characterizing Russians and Russia as uncivilized continued to seep into discourse among Americans in the inter-war period. It is indicative that Dr Henry Owen Eversole, acting chief executive of the Petrograd Children's Colony Expedition, who accompanied the Russian children on the "Kiddie Ship" to San Francisco in 1920 (chapter 2), wrote the following in his report to superiors describing the Russian children in his care:

> Great numbers of the children are of good families and most of them have good mentalities, and with the proper reasoning and with the proper influence, will make fine men and women. Without this influence *I feel that many of them would have been better of* [sic], *and the world at large would have been better, had they been allowed to perish in Siberia.*[8]

Given Eversole's work during the Civil War in Siberia directing a "sanitation and quarantine" program for the American Red Cross on the Trans-Siberian railway line, he had to have had some comprehension of the extreme circumstances these children had faced prior to the Red Cross transporting them to the Far East: abandonment, starvation, and abuse, as well as witnessing the horrific violence of the war. Moreover, he was aware of incidents of abuse towards the children by the crew aboard the S.S. *Yomei Maru*, the ship on which Eversole accompanied the children to San Francisco.[9] Whatever the "mental condition" of the children, Eversole's conclusion that the world would have benefited by their deaths is difficult to fathom. Eversole did not reference the children's Russian ethnicity per se, but the subtext implied the "uncivilized" nature of the children, a referencing of unruly or even violent behavior to which other (perhaps "American") children may not have descended. His conclusion, however, remains inexplicable.

Though Russian émigré parents were (most likely) unaware of this particular report, they were certainly aware of rhetoric in American public discourse that negatively or inaccurately referenced Russian history, culture, or people. That discourse often spoke to the perception of foreign, and particularly Russian "backwardness" in contrast to American modernity. The notion that Russians came from a primitive country, along with commentary about the generally alien and backward nature of

Eastern Europeans and Slavs, permeated public discourse in juxtaposition to modern America.

The promise of America as a "modern" nation, however, reinforced the perception that marginalized people (i.e., new immigrants) perhaps bore the brunt of shortfalls or even missteps. Russian adults certainly experienced the negative aspects of modernization and industrialization with respect to working conditions. Children remained at risk as well in this new world with some cases shaking newcomers' faith in modern America. The death of four-year-old Natalie Rojnovsky was a case in point. In February of 1935, a San Francisco doctor administering anti-diphtheria injections to a group of children misread a bottle label and mistakenly injected five of them with a toxin. Two of the children, Natalie and six-year-old Lois Bowden, died several days later. The incident received nationwide attention, but local coverage focused on the safety of diphtheria vaccinations in order to soothe public fears. Authorities insisted that the previous work of the intern had been beyond reproach. She was expeditiously exonerated in an inquest held two weeks after the deaths.[10] Children were at risk of dying of illnesses, such as pneumonia or meningitis, but the manner of Natalie's death was horrific, not only a victim of negligence by an American-educated medical doctor, but also of advanced technology: the toxin with which the children were poisoned was used for laboratory experiments.[11]

Consequently, Russian parents may have felt the helplessness of marginalized people who could not depend on authorities to protect their children. The case of Natalie's death was particularly egregious, but fears for children in an atmosphere of defensiveness about Russian culture developed early on, and taking charge of children's education and cultural upbringing was a way of exerting some control. Adults feared as well that American educational institutions would provide Russian children with disinformation about Russian culture and history. Their immediate efforts to establish schools informed their struggle to circumvent blanket assimilation for their children, beyond simply maintaining cultural heritage in the form of traditions or artistic expression. Nevertheless, they recognized that to survive, much less thrive, in America, they and their children had to understand the American way of life.

The decisions about how to raise children in America were not static. They evolved in the face of the realities of diasporic life, with some parents deciding to privilege Americanization, stressing assimilation rather than acculturation, given that return to Russia was likely not a viable option in their lifetime. Stressing the notion that Russians were sojourners, some parents believed, was harmful to future chances of success. The Russian community founded and maintained a multitude of groups and institutions to provide intellectual and spiritual solace for adults in their "little Russian world," but they also had to make critical choices for their children, balancing the desire to maintain heritage with acknowledgment that their children might well live out their lives in America. Some of those choices were evident in the decisions émigrés made with respect to taking American citizenship, for example, or changing their names. Loyalty to the Russia of their memories did not necessarily preclude practical considerations.

Émigré women, who played a critical role in the decisions and processes of Russian children's education, faced unfamiliar societal and straitened economic conditions. Their life choices in San Francisco in the context of 1920s American society were, on the one hand, limited by economic realities, but, on the other, varied in comparison with what had faced them as refugees in China or even in their past lives in pre-revolutionary Russia. Arriving to a country with which they were unfamiliar, and where the American gaze targeted them as exotic and alien, they acculturated in a society in flux with respect to gender roles and previously accepted social norms.[12] Women had begun to inhabit previously forbidden American urban public spaces at the turn of the century and, by the 1920s, existing norms and standards regarding the role of women in both domestic and social life were both in question and undergoing rapid change.[13] The business environment of San Francisco had its own historical peculiarities, as noted by Edith Sparks in her study of early-twentieth-century female proprietorship: a "phenomenal demographic and economic growth," and a historically skewed male population that provided opportunities for women in certain industries, such as accommodations.[14] Renting rooms to boarders was a way Russian women earned an income, but they were also creative about using the skills they developed as a result of their upbringing and education, such as needlework, artwork, and musical arts, to earn money or to run their own businesses, such as shops or restaurants.[15]

During the war, the ensuing revolutions, and civil war, Russian women learned to adapt quickly to new conditions to survive and chose their livelihoods in San Francisco based on a combination of chance opportunities, innate talents, and economic realities. Whether single, married with children, or childless, émigré women, unequivocally benefitting from their educated status, took on the herculean task of molding their lives to survive in a completely new environment while remaining "Russian in spirit," a phrase the writer of a biographical sketch of Eugenia Isaenko used to describe her.[16] They weathered the burdens of immigration and economic hardship while preserving their Russian identity and a rich inner life beyond the everyday, whether through their employment, their creative work, and/or through activity in émigré organizations and associations.

Education and Religion

In 1923, Russian community leaders organized a Society for the Protection and Education of Pre-School Russian Children, subsequently opening a day home for children who had no parent at home during the day.[17] The focus on a day home underscored the reality that a substantial number of Russian émigré women worked outside the home. Such a day home served the interests of the community in two ways: it helped Russian families who were struggling to stay afloat economically by allowing both parents to work, and it addressed the core issue of "denationalization" of children.[18] The goal of the society was to "make a small but real step on the path to preserve Russian culture, religion, and customs inasmuch as the impressionable children's soul is able to perceive such things."[19] Several people who arrived on USAT *Merritt* had a hand in organizing the Children's Home, which also later absorbed the children from a pre-school, Children's World (*Detsky mir*), run by prospective student Xenia Bielinskaia (1902–1995).[20]

The official opening of the Russian Children's Day Home and Nursery took place in the heart of the Fillmore in November of 1925 at 1180 Turk Street. A little over a year later, in December of 1926, the society, after raising funds through events and donations, purchased a house further northwest at 2174 Post Street, where the day home remained for the next several decades, integrating into the neighborhood dynamic (figures 6.1 and 6.2).[21] A leading figure in the organization and running of the home for the next twenty-five years was Dr Antonina Maximova-Kulaev (1890–1988), also president of the Society for the Protection of Children for twenty-two years. Born in Tyukalinsk, near Omsk, Dr Maximova-Kulaev earned a medical degree at St Petersburg Medical Institute in 1914. She worked as a surgeon's assistant during the war both in St Petersburg and Serbia, came to San Francisco in 1922, and married Vladimir P. Kulaev (1881–1962), an engineer from Tomsk. Dr Maximova-Kulaev earned an

American medical degree and had a license to practice medicine by the end of 1923, no small accomplishment given the difficulty Russian-trained doctors had in establishing their credentials in the United States, in view of the language barrier.[22] Student Varvara Loschilova (1900–1966), who received a scholarship to Mills College in Oakland and studied bacteriology and chemistry, worked as a social worker at the Day Home. Both women dedicated their professional lives to that Russian educational institution that lasted for forty years.[23]

Another key figure in the educational effort was Nikolay Borzov, a teacher and administrator, originally from Glazov, northeast of Moscow. His mother, a teacher, was plunged into poverty when her husband, a mid-level official, died, and Borzov worked as a tutor through secondary school and university, graduating from St Petersburg University with honors. He relocated to Harbin in 1905, holding positions as the director of the Harbin Commercial School and organizer of a school at the CER. Forced out of his position in 1925 due to pressure from the Soviet government, he brought his wife and seven children to Berkeley, California, returning to Harbin briefly to head the Harbin First Practical School. Upon permanent resettlement in America, he plunged into educational, social, and charitable work in both the Russian Orthodox and Spiritual Christian communities, holding numerous administrative positions, including permanent chairman of the board of directors of the Kulaieff Educational and Philanthropic Foundation, set up in 1931 by Ivan V. Kulaieff (1857–1941), a wealthy industrialist from Siberia who contributed generously to educational and children's institutions of the Russian diaspora.[24] Borzov founded several schools, from kindergartens to adult schools in San Francisco and Berkeley, headed the Children's Society for a number of years, and organized the annual long-running "Day of the Russian Child" charitable event, beginning in 1932, to benefit needy children in Russian diasporic communities around the world, editing a "very well-received literary journal" to raise funds for Russian children abroad.[25]

As a community leader, Borzov also helped bridge the divide between the Fillmore/Green Street and Potrero Hill "colonies," attending and leading meetings of the Society of Russian Literacy organized by the latter group to discuss the organization of an evening school for children and adults.[26] His perspective on diasporic "Russianness" in the inter-war period was fundamentally inclusive and likely had a great influence on the community as a whole, given the universal respect for him and his work.

Figure 6.1 (*above*) Children's Day Home, 1929, at 2174 Post Street. Note the sign in both English and Russian at the front of the house, a rare example indicating a Russian presence in the neighborhood through signage.

Figure 6.2 (*right*) Children's Day Home, ca.1933 at 2174 Post Street. The building was an educational center as it also housed the night school and other organizations. The adults are Daria Zaitceff (1885–1969), at the door, Dr Antonina Maximova-Kulaev at top of stairs in hat, Nina Rubanow (1904–1999) also at top of stairs, and Barbara Menshikoff below. Of the twenty-five children, fourteen are Russian, six are Mexican American, one is of Columbian/Italian heritage (ascertained from census information), and four are unknown.

Literacy and heritage maintenance were concerns for most Russian families, and even those who did not have children or who lived outside the émigré milieu reacted to how the American educational system portrayed Russia. Peter Balakshin, who was editor of *Russian News-Life* from the late 1930s to the early 1940s, pointed to American textbooks invariably beginning discussion of Catherine the Great's rule as one that "was distinguished by loose morals [and her] countless lovers" and identifying "Siberians" as "czarist-era convicts," interpretations of Russian history that were patently offensive to émigrés.[27] A resident of Potrero Hill, Barbara Jacoob (1876–1963), commented on the skewed portrayals in children's textbooks, reinforcing the notion of Russian backwardness: "Do you know in their geography book they've only one picture devoted to Russia ... a few huts with roofs of straw. That is giving ... [Russian children] ... a strange idea of their forefathers' country."[28]

The concerns continued. One of the four goals of the Russian Historical Society in America (chapter 5), was to ensure that Russian youth learn the "true history of the Russian State," its development, and the "genuine spirt of the Russian nation."[29] Baron Boodberg and Sergei Kovaleff, who were involved in numerous educational and social groups, concerned about what they considered "hostile and sordid" materials utilized "in regular schools" to discuss Russia, published a Russian history book in 1939 to distribute to students and teachers in order to counter such narratives.[30] Konstantin Barskii (1894–1975), Russian Center president in the 1940s, noted that American schools provided Russian children with "only scanty and biased information" about (pre-Revolutionary) Russia.[31] The problematic nature of raising Russian children in an educational system that marginalized their cultural heritage preoccupied the community for good reason: the generation of Russian youth in the inter-war period who were on the cusp of entering into marriage and starting families bore the brunt of either negative or non-existent depictions of Russia and Russian history. Whether or not they maintained any link to the community would influence their decisions on how they raised their own children.

Russian community educational efforts focused on heritage maintenance within the context of education. The children's day home program, geared toward preschool children, eventually included a program for school-age children (five to nine years old) to attend after school, and focused particularly on Russian culture, language, and history. The preschool had thirty to forty children attending by July of 1926.[32]

Figure 6.3 Dr Antonina Maximova-Kulaev seated at table at an exposition of all Community Chest agencies in San Francisco, 16 June 1934. The woman seated at left may be Anna Kovaleff (1904–2001) and the woman standing is possibly Nina Rubanow. A photo of the children's home building is displayed, and a meal menu posted in front. Note the announcement at right for diphtheria vaccinations.

The charter specified that the purpose of the school was to prepare children for entry into both Russian and American schools.[33]

Nevertheless, the very atmosphere at the preschool promoted a sense of Russianness as virtually all the employees spoke Russian as their first language. Tuition was on a sliding scale based on parents' income; in extreme cases of poverty, the school waived tuition. Activities included various art and crafts, music and dancing, and physical education.[34] It is indicative that educators included a broad range of non-academic subjects to make that significant "impression" on young children's minds.

In 1928, the day home began to admit "children of all nationalities." In 1929, the San Francisco Community Chest, a fund pooled for charitable activities, began to provide a subsidy to support the facility, acknowledging its important role in the community, not just for Russian families but for all families in need of childcare in the immediate and adjacent neighborhoods (figure 6.3). Several Mexican-American families in the neighborhood sent their children to the school in the early 1930s.[35] In a 1932 article in *The Slavonic Pioneers of California*, Dr Maximova-Kulaev expressed hope that the school would serve not only Russian and American children but "all children of Slav population [*sic*] of San Francisco," distinguishing Russians from Americans but also distinguishing non-Russian "Slavs" from both groups, perhaps having in mind newly arrived eastern Europeans.[36]

Borzov also led an initiative to open evening schools for Russian youth, the first such, as noted, organized by the Society of Russian Literacy on Potrero Hill in the 1920s, and a second evening school at the Post Street location in the fall of 1931, based on the model of a Russian "gymnasium" or secondary school. The school also provided instruction in drawing, singing, and the organization of the first San Francisco Russian youth orchestra.[37] True to form, the organizers focused on cultural education as well as academic subjects, recognizing their importance in developing children's minds while maintaining a cultural connection to the homeland. That focus on cultural education and the arts likely had a role in the success of children retaining both language and cultural awareness despite pressure to assimilate.

Religious education was the focus of Holy Trinity's Church Parish School, initially the only Orthodox church school in San Francisco, but the curriculum included academic subjects focusing on Russian history, geography, and literature as well as cultural studies, particularly choral singing, a critical aspect of Orthodox church services.[38]

A crisis within the Russian Orthodox Church in 1926, the spiritual institution of "Russia Abroad," however, did not leave the San Francisco Russian community unscathed, with the schism causing a rift in the parish and the subsequent founding of a second Orthodox church, parish, and school. That rift may have had its roots in earlier efforts of émigrés to influence the practices at Holy Trinity. An unidentified congregation member put forward a proposal in February of 1924 to hold services in Russian only, "but it became evident that among the congregation there are many who belong to other nationalities, such as Syrians, Serbs, Galicians, Greeks, and Americans, who do not know the Russian language and are nevertheless more devoted to the church than the Russians themselves."[39] The move to Russify the church service certainly came from newly arrived Russian émigrés, but rejection of the proposal indicated they were receiving pushback from non-Russian, and possibly Russian non-émigré, congregation members who made up a substantial-enough

Nostalgic Homelessness and Dual Lives

proportion of the parish and opposed the change. Those who sought Russification therefore may have taken advantage of the situation in 1927, when Metropolitan Platon in New York, head of the North American Diocese, refused to recognize the authority of the Holy Synod of Bishops of the Russian Orthodox Church Outside of Russia (ROCOR) in Sremski-Karlovci (Serbia). Bishop Apollinary (Koshevoy, 1874–1933), the vicar bishop assigned to Holy Trinity in February of 1926, subsequently refused to support Metropolitan Platon, who then "fired" the bishop, sending a telegram to San Francisco with a directive ordering that the bishop be evicted from his quarters at the cathedral.[40]

Effectively penniless and homeless, and in ill health, Bishop Apollinary did, however, have his supporters. Émigré community leader Major-General Georgy Kiyaschenko (1872–1940), along with Holy Trinity priest Father Pavel Razumoff (1868–1931) and other congregation members, met Bishop Apollinary at the train station when he returned from New York. The Kiyaschenkos gave the bishop shelter in their home, also raising money for him. Rear Admiral Boris Doudoroff also supported Bishop Apollinary. He asked the Russian community to put "aside for now the question of who is right in the canonical argument" and view Bishop Apollinary as a human being who was suffering for "honestly and openly following his convictions despite knowing that he would be removed."[41] The bishop founded the Holy Virgin, Joy of All Who Sorrow Church and Parish in June of 1927 with its first location at 3573-5 Sacramento Street (the Kiyaschenkos' apartment). Many of those who initially contributed funds to assist the bishop followed him to his church.[42]

The reasons why members chose to leave with Bishop Apollinary or remain at Holy Trinity Cathedral, however, appeared to be personal, since a substantial number of Russian émigrés remained at Holy Trinity. In other words, the split was not between the pre-1918 congregation and new arrivals. There was no clear-cut division between the two congregations. Though Russian émigrés founded the Holy Virgin Church, the congregation in the 1930s included Serbs and Orthodox Americans of ethnic Russian heritage who had migrated from Pennsylvania, for example.[43] In any case, people continued to socialize irrespective of which church they attended in the inter-war period with organization of many jointly sponsored events. Judging by the outpouring of support for the bishop, a contingent felt that he had been badly treated by the Metropolitan in a very "un-Christian" manner. At the same time, the causes of the church-wide schism spoke to deep divisions within the Russian Orthodox

Church abroad.[44] The tensions played out in virtually all Russian émigré communities with localized conflicts and disagreements having a role in those tensions, blurring the lines between religion and politics, as noted by Catherine Andreyev and Ivan Savický, for example, in how the schism played out in Czechoslovakia.[45] Nevertheless, the dynamic of the San Francisco community in the inter-war period showed a tendency towards inclusiveness within community institutions. The earlier push by one contingent to hold services at Holy Trinity in Russian (thus alienating all Orthodox who did not speak Russian) garnered sufficient push-back to be rejected. Moreover, the Protection Society board had removed the word "Orthodox" from the name of the Children's Nursery prior to opening in 1925, ensuring that it was "opened to all Russian children needing care without question as to whether parents are Orthodox."[46]

The church schism was sufficiently disruptive that Doudoroff, in a plea to all parents to unify on the question of education in 1929, wrote that whatever disagreements people had with respect to the church, the community needed to pay heed to the issue of whether "Russian nationality in America" would survive – and that survival hinged on children's education. Doudoroff suggested founding a single Russian school outside the church and Borzov did open the gymnasium-style night school in 1931, but it nevertheless remained one of several émigré educational institutions, indicating, once again, that no one individual constituted a "leader," setting policy or an agenda.[47]

American Life Choices

Time, rather than money, was the valuable commodity that parents were able to contribute in the struggle to maintain Russian heritage among the youth. Natalia Kiyaschenko (1881–1960) worked in a factory but also ran a school of Russian and American dance in the 1920s and ran youth performance programs. The latter activities may have earned her some money, but the main purpose was to provide cultural engagement for Russian children.[48] Growing up in the Fillmore District, Eugenia Bailey took piano and ballet lessons, noting that the community effort for children's cultural enrichment played an important part in her life, commenting as well that girls were "expected" to study piano and ballet.[49] Georgy Kiyaschenko, on his part, held multiple memberships in organizations benefitting both children's education and culture (as well as in the Church Parish Societies and the Society of Veterans) throughout the 1920s and 1930s. He initially sat on the Children's Society board and was president of the Holy Trinity Parish School parents' committee.[50] The Kiyaschenkos' daughter Nina, born in 1917, attended the preschool and went on to become an accomplished dancer, performing at events including benefits for the preschool and in an Adolph Bolm production of Rimsky-Korsakoff's "Coq d'Or" in the 1930s. Yefim Beliaeff (in a rare positive assessment) described her as a "talented young ballerina."[51]

General Kiyaschenko combined a fervent support of Russian cultural and educational programs with a practical acknowledgment that return to Russia was unlikely, making arrangements for his family to become US citizens as soon as possible. The Kiyaschenkos were from western Russia and left for Siberia in October of 1917, where the general served in Admiral Kolchak's army.[52] When the Civil War ended, the family departed Russia, living a "nomadic" existence in China and Japan until they came to Seattle "in steerage, like the animals," in Nina's words, in October of 1923.[53] Her father applied for their first papers the day after their arrival. He worked at odd jobs and retired from a janitorial/night watchman job at age sixty-seven. Natalia worked in a sewing factory and a laundry, struggling to make ends meet, and sacrificing, in the words of their daughter, to scratch out a living in America, to provide their children with education and opportunities.[54]

Their son Evgeniy's (1913–1990) decision to join the US military, serving in the Marines after graduating from high school, and enlisting in the US Army to fight in World War II, was a common one for Russian émigré young men who could not afford a university education. Early on, Evgeniy changed his surname to "Eugene Kayes." Immigrants with Slavic names provided different reasons for changing their names in the first half of the twentieth century but the underlying cause was certainly pressure to "Americanize," hidden behind explanations regarding the annoyance of constantly having to correct pronunciation or spelling.[55] Having a surname difficult to pronounce, like Kiyaschenko, no doubt spurred Evgeniy to become "Eugene Kayes," an American identity on which no one would remark and which did not require explanation.[56]

Evgeniy, Nina, and their mother Natalia participated in a large-scale 1937 celebration of the completion and opening of the Golden Gate Bridge, a staged performance of the history of Fort Ross (chapter 8). Zoya Petroff (1918–1999), Eugene's first wife, and Boris Koodrin (1915–1976), Nina's first husband, were also in the performance and the couples married after the event. Participating in events focusing on Russian culture successfully brought together young people of Russian background, something the elder members of the community encouraged as it fulfilled the goals of maintaining heritage through familial relationships. The end results, however, often deviated from what "traditionally minded" elders may have envisioned. Zoya and Eugene christened their son at the Holy Virgin Cathedral in 1943, but by 1945 were divorced. Nina divorced Boris soon after giving birth to their daughter and married émigré Georgy Zepaloff (1912–2003) in a ceremony at the Holy Virgin Cathedral in 1942. They had a daughter together, but Nina divorced Zepaloff in 1947, citing his abusive nature. Nina owned beauty shops in San Francisco, later moving to Healdsburg in Sonoma County, where she opened a shop, supporting herself and her daughters.[57] She married twice more, outlived all of her husbands, and passed away at the age of ninety-nine.

The two younger Kiyaschenkos and their spouses, then, exemplified the complicated nature of family relationships in emigration. The fact that the family maintained a connection to the Orthodox Church, with the elder Kiyaschenkos even having a role in the founding of a new arguably "more Russian" parish, and holding important ceremonies there, indicated a desire to maintain their Russian identities in the inevitable acculturation process (figure 6.4). The views of the younger members on family and marriage, however, clearly encompassed a modern and practical view. Divorce was legal in the United States. If the marriage was failing, why prolong the agony? Nina later provided her succinct perspective on life in inter-war San Francisco for Russian émigré youth: "Some of these young lives were wilder then than the lives of the young today. But they had so little money, their future was so uncertain, they needed adventures and were often reckless in searching for it."[58] That need for adventure may have led to impulsive marriages, later regretted. Russian young people may not have felt completely at home in either the American or Russian milieus, adding to the stresses, pressures, and consequent disorientation with respect to marital and family life.

The Russian Orthodox Church perspective on divorce was multi-layered: as a sacrament, marriage was "an unbreakable bond upon which all social relations" were based, and the church considered (and considers) divorce a "grave sin." But "the Church never failed in giving to sinners a 'new chance.'"[59] In fact, according to Orthodox canon, the church allows three marriages if parties obtain a divorce through the church. In practice, however, in pre-Revolutionary Russia, according to Gregory Freeze, the "cumbersome procedure made divorce virtually impossible."[60] In the early

Figure 6.4 Wedding photo of Oleg Vassiliyevsky/Vassil (1899–1965) and Olga Afanasieff (1907–2003), who were married on 3 March 1940, at the Holy Virgin Cathedral on Fulton Street. Seated from *left to right* are: Olga Rubanow (1872–1962); Oleg and Olga Vassil; and Father Vasily Shaposhnikoff (1877–1952). Standing *left to right* are: Nina Rubanow, later godmother to one of the Vassils's children; Leonid Doronin (1909–1999); mother of the bride, Klavdia Afanasieff (1875–1964); Konstantin Rubanow (1902–1985); choir director and Doronin's uncle, Valerian Looksha (1885–1966); his wife, Natalia Looksha (1894–1986); Galina Shatz (1918–2007); and unknown.

twentieth century, secular officials and Orthodox clergy were in a process of attempting to reform divorce law.[61] Freeze asserts nevertheless that, based on actual divorce files, the Russian conception of marriage among Orthodox faithful was much more secular than "sacred," indicating a practical outlook about ending marriages, despite the difficulty in obtaining divorces.[62] Though émigrés experienced a traumatic break with the past, which, in one sense, reinforced the importance of Orthodoxy to their Russian identity outside the homeland, that "secular" view of marriage remained prevalent among the San Francisco community. Multiple marriages were very common in the inter-war period, whether those marriages and divorces took place in the church or outside it. Since church canon did allow three marriages, clergy in exile appeared to take the path of least resistance, realizing that forbidding, or even attempting to discourage, divorce would only lead to parishioners leaving the church.[63] That being said, some émigrés held to the view that "easy divorces" in the United States led to immorality – a "Mr Sh," interviewed as part of the "ethnic project" series in the mid-1930s, who had been born in 1896 in Ufa and who was the first generation of this family to receive a higher education, specifically mentioned the high divorce rate as problematic in his assessment of American society (he was married with one child).[64]

The life of Father Sergei Denisoff (1886–1963) provides some perspective about attitudes, norms, and mores within the Russian émigré community as well as intra-émigré conflict, whether rooted in class divisions, personal disagreements, or a combination of the two, which played out in congregational rifts. Father Denisoff's marital history, particularly since he was an Orthodox priest, sheds light on how those norms and mores evolved or altered in the environment of living life disconnected from a perceived central Orthodox Church authority, and, consequently, a tendency to ignore established procedures or traditions in favor of practical concerns or personal desires.

Father Denisoff was born in St Petersburg and arrived in San Francisco on USAT *Merritt*, joining the clergy at the Holy Trinity Cathedral where Father Vladimir Sakovich was rector. Denisoff began to agitate for a promotion from psalm reader to second priest at the cathedral, setting the congregation on edge. The decision to promote Denisoff, however, lay with Metropolitan Platon in New York. In fact, Father Sakovich had petitioned to the Metropolitan to promote Denisoff to second priest, but the Metropolitan had chosen to appoint him as psalm-reader with the right to conduct church services, likely to test Denisoff's qualifications as he was unknown to the Metropolitan and apparently had no documentation attesting to his ordination.[65]

Student Feodosy Jouravleff (1894–1988), in the course of relating the above history in 1925, asked rhetorically, "Who is Father S. Denisoff?" Jouravleff noted that "all we know is that he came here in 1923 with the Stark group and found a hospitable welcome at our church." Prior to his arrival, Jouravleff insisted, church members had lived in peace for "six years," overcoming difficulties through the good management of Father Sakovich, but that tranquility had been disrupted by discord because of Denisoff's demands. The reference to "six years" of peace seemed to encompass the period when émigrés began to arrive and Father Sakovich's tenure beginning in 1918. Denisoff also refused his assigned duty to hold services at the church in Berkeley, across the bay, as he considered it a backwater and "threatened that the 400 Stark" members of the congregation "supported" him, implying they could take over the Holy Trinity Cathedral. The timing of that threat coincided with the previously noted demand to hold services in Russian only.[66]

The continuing discord played out it in letters to the editor throughout the first half of 1925. Student Ivan Elovsky stated that he loved and respected both Father Sakovich and Father Denisoff equally. Students working in Westwood, Lassen County, however, wrote in unanimous support of Father Sakovich and the church committee headed by Baron Boodberg.[67] Holy Trinity choir conductor Mikhail Krinoff (1878–1933) wrote a lengthy point-by-point refutation of church council member Nikolay Chabanoff's (1874–1942) accusations against Father Sakovich. One of the accusations was that Father Sakovich underpaid Denisoff, directing Chabanoff to throw Denisoff out into the street in vulgar language. Krinoff noted that Father Sakovich, by his very nature, was incapable of using such language, publicly labeling Chabanoff a liar. Denisoff's supporters, however, attempted to smear Father Sakovich with accusations of malfeasance, dancing at balls, and selling vodka.[68] Father Sakovich's supporters shouted them down in the press and Denisoff did not conduct any services at Holy Trinity for the next two years, but the incident disrupted the church considerably.[69]

The discord between the two groups, largely playing out with the Stark arrivals against a contingent of students and likely long-time (pre-1918) Holy Trinity congregation members, indicated both a struggle for dominance within the only Orthodox church in San Francisco at the time and the conviction of either group that "their" priest was the better choice to lead the congregation. However, a parishioner in Berkeley, Vladimir Vesninsky (1872–1934), declared that the troubles began due to the former head of the church committee, Chabanoff, who, in Vesninsky's words, was a man of means voted out of the committee, taking his revenge by utilizing the vanity and desire of Father Denisoff.[70]

How class affiliation played into this conflict is difficult to ascertain since the schism that involved the creation of the new Holy Virgin Parish, which occurred subsequently, did not result in any clear-cut division between émigrés: some members of the Stark group did leave Holy Trinity to join the new parish, but others remained. The role of Chabanoff, an émigré with "means," seemed to indicate both class and ethnic bias, with his opposition to Father Sakovich, who was not an émigré per se, and, perhaps, the non-Russian pre-1918 congregation. On his part, Denisoff continued to demonstrate a somewhat non-traditional and "non-Orthodox" mindset, which higher clergy in Russia would not have tolerated.

Denisoff married three times, divorcing at least twice, despite the fact that divorce is not an option for Russian Orthodox clergy, and even widowed priests may not re-marry, thus "finding a wife precedes taking on clerical office."[71] Widowed priests may be tonsured to the monastic state, which allows them to move up in the church hierarchy (only "black clergy," i.e., monastic priests, are allowed to attain the rank of bishop or above).[72] In San Francisco, Denisoff married twice: in 1927 to Dora Dedenko (1882–1950), a widow with three children, divorcing several years later, and the second time in 1938, in Reno, Nevada, to Irina Jakova (1917–1980), with whom he had a son.[73] They also divorced and he later "retired," moving to Sebastopol in Sonoma County with a "friend," Olga Krantz.[74]

Father Denisoff's enthusiasm for marriage and/or cohabitation with female companions, despite his status as a member of the clergy (though it is not clear when or if he was ever ordained as a priest), did not seem to cause him any problems within the Russian community. He and Irina even married again in a church ceremony in 1939 at the Holy Virgin Cathedral, indicating that the bishop had no objection.[75] Denisoff seemed to have been quite comfortable forging his own path in America both with respect to his calling as an Orthodox priest and to Orthodox traditions and conventions relating to family life.

Foreignness and Citizenship

Taking advantage of the secular nature of American life (e.g., marrying in Nevada if a church wedding was not desirable or feasible) was a step in the Americanization process, as secular marriages had not been recognized in pre-revolutionary Russia.[76] Accepting American legal institutions, rather than the Orthodox Church, as authoritative in the formation of the family structure may have also been linked with decisions to quickly naturalize. The issue of citizenship for émigrés was paramount despite the common narratives in émigré publications regarding the expected fall of the Soviet regime and commensurate anticipated return. Georgy Kiyaschenko, for example, took up a leadership role in the émigré community upon arrival, not uncommon for high-ranking military officers, given that those accustomed to commanding felt comfortable in taking up such roles. He was also a "legitimist," the most conservative faction of monarchists in Russia Abroad and published a newsletter, *Vera I Pravda* (Faith and Truth), which espoused a monarchist and conservative point of view.[77] And yet, Kiyaschenko took eminently practical steps for the benefit of his children's future in the United States, literally the moment he arrived on US soil, by taking out his first papers to ensure that his family became US citizens as soon as possible, indicating that he considered monarchist rule as appropriate for Russia but appreciated the benefits of living in a democracy when it came to his own family.

In contrast to Kiyaschenko's decision regarding American citizenship, Baron Boodberg, for example, was one of the few who chose not to seek citizenship as he could not bring himself to "renounce Russia," clashing also with his daughter with respect to how to raise her son. Boodberg had a similar viewpoint to Kiyaschenko regarding the importance of maintaining a connection to Russian culture, in anticipation that a return to Russia would take place. That being said, his children were adults when they arrived in the United States and had to apply for citizenship on their own, whereas Kiyaschenko's children were minors, which may have played into his decision. Boodberg's daughter Valentina, however, actively and consciously strove to "make an American" out of her own son, George, born in Russia in 1918, contrary to Boodberg's wishes. Boodberg wished for his grandchildren to carry on as Russians in America, which entailed living a dual life at least to some degree, not as Americans of Russian descent, which de-emphasized cultural, and therefore familial, heritage. Valentina refused, asking, "Why should he feel like an émigré? An outcast?" Her son's surname was "Vernon," the name she and her husband selected to replace "Waripaeff." George joined the US Air Force, reinforcing in her mind that America was his country, particularly since he fought for it in World War II: "why should he mourn for a country [Russia] that doesn't exist?" Valentina asked.[78] In a similar situation, Elizabeth Malozemoff, who arrived in 1920, noted that the first time she felt herself to be "more American than Russian" was in 1942 (although she received her US citizenship in 1926) when she saw her Russian-born youngest son, Andrew, in his US Army uniform.[79] Joining the US military, then, played a great part in Americanizing Russian émigré young men, even in the eyes of their own parents.

Vernon, on her part, wanted her son to be as American as possible, considering that reinforcing any sense of Russianness would "hurt" him in the United States, perhaps referencing the continuing pervading suspicion of Russians. She wanted him to "like baseball, football, basketball, and golf," identifying such pursuits as "American" and therefore acceptable.[80] Her son spoke Russian with an accent, married an American woman, and raised children who did not speak Russian. Tellingly, with respect to the non-acceptance Russians faced in certain circles of American society, Valentina noted that her niece Xenia's American father-in-law opposed his son's marriage "because he wanted his son to marry an American" and a person of Russian heritage did not fit that definition (Xenia was born in the United States), vindicating Valentina's decision to relieve her son of maintaining a dual identity in America.[81]

"Foreignness" was an issue for Russian university students as well. According to a student who attended the University of California at Berkeley in the inter-war period, "[Russian] national politics" on which some individuals focused were "a great interference" for students who took part in them, and such discussions were best avoided, particularly in mixed company, leading to conscious self-censorship.[82]

Antonina Von Arnold interviewed Russian students attending American universities in the Bay Area for her 1938 study, estimating that approximately 700 young people "whose parents are Russian" attended (elementary and/or secondary) schools in San Francisco in the 1920s and early 1930s. Interestingly, however, the students whom she interviewed in 1937, both enrolled and recently graduated, even if they had graduated from American high schools, seemed to feel just as "Russian" as the older people in the groups whose formative years had been spent in Russia. The sample was quite small (seventeen students total), therefore perhaps not indicative in any sense of larger patterns, but the fact that attending American high schools did not erase Russian cultural affiliation was significant as evidence of the persistence of dual identity.[83] Eugenia Bailey recalled identifying as "Russian" at an early age, though she had been born in the United States. She attended Children's World preschool and later Holy Trinity Russian school on Saturdays, which also contributed to her feeling Russian. As she grew older, she began to identify as "Russian American," but noted that she kept the fact of her Russian background mostly to herself, though her surname (Nikonenko) did stand out as fairly difficult to pronounce when "competing," in her words, with less foreign-sounding American names.[84] In her interviews of college-age students, Von Arnold did not discuss the "painfulness" of being "foreign" in the interview because "it was understood," indicating those with whom she spoke were not in any state of "denationalization." To the contrary, despite receiving a higher education in America, they still felt like outsiders.[85]

To Valentina Vernon, in opposition to her father's ideation of a future return, "Russia died ... in February of 1920," reinforcing her firm commitment to making sure her son was not an "outcast" in America. That commitment also spoke to her encountering bias against non-American ways or markers despite her generally upbeat and positive recollections of the first difficult years in San Francisco and the complications of adapting to an alien culture. While making clear that America was a welcoming place, she nevertheless repeated that émigrés were "outcasts" and the only way to avoid being labeled an outsider was to shed Russian cultural markers.[86]

Dual Identity or Dual Lives

The "dual" identity or life concept, as noted, became particularly relevant in the initial decades of twentieth-century nativist America for Eastern Europeans and Slavs who faced a mixed welcome in the United States. As nominally "white," though undesirable, future citizens, children of Eastern European and Slavic immigrants, for example, were able to exercise the dual identity "option," which non-white immigrants in that era could not. The customs and languages of Eastern Europeans and Slavs were sufficiently alien to warrant suspicion, with even American-born children of Eastern Europeans, according to Ewa Morawska, "perceived as racially distinct and inferior." Xenia Boodberg's noted experience confirmed the existence of such a perspective with respect to specifically Russian heritage, notwithstanding class considerations. Moreover, the term "invasion" often referenced Slavic immigration in the rhetoric of the day.[87] Milton Esman notes the significance of "distinctive religious tradition" in adopting a "dual or hybrid identity," and Orthodoxy, critical to Russian émigré identity in exile, remained such in the United States.[88] Abandoning religious practices, a factor that may have come into play for younger people as they observed the conflicts playing out among the Orthodox congregations in San Francisco, also freed them from the burden (if they saw it as such) of a dual identity.

Journalist Eugene Lyons, whose family was Jewish from Byelorussia (now Belarus) emigrating to New York, eloquently recalled "an acute awareness of being aliens and intruders in a nation of Americans." Lyons's reminiscences about his experiences referenced the "double existence" he and his friends lived, and feelings of shame brought on by the "disrespect" for their homeland traditions from native-born Americans. His description of the "American self" as an "overcoat" to be removed at home is evocative of the complex nature surrounding identity for children of immigrants growing up in two disparate worlds.[89] Maria Tulinoff-Roth (1886–1942), an émigré teacher in San Francisco, married to a Swiss national and with six Russian-born children, wrote that Russian children raised in America, in response to mockery, no longer recognized the beauty of the Russian language, and were also losing understanding of Russian Orthodox religious services.[90] Von Arnold, in her social work in San Francisco, observed that American-born children of Spiritual Christian families, as well, "do not like to ask American friends to their homes"; the "younger generation" tended to "be consumed by differences between the home and American life ... and ... the peculiarities of [their] parents."[91] The pull to conformity to American norms overcame the indifference that elder Spiritual Christians had maintained towards those they considered *"ne nashi"* (not ours), including Americans. Unlike émigrés, who were concerned with issues of acceptance, the elder first generation of Spiritual Christians had not attempted to acculturate, nor did they take any interest in what Americans thought of them. Exposed to modern American culture in an urban environment that did not allow for detachment, however, and the constant barrage of negative characterizations of "foreign" traditions, younger members of the community were unable to maintain that sense of confidence.

A communication gap between generations was an aspect of diasporic life as well, particularly in the context of experienced trauma. Some adults chose not to speak of the past to their children to shield them and/or because it was too painful. Eugenia Bailey recalled that her parents never spoke of "their evacuation or their prior life in Russia." Her mother Maria was "bitter" about what she had experienced because of the Bolsheviks, but considered that "part of her life closed." Children often grew up in a vacuum, as they did not share a common background with American children: Eugenia noted that she "felt I was different," but neither did children necessarily receive input from family members to understand why they felt "different," and how to cope with those feelings.[92]

The Ilyin Family: Dual Lives and Acculturation

Being a member of the Russian upper classes facilitated the acculturation process in certain contexts, as noted earlier in the case of Boris Von Arnold (chapter 4). The Ilyin family had a marked presence in the San Francisco Russian community, not just because of their class status, but because a significant number of the Ilyins and related Boratynski family settled there. Kiril (1896–1974) and Olga Ilyin (1894–1991), relatives of artists Gleb and Peter, came to San Francisco in 1923 with young son Boris. Olga was a descendant of Russian poet Evgeniy Boratynski, and followed in the footsteps of her ancestor, writing poetry and prose.[93] She was one of the few Russian émigrés published to modest acclaim in the English language. Her book, *Dawn of the Eighth Day* (1951), was a thinly veiled autobiography of her life in Russia up to the years of the Civil War.[94]

She and her husband joined the Russian émigré Literary-Artistic Group upon arrival, and she published her poetry in émigré publications, pursuing her literary work throughout her life. The group's meeting place was three streetcar rides away from the Ilyins' apartment but, though exhausted after working all day, they, like "starving" people seeking bread (in her words), were determined to find intellectual sustenance. That first literary evening, dedicated to a discussion of Nikolai Gumilev's poetry, had an enormous impact on her as she realized how the years of struggles, worry about survival, and everyday concerns had wiped away any thoughts about the "existence of Higher Meaning" – to her, this higher meaning was poetry, her calling, and related directly to the importance of her "real" versus "everyday" life.[95]

She and her husband, however, did have everyday lives that encompassed most of their waking hours. Olga later worked as a dressmaker, eventually running a salon from her living room and designing clothing. Her husband initially listed his occupations as painter, later working as a bookkeeper and real estate salesman for Andrew Gromeeko (1902–1977), an émigré who owned Metropolitan Realty. By 1940, the Ilyins owned their own home in San Francisco and were doing quite well.[96]

The Ilyins' two sons were born eleven years apart and in different countries: Boris (1918–2014), technically an émigré since he was born in Russia, and Dimitri (1929–2013), a second-generation Russian born in San Francisco. Both maintained a connection to their Russian heritage but both married American women. In fact, Olga's three nieces and her nephew, who all lived in San Francisco upon arrival, married Americans, their class affiliation likely a factor; for Americans, marrying descendants of Russian nobility had cachet. Antonina Von Arnold had noted that her brother's "lineage" and "nobility" eased his entry into American society.[97] On their part, the Russians, by marrying upper-class Americans (all the American spouses, male and female, were college-educated), eased their way into American society, diluting their Russianness to a point where they were not obtrusively foreign while simultaneously maintaining those aspects of Russian identity they wished. Adya (1915–2007), Tatiana (1916–2007), and Nichola Boratynski (1915–1989) married their American spouses at the Holy Virgin Cathedral, and Nicholas and first wife Eleanor christened their son there. A blurb about the marriage of Nicholas and Eleanor touted the "uniting" of a "prominent American family with a prominent Russian one."[98] Adya's marriage to Stanford graduate Drayton Bryant in 1937 garnered attention in the press as an "International Romance." Moreover, the reporter went on to describe Adya, smiling brightly in a photo, as a "Daughter of the Revolution," both romanticizing the event and completely misconstruing its effects on her family.[99]

Boris Ilyin served in the US Army in World War II, attaining the rank of Lieutenant Colonel, earned a master's degree in English and creative writing from Stanford, taught English at Stanford and Pomona Colleges, published a novel, *Green Boundary*, and then joined the US Foreign Service, serving for nineteen years until retirement.[100] In his first novel, in which the main character is "Major Radonov," a US Army officer of Russian heritage stationed in post-World War II Germany, Boris wrote:

> Thomas would ask him ... how it was that Radonov spoke Russian. Then Radonov would reply that he was White Russian, and that his parents had brought him to the United States when he was four years old. These were all old phrases to him. "I was born in Russia": "My father was a White." He would probably have to explain what he meant by White ... He dreaded explaining all this. He had been explaining it all his life.[101]

The description clearly referenced Boris's own experience as a member of the US military of Russian background, especially given the resemblance of his main character to his own life (he arrived with his parents at the age of four, his father served in the White Guard, Boris served in the US military and fought in World War II). Particularly telling are the sentences "He dreaded explaining all this. He had been explaining it all his life." The constant demand of immigrants and their children to explain their identity was not limited to White Russians, of course, but here Boris's immediate mention (on page 2) of that aspect of Russianness in America is indicative of the weariness many émigrés felt. The critical factor here was a feeling that, even after decades of living in the United States, White Russians had to satisfactorily explain their disconnection with and opposition to Soviet Russia, something that became more, not less, important as the Cold War began after World War II.

Dimitri's maintenance of cultural heritage remained as strong. He earned a JD, served in the military, and practiced law until retirement in 2012, acting as executor for many Russian émigré families. Among other interests, he focused on Fort Ross preservation.[102] Neither brother changed their surname. Admittedly, a surname such as "Ilyin," though still difficult for Americans to pronounce, is less cumbersome than, for example, "Kiyaschenko." Keeping Russian names and surnames may have helped to maintain Russian identity by maintaining that identity on display, despite the commensurate weariness of constant explanation. In doing so, it seemed the Ilyins did not feel like "outcasts" in their American lives, but their class status, as well as their penchant for marrying Americans, also eased their path into American society.

Women in and out of the Workplace

Emigrating with family indubitably had its advantages as well in terms of easing economic and social burdens of settlement in a new country with limited resources. The Ilyin and Boodberg families were fortunate in that their emigration experience was multi-generational. Pavel and Maria Nikonenko, on the other hand, like many of the people who arrived on USAT *Merritt*, had no family in the United States, and their daughter recalled that the circumstance of not having family support took a psychological toll.[103] Valentina Vernon noted, however, that despite having her entire family with her, her mother worked herself to death, indicating her feelings that an undue burden had been placed on her mother, perhaps because Vernon's father did not work. Baron Boodberg's role as a community leader, his age and prior service, may have excused his placement of that burden on his wife in the émigré community, but Vernon clearly did not excuse it, given her veiled comments. Vernon, unlike her three brothers, did not attend university, also indicating the commitments placed on her as a mother and wife. She and her mother first opened a "refreshment stand" on El Camino Real, a major thoroughfare in Menlo Park, south of San Francisco, which was quite successful, prompting a move to the city.[104] She worked for a time as a waitress at a teashop near the corner of Van Ness Avenue and Green Street, which the owner sold it to her for a nominal sum, starting her on the road to becoming a successful restauranteur.[105]

Vernon, as noted earlier, created her version of a Russian Tea Room that allowed her to maintain her Russianness while running a business that catered to Americans, first on Russian Hill and then downtown in the business district. She bought all the equipment she needed on credit from a hotel supply company, noting that the manager "didn't ask me where I was born or anything," referencing her Russian accent and her "foreignness." Here, she obliquely expressed gratitude that the American manager did not question her about her origins. Vernon weathered the Depression by coming to agreements with her twenty-five employees – Russian émigré chefs and Filipino wait-staff – about cuts in wages in order not to lay anyone off. In contrast, at least two other Russian restaurants, Katenka (noted in Introduction) and the Volga Café and Cabaret, opened outside the Fillmore enclave in the inter-war period and failed within two years.[106]

The economic realities of American life, particularly as the Depression worsened in the 1930s, also influenced perspectives about valuing non-monetary versus monetary familial contributions. Taisia Bazhenova addressed that circumstance in a short story, situating a group of women sitting "in the square on Post and Steiner Streets" near the Children's Day Home. The women recounted their experiences after arrival from Harbin with sons and daughters-in-law who resented having to support them. The story's narrator observed how the eyes of fictional character "Olga Petrovna," who lived with her son, daughter-in-law, and granddaughter, had "dimmed" since she arrived from Harbin; her "kind and sweet smile" no longer evident. "Affection flourishes amidst tranquility," mused Olga Petrovna, adding that her son and his wife saw and heard nothing beyond the everyday grind, their menial jobs stultifying them. Her efforts to help were not sufficient either in her daughter-in-law's eyes or her own. Her friends with older grandchildren, meanwhile, saw that the younger generation had no use for grandparents, the children no longer speaking Russian and refusing to go to church, referring to the deacon as "some guy with long hair shouting" about something or other.[107] The children resented and despised the traditions of their ancestors, including the distinctive, and perceived foreign, aspects of Orthodoxy, seeing these traditions as barriers to becoming "real" Americans. The inability of the older generation, often lost in America as well, to connect with the younger, left a void between the generations as youth quickly adapted and adopted mannerisms and ways that were not only foreign but offensive to their elders, to which Lyons had also alluded from his own experience: "The Americanism that ... [the average boy] ... acquired ... was the loud, vulgar, surface – the slang, the sporting page, the crude success ideals of the movies and yellow journals – and nothing of the grandeur at the core of America."[108] Rejecting Russian customs and traditions, the younger generation inevitably adopted the outlook and values of modern American consumerism and popular culture. The "grandeur" of abstract principles important to the foundations of American democracy garnered less or no attention in the effort to conform and attain "crude success ideals." Nadia Shapiro, for example, referenced the fact that Russian children growing up on Potrero Hill in 1923 were "real Yanks," implying that they had adopted brash and vulgar American mannerisms. Her interviewee, Barbara Jacoob, wondered mournfully whether her two young sons would "even remember their Russian grandparents" when they grew up.[109] Young people were faced with bridging an enormous divide if they were to maintain a dual life, and some of them sought to Americanize quickly and fully to avoid the stresses such a dual life entailed. In her story, Bazhenova integrated information from actual events in the community, noting that Father Pavel Razumoff planned to establish a home for elderly indigent women in San Francisco (which he did do in 1930 at 1761 Turk Street) and implying that women, such as those portrayed in her story, unwanted and rejected by their children or grandchildren, were likely going to end up there, despite having family in America.[110]

Many older women who were unmarried or widowed did live a precarious existence, and the decision to open a home for indigent women indicated the critical need. Olga and Kiril Ilyin listed Katherine Krivoblotsky (1864–1942) as a "servant" in their household in 1930 and as a "lodger" in 1940. Perhaps she did help with keeping house, but the relationship was likely more than that of just servant and employer. Krivoblotsky, who arrived in 1925, likely would have had to apply for assistance to the émigré community's home for indigent women without the Ilyins' assistance.[111]

Bazhenova's pessimism spoke to her own personal experience as well: a budding poet in Siberia and Harbin whose poems brought her acclaim in youth, she worked in a garment factory pressing dresses in San Francisco and "feared to think about poetry" as the distraction might have caused her to burn the dresses. Though she worked for émigré newspapers as a correspondent, her creative spark, she implied, faded away amidst the dreary *byt* of marriage, housekeeping, and factory employment. After years of hard work, Bazhenova and her husband had tiny pensions which could not support them, so her husband continued working long after he should have been able to retire. Suffering from various ailments, she wrote that she was left with nothing to show for all those years of struggle, commenting: "It's strange to me when others joke and laugh."[112]

In direct contrast with Bazhenova's perception of language and culture loss among the young, Antonina Von Arnold had noted, in her discussions with the Russian university students, that the "younger generation" knew and used the Russian language well "in contrast with some of the other nationalities of recent foreign extraction." In her perspective, among the students with whom she spoke, there was "relatively little second-generation conflict," meaning that they did not reject the values of their parents.[113] She ascribed this to the fact that the parents of the group were well-educated, but Bazhenova moved in the same social circles as Von Arnold and observed a desire for quick assimilation. The critical difference may have been access to higher education. If economic circumstances precluded a university education for young people, they felt an urgent need to assimilate in order to find something other than the menial jobs that were the only options open to their parents, and that meant wholesale rejection of any indications of "foreignness."

Tellingly, students told Von Arnold that simply having a "foreign name sometimes interfere[d]" with getting a job.[114] Young people, then, likely began to change their names if their parents had not done so, deliberately disguising their Russian identity as they entered the workforce, eventually, perhaps, losing that identity, depending on whether or not they continued to associate with the Russian community. That process continued into the post-World War II period, for example, in families with a Russian father and an American mother. Student Nicholas M. Protopopoff (1907–1993) kept his surname and married his American first wife, Mary, at St John the Baptist Orthodox Church in Berkeley in 1934. The Protopopoffs' son Michael, born in 1935, changed his surname to "Proto" after World War II.[115] Painting contractor Orest Streltzoff (1905–1980) and his Mississippi-born wife married in the early 1930s and had two sons, both born in San Francisco. Eldest son Orest Jr became "Donald" after the Streltzoffs divorced and subsequently became "Don Strel" in adulthood, also effectively obscuring his Russian roots.[116]

That obscuring of Russian roots in the Americanization process followed a similar path when Russian émigré women married Americans, despite efforts to maintain links to Russian identity. Olga Kemarsky

(1916–1994) arrived in San Francisco with her parents in 1929. In 1937, she married Texas-born James Hunt at the Holy Virgin Cathedral, and they baptized their three sons there. After World War II, the family relocated to the Eel River Valley in Humboldt County, running a gas station and a nursery. Their sons therefore had no ties to the San Francisco Russian community in adulthood. Olga's younger brother Rostislav, born in Shanghai in 1921 and a radio technician in the US Naval Reserve, was killed in action during World War II.[117] Her parents divorced, and her mother relocated to Eureka to live with her daughter in 1969. The circumstances of Olga Hunt's life – marriage to an American, loss of family, relocating to a rural area and no consistent contact with a Russian community – contributed to a situation where her children likely found it difficult to maintain a link to their Russian roots, despite the effort to establish that link through baptism in the Orthodox Church.[118]

In terms of generational differences in acculturation, the Russian students who arrived in the United States in the early 1920s specifically to attend university (i.e., men and women generally in their twenties) and who successfully completed a degree, were generally best able to find a balance between an American career and a Russian identity, whether or not they chose to change their names. The majority of those who achieved professional careers after university study in the United States were men, in line with gender norms of the period, but women did as well. Von Arnold herself was an example.

Antonina Von Arnold (1896–1988) provided a unique perspective of an émigré who documented and analyzed her immigration experience, and thoughts and feelings about the process. Arriving as a student, she studied English and stenography, subsequently working at the California Academy of Sciences as a stenographer. She also worked for the YWCA but, by 1933, she felt the secretarial work she was doing "began to appear as a mere performance of somebody else's ideas and orders." Art was her passion and she enrolled at the California School of Fine Arts, studying painting. After marrying an American, Ignatius McGuire, in 1941, with whom she had been involved intermittently, and moving to Washington, DC, she left him after two months and returned to San Francisco. She completed her master's degree in social work at the University of California at Berkeley in 1942. Her work in social services placed her in a professional position vis-à-vis members of both the Fillmore and Potrero Hill Russian communities. In the late 1940s, she began a relationship with Sergei Scherbakoff (1894–1967), a well-known émigré artist.[119]

Despite Von Arnold's intention early on to make a life for herself in America, she recognized how being foreign imparted a certain persona to her: "My playful bubbling and amusing intelligence practically was submerged in the scarcity and simplicity of my limited English." Husband McGuire had viewed her as a romantic and commensurately exotic figure: "At times I think I was not a real person to him but rather a fanciful figure of a romantic Russian exile girl."[120] Von Arnold, then, experienced a very personal version of the dominant culture view of Russian women in immigration in the United States and, what was rare, documented it, given her inclination for self-analysis. The motivation to document her impressions spoke, at least in part, to recognition of the trauma of displacement, which was ever-present but not often specifically discussed in Russian public discourse, because it was understood, just as feeling "foreign" was understood. She met a "jolly" Russian girl at the YWCA, where she lived for a time, and initially thought "here at last is a Russian who went through revolution and immigration and preserved [her] nerves in perfect condition." Later, however, Von Arnold was disappointed to realize that her new acquaintance was obsessed with illness and death.[121] Von Arnold's pleasure of "at last" encountering a Russian person who initially appeared to be mentally "healthy," spoke to the fact of conscious understanding of that collective trauma, which informed so much of Russian diasporic life in exile.

Her long-term relationship with Scherbakoff, which began when she was in her early fifties, served both to reinforce connections to the Russian community and provide a certain emotional security. The Scherbakoffs built a *dacha* (summer cottage) at Russian River. She brought her mother from Harbin, thus creating a sense of family life (she did not have children). Though she had briefly drifted away from the Russian community, Von Arnold returned to the comfort of a group that did not think her a romantic "fanciful figure," but a professional woman and artist in her own right, where she felt accepted on her own terms, with no need to explain herself. Interestingly, neither was Von Arnold in the camp of those who refused to recognize the legitimacy of the Soviet Union. Sergei Scherbakoff became involved in War Relief activities with the American Russian Institute in 1942 along with Victor Arnautoff (chapter 8). After Scherbakoff's death, Von Arnold donated his paintings to an institution in the USSR, also visiting there as a tourist.[122]

Von Arnold's decision not to have children (and she explicitly stated her lack of desire for a conventional life that included children) was not unusual. Upwards of 50 per cent – and perhaps as many as 60 per cent – of Russians who arrived as students between 1920 and 1925 (about 550 people) did not have children. Those who did not marry, of course, did not have children out of wedlock as the changes in traditional norms, whether Russian or American, did not extend to openly having children outside of marriage. Married couples, however, even those who seemed relatively stable economically, often did not have children either and the incidence of being "child free" seemed too frequent to be coincidental. Of a family of five cousins who settled in San Francisco by 1940, for example, only Tatiana Telbukoff-Hilkovsky (1904–1949) and her first husband, Alexander (1904–1974), had a child. Galina Zekhova (1896–1983), Nadejda Ilyin (1894–1977, spouse of Peter Ilyin), Barbara Kalbus (1892–1983), and Sergei Komov (1904–1988), all married, did not have children. As the subject was not one most people wrote about per se (Von Arnold was an exception as she wrote about deeply personal matters), the reasons for choosing not to have children and the methods to avoid pregnancy are unknown. The UORW had, in fact, sponsored lectures by Dr Constantin Lapidewsky in the 1920s for the Russian community on Potrero Hill, and the topics ranged from "the ideal sex life" to "abortion and its effect on sexual and general health," but whether émigrés attended the lectures is also unknown.[123] The high incidence of childless couples may have been, at least in part, a symptom of the trauma of displacement and the stress of émigré life on women. Their responses to that stress may have been obscured within actions they took within the family unit (i.e., exercising options that they may not have taken in Russia due to existing social pressures from family members). As those family members were either not present in the United States or were experiencing their own stresses in immigration, women forged their own paths. Options included divorcing a spouse (or multiple spouses) to leave unsatisfactory marital situations, choosing not to have children, or perhaps even terminating pregnancies. "Notorious" San Francisco resident Inez Burns (1886–1976) ran an "abortion" clinic at 327 Fillmore Street, just south of the Russian neighborhood, throughout the inter-war period, and purportedly performed as many as 50,000 abortions during that time.[124] Peter Balakshin referenced the fact of its existence in a short story, relating through various vignettes the difficult lives of the Fillmore's residents in terms of labor conditions. In one scene, a young woman standing at Third and Market Streets, listening to a Salvation Army group choir, thinks back to her experience two months earlier when she almost died, lying in a pool of her own blood, alone in a room in the "dreary house of death on Fillmore Street."[125] The description, made somewhat in passing, indicated an acknowledgment of the realities of women's lives.

Maintaining a creative life and participating in Russian community efforts was a goal for those women who had to settle for jobs that provided a living but no spiritual or intellectual sustenance. Eugenia Isaenko née Pechatkina was a leading figure in the community, in terms of literary and theater work as well as community efforts, though her "everyday" life was an office job at Pacific Gas and Electric Company. She arrived in 1923 as a student, studying natural sciences and music at Pomona College, but dropped out for financial reasons, working as a maid, dishwasher, waitress, factory employee, and seamstress to make ends meet.[126]

Isaenko and her first husband, Andrew Soorin (1898–1983), whom she had married in Harbin a few months prior to departure, went their separate ways soon after arrival in San Francisco and she married Alexis Isaenko (1894–1957). As a couple, they devoted themselves to Russian cultural affairs and were founding members of the Russian Club.[127] Alexis was the librarian both for the Russian Club, and later, the Russian Center. Eugenia wrote for *Russkaia zhizn'*, among other publications, and was a member of numerous émigré organizations including the Literary and Art Society and the ART theater society, performing on stage into the 1960s (figure 6.5). Eugenia wrote and published two Russian-language novels to some acclaim: *Perekati-Pole* (Tumbleweed) in 1953 and *Petr Ivanovich* in 1961. Von Arnold noted that Eugenia frequently explored child psychology in her writings, but Eugenia, like Von Arnold, did not have children. A biographical sketch of her noted that Eugenia "remained Russian in spirit" in America, a factor clearly important both to her and the people who valued her work.[128]

The experiences of women who arrived as students from Harbin between 1921 and 1925 were varied in terms of life paths. Despite the fact that seventy-seven of the eighty-seven women of the Harbin student group were between the ages of eighteen and twenty-six in 1922, at least 50 per cent of the group remained childless. Approximately 30 per cent enrolled in higher educational institutions but only 17 per cent graduated with a degree. At least 75 per cent of all the women reported working outside the home or at jobs other than as housewives at some point in the inter-war period. 88 per cent married at least once, and 25 per cent of those were divorced at least once.[129]

Figure 6.5 A 12 April 1959 matinee performance of a scene from Nikolai Gogol's satirical play *The Inspector-General* at the Russian Center at 2450 Sutter Street. Eugenia Isaenko is in the center, playing the role of Anna Andreevna. The male actor was B.F. Dmitriew as Ivan Khlestakoff, and the younger woman, Marina Ukhtomsky (author's mother), playing Maria Antonovna. Both Dmitriew and Ukhtomsky were post-war arrivals in San Francisco. The caption states: "A matinee in memory of writer Nikolai Vasilievich Gogol."

The focus of the Russian community on educating their children about their heritage spoke to that community's realization that everything they had lived and experienced meant little if their children did not understand their past. At the same time, parents struggled to ensure that their children would thrive in America. Concurrently, many were troubled by American values and culture. Émigrés sought to provide a solid cultural foundation for their youth, which, in their view, would allow them to negotiate that complicated path of being Russian in America. Clearly, there was no unanimity of purpose. Parents like Valentina Vernon decided that such efforts, leading to the necessity of dual identity, were detrimental and endangered the future of young people, forcing them to continue living as "outcasts" in America. Though the Orthodox Church inarguably remained an important factor in émigré spiritual life, its significance in the lives of young people waned for those who sought to assimilate. Even a member of the clergy in San Francisco, after all, Father Denisoff, chose to reinterpret church canon to suit his "American" life.

Approximately 30 per cent of those who married at the Holy Virgin Cathedral between 1931 and 1948 married non-Russians, and those who married outside the church likely included a much higher percentage of intermarriage with non-Russians, indicating a certain pull for younger émigrés to live their lives outside the émigré milieu.[130] Yefim Beliaeff, commenting on the Americanization of Russian youth who did not participate in émigré art, literature, and theatrical groups in the 1930s, said that "today's youth is inclined to respond to more practical utilitarian goals," the implication being that by doing so they were no longer "Russian in spirit."[131] Despite such assumptions, however, some who married Americans baptized their children in the Russian Orthodox Church, indicating ambiguity of intentions with respect to how they planned to raise their children.

The struggle to build lives in the perennially economically competitive environment peculiar to American life took its toll on families, however, at times dividing them, leaving already vulnerable members, usually older women, without emotional or material support, a factor that the church leadership recognized given the effort to establish a home for indigent or impoverished women early on. Women who did have children also took on the burdens both of maintaining family life and working outside the home in large numbers among the Russian emigration. Those who obtained advanced degrees and pursued careers were able to do so largely because they chose to eschew family commitments.

Among both men and women, Russians recognized that maintaining a Russian cultural self in America meant a lifetime of explanation of one's identity and, critically, the subtext of questions, such as those that Boris Ilyin referenced in his novel, always contained an assertion of foreignness (suspicion of ethnic difference), exoticism (generally in the case of women), or worse, an imputation of disloyalty (suspicion on political grounds). The choices they made for themselves, and their children, reflected these struggles, and remaining Russian in America was too heavy a burden for some.

Russian immigration from the Far East continued through the 1930s, a decade when Russians were faced with a change in their deportation status: once the United States recognized the Soviet Union, Russians became legally deportable to that country. Prior to 1933, immigration authorities did not focus overmuch on finding in-country Russians in the United States who had entered or remained without legal sanction due to the inability to deport Russians to the Soviet Union (debarring/excluding people at the border upon attempted entry was the prevalent method of controlling Russian immigration). The flow of Russians into the United States, however, utilizing various routes, and at times entering without legal sanction due to the decreased quotas, did continue through the 1930s, complicating their status overall and requiring steps to "legalize" that status as the 1933 deadline loomed.

—7—

"WHITE RUSSIANS IN THE 'NEW WORLD'"
Marketing and Monitoring Identity

But then what do we KNOW about the Russian mind?
We have always found it irrational, inexplicable
BY OUR STANDARDS ...
Of course we do NOT "know" the Russian mind.
It is a completely ORIENTAL mind.

SAN FRANCISCO EXAMINER editorial, 1944[1]

On 25 October 1931, fifty-year-old Lydia Kopiloff crossed into the United States from Mexico, crawling under the border fence at an isolated spot near the two border towns of Nogales. Kopiloff later became a US citizen, a beneficiary of an amendment to the Registry Act of 1929 enacted by Congress in 1934, which both officials and its beneficiaries often referred to as the "White Russian Bill."[2] "A well-educated woman with white hair and dark-gray eyes fringed with black lashes," according to Nadia Shapiro, Kopiloff had begun her journey to the United States almost a decade prior to entering the country, leaving Siberia for Japan with her son during the Civil War. By the time she entered the United States, she was without family, having lost her son to illness while they were living in Mexico. In San Francisco, she worked as a seamstress and house maid, registered as a Democrat upon obtaining US citizenship in 1940, and lived alone in an apartment in the heart of the Fillmore. She died in 1941 and was laid to rest at Cypress Lawn Cemetery in Colma, south of San Francisco. Did anyone visit her grave over the years? Widowed prior to leaving Russia, it seemed she had no family in the United States. As such, her life experiences, incredible in the telling, might have been lost to both memory and history, the only evidence of her existence a few official documents and, thankfully, Shapiro's draft copy of her interview with Kopiloff in 1934.[3]

The initial inflow of thousands of Russian émigrés to San Francisco and the west coast of the United States in the early 1920s was only the beginning of a continuing stream of people pushed out of Russia as well as out of places they had initially settled. The flow continued until 1941 when immigration halted due to the US entry into World War II. Victor Kolokolnikoff, president of the Harbin Committee to Aid Russian Refugees, warned in 1930 that the "flow of people fleeing from the USSR is not decreasing in view of growing famine and terror in the Far East [of the USSR]. In addition, economic opportunities ... [in Harbin] ... are decreasing catastrophically day by day."[4] Various circumstances pushed Russians out of China and Japan in the 1920s while the global Depression and the Japanese occupation of northern China complicated the situation further in the early 1930s, the former for Russian migrants who had settled in Mexico, and the latter for those who still lived in Harbin.

As the American economy continued to deteriorate, Russians in San Francisco faced new challenges to survival, while more Russians continued to arrive via increasingly circuitous routes, at times involving extended residency in Mexico. Yet another critical factor for Russians in the United States, the recognition of the Soviet Union in 1933 signaled danger, as a barrier to deportation technically fell once the United States established diplomatic relations with the Soviet Union.[5] The Russian community in San Francisco embarked on an effort to persuade Congress to pass the Russian Refugees (White Russian) Bill – an amendment to the Alien Registry Act of 1929 that would provide an amnesty for those Russians in the United States who were undocumented. That process highlighted the necessity to "market" Russian identity as suitable: specifically, elite Russian men who were productive in the US economy, who had married American (i.e., Euro-American, non-Russian immigrant) women, and whose anti-communist credentials were above reproach – an identity, at least in terms of the first two categories, that did not encompass people such as Kopiloff, migrating without legal sanction into the US in the early 1930s. As such, Russians took advantage of the long-standing "White Russian aristocrat" trope to facilitate passage of the bill, while Russians who did not fit into that trope complicated those efforts. Simultaneously, US officials questioned the ethnicity of Russians who were not, in their eyes, quite "white" enough.

The White Russian Bill

The hopes of émigrés that the Soviet regime would fall before the United States moved forward with diplomatic recognition crumbled after Franklin D. Roosevelt's election in 1932. His administration set the date of 16 November 1933 for the event, which reinforced the permanent nature of White Russian exile. The act also brought a new threat: US officials considered "subjects of the former Russian Empire ... a most conspicuous example" of persons not deported in the late 1920s and early 1930s.[6] Due to a concerted effort by Russian community organizations, however, American officials became persuaded that deporting Russians to the USSR would likely mean their death or imprisonment. The efforts were largely led by Russian émigrés in San Francisco who mobilized early, assisting those who feared applying for citizenship due to discrepancies in their paperwork or their undocumented status. Anatoly Gavriloff (1898–1940), who arrived in 1926 under the quota, wrote a note to Nadia Shapiro in December of 1932 explaining that he had organized a committee to address the issue of "legalizing Russian students, tourists and illegal [residents]," and asking for her assistance to address the matter in the American press. He contacted her in his capacity as an official member of the Consolidated Committee of Russian National Organizations (hereafter, "Committee"), then based at the Russian Club at 1198 Fulton Street (figure 7.1).[7]

The Committee, headed initially by Gleb Ilyin, set out to explain the status and situation of members of the Russian diaspora who had "no country" or "consular protection" to US officials.[8] Ilyin, by now well-known as he had painted Lou Henry Hoover's portrait in 1930, was a logical choice to promote and lead the cause of the "White Russians." His name and status carried weight, playing into the Russian aristocrat trope. The Committee, however, encompassed the church societies and sisterhoods at: Holy Trinity and Holy Virgin Cathedrals, St John Church in Berkeley;[9] the Russian Club, Russian Former Naval Officers' Association, the San Francisco Post of Russian Invalids of the World War; the Russian Society for Care and Education of Russian Children; the Russian University Club, the Russian Engineers' Society, the Russian Relief Society, the RNSA, the Russian Dramatic Circle, the Russian Musketeers' Union, the Russian Relief Committee for the Far East, and the Russian Athletic Club.[10] In other words, Committee membership spanned a broad range of social groups based in San Francisco whose members had, by

Marketing and Monitoring Identity | 215

Figure 7.1 The Westerfeld House, 1198 Fulton Street, n.d. The Russian Club was located here from 1928 to 1937. From the 1930s to 1950s, Russian émigrés also listed it as a home address indicating they rented rooms there. On the verso, the building is labeled: "Old Russian house between McAllister + Fulton," identifying it as linked to the Russian community, but not, in this case, as a consulate or embassy.

and large, arrived in the early 1920s under the quota and who had become US citizens as soon as they were able (generally, after at least five years of uninterrupted residency).

Committee Secretary Basil Antonenko (1890–1975) sought to mobilize Russian students to act, collecting signatures and involving professors from the University of California's Slavic Department.[11] Those students who were not citizens had much to lose if the legislation did not pass; concurrently, they were examples of model Russians for the purposes of good press, as they were striving to attain a higher education. At this juncture, a decade after Russian students had first begun arriving from Harbin, the narrative had altered 180 degrees: students no longer spoke of returning to Russia upon completing their education but were actively involved in the effort to avoid possible deportation to the Soviet Union. The students did propose in a letter to Secretary of Labor William Doak that Russian students educated in the United States would be of valuable assistance as "intercessors ... should conditions in Russia change."[12] The students also wrote to Harry Hull, commissioner general of Immigration, and the Committee included both President Herbert Hoover and

President-Elect Roosevelt on its list of addressees in the letter-writing campaign to pass the amendment providing an avenue to citizenship for White Russians in the United States.[13]

Admitting that many Russians were in the United States illegally, the Committee stressed their refugee status as persons whom no country would accept given the situation of the worldwide depression, and who would be executed "immediately" if deported to the Soviet Union.[14] Focusing their letter-writing efforts on US officials, with no large-scale resources or wealthy patrons to contribute funds, the organization spent about $45 over the course of the two-year campaign, according to Antonenko, which was basically the cost of postage. Shapiro credited the passage of the act largely to the Committee, although she noted that "Americans of Russian descent and their American friends" provided "tens of thousands of signatures" on petitions to "legalize 'White' Russian refugees."[15] Social, familial, and kin relationships facilitated Russian community efforts in the endeavor. Recognizing that "legality" and "illegality" were terms that masked the often-arbitrary nature of the processes that dictated the fates of immigrants, Russians who had been fortunate enough to obtain legal entry into the United States mobilized to assist their countrymen and women.[16]

The term "White Russian" though, generally incorrectly understood by almost everyone who was *not* White Russian, was helpful in the process to pass the very specific amendment to the Registry Act of 2 March 1929 to allow "bona fide political and religious refugees" to apply for citizenship, despite the fact that they had remained in or entered the United States illegally.[17] The amendment allowed them to register as resident aliens but there was no blanket amnesty – they had to "prove by witnesses that they …[were] … law-abiding person[s] of good moral character."[18] US official fears of Russian communist infiltrators taking advantage of the act were assuaged by the stipulation in the bill that citizenship was not automatic and that questioning of potential candidates would weed out political undesirables.[19]

The persistent notion that White Russians were aristocrats, targeted and victimized by the Bolsheviks and therefore certainly opposed to communist and anarchist beliefs, also provided positive impetus in an effort among congressional and other officials, responding to the letter-writing campaign, to save them from an at best uncertain fate at the hands of Soviet authorities. If these aristocrats or members of the nobility had inadvertently violated US law in their yearning to live free in America, their status as elites made that violation less egregious in American officials' eyes than if they had been illiterate peasants. The amendment to the Registry Act, unofficially the "White Russian Bill," was so narrowly crafted that other groups who also technically qualified as refugees under international law in this tumultuous period (particularly Jews attempting to get out of Germany) could not enter based on the amendment's criteria, which specifically stated that applicants had to have entered the United States before 1 July 1933 *and* "in whose case, there is no record of admission for permanent residence" *and* "who prior to that date could not be deported to any country to which it was lawful to deport him" (i.e., the Soviet Union), with which the United States had no diplomatic relationship until November of 1933.[20] US immigration officials, on their part, upon passage of the amendment on 8 June 1934, made their own inquiries into the USSR penal code, satisfying themselves that a law Soviet authorities had passed on 21 November 1929 declared those Russian citizens who had not returned to the USSR by that date "outlaws" to be shot "within 24 hours of identification" if they dared to enter the country henceforth.[21]

Shapiro published an editorial in the *Christian Science Monitor* on 30 October 1934, after the amendment was enacted, to express the relief of, by her unofficial estimate, 2,000 Russians in the United States "saved ... from life-long misery and possible violent death." Conceding that "these Russian refugees were lawbreakers," she wrote that "the measure that has lifted them from the class of pariahs slinking away at the approach of a uniformed policeman to that of desirable future American citizens is the S. 2692, commonly known among legislators as the Russian Refugees Bill."[22] The official number of applicants taking advantage of the bill was 1,425 nationwide, but "many more" undocumented Russian refugees were reported to be in the United States.[23]

Shapiro's characterization of how undocumented Russians lived indicated that fear of discovery by authorities existed. Russians made efforts to avoid interaction with authorities as lack of English-language skills or telltale heavy accents identified them as foreigners. Boris Shebeko, for example, recalled an incident when Colonel Avenir Efimoff was hit and badly injured by a speeding driver while crossing the street in San Francisco, but was "so afraid that he might have committed some crime like obstructing traffic" that he apologized to the driver and pretended that he was not hurt. That was "how unsure" of themselves Russian émigrés had been "in those first days" after arrival (even, as in the case of Efimoff, if they had entered legally).[24]

The many émigrés who worked as laborers or domestics blended in as faceless "generic" workers who did not draw notice if they remained under the radar. Slavs as a group, however, became targets of police brutality in San Francisco by the early 1930s, as authorities identified them with labor unrest. In a 1932 letter to the RNSA, a Slavonic Alliance of California organizing committee member described how a San Francisco policeman kicked to death a Croatian man for supposedly resisting arrest. The Slavonic Alliance was successful in getting the police officer dismissed from the force, but the writer urged the RNSA to rejoin the alliance in order to empower Slavs to preclude such targeting.[25]

The bulk of Shapiro's editorial focused on the story of Lydia Kopiloff, noted above, whom Shapiro, significantly, did not identify by name in the article. Kopiloff and her son Alexander were forced to leave Japan after the massive earthquake in September of 1923 destroyed much of Japan's infrastructure, booking passage to Mexico, and settling in the coastal town of Mazatlán. In 1930, they resided there with the Leonoff family; Victor Leonoff (1899–1950) had arrived on the same ship with the Kopiloffs. He and Maria Sinitzin (1895–1975), a native of Petrograd and a widow with three children, were married in Mexico in 1924. Sinitzin had also lived in Japan with her family, but her husband passed away and she arrived in Seattle with her children in November 1923. Sinitzin had a transit visa, stating that her destination was Latvia, and the family was admitted provisionally, but migrated to Mexico instead.[26]

Circumstances forced the eventual migration of Lydia and Maria and her children to the United States. Alexander Kopiloff worked as a radio engineer, but fell ill and died of a "tropical ailment" in 1930. Victor Leonoff departed for China as the political and economic situation in Mexico worsened and the two women with Maria's now four children (the youngest born in 1925) moved to Nogales, Mexico. Lydia became a grandmother to that youngest boy (also named Alexander). Unable to find work, Kopiloff started a business selling homemade *pirozhki* (meat or vegetable-filled fritters) but, in response to American forced repatriation of people of Mexican heritage when the Depression began, the Mexican government banned foreigners from running businesses, and authorities in Nogales forbade Kopiloff from selling her wares. Kopiloff noted that American rhetoric against Mexican people in the United States contributed to the reaction against all "foreign" business concerns by the Mexican government.[27] In desperation, she and Maria went to the US Consulate in Nogales, but the consul, refusing their visa requests, stated that they "would be unable to support ... [themselves] ... in the United States." In January of 1929, the US Department of State had sent instruction to consuls in Mexico "to interpret the immigration law more rigorously," and the LPC clause was one of the several bases to deny visas.[28] The consul joked that they might "do as some of the Chinese are doing and jump the frontier fence," referencing the fact that Chinese merchants had also been forced out of business in Mexico and some were leaving for the United States in such manner as they were not legally allowed to enter.[29] Unlike in Harbin in the 1920s, where US Consul George Hanson understood the desperate circumstances of the Russians and issued visas despite disapproval of US Departments of Labor and Justice officials, the consul in Nogales followed orders to exclude undesirables (in this case, older Russian women unaccompanied by males).

Maria, however, had a permit allowing her to make day visits to Nogales in Arizona and her sixteen-year-old son, Vadim aka Joaquin, had fixed up an old truck in which they crossed over. Kopiloff had lost her own permit, but her landlady's son showed her a place to crawl under the border fence one "starry night." She then, in her words, "strolled nonchalantly" into Nogales, Arizona, and joined the Leonoffs, traveling with them to Los Angeles, subsequently migrating to San Francisco.[30]

The odyssey of the women and children not only highlighted the lengthy and circuitous journeys many Russians traveled on their way to America, but the vulnerability of people who were "stateless." Both their routes and extended stays in Mexico differed from that of the majority of émigrés who came to the west coast of the United States directly from the Far East, but they were by no means the only Russians to have lived in Mexico and entered the United States at the US-Mexico border, whether migrating through Nogales or Douglas, Arizona, by Calexico, San Ysidro, by San Diego, California, or by El Paso, Texas.[31] Kopiloff's experience also indicated that finding a place where Russian refugees could survive with whatever remaining family they had was of primary importance as she had remained in Mexico with her son and had developed kin relationships with Maria and her children. In other words, she was looking for a place where she could peacefully live out her life, knowing that any attention cast upon her, as a "stateless" person, with no consular assistance available, might endanger whatever stability she may have found.

Russian consular agent in San Francisco Arthur Landesen and Seattle's Russian consul general Nicholas Bogoiavlensky (1867–1945) received letters of inquiry and pleas for assistance from Russians both in the United

States and in Mexico in the late 1920s and early 1930s about travel and immigration issues in a constantly changing environment. Kopiloff's entry into Mexico prior to its recognition of the Soviet Union in 1924 may have been facilitated as she had a travel document, likely a Nansen passport, issued by a Russian consul in Japan. After Mexico established diplomatic relations with the Soviet Union in 1924, however, the Mexican government gradually tightened the rules on entry for Russians without Soviet passports, refusing entry to Russians with Nansen passports or post-Civil War consular-issued documents that attested to their identity.[32]

Correspondence between Landesen and émigré Helen Lebedeff (1900–1975) in San Francisco in 1929 pointed both to ongoing Russian migration via Mexico to San Francisco and/or decisions to remain in Mexico until it became impossible to do so amid the growing global economic crisis and ensuing difficulties for foreigners noted earlier.[33] Helen's husband was Michael Lebedeff (1898–1935), brother of Victor (1900–1967) and Boris (1911–1976) who, along with their American-born wives, founded the Fort Ross Initiative Group in the 1930s (chapter 5). The Lebedeff family, parents Paul (1867–1943) and Nadejda (1877–1941), and six children in all, from Orenburg, left Russia in 1922. Some family members obtained immigration visas and arrived in San Francisco or Seattle in 1923. Others, along with members of Helen's family, the Miakinkoffs, also from Orenburg, headed to Mexico from Japan, arriving in Ensenada in January of 1925, subsequently settling in Mazatlán.[34] Obtaining visitor's visas at the US border was a possibility for those who could afford to pay a bond, so family members traveled back and forth over the years. Boris, a minor when he arrived with his mother Nadejda in Mexico, traveled to San Francisco from Mazatlán in November of 1927, and supposedly went on to Canada but was living in San Francisco with his family when he received his entry visa in 1930, at which time he officially "entered" the United States at Blaine, Washington.[35]

The experiences of Russian families in the United States, China, Mexico (and to some degree, Canada) paint a complex and deliberate strategy in their process of immigration to the United States, which, for some, from embarkation from Russia to final settlement in the United States, took almost a decade. Like Kopiloff and the Leonoffs, members of these families settled in Mazatlán, indicating a Russian community. Lydia and Maria, as women "without men," had no options to enter the United States, however, while the Lebedeff family network, which included males, utilized various available options over time to facilitate travel to and from

Marketing and Monitoring Identity | **221**

the United States, culminating with all family members eventually gaining sanctioned entry.[36]

Without in-country consular representation, stateless Russians were extremely vulnerable to bureaucratic hostility and indifference as well as changing political winds. Though both Landesen and Bogoiavlensky did their best to assist stateless Russians, their options were limited. To obtain any type of visa to the United States while in Mexico, foreigners had to prove two years' residency in Mexico, and a visitor's visa did not allow visa holders to remain in the US permanently or change their status while in-country.[37] In 1926, Bogoiavlensky was still issuing what he considered official Russian "passports" to people who were able to provide proper documentation along with a Nansen passport (i.e., certificates of birth, marriage, and photographs). Bogoiavlensky claimed that the American consul in Vancouver, Canada recognized as official only those Russian passports that Bogoiavlensky issued.[38] For Russians in Mexico, however, the situation seemed more complicated. Erstwhile teacher and pastry chef Alexander Evtikhieff (1883–1955), who arrived in Mexico in 1925, received such a passport in 1926 intending to come to California. He wrote to Landesen several months later, however, about obtaining a visa to work on a farm because had he had not been able to obtain a visa with the Russian consul-issued passport. He noted difficulties in getting information from American consular authorities because he spoke poor English and the American officials "were distrustful of Russians."[39]

The fact that more than 1,400 Russians took advantage of the 1934 amendment to the Registry Act to apply for citizenship indicated that Kopiloff's experience of crossing the border by crawling under a fence in the dead of night was not an isolated occurrence. In a June 1928 inquiry to the Naturalization Bureau in San Francisco, Landesen noted that "there are many Russians [in San Francisco] whose families [have been waiting for several years] … in Harbin, Manchuria and other cities of China [and] also Mexico" for immigration visas.[40]

In Shapiro's account about how the bill passed, she noted how the congressional representative speaking in support of the bill focused on the fact that "there are few [Russians] in this country" and that "five or six hundred" were in need of the act, indicating that the United States could afford to be magnanimous because of the small numbers.[41] Such reasoning spoke to perennial fears of dominant culture representatives and eugenics proponents, who feared "hordes" of Southern and Eastern Europeans damaging the American gene pool and polluting the cultural heritage of European Americans. The Russians, however, though admittedly law-breakers with respect to immigration law, were purportedly of aristocratic origins and had, according to the representative, "proven themselves good and law-abiding citizens" otherwise, with "many" having "married American women," therefore having American-born children, which would make their deportation difficult.[42] Perception of Russians with respect to gendered profiles had altered (i.e., Russian men of the appropriate class status were capable of contributing to the labor pool) in contrast to previous perspectives that they were either a threat to American wages or dangerous radicals. The trope of the quintessential Russian émigré as a feminine aristocratic figure (perhaps with a stash of jewels sewn into her clothing seams so that she would not become public burden) had receded over the course of the decade as officials encountered women who were impoverished, middle-aged or elderly, and who did not fit their romantic notions of beautiful noble-born Russian émigrés.[43]

The Burden of Respectability

Promoting the White Russian aristocrat trope for the purposes of passing the bill was a clear strategy of émigrés in San Francisco. Major-General Sergei Iserguin (1875–1946) replaced Gleb Ilyin at the helm of the Committee in 1933; his connections to Baron Boodberg, a titled personage, as well as membership in the Veterans' Society, helped reinforce a respectable public face of the Russian community in the period surrounding the push for the amendment, which was indubitably helpful in gaining support. American veterans' groups had invited members of the Russian Veterans' Society in San Francisco to take part in a ceremony dedicating the newly built War Memorial Veterans Building in San Francisco in November of 1932, and the Russian Veteran's Society subsequently held a concert ball there. Captain Vladimir Velikoselsky (1895–1984), a Veterans' Society member and "leader of the local Russian colony," according to reporters, was also, they noted, a "Count."[44] The mutual respect of veterans' groups contributed to the notion of the respectability of White Russians, overshadowing past narratives of anarchistic or, as in the 1920s wanted poster (figure 7.2), violent Russian males.

The realities of life for immigrant men, however, particularly in the Depression era, indicated an alternate narrative existing in parallel with the types of activities émigré community leaders emphasized in public discourse. Unlawful or criminal activity among White Russian émigrés

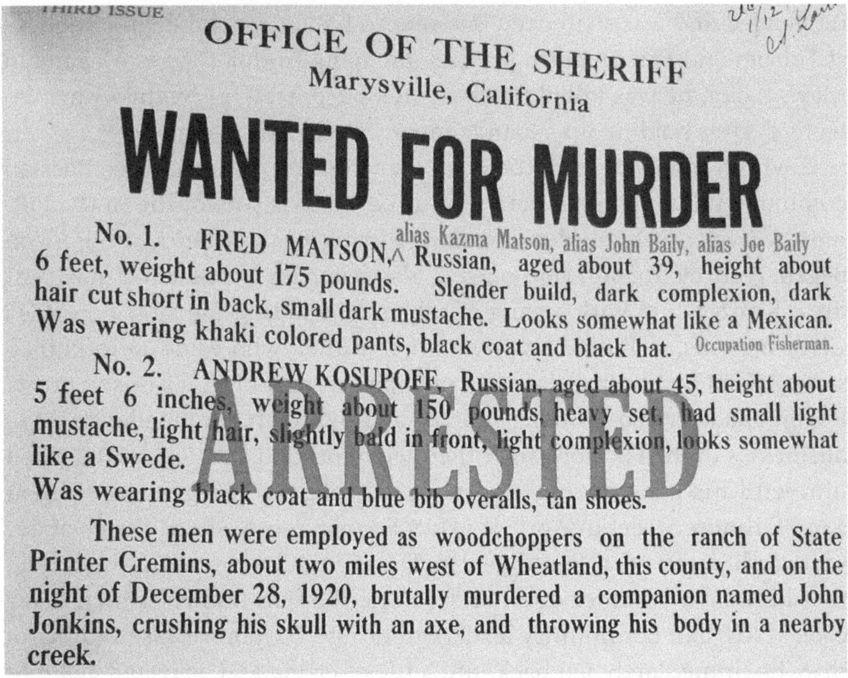

Marketing and Monitoring Identity | **223**

Figure 7.2 Excerpt from a Marysville Sheriff's Office wanted poster seeking Russians Fred/ Kazma Matson and Andrew Kosupoff. On 28 December 1920, they robbed and murdered John Jonkins, throwing his body into a creek at a ranch where they were employed as woodchoppers. Matson was described as looking "somewhat like a Mexican" while Kosupoff looked "somewhat like a Swede," indicating the ethnic ambiguity of Russians to American law enforcement. Further, the men were "hobo types" who camped "in jungles" and would "undoubtedly seek Russian camps and resorts." What jungles or Russian "resorts" is unknown. Russian men did work as fruit pickers in Marysville and may have lived in camps.

was uncommon but not unknown, ranging from traffic violations to serious crimes up to and including armed robbery and murder. Despite Prohibition, Basil Telepneff (1894–1951), for example, was arrested in March of 1926 for reckless and drunk driving after he hit a parked car at Van Ness and Turk Streets.[45] On the other end of the spectrum and labeled a "four-time loser" by newspapers, Gabriel Gavriloff used "American" aliases (William Scott and William Eric Courtney III), obscuring his ethnic background. Born in 1919 in Harbin, he arrived with his parents in 1923, and was first arrested for "joyriding" at the age of fifteen, later passing bad checks in Baltimore and Wyoming, where he was incarcerated. Returning to San Francisco in 1940 (where his mother lived), he again reoffended and was sentenced one year to life for second degree robbery at Folsom and San Quentin prisons. Escaping from a road work gang in May of 1942, he was killed that year in a purported "gunfight with a detective" after holding up a loan company in Omaha, Nebraska.[46]

Gavriloff's violent death took place far from the San Francisco Russian community, but criminal activity was certainly a part of life in the Fillmore. Giving up on the idea of making a living legally after the Depression began, Andrey Rogojin (1903–1979), also using an "American" alias, Andrew Kraft, fell in with a gang of robbers, including the later notorious Clyde Stevens, a "Public Enemy Number One," who went on to kidnap several San Quentin parole board members as part of a 1935 prison break. Rogojin had arrived on USAT *Merritt* and by 1931 had robbed a series of businesses in the Fillmore and other neighborhoods. Police apprehended him with his gang during an attempted robbery of a grocery store at 2400 Fillmore Street in April of 1931.[47] Rogojin received a sentence of five years to life, served at San Quentin. During the legal process, he let slip that he was "a member of an aristocratic Russian family," which likely caused Russian community leaders to cringe.[48] Upon release in May of 1936, he immediately fell back into a life of crime and, arrested again in November, spent eight years in prison (figure 7.3).[49] Though none of the businesses he and his gang robbed were specified as Russian-owned, they certainly may have been (produce and food stores, gas stations, drugstores among them). In his 1942 draft card, Rogojin noted "no one" when asked for a contact just prior to his second release from prison, indicating he may have burned his bridges in the community.[50]

Some Russian men, unable to make ends meet legally in the Depression era, may have taken part in less visible unlawful activity. Sergei Valenko's grandson recalled that Valenko (1901–1992, originally Odnovalenko), who also arrived on USAT *Merritt*, was proficient in the use of "both blunt and sharp objects," such as "saps, knives, small pistols and brass knuckles," and had a reputation for "enjoying violence." His "neighbors feared him." He was never "short of money," even during the Depression, sending his wife, Dina (1903–1977), and daughter, Anna, born in San Francisco in 1924, to resorts in Calistoga for the summer (figure 7.4). Despite such a reputation (or perhaps because of it), friends Stephen (1903–1952) and Helen Shesterikoff/Chester (1898–1952) asked Valenko to be godfather to their son Dmitri/James in 1939. The parental-godparental relationship (*koomoviya*) was traditionally as strong as one of blood ties, and therefore not embarked upon lightly; whatever his activities, then, Valenko remained

Marketing and Monitoring Identity | 225

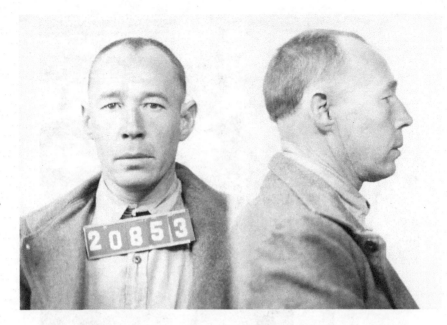

Figure 7.3 Folsom Prison photo of Andrew Rogojin/Kraft aka Rogozinski taken 18 February 1937 during his second prison term.

a member of the community.[51] Valenko's grandson noted that he mellowed in his old age, but never trusted banks, keeping "rolls and rolls of cash at home."[52]

Illegal activities may have included running stills during Prohibition, which ended in 1933, or loansharking. In April of 1923, I. Kaliakin of Sacramento was fined $300 for making moonshine, according to a blurb in *Russkaia zhizn'* (a warning to new arrivals who were considering such activity).[53] A case of loansharking led to the deaths of two men in December of 1933. Michael Osetinsky (b. 1879), a farmer in Santa Rosa, north of San Francisco, in debt to fellow émigré Ivan (John) Ugolnikoff (b. 1883), shot and killed him and then committed suicide after Ugolnikoff threatened to foreclose on Osetinsky's farm. Osetinsky left behind notes explaining his action, adding: "God bless the President of the United States. I have been a good American and have done my best to pay debts and have been loyal to President Roosevelt who is our greatest national hero." The tragedy, highlighted in newspapers as far away as Missouri, likely due to the circumstance of a farmer killing his creditor during the Great Depression, indubitably stemmed from past relationships and grievances

Figure 7.4 Dina Valenko (1903–1977), Sergei Valenko's spouse, *at left*, and two of her friends in the late 1920s in San Francisco. Dina and Sergei's grandson described the unidentified male as "Sergei's gangster associate."

between the two men. Ugolnikoff, supposedly a nobleman "in the Czar's regime," became a "San Francisco moneylender," while Osetinsky had been a bank official in Russia. The two had known each other at least since their sojourn in Harbin. The murder-suicide did not appear to be premeditated but occurred in a fit of rage as Osetinsky's wife and adult children were on the way home from San Francisco to celebrate the holidays together and discovered the horrific scene upon arrival.[54] To some extent, the suicide in this case spoke to the consciousness of the importance of respectability for Russian émigrés. Osetinsky wrote the note to make clear his state of mind: supportive of the American president, America, and its ideals, to the end, so that his family would not suffer any repercussions for his act. Taking his own life also protected them from the stigma of a family member's incarceration.

The case of Ivan Zorin (1899/1903–1935), who made one unfortunate decision after another, also ended with his death. Zorin had served in Admiral Kolchak's army and arrived in Seattle in 1923 with the intention of attending the University of California, Berkeley. In 1929, however, he was working as a mechanic at Russ Garage in Oakland. Apparently bored, he borrowed the manager's car and drove off on a tour of the "middle west," returning the car months later "because it was too cold." The owner pressed charges and Zorin went to prison for three years, incarcerated at McNeil Island Federal Penitentiary in Washington.[55] Upon his release, he began smuggling people into the United States from Mexico. In March of 1935, he was killed near San Diego, along with a Japanese couple he was bringing over the border, while fleeing border agents. He crashed the vehicle "while traveling seventy miles an hour in an effort to escape a rain of bullets from Federal Men."[56]

Russian men engaging in criminal activity contradicted the narrative about Russian émigré identity both in American and Russian émigré public discourse. These were not political crimes (i.e., labor violence or anarchistic activities) in which Russian malcontents took part, in the perspective of law enforcement, nor did the behavior fall in line with how Russian community leaders attempted to portray themselves in terms of respectability to outsiders. The above cases, all differing in circumstances, also indicated the cross-generational circumstance of unlawful, criminal, or violent behavior. Moreover, the biographies of these men did not vary from the general experience of émigrés: Gavriloff arrived as a child with his parents; Rogojin and Valenko arrived on USAT *Merritt*, both listing their occupations as seamen; Osetinsky and Ugolnikoff arrived as immigrants from Harbin; and Zorin, a veteran, was a prospective student. Gavriloff experienced poverty growing up, but so did many Russian émigré children (some were even placed temporarily in orphanages by parents unable to cope during the Depression).[57] Men like Rogojin and Zorin likely saw no hope for improvement in their situations; initially, language difficulties relegated them to menial jobs, while the Depression may have interfered with progress they may have made. Admittedly, making initial poor choices led to a road of no return as incarceration was a circumstance difficult to overcome, as in the cases of Gavriloff and Zorin (Rogojin, however, was rehabilitated and pardoned by California's governor in 1955).[58]

The local perspective about "White Russians" remained variable in the inter-war period with recognition of a "White Russian colony" in San Francisco's urban space arising in connection with incidents of violence, whether suicide (as noted in chapter 4), or, much rarer, violence against others. A case in point was the 1940 murder of émigré Vera Frederick (Fedoroff), a young married woman who became the object of obsession of student Leon Ignaotff/Ignoff. His first marriage ended because Ignoff began stalking Vera, who swore out a "disturbing the peace citation" against him. He subsequently accosted her outside the candy factory where she worked, pursued and shot her, then committed suicide. The *San Francisco Examiner*, not wasting an opportunity to capitalize on the tragedy, referred to Ignoff as a "hot tempered White Russian," and the events leading up to the killing as a "Triangle in [the] White Russian Colony," going so far as to morbidly juxtapose photographs of the victim, who was pregnant with her first child when she was murdered, and her killer together on a skiing vacation in happier times, with a photograph of Vera's husband, Nick, weeping over her lifeless body.[59] The reporting acknowledged the existence of a "White Russian" colony only to reinforce the notion that the violent act had something to do with the nature of "White Russians," Slavs unable to control their baser instincts, implying as well that Vera had somehow been complicit in the violence as she had a previous (undefined) relationship with Ignoff. The issue of citizenship was not specifically in question at this point as the debates about the White Russian Bill were long past, but the questionable desirability of White Russians (or any Russians) as candidates for citizenship was an issue that remained in play into the post-war period.

The complicit focus on respectable noble Russian men as the only candidates needing citizenship during the earlier debates on the national level about the bill also obscured the fact that those in need of paths to citizenship were in similar circumstances to Kopiloff, who had not been allowed to enter the United States legally due to her ethnic background (quota limitations), gender, and age (an "older" woman, and therefore a likely public burden). Kopiloff was successful in gaining unsanctioned entry to the United States and even becoming a citizen, but her story demonstrates the chance circumstances that could have very well led to a different ending in her case, and which may have been the ending for people whose fates remain unknown.

Continuing Migrations

A "steady influx" of Russians continued to arrive in San Francisco until the end of 1941 when immigration halted due to US entry into the war. Antonina Von Arnold, citing Elizabeth Malozemoff, noted that "these late arrivals are said to be significant additions to the community's cultural resources both as social forces and talents, as well as being representative of distinguished families ... Thoughtful observers of community life ... [felt] ... the colony was enriched considerably by this recent influx."[60] Von Arnold and Malozemoff focused their comments on "distinguished" (i.e., respectable) émigrés. Those Russians able to come in under the tiny quota, or as non-quota immigrants, often had relatives in the United States or friends who assisted them through the process. Some had financial means: Russians who had businesses in Shanghai anticipated further serious economic and political instability in China, particularly given the occupation of northern China by the Japanese in 1932, and departed after selling off assets.

Excluding Russians on the basis of gender and age, as in the case of Kopiloff, was not the only tactic immigration authorities utilized. Efforts to exclude Russians based on ethnicity, either covertly or openly, continued as well. When famed choir director and master of choral music Ivan (John) A. Kolchin (1893–1963) and his wife Olympia (1899–1985) arrived in San Francisco from Shanghai in June of 1940, immigration authorities attempted to deport them, although they held quota immigration visas. The justification for exclusion was that their passage had been paid for by Holy Trinity Cathedral, where Kolchin was to serve as choir director, but Kolchin had "admitted to an immigration inspector that he did not sing himself."[61] The purported basis for exclusion was the charge that such payment indicated that Kolchin had come to the United States "by reasons of ... offer, solicitation, promise, or agreement, expressed or implied, to labor in the United States" as prohibited by the 1885 Alien Contract Labor Law and was not a "member of a learned profession." That law had been enacted just after the Chinese Exclusion Act of 1882 to further hinder Chinese, as well as undesirable European, immigration.[62] Both Kolchin and his wife, as well as at least twenty other passengers on the ship, many of them Russian, were also all detained as "LPCs." Most were released the next day, but Kolchin's detention continued as a prohibited "Contract Laborer." The Russian community, up in arms, involved the mayor of San Francisco Angelo Rossi, as well as Senator Hiram Johnson and Congressional Representative Franck R. Havenner, even writing a lengthy appeal to Eleanor Roosevelt as the official hearing on the case was to be held in Washington, DC. Havenner sent a telegram to the Kolchins' attorney Nathan Merenbach noting receipt of the appeal and anticipating a decision in a day or two.[63]

What exactly convinced immigration authorities to allow entry is not clear from the passenger manifest, but the Kolchins were "admitted on appeal on June 26." Handwritten notations on the ship's manifest under Kolchin's name, "Russian nat. Chinese citizen" and "naturalized citizen of China" indicated some uneasiness with Kolchin's status. It is unclear whether the notes were clarifying his citizenship status or attempting to reinforce the immigration agent's position on that status. The decision to detain the Kolchins was based on an arbitrary assessment by local officials, who were uncomfortable with the ambiguity of Kolchin's citizenship (of a country whose citizens were not allowed into the US) and decided to exercise their authority in barring his entry into the United States.[64]

Public discourse and narratives about Russians in the inter-war period reinforced the notion that Russian ethnicity or "race" included certain specificities, distinguishing them from Western Europeans. In a 1936 California court case where the judge had to assign custody of two orphaned girls, Olga and Leanna Boellaard, the judge focused on nationality as well as "race" in making his decision about who would get custody of the girls. The parents had been killed at a railroad crossing in San Mateo in July. The girls' father, John Boellaard, was Dutch, while their mother, Maria, was Russian. The judge deemed the Russian ethnicity of the girls as the most important factor in selecting Alexander (1899–1968) and Nina Ivanoff/Ivars (1890–1956) as temporary guardians. The childless couple were "members of the San Francisco White Russian colony," but had not known the Boellaards, while the other couple asking for custody, Victor Hugo and his wife, who were not Russian, were friends of the family. The judge's decision was based in part on the fact that the Ivars were the "same nationality" as the girls. Prior to the judge handing down the final decision, in fact, newspapers described the custody battle as one of "Love Versus Race," noting the judge's comments that he would weigh the emotional attachment and financial stability of both couples but also consider the importance of "racial preference." Though only half-Russian, the ethnicity (or "race" in the language of the time) of the girls took precedence over a previously existing relationship, in the court's eyes. The father's Dutch background, as Western European, on the other hand, was irrelevant and did not initiate commentary about finding Dutch guardians.[65]

The experiences of Alexander V. Altman (1901–1958), who later became a Russian Center board member, during his immigration process, spoke to the complications for some Russians based on ethnic background, perceived as Asian, which continued into the post-World War II period (chapter 9). Altman emigrated from his birthplace, Harbin, in July of 1929, later specifying in his naturalization application that his parents were Russian, a notation common on declarations of intention of China-born and stateless Russians, given the continuing restrictions on Chinese immigration to the United States in the inter-war period. AIIS inspectors raised numerous hurdles for Asian arrivals and, in Altman's case, apparently decided to question his ethnic background, presumably based on his physical appearance.[66] Altman's "race or people" on the ship's passenger manifest was listed originally as "Russian," but the inspector crossed it out and wrote "Chinese" above it. Another handwritten note below indicated that Altman was examined by the inspector and "held" as he had "Chinese blood." His name was subsequently included in a ledger listing Asian incoming passengers with a notation stating "one-eighth Chinese, entered in this book by error." Though "an error," Altman's case warranted a case number (77-875) and a decision allowing his admission as a European of "1/8 Chinese" background. Altman was released from custody on 29 July 1929 (the ship docked on 19 July), but the date of case disposition was 6 March 1930, indicating his release may have been conditional.[67]

Altman's associations spanned both San Francisco Russian communities. He listed his grandmother, Katherine Laschenko (1866–1935), as a contact. Laschenko had been born in Kherson (now Ukraine) and immigrated to Hawaii in 1909 from Harbin, with her husband and younger children, subsequently relocating to San Francisco. From 1910, they lived in the Potrero Hill neighborhood among the largely Spiritual Christian community.[68] Altman lived with her for a number of years but gravitated to the Green Street community, joining the Union of Musketeers, a right-wing émigré organization whose slogan was "For Faith, the Czar, and the Fatherland!" indicating in his writings that he retained implacably hostile views towards the Soviet Union.[69] Moreover, he had some connection to Russian Fascist Party leader Anastase Vonsiatsky, at least according to the FBI, as they questioned Altman in 1942 when Vonsiatsky was arrested.[70] Altman subsequently enlisted in the US Army and left for Europe. He had been naturalized in 1935 and apparently no one had questioned his declaration in his naturalization petition that he was "white." The draft board also considered him "white" in 1940. He died in 1958 in Bridgeport,

Texas, in a mid-air collision of two military aircraft. His death certificate listed him as "Caucasian," a classification for Euro-Americans, including Slavs, that developed in the wake of the passage of the Johnson-Reed Act in 1924.[71] Altman's journey to become Russian American involved dealing with assumptions about his ethnicity that might have precluded his entrance into the United States. Perhaps to compensate, he adopted a firmly militant anti-communist stance to prove his worth as a potential American citizen and joined an organization (the Union of Musketeers) that celebrated Russian "national" culture. His experience with authorities with respect to how American dominant culture perceived his "racial" status upon arrival in California underscored broader anti-immigrant efforts that encompassed, ironically, both Slavs and Asians.

Another émigré whose "racial" background came into question was well-known composer Vladimir Ussachevsky (1911–1990). Ussachevsky, born in Hailar, China, arrived in California in 1930, following brother Leonid (1898–1976), also a student, who came to San Francisco. Ussachevsky earned a BA in music studies in 1935, and then a PhD at Eastman School of Music in Rochester, New York. He then returned to California to care for his mother and lived with her in Los Angeles until her death in June of 1941, teaching high school and junior college music classes.[72]

In September of 1940, the United States instituted draft registration (Selective Training and Service Act) and Ussachevsky dutifully registered with Local Board No. 236 in Pasadena on 16 October. The registrar marked "white" for race, "brown" for eyes, "black" for hair, and "light brown" for complexion. On the back of the card, a boilerplate statement read, in part, "I have witnessed ... [the registrant's] ... signature or mark and ... all of his answers of which I have knowledge are true, except as follows," under which, in careful printed hand, the registrar wrote "white race doubtful," followed by "verified by Board of Education as Russian."[73] Why the registrar felt it necessary to question Ussachevsky's "race" despite marking the "white" box is unknown (the options apart from "white" were "Negro," "Oriental," "Indian," or "Filipino"). Ussachevsky enlisted in 1942, served until the war's end, worked for US Army Intelligence, and went on to a stellar career as a professor at Columbia University and the founder of the Columbia-Princeton Electronic Music Center in New York City, among other achievements.[74]

Ussachevsky's experience with the draft board registrar may have been a small blip in an otherwise quite successful life in the United States, not only in material but professional and personal terms, judging from his biography. The fact that he faced an official confrontation with respect to his "racial"/ethnic background, however, spoke to the arbitrariness of the processes classifying people by supposed "race," even as they were registering to fight in a war for their country.

In a similar case, the Idaho registrar documenting émigré Alexis Dechenko's particulars on his draft card wrote "Doubtful about race." Dechenko, born 1918, had emigrated to San Francisco with his mother and siblings in 1923 and later earned a cosmetology license, but, in 1940, when he registered for the draft, he happened to be in Blackfoot, Idaho, working on a Union Pacific Railroad gang. The registrar did, in this case as well, despite their doubts, mark Dechenko's race as "white," and his complexion as "dark brown." Dechenko had been born in Harbin, a factor that, again, may have also played into those "doubts." Notwithstanding the "confusion" about Dechenko's "race," he enlisted in the army in January 1941. He departed for Europe, received a promotion to sergeant during the war, and was killed in action in Germany on 5 April 1945. His family brought his body home to the United States in 1948, and he is interred at Golden Gate National Cemetery south of San Francisco.[75]

Russians' "Oriental" Nature

When facing immigration barriers, such as in the case of Kolchin, Russian community members likely saw the attempts to bar his entry as a "misunderstanding." Émigré discourse chalked up broader anti-Slavic or anti-Eastern European rhetoric, if addressed at all, to American ignorance about Russian culture. Facing race-based barriers was an uncommon factor in Russian immigration, given their nominal European status in official American eyes, but individual officials did raise such barriers to target Russian people as they saw fit. Those who faced such monitoring and risk of exclusion likely did not advertise the issue to their Russian compatriots. The fact that an official representing the American government considered them something other than "white," and therefore unacceptable or inferior, was an experience they likely chose to conceal but, once again, the experience reinforced the conviction among arrivals that being anything other than "white" was problematic in American society.

On the other end of the spectrum, one Russian émigré woman, Galina Lissivetz/Liss (1909–1953), chose to flout American conventions, and even laws, with respect to race, by marrying Ray Wise Mala (1906–1952), a cinematographer and Hollywood film actor, who was of Native Alaskan and Russian Jewish descent. They married in 1937 in Mexico because interracial marriage remained illegal in California at the time.[76]

Moreover, public discourse in San Francisco placed the question of Russian whiteness front and center during World War II. The *San Francisco Examiner* published an editorial on 14 February 1944, titled "The Oriental Mind," which included photographs of three Russian (i.e., Soviet) generals: Gen. Ivan Koniev (Konev), Gen. Nikolai Vatutin, and Gen. Ivan Bagramyan. The caption under the photos ran:

> Inscrutably oriental are the features of the three outstanding Russian generals pictured above … Their military successes against the Nazis have been largely the result of strategy based on oriental craftiness. The Russians as a race are in the main as oriental as the Japanese – spiritually, morally and culturally oriental.[77]

Both Konev and Vatutin were ethnic Slavs (Russians), while Bagramyan was Armenian. Describing them as "oriental" and "spiritually, morally and culturally" Japanese was a way of cautioning the "West" that Russians had little or nothing in common with "Western" peoples. The actual point of the editorial was to warn against the possibility of "Russia" (i.e., the Soviet Union), allying with the Japanese "after the European war is successfully concluded." The author wrote (capitalization and italics in original):

> The faces of the three eminent Russian generals, as the vivid photographs from the "Illustrated London News" impress upon us, are strikingly ORIENTAL FACES.
> Indeed, the Russians as a race are in the main as oriental as the Japanese.
> We have never been able to understand the Japanese or to rationalize their acts, and have always been foolish to try to do so, and have always been wrong in our conclusions about them.
> The Russians are as inscrutable to us as the Japanese and for the same reasons.
> We do not know what they THINK or understand what they DO …
> Russia is racially and spiritually, morally and culturally oriental …
> Of all the nations in this war, only Russia and Japan have found it possible and logical and rational and advantageous TO BE FRIENDS WITH THE ENEMIES OF THEIR FRIENDS.
> Only the oriental mind is capable of that.

Marketing and Monitoring Identity | **235**

> And the Russian and Japanese minds ARE oriental. *A FACT THAT WILL HARM US LEAST IN THE LONG RUN IF WE RECOGNIZE IT NOW.*[78]

The author's goal was to cast suspicion on the trustworthiness of the Soviet Union as an ally, not, in this case, because the Soviet Union was a communist country opposed to the capitalist United States, but because the Soviet Union was actually "oriental" Russia: "irrational," "inexplicable," unfamiliar with "western" values, historically lacking "Europeanness," and therefore whiteness. Konstantin Barskii, then president of the Russian Center (chapter 8), shot off an outraged letter to the newspaper objecting to the characterizations of the Russian people. Barskii noted in passing the "unexpected" comparison of the "cultures" of Russian and Japanese people, either inadvertently or deliberately misunderstanding the focus on race per se, but, directly addressing "Mr. [William Randolph] Hearst," objected to the "unjust, unscrupulous and [i]ndecent attacks" on "Soviet Russia" and "the Russian race as a whole." Barskii did not insist on the "European" (non-Asian) nature of Russians. His main argument highlighted the "high morals" and "spiritual and cultural achievements" of the Russian people and the sacrifices of (Russian) soldiers "even under the Soviet regime" – sacrifices, Barskii pointed out, that allowed Americans "to enjoy almost the [*sic*] former comfortable and happy life" during the war. Barskii carefully noted in his conclusion that the members of the "Russian Center of San Francisco, Inc. ... are mostly American citizens." That clarification about citizenship spoke to the possibility that the Russian Center's official protest might have engendered a backlash against the Russian enclave by drawing attention to its existence in a context of dominant culture race-baiting. As a whole, however, Barskii's response mainly addressed Hearst's effort to portray Russian people as enemies in American eyes rather than attempting to argue their "non-oriental" nature.[79]

The focus on Japan in this editorial had to do with the fact that Japan was the enemy of the United States during World War II and Hearst (correctly) surmised that the Soviet Union would be an adversary as well after the war. By couching the possible future actions of "Russia" in racial terms, his purpose was also to emphasize the insurmountable differences that existed between "European" America and "Asian" Russia and Japan. Just as the United States had to go to war with Japan to save the world, particularly since the Japanese government had initiated a surprise attack on the United States on 7 December 1941, so would the country have to go to war with the Soviet Union sooner or later, given the "spiritually, morally and culturally oriental" nature of Russians. Thus the warning to recognize the non-Western nature of Russians before it was too late.[80]

Russians, like all immigrants, were subject to "push and pull" factors in the migration process. Not only were they pushed out of Russia but also out of China and Japan, and subsequently Mexico, by circumstances beyond their control: economic and political issues, and even a natural disaster. The pull to the United States under these circumstances was certainly understandable. Tens of thousands of Russians had settled in what is now the Greater Bay Area by the early 1930s, and even with the economic downturn of the Great Depression, San Francisco had become a very attractive place for stateless refugees.[81] The developing Russian community with its spiritual, cultural, and commercial facets, kin relationships, and Russian neighborhoods, encouraged a continuing flow of people. Some arrived under the now decreased (post-1924) quota or as non-quota immigrants. Others, like Lydia Kopiloff, turned away, decided to take the risk of crossing the border without sanction.

Respectability under the American gaze continued to be a factor of importance, particularly in view of the efforts to pass legislation specifically directed towards Russian paths to American citizenship. Utilizing existing tropes about Russian aristocrats worked in their favor but erased the identities of women, the elderly, and the "ordinary" Russian with no elite status of which to boast. Many were able to obtain a higher education, begin to build careers, and establish financial stability. Just as many, however, had to make do with low-paying jobs (or no jobs as the Depression worsened), choosing paths for survival that were not all "respectable." Moreover, as in the nineteenth century, not only did Russian people remain on the edge of the cultural order in San Francisco, questions arose among dominant culture representatives with respect to Russians and their "classification" in terms of "race" – William Randolph Hearst's diatribe in 1944 resurrecting the "oriental" nature of Russians as unsuitable candidates for political alliances, and therefore, by extension, as American residents, much less citizens. Such questioning, particularly about race and ethnicity, reinforced the notion among people of Russian heritage that being white in America took precedence over any cultural markers they previously held as significant in terms of their identity as Russian Americans. The process of achieving a state of whiteness continued over decades. In the course of that process, Russians in San Francisco continued attempts to explain their culture to Americans, but perhaps succeeded chiefly in reinforcing existing impressions of the foreignness and exoticism of that culture, the subject of the following chapter.

—8—

CONSTRUCTED MIRAGES
Authentic and Imagined Russian Enclaves

> This matter of gathering Russians together should concern us
> because only when congregated, not dispersed, will we preserve that
> which we can call our culture. This term, "Russian culture," should
> not confuse anyone; it is, after all, nothing other than a term that
> characterizes the distinctive attributes of Slavic peoples, both the
> external and the spiritual.
>
> GLEB ILYIN, 1932[1]

The desire for a purely Russian enclave inspired artist Gleb Ilyin to propose
building a Russian-style village in the early 1930s, Novograd, literally "New
Town," north of San Francisco, in the area of Russian River in Sonoma
County. He had bought land there and had "completely instinctively"
built a "small imitation village log cabin."[2] "For Russian Americans, Russian
River is a symbol of faraway never forgotten Russia ... no wonder
Russians go to Russian River in summer in ever large numbers, saving
money to buy a small piece of land near the River," Bazhenova wrote in
the inter-war years.[3] The growing Russian community of summer cabins
was a first step to preserving their Slavic culture and maintaining their
Russianness in the face of pressures to assimilate, indicating resistance
to complete assimilation as a desirable option for Russians in America.

Ilyin compared the urban enclave of San Francisco's Chinatown to
what he envisioned, noting its importance to the Chinese community as,
in his perspective, if Chinese people were scattered all over San Francisco
they would lose the cultural benefits of daily social interaction within
their own community. Ilyin's reference to the success of Chinese cultural
autonomy in San Francisco's Chinatown missed the point that Chinese

people were initially (prior to 1906) relegated to living in a specific part of town at the behest of Euro-American city fathers. They then established a community in that space, "Chinatown." After the 1906 earthquake, James D. Phelan, an anti-Asian immigration proponent, led a group advocating for the relocation of Chinese residents outside the city proper, but met substantial opposition. The post-earthquake architecture of the rebuilt "Chinatown" section was a "hybrid architectural style unique to San Francisco, referred to as 'Chinese Renaissance,'" and though it did remain a Chinese residential and business neighborhood, attracting tourist revenue was an integral and deliberate aspect of the plan.[4]

Ilyin's vision, however, took the Russian community out of urban space, seeing rural isolation as a positive aspect for Russian cultural autonomy, reminiscent of Dukhobor, Old Believer, and, in some cases, Spiritual Christian efforts in the United States, groups who specifically sought rural isolated locations in order to live separately from host societies.[5] His discussion also focused on the importance of decorative and Russian-style architecture, noting that Slavic/Russian "architectural forms" were not represented in San Francisco and with the surfeit of Russian artists and craftsmen in California, they would be able to create a "lovely harmonious hub" in the Russian style, indicating that Russians did not have the freedom to build structures in forms amenable to them within urban space.[6] In his ruminations, noted in the epigraph, Ilyin appeared to be looking for an inclusive interpretation of "Russian culture," defining it as an aspect of being "Slavic," broadly construed. Nevertheless, his focus on a "village" spoke to nostalgia for a Russia he remembered but not a Russia he had necessarily experienced; Ilyin, after all, was of a noble family and likely had not lived among peasants in Russia. In any case, his idea seemed to die on the vine, perhaps because most people were experiencing economic reverses in this period.[7]

Although the Great Depression dominated the overall economic and political landscape in 1930s America, the Russian community nevertheless came into its own as a social and cultural group with a strong sense of their historic past. US recognition of the Soviet Union in 1933, however, played a part in the evolution of émigré and sojourner identity to Russian-American identity. The way home was closed, the Russia they had lost now definitively gone forever. Interactions with Russian groups who held to other religious confessions and customs within a dominant culture that generally marginalized Slavs and Eastern Europeans also reinforced a sense of unity among those who valued common aspects of that culture.

Following a healing of the 1927 schism of the Orthodox Church in 1935, in the larger context of Russia Abroad, the so-called "Green Street" Holy Trinity-centered community, along with the members of the subsequently-formed Holy Virgin Parish, joined with Spiritual Christians and other Russian communities in California to showcase Russian culture in a series of events.[8] Both of the Orthodox communities included people who were of other religious confessions in the inter-war period, whether through participation in organizations and events or family ties. That diversity contributed to the broad assemblage of groups and individuals who took part in planning, organizing, and participating in a series of fairs at Sigmund Stern Grove in April of 1936, and May of 1937 and 1938. The 1937 event was significant in particular because it was part of a city and state "Golden Gate Bridge Fiesta," celebrating the opening of the newly constructed bridge, a modern marvel, which also provided a direct route from San Francisco across the bay to the regions "pulling" Russians north.

By the mid-1930s, émigrés, now Russian Americans, had become comfortable enough in English to express their perspectives about their culture and history, as well as current views, to Americans who inquired. Becoming Russian American led as well to the group effort to acquire a permanent structure to house a Russian Center in 1939 on Sutter Street, which eventually became the home of the émigré archive. Recognition that the way home was closed reinforced the perspective that Russian culture, including, importantly, material culture, required a sanctuary where at least some part of Russian émigré history would remain shielded, whether from appropriation or erasure.

International events also had a role in cooperative efforts between Russian communities, despite varying perceptions of the Soviet regime. The Nazi German invasion of the Soviet Union in June of 1941 spurred both the Russian Orthodox and Spiritual Christian communities to send wartime assistance to a country that US officials viewed as an adversary and instigator of social unrest, despite diplomatic recognition. When the United States entered the war in December of 1941, however, the Soviet Union became an ally. Cognizant that political winds changed direction in response to international events, and that Russians continued to be targets of suspicion in America, the leadership of the newly founded San Francisco Russian Center exhibited caution about their involvement in the process of sending aid, demonstrating foresight, but also fueling feelings of paranoia, which would intensify in response to the continuing suspicion of people of Russian and Slavic heritage in a period of McCarthyist hysteria.

Performance of Culture and the 1936 Fair

The Russian Musical Society, headed by pianist Sergei I. Mihailoff (1898–1978), led the effort to organize a one-day music festival at Sigmund Stern Grove, on the southwestern side of the San Francisco Peninsula, on 26 April 1936 (figure 8.1). The main purpose of the fair was to fund a presentation of Mikhail Glinka's opera, "A Life for the Tsar," in December. Those who participated utilized the fair as a way to make some money in an economically depressed period. The park-like setting, away from urban congestion, and previously unknown to the Russian communities, was also a different "milieu," in the midst of stands of eucalyptus and redwood trees.[9] The organizers of the fair, according to one observer, had transformed Stern Grove, a thirty-three acre site at Nineteenth Avenue and Sloat Boulevard, into a "Russian mirage," an apt representation, as the "Russianness" was somewhat illusory, geared towards entertainment and attracting crowds. Nevertheless, it provided respite from their everyday lives.[10]

The fair included an Orthodox prayer service, but Russians of all confessions were represented at the fair both in terms of attendance and participation. Two thousand people were already present at the fair by the time of the service (at 12:00 noon): "crowds of people, both Russians and Americans, began to arrive at ten o'clock in the morning continuously by streetcar and automobile."[11] Father Konstantin Lebedeff (1877–1943), the rector at the Women's House of Mercy, led the service and followed it with remarks marking the immense cultural contribution that Russians had made to America, reinforcing a theme that organizers would emphasize as well in their advertisement of the following year's event in the same space.[12]

Bazhenova, who covered the fair for Russian newspapers, was lukewarm about the event, opining that insufficient funds made the event a "picnic," rather than a fair, and noting that there were only ten "modest" kiosks. The modest nature of the celebration, in her eyes, may have reflected the continuing poverty of Russians in America; marginalization due to economic circumstances perhaps led to participation in events where Americans recognized Russians only in terms of entertainment or spectacle, a situation Russians encouraged, inadvertently or not.[13]

Shop owners from all the Russian communities sold their products at the fair. John Astredinoff (1884–1958), a Baptist and owner of Astra Russian Confectionary, and Horen Markarian (1888–1963), who was Armenian Orthodox and proprietor of the very popular Markarian Confectionary,

Figure 8.1 The crowd at the April 1936 fair at Stern Grove after the church service, awaiting the beginning of the entertainment program. Handwritten text on verso incorrectly identifies the year as 1939.

sold candy, sweets, and pastries, while another Baptist family ran a booth selling home-baked goods complete with a samovar brewing tea. Other shop proprietors and individuals sold clothing, books, crafts, and other items. The Russian Music Society had a booth with "Russian items" on consignment, indicating the persistent economic effects of the Depression, which spoke to Alexander Farafontoff's timely warning about loss of heritage due to impoverished Russians selling items of value to get by.[14]

Performers included a broad range of musical talent, while the overall tone of the event addressed the multi-ethnic history of the Russian Empire, both in the sphere of the arts and food culture. Boris Kramarenko's (1899–1971) Great Russian and Russian Balalaika Orchestras performed (figure 8.2).[15] Another orchestra played Russian and American dance music at a special pavilion, which appealed to all. The main program, with an audience of 3,000 people, included mezzo-sopranos Elena Burskaya (1891–1979) in "Malorussian" (Ukrainian) costume and Tatiana Popow (1900–1999) in Russian costume, while Sophia Samorukoff (1894–1979) sang "The Hills of Georgia," in introduction to the climax of performances of Mikhail Ippolitov-Ivanov's Caucasian Sketches, orchestral suites that the composer wrote after his years as director of the music conservatory in Tbilisi, Georgia (figure 8.3).[16]

Figure 8.2 Boris Kramarenko (seated second from right) and his orchestra on 26 April 1936. Handwritten text on verso identifies the group as the "Russian Balalaika Orchestra in Stern Grove at Russian Fair."

Figure 8.3 At the 1936 Fair at Stern Grove. Paul Shulgin, conductor and composer, in the center. Tatiana Pdpow, identified as the "only" singer in San Francisco who performed Russian folk songs, in Russian costume. The two unidentified men on either side are wearing Caucasian attire, *cherkeskas* and *papakhas*.

The festival differed from the Russian participation in the 1925 Diamond Jubilee parade because of a conscious focus on folk culture rather than on czarist symbols and pre-Petrine *boyar* nobility that had dominated visually: *"Russian folk life* as it was in the pre-Revolutionary days, will be depicted in dance, song and the instrumental music of Balalaika orchestras."[17] The only "tsar" and "boyars" mentioned were in a skit of "Sleeping Beauty." Russians at the fair dressed in a variety of ethnic costumes, which did include the elaborate *boyar* gowns and headdresses, but also in peasant clothing, Ukrainian embroidered shirts, and Caucasian attire. The multicultural and multi-ethnic history of the Russian empire meant that this appropriation of attire was not necessarily gratuitous. Russians came from a variety of backgrounds, and their choices as to dress and performance may have had some relation to their own familial ethnic history.

The Golden Gate Bridge Fiesta of 1937

The success of the first Russian fair at Stern Grove provided impetus for planning the following year's event, which was many times larger as it celebrated the recently completed Golden Gate Bridge. The three-day fair, this time officially billed in English language publications as a "Russian *Yarmarka*" (Fair), was part of a larger week-long "Golden Gate Bridge Fiesta" organized by city and state officials with venues around San Francisco. The Russian organizing committee in charge of the fair stressed to the Russian community that it was "especially important that the *Yarmarka* be gay, beautiful, and that it make a wonderful impression on everyone."[18]

The committee put out a call to "all" Russians throughout the state of California to come to the fair to showcase Russian culture including rural areas where Spiritual Christians had settled as well as émigrés who had migrated out of the urban enclave: "from Eureka and Los Angeles, from Sacramento and Stockton, from all lumber mills and farms ... [Russians were invited] ... to come to the fair and make it a real Russian celebration."[19] Regional representatives were the points of contact for people outside San Francisco: Alexander Rodochey (1900–1973) lived in Bryte, east of San Francisco; Mary Klochko (1888–1962), wife of blacksmith Peter, lived in Eureka (nearer to the Oregon border); in Sonoma County, Vladimir Fedoroff (1891–1947) was a farmer and egg wholesaler in Santa Rosa, arriving from Persia in 1921; and Timothy Corneyeff (1874–1941) in Petaluma was a poultry farmer and member of the First Russian

Figure 8.4 A group of girls and women at the 1937 *Yarmarka* at Stern Grove. *From left to right*: Eugenia Nikonenko, who was born in San Francisco a few months after her parents arrived on USAT *Merritt*; Irene Podsosoff (1925–2010); Nina Parfenoff (1924–1971); Mary Rose Borg (1923–2017); Nadia Kvitko (1922–2017); Barbara Tochilin (1899–1977); unknown (standing in front in coat); Mila Starostin (1923–2016). All, except for Borg, were Russian. Identification of individuals by Eugenia Bailey (nee Nikonenko).

Baptist Church in San Francisco.[20] In other words, an even broader range of California's Russian residents outside the Orthodox community were involved in the organization of the event (figure 8.4).

Using the success of the previous year, organizers included as many aspects of cultural life as possible, attempting to create an even more festive and authentic atmosphere for visitors unfamiliar with Russian culture. The Russian community promotion of the fair was so successful that during the weekend of the fair, streetcar conductors of the number 17, 12, and K streetcars "learned to announce the Stern Grove stop as 'Russian *Yarmarka*.'"[21]

The event aimed at interactive contact between Russians and non-Russian fair visitors in view of the previous fair's success, but, as much as it was an opportunity for Russians to celebrate their culture, an underlying thread in the exhortations spoke to a response to how Americans perceived Russians, not only in public discourse, but in other Russo-American interactions. Eugenia Isaenko wrote somewhat acerbically years later, when reminiscing about the event, that the Americans who came were mostly just "curious to eyeball the oddball Russians."[22] Isaenko had a leading role in the community throughout her life with respect to the organization of, and participation in, cultural and artistic events, and often donned the elaborate costumes that drew attention, but appeared to look back on playing the part of the exotic Russian with a degree of weariness, or even cynicism, perhaps in recognition that such events drew attention to Russians as performers and exotics. The relatively constant drumbeat of Russian cultural oddity and intellectual inferiority both in public discourse and in personal interaction inevitably had an influence on whether Russians felt like "outsiders" in America and whether they consequently chose to exhibit, conceal, or eliminate Russian cultural markers outside of deliberately performative events.

Some non-Russian spouses exhibited not only acceptance but appreciation for Russian culture. Dimitri Ilyin's American wife Donna Hewitt, for example, who was of Scottish extraction, spoke fluent Russian (albeit possibly because she was involved in "intelligence work" in post-World War II Germany) and converted to Orthodoxy.[23] On the other end of the spectrum, Nadia Shapiro described her close friend Boris Volkov's unhappy second marriage, characterizing his "stuffy" wife Bessie Townley as a "proud" descendant of Puritans who arrived on the Mayflower. Baldwin's ancestors later chose the wrong side in the American Revolution and fled to Canada where they "stayed sulking," in Shapiro's words, for 150 years. Bessie forbade her husband to continue his associations with any of his Russian friends, including Shapiro, who had known Boris from childhood in Irkutsk. Moreover, Bessie, a teacher of special needs children, "maintained" that "foreigners, especially Italians and Russians, were contributing the lion's share of children to her classes for morons," which may have been her personal outlook, but one she felt free to disclose.[24]

In reaction to such characterizations, perhaps, the language of the *Yarmarka* program (written by Russians in English) focused particularly on the Russian role in founding Fort Ross, stressing, in a dig towards Anglo/Euro-American dominant culture representations, how Russians as a group were not only integral to early California history, but that their presence pre-dated that of most Euro-Americans:

Russians participated in the history of California from its very beginning when in 1812 they built Fort Ross. At present many thousands of Russians reside in all sections of the State and *take an active part in the civic and artistic life of California.* Thus, it is very appropriate that Russians take a prominent part in a great event of California: the opening of the Golden Gate Bridge.[25]

The narrative stressed the contribution of Russians to contemporary American life: Russian culture and history, the program emphasized, was integral to Russian-American identity and provided positive input into American culture, pointedly challenging the views of people like Bessie Townley-Volkov who viewed Russians as inferior.

The Fiesta program included a re-enactment of how the Russians founded Fort Ross in the "Span of Gold" pageant, a performance about the history of California. Out of the almost ninety people listed as actors or participants in the performance titled "Fort Ross–Russian Period," all but a handful had Russian surnames. Of the Russians, most were Orthodox but included representatives from the Molokan, Jewish, and Baptist communities.[26]

The re-enactment focused on the Russian cultural stamp on Fort Ross, likely obscuring the role of Indigenous residents, but at least one San Francisco Russian family, in fact, traced their heritage back to Alaska. Alexander Hilkovsky (1904–1976), who arrived in San Francisco as a student in 1923, completed a circle of migration, which his grandmother, Katherine Karlovna, had begun in 1867. Born in Alaska, of Russian and Native Alaskan heritage, she married Russian Army officer, Ivan Hilkovsky, the last imperial garrison commander of Sitka. They departed for Russia with son, Valentin (1865–1936), born in Sitka, who, in turn, joined his son Alexander in San Francisco in 1929.[27]

Becoming Russian Americans:
Class Considerations and Political Affiliations

The decision not to focus overmuch on Russia's czarist past during the *Yarmarka* reflected the heterogeneity of perspectives in the émigré community, which, in the 1930s, however, did indicate a hardening dichotomy in certain circles with respect to how former émigrés thought about the monarchy, its place in Russian history, and its role in Russian-American identity. As noted previously, the perspectives of many émigrés about the monarchy related to their cultural nostalgia rather than political affiliation or outlook.[28] Moreover, for many the monarchy represented the Russian past while contemporary celebrations of culture reinforced an intent to remain Russian in America.

Most importantly, however, adherence to "monarchist" symbols remained a safe option in American society, where émigrés continued to encounter hostility both for socio-cultural and political reasons. A monarchist, by definition, could not be a communist or an anarchist, two groups US government officials had targeted in the first Red Scare. Therefore, the public identification with the Romanoff monarchy as a unifying socio-political entity for émigrés utilizing monarchist symbols, as during the 1925 parade, were safe outlets for expression of national feeling in the inter-war United States. Identification with the monarchy also became a fallback position that did not require explication of identity to non-Russians. The American fascination with royalty or aristocracy helped entrench the idea that Russians were, by virtue of their status as exiles, monarchists.

By the late 1930s, however, many émigrés, now US citizens, were comfortable enough with their new identity as Russian Americans to definitively explain to a reporter during a November 1938 event that they were not monarchists. The gathering took place after a performance of excerpts from the opera and ballet, "Ruslan and Ludmila," at a benefit for disabled World War I Russian Veterans, the annual Russian "Invalid Ball."[29] Though the reporter, Carl Latham, began his article with the statement that "Imperial Russia is not dead" and waxed effusively about "the land of the tsars" and "glittering courts at Petersburg" coming to life with "mammoth piles of strange looking food" at the reception, he noticed that the symbols and decorations omitted the "double eagle emblem of the Tsar." The emblem was one he had come to recognize and identify with White Russian identity. Those at the event included "former officialdom represented by" Prince and Princess Vasiliy Romanoff, General A.P. Boodberg, Rear Admiral B.P. Doudoroff, and Former Imperial Consul General A.M. Wywodtseff. Attendees whom he did not identify by name, however, told him that "though the *majority* of them fought against Bolshevism, they recognized the social injustices of … [autocratic monarchy] … and are not monarchists." In fact, Latham noted, many at the gathering were supporters of President Roosevelt and were "staunch Democrats."[30]

Authentic and Imagined Russian Enclaves

The Russian Americans present who chose to clarify their position in terms of their political perspectives may have been indicating a watershed moment in their community history. Their comments spoke to divergent views within that community, which now included voting citizens with political viewpoints about their new homeland, who simultaneously maintained a connection to Russian cultural events and causes. In choosing to support Roosevelt, they stepped away from a position of knee-jerk negative reaction to perceived "socialist" programs to one of independent political thinking. If consistently walking in lockstep and considering "anti-communism" as the most important factor in how they interpreted the American political scene, they should have rejected Roosevelt both for his administration's recognition of the USSR and the "socialist" tenor of the New Deal.

The Russian community included more Democrats than Republicans in the inter-war period, however, with husbands and wives at times registering under different parties. Alexander Varguin (Russian Center president), for example, was a registered Republican; his wife, Nadejda (1894–1985), a Democrat.[31] In a sample of 550 students who arrived in the 1920s, the voting registration records of 303 were available in the inter-war period. 42 per cent registered as Democrats, 28 percent as Republicans; 22 per cent of the Republicans switched to Democrat as the Depression took hold.[32] Support for Roosevelt, however, emerged early on, indicating that the overwhelmingly anti-Bolshevik perspective of émigrés did not overly influence them despite the Roosevelt administration's recognition of the Soviet Union.

The support for Roosevelt was certainly not across the board in the Russian community. Baron Boodberg, according to Valentina Vernon, who shared his opinion, decried Roosevelt's "interference" in the economy, citing the WPA. Under the program, Vernon felt, people would become accustomed to getting "something for nothing."[33] Vernon was registered as a Democrat in 1935 and as a Republican in 1938, the opposite of most émigrés who switched parties in this period.[34] Her perspective as a business owner and employer likely informed her views on labor/management relations, ignoring the fact that many émigrés in San Francisco held WPA jobs during the Depression, which kept them employed, even if on the edge of poverty.[35]

A few high-ranking officials had the advantage of arriving with financial resources which set them apart, perhaps influencing future political affiliations but also contributing to characterizations of White Russian elite status among Americans. Admiral Boris Doudoroff, noted earlier, arrived in 1923 with $30,000 at a time when many people arrived with $50 or $60. Doudoroff bought a hotel in San Francisco and later opened Homer Market in Palo Alto where his brother-in-law Nicholas Shulgin (1898–1988) also worked. Boris's wife Natalia (1889–1976), an accomplished poet, did not work at a factory job upon arrival, as did many Russian women in San Francisco. Their two sons, Michael and Peter, attended university and went on to brilliant careers as scientists. All naturalized family members were registered Republicans in the 1930s.[36]

The previously noted initial experiences of many Russians as laborers likely had a hand in forming their political ideologies with respect to labor politics and social equity in the United States. Moreover, discriminatory or perceived discriminatory practices based on their Russian ethnicity reinforced the idea that conformity (Americanizing names, for example) was imperative to succeed. An anonymous interviewee, "Mr X," who arrived in San Francisco through a circuitous route as a seaman in 1929, and who was not an émigré (his father had been involved in revolutionary work in Odessa and sent to Siberia prior to 1917), stated that his own "revolutionary" activities in San Francisco, which included selling the *Western Worker* and *New Masses* for a living, were spurred in part due to "adverse ... discrimination against him because of his Russian birth" in the United States and "experience of bad conditions on American ships."[37]

The perspective of pro-Soviet Spiritual Christians in the 1920s that laborers in the United States were largely disempowered in everyday life may have been heresy for émigrés in view of the careful narrative of gratitude for opportunities allowed them in America. Though unstated for public consumption, however, some indubitably agreed with that perspective, particularly given union membership, leadership, and activism (e.g., George Valter, chapter 4). Almost all White Russians continued to view the Soviet regime as oppressive, but their lived experience in the United States also informed their perspectives about social justice under the socio-economic system in which they now lived, and they did not necessarily adhere to exhortations about the superiority of market economics and competition, particularly as the Depression worsened.

Others, however, considered maintaining a strict anti-communist stance to be the overwhelmingly critically important factor in their identity as Russian-American citizens of the United States. Men like Alexander Varguin, who did work as a laborer initially then owned a grocery store, and Konstantin Barskii, who held jobs as a janitor and clothing presser, joined the Republican Party, and focused their political and social efforts on leading the anti-communist crusade, a crusade that would become the hallmark of San Francisco's Russian Center after World War II, walking in lockstep with McCarthyism. Retaining an ideological loyalty to the monarchy became part of that crusade, not only because it was a safe outlet for expressing Russian nationalism in the United States, but to create, and to a certain extent, impose, a uniform Russian-American identity under that banner of anti-communism (chapter 9).[38]

In direct opposition, a few Russian émigrés experienced intense disillusion with the American way of life, rejecting it as obsessively materialistic, meanly competitive, and consequently restrictive and oppressive for those who sought to escape the monotonous and deadening routine of *byt*. That rejection led to radical swings to the left for some, despite nominal "White Russian" identity. Victor Arnautoff, noted earlier, a White Army officer, joined the US Communist Party, and repatriated to the Soviet Union in the 1960s. George Bratoff (1891–1956), also a White Army officer, was, as noted, a playwright and poet. He arrived in Seattle in 1923 with wife Vera and three stepsons, relocating to San Francisco in 1926.[39] Bratoff "united the best amateurs and began to stage shows independently, which soon brought renown to the entire troupe."[40] He staged a wildly successful play titled "Arrival" (*Priyekhali*), depicting the experiences of a family of a Russian émigré CER official who decide to come to the United States by inertia because "everybody is coming to America." The play, a "witty satire" and a "tragi-comedy," poked fun at émigrés who floundered upon arrival amidst the confusion of attempts to acculturate. The play's success stemmed from the fact that the audience recognized themselves in the characterizations and reactions, seeing the humor in disturbing or traumatic situations, which they had all experienced.[41]

Bratoff's job options were limited due to health problems, and he opened a cafeteria in 1927. *Russkaia zhizn'* editor Pavel Karelin urged Russians to patronize Bratoff's establishment to support him: "a talented individual driven by circumstances into the clutches of poverty."[42] By 1930, the cafeteria had failed and Bratoff was working as a janitor. He nevertheless remained a driving force in the Russian community dramatic arts scene throughout the 1930s, organizing an Actor's House under the auspices of the popular theater Kolobok in the 1930s, and staging Leo Tolstoy's "The Living Corpse" successfully at San Francisco's Community Playhouse in 1933. He also took part in almost all major cultural events, including the 1930s fairs, and continued his work staging and directing productions.[43]

In the late 1930s, Bratoff began "to turn to the left." Eugenia Isaenko ascribed his abandonment of theater to his decreasing popularity, noting that he began to "play at politics" and joined "some kind of leftist organizations."[44] Bratoff joined the American Civil Liberties Union and become vice-president of the Russian-American Society (discussed further below) in San Francisco in 1941, which had a major role in aid and relief efforts to the Soviet Union during World War II, and which caught the attention of the FBI, as did the president of the society, Arnautoff, also under surveillance.[45] Isaenko opined that Bratoff's "habit of posing and showing off was now expressed in eccentricity." He grew a mustache and beard, also growing his hair down to his shoulders, "consciously" becoming a "beatnik," which was prior to anyone even knowing what a "beatnik" was, as Isaenko noted. "Gradually he became strangely disappointed with America and became consumed with nostalgia, even dreaming of going to the USSR."[46] Isaenko's assessment, written in the post-World War II period, included the judgment that those who allowed nostalgia to consume them were doomed to discontent in the United States, similar to Parisian émigré writer Nadejda Teffi's defining nostalgia as a "disease" émigrés suffered, turning "passive" and indifferent, even dying as a result.[47] Isaenko recognized that nostalgic dreams may have initially sustained people, but precluded their ability to conform to the American way of life. Indirectly, Isaenko was critiquing that way of life: survival necessitated conformity. Undeniably talented and dynamic, Bratoff's disillusionment with life in the United States was likely related to the unending struggle for survival and the realization that he neither wanted to nor could conform, which, rather than nostalgia per se, eventually drained him of enthusiasm for practicing his art. Bratoff, after all, rather than turning passive, had attempted to turn that nostalgia in another direction, attempting to reconnect with Russia in its incarnation as the Soviet Union. Unlike Arnautoff, however, who eventually did repatriate, Bratoff chose not to take that step.

Founding the Russian Center: A "Russian Corner"

As problematic as nostalgic dreams may have been in terms of accepting the new reality of American life, they were critical in the drive to maintain Imagined Russia in California, which included establishing a physical repository for Russian culture in terms of both intangible (creative effort, performance, social interaction) and tangible (relics,

Authentic and Imagined Russian Enclaves

| **253**

artifacts, documented history) aspects. The first initiatives to found such a central institution in 1926 had not been successful.[48] Subsequently, the Russian Club at the Westerfeld House became a community center with a library, but the focus remained on arts events and entertainment.[49] The fact of its founding and lengthy period of existence in that space (1928–1937) led to a firmer commitment to purchase a building to ensure the preservation of cultural heritage and relics, which were in danger of being discarded. The Russian Club, as an entity, closed on 1 January 1938, and sold its library to the Holy Virgin Cathedral Sisterhood. Income from sale of property, a total of approximately $140, went into the existing fund for creation of a Russian Center.[50]

In the meantime, the Russian Historical Society approached San Francisco City Hall in 1937 to ask for a space to preserve their growing archival collection and received offers of buildings in both Golden Gate Park and the Presidio. Alexander Farafontoff, however, came to fear that moving into a municipal building might subject the society's property to risk of appropriation, and refused. He noted the uncertainty of émigrés, who felt that "living in these times … [one did not know what might] … happen in the next minute much less the next day."[51] That uncertainty was combined with the understanding that they remained foreign in American eyes, and what they considered of value with respect to their heritage made it all the more alien to Americans. After all, some of the emigres' own children, already estranged from their past, moving in the direction of complete Americanization, were taking part in the process of commodifying that heritage and discarding items that had no monetary value. The society therefore settled for the Holy Trinity Cathedral basement to locate a small museum and archive. With receipt of items from families whose elder members had passed way, that space quickly became inadequate.[52]

The Consolidated Committee, still in existence in the 1930s, took the lead on efforts to purchase a building, which the Committee envisioned would include a shelter for elderly and disabled people, free medical care and legal aid, employment assistance, and other services. Russian elderly, disabled, and unemployed often lived, according to advocates for the center, in the damp basements of San Francisco's buildings with no amenities and in terrible want. In other words, the members of the Committee initially envisioned a social services center rather than an arts and entertainment center, unlike the Russian Club. As the concept evolved, however, input from community members indicated they also wanted a place for Russian youth, who otherwise patronized "beer joints" and card rooms where they spent and lost all their money. Activities at a center would include gymnastics, chess, billiards, and music appreciation – wholesome, respectable, intellectual, or cultural activities to maintain high moral standards. To raise money, they held events: a "Russian Day" at the California Women's Club in May of 1936, and a Tatyana's Day concert and ball in January of 1937 (the RNSA, the originator of the latter event, had dissolved in 1936).[53]

The Committee rallied Russians across the board in a concerted effort to raise more money. The clergy and parishioners of the two Orthodox Cathedrals supported the venture and donated money from church collections to the fund.[54] Russian families were urged to donate one dollar a year to the fund, a report on the progress of collections noting that in San Francisco alone there lived more than 5,000 Russian families in 1936. In 1939, the total net amount collected for purchase of a Russian Center building was $1,025.49. Most of the money came from revenues from dance balls ($531.47). Donations from individuals and families added up to $158, indicating that few families had answered the call to contribute a dollar a year. Konstantin Barskii explained the dismaying lack of enthusiasm as due to "our passive attitude and general distrust of community activities." "Distrust" in this context seemed to mean that Russians had heard speeches about grandiose plans that remained unfulfilled and therefore had a jaundiced view, not willing to donate hard-earned cash during the Depression era for causes that vanished without coming to fruition.[55] Nevertheless, the Committee moved forward with the plan to purchase Turn Verein Hall at 2450 Sutter Street (figure 8.5).[56]

Further evolution of the concept of a Russian Center firmly stressed the apolitical nature of the endeavor (just as the Russian Club's charter had stressed its apolitical nature), but also its role as a center of Orthodox Russian Culture and Arts, markedly identifying the venture as one that celebrated not just "Russianness" but Orthodoxy, indicating a critical narrowing of both purpose and identity. Further elaborating on their mission, the provisional Russian Center board alluded to the need to dispel "prejudices against Imperial Russia" in the United States.[57] The focus on "Imperial" Russia was also a shift from a general focus of combating bias or stereotypes of Russian culture and history, and likely further alienated the Spiritual Christians.

Realtor Pamphil Tesluck arranged for the purchase of the building for $30,000 and the transaction was completed 9 April 1940. The formal

Figure 8.5 Turn Verein building, 2450 Sutter Street. The building was completed in 1911 and the sign announcing its opening indicates that is likely the year this photograph was taken. The building was later renamed Sciots Hall. The Russian community purchased the building in 1939 and it became the Russian Center.

opening with church liturgy and banquet took place that May with Archbishop Tikhon (Troitsky, 1883–1963) of Holy Virgin Cathedral conducting the service. The Holy Virgin Cathedral choir, conducted by Valerian Looksha (1886–1966), recently arrived from Harbin, sang at the service and at the opening ceremony. Approximately 1,000 people visited the center's open house event. The archbishop presented Varguin with an icon of St Tatyana; as the St Tatyana's ball held in January had raised a significant amount of money for the cause, St Tatyana became the Russian Center's patron saint.[58] Though a secular institution, the involvement of the Orthodox Church in all aspects of the founding and opening of the center indicated the predominant religious affiliation of the founders and leading members.

Once the center opened, the feared indifference of the Russian community transformed, at last initially, into enthusiasm, and many came to participate in the myriad activities, classes, and groups. In an article about the center's popularity, Ivan S. Guz (1891–1982) referred to it as a "Russian corner" – a place where Russians could take comfort in knowing they were not alone in the often-harsh circumstances of life in emigration, indicating a continuing uneasiness about life in America. He compared the Russian Center to "Mecca," drawing in members of the "Russian Colony" to this small piece of "our never-to-be-forgotten treasured Motherland," identifying the space in both religious and nostalgic terms.[59]

Situated several blocks northwest of the O'Farrell "Russian center" neighborhood, the building was in an area that was undergoing some demographic changes in 1939. In fact, in a Russian newspaper article about the pros and cons of purchasing the building, the author referred to concerns of certain board members that the building was in a neighborhood in which large numbers of people of "colored races" had begun to settle in recent years. Such concern was linked directly to the prevalent practice of banks of "redlining." The writer continued: "due to ... [the changing demographics], banks and other financial institutions are even refusing to issue or are greatly reducing mortgages for homes located in this area." In other words, the concern was that Russians would not be able to buy homes in the area because of issues with obtaining financing. The low price for the building, then, was explained by this circumstance.[60] The seller apparently felt that no one except "foreigners" would buy the building in a neighborhood with such a shifting demographic. The Fillmore and Western Addition, however, had included a diverse community throughout the 1920s and 1930s while Russians lived there. Therefore, the circumstance of non-whites moving into the specific area around the intersection of Sutter and Divisadero did not seem new. What was of concern was the feared effect on economic well-being of Russians who might want to live near the Russian Center. The writer went on to say that other members felt it did not matter who lived in the neighborhood. The matter-of-fact acknowledgment of redlining, however, indicated that in the almost twenty years that most of these émigrés had lived in San Francisco, they had become familiar with how the racial hierarchy in the United States functioned. Though the writer did not use the actual term "redlining," they were clearly aware of its existence, purpose, and targeted populations. As some émigrés had been involved in the real estate business for years, they would have been even more cognizant about how the mortgage industry operated.[61]

Konstantin Barskii, who was vice-president and later president of the Russian Center board, also raised the issue of demographics bluntly, but somewhat ambiguously, stating at one of the meetings discussing the purchase that "there has been much talk in the Russian colony about the purchase of Sciots Hall with respect to the Negro neighborhood," noting that this was the only neighborhood in San Francisco where a building of such size could be purchased for $30,000. The account of that meeting did not indicate whether there was any reaction to Barskii's comment. It is indicative that his phrasing obscured who exactly was doing the "talking" and in what context. In other words, the issue of neighborhood demographics appeared to concern him, but perhaps to avoid casting himself in a negative light, he couched the statement as a general concern of some nebulous group. At the same time, both his articulation about the issue and the matter-of-fact mention of redlining may have indicated a perspective that spoke both to the continuing process of Americanization as well as lingering émigré perspectives that complemented one another. The discrimination against people of color was an "American" practice and, given the economic hardships most Russians experienced, their view of social policy, in the context of their own experience, acknowledged the competitiveness of the American economic and social order. Therefore, taking advantage of one's opportunities was the "American" thing to do (i.e., buying the building for a good price because no one else would). Moreover, discriminatory policies based on race, though morally wrong, were an "American" problem. Russians felt their own sense of alienation. Alexander Varguin, in fact, later articulated his concern that non-Russian groups who had been renting space in the building might leave once Russians purchased it, indicating his feeling that Americans did not accept Russians as Americans (notwithstanding how long they had lived in the United States), and therefore certainly not as landlords.[62]

The buffer of the mental territory in which émigrés lived also worked to insulate them from the experiences of those who were not part of their "little Russian world." Newly created ethnic (as opposed to cultural) cohesion, in an environment that prized competition, had begun to dictate how some Russians viewed American society, particularly those that did not have children. Given that Americans would never accept Russians who maintained their cultural attributes as bona fide Americans, there was no point in making an effort to fully Americanize. Barskii's comments indicated his possible adhesion to these perspectives. Relatively young when he arrived in the United States, he nevertheless did not pursue an American higher education, working for most of his life as a clothing presser. He and his wife had no children. The focus of his "real" life was the social/organizational and, later, the political circles of the Russian community. He became president of the Russian Center in 1943, when Varguin stepped down due to health reasons, and the center began to experience internal conflicts and withdrawal of participation, in part due to Barskii's style of leadership (chapter 9).[63]

Aiding the Russian People

The Russian Center became one of the focal points in the Russian-American community in organizing aid to the Russian people when Germany invaded the Soviet Union. The global political situation had already begun to change as émigrés prepared to purchase the Sutter Street building in 1939. On 1 September 1939, a week after signing the Molotov-Ribbentrop Pact, Hitler and Stalin invaded Poland; Britain and France subsequently declared war on Germany. The uneasy peace between Germany and the Soviet Union ended on 22 June 1941 when Germany launched Operation Barbarossa; six months later, on 7 December 1941, Japan attacked the United States at Pearl Harbor. In the course of two years, the Soviet Union's position as a complicit partner to Nazi German aims in Europe, particularly in the partition of Poland, altered to being an ally of the United States in the war against the Axis Powers.

The continuing influx of émigrés throughout the decade prior to World War II from various backgrounds and with differing experiences, ongoing conflicted interactions with US immigration authorities, and the dynamic global situation contributed further to the heterogeneity of political viewpoints among Russians in San Francisco. At the same time, almost inevitably, the Russian Center's mission became ever more politicized, despite the initial intentions to remain apolitical. A document marked "not for press" compiled by Varguin, dated 2 September 1941, divided San Francisco's community into groups based on level of opposition to the Soviet Union. Varguin recognized that lived experience often dictated the extent of hostility (or lack of it), also acknowledging that perspectives may have changed over time, particularly given the German invasion of the homeland.[64]

Varguin's analysis, however, did not take into account, at least overtly, the experiences of Russians once arrived in the United States and how those experiences might have influenced their outlook. In other words, the economic difficulties, consequent marginalization, and dominant culture hostility that many experienced may have influenced perceptions of both the Soviet Union and the United States, as well as their own identities. His

Authentic and Imagined Russian Enclaves | **259**

analysis of the San Francisco community, however, recognized the difficulty of developing a platform with respect to sending aid to the USSR, even if such aid specifically targeted the people of the country rather than the regime.

During the six-month period between the invasion of the Soviet Union by Nazi Germany in June of 1941 and the Japanese attack on Pearl Harbor, the Russian Center leadership attempted to define the "White Russian" position on what action to take, if any, to assist Russia, continually emphasizing that clear distinction between the Soviet regime and the "Russian People" (often written in capital letters). At a September 1941 semi-annual board meeting, Varguin noted the "agonizing" of Russian Center members since the Axis powers had declared war on the USSR two and a half months prior. With 400 members and approximately 1,500 people involved in Russian Center activities and events, the center had a significant force to pursue whatever course they might choose to take. At the same, there was no unity in Russia Abroad (either in San Francisco or around the world), much less among Russian expatriates who made up many different groups with varying perspectives about the USSR, from intensely hostile to the regime, to indifferent, to well-disposed.[65]

In the interests of inclusivity and positive action, the board approved Varguin's resolution, presenting it at the following day's General Meeting. The resolution stated a goal of the Russian Center to reinforce the high ideals of American citizenship among members; as firm defenders of the national *and* democratic ideals of the Russian people, Russian émigrés were deeply devoted to the principles of the American Constitution and would always support the people and government of the United States. That being said, "we, members of the Russian Center" were "linked through blood ties with the Russian people," and recognized their great suffering in the battle for their homeland and national ideals. The board thus decided to create a "Fund to Aid the Russian People" with donations disbursed through the American Red Cross.[66] Varguin, cognizant of the complicated position émigré Russians were in at this juncture, attempted to anticipate any future difficulties that might arise as a result of sending funds to a foreign power, which, a short time ago, had been the focus of American hostility, the emphasis on "Russian People" notwithstanding. Such calculations spoke to the ongoing pressures Russians experienced in American society as a politically suspect group: the House Un-American Activities Committee (HUAC) had been formed in 1938, and though its activities temporarily decreased after the United States entered the war as an ally of the Soviet Union, the activities of the FBI did not.

FBI agents paid close attention to any organization that had a connection to the USSR, but fundamentally misunderstood Russian-American group divisions and affiliations. An FBI report on the "Russian-American Society for Assistance to the USSR and Great Britain in the Struggle against Hitler's Fascism," which Victor Arnautoff and George Bratoff, by then Communist Party members, helped organize in 1941, stated that the organization "is a typical Communist front organization and is an attempt to have a patriotic appeal for the White Russians in this country and to draw them into this Front organization either because of that appeal or for failure on the part of this group to realize the ultimate purpose of the Society."[67] The idea that White Russians as a group, many of whom viewed even the most benign commentary about the Soviet Union as communist propaganda, would be drawn into an organization affiliated with the Soviet government (given the enthusiastic support of the Soviet Consul for its activities) indicated the lack of comprehension regarding White Russian perspectives even at this juncture. Arnautoff's and Bratoff's nominal affiliation with White Russians certainly muddied the waters but both had been openly (not secretly) sympathetic to the Soviet Union for years.[68]

A subsequent summary report quoted a source who claimed that until January of 1942, "numerous White Russians" were members of the Russian-American Society until "Communists" started to distribute "Communist propaganda," at which time the White Russians left and formed the "United Russian Society."[69] That latter society, however, was actually the Russian United Relief Society, founded by Spiritual Christians on Potrero Hill, not "White Russians."[70] Apart from Arnautoff, Bratoff, and Sergei Scherbakoff (who was a member of the executive board), there were likely no "White Russian" members in the Russian-American Society. Both the Russian-American Society and the United Relief Society, in fact, refused to participate in an April 1942 "All Russian" effort sponsored by the Russian Center.[71] Whether the informant used the term "White Russian" or whether the FBI handlers made the erroneous assumption that the source meant "White Russian" is unknown, but previous communications indicated officials' confusion about the appellation.[72] Moreover, the subtext of the FBI report implied that "White Russians" were at best naïve and at worst untrustworthy in the event of a situation requiring them to choose between Russia and the United States.

The conflicts between the different groups were exacerbated by the editors of *Novaya Zarya* newspaper, a Russian émigré daily, who, taking

Authentic and Imagined Russian Enclaves | 261

their role as members of a free press seriously, made it their mission to criticize every decision of the Russian Center's leadership from the day of its organization. Gregory (1896–1987) and Matrena Soohoff (1899–1999) started the paper in 1928 and it remained in conflict with the Russian Center in the post-war period, earning it accusations of not just pro-Soviet sympathies but of Soviet government funding.[73] The constant barrage of criticism was a factor in the Russian Center buying out Peter Balakshin, who had been publishing *Russian News-Life* newspaper, and running the paper as the new version of *Russkaia zhizn'* out of the Russian Center beginning in 1942, which led to a new host of financial problems.[74] Commenting on the conflict, Nadia Shapiro noted that the Russian Center, the "union of all Russian anti-Bolshevik societies in San Francisco, has decided to launch a paper to break the monopoly of Gregory Soohoff" who "has maneuvered himself into a situation where all other Russians are gunning for him."[75]

The disagreement about how to approach the aid question at the Russian Center had continued throughout the fall of 1941, with some Russian Center members objecting to working with the Russian War Relief Board, as that board made no distinction between aid to the Soviet regime and the Russian people. Varguin had addressed his meeting with the board regarding transfers of raised funds on the day preceding a fund-raising ball at the Russian Center for aid to the Russian people.[76] Four days after that board meeting, Japan had attacked Pearl Harbor, taking the United States into the war, further complicating the task of the Russian Center, but also providing it with opportunities to take part in San Francisco's patriotic activities in the areas of civil defense, citizen involvement, and public health.[77]

Fund raising continued but the Russian Center maintained its distance from the Russian-American Society on the grounds that the leadership of that organization was intent on bringing politics into the humanitarian aid effort. Russian Center leadership continued to insist on its apolitical status, a position that would change 180 degrees immediately after the war.[78] Shapiro elaborated on the conflicted situation in which White Russians found themselves during the war:

> [White Russians have] remained bitterly anti-Bolshevist ... [and] ... at the same time they're hotly patriotic. This leads to such situations as when a friend of mine buys out of her meager earnings wool to knit sweaters for the Red Army and then runs around town looking for a

neutral American friend to turn the stuff over to the Soviet Consul since she cannot be, and will not be, on speaking terms with a representative of the Soviet Government! [79]

Shapiro saw this conundrum as both "funny and pathetic." Knitting a sweater or sewing a garment provided a sense of connection to Russians suffering the hardships of war. The fact that Russians in America avoided direct contact with Soviet representatives, however, likely spoke as much to apprehension about American perceptions of Russians as untrustworthy, given, for example, the editorial that ran in the *San Francisco Examiner* in 1942 (chapter 7), as it did to moral principles precluding "speaking" to Soviet representatives. Using a "neutral American friend" as an intermediary provided a buffer to avoid possible repercussions. To wit, when San Francisco Soviet Consul A.A. Skoriukoff requested that the Russian War Relief administration assist him in collecting information about local Russians participating in the effort to aid the Soviet Union for a post-war exhibit in Moscow, the Russian Center board left it "up to individual members" to provide the information, indicating both apprehension as to how this participation would be perceived by American authorities, as well as suspicion of Soviet motivations. [80]

As noted by Johnston, the Russian émigré response in Europe to the attack on the Soviet Union by Nazi Germany ranged from a "suspension" of hostilities to outright calls for reconciliation, while a "small handful of individuals" aligned with the Nazi regime, similar to the range of responses in the San Francisco community. [81] Russians who had arrived in the inter-war period, however, had, by this time, almost universally naturalized. Those who had held out, perhaps still hoping for the possibility of return, generally submitted their papers once the United States entered the war, due to the problematic nature of remaining "stateless" in wartime. After Japan's attack on Pearl Harbor, Russians witnessed the repercussions on Japanese Americans and Japanese nationals firsthand as they were forced to leave their homes in the Fillmore for internment camps. Allies or no, the future, as always, was uncertain, and Russian Americans supporting the Soviet Union also foresaw their own continuing residence in a post-war America.

The attack on the Russian homeland by fascist forces simultaneously mobilized the Potrero Hill Russian community with Fred Sysoeff, as politically active as ever, leading organizing efforts in tandem with Arnautoff and Bratoff. Their response did not go unnoticed, with the Soviet

Authentic and Imagined Russian Enclaves | **263**

ambassador in Washington, DC sending a letter of thanks for their support, and renewed FBI monitoring of the Potrero Hill Neighborhood House on De Haro Street, a center of aid activity.[82] In July of 1941, the director of the Neighborhood House had informed the FBI about the formation of the Russian-American Society, which, as noted, supposedly initially included a significant "White Russian" contingent.[83] The Neighborhood House was "the center of Red Cross activity in the Russian colony," eclipsing the émigré effort. Not only did women knit and make clothing, the Molokan Russian Mothers' Club led efforts rolling bandages at the Molokan church on Carolina Street, raising funds for Moscow hospitals, and groups ran blood drives. There were no hesitations about meeting with the Soviet consul and, upon Soviet consul Jacob Lomakin's departure from San Francisco in 1944, the Molokan community honored him with a farewell dinner.[84]

Both communities, then, mobilized to help the Russian people. Despite the negative experience of some Molokan families upon their attempted return to Russia in the 1920s, the bond to the homeland under attack was such that they recognized Soviet representatives as Russians. The Russian Center and the community supporting it, however, attempted to maintain a clear dividing line between their support of the Russian people and opposition to Soviet officialdom (and commensurately any "communist" groups) in what was now a Russian-American community rather than a Russian "colony."

Critically, however, both Arnautoff and Bratoff had both been on a list of lecturers the Russian Center invited to speak as late as August of 1940. In other words, the immediate pre-war environment in the Russian community remained tolerant of alternate political viewpoints in the artistic and social context; the topic of Arnautoff's proposed lecture was icon painting, while Bratoff was to speak to youth about theater arts.[85] Moreover, émigrés overwhelmingly considered a victory over fascism as critical, supporting the work of the Russian-American Society (even if they were not members) in the society's newsletter, "Za Pobedu [For Victory]," despite its pro-Soviet rhetoric. Boris Von Vakh (1888–1958), a White Army colonel, a member of the Society of Russian Veterans, and a registered Republican in 1936, even contributed an article to the newsletter about the progress of the war in the April 1942 issue, an issue that included an editorial attack on White Russians for harboring "secret fascists."[86]

Both domestic and international events in the 1930s and early 1940s influenced the continuing evolution of the Russian community ethos in

San Francisco, now largely identifying as "Russian-American." That identity was not uniform and the multiple events Russians in San Francisco organized together in the 1930s indicated a multicultural perspective with respect to "Russianness" in America. Remaining "hyphenated" Americans, however, reinforced the notion of cultural difference: even as Russians presented their culture to Americans and created their own narratives about their place in American history and society, they realized that maintaining any part of their Russian identity in any visible way would require a lifetime of explanations and battling suspicions. First-generation Russians may have been willing to accept that requirement, but their children often did not, whether they were members of the "Green Street" community, the Holy Virgin Parish, or residents of Potrero Hill. The price of authenticity was often alienation and, over the course of the 1940s, some members of the Russian communities chose to distance themselves both socially and geographically from their respective Russian communities.

The fractious period during the war contributed to such distancing as well, with both covert and overt monitoring by the FBI of any "Russian" activities per se. At a time when San Francisco urban space included two distinct Russian neighborhoods, three Russian Orthodox cathedrals, Russian churches of various denominations, a newly founded Russian Center, and a Russian Historical Society, the Russian community centered in the Fillmore District began its inevitable dispersal. Part of that dispersal had to do with changing economic circumstances, with people buying homes in the Richmond and Sunset Districts in the city or moving to surrounding areas, particularly Sonoma County. Others found ways to make a living outside the urban enclave. The Dobrovidoffs, who owned a clothing store and beauty shop in the Fillmore in the inter-war period, relocated to Calistoga in Napa County, known for its restorative waters, by the late 1930s, where they ran their summer resort, which they named Dobr Mineral Springs.[87] That migration north had a role in the steady dispersal of the community and the consequent withdrawal of some members of the inter-war contingent from participation in San Francisco organizations and events. The increasingly dictatorial tone coming from the Russian Center leadership, however, discussed further in chapter 9, was also a factor influencing whether people continued their participation going forward.

The post-World War II wave of Russians coming to San Francisco would mitigate the dispersal of the community, as thousands of Russian

Authentic and Imagined Russian Enclaves | 265

refugees and displaced persons streamed in from camps in Tubabao in the Philippine Islands, from China, and from Europe. The ideology of the vast majority of the newcomers was militantly anti-Soviet, and the collectively nostalgic ideations about Russia that had previously informed émigré life and artistic endeavors shifted in response. Political activism, which inter-war émigrés had almost uniformly eschewed, began to have a central role in all Russian community activity. In the inter-war period, émigrés had mourned the loss of their motherland, but the narrative of loss altered in the post-World War II era to match the militant outlook: Russians had not lost Russia according to that perspective – Russia had been taken from them.

—9—

PAWNS ON A CHESSBOARD
The New Exodus and the Post-War Russian Community

A new exodus has taken place. An exodus in its scope even
more significant than that of 1920 when the Russian emigration
appeared abroad.

NIKOLAI A. TSURIKOV, Russian DP Camp,
Füssen (Allgäu), Germany, 29 June 1946[1]

Russian [academic] subjects are beginning to come under question.
They are unpopular. There is considerable apprehension with respect
to having any affinity for Russian culture. A bad sign:
the shunning of both Russian subject-matter and Russian people may
become a dreadful fact.

GEORGE GREBENSTCHIKOFF
to Alexandra Jernakoff-Nicolaeff, 1949[2]

Part of the terror was that if you grow up in the United States and
you go to school in the United States and you read American history
and you admire this country, you are not only mystified but totally
taken aback to experience something as bizarre and as corrupted and
as vicious as this, in the United States. You're utterly unprepared.
This is not the country that you know.

VLADIMIR I. TOUMANOFF, 1999[3]

In May of 1950, the International Refugee Organization (IRO) director
in Washington, DC forwarded a cable from IRO headquarters in Geneva to Russian Orthodox Archbishop John (Maximovitch, 1896–1966)
in New York. The cable concerned the children of St Tikhon-Zadonsk

Orphanage, founded by the Archbishop in Shanghai in 1935. The IRO had evacuated approximately forty children and young people, aged seven to eighteen years from that orphanage to the island of Samar in the Philippines in 1949 as part of a massive effort to resettle almost 6,000 refugees fleeing Shanghai in the final stages of China's civil war. The cable read:

> Chances of resettlement in the States or British Commonwealth extremely remote. We will use best efforts to resettle children but point out group resettlement may not be possible; therefore we will explore possibility of *dispersal of children* in Western Europe. Certain number children will undoubtedly *be left Philippines.* Has Archbishop John any plan or program of longtime care for them in Philippines? If so we will assist. If not we will need to make alternative arrangements such as placement in Red Cross orphanages in Philippines.[4]

The fates of the children, casually dismissed in this cable from IRO headquarters, depended, as did the fates of all the refugees at Samar, on bureaucratic decisions over which they had no control. Concurrently, officials, including those from aid agencies, wreaked havoc on the emotional and mental state of the refugees, already traumatized by years of conflict, statelessness, and marginalization, but forced into yet another displacement. The reference to "dispersing" the children, who had been living together as a family at the orphanage, spoke to a lack of empathy by officials and a willful incomprehension of the consequences of their proposed solutions to the resettlement problem. Almost all the children in the orphanage, in fact, contrary to the pessimistic view of the IRO official who wrote the cable, did make it to San Francisco, primarily due to the persistence and indomitable will of the archbishop and his supporting network of Russian émigrés both in Tubabao, on the island of Samar, and San Francisco. Many refugees, however, did not. At least 1,000 were left behind in Shanghai in the chaos of evacuation; of those who made it to Tubabao, approximately 1,300 went to Australia; hundreds of others scattered into various countries in South America and the Caribbean where living conditions were often just as problematic as in Tubabao; and a group of approximately 500, including one of the orphans, diagnosed with tuberculosis or other diseases, ended up in sanitariums in Western Europe.[5]

Efforts by San Francisco's Russian community to facilitate the path of Russian refugees to America began immediately upon the conclusion of the war, with the creation of a Federation of Russian Charitable Organizations in the United States focused initially on assisting the thousands of Russians displaced from Shanghai to a refugee camp at Tubabao. Russian émigrés also continued to arrive in San Francisco from Europe and from Harbin into the 1950s, and re-migrated from third countries in South America and elsewhere, where they had initially settled after the war, into the 1960s.[6] The migrations were in tandem with the rise and fall of McCarthyism in the United States and Russian-American efforts were, at times, at cross-purposes with the goals of politicians, who conflated anti-communism with anti-immigration policy. Russian Americans, however, also sought to emphasize the dangers of communism to Americans, despite the fact that fear of "communism" played a role in precluding entry for thousands of Russians in the increasingly xenophobic atmosphere engendered by McCarthyism. The uneasiness about Russian, or any excessive Eastern European immigration, reinforced fears of a "fifth column" of Soviet agents attempting to gain entry into the country.

The politics of anti-communism in the newly bipolar world, dominated by Soviet-American hostilities, influenced the shaping of Russian-American identity. Inter-war San Francisco Russian community efforts to keep their institutions apolitical were swept aside by demands for active opposition to the global communist threat and Russian community leaders undertook efforts to emphasize Russian American patriotism and loyalty to the United States and its credo, particularly salient given the global acknowledgment of the post-war "polarization of East and West."[7] The ensuing demands to walk in lockstep created conflict, particularly within the Russian Center, founded in 1939 as a cultural rather than a political institution, but re-branded a "Russian-American Anti-Communist Organization" by the end of 1945.[8]

The processes of Americanization among inter-war émigrés, who had obscured their Russian identity in many contexts, influenced their perceptions of how to live as Russians in America in the post-war world.[9] Some saw the anti-communist crusade, popularized by political figures and institutions in the McCarthyist period, as a way to maintain a Russian identity in an increasingly Russophobic environment. In tandem, post-war arrivals, experiencing their own trauma in the course of multiple displacements, saw their role in America as anti-communist warriors. Strident anti-communism equaled American patriotism, in their view, contributing to a dynamic of paranoia and suspicion, generally prevalent in McCarthyist America. An ideological mix of fervent anti-communism and neo-monarchism also began to prevail as the accepted form of Russian-American identity. The militant nature of this developing Russian-American identity was defensive in nature, and rooted in paranoia, altering the nature of the community, but also facilitated a path to joining the burgeoning post-World War II American white middle class.

McCarthyism and the US Response to the Refugee Crisis

McCarthyism, or the search for a fifth column, particularly in US government agencies, the US military, educational institutions, and Hollywood, was the post-World War II iteration of a process that had begun in 1918 with the first Red Scare. As discussed previously, the creation of the American surveillance state focused specifically on infiltration or direction from "Moscow" in the inter-war period. HUAC, founded in 1938, was a targeted response to fears of communist infiltration of American society at a time when many Americans, both working class and intellectual, sought non-capitalist solutions to the heretofore greatest economic catastrophe to occur in the United States – the Great Depression.

The California Un-American Activities Committee (CUAC), formed in 1941 and headed initially by California Senator Jack Tenney, targeted communists, and perceived sympathizers in that state, with the late 1940s and 1950s its most intensive period of activity, in tandem with the efforts of HUAC and Senator Joseph McCarthy. The running narrative about the threat of communist infiltration kept the terms "Red," "Russian," and "Communist," all interchangeable, on the front pages of newspapers and the fear of that threat, one that many Russian Americans promulgated as well, served to complicate the very task they were trying to achieve: to bring their Russian compatriots to the United States.[10]

Reinforcing the dangers of communism to America made the tasks of assisting Eastern European refugees, categorized by United Nations Relief and Rehabilitation Administration (UNRRA) as "displaced persons" (DPS) even more difficult, as did the continuing reluctance of US authorities to admit immigrants of unclear ethnic origins, and, in the case of Russians, those who were of "Asiatic descent." Such questioning of ethnic origins among officials in both refugee/aid organizations, as well as US immigration agencies, referenced Russian refugees in the Far East specifically but, as Susan Carruthers points out, during the McCarthy era, "nativism and anticommunism found common cause" in reaction to Russian and Eastern European immigration, whether from Europe or Asia.[11]

The Russian refugees who came to San Francisco following World War II were in large part émigrés who had remained in China and Europe during the inter-war period, but also Soviet citizens who had left the Soviet Union during the war. As in the inter-war period, the largest group to come to San Francisco was from China, particularly Shanghai, where Russians had formed a community, disrupted first by Japanese occupation in the 1930s, then the war, and the Chinese Civil War. The continued circumstances of being stateless and living in conflict zones in a world where, more than ever, papers defined a person's identity, played on the existing insecurities and fears of the refugees, compounded by a reality that few governments welcomed them.

In Europe, Russian émigrés who had barely been eking out a living in the inter-war period, literally displaced from their homes, lived in DP camps, not only destitute, but fearing Soviet arrest. A group of émigrés living in Prague, for example, were arrested at the end of 1945, "according to lists … compiled by Soviet authorities."[12] DPS also included Soviet citizens who had either been forcibly transported out of the Soviet Union as *Ostarbeiters* ("Eastern workers," at least two million of whom were from Soviet Ukraine) by the Nazi regime, POWS, and those who had left the Soviet Union, voluntarily or involuntarily joining the German Army in its retreat as the tide of the war began to shift. Western European and American authorities forcibly repatriated ethnic Russians to the Soviet Union from 1945 through 1947. Growing outrage, largely due to information disseminated by émigré activists, and the pleading of Metropolitan Anastasii, the head of the Russian Orthodox Church abroad in Europe with then-General Dwight D. Eisenhower to cease the repatriation, led to a halt on the part of the Americans.[13] The nominal reason for repatriations was the Yalta Agreement between the three heads of state, Franklin D. Roosevelt, Winston Churchill, and Joseph Stalin, in which Stalin specifically stipulated, with Roosevelt and Churchill acquiescing to his demand, that all Red Army POWS, forced laborers, and other Soviet citizens (in other words, people of various nationalities) be returned to the Soviet Union after the war. The brutality of the methods of repatriation by British and American authorities, however, which included rounding up people, including thousands of Russians "who had never been Soviet citizens," and forcing them under arms into train cars, indicated to

The New Exodus and the Post-War Russian Community | **271**

Russian Americans that the Western powers saw the removal of DPS as a way to cleanse Western Europe of "foreign" refugees.[14] Cognizant of the tenuous positions of DPS, Russian Americans took care in how they characterized US actions: inter-war émigré Gregory Tschebotarieff, for example, noting the terrible consequences of forced repatriations in his correspondence with Senator H. Alexander Smith in 1951, was careful to absolve US authorities of responsibility, labeling the policy a "monumental and tragic blunder" as if US officials simply had not known any better.[15]

Opposition to the resettlement of DPS in the United States was both immediate and virulent. Texas Representative Ed Gossett made the following statements in 1947 in opposition to the first version of the Displaced Persons Bill, which would have allowed 400,000 eligible refugees from the camps to enter the United States:

> When there were frontiers to conquer and jobs to fill, immigrant blood meant strength. The blood now offered means weakness and pollution. The Germans, the Irish, the Norwegians, the immigrants from northern and western Europe who came here in the last century are among our best citizens ... Many of [the displaced persons] have come from Russia and countries under Russian domination. While a few good people remain in these camps, they are by and large the refuse of Europe. The camps are filled with bums, criminals, black-marketeers, subversives, revolutionists, and crackpots of all colors and hues ... Doubtless many persons have been planted in these camps to infiltrate the country and to serve alien causes ... Hundreds of dangerous persons have entered this country in recent years, and many are still coming. Other hundreds of potential fifth columnists sit in the DP camps and await passage to America.[16]

Gossett was essentially repeating the nativist and eugenicist arguments from earlier years adding a new spin about fifth columnists as a "virus": Northern and Western Europeans, wholesome and desirable immigrants, had built America. Eastern Europeans were, at best, aliens, incompatible with the American way of life and, at worst, communist infiltrators: a dangerous "foreign virus." His reference to "all colors and hues" indicated a belief that Eastern Europeans were not quite white enough to qualify for entry into the United States. His hyperbole sought to forestall any disagreement: if not subversive, then the DPS were criminals; if not criminals, they were mentally ill. At the root was a "weakness and pollution" of the blood, raising imagery of defective and impure populations, not suitable for America, mimicking, as it were, Nazi German rhetoric. Gossett also insisted that there was no evidence that repatriated people were persecuted in the Soviet Union.[17] Despite the opposition, Congress passed the first Displaced Persons Act in 1948 (decreasing the number of refugee slots from 400,000 by almost half, however) and President Harry S. Truman signed it on 25 June 1948, the first such law to distinguish refugees from immigrants.[18]

Russian Refugees and DPs in Asia

In Asia, the issue of resettling refugees took on urgency by 1948 in response to the growing realization that Chinese Communist forces were likely to be victorious over the Nationalists in the Chinese Civil War, which had resumed in 1945 after a hiatus during World War II. Approximately 7,000 White Russians were in Shanghai as of November 1948 and an unknown number overall in China.[19] The Russian Emigrants Association (REA), formed in Shanghai in April of 1946, evacuated approximately 4,000 Russian émigrés (included in a total of 6,000 people) to Tubabao in 1949, with the assistance of the IRO, as Communist forces neared the city. Alexander Lenkoff (1899–1975), living in the city of Tientsin, "abandoned everything," and fled with his family to Shanghai in 1948, assisted by American forces, because the "Communist Eighth Army" was headed their way. The Lenkoffs came to San Francisco in February of 1953 from Tubabao, in one of the last groups to depart.[20]

Philippines President Elpidio Quirino had agreed to provide temporary refuge to evacuees in Tubabao, but the location held no structures or amenities, apart from the foundations of huts erected by Americans during World War II. The initial agreement allowed refugees to remain there for no more than four months because the area lay in the path of storms during typhoon season. Nonetheless, approximately 3,000 people ended up living there, in tents and makeshift barracks, for at least one year, many for two years, and some until 1953, as the IRO was woefully unprepared in the efforts to arrange for permanent resettlement.[21] Archbishop John evacuated from Shanghai with the refugees to Tubabao, departing to New York after a short stay in July of 1949, when it became clear that the assurances of IRO officials of expeditious resettlement had grossly underestimated the complexity of the task. Moreover, IRO officials had implied in 1948 that processing visas for Russian refugees to the

United States, Canada, and Australia would be a mere formality, which was certainly not the case.[22]

For the next two years, Archbishop John traveled back and forth from New York to Washington, DC, maintaining contacts with American officials, as Congress began the process of amending the 1948 Displaced Persons Act to include a broader range of groups. The archbishop also corresponded with REA president Colonel Gregory K. Bologoff (1895–1976) in Tubabao, apprising him of the twists and turns of the American legislative process. The archbishop, understanding the complexities of that process, made clear to Bologoff, whose sense of drama placed White Russians in the center of the refugee crisis, that they were but a small pawn in the game of politics. The archbishop emphasized the criticality of ensuring that someone did not remove, inadvertently or otherwise, that small pawn from the larger chessboard that was the amended DP Act.[23]

Bologoff, in turn, maintained correspondence with Russians in San Francisco, particularly Victor Borzov, who was the executive director of the Federation of Russian Charitable Organizations in the United States (hereinafter "Federation"), a compilation of approximately thirty Russian émigré organizations in San Francisco, Berkeley, Los Angeles, Seattle, Portland, and New York certified by the US Department of State in September of 1950 as the central aid organization assisting DPS of Russian nationality in China and the Philippines to resettle in the United States. More than 90 per cent of the refugees remaining in the camp in the Philippines, after some initial departures, were Russians.[24]

The headquarters of the Federation was in San Francisco and the geographic division was, in part, a conscious effort at attempting to efficiently manage the tasks at hand – the ships and airplanes transporting the DPS from the Philippines docked and landed at San Francisco. Although the Russian community there also took part in various aid efforts for DPS in Europe, the Tolstoy Foundation and the Russian American Union for Protection and Aid to Russians Outside of Russia, both based in New York, led the European effort. Countess Alexandra Tolstoy headed the Tolstoy Foundation; Prince Sergei Belosselsky-Belozersky headed the Russian American Union; and Lev Nikolaevsky (aka Leon Nicoli), a Russian Imperial Army colonel and of a noble family noted in chapter 5, was president of the Federation in San Francisco, lending credence once again to the notion of the prevalence of Russian nobility among émigrés.[25]

The Tolstoy Foundation and Los Angeles aid group Humanity Calls were not included in the final roster of the Federation's member organizations. Alexandra Tolstoy felt that the New York organizations were too politicized for aid work and refused to join, while émigré Leo N. Kay, founder of Humanity Calls, publicly accused UNRRA of carrying out a pro-Soviet agenda, writing letters to the US attorney general to that effect and interfering with the recognition of the Federation. CUAC's Jack Tenney, however, was an enthusiastic supporter of Humanity Calls, in line with one of the organization's main goals to aid the "victims of communism."[26]

The mutual political interests of Humanity Calls and CUAC bolstered the aid organization in its initial efforts to draw attention to the crisis involving displaced Russian people but was ultimately detrimental to the overall resettlement effort. Tenney wrote to California Governor Earl Warren in 1948, urging him to include a representative of the "Greek Orthodox Church" on a committee of "California citizens on the settlement of displaced persons in the State of California." Tenney noted that since most of the DPS coming to California were likely "Russians of the Greek Orthodox faith," they should have their own representative along with the "Protestants, Catholics, and Jews" on the committee.[27] Tenney, who was openly anti-Semitic, affiliating Jews with communism, saw anti-communist and Christian White Russians, though a tiny minority in the United States, as a worthwhile ally in the effort to ferret out Soviet spies. Kay's assurances about "screening out all the undesirables, or people of doubtful political standing," however, reinforced the notion that DPS were a danger, particularly if they were Russian.[28] That emphasis on danger backfired on DPS and Russians in America as McCarthyist hysteria began to dominate both political discourse and the drafting of national security legislation in the coming years.

The Anti-Communist Crusade Network and Slavic Americans

Tenney, in his role as co-chairman of CUAC (1941–49), utilized techniques to find subversives that Senator Joseph McCarthy would later take up, using operatives to ferret out information on suspect individuals or organizations in California. Sometimes, in the spirit of denouncing enemies of the state, concerned citizens sent letters to Tenney. In 1949, for example, "young Republican" Virginia C. Anderson of Hollywood, California, wrote to CUAC about her fears that communists had infiltrated her folk dancing group, and asked for help to "combat the commies."[29]

Communist infiltration of folk dancing groups was only one of Tenney's foci and his investigators collected materials based on peoples' ethnic background, notably Slavs. A 1949 copy of *The Slavic-American Quarterly*, admittedly a politically left publication, was as suspect to Tenney as 1948/1949 Los Angeles Russian Theatrical Society programs, including children's picnic announcements, all items in his files.[30]

Then-Congressman Richard M. Nixon, a member of HUAC, sent twelve copies of the "Report on the American Slav Congress and Associated Organizations" to Tenney in 1949 (the American Slav Congress published the *Quarterly*), indicating a community of purpose in their targeting of Slavs. Nationwide, Slavic groups had formed numerous ethnic fraternal associations by World War II, whose membership was largely made up of workers in heavy industry and who were closely linked with the Slav Congress, formed in 1942.[31] HUAC put out a statement that the Congress was a "Russian weapon" intended to "subvert" ten million "Slavic Americans" with "poisonous and lying propaganda."[32] Even Nikolay Borzov, a leading member of the San Francisco White Russian community for more than twenty years and hardly a leftist, received correspondence from the Slav Congress in 1945, likely because he was on a mailing list, but nevertheless leaving him open to possible accusations of communist sympathies.[33] Nor did anti-communist demagogues have any compunction about casting suspicion on "White" Russians as fifth columnists: radio broadcaster Fulton Lewis Jr declared that 300 White Russian refugees seeking to gain entry from the Philippines (Tubabao) in 1951 "might suddenly turn Red" upon entry into the United States.[34]

Ironically, the idea that ferreting out enemies of the state by any means necessary was of more importance than maintaining individual civil and constitutional rights in the United States was one that many Russian Americans came to share. The paranoia and hysteria during the McCarthy era depended in great measure on politicians stoking the fear of an outside force threatening the American way of life. Moreover, McCarthy used fear of communism as a boost to his own political recognizability: "[McCarthy] has made no secret of the fact that he considers himself Presidential timber for 1956."[35] Reporters concluded after "an extensive investigation" of McCarthy: "communism is largely the instrument of his personal ambitions."[36] Russians in America, however, perceived him as a crusader against the forces that had sent them into exile and were now a global threat. Adopting the role of Cassandras to whom no one listened as they warned the world about the evils of communism, they took McCarthy's aggressive seemingly pro-American stance at face value, particularly since one of the few American politicians who did assist in the effort to bring Russian refugees to America was another Republican, California Senator William Knowland.

Russian Displaced Persons and the IRO

Largely due to the lobbying efforts of émigrés in the United States, who engaged Senator Knowland in their cause, Congress specifically included up to 4,000 immigration visas for DPS residing in China as of 1 July 1948 or who had left China but remained without a "permanent residence" in the 1950 amendment to the 1948 Displaced Persons Act.[37] The language was directed to assist the Russian DPS in Tubabao, and those remaining in China, in acquiring US visas. Importantly, that amendment also included a change to an eligibility requirement regarding a DP's location in Europe during and after the war, extending the timeline to include any DP in occupied zones in Western Europe as of 1 January 1949, thereby including persons who had fled Soviet persecution after the war.[38]

Senator Knowland's assistance was particularly significant since Russians coming from Asia received little notice, given relatively small numbers in comparison with DPS from Europe, or, alternatively, as noted above in Fulton Lewis Jr's comment, received negative attention. Highhanded treatment by IRO officials, combined with the lack of foresight and planning, contributed to an already existing sense of aggrieved alienation and persecution among the Russians as their stay in Tubabao lengthened. Incidents highlighted in Bologoff's retained correspondence indicate actions by IRO directors and staff at the camp that pointed to, at the very least, a remarkable lack of sensitivity towards a group of people that had been stateless and therefore effectively homeless for a generation.[39]

Bologoff regularly clashed with E. Bogen, the IRO resettlement officer, in Tubabao. A point of conflict was the process of obtaining US visas, which Bogen claimed were the responsibility of the individual, while simultaneously limiting refugees' ability to communicate with American consular officials.[40] The US immigration quota for Russians, whether they were Soviet citizens, Chinese citizens (referred to in official documents as "China White"), or stateless (the majority), was very small and backlogged, while the 1948 Displaced Persons Act in effect when the evacuation from Shanghai had taken place applied only to refugees in Europe.[41]

Further, IRO officials had made no cautionary statements to refugees, according to Bologoff, about age restrictions. Most male heads of families were World War I and Russian Civil War veterans, thus over forty-five years of age. Australia categorically refused to take men over forty-five and women over thirty-five years of age at the time (the term utilized by IRO officials was "over-aged").[42] Upon realizing Australian restrictions, Bogen told refugees in August of 1949, after several months in Tubabao when it became clear that many of the refugees would have trouble finding a recipient country, that the only option would be to resettle them in camps in Germany and Italy.[43] Russian diaspora networks around the world, however, considered that option unacceptable given attitudes towards Russians in Europe. Austrians, for example, refused to hire Russians even if work was available, and DPs opined that such refusal was a method to force them to go to the Soviet Union.[44] Moreover, émigrés were well aware of the repatriations of both Soviet and non-Soviet Russians, notably at Lienz in June of 1945, when British troops had forcibly repatriated thousands of Cossacks, leading to mass suicide. As many as 1,500 of the Russians at Tubabao were Cossacks, according to Bologoff.[45]

Although the refugees on Tubabao had built an array of facilities in the camp including two hospitals, dining rooms, a theater and cinema, police and fire departments, churches, a mosque, and schools, and had orchestrated a system of running water and electricity, overall conditions began to worsen almost immediately in the summer of 1949 because no plan had been put in place in the event of failure to resettle everyone within the stipulated four-month period. Bologoff noted that the tents IRO had provided were falling apart and did not protect from the elements.[46] IRO officials soon cut food rations by one third and the quality of food contributed to worsening health of even healthy people.[47] Everyday discomforts included insect infestations, lack of sufficient latrine facilities (two for every 500 people), and the lack of privacy, particularly for couples, who had to retreat to the jungle for intimate encounters, perilous due to the large number of insects and snakes, which "lacked any romantic sensibilities."[48]

The compromised health of some DPs, exacerbated by the conditions, was also a cause for concern as the United States, Canada, and Australia refused to accept immigrants with contagious diseases. Health care provided at the camp was often rudimentary and tuberculosis a common ailment. It is indicative that the DPs had to establish a cemetery upon arrival.[49] Pundit Fulton Lewis Jr, however, in cautioning Americans about allowing Russians at Tubabao to come to America, trivialized their plight, in addition to casting suspicion on their political affiliations, noting that they wanted "to get out of the Philippines" because "they have a fear of tropical diseases," as if they were free to travel about at will.[50] Archbishop John had noted, in fact, that the refugees were essentially prisoners, as they were not allowed out of the camp area. Moreover, an atmosphere of suspicion, exacerbated by IRO officials, affected morale. IRO officials censored mail and camp residents could only write outgoing mail in English.[51] A letter from Peter Tretiakoff to his captain (both Cossacks) stated that he discovered piles of intercepted mail by Bogen's hut.[52]

Refugees of Asiatic Descent

In mid-1950, approximately 2,500 of the original 6,000 people remained on Tubabao, and the process of amending the 1948 DP Act was one they followed closely. Senator Pat McCarran, the main author of the 1950 Internal Security (McCarran) Act, repeatedly attempted to quash the amendment, fearing that the bill would allow fifth columnists disguised as DPS to enter the United States.[53] Once the bill did pass, President Truman signed it into law on 16 June 1950, and approximately 140,000 eligible DPS had to find individuals or organizations to sponsor them either through assurances or affidavits, forms of visa support.[54]

Language in the legislation that referenced people of "European" origin became a source of concern for some refugees in Tubabao, who asked Bologoff to clarify the issue of "Asiatic descent." That issue, however, had already arisen in May of 1949. Major General John S. Wood had written to the DP commissioner in Washington, DC:

> In response to your inquiry of 22 May, I can now report on the basis of a cable which we have received yesterday from our office in Philippines that "Refugees of Asiatic decent [sic] and refugees not holding valid national passports had been informed that, until bill is passed, no information as to eligibility to immigrate in [sic] America could be given."
> This cable also states "no refugees informed that he is INELIGIBLE under the I.R.O. or ineligible immigration America account Asiatic origin."

The New Exodus and the Post-War Russian Community | **279**

> With specific reference to Marguerite Art[a]monoff, this cable reports
> that she had "registered in 1946 China white quota and when she
> herself requested information whether eligible China racial quota
> [o]n account Asiatic origin, consul replied "yes.""[55]

Wood referenced both ethnic/racial origins and citizenship status (i.e.,
national passports) here, which were two different issues. The first was
an issue of continuing discriminatory policies with respect to allowing
entrance of Asian people into the United States, while the second had to
do with the "stateless" nature of most Russians. By 1949, some Russian
émigrés in China had taken Chinese or Soviet citizenship, and the latter
would be a problem for security reasons for those wishing to enter the
United States, particularly after the passage of the 1950 Internal Security
Act. US State Department official H.J. L'Heureux assured Archbishop
John, in response to the latter's inquiry, that persons who had held
Chinese or Soviet passports as of 1 June 1948, but who renounced those
citizenships, were eligible to receive US visas under the amended DP Act.
In practice, however, US officials considered Soviet passport holders
security risks.[56] By this time, however, US immigration officials were
familiar with ethnic Russians who held Chinese citizenship. The specific
reference to Marguerite Artamonoff indicated that she was uncertain
about her status on "account [of her] Asiatic origin" despite having
registered as an applicant for a US quota immigration visa (likely at the
US consulate in Shanghai) in 1946.

In May of 1950, Archbishop John wrote to Senator Knowland, informing him that the IRO representative at Tubabao had called "every person
in alphabetic[al] order for the questioning of their origin," and "Mrs. M.
Artamonoff née Choglokoff was officially informed that she cannot be admitted according to the new law as she was born in China." The archbishop
went on to say that Artamonoff had been born to a refugee family in China
after the Russian Revolution and graduated from the Russian high school
in Shanghai.[57] His support of her as a person of Russian heritage, however,
mentioned nothing about her citizenship and it is therefore unclear why
she, specifically, was singled out: as noted, many Russians had been born
in China since 1900 and a substantial number had already immigrated to
the United States in the inter-war era. Therefore, the actual issue here had
to have been the perception that Artamonoff did not "look European," and
IRO representatives utilized her case as a warning that stateless Russians

born in China who possibly had "Asiatic origins" based on physiognomy would be barred from entering the United States. The archbishop, in his response, focused on proving that Artamonoff was a China-born member of the Russian community (e.g., she attended a Russian high school), ignoring the reference to ethnicity (i.e., possible "Asiatic" descent).[58]

A copy of that same letter from Wood to Rosenfeld but re-dated May of 1950 appeared to have been sent to Bologoff in the period when IRO officials at the camp were interrogating Russians with respect to their "origins." On that copy, a handwritten notation in Russian beneath the original text stated: "According to a verbal explanation from the IRO, there are no restrictions for individuals with Chinese blood." Further, a typed phrase in English on the bottom of the letter added "IRO from Geneva informed children under 21 considered eligible by IRO and IRO representative on Philippines properly advised," which, given the context, refers to people under age twenty-one who might have been of "Asiatic" origin.[59] Nevertheless, Bologoff again wrote to the archbishop in June 1950 asking him to clarify the matter despite a telegram from Senator Knowland stating that all the refugees on Tubabao, regardless of race or ethnicity, were eligible for admission under the new DP law. Bologoff likely feared, given past issues with IRO personnel, that "verbal" assurances meant little and that, depending on the interpretation of the language as he read it, people of Asian background might be excluded. His own interpretation of "Asian background" seemed to include those Russians born in China, but some Russians residing in China, whatever their place of birth, were not necessarily of Slavic (i.e., "European") origin alone. He added that "one might come to the conclusion that we are not included at all," seeming to refer to the fact that the Russians at Tubabao were generally from geographic Asia (i.e., Siberia) or China by birth, and therefore not "European" in this interpretation.[60]

As it happened, Marguerite Artamonoff and her husband were among the first in a group to get their visas, and departed from Manila in September of 1950, settling in San Francisco.[61] Artamonoff's concerns, exacerbated by IRO officials, about not being allowed entry into the United States, then, were happily unfounded, but why those concerns kept re-emerging on Tubabao indicated the uncertainty of IRO officials about the status of persons whose "European" origins were somehow under question. These officials further exacerbated paranoia and fears of refugees through miscommunication about their status vis-à-vis entry into the United States when their ethnic/racial background was not

The New Exodus and the Post-War Russian Community | **281**

sufficiently "European," or in American terms, "white," at least in the eyes of those officials.

That uncertainty and miscommunication, as well as a tentative effort to avoid the entire question by leaving people of possibly Asian origins in the Philippines, was particularly relevant when considering the cable cited at the beginning of this chapter from IRO headquarters in Geneva and the sentence added on to Major General Wood's letter to the DP commissioner referencing refugees under the age of twenty-one. Those refugees in question were the orphans of St Tikhon-Zadonsk Orphanage, to whom camp officials persisted in referring as "unaccompanied," spurring Archbishop John to send angry letters and cables objecting to that term to IRO officials, as it indicated, in his view, the initiation of efforts to break up the orphanage in anticipation of closure of the camp.[62] Those efforts began to take shape in May of 1950, with Bologoff noting pressures exerted (by unspecified parties) on the orphanage school. Bologoff added ominously that it was not yet a case of "open conflict," but that he would send a telegram to the archbishop if things changed.[63]

Soon after, in the summer of 1950, Hieromonk Modest, a member of the Russian Orthodox clergy and orphanage employee at Tubabao, engaged in a running battle with IRO officials David Karber, the camp's welfare officer, and Percy Snape, the camp director, regarding the care of the children. Snape and Karber issued orders to effectively break up the orphanage, moving the older children out. Archbishop John, informed of their efforts, declared the attempts to destroy the unity of the church's institutions as an attack on the church, while eleven of the orphanage children signed a letter to Snape asking to remain at the orphanage, noting that he was "ignorant of our way of living." Snape, referring to the children as "unfortunate," and including a veiled threat that the IRO was paying for their accommodations, food, and clothing, claimed that his measures would improve the children's "education and morals," implying that orphanage personnel were not doing their job in that regard.[64]

The archbishop had correctly surmised from these exchanges that officials did not want to take any chances that some complication with resettlement of the children might interfere with the planned closing of the camp (in place long after the original four-month stipulation), and splitting up the children would facilitate placing them in institutions in the Philippines or elsewhere if they were not allowed to enter the United States. The added sentence in the text of Wood's letter about acceptance of all persons under aged twenty-one notwithstanding, the varied ethnic backgrounds of the children seemed to concern someone in the IRO chain of command.

In order that all the children gain entry into the United States, the narrative to which Russian orphanage officials had to adhere was that they were orphaned children with at least one biological parent an ethnic Russian. The actual case for some of the children, however, was that both parents may have been ethnic Chinese. Several of the orphans, for example, had been "brought to the orphanage" during World War II as their parents had either been killed or had disappeared.[65] The situation in China under Japanese occupation in the 1930s and during the war was horrific, with rampant violence against Chinese civilians by Japanese authorities, including Japanese-run concentration camps.[66] The Tikhon-Zadonsk Orphanage had cared for approximately 1,000 children since its founding, and the archbishop personally searched for abandoned infants in the streets of Shanghai, bringing them to the orphanage.[67] As the children were in the orphanage at the time of evacuation in 1949 because they had no family able to take them, the archbishop refused to leave any of them behind in the midst of a civil war, and their ethnic background, in his view, was completely irrelevant.[68]

Archbishop John's resistance to breaking up the orphanage ensured that the children did come to San Francisco, where they initially lived at the newly established St Tikhon's orphanage on Balboa Street and 15th Avenue, the building housing St Tikhon of Zadonsk Russian Orthodox Church today.[69] Twenty-one of the children traveled together on the USNS *General W.G. Haan*, docking in January 1951 (table 9.1). Unlike the conflicted atmosphere on Tubabao, the relationship with IRO officials on board ship appeared to be friendly on both sides. The passengers published a newsletter "Our Herald" in which the IRO escort officers wrote fond notes to them.[70]

Adjustment to life in the United States was difficult for the orphans, however. Interviewed by a reporter several months after arrival, Sergei Grigorieff said that he liked "Shanghai better" than San Francisco. The Perieff brothers expressed a desire to join their mother in Australia. The reporter noted erroneously that the children had been "born in Shanghai of Russian parents or Russian fathers and Oriental mothers," an assumption which apparently explained to his satisfaction why many of them were (in his view) Asian despite having Russian surnames, an echo of the discussion regarding the ethnic heritage of Native Alaskan and Creole boys in San Francisco in the 1890s who had "Russian" names. Commenting

The New Exodus and the Post-War Russian Community | **283**

Table 9.1 Transports carrying Russian displaced persons
from Philippine Islands, 1950–52

Vessel	Date of arrival, SF	
SS *General W.H. Gordon*	23 September 1950	Included small number of DPS
USNS *General H.I. Hersey*	30 November 1950	IRO charter/carrying 620 DPS
USAT *General W.G. Haan*	25 January 1951	IRO charter/carrying 1106 DPS
General Black	14 June 1951	IRO charter/carrying 490 DPS
Flying Tiger Aircraft	28 July 1951	IRO charter/carrying 50 DPS
Flying Tiger Aircraft	8 November 1951	IRO charter/carrying 69 DPS
Approximately 80 DPS arrived on various other transports in 1951 and 1952		

Sources: 1950–51 Report, Federation of Russian Charitable Organizations Records, Box 1:5;
Borzov Papers, Box 18:2, HIA.

that the children were slow to smile, he blamed the "dreary routine" of their lives at the orphanage where they had to work and go to school year-round to catch up and learn English.[71] The reporter, however, inadvertently touched on an issue that affected all Russian refugees. Years of uncertainty, displacement, and trauma were not wiped away simply because they had managed to get into the United States. For the orphans, the process of obtaining visas had also been tainted by racist attitudes and policies of US officials, which, at least at some point, they must have encountered first-hand.

The subtitle of the reporter's article, "Displaced youngsters have hard time getting adjusted in Orthodox Home," implied that it was the "Orthodox home" that was the problem for the orphans, when in actuality it was likely everything else: a new environment, a new language to learn, and a sense of isolation in an alien country.[72] A few of the older orphans left the home almost immediately, with some of the boys joining the military and several of the girls marrying. Some remained in San Francisco and continued involvement in Russian community institutions and events. Others married non-Russians and/or moved away, losing contact with the community, but all, by and large, remained in the United States despite the initial lack of enthusiasm.[73]

Three Perspectives on Russian Americanism

Nikolai Massenkoff (1938–2020), the youngest of three siblings at the orphanage, built a successful performing career that spanned five decades. His command of English was very poor initially and he spent his first years in school in San Francisco in a state of confusion. There were no bilingual programs and he felt "very lost." By the time he enrolled at George Washington High School, however, a school many Russian teenagers attended, he felt comfortable speaking English. He also attended the church school at the Fulton Street Holy Virgin Cathedral, maintaining his Russian language skills. After high school, he worked at as series of jobs: as a theater usher, a bicycle delivery person, and a busboy at Manning's Coffee Café to earn money to go to San Francisco City College where he studied music and drama. He was student director of the orchestra and earned a teaching credential. In the 1960s, he joined the reserve as he did not wish to fight in the Vietnam War, and he was assigned to the psychological warfare unit at the Presidio in San Francisco.[74]

The 1960s in San Francisco, with the compelling manifestations of the Black Power and Chicano Power movements, which spoke to empowerment of marginalized groups, motivated him to dedicate himself to his professional performing career, wishing to "express Russian musical culture to the world." Massenkoff's identification with the noted political movements, movements that likely filled many Russian Americans with horror in view of their connection to radical ideologies, may have been linked to his own heritage. His mother was of Indigenous Siberian heritage and his father was of Russian and Mongolian ancestry.[75] Massenkoff identified as Russian, and was Russian culturally and ethnically, but perhaps felt a connection to groups who were expressing their dissatisfaction with marginalization in American society, indicating an acknowledgment of exposure to racism in his own life.[76] His perspective varied considerably from the developing conception of Russian-American identity that began to prevail in the Russian community at large in the post-war period.

The prevailing nostalgic narrative of the San Francisco inter-war community dominating cultural remembrance, which had included a marked sense of repentance with respect to how Russia had been "lost," receded in the post-war period in the face of a narrative that Russia had been "taken" by satanic forces, bent on destroying true Russian culture. For some who had arrived in the inter-war period, even with acculturation America remained an alien land and, as adults, their sense of not quite

The New Exodus and the Post-War Russian Community | **285**

belonging evolved into resentment of having to live their lives as out-siders. In this narrative, the evil forces that had driven their parents out of a putatively benign imperial hegemony were now setting their sights on the rest of the world, including America, while political figures such as McCarthy were rightfully attempting to stop them. Viewing an au-tocratic monarchy as the "natural" form of government for Russia had permeated narratives among monarchist groups, such as the Mladorossy, for example, who had a small contingent in inter-war San Francisco. In the post-World War II period, new arrivals reinforced that militant and neo-monarchist stance, envisioning yet another world war as a precursor to the overthrow of Soviet power and a neo-monarchist Russia rising from the ashes. The neo-monarchist outlook went hand in hand with the per-spective of inter-war community leader General Kiyaschenko (chapter 6), for example, who compartmentalized his nostalgic recollections of Rus-sia as indivisible from autocratic monarchy.[77]

While the concept of Russia "out of time and space" spoke to reflective nostalgia, as discussed by Boym, neo-monarchist ideations viewed the past through the prism of restorative nostalgia, as a "perfect snapshot": an Imperial Russia frozen in time to be restored to glory.[78] As Boym notes, these "two kinds of nostalgia are not absolute" but are "tendencies," with one or the other dominating amongst émigrés as they sought to make sense of their longing for the homeland against the reality of no return.[79] Both tendencies allowed for maintaining a link to that homeland through intra-émigré discourse, telling "different stories" about the history and future of Russia.[80] Reflective nostalgia tended to focus on continuing cultural practices to preserve a "Russian self" (i.e., a persona that was "Russian in spirit") both within family units and the émigré community at large. Such practices, including, for example, the education of children in Russian schools to preserve language and cultural heritage; maintain-ing traditions, such as celebrating Orthodox holidays (e.g., Christmas, which falls on January 7 in the Julian calendar) in addition to "American" holidays; and baptizing children in the Russian Orthodox Church, even when one spouse was not Orthodox. These practices fell as well within the purview of restorative nostalgia, along with the utilization of monar-chist/nationalist symbols, interpreting Orthodoxy as a faith historically and integrally intertwined both with the Russian monarchy and, impor-tantly, with "real" Russian identity. Groups such as the Russian Scouts (discussed further below) blended homage to pre-revolutionary Russian institutions, reinventing a form of Russian nationalism and combining monarchist symbols with the American flag as part of a unifying credo in the post-World War II period, which involved a firm political anti-Soviet (and commensurately pro-American) stance within the Cold War paradigm. These were, in effect, the "new traditions" of which Boym speaks, "conservative" in their rooting in the "old" or "real" Russia in "modern" America, and "selective" in their representations of that Russia to the generation that had never experienced it but knew it only from the memories of their parents or grandparents.[81]

The prevalent inter-war narrative of a "lost" Russia had spoken to a sense of personal responsibility among the adult first generation – people who had lived under the old regime did not consider themselves disconnected from the series of events leading to the Bolshevik seizure of power. Perhaps through inaction or inertia, Russians in exile, in their perspective, had failed in their duty and "lost" Russia. Theodore Olferieff, a military officer from a noble family, described "the odor of death from a decomposing regime [of Nicholas II]," referencing the theme of Leo Tolstoy's play "The Living Corpse." Olferieff was convinced that "there was neither vision, nor belief, nor creative growth" in Russia during that regime. At the same time, he took responsibility, as a member of the elite, for the "sin" of maintaining a "long-dead system of government that exploited 150 million people."[82] Nikolay Borzov wrote to George Grebenstchikoff in response to the latter's nostalgic writings about the beauty of the Crimea: "you compel us to repent; you compel us to think about what was done."[83] The ideation of an Imagined Russia, existing as a mental territory in the perceptions of Russian émigrés in San Francisco, had provided comfort, as did the nebulous idea of "return" to the motherland at some undefined point in time.[84] The understanding that the destruction of their homeland had taken place on their watch, however, remained as an undercurrent in their narratives about that past. Hilary Teplitz, for example, noted poet Anna Akhmatova's condemnation of "Russian intellectuals" who left Russia as "betrayers of the Russian nation, the Russian people and themselves," a perspective which may have played upon feelings of guilt, responsibility, and repentance among some émigrés.[85]

That perspective began to lose ground in the face of the militant point of view among many Soviet DPs who understood first hand the role of terror in maintaining control in the USSR and who had suffered the trauma of living under that regime, as well as the trauma of displacement. Dubinets notes that "second-wavers ... felt only disdain – not a shred of nostalgia – for the Soviet regime."[86]

A similar perspective existed among incoming émigrés from Shanghai, many from military and/or Cossack families, who, like all those who experienced the Civil War, remembered the atrocities, and who had also spent the last twenty-five years as stateless, and therefore marginalized, persons and real or perceived targets of Soviet intelligence agencies. That perspective dovetailed with that of a certain contingent of San Francisco inter-war émigrés such as Victor Borzov and his brother Boris (1910–1979), who had arrived as young men, had chosen not to assimilate, and who, in the post-war period, began to view their Russian identity chiefly through the prism of an ideology of negation, "anti-communism," rather than through the identification with Russian cultural achievements that had been so critical to the inter-war community. Victor had graduated from UC Berkeley with an engineering degree and had a successful career. He referenced his efforts, however, to battle false narratives about pre-revolutionary Russia and Russian culture in America. His experience in the United States since his arrival in 1920, therefore, had exposed him to such narratives and stereotypes, a factor in causing feelings of alienation despite a relatively smooth path to financial/material stability and security, particularly when compared to those who were not able to enter the United States in the inter-war period.[87] As the Cold War ramped up, Russians in America acknowledged that wishing the Bolsheviks away had not worked, requiring a militant aggressive stance that went hand in hand with feelings of alienation or resentment.[88]

The two Borzov brothers exemplified the experience of many Russians arriving in San Francisco as young men or women with little or no personal memory of Russia. Although Russians who had been born in China identified as Russian, often living in Harbin, a city very "Russian" in character in that period, their memories of Russia and the accompanying nostalgia were nevertheless inherited, thus mytho-poetic as nostalgic reminiscences of a lost homeland tend to be.[89] Victor had been born in Russia but had left with his family for Harbin as a child, where Boris was born, leading to varying nostalgic ideations about Russia, learned from parents and their community.[90] Boris's inherited memories and absorbed nostalgic recollections did not include the repentance some older émigrés felt. His was a nostalgia fueled by resentment and a sense of alienation for having to live in America – to some degree, even, a resentment against his elders, who had "lost" Russia.[91] Boris never took US citizenship, and worked as a laborer, baker, and machinist. He also wrote poetry, much of which dealt with Russia under the yoke of communism: "Not for ourselves but for Russia of the future / We pray for the great day / When the Bolsheviks' lies are forgotten / Incinerated like a manuscript by fire"; "I do believe that evil shall not last / The day will come when evil shall be destroyed / And once again all our people shall turn to God / And the bells shall ring." In this poem, the destruction of evil is undefined; somehow the Bolsheviks would magically disappear, and church bells, symbolizing a return to the Orthodox faith, would ring once more. Boris also addressed his feelings of injury and alienation: "How many lies and how much ridicule we've heard / How many coarse and fatuous insults / We've suffered it all in the abroad / Our Russian heart aches with pain."[92]

By the late 1950s, Boris's focus became actively political, citing a speech in his writings, for example, about communist subversion in the United States by HUAC member Richard Arens and the Christian Anti-Communist Crusade as critical rallying points for Russians in America. Boris called on fellow Russians to liberate their brethren and proclaim their irreconcilability with those who had "taken our Russia from us."[93] In post-war narratives, the bitterness of loss, which Bazhenova had referenced in the context of healing in "Imagined Russia" among the natural landscapes of California, had not receded. Boris wrote of having to spend "our entire lives ... in foreign lands"; "And a bitter thought comes to me / I will not see Rus'... ever / I am fated, a sinful servant / To sleep on alien, not Russian, soil / And dreams of my beloved Russia / Fade away in the darkening gloom."[94] That bitterness fueled enthusiasm for militant action in the Cold War environment, which, ironically, targeted Russians and Slavs as untrustworthy.

In the developing perspective of some of those who had come of age in America, they now had to take a proactive role in the war against communism. That call to action found willing adherents in the Russian community and positive reinforcement from demagogues such as Tenney, or politicians such as Knowland, who saw Russian Americans as a small but dedicated contingent supporting the anti-communist cause. Russian young men who had arrived in the inter-war period and had been of age to serve in the US Armed Forces during World War II were another contingent in this new proactive anti-communist movement; in this case, both assimilating and taking on the anti-communist cause with fervor under the banner of American patriotism. Benjamin Lashkoff was born in the Amur region in 1921 and came to San Francisco with his mother and a brother in 1926. Three other brothers had arrived on USAT *Merritt* in 1923. Their father, a priest, and another brother had been killed in the

The New Exodus and the Post-War Russian Community | **289**

Soviet Union in 1924, reinforcing the narrative of the impossibility of reconciling with a brutal regime.[95]

Lashkoff's life choices indicated conscious efforts to maintain his Russian heritage as an American actively working against disruptive anti-American communist influences. Lashkoff and two of his brothers joined the US Army and fought in World War II. He then joined the San Francisco Police Department, earning "numerous commendations" for rescuing people from burning buildings and capturing criminals. He had a "reputation for unimpeachable honesty, integrity and hard work" and some even described him as "heroic." He also "worked in liaison with government agencies, including the FBI," and conducted surveillance of "militants and 'revolutionaries.'" In 1969, he, as an "intelligence expert," testified before the US Senate Permanent Sub-Committee on Investigations about Black Panther propaganda, which, in his testimony, "taught hatred, violence and revolutionary tactics to black children at breakfast meetings" in a San Francisco Catholic church. Lashkoff's work in intelligence and his testimony about the violent revolutionary aims of the Black Panthers spoke to official and public fears of the dangers of radical organizations in a time of great social upheaval. Protests against the Vietnam War, a war that politically conservative coalitions (with Russian Americans often among them) generally characterized as necessary to combat the spread of communism around the globe, were in full swing in this period. Lashkoff's efforts indicated that he felt his work in monitoring radical groups was both necessary and justified, both as a person of Russian heritage and as an American law enforcement officer.[96]

Of the Lashkoff brothers living in the Bay Area, Benjamin, whose wife was Lutheran, was the only one to baptize his son at the Holy Virgin Cathedral, indicating his adherence to Russian cultural traditions. He died of cancer in 1974, and the *panihida* (funeral service) was also held at the Holy Virgin Cathedral. He was interred at Serbian Cemetery as was his eldest brother Pavel, who was godfather to Benjamin's son.[97]

As an immigrant who was, in fact, a "victim of communism," who had fought for his adopted country, gained citizenship, and joined a law enforcement organization that upheld dominant culture norms, Benjamin likely considered that methods of illegal surveillance, utilized by the FBI in its Counter Intelligence Program (COINTELPRO, 1956–71) in which local police departments were involved, were justified in a period where American freedoms were under threat. The fact that those freedoms had historically not existed for all Americans, based on their identity as people of color, was of lesser importance, in his view, in the face of battling the communist evil.[98] By the time of the war in Vietnam, many Russian Americans in San Francisco, in the midst of the political and social unrest of the 1960s, likely agreed with him. In contrast, Massenkoff, whose own life had also been negatively impacted by the Bolshevik Revolution and the ensuing chaos, and who was also unequivocally loyal to his adopted country, nevertheless did have sympathy for historically oppressed Americans who sought social justice and equal treatment before the law, as noted in his recollections of the impact of the Black and Chicano Power movements on his own identity. At the root of this dichotomy in the perspectives of two people who both identified as Russian was the issue of race: Lashkoff's "whiteness" had likely never been in question, while Massenkoff's likely had been.

The Work of the Federation

According to Victor Borzov, the response from Russian Americans to help with sponsoring Russians remaining in Tubabao in 1950 was less than encouraging, with very few people willing to provide either assurances or affidavits. He interpreted this lack of enthusiasm as a character failing of Russian Americans, something with which Archbishop John agreed, noting that most Russians he had encountered in New York had "forgotten" that they were Russian, noting he was "stunned at the cold attitude of people, even those one would think would empathize and help."[99] Borzov's assessment was even more condemnatory, explaining it as a failing of Russians to unite, but the subtext implied that American values, which Russians had adopted in the Americanization process, were at the root of this failure to empathize with those less fortunate.[100] He saw the lack of engagement as a sign of the moral decline of Russians in America, using the circumstance to emphasize to Bologoff in his correspondence that he, Victor, was Bologoff's only hope because Victor, unlike other Russian Americans, had not "forgotten" that he was Russian.[101] Borzov's characterization omitted mention of those who did act as sponsors. Leonid Benthen, for example, who had arrived from Shanghai with his family in 1938, owned a successful jewelry and watch repair shop in the Fillmore and sponsored so many people after the war that the State Department forbade him to sponsor anyone else.[102]

A factor leading to a lack of enthusiasm for sponsorship may have had to do with the increasingly tense McCarthyist political environment.

The New Exodus and the Post-War Russian Community | 291

Even Russians who were citizens may have felt that getting involved with persons unknown to them might jeopardize the situation of their own families – what if they sponsored someone who drew the attention of the FBI? The McCarran Act had, among other things, expanded "the state's powers of deportation" and those who had recently obtained citizenship might have felt lingering insecurity.[103] The legacy of fear was not limited to Russian Americans: as late as 1961, New York residents, fearing persecution as possible communists, declined to sign a petition to stop the spread of nuclear weapons even though they supported it in principle.[104] Russian Americans, however, felt even more pressure to not only publicly display unwavering loyalty but to avoid any encounters with government agencies.

The Federation, despite the difficulties of running what was, in essence, a "shoestring operation" in San Francisco, was nevertheless successful in its efforts to find sponsorship for most (though not all) of the remaining Russian DPS on Tubabao, as well as other refugees in the Far East.[105] Once refugees came to San Francisco, the Federation provided loans and paid for initial hotel and maintenance costs through the San Francisco branch of the Russian-American Union. The Federation established close contacts with other organizations involved in resettling Displaced Persons, notably Church World Services, and the National Catholic Welfare Council.[106]

Cognizant of anti-DP and anti-Russian feeling, Borzov contacted American press agencies to cover the arrivals of the refugees, as an "anti-communist" contingent. Consequently, he asserted, "all the refugees were welcomed with joy and people made efforts to help them," the three largest ship transport arrivals receiving positive coverage.[107] A reporter covering the first group arrival, however, true to form, noted that "aristocrats and peasants alike" lived together in the camps at Tubabao although few, if any, of either class were part of the group.[108]

Despite the public welcome, individuals were detained due to security issues, and Borzov admitted that it was "sometimes impossible" to help them, implying that such cases led to exclusion.[109] The Saranin family arrived in San Francisco directly from Shanghai, for example, in May of 1950. Held for thirteen months as "bad security risks," they claimed to be victims of "malicious gossip." Their appeals were denied, and they were deported to Hong Kong.[110] Borzov also asserted, however, that people were "quickly released" *unless* there was a security issue, but that was not necessarily the case and, due to a lack of transparency, reasons for detention were not clear.[111]

Immigration authorities detained sixteen people "for secondary inspection" among those who arrived from Tubabao on a chartered *Flying Tiger* aircraft in November of 1951. Although security issues may have been in play for some, the detention of women traveling alone who were over forty years of age seemed to indicate other concerns having to do, once again, with gender and age (see table 9.2). Anastasia Volhontseff arrived alone as she had remained in Tubabao to make arrangements for her daughter, who had to go to Japan for TB treatment. Anastasia's husband and other children had arrived previously, and, though detained, she was released the following day. Other women traveling alone, however, all fifty years old or older, were detained for three to eight months or more.[112]

In February of 1952, thirty-three people in the immigration jail in San Francisco signed a letter directed to Archbishop Tikhon at the Holy Virgin Cathedral begging for assistance in obtaining release – immigration authorities had not told them why they were being held or for how long. Some had been in detention for eight months. At least two families in detention included minor children. A few people were released at the end of February, possibly in response to inquiries into the matter from Senator Knowland's office: a letter to Archbishop Tikhon noted that that the situation was "receiving the Senator's careful attention."[113]

The Politics of Russian Refugee Resettlement

The "success" stories of those who negotiated the circuitous path to US residency (i.e., families who arrived safely) were expeditiously admitted, obtaining housing and employment, overshadowed the stories of those whose path was rockier. At times the actuality of arrival for Russian DPs seemed deliberately obscured in public discourse. Tatiana Radina, for example, who arrived in July of 1951, was the focus of a newspaper article story titled "41 White Russ Refugees Find Freedom Here," including a photo of her smiling happily and shaking the hand of the pilot who had flown a Russian group from Manila on the last leg of their escape from the "Red terror." Radina, however, was detained in jail until 27 February 1952, a detail not publicized. According to the article, Radina had been "seriously ill," which may have been a factor in her detention.[114]

Alexandra Tolstoy, whose organization had a role in the resettlement of the above group, eschewed politicizing the refugee crisis, recognizing, perhaps, the danger of making disempowered people "pawns" among competing narratives that politicians utilized to pursue a particular agenda,

Table 9.2 Displaced persons arriving from Tubabao detained prior to US entry

Name and age (if relevant)	Arrival	Date entered US/ period of detention
Lebedeff family	USNS *General Black*, 14 June 1951	18–19 March 1952 (9+ months)
Zolotovsky family		3 March 1952 (8+ months)
Sentianin family		27 February 1952 (8+ months)
Vedensky family		28 February 1952 (8+ months)
S. Drobishovskaya-Kalinkina, 62		In custody as of 20 February 1952 (8+ months); release date unknown
T. Radina, 48	Flying Tiger airplane, 28 July 1951	27 February 1952 (7+ months)
V. Martinoff		In custody as of 20 February 1952; release date unknown (signature on letter to Archbishop Tikhon but no other identifying information)
Shtogrin family	Flying Tiger airplane, 8 November 1951	24 March 1952 (4+ months)
S. Gladkoff, 56 (wife Anna and children arrived on *General Black* 14 June 1951)		27 February 1952 (3+months)
Sheveloff family		3 March 1952 (3+ months) (husband)
		30 November 1951 (22 days) (wife and child)
G. Sheveloff (spouse arrived on *General Black* 14 June 1951)	Philippine Airlines flight, 7 November 1951	28 February 1952 (3+ months)
K. Sheveloff, 66		Unknown
E. Petrikina, 50	Flying Tiger airplane, 8 November 1951	27 February 1952 (3+ months)
S. Raudsoo, 47		28 February 1952 (3+ months)
N. Mazurkevich, 45 or 53		Released prior to 20 February 1952: length of detention unknown
Veretennikoff family		26 November 1951 (18 days)
A. Klukhanoff, 53 (spouse arrived on *General Haan* 25 January 1951)		9 November 1951 (1 day)
A.Volhontseff, 43 (spouse, children arrived on *General Black* 14 June 1951)		9 November 1951 (1 day)
T. Narewski, 61		Detained; release date unknown

Table 9.2 (continued)

Zoob family	*President Cleveland*, 6 or 11 December 1951	15 May 1952 (5+ months)
A.Petrenko (?), 67	Unknown (with spouse on passenger manifests from Tubabao to the Dominican Republic in 1949 but both later in San Francisco as death records indicate they both passed away in California).	In custody as of 20 February 1952; release date unknown (signature on letter to Archbishop Tikhon).
Petrenko family	ss *William Luckenbach* scheduled to leave Manila, P.I. 21 June 1951; arrival in San Francisco July 1951?	18 March 1952 (8+ months if arrived in July 1951)
Rubanoff family		27 February 1952 (7+ months if arrived July 1951)
A. Sokoloff	Unknown	In custody as of 20 February 1952; release date unknown (signature on letter to Archbishop Tikhon but no other identifying information)
N.I. Sokoloff		"
N. Tetsheff (?)		"
D.K. Loh???		"

Sources: Signatories of letter to Archbishop Tikhon, 20 February 1952. Archbishop Tikhon (Troitsky) Papers, Box 2:73, wda; "Passenger Lists of Vessels Arriving at San Francisco, California," nai 4498993; "Passenger Manifests of Airplanes Arriving at San Francisco, California," nai 2945502.

leading to possibly baseless detention. In contrast, Prince Sergei Belosselsky-Belozersky wrote to Leon Nicoli in 1951: "I am in complete agreement with you that philanthropy should not be disassociated from politics. On the contrary, I believe that we will be able to interest the American public in the matter of assisting Russians only when [the American public] understands that by assisting victims of communism they are assisting in the battle against communism."[115] Belosselsky's and Nicoli's hopes did not come to fruition as the American public largely ignored the plight of the "victims of communism" (Russian DPs) to which Belosselsky referred. Official and public fears of communist infiltration were playing out in public discourse and taking precedence over humanitarian concerns. Both Russian immigrants and Russian Americans were often targets of suspicion.

The New Exodus and the Post-War Russian Community | **295**

Admittedly, as San Francisco had had a long-time White Russian community, local government officials did acknowledge their plight in China. In December of 1948, San Francisco supervisor Chester Macphee had proposed a resolution to aid White Russians in China by including them in the category of DPs. As uplifting as that may have been for the Russian community, the resolution carried no real weight, simply asking "Congress to help in removing White Russian refugees from the path of the Communist advances in China," which happened two years later when the 1950 DP Act was passed.[116] It is a testament to the efforts of Russian Americans that the US Congress passed the legislation specifically to allow Russian DPs to apply for US visas, but it was largely just that, a Russian-American effort. The board president of the International Institute of San Francisco acknowledged in 1945 that "American Russians of San Francisco" raised awareness about Russian refugees both in Europe, and particularly Asia, among government officials and aid organizations.[117] There was no sense of urgency among those officials, however, leading to a disjointed global humanitarian aid response and commensurate chaos in the evacuation from Shanghai. Tellingly, in direct contradiction to the board president's earlier recognition of Russian-American efforts, a 1951 International Institute report took primary credit, along with the Travelers Aid Society, for bringing Russian refugees from Tubabao to the United States, noting, in passing, that "many Russians were involved," but omitting any mention of the Federation.[118]

Institute officials, in fact, long involved in social work in San Francisco, "experienced great difficulties in trying to interest Americans to become members of the [Russian-American Advisory] Council" in 1945 when the effort to assist Russian refugees began to gear up.[119] The initial purpose of the council was to address existing social problems, including poverty and unemployment, of the Russian community, but after the council formed, the issue of helping Russian refugees dominated its efforts. A rough draft of an Institute report, written by Irina Obolianinoff, an émigré who arrived in San Francisco in 1939, illustrated bluntly what socially conscious Americans, presumably those the Institute invited to join, thought about Russians in 1945:

> As it usually happens, the Americans who were interested in Russians were more concerned about the present Russians of [the] USSR and would not accept the membership ... in ... the Council when they found that the Council was to work with ... [Russian Americans].

In their opinion the Russians of SF were not colorful or picturesque enough. For others the problems of the Russians of SF did not seem urgent enough ... Other Americans felt the problems of Russians are of chronic nature and there was nothing spectacular in helping them. There were also Americans, who not being familiar with the Russian community in SF, refused to serve on the Council for fear of getting "mixed up" in something Russian. It did not matter to them whether these Russians were immigrants or Communists; *to these Americans all Russians were dangerous* ... Those Americans who usually took interest in foreign groups were liberal. At the same time, they were a group that would rather be interested in modern Russia's latest developments than in the Russian community in SF which by its nature was a group of conservative Russians vs. the Russians of USSR.[120]

Obolianinoff's assessment encapsulated many of the attitudes about foreigners among Americans, which Russians, many of whom had been living and working in the San Francisco Bay Area for more than twenty years, still were in their eyes. Now, however, outside of parades or entertaining events, Russian Americans were no longer sufficiently "colorful and picturesque." Further, their problems were "chronic" and therefore likely their own fault: groups with "chronic" problems clearly had not assimilated and therefore could not function effectively in American society. Significantly, "all Russians were dangerous" to some Americans, who saw them as either perennial outsiders or radicals. The "danger" was political as early as 1945, despite the fact that McCarthyism as a political force had not yet come into play, feeding into later paranoia. The perception of the political unreliability of White Russians escalated in line with increasing McCarthyist rhetoric: in 1953, those who had recently arrived in the Bay Area, according to a reporter, were "having a rough time finding jobs and convincing some Americans that they are not Communists."[121] On the other side of the political spectrum, as noted in Obolianinoff's report, liberally-inclined Americans had no interest in associating with the perceived reactionaries that émigrés supposedly were – an assessment that Obolianinoff, who had not experienced the Russian community in the inter-war period, echoed, indicating that the heterogenous nature of that community was already obscured.[122]

Suspicion of Russians

Public discourse about the "Red" threat permeated newspaper coverage, spurred by the deteriorating relationship with the Soviet Union, the war in Korea, the communist victory in China, and by the rise in and focus on McCarthyist tactics within the United States to ferret out spies and communist agents.[123] None of these issues, however, connected the plight of Russian DPs with the battle to stop the spread of international communism. Moreover, if "White Russians" were mentioned at all in popular culture, it was in the context of untrustworthiness and Cold War espionage. Philip Wylie, author of novel *The Smuggled Atom Bomb* (1951), wrote: "any Russian is suspicious, even those who claim to be White Russian."[124]

Locally, an art exhibit review by watercolor artist and *San Mateo Times* columnist Nadia Didenko, prompted a reader to accuse Didenko of forcing "abstract things down American throats" in the manner of "Russian Communists." The reader clearly drew a connection between Didenko's Slavic surname and her supposed affiliation with "Russian communists."[125] Didenko had arrived in the United States in 1920 as the bride of American Expeditionary Force soldier George Washington Graham, almost forty years prior, and had used her married name, despite divorcing Graham early on, until she began working as an artist later in life.[126] Reverting to her family surname may have been a way to reconnect with her heritage, but was a lightning rod for those who equated people of Russian heritage with "Communists," implying that she was attempting to further the agenda of the Soviet Union through her art.

Moreover, any links to Russian language material became problematic. Nadia Shapiro, who did not scare easily, and worked for the US government after World War II, nevertheless chose not to subscribe to Russian-language publications after unknown parties began to interfere with deliveries of Russian-language newspapers to her home, deliberately mangling them. She took the path of least resistance, and her action indicated the self-regulation Russian Americans undertook to avoid scrutiny in everyday life.[127] But even as early as 1937, Gregory Tschebotarieff, noted earlier, a civil engineer hired by Princeton University, recalled that "because of my Russian origin, I deliberately steered away from classified subjects" when selecting research projects.[128] His self-restriction to forestall possible problems existed even then, indicating an acute awareness of Russians' tenuous position in inter-war America, which only increased after the war.

US State Department employee Vladimir Toumanoff, who came to the United States with his parents from Constantinople in 1923 and grew up in Boston, was targeted by McCarthy's Committee in 1953 based on his Russian surname. First interrogated by McCarthy's staff, Roy M. Cohn, Donald Surine, and G. David Schine, in a "windowless room somewhere down in the basement of the Capitol building," he was questioned about his family and personal history. The ensuing "investigation" led to nothing, but his career stalled, his family receiving anonymous threatening phone calls. Toumanoff's uncle, Leo, a librarian, was a witness on the naturalization petition of Lev Zaitzevsky, a Russian student who came to San Francisco in 1923, and who attended MIT in the 1930s, indicating the interconnected nature of the diaspora and consequent facilitation of communications about such incidents amongst Russians in America.[129]

The "victims of communism," émigrés and DPs trying to come to the United States, suffered the brunt of paranoia, intertwined as it was with xenophobia, with instances of Soviet DPs refused US visas based on their possible untrustworthiness.[130] Moreover, efforts to avoid forced repatriation to the Soviet Union and commensurate efforts to get out of Europe led to the necessity of elaborate deceptions about DPs' backgrounds, complicating their lives even once they reached America. The case of Rodion Beresov (1896–1988), who lived in San Francisco intermittently in the 1950s, illustrated the complexity of a DP's position in every stage of the immigration process. Born to a peasant family in Samara in 1896, Beresov served in the Red Army in 1941, when he was captured by the Germans and sent to a POW camp. He left the camp ahead of advancing Soviet forces, crossed the border into what was then Byelorussia, and continued to Austria, living in a DP camp after the war. With the assistance of inter-war émigrés, who forged documents or coached their Soviet brethren, he and other DPs avoided repatriation by claiming to be inter-war émigrés.[131] Beresov told interrogators that he had surreptitiously crossed the Soviet border near Minsk in 1937, afterwards living in Vilnius. He went through several interrogations, both by Soviet authorities and the American Counterintelligence Corps, but finally obtained a US visa and arrived in New York in 1949.[132]

Beresov received an offer to work at the Army Language School in Monterey, California upon arrival and flew there at his own expense. A religious man, he was stricken with guilt for entering the United States under false circumstances and decided to confess, telling his employers at the school that he wanted to start his life in America with a clean slate.

The New Exodus and the Post-War Russian Community | **299**

They promptly fired him and sent his papers to the INS office in San Francisco. The INS official later told Beresov, to his horror, that confessing had been a quixotic thing to do, acknowledging the hypocritical nature of the entire process on the part of American authorities.[133]

In the next six years, Beresov was jailed, released on bond, tried, convicted of visa fraud, and ultimately received a notice of final deportation. He worked an impressive array of low-paying jobs, wrote and published several books, and traveled around the United States and even Canada. His case was distinctive enough that he testified to Congress in May of 1956 in support of a law sponsored by then Senator John F. Kennedy to allow DPs, who had falsified their biographical information for fear of forced repatriation, to correct their records and remain in the United States. Beresov became a US citizen in 1958. Throughout his ordeal, Beresov maintained that he understood why American officials had to vet immigrants, either not realizing or declining to point out the hypocrisy of the process. Nevertheless, that process had a great impact on his mental health. American authorities had been integrally involved in his fate since 1945, wielding the power, if they chose to do so, to send him back to a regime that US officials proclaimed a seminal threat to human rights and freedoms.[134]

Not all DPs could "pass" as inter-war émigrés in Europe, and many from the Soviet Union claimed Polish nationality to avoid repatriation, altering vital information and ethnicity as necessary. Gregory Bogdanoff (1926–2006), an *Ostarbeiter* in Germany during the war who had been born in a small village in eastern Ukraine, provided the city of Luck (Lutsk), then in Poland, as his place of birth in his 1945 DP registration record. He identified as "Polish Ukrainian" and noted Ukrainian as his native language. He did not write in English in 1945 so someone else filled out the initial document for him, likely selecting Lutsk arbitrarily. By the time he emigrated to the United States, he had become "Russian," possibly because he had lived at Fischbek, a DP camp near Hamburg with a mostly Russian DP population. His brother Yefim, who emigrated in 1949, remained "Polish" in his papers. Gregory shortened his surname, changed his date of birth, and provided false parental names. In his 1957 US naturalization petition, Gregory changed his place of birth to Kharkov. Apart from avoiding repatriation, falsifying information served to protect family still in the Soviet Union, with whom, incidentally, Gregory did not initiate contact until the late 1990s, after the dissolution of the USSR. Gregory's *koom*, Igor Prohoda (1924–2011), born in Poltava, Ukraine, gave his place of birth at US naturalization as Kraków, Poland.

He indicated that the weight of the guilt of providing false information when he naturalized remained with him throughout his life, since he, unlike Beresov, chose not to "confess."[135]

In the debates about then Senator Kennedy's proposed law, the main point in favor of its passage was that DPs were vulnerable to blackmail by Soviet agents who might threaten to expose them, not that the Yalta Agreement forced people to lie to avoid repatriation to a regime that routinely violated human rights. DPs certainly understood the hypocrisy of the process but feared to criticize US policies due to their untenable situation. Nevertheless, a Russian émigré journalist pointed out that Americans interrogating Russian DPs utilized "what smelled like Chekist [Soviet secret police] techniques a mile off." Such discourse was limited to those who had no intentions of applying for a US visa, or who were confident in their anonymity.[136]

The Russian Center under the American Gaze

Avoiding criticism of US policy to preclude accusations of anti-Americanism became part of Russian-American narratives reinforcing and unquestioningly supporting the good vs evil US/Soviet binary that characterized the Cold War. Since the Americans were the "good guys," everything about American life was good and those who thought or spoke otherwise were malcontents or subversives within that narrative. Moreover, as early as 1948, US policymakers considered any opposition to Cold War policies, including in the context of the peace movement, "by definition subversive."[137] Events within the San Francisco Russian community reinforced the logic of adhering to the stance supporting the binary to avoid any accusations of disloyalty.

St Tatyana's Day Ball at the Russian Center in San Francisco in 1949 included some unexpected guests: five officials from the Board of Equalization came to the event on 28 January to investigate a charge that the center was selling hard liquor without a license. According to Nickolas Bikoff, then-president of what had become a "Russian-American Anti-Communist Organization," a "denunciation" to the Board of Equalization also stated that a "group of Reds had organized festivities at the Russian Center and were planning to send the funds collected to Soviet Russia."[138] Though "communist" activity was not a Board of Equalization concern, the allegation likely piqued the interest of officials who shared such information with the FBI, which was most interested in "Red" activities.

The Board of Equalization visit was not the only visit by authorities to the Russian Center in the 1940s, and the characterization of that underlying complaint was incongruous given the center's openly anti-communist politics in the post-war period. The Russian Center had, in fact, morphed from a cultural and social institution to one that advocated a clear political anti-communist stance specifically to preclude such attention. Official and unofficial rhetoric, however, that all Russians were suspect as fifth columnists fueled paranoia, rampant by 1950. That paranoia, in turn, contributed to a kind of hysteria among the leadership of the center, with almost non-stop clashes and mutual accusations among board members of secret Soviet sympathies. The measured and careful navigation by Alexander Varguin during the war, attempting to anticipate any unwelcome attention to Russians as undesirable residents in America, appeared to be for naught as actions by local law enforcement led to mutual accusations among members of both wrongdoing and political unreliability, culminating in a lawsuit of warring Russian Center boards in 1952.

The enemies of the Russian Center "did not sleep," in the words of Bikoff, in their efforts to interfere with and harm the center. Immediately prior to the Board of Equalization visit in January of 1949, two SFPD officials, also acting on a tip of illegal activity, had come to the center to demand that management stop poker games. The center closed the card room, making changes to procedures, but these were not sufficient in satisfying either the authorities or the unknown informant who continued to provide them with information about gaming violations, and subsequently "upping the ante," made subsequent denunciations about "Red" activity.[139]

Less than two months later, on 3 March at 11:00 p.m., the San Francisco Police Department, again acting on a tip, raided the Russian Center's club room, where patrons were playing cards. They arrested all those present including the club room manager, Vera Udaloff (1902–1990). Authorities dropped all charges against sixteen detained card players, but charges against Udaloff remained in force. As the club room manager, she, in the eyes of police, was responsible for any illegalities. The Russian Center's attorney, Andrew Bodisco (1912–1963), took up her defense. District Attorney Edmund G. Brown, reluctant to prosecute Udaloff, and interpreting Section 288 of the police code on gambling as applying only to "commercial establishment," not private clubs, argued that gaming was legal if the club "was not operated for the primary purpose of gambling." The head of the vice squad, however, claimed that the patrons almost all said they had "joined the club for the sole purpose of playing poker," and draw poker had, by that time, been banned by the city.[140]

Apart from the original tip to the police about illegal gambling in the Russian Center club room, Bodisco told Russian Center officials that police had received two other anonymous (unspecified) "denunciations" against Udaloff and another woman playing cards that night, indicating an informant who had first-hand knowledge about card room operations and the patrons. Udaloff was convicted of "keeping a gambling house at the Russian Center Social Club," receiving a suspended sentence of thirty days.[141] Udaloff refused to appeal the conviction, despite the fact that the Russian Center intended to pay her legal costs because she felt further focus on the incident would harm the center, and therefore the community.[142] Russian Center officials changed the methods of playing draw poker and of collecting money and reopened the room in June.[143]

The Russian community in San Francisco became somewhat of a microcosm of American society during the intense and charged environment of the McCarthy era. The uneasiness of maintaining Russian identity in an atmosphere characterized by nativism and political suspicions, which informed much of how Russians acculturated in the inter-war period, morphed into a full-blown paranoia in the post-war period, reinforcing the notion that obscuring Russian heritage in everyday life was a necessity just as or even more critical than in the inter-war period. A notation in the 1954 funeral instructions for Kenneth Braves, aka Innokenty Brevnoff (b. 1901), a student who had arrived in 1923, stated "do not mention a native of [Russia]" with respect to information to include in his obituary. Brevnoff had officially changed his name upon naturalization in 1942. The instructions to omit mention of his native country seemed a deliberate, and ultimately successful, attempt to conceal his heritage. Inter-war émigrés advised post-war arrivals to change their names, based on their own experience but the increasingly Russophobic atmosphere in the McCarthyist period was also a factor.[144]

The continuing police attention at the Russian Center damaged confidence in its leadership, splintering the community further. Nadia Shapiro wrote to Peter Balakshin in 1953 on the various new and regrouped factions:

> Russian San Francisco, they say, has broken apart into mutually feuding groups: the old, the very old, the new, the newer, and the newest emigration, into monarchists, solidarists, republicans, Russian centrists, anti-Russian centrists, homeowners, and all kind of other Tubabaons and old Shanghaians. Nevertheless, almost everyone shows up at the Invalid and other charitable balls for which much is forgiven them. [145]

Some of the resulting discord had to do with the large number of newcomers, the so-called "Shanghaians" (who arrived directly from Shanghai or via Hong Kong) and "Tubabaoans," whose experiences reinforced the need to display militant anti-communism. Paranoia also engendered feelings of intensified persecution in response to real or perceived attacks: the enemy was everywhere and nowhere, lurking outside the community looking in, but apparently blending in within the ranks at times, causing discord and distrust. "Dark forces" and "enemies," tasked by "Moscow," were bent on harming "the Russian name" and the Russian Center, as an anti-communist institution.[146] A certain viciousness began to inform conflicts in the center, indicated by the perennial "denunciations," which both stemmed from and thrived on paranoia. Newly developed suspicions about motivations of Russian community members, who had known each other for decades, also mirrored the American suspicion of all Russians as "Reds" with Russians now accusing one another of "secret" Soviet sympathies. The practice of "denunciations" to authorities was something new, fomenting an attitude of fear and distrust not apparent earlier. As much as the inter-war community had squabbled, there had been an attitude of camaraderie among people with differing perspectives coming together to maintain and celebrate Russian culture. Accusations of "monarchism" by opponents of émigré groups in the 1920s, made in the Russian press, though perhaps damaging to the image of émigrés as elitists, were nevertheless not the type of accusations that led to visits from law enforcement agencies seeking out spies. Even with respect to disagreement on political issues, it was one thing for Russians to make "in-house" accusations amongst themselves of insufficiently anti-communist views in the émigré press, while it was quite another to make anonymous denunciations of Soviet sympathies to authorities – a practice eerily reminiscent of life in Stalinist Russia, where people had learned to fear denunciations from their neighbors.[147]

Russian community leaders such as Alexander Varguin played an important role in the processes of formulating a neo-monarchist/anti-communist ideology in the Cold War environment to explain Russian-American identity to outsiders and his efforts to do so aligned him with the incoming wave of Russians. The post-war iteration of public Russian-American identity narrowed to a certain acceptable form, rejecting deviation, and was, to a great degree, dictated from "above" by Russian Center leadership. Cold War ideology, McCarthyist paranoia, and the expansion of communism, by 1950 the state ideology of two of the largest countries in the world (both, as it happened, countries to which Russian émigrés had nostalgic connections), served to reinforce fears in the Russian community that they were targets of both Soviet and American intelligence agencies. The first sought to disrupt and destroy them while the latter's interactions with the community was a reminder that Russians in America might well become targets of hysteria in the event of war with the Soviet Union. Just a few years prior, after all, US agencies had targeted California's Japanese communities, including those living in the Fillmore District, side by side with Russians, and all people of Japanese descent were summarily removed from the area and forced to live in concentration camps.[148] Witnessing the removal of Japanese Americans had been yet another reinforcement to Russians of the protections "whiteness" granted in America.

The campaign against the club/card room was one that *Novaya Zarya* newspaper had spearheaded earlier – the police had first raided the card room in 1944, after an anonymous tip of illegal gambling practices, and arrested twenty-nine card players. The paper's editors, the Soohoffs, had gleefully covered that raid in their newspaper, but their complaints centered on the inappropriateness of gambling in what was supposed to be a cultural center, and the commensurate practices to keep revenues up, such as loaning money to those who lost at cards so they would keep playing, allowing non-members to play, and, generally, taking money from the pockets of "working people." The police came in force in several vehicles on the day of the raid and asked people for member cards, which only one person was able to provide. The attorney for the room manager, Ben Lador (aka Veniamin I. Ladov, 1894–1959), however, made the case that draw poker was not illegal at the time under city or state statutes and the case, as a first violation, was dismissed.[149]

The fact was that income from the card room became very important to Russian Center financial survival, indicating that other less problematic sources of income, such as dues, were not increasing despite more Russians arriving in San Francisco. As early as 1940 Konstantin Barskii had noted the importance of cards as a source of income and, in 1943, income from the card room had increased to $8,850.74 from the $3,766.70 of 1940.[150] Board members did not want to tamper with that success even if certain practices spoke to exploitation of people's addictions, but other center members, such as inter-war arrival Peter Constantinoff/Coff (1890–1954), excoriated the focus. Constantinoff, Museum of Russian Culture president from 1949 to 1954, also noted to Varguin in 1943 that youth groups had left the center, as they could not stand the regime (of Barskii, then president). Ivan Kolchin's choir had left for the same reason, as had the fishing and hunting club, the chess club, the historical society, and the athletes. Did the Russian Center even have the right to call itself a cultural center, he asked, when board members had reduced cultural matters to a method of making money?[151]

The raids at the center and other issues incoming Russians faced upon arrival in San Francisco (unemployment, under-employment, lack of English-language skills) promoted an image of Russians as undesirables, combined with their possible "communist" affiliation. A 1951 International Institute report noted that, with the arrival of the Samar refugees, "the community problems of the Russians are magnified." Further, "it has been brought to the attention of the Institute also that now the Russians have an increasingly 'bad press.'"[152] The report spoke to a lack of respectability, a respectability that the Russian Center leadership had actively cultivated since its opening in their efforts to participate in local events, organizations, charitable and wartime efforts, maintaining relationships with local political leaders and institutions. Raids by police interfered with that mission and Varguin's continual circulating back to the post of Russian Center president indicated the community's trust in him to take control of the situation and resolve outstanding issues (see table 9.3).[153]

Table 9.3 Russian Center board presidents to 1964

Russian Center board presidents	Years served	Place of birth/arrival in US/departure point
Alexander N. Varguin (1884–1953)	1939–July 1942	Orenburg/1922 in SF/Harbin
Konstantin P. Barskii (1894–1975)	1942–1945	Taurida/1923 in Seattle/Shanghai
Peter A. Tray (1881/3–1964)	1945	Novorzhev/1923 in Seattle/Shanghai
Alexander N. Varguin	April 1945–September 1947	
Nicholas I. Zvonareff (Bell) (1893–1951)	1947	Blagoveshchensk/1923 in Seattle/Harbin
Nicholas E. Bikoff (1896–1983)	1948–February 1952	Barguzin/1923 in Seattle/Harbin
Alexander N. Varguin	February 1952–May 1953	
Victor N. Korosteleff / Korostylev (1903–1990)	1954–1955	Khabarovsk/1940 in San Pedro/Japan via Buenos Aires, Argentina
Michael V. Shastin (1890–1961)	1956	Kazan/1951 in SF/Shanghai via Tubabao
Anatole G. Semenov (1902–1977)	1957–1958	Harbin/1925 in SF/Harbin
Gregory K. Bologoff (1894/5–1976)	1958–1964+	Irkutsk/1951 in SF/Shanghai via Tubabao

Sources: Slava, Khvala, Chest' (1964), MRC; "Passenger Lists of Vessels Arriving at San Francisco, California," NAI 4498993; "Petitions for Naturalization, 8/6/1903–12/29/1911," NAI 605504.

Warring Russian Center Boards

"Bad press," however, seemed a catch-all term to indicate the problem of identifying as Russian in a Russophobic environment, with public discourse and rhetoric characterizing all Russians as not only unassimilable but as Soviet spies. Being passively anti-communist, therefore, was no longer sufficient. To preclude any future negative attention, it was important to be vocally anti-communist, while also promoting an image of respectability and good citizenship. Herbert Vantz, who had led the small Russian Fascist Party faction in San Francisco in the inter-war period, reviewed the first "Tragedy of Russia" event at the Russian Center, held by a newly formed young Russian Scouts group in November of 1951.[154] Russian Scouting groups in Europe had started the event as a response

The New Exodus and the Post-War Russian Community | **307**

to the Soviet celebration of the Bolshevik Revolution, holding it the first Sunday after November 7. Scouting advocate Mikhail Zalessky explained it as a critical event for Russian youth abroad as they searched for meaning in their lives and took part in the struggle against communism, in tandem with a struggle for the "soul" of the Russian people, and particularly the souls of Russian youth. Dressed in their scouting uniforms, young people performed songs and recited poetry elucidating the suffering of the Russian people under the yoke of communism and hope for a future in which the Soviet regime was (somehow) overthrown.[155] Vantz noted afterwards that some people "in the Russian colony in San Francisco began to show more active opposition to communism, which a patriotically-oriented American society can only welcome."[156] The message was that Russians had to be *actively and openly* anti-communist in order to be perceived as patriotic and to claim their place in American society as acceptable citizens.

Commensurately, minimizing the role of the Russian Center in its aid efforts to the people of the Soviet Union during the war also became a factor in demonstrating appropriate anti-communist outlooks. Varguin had been careful in crafting the original statements about the purpose and beneficiaries of Russian-American aid in the war effort, foreseeing possible future repercussions against Russian Americans.[157] Nickolas Bikoff, however, who had openly served in an official capacity on the aid committee (unlike those who surreptitiously knitted sweaters), became a target of accusations of "secret" pro-Soviet views in the increasingly paranoid post-war environment. A few White Russians from the San Francisco community, notably Arnautoff and Bratoff, had become open advocates of communism, perhaps opening the door to the suspicions that "subversives" might indeed exist in the heart of the community. On the other hand, both men were openly and vocally pro-Soviet. In Bikoff's cases, an accuser had labeled him a *"secret* Bolshevik" because he had chaired the Russian Center's committee to aid the Russian people, despite the fact, as Bikoff pointed out, that Varguin himself had approved the creation of the committee.[158] Varguin, however, had also, in April of 1945, taken the lead in establishing the center as an anti-communist bastion, retiring again in September of 1947.[159]

In February of 1952, during a general meeting at the Russian Center, members led by Varguin, emerging yet again from retirement, ousted Bikoff as board president along with his supporters on the board, electing Varguin to head a new board. Both sides accused one another of Soviet sympathies. The reasons for the "coup," however, lay in a series of incidents under Bikoff's leadership, which included the police raids, as well as a staged robbery in August of 1951 by the building manager, Nicholas Tarasoff, hired in 1949 upon arrival from Shanghai.[160] Though those incidents certainly may have caused members to lose confidence in Bikoff, the insistence in framing the conflict in Cold War terms (i.e., each side accusing the other of "secret Red" sympathies) likely began as a ploy of intimidation so that Bikoff would "leave quietly," which he did not.[161]

Bikoff placed the conflict into a global Cold War context in his correspondence with Varguin and published articles, writing that only the Soviets would benefit from the destruction of the Russian Center and its newspaper *Russkaia zhizn'*.[162] Utilizing Cold War rhetoric and implying that the San Francisco Russian community was a target of Soviet intelligence agencies, he noted that Politburo members in Moscow were "rubbing their hands in glee" because "Judases" had fulfilled their "socialist orders" in exchange for "pieces of silver."[163] Varguin, on his part, implied that Bikoff was a communist agent who had interfered with Varguin's goals to elevate "the Russian Center to its proper place among American national organizations that were helping the US government in the battle against communism." Who but the enemies of the anti-communist movement would reap the benefits from damaging the "Russian name?" Varguin asked rhetorically. He reminded members that to be a "worthy" member, one was obligated to support the mission of the Russian Center, which included not only safeguarding the best traditions of Russian culture, but also – making a novel public argument about Russian-American identity – "*venerating the memory of the murdered Czar Nicholas II*." That argument seemed to be an important factor in the dispute as Varguin had just founded an organization of "devotees" to the memory of Czar Nicholas II in 1951.[164]

Venerating the last czar of Russia and advocating for the reinstatement of the monarchy in a post-Soviet scenario became the prevalent religio-political focus for both adult and youth Russian groups in the post-war period. Though the murder of the czar and his family in July of 1918 had become a sorrowful anniversary marked by a church service and commemorative events for many in the Russian diaspora, creating an organization of "devotees" spoke to an effort to both reformulate Russian-American identity and alter the narrative to declare uniformity of émigré belief since 1918 (the year the Bolsheviks executed the Romanoff family and the beginning of the Russian Civil War).[165]

The New Exodus and the Post-War Russian Community | 309

Moreover, the organization of devotees to the memory of Czar Nicholas was only one of several newly-organized monarchist groups. Whereas the overwhelming trend in the inter-war period had been to celebrate and disseminate Russian cultural achievements in the fields of art, literature, and drama, discourse and gatherings in the post-war period began to focus on the immutable criticality of the monarchy to Russian history and culture, past, present, and future. Commensurately, a number of Cossack groups formed as well to keep their history alive, also in the context of unity under and loyalty to the Russian Empire, ignoring the separatist stance of several Cossack groups in the wake of the dissolution of the empire (see table 9.4).[166]

The overwhelming majority of founders/representatives of the new organizations listed in table 9.4 arrived in San Francisco after World War II and most were born prior to 1900, therefore getting on in years, which likely explained why many of these organizations did not last past the 1960s. Nevertheless, the push to place emphasis on the criticality of the monarchy to Russian identity imbued the Russian Center with a certain atmosphere that some Russians, such as those from the Potrero Hill community, would find unwelcoming.

Russian Americans may have felt sorrow about the tragic history, but transforming that sorrow into a political ideology held little appeal for those who had lived in the United States for decades, had built lives and careers and, importantly, whose children identified, at most, as Americans of Russian background. Attending church services to pay their respects on the anniversary of the royal family's murder did not mean seriously entertaining the idea of Vladimir Kirillovich Romanoff's claim to the throne (the self-proclaimed Head of the Imperial Family until his death in 1992 in Miami, Florida). What was important to them was the celebration of their culture: family gatherings, secular and church events and holidays, supporting the maintenance of Fort Ross, and maintaining traditions. Imposing a belief system that was out of touch with the reality of their life in what was supposed to have been a Russian cultural center likely alienated some members of the community.

Moreover, the "Shanghaians," who had begun arriving immediately after the war, some with significant financial resources (in comparative terms), did not endear themselves to the community from the outset. Victor Korosteleff, who arrived in 1940 from Argentina, wrote to Bologoff in 1950 that "your Shanghaians who came to America have not engendered any sympathy." Among other things, Korosteleff noted, they did

Table 9.4 Organizations formed after World War II

Name of organization	Founders/presidents in the 1950s
Supreme Monarchist Council Representative	**P.I. Malkov** (1896–1975): POB Nerchinsk; arrived 1950 from Tubabao.
	M.S. Kingstone (Krapivnitsky née Pechatkina) (1902–1980); POB Ashkhabad; arrived 1923 from Harbin.
Union of Devotees to the Sacred Memory of Czar Nicholas II	**A.N. Varguin** (1884–1953); POB Orenburg or Kiev (identified as Orenburg Cossack); arrived 1922 from Harbin.
	V.A. Presniakov (1883–1961); POB St. Petersburg (?); arrived ca. 1950 from Germany.
	N.V. Borzov (1871–1955); arrived 1925 from Harbin.
Monarchist Association "For Faith, Czar and Fatherland"	**P.I. Malkov**
All Monarchist Association	?
National Monarchist Movement	**M.S. Kingstone**
Union of Nobility	**V.A. Presniakov**
Committee to Aid Russian All-Military Union	**A.N. Varguin**
Imperial Army and Navy Corps	**N.N. Nikolayev** (1884–1965) POB Russia; arrived 1951 (?) from Shanghai via Tubabao.
Crusade for Truth	**N.M. Neckludoff** (1898–1985) POB Smolensk; first arrived 1923; returned to China by1925; re-immigrated 1947 from Harbin.
	A.D. Bilimovich (1876–1963/1968) POB Zhitomir; arrived 1948 in New York.
Anti-Communist League	**A. Arseniev** (1927–2014) POB Belgrade; arrived 1956 in NY from Rome.
	D.T. Arseneff (1902–1978), POB Tver; arrived 1939 from Harbin.
Russian National Association in San Francisco, branch of All-Russian National Representation (in NY)	**Head of San Francisco branch: K. Barskii** (1894–1975) POB Taurida; arrived 1923 in Seattle from Shanghai.
Knights of the Order of St George the Dragon Slayer	President: **Major-General M.M. Sokoloff** (1885–1985) POB St Petersburg; arrived 1951 via Blaine, Washington from Australia; prior to that in Shanghai.

Association of former Drozdovsky troops (named for White Guard Major General Mikhail G. Drozdovsky, a monarchist and supporter of the Romanoffs, killed in battle in 1919)	President: **A.M. Nizovtseff** (1895–1959); POB Baikal region; arrived in U.S. after 1945 from Bulgaria.
Association of Vlasovites (supporters of General Andrey Vlasov, head of the Russian Liberation Army during World War II; hanged by Soviet government for treason after the war).	**Dr A.A. Efimov** (1898–1955) POB Tambov; arrived 1949 in NY.
Mutual Aid Society of former Nikolayev Cavalry School Pupils	**Colonel S.K. Poliakoff** (1886–1977) POB Novocherkassk; arrived 1949.

Society of Former Cadets (of Russian Imperial and Russian émigré military schools). According to Society website: most of the Cadets in San Francisco in inter-war period were from Siberia and Khabarovsk. There was one Siberian Cadet organization prior to 1950, which joined the Society when it formed in 1951.

Presidents:

(1951–1952) Colonel N.I. Mamontoff (1886–1958) POB Krasnoyarskaya Camp; arrived 1927 from Harbin.

(1952–1953) V.P. Ochlopkow (1889–1956) POB Russia; arrived 1952 in New Orleans from Germany.

(1953–1956) V.S. Daniloff (1903–1990) POB Voronezh; arrived 1950 in NY; previous residence Yugoslavia.

(1956–1964/1969–1970) Colonel A.A. Linitsky (1895–1977) POB Kharkov; arrived 1956 in NY.

All-Cossack Union	**Colonel G. Bologoff** (1895–1976) POB Irkutsk; arrived 1951 from Shanghai via Tubabao.
All-Cossack Unit (*Kuren*)	**L.K. Tooretsky** (1875–1965); POB Romania; arrived 1923 in Seattle from Shanghai via Canada; resided in Detroit and SF; in SF permanently from 1933 (identified native language as Ukrainian in census).
Representative of Amur Cossack Ataman	**N.I. Borodin** (1879–1963); POB Konstantinov; arrived 1950 from Shanghai via Tubabao.
Amur Cossack Stanitsa *	**N.N. Makarov** (1897–1973) POB Unknown; arrived 1950 from Tubabao.

* "Stanitsa" is variously translated as Camp, Station or Village and always references Cossack settlements

Don Cossack Stanitsa	**V.A. Beltsevshin** (?)
General Zbovrovsky Kuban Stanitsa	**N.L. Kissil** (1889–1964) POB Yekaterinodar (now Krasnodar); arrived 1951 in NY from Germany/Yugoslavia.

General Korniloff Siberian Cossack Stanitsa/ Authorized Representative of Siberian Cossack Troops	**I.E. Picoulin** (1894–1967) POB Akmolinsk (now Nur-Sultan, Kazakhstan); in transit 1950 from Shanghai via Tubabao (to Canada?); arrived 1952 in Blaine, Washington.
	Fedor Maksimovich (?)
Ataman Dutoff Orenburg Cossack Stanitsa/ Representative of Orenburg Cossack Troops	**P.K. Kouznetsoff** (1901–1986) POB Orenburg; arrived 1950 from Tubabao.
	A.A. Dmitrieff (1893–1974) POB Orenburg; arrived 1950 from Tubabao.
Baikal Cossack Stanitsa/Chief Representative of Baikal Cossack Troops	**V.V. Ponomarenko** (1902–1962) POB Chita; arrived 1949 from Shanghai.
	N.I. Mamontoff
Yenisei Cossack Stanitsa	**A.G. Yushkoff** (1895–1970) POB Krasnoyarsk; arrived 1951 from Shanghai via Tubabao.
Ussuriisk Cossack Stanitsa	**A.I. Zhigalin** (1921–2000) POB Harbin; arrived 1951 from Tubabao.

Sources: RC Papers, Box 26:1, MRC; "Passenger Lists of Vessels Arriving at San Francisco, California," NAI 4498993; "Passenger and Crew Lists of Vessels Arriving at New York, New York, 1897–1957," Microfilm Serial or NAI T715; "Petitions for Naturalization, 8/6/1903–12/29/1911," NAI 605504; History of the Association, http://www.ruscadet.ru.

not donate money for gifts for children in Tubabao: "many Shanghaians, clearly well-off people, categorically refused." Korosteleff pointed out to Bologoff that many people who donated money for the Tubabaons were "Jews, Tatars, and others" (i.e., non-Orthodox Russians) in the San Francisco area.[167]

Bikoff pointed out as well that the "Shanghaians" all joined the congregation of the Holy Virgin Cathedral, indicating their rejection of any recognition of the Moscow Patriarchy of the Russian Orthodox Church as a legitimate church institution. In 1946, the unity of Metropolia/OCA (Holy Trinity Cathedral) and ROCOR/ROCIA (Holy Virgin Cathedral) ended when ROCOR Archbishop Tikhon in San Francisco terminated ROCOR association with the Metropolia after the Seventh All-American Council recognized the Patriarch of Moscow and All Russia as the spiritual head of the Russian Orthodox Church.[168] Many post-war arrivals gravitated to the Holy Virgin Cathedral based on its firm anti-Soviet stance, and, for many of those from Shanghai, Archbishop John, a ROCOR clergy member, was their spiritual leader. In their view, there was

The New Exodus and the Post-War Russian Community | 313

no middle ground: by not cutting ties with the Moscow Patriarchy, the Metropolia took on a "reddish" tint in their eyes.

The "Shanghaians" also, Bikoff insisted, then had a part in pushing for his removal as they aligned with the Tubabaons. Colonel Bologoff, Bikoff claimed, had brought his faction to the 1952 general meeting and they had thrown their support behind Varguin, now openly advocating for a Russian Center whose mission was not only to fight communism but to advocate for the historic and symbolic importance of the Romanoff dynasty to Russian-American identity. Board members agreed that "Varguin's words will be the platform upon which the new board will base its work."[169]

Not willing to concede his loss, Bikoff filed suit against the new board in March of 1952. The court eventually found in favor of the defendants, however, and the new board promptly suspended Bikoff and two other board members who supported him, Victor Bryditzki (1895–1958) and Pavel Zaitseff (1883–1953) for one year. Bryditzki was an inter-war arrival while Zaitseff (bucking the general trend of the post-World War II group) had arrived in 1948 from Shanghai.[170] Bikoff had other supporters who felt that he had been treated unfairly simply for having a "differing view" from the majority. Two inter-war arrivals, Ivan Guz and Alexander Mooromsky (1897–1970), both of whom were deeply involved in the Russian Center's founding, asked Varguin to overturn the punishment but he refused, reinforcing the authoritarian nature of the leadership.[171] The hostilities therefore continued, creating a foundation of resentment that would play out time and again in the 1950s, with conflicts amongst different factions, culminating in yet another lawsuit between warring groups in the early 1960s related to the construction of the new Holy Virgin Cathedral on Geary Boulevard.[172]

Russian Youth

The post-World War II conflicts in the adult San Francisco Russian community notwithstanding, concerns about denationalization of Russian youth remained in the forefront, just as in the inter-war period. Attracting steady youth participation at the Russian Center had been a goal of the board from the outset but remained problematic. Young people came to the Russian Center after its opening in 1939 to participate in athletic activities or dances but, as noted previously, clashed with Konstantin Barskii during his tenure – a sign of generational, cultural, and, to some extent, perhaps, ideological, conflict. Despite the stated goals of the older

Russian generation to attract youth, economic perspectives were not necessarily in sync. Money was tight, while competing needs, particularly maintenance for a very large building, meant that requests, such as investing in mats for wrestling, for example, or radios for entertainment, may not have been honored.[173] In 1940, board member Alexander Martynoff spoke against remodeling the youth group room as it was not a priority.[174] The marginalizing of youth activities at that time by a board member spoke to the lack of agreement as to the role of the center both among leadership and the community at large – was the main purpose to create a future Russian-speaking and culturally Russian generation in America or to preserve Russia's imperial, monarchist, and cultural heritage to pay homage to that past?

The end of the war brought the question of youth participation to the forefront once more and the board held a special meeting in October of 1946 to discuss the youth question where various members raised the same concerns about how to attract young people. George Guins (1887–1971), then editor of *Russkaia zhizn'* and later professor at UC Berkeley, characterized the issue as the "old problem of 'fathers and children,'" which had become more acute with increased antagonism between the generations:

> We see how "the children" are straying further away from their "roots," from our Russian origins. But even if Russian youth become more Americanized outwardly, acquiring and adapting a new polish, new habits and tastes, in their souls they will always remain Russian and will have ... "two worthy identities" within them which is of value for America and Americans.[175]

Here, Guins acknowledged the necessity of dual identity for Russian youth if they chose to remain within the Russian community and framed his comments in a way that recognized both the complexity of the problem as well as the possibility of advantages in drawing from and contributing to both cultures.

Russian young people in post-war America, however, continued to face obstacles when it came to understanding and being understood by Americans. Being "Russian" in America in the 1950s (even into the 1960s) meant facing accusations of "communism" as early as in elementary school. Natalie Sabelnik, who came with her parents from Tubabao in 1950, recalled how schoolchildren as young as five accused her of being a "Red" and a "commie" in elementary school. Natalie noted that no five-year-old had any understanding of what such accusations meant, clearly picking it up from parents who equated "Russianness" with communism.[176] Logically, being anti-communist then meant being anti-Russian for those with no interest in or knowledge about Russian history, putting children and young people into very difficult positions with respect to expression of their identity.

The established Russian church and secular schools in San Francisco, experiencing drops in enrollment as the inter-war generation grew up, benefitted from the arrival of the thousands of newcomers after World War II, as many had school-aged children whom they enrolled at the Holy Virgin Cathedral school. In 1947, Hegumen Afanasy Stukov from Shanghai reorganized the school under the name "Saints Cyril & Methodius," beginning a three-day per week lesson program. By 1951, with the incoming wave of post-World War II Russian refugees, the school had more than 140 students, thus carrying over the inter-war institution into the post-World War II period and beyond.[177]

Bologoff, as the nominal leader of the "Tubabaons," and later president of the Russian Center, continued in his role as a warrior in the struggle against communism and also saw the children as the vanguard who would carry "the torch with its holy flame" back to the motherland at the appointed time, as he wrote to his friend, Scout leader Oleg Levitsky, in 1952.[178] To understand the "Tragedy of Russia," the younger Russian generation had to maintain its Russianness in America. Apart from school enrollment, the community turned to establishing groups, such as the Scouts, specifically geared towards inculcating pre-revolutionary Russian cultural ideals and Russian Orthodox precepts in Russian youth, reinforced, however, by patriotism to America, the bastion of anti-communism in the post-war world. Bologoff's idea of return, in a context that differed from the inter-war narrative, viewed America as the means by which the Soviet regime would be destroyed. The Scouts/ Pathfinders, a youth organization founded in pre-revolutionary Russia and an important part of most diasporic communities in the inter-war period, became a significant part of the San Francisco community in the post-war period.

The Russian Scouts

Based on British Army Officer Robert Baden-Powell's Boy and Girl Scout Movements founded in England in 1907, the scouting movement began in Russia in 1909 under the leadership of Colonel Oleg I. Pantyukhov and quickly expanded. Scouting organizations were labeled "bourgeois" under the Soviet regime, however, and "forcibly dispersed" after the Civil War in favor of Red Pioneers. Inter-war diasporic communities carried on scouting all over the world, their precepts intrinsically intertwined with Orthodoxy.[179]

The San Francisco community had founded its first scouting chapter late in the inter-war period, in 1939. With the support of the clergy, Russian community leaders met at the Children's Pre-School on Post Street and organized a National Organization of Russian Scouts (NORS) chapter.[180] The focus of scouting in its first iteration in San Francisco was largely recreational and nature-oriented, although patriotism both to Russia (in the conceptual sense) and the United States, as well as religious faith, were all integral to the organization. By 1940, scout troops (*druzhinas*) based in San Francisco spent summer months at camps at Clear Lake and Jordan Park (in Cobb Valley) in Lake County.[181]

The scouting movement in San Francisco experienced a hiatus due to the entry of the United States into World War II in 1941, likely because all the scouting leaders joined the US military.[182] In 1953, however, émigré Bonifatij Kucevalov (1893–1981), a Russian Center board member, provided an alternate interpretation, opining that "harmful influences" had a hand in contributing to the San Francisco scouting group's dispersal during the war, referencing the softening stance toward the Soviet Union as an ally of the United States among Russians in San Francisco. As Kucevalov, a professional singer who worked on ships, permanently settled in San Francisco only in 1944, his knowledge of events about the organization prior to that time was hearsay.[183] Herbert Vantz also ambiguously noted that the inter-war scouting group broke up "under the pressure of events," without further clarification.[184]

A prior call to sign up for scouting activities in 1950 did not reference the inter-war group at all: Vsevolod Selivanovsky, Kucevalov's son-in-law, called on children and young adults from seven to nineteen years old to join, noting that experienced scouting instructors had arrived from both Europe and China (in other words, not members of the inter-war San Francisco community).[185] Among them was Scoutmaster Lev Gishizky

(1925–2001), born in Pančevo, Yugoslavia, who arrived in 1950 and organized the Organization of Young Russian Pathfinders (ORUR) Kiev *druzhina* (troop); and, later, Scoutmaster Alexei Kniazeff (1909–1993), born in China in 1909, who came from Tubabao in 1951, becoming head of the North American division of the National Organization of Russian Scouts-Pathfinders (NORS-R), indicating an existing divide in Russian scouting abroad.[186] Other scouting leaders re-migrated later from South America. The "Tragedy of Russia" event was part of a directed effort to integrate youth groups into events with an anti-Soviet focus, which, as noted, had the effect of reinvigorating general community participation.

Orientation towards monarchism was incorporated into the new postwar iteration of scouting in San Francisco. Not only did Scouts study the history of the "bygone czars," "but the Russian Orthodox Czar" was the unifying figure of the organization with the slogan "for faith, the czar, and fatherland" part of the scouting credo.[187] Reinforcing the dedication to pre-revolutionary czarist Russia in particular, émigré Dmitry Shishkin declared in an article aimed at parents of Scouts: "the generation that allowed the bloody All-Russian upheaval and had a part in that upheaval in significant measure has, too late, repented for what it has done," obliquely referencing those émigrés that had espoused "liberal" views and supported the abdication of the czar, thus sending Russia down the slippery revolutionary slope into communism. The call for repentance here was an accusation referencing the responsibility of the generation that had, in this narrative, facilitated the work of the Bolsheviks. Shishkin went on to write that the "scouts-pathfinders are the vanguard of the current generation" and "love for Russia, passionate faith in its future and *readiness to do battle* for its resurrection will bring victory over the communist evil," reinforcing the call for militant action. Shishkin arrived from Tubabao in 1951 at the age of sixty-seven; his wife had died in China in 1945 and he did not know the whereabouts of his only daughter. Shishkin's perspective was of someone who had lost his homeland and his entire family. His condemnation of those who had passively or actively contributed to the seizure of Russia by satanic forces, thus leading to his own loss of family, likely spoke to the bitterness of émigrés whose experiences of loss informed their view as participants in a crusade.[188]

The youth of the Russian diaspora, born in exile in communities that maintained Russian culture and tradition as well as the Orthodox faith, infused the San Francisco community in the post-World War II era with a certain energy, which was likely exciting for those who feared the erasure of their contributions to the maintenance of Russian culture abroad. That energy had certain very specific directions, however, as Russian young people were enjoined to take up the militant stance against Soviet and international communism, now a global threat. The Scouts (both boys and girls), who wore uniforms, learned survival techniques, and militarily useful skills such as the Morse Code, maintaining Russian traditions and the Orthodox faith, represented a movement that would one day return to Russia to rebuild it, mimicking the narrative of the Russian students in the inter-war era but with new implications. Yet another world war was necessary to facilitate that return, fitting neatly in with McCarthyist rhetoric focusing on the importance of ferreting out enemies and preparing for battle.[189]

The younger generation, however, unlike those in the inter-war Russian community, had not experienced the Civil War personally, and though raised to honor the memories of those who fought and perished in that war, nevertheless could not comprehend its actuality. The experiences of the second- or third-generation diaspora, who had never seen the homeland but were familiar with it based on the narratives of their parents, grandparents, or teachers, necessarily altered the meaning of the original experience despite a conviction that the new generation carried on to serve the same cause. The sense of repentance that informed much of émigré recollections among the San Francisco's inter-war diaspora, which spoke to remorse at failure to affect positive change in what Olferieff had called "a long-dead system of government," was replaced with rhetoric placing blame on those who had not done their duty to defend that system of government, leading to Bolshevik victory, a position that might have been offensive to those who had actually fought in the Russian Civil War.[190]

The arrival of thousands of Russian people to San Francisco in the post-World War II years was the culmination of the efforts of a network of Russian Americans and émigrés working for that common cause. As often as not, however, people were working at cross purposes. Many people who might have otherwise obtained visas to the United States did not because of the reiterated exhortations, among both American politicians and Russian Americans, that the threat of a fifth column undermining American democracy was real. As late as the 1960s, Russians in America had to address the issue of their "anti-communist" affiliation and identity: Valentina Vernon opened a restaurant in Carmel, California in 1961, naming it a "A Bit of Old Russia" specifically to clarify that "there was no communist affiliation."[191]

The process of immigration in the immediate post-war period also highlighted the racism permeating American institutions. Anxieties about Russians of "Asiatic" descent were clearly present, and Russians involved in the process of bringing refugees to the United States, rather than decrying the inherent racism in those institutions, had to find ways to work around that racism. Once arrived, those people who had to bear the brunt of such anxieties went on to live their lives in America, likely burying their emotions about negative experiences under the cover of expected gratitude. After all, many Russians, whatever their ethnic background, were barred from entering the United States at all. Only hints of the trauma experienced are evident in Nikolai Massenkoff's story, for example, as in his identification with political movements of historically oppressed people in the United States.

Identifying as white in America, rather than as Russian American, precluded the necessity of explanation: a "white" person did not need to clarify that they were "White Russians," not "communists" or "Reds." Those who kept their Russian surnames, however, also retained the identity of foreigner, or at least immigrant, no matter how long they had lived in America and that factor contributed to insecurity and defensiveness as issues of racial discrimination arose in the changing post-war environment. The prevalence of discriminatory practices in San Francisco's building and real estate industries for example, which had come up peripherally in the 1939 debate over the purchase of the Russian Center building, arose again in the 1950s.

In 1957, African-American baseball player Willie Mays, already a household name, relocated to San Francisco from New York with the Giants, but found hostility when attempting to purchase a home. A first bid on a house resulted on the house "mysteriously taken off the market," and a bid on a second home in one of the toniest neighborhoods in San Francisco, St Francis Wood, revealed, in the words of Mays's biographer James Hirsch, "the insidious but standard" practices among all participants in the real estate industry to keep African Americans out of certain areas.[192] The home belonged to builder Walter Gnesdiloff (1908/1912–1996), who had arrived in San Francisco with his parents and siblings in the 1920s. His family was from Orenburg, his father a "wealthy merchant" in Russia."[193] Gnesdiloff worked a variety of jobs, entered the trades, which required union membership, and, in the 1950s, built the home he was selling. After Mays and his wife Marguerite made their offer (at asking price), neighbors began calling Gnesdiloff urging him not to sell because an African-American homeowner would cause, in their view, lowering of property values. Hirsch describes the events in detail in his biography of Mays. At the time, newspapers across the country picked up the story, which came to a resolution within twenty-four hours when Gnesdiloff agreed to go forward with the sale, but San Francisco's reputation as an "enlightened" city became irrevocably tarnished.[194]

Gnesdiloff's ethnic heritage received no mention despite his obviously Slavic surname, as it was irrelevant in this context. As a middle- or upper-middle-class white American, Gnesdiloff was urged by Martin Gaehwiler, a property owner and builder in the neighborhood, to "use his own conscience," presumably in the context of being a white person who was duty-bound to support the white cause of racial segregation, threatening that Gnesdiloff would "get a bad name" if he did not toe the color line. Gaehwiler then doubled down, stating in the presence of reporters that he (Gaehwiler) would "lose a lot if colored people moved in [to the neighborhood where he owned houses]" and, further, that he "wouldn't like to have a colored family" living anywhere "near" him. After a series of meetings with officials and a shouting match with Gaehwiler, Gnesdiloff sold the home to the Mays family. In a further indication of prevalent attitudes, Gnesdiloff's realtor refused to participate, foregoing his commission to avoid doing business with an African-American person.[195]

Gnesdiloff's ethnic background did come up in the aftermath when he received "anti-Semitic" mail from opponents of his decision. The assumption, then, from such opponents, was that Gnesdiloff, whose surname identified him as Eastern European, was Jewish (he was not). Edward Howden, the director of San Francisco's Council of Civil Unity, who took a leading role in persuading Gnesdiloff to go through with the sale, described him as "naïve," as he interpreted Gnesdiloff's hesitation as a lack of understanding of the "matter's significance" (i.e., an "American hero" facing discrimination in "tolerant" and "sophisticated" San Francisco). The implication here was that Gnesdiloff's failure to grasp that "significance" was due to his status as an immigrant, which remained unsaid but stemmed from the "foreignness" of his surname. Howden's point was that the "image" was all important and the underlying hypocrisy less so – after all, if Mays had not been so famous, the incident would have received no attention at all. Gnesdiloff, however, probably

The New Exodus and the Post-War Russian Community | 321

understood all of the issues at hand quite well – he had lived in the US since 1923, after all – but was in a vulnerable position as he feared future repercussions from the entrenched real estate/building establishment, noting initially to reporters that he would "never get another job" in the building industry if he went through with the sale, indicating his comprehension of the pressure to support white supremacy. Gaehwiler, on his part, born and raised in inter-war San Francisco to Swiss immigrants, who went on record in unapologetic support of racial discrimination and segregation, made a point of distinguishing Chinese and Filipino residents of the neighborhood as acceptable, reinforcing the notion of existing hierarchies of race, which shifted as needed: in this case, to keep African Americans out of St Francis Wood.[196]

Russians, then, remained on the periphery of the cultural order in San Francisco in the 1950s, in part because those émigrés, like Gnesdiloff, who had Americanized sufficiently to be successful within the American economic paradigm, and accepted their privilege as white people, nevertheless felt discomfort when confronted with the notion that their success may have come at a price that others had to pay. Their inclusion as Americans stipulated that they identify with white supremacist ideology and that entailed their participation in maintaining the racial status quo. Otherwise, they could get a "bad name," in Gaehwiler's words. Gnesdiloff ended up on the right side of history, but the fact that he hesitated initially to go through with the sale indicated the enormous weight and pressure brought to bear on him from his peers, his neighbors, union members or officials, and his potential employers (like Gaehwiler) to maintain the status quo.

Not only domestic but international post-war political developments played a role in the molding of Russian-American identity. The leadership of San Francisco's Russian Center rebranded it a Russian-American anti-communist organization, in effect throwing down a gauntlet. Russians, if they wished to be part of that organization, could no longer be apolitical. Indeed, their politics had to fall in line with the advertised position. The position of Russians who wished to politicize their most publicly visible organization was bolstered by the fact that Republicans like Senator Knowland had actively helped Russian refugees come to the United States (ignoring the fact that other Republican politicians, such as Senator McCarran, had tried to stop them). Notwithstanding the effect of the global Cold War on that identity, however, the re-branding of a cultural institution into a political one was a direct result of anti-Russian feeling and an attempt to forestall attacks on the center in the increasingly hostile domestic environment.[197]

At the same time, Russians remained foreign in American eyes, and the history of the White Russian emigration remained obscured within the broader historical context of Soviet-American relations. Russians in America still had to explain themselves even after decades of living in the United States. Though past tropes had contributed to turning Russian people into caricatures, Russians could and did use them for their own purposes in the inter-war period. The increasing trend of interchanging the terms "Russians," "Reds" and "Soviets," however, thus identifying any Russian as a possible fifth columnist, was not a stereotype Russians could manipulate to their benefit.

Moreover, in view of factors such as "bad press" in San Francisco and persistent negative attention from law enforcement agencies, identifying as strident anti-communists (a factor which became even more significant, in terms of identifying with whiteness in the 1960s when government authorities labeled civil rights groups as tools of communists) to ensure safety was a logical choice for Russian Americans. They could then maintain those cultural attributes important to them: religious faith, language, and tradition within the community, combining them with an adherence to narratives of America's new role as the leader in the war against communism.

The Russian Center, therefore, despite its visible role as a representative organization of Russian Americans, served as an institution for a certain contingent, who, in effect, set out to make it exclusive and exclusionary rather than a pan-Russian center. Being assertively "anti-communist" required a constant adversary with whom to do battle. When no such adversary existed, people turned on one another, as evident from the struggles at the Russian Center.

Moreover, Potrero Hill community members seemed to take little or no interest in Russian Center activities during the McCarthy era and Jewish Russians like Jacob Boxer, who had contributed funds to the purchase of the Russian Center building in 1939, were notably absent from post-war Russian Center events. Russian Americans from the inter-war emigration were divided about the center and its evolving role. The reasoning to create a certain Russian-American identity may have been logical in view of perceived Russian vulnerability in an environment where "Soviet" and "Russian" were interchangeable in almost all discourse, but the direction nevertheless did not sit well with everyone. The constant issue of insufficient funds, thus the dependence on gambling revenues, spoke to the lack of financial support for an institution that many in the Russian community at large felt did not represent them.

In the post-war experience in San Francisco, new arrivals had an advantage of institutions that already existed, particularly the Russian churches and their schools, the Russian Center, and the established network of artistic and cultural groups. That network, combined with the fact that they had maintained their culture for so many years living outside of Russia, reinforced a desire to raise their children as Russian Americans. Thus, the focus on sending children to Russian schools and maintaining Russian youth groups that focused not only on Russian culture but on a new battle to defeat communism, now a global threat.

As the Cold War intensified, being a loyal American meant being anti-communist as a matter of course and for Russian Americans that loyalty and patriotism had to be publicly proclaimed. The new American reality, however, was a negatively charged political atmosphere, which demanded, particularly for Russians, the constant proving of loyalties. If Russians wanted to maintain any part of their cultural traditions in the United States, publicly proclaiming first loyalty to the United States was imperative. Unquestioning acceptance of dominant culture narratives about American history and culture, including those about American ethnic and racial history, was included in that loyalty and patriotism. The post-war world was divided into the "good": the United States representing freedom and democracy, and the "evil": the Soviet Union representing oppression and totalitarianism. Russian Americans incorporated that binary into their public expressions of identity as anti-communist warriors. In that binary, there was no room for nostalgic ideations of a land "out of time and space." As such, the creative life outside of *byt* that was so important to members of the inter-war community was overwritten by a desire to join the American middle class – a purely American dream. To strive for economic success and to support the dominant culture narrative, including exceptionalist mythologies relating to immigration, social justice, and equality, was to be a patriotic American. The "Tragedy of Russia," an ideation about a war still to be fought, replaced "Imagined Russia," a place of refuge for the exiled, as the central tenet of being Russian American in San Francisco.

CONCLUSION

Only our love for great Russia gives meaning to our existence.

ÉMIGRÉ NIKOLAI ALL, 30 December 1926[1]

Nikolai All's reference to "great Russia" spoke to a concept of a mental territory which existed, as Nadia Shapiro had said, "out of time and space." Relics from a Russian imperial past remaining in northern California provided that link across time and space to the Russian earth. The nostalgic yearning for Russia encompassed an idea, a mythology, a legacy, and an identity. In San Francisco, that conceptual Imagined Russia existed to a sufficiently significant extent that émigré Ivan Stenbock-Fermor, as noted in the epigraph prefacing the Introduction to this book, considered San Francisco the "greatest" and "only" Russian city outside of Russia. He made his observation in the 1970s, looking back through layers of accumulated impressions, memories, and nostalgic reifications of Russia by Russian diasporas who sought meaning in their experiences of exodus and settlement outside of their motherland.

The physical space of northern California where Russian émigrés landed, contained objects and landscapes – temples, relics, and sacred spaces – that provided a link to their lost homeland, bringing them solace and providing impetus to find meaning in that exile through exploration of history and efforts to maintain heritage for future generations. Their educated status set them apart from most immigrant groups even though their "everyday" lives were those of immigrants struggling to survive and working at jobs that, among other things, made them invisible. The "visible" Russians were the aristocrats and those who consciously played up the exotic aspect of being Russian because such visibility was advantageous. Nevertheless, those choices assisted in promulgating the trope of a particular White Russian identity, effectively erasing swaths of people in San Francisco who identified as Russian in the inter-war period.

Conclusion | 325

As political exiles in the 1920s, many émigrés initially considered themselves not immigrants, but sojourners in America, which had some impact on how they interacted with Americans initially. The processes of either selectively acculturating or assimilating were conscious, though often coerced, choices of both émigrés and their children, and involved actions that seemed to be in direct contradiction to their philosophical outlook. These included the immediate alteration and Americanization of names, a critical marker of identity, and application for US citizenship despite the fact that discourse within the community continued to reference return to Russia as imminent. That possibility of departure and the option of leaving behind their American identity (or "overcoat") if they returned to Russia likely informed the choices to avoid the label of "foreigner" and to fit in, at least on a superficial everyday level.

The dream of possible return mitigated the sorrow of obscuring their ancestry to suit the norms of an alien society. As the years of exile went by with that dream fading, members of both the first and second generation of the inter-war group, upon experiencing the reality of the racial hierarchal structure predominant in the United States, actively set out to attain a "state of whiteness," which, in its turn, had a role, ironically, in negating their own cultural history, a history that they had valued above all else. Boris Shebeko noted in 1961 that the French and British in inter-war Shanghai considered "manual work" to be "degrading to the white race," in the context of the difficulty Russians had in making a living there. Shebeko foregrounded the whiteness of Russians in his recollections, reframing Russian identity as white prior to arrival to comply with the American paradigm in which, as W.E.B. DuBois wrote, those who benefited from the system accepted the "public and psychological wage" of whiteness.[2]

The Fillmore neighborhood in the inter-war period was a short-lived but real experience in living in a multi-ethnic and multicultural environment where the playing field, though certainly not even in view of American racial history, provided a glimpse of life in a neighborhood that was quite diverse in terms of residents' backgrounds and experience. Commonalities among the residents were that they were newcomers to San Francisco, had little in terms of material wealth, but enjoyed a richness of cultural heritage, which they all brought to the table. As such, however, such a community was unsustainable, given social, economic, and actual physical alterations to the space in the post-war period.

Poverty, as Nadia Shapiro had pointed out, is romantic only for those who have not experienced it.

The Russian experience in America also included an ever-present political connotation. In recognizing the necessity of gaining American "trust" upon arrival, as Vladimir Peshehonov noted in 1925, Russian émigrés performed their culture publicly, utilizing symbols of a society no longer in existence, thus creating mixed messages for American observers, who often placed Russians in America in the category of quaint and picturesque "aliens" exhibiting a vanished past. Under the American gaze, then, the display was simply spectacle, which had no place in modern American society except as a curiosity or entertainment. Both authenticity and cultural autonomy remained in the balance for the White Russian community, particularly within the urban landscape where they had settled. Their efforts to maintain that autonomy were successful because they grasped the need to definitively claim space within the built environment and to actively preserve material culture given the circumstances of their exodus from the homeland. Nevertheless, continuing manifestations of anti-Russian feeling, both for nativist and political reasons, served to reinforce a defensiveness among Russian émigrés, causing many who arrived in the inter-war period to acculturate to a point just short of total assimilation and the subsequent complete assimilation of their children. This process was facilitated by the fact that so many people changed their names early on as well as by the dispersal of that community from the Fillmore, followed by the physical erasure of the Fillmore in the post-World War II redevelopment projects. The descendants of the diaspora dispersed even further, outside of San Francisco, with many of the second and third generations often settling throughout the American West.[3]

The Russian Fillmore No More

By 1960, the notion that Americans had needed a Russian interpreter when visiting the Fillmore neighborhood seemed unlikely. The idea that a Russian émigré, standing on the corner of Eddy and Buchanan Streets after eating his dinner of *shchi* and beef tongue, envisioned a "bearded Moscow cab driver" rolling out of the fog to the sound of imagined ringing church bells, no doubt seemed far-fetched even to post-World War II Russian arrivals. The demographics of the neighborhood changed several times over and, by the 1960s, urban renewal projects

Conclusion | 327

had largely obliterated the neighborhood: Fillmore Street turned into a "redevelopment-gutted boulevard."⁴ The remains of the "Russian center" of stores and businesses encompassing the O'Farrell/Eddy/Ellis/Turk and Steiner/Fillmore/Webster/Buchanan section disappeared completely.

The built environment that the inter-war Russian community had adapted for its needs or outright acquired to provide a physical foundation for their cultural activities, and to practice their religious faith, remained, however, providing clues to what had been. The Russian Center building on Sutter Street is among the prominent structures remaining, as is the old Holy Virgin Cathedral on Fulton Street, and the Westerfeld House, steeped in urban legends. The Holy Trinity Cathedral, at the foot of Russian Hill, outside the borders of the Fillmore, also remains as a testament to the longevity of the Russian and Orthodox presence in San Francisco. Despite Holy Trinity's significance, both architecturally and historically, it is the Richmond, however, that writers today identify with Russians, if they do so at all; Solnit includes the Holy Virgin Joy of All Who Sorrow Cathedral at 6210 Geary Boulevard in her Treasure Map of "the forty-nine jewels of San Francisco."⁵ If not for the built environment that remained to testify to their presence, the history of inter-war Russian San Francisco might have been erased completely. It is indicative that in 1957, in the midst of the Cold War, the residents of Russian Hill moved to change the existing name in favor of one "honoring a San Franciscan," claiming that the existing appellation "was held up to ridicule and scorn." Because then-Mayor George Christopher was expecting a visit from Soviet Premier Nikita Khrushchev and did not want to cause a diplomatic incident (not because of the history of the Hill), he refused the request. That history was irrelevant to San Francisco residents in light of Cold War concerns: "Russian" Hill, in their eyes, was not an "American" appellation.⁶

White Russians to White Americans

The pull to homogenize, sanitize, and neutralize is not specific to American society. It only seems incongruous because of the myth that American society and culture celebrate both heterogeneity and individuality. Russian émigrés were an interesting foil for the pull to homogenize American society in the inter-war period because they often resembled the kind of people American eugenicists and immigration opponents held up as examples of the "right kind" of immigrant: nominally

"European" and well-educated. At the same time, however, they exhibited cultural markers that did not fit in at all: a language that, as a nineteenth-century American described (chapter 1), was "barbarous," a religion that was "Oriental," a history and culture that was at best "Byzantine," and, at worst, in the eyes of eugenicists such as Madison Grant, "Asiatic." If Russians shed those markers, they could blend in and eventually they and their descendants did indeed become "white" people, in the process negating the ethno-cultural history of Russians who did not fit into that "whiteness" paradigm.

The atmosphere of the post-World War II Cold War period in the United States, which did not allow for disagreement or even debate without accusations of Soviet sympathies, contributed both to paranoia and an even more intensive pull to conformity. The paranoia was much more intense than in the inter-war period, when émigrés had perceived the Bolshevik regime as an anomaly of history that might end in their lifetime. Decades of displacement, uncertainty, and consequent trauma had made their mark on new arrivals. The core San Francisco Russian-American community of the post-World War II period, which built its institutions on the foundation constructed by a heterogeneous inter-war diaspora, developed into a model American middle-class politically conservative social group, one that was particularly comfortable in that identity because of broad middle-class support of Cold War ideology, intrinsic to what Boym calls the Manichaen and "conspiratorial worldview."[7] The nostalgic ideations that informed memories of the Russia "we lost" devolved into a victimization narrative: the Russia that "was taken from us." The latter narrative was driven by perceptions of real or perceived injustices informing the processes of forced exodus, immigration, scrutiny, and assimilation to American society of people traumatized and re-traumatized through every stage in these processes. Unlike Orthodoxy, which, in many historical instances, functioned as an inclusive identity in America, Russian-Americanism, based on a particular "White Russian" past, came to be an exclusionary one with strict delineations of acceptable political ideology and a preference for the values and norms of the American (white) middle class, which, notably, experienced unprecedented economic prosperity in the decades following World War II.[8]

The role of trauma, an aspect of the migration process in any context, combined with the post-World War II atmosphere of fear and paranoia, was indubitably instrumental in creating that Russian-American identity. The history of displacements, statelessness, and uncertainty had both

Conclusion

| 329

an individual and collective influence on both mentality and psyche. In other words, were the people who finally arrived in America in the 1950s (some of whom experienced yet another episode of detention prior to entry) the same people who left whatever homeland in which they were born? Was the pull to Americanize and exhibit almost frantic patriotism among the post-World War II arrivals a function of exhaustion rather than enthusiasm?

The evolution of Russian-American identity in the post-World War II period was also, as in the inter-war era, a negotiation and a function of cultural survival – a recognition that to maintain cultural traditions in an organized way (churches, schools, institutions, and events), Russians, in the dangerous period of McCarthyism, when a Slavic surname drew unwanted attention, had to take great care in how they expressed themselves. In this second iteration, however, dissenting views about that Russian identity were suspect. The Russian Center leadership, representing the "public" face of one Russian-American community in that post-World War II period, then, defined Russian-American identity as a combination of white middle-class values and a neo-monarchist ideology espousing Russian nationalism, a nationalism that now encompassed an American conceptualization of "whiteness."

The continuing defensiveness of Russian Americans, referenced by Glazunova in her thesis, culminated in the 1970s in the founding of the Congress of Russian Americans (CRA) to address "Russophobia" in American public discourse. The tendency of the CRA, at least prior to the collapse of the Soviet Union in 1991, to frame their discourse in overwhelmingly Reagan Republican terms (i.e., Russians living in the United States were good and loyal Americans *specifically* because they were politically conservative) promoted a new trope about the homogeneity of Russian-American identity that began in the immediate post-World War II era. That shift in thinking had occurred among some inter-war émigrés. In an early example, Elizabeth Malozemoff, who was a Social Democrat in pre-revolutionary Russia (though living a privileged life due to her husband's noble status despite exile in Siberia), registered as a Democrat upon naturalization in 1926 but was a Republican by 1932, "fearing," in her words, "revolution" in the United States.[9] Later in the timeline, a 1965 paean to Prince Belosselsky's activities in the Russian-American community and anti-communist credentials stressed that he was "an active member of the Republican Party."[10] That identity became so exclusionary that Nikolai Massenkoff, a Russian American who had conceived of

America as a "dreamland," where his dreams did, in fact, come true, was denied membership in the CRA in the late 1970s: he had visited the Soviet Union for an artistic competition and the organization returned his application because of his supposed "communist" sympathies.[11]

The dreams of return to rebuild their homeland were not fulfilled for the post-1917 Russian diaspora. The difficult but largely successful struggle to adapt and build lives in America may have assuaged that loss for some, particularly since they were able to experience the mental territory of an "Imagined Russia" in California. A core group also persisted in creating a foundation meant for the next generation, many of whom, however, were in the process of assimilating into American culture, wearied by the burdens of a dual life. Nevertheless, that foundation enabled the preservation of cultural heritage even as that inter-war community dispersed and much of the physical evidence of their milieu "disappeared into oblivion."

The post-war McCarthyist reality in America underscored a perceived necessity of re-formulating Russian-American identity into its Cold War iteration, an identity that would help ensure the safety and security of future generations of Russians in America. In accepting and adopting the values of the white American middle class, Russians secured a place for their children within the reality of American life. The end of the Cold War gave rise to what turned out to be a false hope for Americans of Russian heritage that they, like the descendants of other immigrant groups, could, if they wished, maintain a connection to their ancestral history through both cultural ties and familial and kin relationships in the homeland. The wars of aggression perpetrated by the current Russian government, culminating in the war against Ukraine in 2022, put an end to those hopes, and spurred yet a new wave of hostility towards manifestations of Russian culture in America, the consequences of which will indubitably affect future generations of Americans of Russian heritage.

NOTES

Introduction

1 Ivan Stenbock-Fermor, "Memoirs of Life in Old Russia, World War I, Revolution, and in Emigration," oral history transcript (1976), 1102–3.
2 Solnit, *Infinite City*, 66. Westerfeld House model labeled "Russian Consulate": San Francisco Russian Ephemera (SFRE) File, SFHC, SFPL.
3 US Census, 1940/1950, 1198 Fulton Street, San Francisco Assembly District (AD), 26.
4 Minutes, RC GM, 7 February 1940. Russian Center (RC) Papers, Box 6:2, MRC.
5 A.P. Farafontoff's report to GM, 30 March 1940. Loukashkin Papers, FR/Alaska File, MRC.
6 Russian elites fled Petrograd after the February 1917 revolution, which installed the Provisional Government (after the abdication of Czar Nicholas II), as life there became "chaotic," moving to the Crimea or Finland, among other places. Vassiliev, *Beauty in Exile*, 47. The vast majority of Russians, however, left the country after the Bolshevik seizure of power in October of 1917 or during the ensuing Civil War.
7 WPA Federal Writers' Project, *San Francisco in the 1930s*, 285.
8 Selunskaia, "The Integration of the Russian Émigré Community," 12.
9 Ibid., 13.
10 Wagner, "Ideology, Identity, and the Emergence of a Middle Class," 163.
11 Barrett and Roediger, "Inbetween Peoples," 3–44.
12 Roediger, *The Wages of Whiteness*; Roediger, *Working toward Whiteness*.
13 Hassel, "Russian Refugees," 1–2.
14 Dubinets, *Russian Composers Abroad*, 172. On demographics of San Francisco's Russian émigré population in the inter-war period, author's examination of thousands of immigration and naturalization documents.
15 For the legal and social construction of race and gradations of whiteness, particularly among Eastern Europeans in the United States, see: Jacobson, *Whiteness of a Different Color*, 19–44; Feagin, "Toward an Integrated Theory of Systemic Racism," 211–16; Roediger, *Working Toward Whiteness*, especially Part II, "Inbetweeness." On the development of the hierarchical racial paradigm in the United States, see, among others, Allen, *The Invention of the White Race*.
16 Bodnar, *The Transplanted*, xv; Sadowski-Smith, *The New Immigrant Whiteness*, 12–13; Warne, *The Slav Invasion and the Mine Workers: A Study in Immigration*, 1904.
17 Van Nuys, *Americanizing the West*, xii.
18 Sadowski-Smith, *The New Immigrant Whiteness*, 6.
19 On Slavs becoming "Caucasian" in the inter-war period, see Jacobson, chapter 3: "Becoming Caucasian, 1924–1965," in *Whiteness of a Different Color*.
20 Sadowski-Smith, *The New Immigrant Whiteness*, 8. Gubanova specifically refers to American "middle class patterns" as being "of largely white, Anglo-Saxon origins." Gubanova, "Adjustment Process of Russian Immigrants," 2.
21 Bushkovitch. "What is Russia?," 144–61.
22 "Russian Writers," Shapiro Papers, Box 7:3, HIA.

332 | Notes to pages 8–13

23 Kappeler, *The Russian Empire*, chapters 1–4; Cross, "Them," 80; Black, *Russians in Alaska*, chapter 12. Author excludes discrimination against the Jewish population in the Russian Empire in this overview as those policies were based on religious grounds, rather than race per se.

24 Vinkovetsky, cited by Luehrmann, *Alutiiq Villages under Russian and US Rule*, 117. Miller, *Kodiak Kreol*, on Russian imperial perspectives of racial fluidity and categorization of race/ethnicity in Kodiak, Alaska.

25 Luehrmann, *Alutiiq Villages under Russian and US Rule*, 117, referencing Black, "Creoles in Russian America."

26 For example, in *Houston Bound*, Tyina Steptoe explores the fluidity of ethnic and racial identity in Houston among "Creoles of color" in the inter-war period as Louisiana Creoles migrated to that city, challenging concepts of fixed racial identity.

27 Oleksa, *Orthodox Alaska*, 150.

28 US Census records, 1910–1930, Sitka, Alaska. Luehrmann cites census reports of Ivan Petroff, 1884, and Robert Porter, 1893. Petroff, a Russian-born American, used "Creole" when conducting the census in Alaska in 1880 while "in 1890, the census categories were 'White,' 'Mixed,' 'Indian,' 'Mongolian,' and 'all others,'" *Alutiiq Villages under Russian and US. Rule*, 151n2. Kan, "Guest Editor's Introduction," 351–61, on American interpretation of "Creole" in Alaska.

29 Ngai, *Impossible Subjects*, 30, 37. US Census counts in Alaska, 1890–1920, arbitrarily categorized residents as "Indian," "Mixed," or "White." In 1920, authorities designated eighty-four of eighty-seven residents of a community "mixed" although some of those were ethnic Russians and others Native Alaskan. Luehrmann, *Alutiiq Villages under Russian and US Rule*, 119.

30 Wollenberg, "Immigration through the Port of San Francisco," 143–4.

31 Hieromonk Sebastian, 12 February 1897, *American Orthodox Messenger* 15 (1–13 April 1898), 455–60, 16 (15–27 April 1898), 479–82; Kroll, *Friends in Peace and War*, 130-1; Afonsky, *A History of the Orthodox Church in Alaska*, 77n7 (author's emphasis).

32 Haney López, *White by Law*, on history of racial categories in America. References to Syrians, 1–5.

33 Tripp notes 350 Orthodox in 1891, "Russian Routes," 71; "Data and status of Alaskan Diocese as of 1879," Alaska Russian Church records, reel 300, ASML.

34 Ciment, *Encyclopedia of American Immigration*, vol. 3, 968.

35 Slobin, *Russians Abroad*, 25–6; Johnson, "'New Mecca, New Babylon,'" 5; Dubinets, *Russian Composers Abroad*, 172–3; Williams, *Culture in Exile*, chapter 3.

36 Tripp on Serbian community and businesses in nineteenth-century San Francisco in "Russian Routes." Death notices of Serbian Americans referenced funerals in a "Russian" cemetery in the 1880s and 1890s. *San Francisco Call* and *San Francisco Chronicle*.

37 Vassiliev, *Beauty in Exile*, 57.

38 Lee and Yung, *Angel Island*; Barrett and Roediger, "Inbetween Peoples."

39 Berglund discusses that process from 1846 to 1906 in *Making San Francisco American*.

40 Barkan, *From All Points*, 2, 241–2.

41 See Said, *Orientalism*, for a historical contextualization of the "occidental" as the norm and "the Orient" as the "other."

42 "The Review Stands Pat," *Bisbee Daily Review*, 29 May 1903.

43 Barkan, *From All Points*, 7. "Bohunk" was a pejorative term derived from "Bohemian" and came to reference eastern Europeans. Bohemia was region in the Austro-Hungarian Empire from where Slovak immigrants, among others, immigrated (now in the Czechia). Roediger cites Wtulich on history and the meaning of the term in *Working Toward Whiteness*, 43–4.

44 Guglielmo, *White on Arrival*, chapters 3, 8; Hirsch, "E Pluribus Duo?"; Barrett and Roediger, "Becoming American and Becoming White," in *Major Problems in American Immigration History*, 324–6; Barrett and Roediger, "Inbetween Peoples."

45 Berglund, *Making San Francisco American*, 224. Sadowski-Smith utilizes the term "insisting" on whiteness in characterizing European immigrant efforts. *The New Immigrant Whiteness*, 156.

Notes to pages 14–21 **| 333**

46 Johnson, *New Mecca, New Babylon* (Paris); Andreyev and Savický, *Russia Abroad* (Prague); Shlegel, *Berlin: Eastern Station*.

47 A. Cohen, "Oh, That!" 72.

48 Slobin on the role of literature in defining a national identity for Russian émigrés, specifically in Europe in the inter-war era. *Russians Abroad,* Introduction.

49 Glazunova, "Bay Area Russian-American Community," 62–3 (capitalization in original); theses by Tripp, "Russian Routes"; Gubanova, "Adjustment Process of Russian Immigrants in California."

50 See Gramsci on defensiveness of subaltern groups. *Selections from the Prison Notebooks*, 54–5.

51 Hardwick, *Russian Refuge*, 12.

52 R. Cohen, *Global Diasporas*, 13.

53 Slobin, *Russians Abroad*, 19–21.

54 Hardwick, *Russian Refuge*, 28–31. "Molokan" is derived from the Russian word *moloko*, which means milk. Molokane adhere to Mosaic dietary laws and do not follow Orthodox fasts which prohibit consumption of dairy products during Lent, 29.

55 Russian émigré "Petitions for Naturalization [PFN], 8/6/1903 – 12/29/1911," National Archive Identifier (NAI) 605504, *Records of District Courts of the United States* (USDC), *1685–2009*, RG 21, National Archives (NARA) at San Francisco, San Bruno, California.

56 Language in naturalization petitions, 1927–1942. The country to which Russians renounced fidelity in the documents was "Russia," not the USSR, indicating the interchangeability of the two in the minds of US officials. On remaining an intact diaspora, see Slobin, *Russians Abroad*, 21–2.

57 Boym, *Common Places*, 29–40; *The Future of Nostalgia*, chapter 5.

58 Rosińska, "Emigratory Experience" in *Memory and Migration*, 31.

59 Van Der Kolk, *The Body Keeps the Score*, 21.

60 Ed Gossett, Texas, HR, "A New Fifth Column or the Refugee Racket," 2 July 1947, 1–5, CUAC, Box 21:6, CSA.

61 Most noted Yiddish as their first language in census records.

62 Morrissey, *Mental Territories*, 15.

63 The dangers presented by the Soviet government in Europe included kidnappings of White Russian generals, for example. Slobin, *Russians Abroad*, 27.

64 Nadia Shapiro's characterization in "Girl Reporter: Russian Refugees," undated article draft (ca. late 1920s), Shapiro Papers, Box 5:36, HIA.

65 Dubinets, *Russian Composers Abroad*, 173.

66 Rosenbaum, *Cosmopolitans*, 2–3, 197–8. The other Jewish neighborhoods were south of Market and the San Bruno Avenue area, according to Rosenbaum, which also included contingents of Russians and other ethnic groups, 2–3, 207–9.

67 Glad, *Russia Abroad*, 227. Statistical reports regarding non-Asian immigrants arriving in San Francisco 1921–1940 have not survived. Sakovich, "Angel Island Immigration Station Reconsidered," 3–4.

68 Clausen and Thøgersen, "The Era of Russian Influence,1898–1932," in *The Making of a Chinese City*, 23–66. Harbin's population throughout its early-twentieth-century history included most ethnic groups from the Russian Empire, and enclaves of Western Europeans. See also Gamsa, *Harbin, A Cross Cultural Biography*, and Wolff, *To the Harbin Station*.

69 Stone and Glenny, *The Other Russia*, 200.

70 Clausen and Thøgersen, *The Making of a Chinese City* (citing Stephan, *The Russian Fascists*, 40, and other sources), 45.

71 On the retreat, see Smele, *Civil War in Siberia*, chapter 6.

72 Information from "Passenger Lists of Vessels Arriving at San Francisco, California (PLV SF)," NAI 4498993, Records of the Immigration and Naturalization Service (INS), *1787–2004*; RG 85, NARA; "PFN," NAI 605504, Records of USDC, NARA.

334 | Notes to pages 21–30

73 Ibid. Pogranichnaya was a locality in China listed in immigration documents. The contemporary town of Pogranichny is in Russia, just across the border from Suifenhe.
74 Clausen and Thøgersen, *The Making of a Chinese City*, 29. The authors note as well that a contingent of prisoners released from czarist-era penal colonies (*katorga*) also settled in Harbin.
75 "PFN," NAI 605504, Records of USDC, NARA.
76 The 1882 Chinese Exclusion Act restricted Asian immigration early on. On Asian exclusion and anti-Asian sentiment, particularly in California, see: Ngai, *Impossible Subjects*, 37–50, 204–6; Lee, *At America's Gates*.
77 Wtulich, *American Xenophobia and the Slav Immigrant*, 68. On immigration laws, Ngai and Gjerde, eds, *Major Problems in American Immigration History*, 190; Ngai, *Impossible Subjects*, 23–5.
78 Schrag, *Not Fit for Our Society*, 122.
79 Ngai, *Impossible Subjects*, 23
80 Behdad, *A Forgetful Nation*, 13.
81 Sakovich, "Angel Island Immigration Station Reconsidered," 245.
82 Ngai, *Impossible Subjects*, 28–9.
83 Johnson, *New Mecca, New Babylon*, 7.
84 Dubinets quoting Kevin F.M. Platt and Giya Kancheli, *Russian Composers Abroad*, 3–4.
85 A California official declared unnaturalized immigrants a danger and a threat "to the very life of the republic," in 1915. Van Nuys, *Americanizing the West*, 3.
86 A.A. Voloshin, "Freedom of the Press," *Russian News-Life*, 7 March 1941. Isaenko Papers, Box 11:2, HIA; Robinson, *Russians in Hollywood*, 16. This book focuses on San Francisco, but the proximity of Hollywood facilitated interaction between the two Russian communities.
87 *San Francisco Examiner*, 30 December 1926.
88 O.O. McIntyre, "New York by Day," *San Francisco Examiner*, 15 June 1927.
89 N. Zelensky, *Performing Tsarist Russia in New York*, 12.
90 Elizabeth Malozemoff, "The Life of a Russian Teacher," oral history transcript (1961), preface by Alton C. Donnelly.
91 Prosvita announcements: *Russkaia zhizn'*, 29 April 1922, 7 March 1924, 16 January 1926, among others.

Chapter One

1 Response to "Russian gentleman" who suggested teaching Russian children the Russian language in San Francisco public schools. Quoted in *Alaska Herald* [AH], 15 April 1869.
2 "St Peter's Chains," *San Francisco Chronicle*, 26 January 1880.
3 "Dramatic Church History," *Examiner* (San Francisco), clipping, ca. 1891. San Francisco Imperial Russian Consulate Records (SFIRC), roll 143, NARA. Formal appellation of Russian Orthodox Church in America in this period was the "Russian Orthodox Greek Catholic Church."
4 WPA Federal Writers' Project, *San Francisco in the 1930s*, 302.
5 Black provides a figure of 468 persons who departed from Sitka for Russia in 1867 and 1868 on Russian vessels. *Russians in Alaska*, 290n52.
6 Ngai, *Impossible Subjects*, 38–44.
7 "A Church Scandal," *San Francisco Chronicle*, 12 June 1891.
8 Ibid.
9 Orthodox carry given names of Christian saints and some descendants of employees maintained Russian surnames, particularly if they practiced Orthodoxy. On cultural history of Russian America, see: Black, "Creoles in Russian America" and *Russians in Alaska*; Kan, *Memory Eternal*; "Sergei Ionovich Kostromitinov (1854–1915)."
10 "Alexine's Foul Dungeon," *San Francisco Examiner*, 8 July 1891.

Notes to pages 30–5 | **335**

11 Ibid., "A Church Scandal," *San Francisco Chronicle*, 12 June 1891; Orthodox church attorney Horace Platt to Russian Consul General G. Niebaum, 17 June 1891. SFIRC, roll 143, NARA. Descriptions of conditions in Orthodox seminaries in nineteenth-century Russia often referenced corporal punishment and egregious conditions. Manchester, *Holy Fathers, Secular Sons*, chapter 5.

12 Berglund, *Making San Francisco American*, 218.

13 "Was Russian Priest Murdered?" *Alta California*, ca. June 1878; Affidavits of Officers Lafayette Stivers and Michael Brickely, SFIRC, roll 143, NARA; "A Case of Murder," *San Francisco Chronicle*, 25 May 1889.

14 Ship employee statement (fragment). *Examiner*, San Francisco, "Dramatic Church History," ca.1891, SFIRC, roll 143, NARA; "A Drowned Prelate," *San Francisco Chronicle*, 15 August 1882; Emmons, *Alleged Sex and Threatened Violence*, 10–11.

15 "A Russian Bishop," *San Francisco Chronicle*, 19 April 1888; "The Russian Church," *San Francisco Chronicle*, ca. 1890, SFIRC, roll 143, NARA.

16 "Russo-Greek Church," *San Francisco Chronicle*, 23 April 1888.

17 Branson, *The Life and Times of John W. Clark*, 150.

18 Tartars (or Tatars) in Russia were/are generally Muslims; how the observer deduced the ethnicity of congregants is unknown. The reference to "colored people ... converted in the South" is also unclear but a Greek Orthodox parish was indeed established in New Orleans in 1864: https://holytrinitycathedral.org/history.html.

19 Ciment, *Encyclopedia of American Immigration*, vol. 3, 966–7. White discusses role of violence in settling of American West in "*It's Your Misfortune and None of My Own*": violence against Indigenous inhabitants of California within that context, 337–40; against Chinese people, 341–2.

20 "Russian Christmas," *San Francisco Chronicle*, 7 January 1894.

21 "Russian Church," *San Francisco Examiner*, 23 May 1889; "A Russian Bishop," *San Francisco Chronicle*, 19 April 1888; "The Russian Church," *San Francisco Examiner*, ca. 1890, SFIRC, roll 143, NARA. Emmons, *Alleged Sex and Threatened Violence*, chapter 2, on Russel/Sudzilovsky and Orthodox community.

22 "Under Espionage," *San Francisco Chronicle*, 7 February 1890.

23 Afonsky, *A History of the Orthodox Church in Alaska*, 82, citing *Tserkovniye Vedomosti*, 1888, no. 26.

24 Bishop Nestor Correspondence, 14/26 January 1880, ARC, reel 304, ASML.

25 "Russian Christmas," *San Francisco Chronicle*, 7 January 1894.

26 "Thanksgiving Service in the Russian Church," *San Francisco Chronicle*, 5 May 1875; "Elaborate Vestments Worn by the Bishop and Priests," *San Francisco Examiner*, 2 April 1900 (author's emphasis).

27 "Spectacular Ceremonial," *San Francisco Examiner*, 1 October 1900; "Unusual Ceremonies upon the Occasion," *San Francisco Chronicle*, 27 January 1891; "A Russian Festival," 7 April 1894, noting incense played "an *unusual* part in every element" of the Orthodox Church service (author's emphasis).

28 *San Francisco Chronicle*, ca. October 1894 clipping, SFIRC, roll 143, NARA; "Russians Open Fair in Aid of Red Cross Fund," *San Francisco Chronicle*, 20 April 1904; "Ladies of Russian Church Celebrate Anniversary," 13 March 1910; "Russian Women to Hold Picturesque Baza[a]r Here," 26 April 1911.

29 On architecture as a medium for conscious public expression, see Gyrisco, "East Slav Identity and Church Architecture in Minneapolis, Minnesota," 199–200. The cathedral was initially consecrated to St Alexander Nevsky, destroyed by 1889 fire, rebuilt and consecrated to St Basil. Bishop Vladimir to St Paul Congregation, 4 June 1889, regarding fire 9/21 May. Alaskan Russian Church Records, reel 118, ASML.

30 "Russian Christmas," *San Francisco Chronicle*, 6 January 1891.

336 | Notes to pages 35–40

31 Tripp discusses the nineteenth-century history of Orthodox societies and the Russian Orthodox Church in San Francisco at length in "Russian Routes," 50–71. Cooke, *A History of the Diocese*, 13.

32 "Bishop's Title Changed," *San Francisco Chronicle*, 13 March 1900; "Bishop Tikhon's See Embraces a Continent," *San Francisco Chronicle*, 21 March 1900.

33 "Raising Money to Build a New Cathedral," *San Francisco Examiner*, 25 January 1903.

34 "City May Buy Russian Church," *San Francisco Chronicle*, 13 April 1905; *San Francisco Call*, "New Playhouse to Open in September," 7 March 1906; "North Beach is to have Modern Theatre," *San Francisco Examiner*, 7 March 1906.

35 "City May Buy Russian Church," *San Francisco Chronicle*, 13 April 1905.

36 Lazarev, *Plavanie vokrug sveta*, 198.

37 The hill was formally named on 10 December 1852, when officials selected a name to document the "town's first official execution" and chose the previously informal appellation. WPA Federal Writers' Project, *San Francisco in the 1930s*, 254.

38 A. Kashevaroff, E.O. Essig Correspondence, and others, 1927–1929, Kashevaroff Collection, ASML.

39 "Russian Hill: Steep, Green Home Place," *Hills of San Francisco*, 38.

40 "Matters of Interest to the Clergy and Laity," *San Francisco Chronicle*, 11 July 1909.

41 Glad, *Russia Abroad*, 25. Glad briefly mentions Molokane settling in San Francisco and Los Angeles, 227.

42 *AH*, 1 June 1871; 15 December 1868.

43 On subsidy, see: Glad, *Russia Abroad*, 99–100; "A California Factor in Russian Revolution," *San Francisco Chronicle*, 23 July 1905.

44 Honcharenko, "Russian Complications," *Daily Morning Chronicle* (San Francisco), 29 July 1869. Tripp notes Honcharenko's mention of migration from Alaska to San Francisco after 1867 in "Russian Routes," 57.

45 Grinev, *Kto est' kto*, 35. Honcharenko later labeled Arkhimandritoff a "Judas Iscariot." *AH*, 15 February 1869.

46 *AH*, 1 July 1868.

47 *AH*, 1 March, 1 June 1868; 1 January 1872.

48 Glad, *Russia Abroad*, 99–100.

49 US Census 1900, Sonoma, California; "Death Summons Mrs. Olga Gordenker," *Petaluma-Argus Courier*, 22 November 1932; Quote from N. Shapiro's translation of Gordenker obituary in *Novaya Zarya*, 22 November 1932, Shapiro Papers, Box 2:20, HIA. Shapiro spelled the surname correctly as "Gordenko," misspelled in English-language documents upon arrival.

50 On Gordenker/Bishop Vladimir hostilities, see Emmons, *Alleged Sex and Threatened Violence*, chapters 2–3.

51 On 1905 revolution and aftermath, see Salisbury, *Black Night, White Snow*.

52 Post, *The Story of the Postnikov Family*, 4–5, 21–47, 181.

53 Nathan Merenbach, "Declarations of Intention for Citizenship," NAI 4713410, *Records of USDC*, NARA; *US, School Yearbooks*, University of California Berkeley, 1918; *US, Department of Veterans Affairs*, BIRLS Death File.

54 "P.F. Tesluck," *San Francisco Examiner*, 14 April 1965.

55 Saroyan and Vinson, *Hilltop Russians in San Francisco*; Hardwick, *Russian Refuge*, chapters 2–3. Groups settled throughout California as well as Oregon, Arizona, and Mexico.

56 Moore, *Molokan Oral Tradition*, 5.

57 Ibid., 9.

58 Hardwick, *Russian Refuge*, 80, 91. That number likely encompasses all Spiritual Christians living on Potrero Hill.

59 Moore, *Molokan Oral Tradition*, 12–13; Breyfogle, "Prayer and the Politics of Place, 224–5; Hardwick, *Russian Refuge*, 28–31.

Notes to pages 40–8 | **337**

60 Ethel Dunn, "Potrero Hill's Russians," *The Potrero View*, 1 December 1971, SFRE File, SFHC, SFPL.
61 "Fled from Siberia," *San Francisco Chronicle*, 14 October 1891.
62 "Hid by Refugee?," *Los Angeles Times*, 1 May 1906.
63 Rosenbaum, *Cosmopolitans*, 189; Zimmer, *Immigrants Against the State*, 116–17.
64 Davis and Trani, *The First Cold War*, 2. See Norman E. Saul's extensive work on the historical Russian-American relationship, particularly *War and Revolution: The United States and Russia, 1914–1921*.
65 On post-World War I unrest in United States, see Murray, *Red Scare*, chapter 1.
66 Grant, *The Passing of the Great Race*.
67 Ngai, *Impossible Subjects*, 22
68 Bierstadt, *Aspects of Americanization*, 35.
69 Zimmer, *Immigrants against the State*, 70.
70 Words from sonnet by Emma Lazarus, "The New Colossus" (1883) on the Statue of Liberty: "Give me your tired, your poor, your huddled masses yearning to breathe free."

Chapter Two

A version of this chapter, titled "Keeping to the Sober Truth: A Jewish Lutheran White Russian in San Francisco," was published as an article in the *Journal of Russian American Studies* (May 2021)

1 "Russia as Ever-Smoldering Racial Vesuvius," *Literary Digest*, 9 March 1918, 70.
2 "The Inrush of the Russians: New York's Topsy-Turvy Colony of Emigres," *New York Times*, 10 June 1923.
3 Nadia Lavrova (Shapiro), "'God's Own Country' Pleases Nadia; But Let her Tell It," *San Francisco Examiner*, 1 April 1923.
4 H.W. Hess, "In Re: 'Harbin Committee Rendering Aid to Russian Students,'" 12 September 1922, File 55605/130 INS Central Office Subject Correspondence and Case Files [COSCCF], Entry 9, Records of the US INS, NARA.
5 "25 Students Held Here from Russia," *San Francisco Daily News*, 30 August 1922.
6 The Bolsheviks shot and bayoneted Nicholas II, his wife Alexandra, and children (daughters Olga, Tatiana, Maria, Anastasia, and son Alexei), and their staff, in July 1918.
7 Lavrova, "Mystery is Better than Peroxide when You're Looking for a Job," *San Francisco Examiner*, 22 April 1923; "How I Came to Write in English: Shapiro Papers, Box 4:14 and 5:11, biographical details: Box 1:1–7, HIA.
8 On the fascination with Russian aristocracy and hyperinflation of numbers of Russian aristocrats in "exile" after the Revolution, see Matich, *The White Emigration Goes Hollywood*, 187.
9 On Chinese community in San Francisco, see Shah, *Contagious Divides*; On Chinese immigration during the Exclusion era, see Erika Lee, *At America's Gates*.
10 Barkan, *From All Points*, chapter 26.
11 Vassiliev, *Beauty in Exile*, 17–28, 72, 101.
12 Kachina notes protests against Russian immigrants in San Francisco in the 1920s due to such fears. "From Russia to America," 61.
13 Lee and Yung, *Angel Island*, 229.
14 Schrage, *Not Fit for Our Society*, 86–7.
15 Murray, *Red Scare*, 197; Schmidt, *Red Scare*, 250; Schrag, *Not Fit for Our Society*, 86.
16 Jensen, *Army Surveillance in America*, 137–49; 167–77; Zimmer, *Immigrants against the State*, 107, 116.
17 J. Davis, *The Russian Immigrant*, vii.
18 "Thoughts about St Tatyana's Day," undated, Borzov Papers, Box 11:3, HIA (author's emphasis); Varneck worked at Stanford University and as a US Department of State translator. Varneck Papers, HIA.

338 | Notes to pages 49–52

19 Jensen, *Army Surveillance in America*, 188–97.

20 "Act to exclude and expel from the United States aliens who are members of the anarchistic and similar classes" approved 16 October 1918. Correspondence, 1920, US Dept of Labor, Immigration Service, US INS, File 71-42 records, Roll 2, IHRCA.

21 Anthony Caminetti, Commissioner-General, "News Release – Deportation Train," 17 July 1920, US INS, File 71–42 records, Roll 2, IHRCA; Blue, *The Deportation Express*, 26.

22 "'Reds' Victim May Recover," *San Francisco Examiner*, 23 February 1920. Cherny cites the *Schneiderman* Supreme Court decision in 1943 as seminal in reducing denaturalization prosecutions. William Schneiderman was a Russian-born American Communist Party member in California who naturalized in 1927 and was denaturalized in 1940, subsequently appealing the decision successfully to the Supreme Court: Cherny, *San Francisco Reds*, 87, 377–80.

23 D.B. Davis, "Responses to International Involvement and Ethnic Pluralism (1918–1948)" in *The Fear of Conspiracy*, 210.

24 Davis and Trani, *The First Cold War*, Introduction.

25 Records of Imperial Russian Consulate in the US finding aid, 1862–1922, NARA. The US government supported Russian consular officials in Portland, Oregon; Philadelphia, New York, Chicago, Honolulu, and Seattle. Baron Th. de Gunsburg to Basil Miles, Department of State, 17 December 1918; Embassy Counselor to Romanovsky, 28 April 1921, SFIRC, Roll 103, NARA. The Russian embassy in Washington, DC, became a "quasi-agency of the American government and reported to it … causing dissension within the embassy staff." Saul, *War and Revolution*, 179.

26 "Secret" Letter No. 3, Acting Russian Consul, San Francisco to Russian Embassy, Washington, DC, 13 November 1919, SFIRC, Roll 103, NARA.

27 Shapiro referenced Potrero Hill as "peasant Russia" and "Russian Mountain" in 1923: Lavrova, *SF Examiner* "Russian Mountain Tots Real Yanks," 23 November 1923.

28 "Secret" Report to Russian Embassy, 26 July 1919. SFIRC, Roll 103, NARA.

29 Missive "To All Workers, Men and Women, in the United States of America," San Francisco Society for the Co-operation with the Russian Revolution. Bluma Yulianovna Zaliaznik documents, SFIRC, Roll 103, NARA.

30 Reports, N.H. Castle, 21 August 1919; 7 August 1919. SFIRC, Roll 101, NARA.

31 Letter No. 3, 13 November 1919. SFIRC Records, Roll 103, NARA.

32 Vladimir Vesninsky, "Under the Church," *Russkaia zhizn'*, 14 September 1926.

33 Romanovsky to Russian Embassy, Washington, DC, 13 November 1919; N.H. Castle Report 7 August 1919. SFIRC, Roll 103, NARA.

34 "Communists in Oakland," *San Francisco Examiner*, 12 November 1919. SFIRC, Roll 103, NARA. Oakland is across the bay from San Francisco.

35 Sakovich, "Angel Island Immigration Station Reconsidered," chapter VI; Lee and Yung, *Angel Island*, chapter 6, on interrogations of Russians.

36 Russian Consul to Russian Ambassador, 3/16 May 1918. Roll 103, SFIRC Records, NARA.

37 Bulletin No. 12, 12 August 1923. Borzov Papers, Box 11:1, HIA.

38 Berglund, *Making San Francisco American*, 130. "Opium smoking was considered to transpire in 'every sleeping-room in Chinatown'" in San Francisco. Shah, *Contagious Divides*, 91. Berglund's study ends in 1906; Shah's work spans mid-nineteenth to mid-twentieth century.

39 Notes (undated), Shapiro Papers, Box 7:10, HIA.

40 "From Royal Robes to Rags," *San Francisco Chronicle*, 16 May 1920.

41 "Finding Odd Jobs for Exiled Aristocrats," *San Francisco Chronicle*, 21 August 1921.

42 "Russians in Exile," *San Francisco Chronicle*, 4 November 1920.

43 "Does a General Wait on Your Table or a Countess Mend Your Clothes?" *San Francisco Chronicle*, 28 May 1922.

44 Ellery Queen, "The Adventure of the Glass Domed Clock" (1933), 109–10.

Notes to pages 53–9

45 Romanticized stories about Russian refugees. For example: "The Love Quest that Triumphed through a Song," *San Francisco Chronicle*, 19 September 1920; "Two Love Calamities Tell the Tragedy of Russia," *San Francisco Chronicle*, 23 April 1922.

46 "526 Czarist Refugees Find Haven Here," *San Francisco Chronicle*, 2 July 1923; *Russkaia zhizn'*, "Arrival of the Stark Group," 6 July 1923; Surname spelled "Klomatovich" in newspaper.

47 "800 Children due in SF Monday," *San Francisco Chronicle*, 31 July 1920; "'Kiddie Ship' Arrives with 800 Refugees," 2 August 1920. Parents' occupations in children's roster, League of Red Cross Societies, The Petrograd Children [*sic*] Colony, American National Red Cross [ANRC] Records, Box 132:1, HIA. For details of journey, see Bogdan, "Between Dreams and Reality," chapter 4.

48 "Armed Russ Dancer in S.F. Ready for Trouble," *San Francisco Chronicle*, 7 April 1922; Tamara Balaeff, "Naturalization Records of the USDC for the Southern District of California, Central Division (Los Angeles), 1887–1940," NARA.

49 Alexander Lawb, "PFN," NAI 605504, Records of USDC, NARA; US Census 1920, San Francisco AD 31.

50 "Passenger Held by Authorities," *San Francisco Chronicle*, 18 February 1918.

51 "Ex-President of Russia is Visitor in SF," *San Francisco Chronicle*, 10 February 1919.

52 "Port Officials Seize Russians as 'Red' Agents," *San Francisco Chronicle*, 19 December 1919.

53 "US Releases Russians Held as Bolsheviki," *San Francisco Chronicle*, 20 December 1919.

54 On 25 January 1918, Acting Secretary of State "requested that immigration officials at all ports of entry send monthly lists of 'all Russians entering the United States.'" File 54277/Gen, Entry 9, NARA, cited by Sakovich, "Angel Island Immigration Station Reconsidered," 151.

55 "Banned Russian Refugees Face Death if Deported," *Washington Post*, 7 October 1923.

56 *San Francisco Chronicle*, 13 July 1923 (author's emphasis).

57 "Earthquake Halts Alien Deportation," *San Francisco Chronicle*, 6 September 1923; "Disposition of 80 Russians Puzzle," *San Francisco Chronicle*, 15 September 1923; "Russians Win Delay on Deportation Order," *San Francisco Chronicle*, 16 October 1923.

58 "Russ Refugees Arrive Here," *San Francisco Chronicle*, 1 August 1921; RNSA application, Borzov Papers, Box 9:4, HIA.

59 Nadejda Vasilievna Vitt, "PFN," NAI 605504, Records of USDC, NARA; Alexander Gavrilovich Nikitin, "PFN From the U.S. District Court for the Southern District of New York, 1897–1944," NAI 575701, Records of USDC, NARA; On Harbin, Clausen and Thøgersen, *The Making of a Chinese City*, chapter 3; Harris, *Factories of Death*, chapters 1–2; Stephan, *The Russian Fascists*, chapters 5–6.

60 "Russ Students Seek Refuge and Education in California," *San Francisco Chronicle*, 1 May 1922; RNSA applications, Borzov Papers, Box 9:4, HIA; Ruzanna Serge Bebenin, "PFN," NAI 605504, Records of USDC, NARA; Vera Nina Reed, Natalie Cooper, *US Social Security Applications and Claims Index*.

61 "25 Students Held Here from Russia," *San Francisco Daily News*, 30 August 1922.

62 On class and social status in late Imperial Russia, see Clowes, et al., eds., *Between Tsar and People*.

63 Notes and reminiscences, Shapiro Papers, Box 1:1, HIA. On Siberian-Alaskan-Californian connections, Shapiro wrote articles for the *San Francisco Examiner*, including "Old Russian Alaska Inspires Romance," 28 October 1923, emphasizing link between Alaska and California. On Orthodox ritual, acquaintance with Father "V" (Vladimir Sakovich at Holy Trinity Cathedral), see "Girl Reporter," Shapiro Papers, Box 5:36, HIA.

64 "Chronicle of revolutionary events in Blagoveshchensk," undated, Box 4:7, 4:16, and biography, 2 December 1924, in letter draft, 12 December 1933, Box 3:29, Shapiro Papers, HIA.

65 Personal Recollections, "Conquest of America," Von Arnold Papers, Boxes 1:3, 3:5–6, 11:11, HIA.

66 Shapiro to Mikhail Vinokuroff, 18 November 1934, Shapiro Papers, Box 3:47, HIA.

67 Shapiro to Mr W.H. Mack, 7 January 1936, Shapiro Papers, Box 3:16, HIA.

340 | Notes to pages 59–66

68 "American vs. Russian," 31 August 1965, Von Arnold Papers, Box 3:6:206, HIA.

69 Willoughby to Merle Crowell, *American* magazine editor, 24 February 1927, Shapiro Papers, Box 3:50, HIA. Barrett Willoughby was a pen name of Florence Barrett.

70 Lavrova, "Alaska's Fighting Russian Priest Helps Win from Reds," *San Francisco Examiner*, 2 November 1924. APK Scrapbook, 1906–1939, ASML.

71 The "modern [Orthodox] Living Church" was under control of the Soviet government. Kedrovsky ultimately won control of St Nicholas Cathedral in New York. Hassell, "Russian Refugees," 54.

72 Lavrova, "Alaska's Fighting Russian Priest Helps Win from Reds," *San Francisco Examiner*, 2 November 1924. APK Scrapbook, ASML.

73 Willoughby spent time in Alaska but was born in Wisconsin. Ferrell, *Barrett Willoughby*.

74 Shapiro to "Billie," 24 December 1939, 3 September 1943. Shapiro Papers, Box 3:50, HIA.

75 Lavrova, "Old Russian Alaska Inspires Romance," *San Francisco Examiner*, 28 October 1923.

76 Though Russians use diminutives when addressing very close friends or children, Willoughby's adoption of this practice in English was patronizing.

77 Shapiro and Willoughby Correspondence 1925 to 1950s, Shapiro Papers, Box 3:49–50, HIA. On visions of America and modernity in the inter-war period, see: Miller, *New World Coming*; Allen, *Only Yesterday*; Dawley, *Changing the World*.

78 Lavrova, "Alaska's Fighting Russian Priest Helps Win from Reds," *San Francisco Examiner*, 2 November 1924. APK Scrapbook, ASML.

79 Pierce, *Russian America*, 217–8.

80 Kashevaroff objected to description of his ancestor as Creole, noting "our family was of pure Russian blood and came to Alaska about 1820." Correspondence, Kashevaroff and E.O. Essig, Kashevaroff Papers ca 1901–1935, Folder 4, ASML.

81 Kan, "Guest Editor's Introduction," *Ethnohistory*, 351–61.

82 Lavrova, "Alaska's Fighting Russian Priest Helps Win from Reds," *San Francisco Examiner*, 2 November 1924. APK Scrapbook, ASML (author's emphasis).

83 Willoughby, *Sitka: Portal to Romance*, chapter 6.

84 Ibid. On Kashevaroff, Pierce, *Russian America*, 215–6.

85 Willoughby, *Sitka: Portal to Romance*.

86 Shapiro to "Billie," 27 October 1941. Shapiro Papers, Box 3:50, HIA.

87 Ibid.

88 On San Francisco's 1920s African-American community, see Broussard, *Black San Francisco*, chapter 1.

89 *Russkaia zhizn'*, 12 February 1926. *Russkaia zhizn'* was published for San Francisco and Los Angeles Russian communities in the 1920s; the editorial office was in San Francisco.

90 "Russians and Americans," *Russkaia zhizn'*, 12 March 1926, 5.

91 *Rupor*, "How We Live in America," n.d. (ca. late 1920s/early 1930s), Bazhenova Papers, Box 2:3, HIA.

92 Cherny, *Victor Arnautoff*, 14–15, 108–12. Arnautoff's accounts of his Civil War military service varied; on service as White Army officer, 26–33.

93 Arnautoff, *Zhizn Zanovo*, 49–50.

94 Cherny, *Victor Arnautoff*, 114.

95 Chepourkoff Hayes, *Michael Chepourkoff*, 107–8, 189–93, 250.

96 "How I came to write in English"; "Journey through Time." Shapiro Papers, Boxes 4:14 and 7:10, HIA.

97 "200,000 Russians in Harbin Face Helplessness under Chinese Rule," *San Francisco Examiner*, 3 June 1923. Shapiro Papers, Box 5:14, HIA.

98 Slezkine notes the expression "*zheltyi vopros*," which he translates as "yellow peril," came in to use by Russians in the late imperial Russian period in the context of colonization and the Russian Far East. As such, it referred to Chinese or Korean peoples (specifically, foreigners as a threat to the empire), not to Indigenous peoples of Russia. *Arctic Circles*, 97.

Notes to pages 66–76 | 341

99 Lavrova, "Admirals of Russia Swab Deck Gladly," *San Francisco Examiner*, 2 August 1925.
100 Berglund, *Making San Francisco American*, 97–8.
101 RNSA Bulletin 12, 12 August 1923. Borzov Papers, Box 11:1, HIA. The argument was not successful; many in this group remained in detention for up to three months.
102 Vsevolod Ivanov, "Russians in Service to the East," *Russkaia zhizn'*, 29 April 1927.
103 On immigrants identifying as white over time, see Guglielmo, *White on Arrival* and Hirsch, "E Pluribus Duo?"
104 Interview with "G" (aka Gleb), Paul Radin Papers, SERA, 1933–2000, Series I/Radin Ethnic Surveys, Box 2, SFHC, SFPL.
105 The "Golden Horde," a segment of the Mongol Empire, established by Genghis Khan, invaded Russia in the 1200s and ruled for two centuries. Martin, *Medieval Russia*, chapters 5–10.
106 Jacobson, "Becoming Caucasian, 1924–1965," in *Whiteness of a Different Color*.

Chapter Three

1 Mezzo soprano Esther Vera Merenbach sang Romany and Ukrainian songs in KFRC radio concert. "Radio Concert of Mrs. Merenbach," *Russkaia zhizn'*, 14 May 1926.
2 Anonymous author on "the struggle to maintain one's identity in the face of the yoke of triviality" (*naiti sily dlia bor'by za svoe ia protiv gneta obydenshchiny*) in America. "Masquerade Ball, 19 Feb.," *Russkaia zhizn'*, 18 February 1927. The author suggested dancing, rather than drink, as a method of escape.
3 T. Bazhenova, *Rubezh*, "Russians in a New Temple," n.d., on Russian choreographer Adolph Bolm's (1884–1951) leading role in organizing and directing San Francisco Opera Ballet School, 1933–1937. Articles (Russian), Adolph Bolm Collection, LOC, author's emphasis.
4 "Russ Artists Find Spirit to Work Here," *San Francisco Examiner*, 24 June 1923. Father Sakovich arrived in 1918 and served at Holy Trinity until his death in 1931 (see chapters 5–6).
5 Buford Gordon Bennett, "Dalgeim's Russians in 'Chat Noir' Rehearsal for their Week at the Curran," *San Francisco Examiner*, 4 November 1923, author's emphasis.
6 Ben-Sira, *Immigration, Stress, and Readjustment*, chapters 1–3.
7 Grinberg and Grinberg, *Psychoanalytic Perspective on Migration and Exile*, 87.
8 Letters to editor from Russian workers' groups in *Russkaia zhizn'*, 1922–1927, which billed itself as "non-partisan."
9 "Russian writers," in "Speeches and Writings," Shapiro Papers, Box 7:3, HIA.
10 Raeff, *Russia Abroad*, 8.
11 Boym, *Common Places*, 29–40.
12 Kelly, "*Byt*," 149.
13 Jean Delage in *La Russie en exil* (Paris, 1930), 64–8, quoted by Hassell, "Russian Refugees," 49–50.
14 Slobin, *Russians Abroad*, 52.
15 Serebrennikova to Volkov, 7 September 1929, Volkov Papers, Box 2:15, HIA.
16 Borzov to Grebentschikoff, 13 February 1946, Grebentschikoff Papers, Box 14:4, IHRCA.
17 "American vs. Russian," 31 August 1965, Von Arnold Papers, Box 3:6:206.
18 E. Isaenko Recollections, "Theater in San Francisco," Isaenko Papers, Box 7:13, HIA. Screenplay by Peter M. Komaroff (1897–1972), cameraman Anatoly V. Anichkoff (1897–1970). The filmed "play," was shown 14 September (likely 1949) at a Russian Center gathering. "'Tuesday' of Museum-Archive," undated clipping, RC Papers, Box 2:6, MRC. MRC staff responded to author's inquiries that no such film exists in their archives.
19 E. Grot, "Den' Russkoi kultury [Day of Russian Culture]," *Russkaia zhizn'*, 22 October 1926.
20 S.S. *Korea Maru*, "PLV SF," NAI 4498993, Records of the INS, NARA.
21 "A Cultural Corner of the Russian Colony in San Francisco" in *Dymny sled* [Smoke wake], (1926), Landesen Papers, Box 1:3, HIA.

342 | Notes to pages 76–82

22 On Russian community in Los Angeles, see H. Robinson, *Russians in Hollywood*. On New York Community, see: Hassell, "Russian Refugees"; N. Zelensky, *Performing Tsarist Russia in New York*.

23 "Russ Artists Find Spirit to Work Here," *San Francisco Examiner*, 24 June 1923; "Kalmykov to Grigory Golubeff, 6 February 1924," *Russkaia zhizn'*, 8 January 1924 (author's note: "January" is a misprint; it is the 8 February issue).

24 Le Heart interview, 15 July 1945, Hollywood, California, E/A file, MRC. Le Heart arrived 1917. Phelan held, among others, posts as San Francisco Mayor (1897–1902) and US Senator from California (1915–1921). He was a virulent and life-long opponent of Asian immigration.

25 *Boyars* were non-hereditary nobility in Russia. Peter the Great eliminated ranking in the early eighteenth century.

26 "Russian Clergy Observe Jubilee," *San Francisco Examiner*, 13 September 1925.

27 "Parade of Nations," *Russkaia zhizn'*, 18 September 1925, E/A file, MRC.

28 Alexander Grigorievich Ignatieff, "PFN," NAI 605504, Records of USDC, NARA; Board of Special Inquiry testimony of Grigorii Ignatieff, Manifest No. 29883/13-8 US Dept of Labor, Immigration Service, 15 December 1930, NARA.

29 "Gorgeous Fete Climaxes Jubilee Week," *San Francisco Examiner*, 13 September 1925.

30 *California's Diamond Jubilee*, 89.

31 "Our Diamond Jubilee," *Los Angeles Times*, 4 September 1925. "Brilliant Parade Ends Jubilee Fete," *Oakland Tribune*, 13 September 1925.

32 Higham, *Strangers in the Land*, 237.

33 Referencing location of Holy Trinity Cathedral on Green Street.

34 "Letter to editor," *Russkaia zhizn'*, 2 October 1925.

35 Flamm, *Good Life in Hard Times*, 72.

36 Valentina Vernon, "Recollections of Life in Russia and in Emigration," oral history transcript (1980), 26–38.

37 P. Karelin, "Russian Center," *Russkaia zhizn'*, 31 December 1926; advertisements, SFRE file, SFHC, SFPL; Joseph Cykman, "PFN," NAI 605504, Records of USDC, NARA.

38 "Russians in San Francisco," (1942), Von Arnold Papers, Box 13:3, HIA.

39 Émigré Nicholas V. Riasanovsky emphasized the factor of geography with respect to anti-Semitism in Russia. Professor of Russian and European Intellectual History, University of California, Berkeley, 1957–1997; interview by Ann Lage (1996), Regional Oral History Office, Bancroft Library, University of California, Berkeley, 1–5.

40 Russian students listed place of birth/religious confession in RNSA applications. Borzov Papers, Box 9, HIA. At least three passengers arriving on USAT *Merritt* in 1923 were initially listed as "Tartars." Mikhail Ganeeff, Samigoola Gareeff, and Fatih Gazizoff, USAT *Merritt*, "PLV SF," NAI 4498993, Records of the INS, NARA.

41 Alexander Grigorievich Ignatieff, "PFN," NAI 605504, Records of USDC, NARA; Board of Special Inquiry testimony of Grigorii Ignatieff, Manifest No. 29883/13-8 US Dept of Labor, Immigration Service, 15 December 1930, NARA; Wolff, *To the Harbin Station*, chapter 3, on population groups in Harbin in early 1900s.

42 "Society of Friends of Russian Freedom," *Novaya Zarya*, circa January 1930; Volkov to Grebenstchikoff, 26 January 1930. Grebenstchikoff Papers, Box 43:3, IHRCA.

43 "To Workers of the Russian Colony," *Russkaia zhizn'*, 22 January 1926.

44 "ROC," *Russkaia zhizn'*, 2 December 1927.

45 Landesen to Phelps, 3 July 1933. Landesen Papers, Box 1:1, HIA. Russian consul general in Seattle Nicholas Bogoiavlensky asked Landesen, Russian vice consul in Harbin (1914–1921), to handle consular duties in San Francisco March 1926. Documents/Correspondence, Landesen Papers, Box 1:1; "Vnezapnaya konchina [Unexpected Passing of] A. Yu. Landesen," *Novaya Zarya*, 14 May 1935, Bazhenova Papers, Box 5:2, HIA.

46 Pavel S. Krasnik/Krasnikov aka Karelin, *Russkaia zhizn'* editor, 1924–1927. Born in Moscow, arrived in 1923; "Death of P.S. Krasnik, Former Editor of Newspaper, *Russkaia zhizn'*,"

Notes to pages 82-8 | **343**

Russian News-Life, n.d. (1939), Bazhenova Papers, Box 5:2, HIA; Paul Sergeev Krasnikov, "PFN," NAI 605504, Records of USDC, NARA.

47 "Letter to my auntie," *Russkaia zhizn'*, 12 August 1927.

48 See, for example, Theodore Roosevelt's comments advocating for "100 percent" Americanism in 1915. Ngai and Gjerde, 319–21.

49 Vassiliev notes penchant for dressing in *boyar* costumes among Russian elites during the reign of Nicholas II, describing the trend as an "upsurge of Russian patriotism." *Beauty in Exile*, 41. The decision in San Francisco spoke more to providing the kind of spectacle American parade officials expected.

50 Photographs show depictions of Nikolay Rezanov and Conchita Arguello (1806), Admiral Popov's visit to San Francisco Bay (1863), and "Russian Contributions" to California. See Zaverukha and Bogdan, *Russian San Francisco*, 35–7; originals: E/A file, MRC.

51 Vladimir Lenin issued a decree in 1921 depriving unreturned Russian subjects of nationality. Hassell, "Russian Refugees," 18.

52 V. Peshehonov, "Russian success," *Russkaia zhizn'*, 9 October 1925.

53 *Russkaia zhizn'*, 2 September 1922.

54 "Russians Here would Return Soviets Told," *San Francisco Chronicle*, 20 March 1922.

55 Lavrova's phrasing on Molokan perceptions, article draft, March 1929, Shapiro Papers, Box 5:26, HIA; on California Commune, Cherny, *San Francisco Reds*, chapter 1; Moore, *Molokan Oral Tradition*, 8.

56 "Troubling News about Molokane in Don Region," *Russkaia zhizn'*, 21 March 1924.

57 Shanovsky, "Among Molokane," *Russkaia zhizn'*, 26 March 1926; 14 January 1927; telegram to *Examiner*; Lavrova article draft, March 1929, Shapiro Papers, Box 5:26, HIA; Cyprian Shanowsky, "PFN," NAI 605504, Records of USDC, NARA. Shanovsky worked at San Francisco's Russian Consulate prior to 1917. Shanovsky to RNSA, 31 May 1932, Borzov Papers, Box 4:3, HIA. Shanovsky referenced the "California Commune" in discussion about those wishing to return, but the Don region commune founded by San Francisco members was not part of the California Commune, according to Cherny, *San Francisco Reds*, 218n17.

58 Bataiff to Shanovsky, 22 December 1925, Shapiro Papers, Box 5:26; Shapiro on Bataiff, Box 8:12, HIA.

59 Lavrova's draft, March 1929, Shapiro Papers, Box 5:26, HIA.

60 Fetesoff's comments, Lavrova's article draft, March 1929, Shapiro Papers, Box 5:26, HIA; S.S. *Ile de France* and S.S. *Paris*, "Passenger and Crew Lists of Vessels Arriving at New York, New York, 1897–1957," NAI T715, Records of the INS, NARA.

61 Album 24, Vrangel Papers, Box 49, HIA; "Russian Club's Program Tonight," *San Francisco Examiner*, 23 July 1927.

62 "Russians in America" *Russkaia zhizn'*, 27 April 1923; "Letter to the editor," 2 October 1925.

63 Russian language "Bank of Italy Russian Department" pamphlet, 44, E/A file, MRC.

64 Weekly Bank of Italy advertisements in *Russkaia zhizn'*, 1922–1927.

65 *Russkaia gazeta*, 5 October 1921. The word "job" was transliterated into Cyrillic. See chapter 4 on jobs.

66 *Russkaia zhizn'*, 26 November 1926.

67 "Cultural work," *Russkaia zhizn'*, 11 February 1927.

68 Gordenker's obituary, *Novaya Zarya*, 22 November 1932, Shapiro Papers, Box 2:20, HIA.

69 *Russkaia zhizn'*, 23 October 1925; Nathan Merenbach, "Christmas Holiday Greetings," *Russkaia zhizn'*, 5 December 1925; "To the Russian Colony," *Russkaia zhizn'*, 5 March 1926; *Russkaia zhizn'*, 15 October 1926; Benefit Concert and Ball program for Russian disabled veterans, 12 November 1938, SFRE File, SFHC, SFPL. The Merenbachs had several offices including in the Fillmore.

70 "P.F. Tesluck," *San Francisco Examiner*, 14 April 1965; Evdokia Tesluck, "PFN," NAI 605504, Records of USDC, NARA; documents on purchase of 2450 Sutter Street building, RC Papers, Box 1:1, MRC.

71 Post, *The Story of the Postnikov Family*, 78–9, 99–100, 116.
72 Ibid., 21–56, 205.
73 Issel and Cherny, *San Francisco, 1865–1932*, 66–70.
74 "The Russian-American Club," *Russkaia zhizn'*, 6 November 1925; 25 December 1925; 8 January 1926. Engineering was the chosen field for many Russian students in the 1920s. The American engineers were Howard Brown and "Beckman" (first name unknown).
75 *Russkaia zhizn'*, January–February 1926.
76 "A brief study of Russian students in the University of California, 1920–1937," Von Arnold Papers, Box 12:2, HIA.
77 N. Zelensky, *Performing Tsarist Russia in New York*, 71.
78 Ibid., 73.
79 W.E.B. DuBois, *Black Reconstruction in America, 1860–1880*, 700, cited by Feagin in "Toward an Integrated Theory of Systemic Racism," 216.
80 N. Zelensky, *Performing Tsarist Russia in New York*, 93; H. Robinson, *Russians in Hollywood*.
81 Johnson, *"New Mecca, New Babylon,"* 6.
82 *In the Name of Russia*, 12–14; 114–22. Notably, Belosselsky-Belozersky's father, émigré Prince Sergei Konstantinovich, also married into a very wealthy Bostonian family.
83 N. Zelensky, *Performing Tsarist Russia in New York*, 98.
84 *Russkaia zhizn'*, 6 November 1926; 4 January 1927.
85 *Russkaia zhizn'*, 21 January 1927.
86 Lavrova, "Russians in S.F. Plan for Self Aid," *San Francisco Examiner*, 31 January 1926.
87 "At the Russian Club," *Russkaia zhizn'*, 29 July 1927; "Russian Club's Program Tonight," *San Francisco Examiner*, 23 July 1927; *Russkaia zhizn'*, 11 March 1927; 1 April 1927.
88 "The Russian Club," *Russkaia zhizn'*, 29 April 1927.
89 Russian Club documents, RC Papers, Box 1:4; Borzov Papers, Box 2:1.
90 Rachmaninoff event clippings, 1942, Bazhenova Papers, Box 4:3, HIA.
91 Russia Abroad recognized some San Francisco émigrés for literary achievements, but they were virtually unknown outside émigré circles (e.g., Boris Volkov in 1933 for *V pyli chuzhih dorog* (In the Dust of Faraway Roads)); Eugenia Isaenko for *Perekati-Pole* (Tumbleweed); and Peter Balakshin.
92 *Russkaia zhizn'*, 1922–1927.
93 Laub advertised in *Russkaia zhizn'* in the 1920s; Ermoloff's activities in Beliaeff's album; studio at 2956 Sacramento Street: CH file, MRC. Both relocated to Los Angeles.
94 *Russian News-Life*, "Concert of E.V. Boris' Students," 17 June 1938, Bazhenova Papers, Box 5:2, HIA.
95 Album 24, Vrangel Papers, Box 49, HIA.
96 For discussions of social changes in Russian society leading up to World War I, see Clowes, et al., eds., *Between Tsar and People*.
97 M. Shevchenko, *Russkaia zhizn'*, 19 March 1926.
98 ART events fliers and reviews, Isaenko Papers, Box 11, HIA.
99 "OMON," *Russkaia zhizn'*, 8 January 1926.
100 On Kolobok, see Lambert, *Natalie Wood*, 16. A "Bohemian Café" aka the "Russian Club Café" opened at 1119 Market Street, outside the Fillmore, in the mid-1920s. "Reopening of the Russian Club Café," *San Francisco Examiner*, 8 March 1925.
101 Album 24, Vrangel Papers, Box 49, HIA. Victor Peshehonov (1878–1950) directed. On Europe, see Avins, *Border Crossings*, 91.
102 Utemoff's professional surname as a dancer, actor, and choreographer was Temoff. Sergei Utemoff, "PFN," NAI 605504, Records of USDC, NARA; "Interview with and Departure of N.N. Ermoloff," *Russkaia zhizn'*, 22 January 1944, Borzov Papers, Box 3:34, HIA.
103 "Assembly Thursday to Feature Baritone, Serafim Strelkoff," *Globe-Gazette* (Mason City, Iowa), 22 April 1950.

Notes to pages 97–104

104 *Freeport Journal Standard* (Freeport Illinois), "'Singing Globe Trotter' Entertains Lions Club: Russian-American Bass Baritone Sings During Noon Meeting Today," 28 March 1939. The Strelkoffs were among the few who repatriated to the Soviet Union after World War II.

105 Anonymous author on escaping triviality of *byt*. "Masquerade Ball, 19 Feb.," *Russkaia zhizn'*, 18 February 1927.

106 E. Grot, "Victims of Troubled Times," *Russkaia zhizn'*, 15 April 1927.

107 V. Voljanin, "Tatyana's Day," *Russkaia zhizn'*, 28 January 1927.

108 "Invalid Committee Formal Meeting," *Russia News-Life*, 26 May 1939, Bazhenova Papers, Box 5:2, HIA.

109 Hassell, "Russian Refugees," 58; N. Zelensky, *Performing Tsarist Russia in New York*, 10.

110 "Russians in San Francisco," (1942): Von Arnold Papers, Box 13:3, HIA.

111 Eugenia Bailey, phone interview by author, 15 November 2021.

112 Russian consuls in Japan issued Nansen passports to émigrés in the 1920s. See chapter 7 on travel documentation.

Chapter Four

Russian war veteran comparing sound of lumber mill machinery to machine gun fire and recalling how soldiers dealt with stress of combat. RNSA Bulletin no. 14, February 1924, Borzov Papers, Box 11:1, HIA

1 On "Muscovite" and "Russian invasions" in New York prior to 1917, see Walter Vogdes, "The Smart Set Must Have a Russian Background Now," *San Francisco Chronicle*, 15 April 1923.

2 RNSA Bulletin no. 14, February 1924, Borzov Papers, Box 11:1, HIA.

3 Obituary of Col V.I. Konevega, who died from injuries in car accident. "Society of Russian Veterans Newsletter" [hereinafter "Newsletter"], June 1934, IHRCA. Author's emphasis.

4 Denning, *The Cultural Front*, 16.

5 "George J. Valter of ILWU Dies," *San Francisco Examiner*, 8 June 1970; Birth, Marriage, and Death Register (1931–1948), HVC Papers, Box 35:2, WDA; *Great Register of Voters, 1900–1968*, California State Library (CSL), Sacramento CA; *U.S. Department of Veterans Affairs BIRLS Death File, 1850–2010*.

6 RNSA application, Borzov Papers, Box 9:4.

7 "Fatal Fumes of Bug Exterminator Kill 2 Men Here," *Daily News* (Los Angeles), 28 July 1924; "Probe Deaths of 2 Men form Cyanide Gas," *Los Angeles Evening Express*, 28 July 1924; "Unavoidable Death Verdict in Case of Victims of Cyanide," *Press-Telegram* (Long Beach, CA), 31 July 1924; "Cyanide Fumes Kill Two," *Los Angeles Times*, 28 July 1924. Less than a month later, another worker, Jesus Perez, was also killed by cyanide fumes in Whittier. "Fumes Kill Rancher," *Los Angeles Evening Post-Record*, 18 August 1924.

8 "The Tragic Death of P.A. Golovinsky," and "Obituary of P.A. Golovinsky" by B. Zonn, *Russkaia zhizn'*, 23 October 1925.

9 A USAT *Merritt* passenger denied entry suffered from "shell shock." "Red Refugees Denied Entry," *San Francisco Chronicle*, 13 July 1923.

10 Dubinets, *Russian Composers Abroad*, 216.

11 "Newsletters" 1926–1936, IHRCA and RNSA records, Borzov Papers, Boxes 3, 4, 5, 9, 11, HIA. Other military-based organizations in 1920s San Francisco were the Naval-Maritime Association, the Cossacks Union, and the Musketeers' Union. See Okorokov, *Russkaia Emigratsia, 1920–1990*, on émigré political/military organizations.

12 Dubinets, *Russian Composers Abroad*, 216; Undated/untitled typescript: Bazhenova Papers, Box 2:2, HIA.

13 "Japan Tired of Russ Refugees," *San Francisco Chronicle*, 12 December 1922; "Beaten and Broken Enemies of Bolshevism Haunted by Their Terrible Memories," and "Russ Odyssey

Tale of Hunger and of Disease," *Honolulu Star Bulletin*, 20–21 June 1923. On flotilla, see: Rear-Admiral Y.C. Stark, "Report on the activities of the Siberian Flotilla during 1921-1922," *The Naval Records*, Association of Russian Imperial Naval Officers in America, Inc., New York, Vol. XIII, No. 2/3, August 1955, 68–81 and Vol. XIV No. 1 April 1956, 53–69, IHRCA; "They've Arrived," *Russkaia zhizn'*, 6 July 1923; "Remnant of White Russian Force Reaches US Haven," *Washington Post*, 2 July 1923; Chzhichen, *History of Russian Emigration in Shanghai*, 22–40; Bogdan, "Between Dreams and Reality," chapter 3.

14 "Russian Refugees to be Admitted," *Los Angeles Times*, 27 April 1923.

15 On Stark, Lada Tremsina, "The Long Journey from the Golden Horn to the Golden Gate," *Russkaia zhizn'*, 16 and 23 June 2018.

16 Consul General to Ughet, 27 April 1923, SFIRC Records, Roll 152, NARA.

17 Ughet to Romanovsky, 1 May 1923, SFIRC Records, Roll 152, NARA.

18 General Secretary, Russian Refugee Relief Society of America to Col Bicknell, Vice-Chairman, Foreign Operations, American Red Cross, Washington, DC, 16 May 1923; Ughet to Romanovsky, 30 April 1923, SFIRC Records, Roll 152, NARA. The Czech and Slovak legionnaires had fought the Bolsheviks in Siberia.

19 Ughet to Romanovsky, 30 April 1923, SFIRC Records, Roll 152, NARA.

20 Sakovich, "Angel Island Immigration Station Reconsidered," 60; Lewis and Schibsby, "Status of the Refugee," 76.

21 SS *Taiyo Maru*, "PLV SF," NAI 4498993, Records of the INS, NARA.

22 "Remnant of White Russian Force Reaches US Haven," *Washington Post*, 2 July 1923.

23 Ibid. "Message from General Heiskanen," *Honolulu Star Bulletin*, 20 June 1923; USAT *Merritt*, "PLV SF," NAI 4498993, Records of the INS, NARA.

24 "Remnant of White Russian Force Reaches US Haven," *Washington Post*, 2 July 1923; "Message from General Heiskanen," *Honolulu Star Bulletin*, 20 June 1923; Erakle Hounkloff, "WWII Draft Registration Cards for California," NAI 7644723, Records of the Selective Service System [SSS], NARA.

25 "They have Arrived," and "Arrival of the Stark Group," *Russkaia zhizn'*, 6 July 1923.

26 Tremsina, *Russkaia zhizn'*, 30 June 2018.

27 Hassell, "Russian Refugees," 11.

28 E. Bailey phone interview, 15 November 2021; US Census, 1930, San Francisco AD 30, block 53.

29 Simpson, *The Refugee Problem*, 85. Based on RNSA statistics compiled by the author: 85 per cent of students were male; USAT *Merritt* passengers' lists: 14 per cent of 526 were women.

30 E. Bailey phone interview, 15 November 2021. On Russian military veterans in Europe in inter-war period, see Robinson, *The White Russian Army in Exile*.

31 From *Russkaia zhizn'*: "Mania of suicide in Harbin," 5 February 1926; "Epidemic of suicides in Harbin," 12 March 1926; "Starvation and suicide await invalids without help ... 68-year-old General Beneskul killed himself in Greece," 19 March 1926; "Thousands of graves unmarked ... suicides," 26 March 1926; Reports of 3–4 suicides a day in Harbin, 30 July 1926; A report of increase in suicides in Harbin, 11 March 1927.

32 Interview with "Mr A" by (Alexander D.) Lifantieff, 26 February 1935, Radin Papers.

33 Register (1931–1948), HVC Papers, Box 35:2, WDA; "Andre George Antonoff Obituary," *San Francisco Examiner*, 16 March 1982; "WWII Draft Registration Cards for California," NAI 7644723, Records of the SSS, NARA.

34 *Russkaia gazeta*, 14 May 1921.

35 Caruth, *Unclaimed Experience*, 65.

36 "St George Greek Orthodox Church," http://www.stgeorgegoc.org/pastors-corner/suicide, accessed 11 April 2020.

37 RNSA Bulletin, 14 February 1924, Borzov Papers, Box 11:1, HIA; Nicolas Nicolach Masloff, *San Francisco Area Funeral Home Records, 1895–1985*.

Notes to pages 109–22 | **347**

38 "Tragic Death," *Russkaia zhizn'*, 16 July 1926; "Hundreds See Beach Suicide," *San Francisco Chronicle*, 14 July 1926; "Bay Man Drowns," *Napa Journal*, 14 July 1926; "S.F. Bay Suicide's Motive is Sought," *Oakland Tribune*, 14 July 1926.

39 "Suicide of S.A. Trinko," *Russian Life-News*, 14 May 1941, Isaenko Papers, Box.11:2, HIA.

40 "'Funny Guy' Ends Life by Dynamite," *Oroville Mercury Register*, 24 February 1937.

41 "Stranger Leaps to 3-Story Death," *San Francisco Examiner*, 15 May 1938; RNSA application, Borzov Papers, Box 9:4, HIA.

42 "Funeral Rites Tomorrow for Student Suicide," *Oakland Tribune*, 5 October 1934.

43 "Finds Hubby Dead," *Napa Journal*, 28 April 1937.

44 "Accidents, Suicides Claim Twelve in Northern California," *Chico Record*, 24 August 1937.

45 Van Der Kolk, *The Body Keeps the Score*, 53.

46 Ibid., 18.

47 US Census, 1940, Mendocino State Hospital, Ukiah CA; San Francisco City Directories, 1931–1934; Seattle City Directory, 1941; Georgia Institute of Technology yearbook, 1929.

48 US Census, 1940, Stockton State Hospital, Stockton, CA.

49 Eugene Nikolaevich Chernigovsky, Nina Alexandrovna Chern, "PFN," NAI 605504, Records of USDC, NARA; US Census, 1940, Mendocino State Hospital, Ukiah CA; Eugene Nicolas Chern, *San Francisco Area Funeral Home Records, 1895–1985*.

50 Van Der Kolk, 21, 43.

51 Sadowski-Smith, *The New Immigrant Whiteness*, 6–7.

52 Lavrova, "Theater of Moods Offered by Chat Noir," *San Francisco Examiner*, 5 November 1923; Bennett, "Dalgeim's Russians," 4 November 1923. On trauma, see Alexander, *Trauma: A Social Theory*, chapter 1.

53 M. Kulakova, "Ghosts of the Past," *Russkaia zhizn'*, 15 April 1927.

54 Balakshin, "Demented Norma's Dance," in *Spring over the Fillmore*, 36–7.

55 Newsletter Nos. 87–88, Aug–Sept 1933, IHRCA.

56 Newsletter No. 86, July 1933, IHRCA. The "cup of tea" was and remains a ubiquitous event spanning all Russian émigré (and later Russian American) organizations: rather than a "cocktail hour," Russians gather for a cup of tea and light refreshments to converse and socialize.

57 Olferieff, *Russia in War and Revolution*, 284. On birthplaces, RNSA student applications, Borzov Papers, Box 9, HIA.

58 Newsletter No. 86, July 1933: IHRCA. Grand Duke Nikolay Nikolayevich, grandson of Czar Nicholas I, cousin to Czar Nicholas II. Russian émigré monarchist groups were broadly divided into "absolutists" and "moderates" with the latter supporting Grand Duke Nikolay Nikolayevich. Veterans considered the Civil War a continuation of the Great War (World War I).

59 Boodberg, "How the Czar was Deceived," Newsletter No. 8, 9 December 1926; "There is no greater love," Newsletter No. 21, January 1928, IHRCA.

60 White Army General Peter Wrangel founded ROVS in 1924 to aid White Guard veterans, with headquarters in Sremski Karlovci in the Kingdom of Serbs, Croats, and Slovenes (later Yugoslavia).

61 Robinson, *White Armies in Exile*, citing "Newsletter," 154/155, Mar–Apr 1939, 1–2, 167.

62 Newsletter 95–6, April–May 1934; History of Society in Newsletter, No. 1, 16 May 1926, 1–6, IHRCA.

63 Newsletter, April–May 1932, IHRCA.

64 K. Parchevsky, "On the Philippine Islands," undated, Isaenko Papers, Box 11:4, HIA. Liubarsky may have immigrated to Australia.

65 Newsletter No. 1, 16 May 1926, IHRCA.

66 Riasanovsky oral history transcript, 8. Pozdnyakov, *From China to America*, 136. Boodberg's children were Valentina (Waripaeff/Vernon by marriage), Peter, Paul, and Alexander, all initially residing in San Francisco after emigration.

67 Newsletter No.1, 16 May 1926, IHRCA.

68 *Russkaia zhizn'*, 2 October 1925.
69 Newsletter Nos. 95–6, April–May 1934. On founding and purposes of committee: *Russkaia zhizn'*, 20 November 1925.
70 Ablova, *KVZHD*, 120.
71 Letter No. 903, Mutual Aid Society, Harbin to RNSA, 3 October 1923, Borzov Papers, Box 4:7, HIA.
72 Borzov Papers, Boxes 4, 9, 11, HIA; Raymond and Jones, *The Russian Diaspora*, 77; Lee and Yung, *Angel Island*, 231.
73 Raymond and Jones, *The Russian Diaspora*, 49–50.
74 Com. Edward White to Com-General of Immigration, 12 August 1922; Com-General W.W. Husband to W.J. Burns, Director, Bureau of Investigation, 10 October 1922, File 55605/130 INS COSCCF, NARA. On interrogations of students Maria Kusmina and Nina Karpova (10 August 1922), see Sakovich, "Angel Island Immigration Station Reconsidered," and Bogdan, "Between Dreams and Reality," chapter 3.
75 Vasily V. Ushanoff, "Recollections of Life in the Russian Community in Manchuria and in Emigration" (1981), oral history, 28–30; RNSA applications, Borzov Papers, Box 9, HIA.
76 RNSA documents, Borzov Papers, Box 4:2–4, HIA; 1922–1923 correspondence of Day, Riley, and students, Borzov Papers, Box 11, HIA. Elovsky on Day's and Riley's assistance, *The Russian Students of California* (1926), 55–6, E/A File, MRC. Professors George Noyes and George Patrick (Russian émigré), among others, at UC Berkeley were on a committee to assist Russian students.
77 N. Merenbach's legal advice column, *Russkaia zhizn'*, 23 October 1925; Hassell, "Russian Refugees," 39. Russian Student Fund directors (under auspices of Institute of International Education in US) "expected its beneficiaries to return to the USSR." Hassell, "Russian Refugees," 76.
78 Com. White to Com-Gen of Immigration, Washington, DC, 12 August 1922, File 55605/130 INS COSCCF, NARA.
79 Report "In Re: 'Harbin Committee Rendering Aid to Russian Students," by H.W. Hess 12 September 1922, File 55605/130 INS COSCCF, NARA.
80 Correspondence, reports of US officials Aug 1922 – May 1923, File 55605/130 INS COSCCF, NARA. Hanson suspended issuing visas March 1923 because annual quota was exhausted and began again in June for July (new fiscal year) quota. Sakovich, "Angel Island Immigration Station Reconsidered," 178.
81 Sakovich, "Angel Island Immigration Station Reconsidered," 158.
82 RNSA Bulletin No. 12, 12 August 1923, Borzov Papers, Box 11:1; Lee and Yung, 232–6.
83 "Last-Minute Writ Unites Russ Family," *San Francisco Examiner*, 8 August 1923; SS *Shinyo Maru*, "PLV SF," NAI 4498993; INS Records, NARA.
84 *Russkaia zhizn'*, 27 July 1923.
85 Day to Dmitrieff, 25 August 1922, File 55605/130 INS COSCCF, NARA.
86 Board of Special Inquiry, Angel Island Station, 10 August 1922, No. 21325/26-13; 17, File 55605/130 INS COSCCF, NARA.
87 Olferieff, *Russia in War and Revolution*, 425. The 1924 Johnson-Reed Act mandated that "aliens" had to have an immigration visa, issued by an American consular officer abroad, in hand to enter the United States.
88 Romanovsky to J. Nagle, Immigration Commissioner, 14 August 1923, SFIRC Records, Roll 143, NARA.
89 E. L. Hoff, Commissioner's office, Angel Island to Romanovsky, 16 August 1923, SFIRC Records, Roll 143, NARA.
90 Undated/untitled typescript, Bazhenova Papers, Box 2:2, HIA.
91 Sakovich, "Angel Island Immigration Station Reconsidered,"47–8, citing Tolstoy's memoir *Out of the Past*, 312–3, and Shapiro's manuscript, Shapiro Papers, Box 6, HIA. Behdad, *A Forgetful Nation*, 140–1.
92 C.W. Riley, Student Friendship Fund to S.P. Kovaleff, RNSA, 4 December 1923, Borzov Papers, Box 4:1, HIA; RNSA student applications, Borzov Papers, Box 9, HIA.

Notes to pages 128–34 | **349**

93 Student correspondence, Borzov Papers, Boxes 4, 5, 9, 11; articles and advertisements in *Russkaia zhizn'*, 1922–25.
94 RNSA application, Borzov Papers, Box 9:5, HIA; Tremsina and Pak, "Mending a Broken Thread after a Century's Time," *Russkaia zhizn'*, 24 August 2019.
95 Day to Russian Students, RNSA Bulletin, 15 September 1922, Borzov Papers, Box 11:1, HIA. Day worked for the YMCA in St Petersburg and other Russian cities 1908–1918. See Miller, "American Philanthropy among Russians," 289–340.
96 Reshetnikoff to Kovaleff, 27 August 1922, Borzov Papers, Box 5:3, HIA.
97 Peter Teodor Reshetnikoff, "PFN," NAI 605504, Records of USDC, NARA.
98 Students also worked in mines in Nevada.
99 Correspondence and RNSA documents, Borzov Papers, Boxes 4, 5, 9, 11; newspaper listings, ads, information on hiring in California, *Russkaia zhizn'*, 1923–1925.
100 *Russkaia zhizn'*, 2–3 October 1925.
101 Day to Dmitrieff, 25 August 1922, File 55605/130 INS COSCCF, NARA. Scholarships available at Redlands University, Occidental College, Pomona College, Whittier College, and College of the Pacific. Day informational letter, 10 May 1923, Borzov Papers, Box 12:4, HIA. Students attended University of Southern California, California Institute of Technology, and Pasadena Colleges in Southern California. Day to Kovaleff, 24 October 1923, Borzov Papers, Box 5:1, HIA.
102 Uteyeff to Kovlaeff, 12 September 1922; US Census, 1930, San Francisco, AD 30, Block 93; 1940, Sacramento.
103 Pashinsky to Kovaleff, 1 October 1922, Borzov Papers, Box 5:3; K. Shishkin to B. Shishkin, 25 February 1923, Borzov Papers, Box 5:5, HIA.
104 Gollandskoff to Kovaleff, 15 September 1922, Borzov Papers, Box 5:3, HIA.
105 (Mark?) Lifshitz to unknown, 23 August, no year (ca. 1923), Borzov Papers, Box 5:1, HIA.
106 *Russkii golos*, "Russians in America," 18 May 1924, Shapiro Papers, Box 9:10, HIA.
107 Nikolai All, "University of California," *Russkaia zhizn'*, 19 September 1926.
108 Correspondence of Knowles, Riley, Kovaleff, September 1923; Bill Stallings, YMCA to Turleminsky, RNSA, 20 September 1926, Borzov Papers, Box 4:7–8, HIA.
109 RNSA charters, meeting minutes, lists of members, Borzov Papers, Box 4:2–4, HIA.
110 Minutes of Joint Meeting of RSC and RNSA committees, 9 October 1921, Borzov Papers, Box 12:5, HIA.
111 Minutes, 9 October 1921, Borzov Papers, Box 12:5, HIA; Solomon Philip Milovich, "PFN," NAI 605504, Records of USDC, NARA.
112 Alexander and Grigorii Ignatieff interviews, Manifest No. 29883/13-8 US Dept of Labor, Immigration Service, Board of Special Inquiry, 15 December 1930, NARA.
113 *Oakland Tribune*, "Elopement Called Off by Mother," 27 February 1931; Student documents, Borzov Papers, Box 4, HIA; US Census, 1940, Contra Costa County CA; "'Iron Mike' Bricksin Dies in Roseville," *Sacramento Bee*, 27 March 1982.
114 Briksin Obituary, *Oakland Tribune*, 8 September 1954.
115 Lease information, history of RNSA, Borzov Papers, Boxes 9:3, 11:3, HIA. Addresses 2110, 2112, 2115 Durant Street.
116 Elovsky, *The Russian Students of California*, 45, E/A File, MRC.
117 Correspondence, Borzov Papers, Box 4:9; RNSA history by S. Kovaleff; St Tatyana's day history by "P.P."; Announcement, Borzov Papers, Box 11:3–4, HIA.
118 RNSA Board to colleagues, undated, Borzov Papers, Box 9:4; Open letters, Kovaleff, RNSA secretary, RNSA Bulletin, 15 September 1922, 12 August 1923, Borzov Papers, Box 11:1.
119 RNSA Bulletin No. 13, September 1923, Borzov Papers, Box 11:1, HIA; Student questionnaire: Borzov Papers, Box 9:8, HIA.
120 "Letter to editor," *Russkaia zhizn'*, 10 July 1925.
121 Boris Shebeko, "Russian Civil War (1918-1922) and Immigration," oral history transcript (1961), 266.

350 | Notes to pages 134–44

122 Shebeko, oral history transcript, 251–60.
123 Elovsky, *The Russian Students in California*, 48, E/A File, MRC.
124 Newsletters Nos. 95–6, April–May 1934; No. 97, June 1934, IHRCA.
125 Victorin M. Moltchanoff, "The Last White General" (1972), oral history; Petroff, *Remembering a Forgotten War*, 279.
126 Shebeko, oral history transcript, iv.
127 Ibid., 253.
128 Ibid., 254–5. Saharov's re-emigration: SS *President Wilson*, "PLV," NAI 4498993, Records of the INS, NARA.
129 *Russkaia zhizn'* ran a weekly sports-related column: 1922–1927; Elovsky on Russian Athletic Society, *The Russian Students of California*, 46, E/A File, MRC.
130 Newsletter, Nos. 95–6, April–May 1934, IHRCA.
131 *Russkaia gazeta*, Editor's note, 23 March 1921.
132 *Russkaia gazeta*, 9 April 1921.
133 *Russkaia gazeta*, 1920–1921.
134 "Occupation" in "PFN," NAI 605504, Records of USDC, NARA.
135 *Russkaia gazeta*, 9 April 1921.
136 Hassell, "Russian Refugees," 50, author's emphasis.
137 Ibid., 87.
138 Bederman, *Manliness and Civilization*, 13. Bederman focuses on interconnection of "civilization" and understandings of masculinity in the United States in noted period, particularly in terms of racial domination.
139 Alexander, *Trauma: A Social Theory*, chapter 1.
140 "Is my brother Boris a prodigal son?" and "Boris goes to university in California" and other writings. Von Arnold Papers, Box 12:3; Correspondence from Boris to Antonina (Dora), Box 7:7, HIA.
141 "American vs. Russian," 31 August 1965, Von Arnold Papers, Box 3:6:206.

Chapter Five

1 "Girl Reporter: Russian Refugees," undated draft (ca. late 1920s), Shapiro Papers, Box 5:36, HIA.
2 Protopriest S. Leporsky, "150-Year Anniversary of the Russian Orthodox Church in America," *Russkaia zhizn'*, ca.1944, Bazhenova Papers, Box 5:2, HIA. Leporsky served in: Wilkeson, Washington; Berkeley, California; and Baltimore, Maryland.
3 Mettini/Metini is the Indigenous appellation for location where Ross structure stands. Author references built environment as "Fort Ross" or "Ross."
4 B. Volkov, "Fort Ross," *Novaya Zarya*, n.d. (1937), Loukashin Papers, MRC.
5 Ibid.; Spring Ball Program, Grebenstchikoff Papers, Box 18:5, IHRCA.
6 Glazunova, "Bay Area Russian-American Community"; Tripp, "Russian Routes"; Gubanova, "Adjustment Process of Russian Immigrants in California."
7 Norá, "Between Memory and History."
8 Gutiérrez, "Migration, Emergent Ethnicity, and the 'Third Space,'"; Innis-Jimenez, *Steel Barrio*, Introduction and Part II; Morrissey, *Mental Territories*, Introduction.
9 The fire destroyed most of the original construction in the city center, about four square miles, spanning the area east of Van Ness Avenue to the city waterfront and stretching south from the Marina to well below Market Street.
10 On émigré communities and conditions in inter-war Europe see on Berlin: Raeff, *Russia Abroad*; Shlegel, *Berlin, Eastern Station*; and Williams, *Culture in Exile*; On Paris, see: Johnson, *"New Mecca, New Babylon"*; Hassell, "Russian Refugees"; Rappaport, *After the Romanovs*, chapter 5–7 and 12.
11 Interview with "T," undated, Radin Papers.

Notes to pages 145–51 | **351**

12 Tweed, *Our Lady of the Exile*, 85–6.
13 Lavrova, "My Home Town," *Los Angeles Times*, 24 September 1933, Volkov Papers, Box 17:13; Shapiro Papers, Box 6:8, HIA.
14 "The Last Journey of Baron Boodberg," n.d. ca. 1945, Bazhenova Papers, Box 5:2, HIA.
15 "ROC [Society of Russian Culture]," *Russkaia zhizn'*, 25 November 1927.
16 Olferieff, *Russia in War and Revolution*, 421.
17 Kivelson, *Cartographies of Tsardom*, chapter 4.
18 Slobin, *Russians Abroad*, 39.
19 Writer Boris Zaitsev, quoted by Slobin, *Russians Abroad*, 25. On bells, see Bogdan, "Between Dreams and Reality," 378–9.
20 Kivelson, *Cartographies of Tsardom*, 212.
21 Bazhenova, "Po sledam nashiskh predkov" [Following the footsteps of our ancestors], *Novaya Zarya*, 1 June 1940, Loukashkin Papers, FR/Alaska File, MRC.
22 Manchester, *Holy Fathers, Secular Sons*, 75, 100.
23 "On the opposite shores of the Pacific Ocean" or "Traveling against the sun." Volkov Papers, Box 16:7, HIA.
24 F. Pashkovsky, "'Old 'Ross' – now Fort Ross," *AOM*, 15–30 April 1905, Loukashkin Papers, FR/Alaska File, MRC.
25 B. Volkov (papers, HIA), T. Bazhenova (papers, HIA), writings in Loukashkin Papers, FR/Alaska File, MRC.
26 Tweed, *Our Lady of Exile*, 85–6; Milligan, "Displacement and Identity Discontinuity,"381.
27 Innis-Jimenez, *Steel Barrio*, Introduction, on "physical and cultural environment."
28 Lefebvre, *The Production of Space*, 35.
29 Landesen and Florence Boon Phelps, 21 June, 3 July 1933; and Jos O'Connor, 6 and 15 November 1933, Landesen Papers, Box 1:1, HIA. The Soviet trade or "Amtorg" representative was the only Soviet official in San Francisco at the time. Soviet Consulate was housed at 2563 Divisadero Street, 1934–1948.
30 Shebeko oral history transcript, 266. On communist activity in the Bay Area, see: Glass, *From Mission to Microchip*, 211–28, 229–46; Cherny, *San Francisco Reds*. On communism in America, see Klehr, *The Heyday of American Communism*.
31 Taylor, *Stalin's Apologist: Walter Duranty*; Johnson, *New Mecca, New Babylon*, 133–4. On the Great Terror, mass arrests, and purges, see Khlevniuk, *Master of the House*. On labor camps and the Gulag, see: Solzhenitsyn, *The Gulag Archipelago*; Alexopoulos, "Destructive-Labor Camps." On collectivization and oppression of the peasantry, see: Conquest, *Harvest of Sorrow*; Fitzpatrick, *Stalin's Peasants*. On the Gulag and interconnection with collectivization and Great Terror, see Khlevniuk, *The History of the Gulag*.
32 Quoted by Slobin, *Russians Abroad*, 207.
33 Balakshin to Shapiro, 17 December 1935, Shapiro Papers, Box 2:4, HIA.
34 Malozemoff, oral history transcript, 2–16, 388.
35 Raymond and Jones, *The Russian Diaspora*, 52–7; Tripp, "Russian Routes"; Gubanova, "Adjustment Process of Russian Immigrants in California."
36 Willson, "Foreign Nationalities in San Francisco *SF Examiner* (Nov–Dec 1923)," manuscript, SFHC, SFPL.
37 WPA Federal Writers' Project, *San Francisco in the 1930s*, 285.
38 On Imperial Chamberlin Nikolay Rezanov's visit to California in 1806, early nineteenth-century Russian Imperial scientific expeditions, and visits of Russian Imperial Naval vessels to San Francisco see, among others: Gibson, *California through Russian Eyes, 1806–1848*; Bolkhovitinov, *Istoriya Russkoi Ameriki, 1732–1867*; Kroll, *Friends in Peace and War*.
39 Shevzov, *Russian Orthodoxy on the Eve of Revolution*, 54–94.
40 "Letter to the editor," *Russkaia zhizn'*, 30 January 1925; A. Kropotkin, "Life Abroad," in "75th Anniversary of the Russian Orthodox Parish, 1868–1943," 53, HTC File, MRC.

352 | Notes to pages 152–6

41 Raymond and Jones on Church, *The Russian Diaspora*, 12; Schaufuss, "The White Russian Refugees," 49.

42 Figes notes the "revival of the Russian faith abroad" among exiles who exhibited "a level of religious observance which they had never shown before 1917." *Natasha's Dance*, 538.

43 Service, *A History of Modern Russia* on church persecution. The number of priests fell from 60,000 in the 1920s to 5,665 in 1941, 203–4; Fitzpatrick, *Stalin's Peasants*, 204–18, on assault on religion in villages (1929–1933); Johnson, *New Mecca, New Babylon*, 44, on émigré view of church persecution. Baptists and Molokane experienced Soviet religious persecution early on. A.G. Chesheff wrote of attacks on and even "executions" of Baptists and Molokane around the village of Tambovka in the Amur region. Chesheff fled across the border to China and asked for assistance to immigrate, noting that he much regretted not coming to America in 1911, when a friend had invited him. *Russkaia zhizn'*, 13 February 1924.

44 "Fate of Patriarch Tikhon," *Russkaia zhizn'*, 6 July 1923; Epistle of Patriarch Tikhon ex-communicating the Bolsheviks, 10 January 1918, History of Russia, the ROC, and ROCOR in the 20th Century Collection, Box 58:3, WDA. Patriarch Tikhon declared attacks on the church by Bolsheviks "satanic." Rumors of the poisoning of the patriarch appeared prior to his death (in April 1925) in *Russkaia zhizn'* on 20 February 1925.

45 On "satanic" regime, see: Veterans' Newsletters; Correspondence, Isaenko Papers, Box 2; Borzov Papers, Boxes, 1, 2, 3, HIA; "Monument to Pat. Tikhon," *Russkaia zhizn'*, 11 June 1926.

46 "Doudoroff at Holy Trinity: A Wandering Pharisee," *Novaya Zarya*, 29 January 1930, HTC file, MRC. The expression referenced hypocrisy or self-righteousness.

47 "Russian Church is Dedicated," *San Francisco Chronicle*, 12 July 1909.

48 "Holy Trinity Cathedral (San Francisco, California), https://orthodoxwiki.org/Holy_Trinity_Cathedral_(San_Francisco,_California), accessed March 2024. The architect is unknown.

49 Zelensky and Gilbert, *Windows to Heaven*, 129.

50 "Editorial," *Russkaia zhizn'*, 2 October 1925.

51 V. Vesninsky, "Under the Church," *Russkaia zhizn'*, 14 September 1926. "*Matushka*" is a term to address an Orthodox priest's wife.

52 The church building that became the Holy Virgin Cathedral on Fulton Street, purchased in 1930–1931 (chapter 6), was a Protestant church. The initial exterior appearance of St Nicholas Church of the Moscow Patriarchy, established in 1934–5 at 433 Divisadero, is unknown. On St Nicholas, see Tripp, "Russian Routes," 105, 153.

53 *Russkaia zhizn'*, 28 August 1925.

54 On cemeteries as consecrated spaces, see "The Russian Orthodox Church in Alaska Historic Ecclesiastical Landscapes Study, 1840–1920," 75.

55 For example, Ushanoff on *Radonitsa* in China, outside of Harbin, oral history, 25.

56 Russian Orthodox in the Bay Area were (and are) often interred at the Serbian Orthodox cemetery in Colma, south of San Francisco, established by the First Serbian Benevolent Society in 1901. Svanevik and Burgett, *City of Souls*, 101–4.

57 In 1920, about 2,400 African Americans lived in San Francisco, mostly in the Western Addition. Broussard, *Black San Francisco*, chapter 1. On other communities, see: Issel and Cherny, *San Francisco, 1865–1932*, 66–70; WPA Federal Writers' Project, *San Francisco in the 1930s*, "The Western Addition," 282–303.

58 Balakshin, Demented Norma's Dance, *Spring Over the Fillmore*, 47.

59 S.R. Martin Jr, *On the Move*, 107, 118.

60 Shebeko, oral history transcript, 250.

61 Zipperstein, *Pogrom*, chapter 3.

62 Rosenbaum, *Cosmopolitans*, 216; *Great Register of Voters, 1900–1968*, CSL.

63 Eisenberg et al., *Jews of the Pacific Coast*, 93, citing Raye Rich oral history with Ava F. Kahn, San Francisco, 12 September 2000, parts 1, 4, 5, and 9, Western Jewish History Center. The Walls arrived in New York in 1910, and lived and worked in the Fillmore. Raye Rich was born in Kiev.

Notes to pages 156–65 | **353**

64 P. Karelin, "The Russian Center," *Russkaia zhizn'*, 31 December 1926.
65 Ibid.
66 Information about businesses from *Russkaia zhizn'* (1922–1927); Clippings, event programs, and other materials in Shapiro, Bazhenova, Isaenko, Volkov Papers, HIA, and SFRE File, SFHC, SFPL.
67 Shebeko, oral history transcript, 251.
68 "Waxman's Bakery," *Russkaia zhizn'*, 8 January 1926; Vernon, oral history transcript, 37.
69 Flamm, *Good Life in Hard Times*, 76.
70 US Census, 1930, San Francisco, AD 22, Block 26; US city directories, San Francisco, 1927, 1932; Van pictured in Bogdan, "Between Dreams and Reality," 387, original in E/A file, MRC.
71 "Russian Restaurant," by "Nikolay-ev" (pseudonym), *Russkaia zhizn'*, 1 January 1926. "Zaporozhiye" was an area of Ukraine home to a large contingent of Cossacks (the Zaporozhian Host) and a Zaporozhian mustache was a luxurious one that drooped down on either side of the mouth; As Prohibition was in effect, no alcohol was openly served, thus the "dream" of beer.
72 A restaurant named "Russkii Ugolok" (Russian Corner) was at 1301 Eddy St on the corner of Buchanan, advertised same page.
73 "The Russian Woman in Emigration," Isaenko Papers, Box 7:23, HIA.
74 E. Bailey phone interview, 15 November 2021; "Cup of Tea," *Russkaia zhizn'*, 5 February 1926; "Sports," *Russkaia zhizn'*, 26 March 1926; "Russian Center," *Russkaia zhizn'*, 31 December 1926.
75 WPA Federal Writers' Project, *San Francisco in the 1930s*, 87.
76 E. Bailey phone interview, 15 November 2021.
77 Balakshin, "Spring over the Fillmore," 236–7 (epigraph in front matter).
78 Balakshin, "Room over the City," *Spring over the Fillmore*, 141–2.
79 V. Anichkoff interview, ca. 1934, Radin Papers; Lavrova, "Russia's Lightning Changes of Useless Paper Money," *San Francisco Examiner*, 4 May 1924; ads in *Russkaia zhizn'*, 1923–1927.
80 Bazhenova, "Alien Shore," Bazhenova Papers, Box 3:4, HIA.
81 *Russian-News Life*, 14 March 1941, Isaenko Papers, Box 11:2, HIA.
82 Board of Special Inquiry, Boxer family, 9 May 1931, NARA; Jacob Paul Boxer, "WWII Draft Registration Cards for California," NAI 7644723, Records of the SSS, NARA; *Novaya Zarya*, *Russkaia zhizn'*, (3?) December 1955; E/A File, MRC.
83 V. Anichkoff interview, ca. 1934, Radin Papers. On Nicolis and business: San Francisco newspaper clippings ca. 1950, Bazhenova Papers, Box 5:2; "25-year Anniversary of Natalia Nikolaevsky's House of Fashion," *Novaya Zarya*, 31 March 1948, Abdank-Kossovskii Papers, Box 25, HIA. The Anichkoff Fund aka Russian Benevolent Trust Fund in memory of V.P. and M.P. Anitchkoff, Russian Center records, 1950s–1960s, RC Papers, Box 26:1, MRC.
84 Norá, "Between Memory and History: *Les Lieux de Memoire*," 9.
85 Norá, "Introduction," *Realms of Memory*, ix.
86 Undated (pre-1937) clipping, Loukashkin Papers, FR/Alaska file, MRC. *The Russian Advance into California* by Flora Faith Hatch, published 1922, indicated aggression via the title as did a Cold War era film, *California Conquest* (1952), about the Russian colonization of California. Robinson, *Russians in Hollywood*, 160.
87 Kalani, et al., eds., *Fort Ross*, 27.
88 F. Pashkovsky, "Old 'Ross' – Now Fort Ross," *AOM*, 15–30 April 1905, Loukashkin Papers, FR/ Alaska File, MRC.
89 Ibid.
90 Parkman, "A Fort by Any Other Name," 1–8. Parkman quoted Russian Orthodox priest Rev. V. Derugin, who wrote to the Fort Ross Interpretive Association in 1991 regarding the marketing of the space to tourists as a center of conflict, 8.
91 Kalani, et al., *Fort Ross*, 46.

354 | Notes to pages 165–71

92 Parkman, "A Fort by Any Other Name," 6–7; "Common Misconceptions Concerning Fort Ross," Russian Historical Society document (n.d., ca. 1950s), Loukashkin Papers, FR/Alaska File, MRC.

93 Tripp, for example, lists 253 people at Ross in 1833 with forty-five Russian men and six Russian women, the remaining population listed as Native Alaskan and Creole (no mention of Indigenous Californian population). "Russian Routes," 40.

94 Kalani, et al., Fort Ross, 5, 13.

95 Honoraria Tuomey, "Priest Chants Services at Fort Ross," The Bulletin, San Francisco, 8 July 1925, Loukashkin Papers, FR/Alaska File, MRC.

96 "Fort Ross," Russkaia zhizn', 3 July 1925; "July 4," Russkaia zhizn', 10 July 1925.

97 Schwartz, "Rethinking the Concept of Collective Memory," 9–21.

98 "Trip to Fort Ross," Russkaia zhizn', 10 June 1927.

99 Shapiro to "Sasha," 23 January 1973, Shapiro Papers, Box 2:15, HIA. The Lebedeffs, founders of the Fort Ross Initiative Group, baptized their son there in 1935. Photo/caption, Lebedeff baptism in "Fort Ross, Outpost of Russia's Past Glory in America: Historic Album, 1812–1937," FRC Library.

100 "Russian Couple Wed at Historic Fort Ross Church," Santa Rosa Press Democrat, 18 April 1934.

101 Photograph verso, April 1934, FRC Library; "Russian Couple Wed at Historic Fort Ross Church," Santa Rosa Press Democrat, 18 April 1934. Holy Virgin Cathedral established in 1931 (chapter 6).

102 Indis Alfred Gray was a son of Nicholas Gray, a Russian-born American citizen who returned to Vladivostok as American consul. "Passport Applications, January 2, 1906 – March 31, 1925"; NAI 583830, General Records of the Department of State, RG 59; "Consular Reports of Marriage, 1910–1949," NAI 2555709, A1, Entry 3001, General Records of the Department of State, NARA.

103 "Woman Prefers Jail to Release without her Lover," San Francisco Chronicle, 16 September 1921. Igor and Vera later divorced.

104 Kalani et al., Fort Ross, 34–5.

105 Ibid.

106 V.P. Anichkoff collection (photocopy), Loukashin Papers, FR/Alaska File, MRC. Americans found "Slavyanka" (Slavic girl) too difficult to pronounce and renamed the river. Other "Russian" locations included: Russian Gulch in Jenner, at one time a train station; the town of Sebastopol (after the city Sevastopol, in the Crimea); and Moscow Road in Rio Nido area, a former railway stop.

107 American author Bret Harte wrote a ballad, "Concepcion De Arguello," and Gertrude Atherton a novel "Rezanov" (1906), about the romance. Other depictions by Victor Arnautoff: Arguello and Rezanov in mural at Interfaith Chapel in Presidio of San Francisco (1936); By Anatoly Sokoloff: two paintings of Concepcion (1960s); By Soviet Russian writer Alexey Rybnikov and poet Andrei Voznesensky: rock opera, "Juno and Avos" (1979). Images in Zaverukha and Bogdan, 10–12.

108 Poems by Bazhenova, Loukashkin Papers, FR/Alaska File, MRC.

109 Shapiro to Jean Helm, 16 October 1934, Shapiro Papers, Box 2:24, HIA.

110 Kalani et al., Fort Ross, 29–39.

111 Text, photos, and captions, "Fort Ross, Outpost of Russia's Past Glory in America: Historic Album, 1812–1937," FRC Library/Loukashin Papers, MRC.

112 F. Pashkovsky, "'Old Ross' – now Fort Ross," AOM, 15–30 April 1905, Loukashkin Papers, FR/Alaska File, MRC.

113 N. Yazykoff, Slovo, 6 June 1937, Loukashkin Papers, FR/Alaska file, MRC.

114 Nashe Vremia, 30 June 1951, Loukashkin Papers, FR/Alaska file, MRC.

115 "The First Russians in America," Rubezh, 2 March 1940, Bazhenova Papers, Box 2:3, HIA.

116 Parkman, "A Fort by Any Other Name," 5–6.

Notes to pages 172–81 | **355**

117 "At Fort Ross," *Novaya Zarya*, 7 July 1942, RC Papers, Ephemera File, MRC. Group included Prince A. Kropotkin and Hegumenia Ioanna, abbess of newly established Uspensky Russian Orthodox convent in Santa Rosa.

118 Russian Historical Society charter; A.P. Farafontoff's report to GM, 30 March 1940, FR/ Alaska file, Loukashkin Papers, MRC; "Letter to editor from A. Farafontoff," *Novaya Zarya*, 30 June 1937, Loukashkin Papers, FR/Alaska File, MRC.

119 Russian Historical Society GM Proceedings, 13 June 1937, Loukashkin File, FR/Alaska File, MRC.

120 Farafontoff to Grebenstchikoff, 29 July 1936, Grebenstchikoff Papers, Box 18:5, IHRCA.

121 Lavrova, "What People Are Talking About," *Russian News-Life*, 26 November 1937, Loukashkin Papers, FR/Alaska, MRC.

122 A.P. Farafontoff's report to GM, 30 March 1940, Loukashkin Papers, FR/Alaska File, MRC.

Chapter Six

1 Lyons, *Assignment in Utopia*, 4. The term "first-generation" refers to immigrants who are "foreign-born," and "second-generation" to children born to immigrants in the United States.

2 Ilyin about first literary evening in 1923 in dimly lit "basement." "First literary evening in San Francisco" in *Russkaia zhenshchina v emigratsii* (The Russian Woman in Emigration). Washington, 1970, 18–20. E/A File, MRC.

3 "Kurlin" (death notice), *San Francisco Examiner*, 15 September 1929; Vera and Olga Kurlin/Kourlin, "San Francisco Area Funeral Home Records," 1895–1985; US Census 1930, San Francisco, Page 21A; Enumeration District, 0032.

4 US Census 1940, San Francisco, AD 22; "George A. Kurlin," National Cemetery Administration. *U.S. Veterans' Gravesites, ca. 1775–2019*; Boulder, CO City Directory, 1951; Kurlin/Richardson marriage announcement, *The Cincinnati Enquirer*, 3 October 1952; Stella Henriette Castellanni/Kurlin/Gamelcy, *U.S. Social Security Applications and Claims Index, 1936–2007*.

5 E. Grot, "Victims of Troubled Times," *Russkaia zhizn'*, 15 April 1927.

6 Higham, *Strangers in the Land*, chapter 9.

7 Von Arnold Papers, Box 13:10–12.

8 H.O. Eversole report, 26 August 1920, ANRC, Box 138:8, HIA (author's emphasis).

9 The Odyssey of the Lost Children," *Swarthmore College Bulletin*, May 1988, ANRC, Box 132:1; H.O. Eversole report, 26 August 1920, ANRC, Box 138:8, HIA; "Californian is Russian Health Work Director," *San Francisco Chronicle*, 8 August 1920.

10 "Wrong Toxin Fatal to S.F. Child; 4 Ill," *San Francisco Examiner*, 15 February 1935. Natalie's father John, estranged from spouse Valeria, died under unclear circumstances in Juneau, Alaska two months after his daughter's death. John Rojnovsky, *U.S. Find a Grave® Index*, 1600s–Current.

11 Register (1931–1948), HVC Papers, Box 35:2, WDA; "Serum Death Blame Sought," *Oakland Tribune*, 16 February 1935.

12 Hoganson, *Fighting for American Manhood*, on shifts in gender norms in period just prior (1887–1919); Miller, *New World Coming*, on social changes.

13 Rabinovitz, *For the Love of Pleasure*, on women in urban public spaces at the turn of the century.

14 Sparks, *Capital Intentions*, on period just prior to Russian émigré arrival.

15 Room rental ads, *Russkaia zhizn'*, 1922–1927; US Census, 1930/1940, San Francisco.

16 Biographical sketch, Isaenko Papers, Box 1:2, HIA.

17 The name of the society was translated by organizers. "Protection" (*pokrovitel'stvo*) was later changed to "care."

18 On denationalization, N. Borzov to Grebenstchikoff, 7 May 1934, Grebenstchikoff Papers, Box 14:4, IHRCA.

356 | Notes to pages 181–7

19 Children's Home pamphlet, CH File, MRC.
20 P. I. Kheiskanen's (Heiskanen) obituary, 22 May 1927, CH File, MRC.
21 Society/Day Home history, CH File, MRC; *Russkaia zhizn'*, 17 December 1926. Society announcements in *Russkaia zhizn'*, 1925–1926.
22 Russian Consul to US Customs office, 5 April 1922, SFIRC, Roll 143, NARA; Antonina Alexandrovna Maximova Kulaev, "PFN," NAI 605504, Records of USDC, NARA; Occupational directory, 1923, CSA, Sacramento CA; Maximova-Kulaev, "The Russian Children's Day Home," in Meler, *The Slavonic Pioneers*, 61. Hassell on problems of Russian émigré acceptance by American medical/legal organizations, "Russian Refugees," 37.
23 RNSA application, Borzov Papers, Box 9:4; US Census, 1940, San Francisco, AD 26, Block 36. Loschilova married Nicholas Menshikoff/Mensh in 1924 in Berkeley, CA, CSA, Sacramento CA.
24 Kulaieff was born in Krasnoyarsk, built a fortune in Siberia, and relocated to Harbin in 1900. Three of his sons attended University of California at Berkeley. He settled in Hollywood in the 1930s. Visa application, SFIRC Files, Roll 143, NARA; Borzov eulogy, Borzov Papers, Box 1:10; Borzov-Kulaieff correspondence, Borzov Papers, Box 2, HIA; *Novaya Zarya*, Kulaieff obituary, 25 November 1941, Grebentschikoff Papers, Box 26:8, IHRCA.
25 Borzov eulogy, Borzov Papers, Box 1:10, HIA; *Day of the Russian Child*, 1952, 1954, IHRCA; "Day of the Russian Child" events, CH file, MRC; Correspondence 1930s–1950s, Borzov Papers, Boxes 1, 2, 3, 14.
26 *Russkaia zhizn'*, 28 October, 4 November 1927.
27 Balakshin to Shapiro, 17 December 1935, Shapiro Papers, Box 2:4, HIA.
28 Lavrova, "Russian Mountain Tots Real Yanks," *San Francisco Examiner*, 23 November 1923. Barbara Jacoob nee Silich (1876–1963) arrived 1911 to join husband William (1876–1939, born Riga), in New Jersey, so family was not White Russian, although Barbara was Orthodox. William's religious affiliation unknown. SS Kursk, "Passenger and Crew Lists of Vessels Arriving at New York, New York, 1897–1957," NAI T715, Records of the INS, NARA; Funeral record, Barbara Jacoob, 12 August 1963.
29 Society description in "75th Anniversary of the Russian Orthodox Parish, 1868–1943." HTC file, MRC.
30 "Book published in memory of the Czar." RC Papers, Box 1:2, MRC.
31 K.P. Barskii, *Russian Center*, "On the Founding of the Russian Center," January 1939, RC Papers, Box 1:2, MRC.
32 CH file, MRC. Periodic progress reports in *Russkaia zhizn'*, 1926–1927.
33 Charter of Society for Protection of Children, 18 July 1926, CH File, MRC.
34 Children's Nursery pamphlet, CH File, MRC.
35 Photos identifying children by name dated 1929–1933, CH File, MRC; US Census, 1930, San Francisco.
36 Meler, *The Slavonic Pioneers*, 61. Publication focused on "Southern Slavs" ("Jugoslavs") from the Balkans.
37 *Russkaia zhizn'* articles, 1926–1927; "History of the organization of the Day Home, 1925–1950," *Novaya Zarya*, 4 October 1935, CH File, MRC; Meler, *The Slavonic Pioneers*, 61.
38 "Russians in America," *Russkaia zhizn'*, 27 April 1923; "Church meeting," 8 January (February) 1924; "Russian Church Parish School," 9 January 1925.
39 "Annual Meeting of Russian Orthodox Church Congregation in San Francisco," by "A Christian," *Russkaia zhizn'*, 8 January 1924 (author's note: correct date 8 February).
40 Telegram, Metr. Platon to Father V. Sakovich, 1 February 1927, OCA Papers, Box 14:1, WDA. The synod subsequently appointed Bishop Apollinary as Bishop of North America and San Francisco (in 1929, Archbishop of North America and Canada). The Russian Orthodox Church in the United States split into the Metropolia (later the Orthodox Church of America [OCA]) headed by Metr. Platon, and ROCOR, aka Russian Orthodox Church in Exile (ROCIA). See "Blagovestnik," June 2002; Parish histories: Holy Virgin Joy of All Who Sorrow (HV) File, MRC; G. Kiyaschenko, "Vera i Pravda," OCA Papers, Box 14:4, WDA.

Notes to pages 187–93 | **357**

41 B. Doudoroff, "Appeal to Orthodox People," *Russkaia zhizn'*, 18 February 1927.
42 Charter of Holy Virgin Orthodox Society, 15 January 1933, Russkii Katolicheskii Tsentr (RKT) Papers, Box 8:1, HIA; *Russkaia zhizn'* coverage of local events including receipt of telegram and actions of HTC church council community members, Feb–Jul 1927.
43 Register (1931–1948), HVC Papers, Box 35:2, WDA.
44 Regarding schism: articles, letters to editor, editorials in *Russkaia zhizn'*, 1927.
45 Andreyev and Savický, *Russia Abroad*, 117–21.
46 *Novaya Zarya*, 28 September 1935, CH File, MRC.
47 B.P. Doudoroff, "Russian Children's Education," *Novaya Zarya*, 5 February 1929, Archbishop Tikhon (Troitsky) Papers, Box 2:2, WDA; "Blagovestnik," June 2002; Parish histories: HV file, MRC.
48 Natalia Kiyaschenko, "PFN," NAI 605504, Records of USDC, NARA; On dance school: "From the Drama Circle," *Russkaia zhizn'*, 18 December 1925, 1 January 1926.
49 E. Bailey phone interview, 15 November 2021.
50 G. Kiyaschenko role/activities in *Russkaia zhizn'*: 9 January/2 October 1925; 12/19 February 1926; 22 October 1926.
51 Album 24, Vrangel Papers, Box 49, HIA; T. Bazhenova, "Terpsichores across the Ocean," *Rubezh*, on Bolm productions in San Francisco, n.d., Adolph Bolm Collection, LOC.
52 On Kiyaschenko's service in Admiral Kolchak's army: Ivan Podvaloff, "In honor of the 75th anniversary of the end of World War II," *Russkaia zhizn'*, 16 May 2020; swolkov.org (Sergei Vladimirovich Wolkov) database of White Army officers and combatants.
53 "The General's Daughter," *Havasu News*, 7 May 2004, https://www.havasunews.com/the-general-s-daughter/article_55c25991-d1da-569a-a8fb-ca742f3335cd.html, accessed 14 January 2020.
54 George Titous Kiyaschenko, "PFN," NAI 605504, Records of USDC, NARA; "The General's Daughter," *Havasu News*.
55 Morawska, *For Bread with Butter*, chapter 8, on feelings of "embarrassment and inferiority" of eastern European children.
56 Register (1931–1948), HVC Papers, Box 35:2, WDA; "The General's Daughter," *Havasu News*; Eugene G. Kayes obituary, *Santa Rosa Press Democrat*, 6 July 1990. Nina also used "Kayes" prior to marriage.
57 Register (1931–1948), HVC Papers, Box 35:2, WDA; Ads, Nina's Beauty Salon, *Russikiye Novosti*, 2 July 1937, Loukashkin File, MRC; Russian Disabled Veterans Benefit Concert and Ball program, 12 November 1938, SFRE File, SFHC, SFPL; Lambert, *Natalie Wood*, 15–20, 65–7.
58 Lambert, *Natalie Wood*, 16–17.
59 Manchester, *Holy Fathers, Secular Sons*, 73; Meyerdorff, *Marriage: An Orthodox Perspective*, 64.
60 Freeze, "Profane Narratives," 148.
61 Wagner, "Ideology, Identity, and the Emergence of a Middle Class," 149–63.
62 Freeze, "Profane Narratives," 162.
63 Author review of thousands of documents indicates high frequency of divorce/remarriage in San Francisco Russian émigré community in inter-war period.
64 Interview with "Mr Sh," 19 February 1935, Radin Papers.
65 Jouravleff letter to editor, *Russkaia zhizn'*, 30 January 1925; V. Vesninsky, "Conflict in the Church," *Russkaia zhizn'*, 20 February 1925; Serge Denisoff, "PFN," NAI 605504, Records of USDC, NARA.
66 Jouravleff letter to editor, *Russkaia zhizn'*, 30 January 1925; V. Vesninsky, "Conflict in the Church," *Russkaia zhizn'*, 20 February 1925. Father Sakovich was instrumental in rectifying the financial situation of Holy Trinity after his arrival, left in straitened circumstances by the previous rector, Father Vladimir Alexandroff, (1871–1945). "Rector is Target of Letter Writer," *San Francisco Chronicle*, 16 July 1915; "Report to Bishop" at "Holy Trinity Cathedral," https://www.holy-trinity.org/history/1918/06.21.Sakovich-Nemolovsky.html, accessed 22 May 2023.

358 | Notes to pages 193–9

67 "Letters to editor," *Russkaia zhizn'*, 6 March 1925.

68 Ibid. Krinoff arrived March 1917 as Russian Consulate attaché. *Russkaia zhizn'*, 6 April 1923. Chabanoff later headed Holy Virgin Church Parish council. "Twenty-five Year Anniversary of the Holy Virgin Joy of All Who Sorrow Cathedral," 1927–1952," 12, HV File, MRC.

69 *Russkaia zhizn'*, January–April 1925; "Father Denisoff Holding First Service in Two Years," *Russkaia zhizn'*, 25 March 1927.

70 Vesninsky, "Conflict in the Church," *Russkaia zhizn'*, 20 February 1925.

71 Kizenko, "Feminized Patriarchy?," 596; Manchester, *Holy Fathers, Secular Sons*, 73.

72 Kizenko, "Feminized Patriarchy?," 596.

73 *Russkaia zhizn'*, 5 August 1927; Register (1931–1948), HVC Papers, Box 35:2, WDA.

74 "Russian Veteran of World War I Dies at Home," *Sonoma West Times and News*, 24 October 1963.

75 Notation in church register states Denisoff's 1939 marriage was his third. Register (1931–1948), HVC Papers, Box 35:2, WDA.

76 Stites, *The Women's Liberation Movement in Russia*, 6. Blood tests or waiting periods were not required for marriage licenses in Nevada.

77 "The General's Daughter," *Havasu News*; Lambert, *Natalie Wood*, 15; "Vera i Pravda," OCA Papers, Box 14:4, WDA.

78 Vernon, oral history transcript, 7–41.

79 Malozemoff, oral history transcript, 351.

80 Russian sports clubs focused largely on soccer though they played other sports, such as tennis; Continued into the contemporary period.

81 Vernon, oral history transcript, 7–40.

82 "A brief study of Russian students," Von Arnold Papers, Box 12:2, HIA.

83 Ibid.

84 E. Bailey phone interview, 15 November 2021, and email correspondence, 9 December 2021.

85 "A brief study of Russian students," Von Arnold Papers, Box 12:2, HIA.

86 Vernon, oral history transcript, 20–2.

87 Morawska, *A Sociology of Immigration*, 21–4. Higham, *Strangers in the Land*, chapter 9. On the "problem" of non-Western European immigration, see: P. Davis, *Immigration and Americanization* (1920); Haskin, *The Immigrant: An Asset and a Liability* (1913); Warne, *The Immigrant Invasion* (1913).

88 Esman, *Diasporas in the Contemporary World*, 109; Morawska, *For Bread with Butter*, on eastern Europeans. In the American West, Orthodox often had to make do without churches, depending on traveling priests, particularly Father S. Dabovich. Farley, "Circuit Riders to the Slavs and Greeks," 1–21.

89 Lyons, *Assignment in Utopia*, 4–5.

90 M.M. Tulinoff, *Novaya Zarya*, "Russian Children's Education," 5 February 1929, Archbishop Tikhon (Troitsky) Papers, Box 2:2, WDA.

91 "Russians in San Francisco" (1942), Von Arnold Papers, Box 13:3, HIA.

92 E. Bailey phone interview, 15 November 2021.

93 Olga Kiril Ilyin, "PFN," NAI 605504, Records of USDC, NARA; Biographical details: *Nashe Nasledie* (Our Heritage), a cultural and historical journal, http://www.nasledie-rus.ru/podshivka/5512.php.

94 O. Ilyin, *Dawn of the Eighth Day*.

95 O. Ilyin, "First Literary Evening in San Francisco," 18–20, E/A File, MRC; *Nashe Nasledie*, http://www.nasledie-rus.ru/podshivka/5512.php.

96 Kiril Ilyin, "PFN," NAI 605504, Records of USDC, NARA; US Census, 1940, San Francisco, Block 24–5; Realty ads in *Russian News-Life*, 25 July 1950, Volkov Papers, Box 19:1, HIA; Caroline Drewes, "The Russians of the Bay Area," *San Francisco Examiner*, 15 September 1981.

97 Register (1931–1948), HVC Papers, Box 35:2, WDA; "Hewitt Wedding October 14," *San Francisco Examiner*, 22 September 1955; "American vs. Russian," Von Arnold Papers, Box

Notes to pages 200–6 | **359**

3:6:206. On American attachment to importance of "lineage": reporters referred to daughter of Russian Princess Xenia Georgievna and American tin empire heir William B. Leeds, Jr. as a "Royal American." "Xenia's Baby Christened," *San Francisco Examiner*, 14 August 1925. Robinson writes of cachet "of the idea of Russian aristocracy" in the "Hollywood mentality," which, as noted in chapter 2, was reflected in public discourse on the topic. *Russians in Hollywood, Hollywood Russians*, 145.

98 "Items from Marin Co. Towns," *Petaluma-Argus Courier*, 2 May 1941; Register (1931–1948), HVC Papers, Box 35:2, WDA.

99 "An International Romance," *San Francisco Examiner*, 31 December 1936. The Boratynskis' father, Dmitry, was murdered in Russia prior to the family's departure. The caption in the noted article stated that he "succumbed during the revolt," as if he had, perhaps, been taken ill. The Bryants divorced by 1950.

100 "Boris Ilyin," *Sacramento Bee*, 19 August 2014.

101 B. Ilyin, *Green Boundary*, 4–5.

102 San Francisco City Directories, 1970–1980; Dimitri K. Ilyin obituary, "Sullivan and Duggan's Funeral Service," https://www.sullivansfuneralandcremation.com/obituaries/DIMITRI-K-ILYIN?obId=12378919.

103 E. Bailey phone interview, 15 November 2021.

104 Ruth Thompson and Chef Luis Hanges, "Eating Around San Francisco," pamphlet (first printed in *San Francisco News*), n.d.; Interview of Vernon in same, ca. late 1930s, SFRE File, SFHC, SFPL.

105 Vernon oral history transcript, 7–40.

106 Ibid. On Katenka (1926–1928), 358 Sutter Street, *Russkaia zhizn'*, 17 December 1926; Notices in *San Francisco Examiner*, 1927–1928; On Volga Café (1932–1933), 267 Powell Street, multiple notices in *San Francisco Recorder, San Francisco Examiner*, 1932–1933.

107 Alien Shore," n.d., Bazhenova Papers, Box 3:4, HIA. Orthodox clergy traditionally do not cut their hair or shave facial hair. Deacons chant the hours, thus the reference to "shouting."

108 Lyons, *Assignment in Utopia*, 5. Allen noted upswing in consumer culture, yellow journalism (sex and confession magazines), "moving pictures," and movie magazines in 1920s, *Only Yesterday*, 86–9 and chapter 7.

109 Lavrova, "Russian Mountain Tots Real Yanks," *San Francisco Examiner*, 23 November 1923.

110 "Alien Shore," n.d., Bazhenova Papers, Box 3:4, HIA.

111 US Census, 1930, 1940, San Francisco; Register (1931–1948), HVC Papers, Box 35:2, WDA.

112 Reminiscences, n.d., Bazhenova Papers, Box 1:11, HIA.

113 "A brief study of Russian students," Von Arnold Papers, Box 12:2, HIA.

114 Ibid.

115 "Obituary for Nicholas Protopopoff," *San Francisco Examiner*, 11 April 1993; California marriage records, CSA, Sacramento, CA.

116 "Obituary for Don Strel," *Albuquerque Journal*, 16 October 2020; US Census 1940/1950, San Francisco.

117 Register (1931–1948), HVC Papers, Box 35:2, WDA; US Census, 1950, Eureka, CA; "*US Rosters of World War II Dead, 1939–1945.*"

118 Funeral record, Nicholas V. De Kemarsky, 24 May 1969; "Five Generations Present at Birthday Party and Reunion," *Times-Standard* (Eureka), 27 March 1969.

119 Von Arnold Papers, Boxes 1, 3, 11, 12, HIA. Von Arnold alluded to McGuire physically attacking her and to his mental illness.

120 "A Russian Story about an Irish Love," Von Arnold Papers, Box 12:1, HIA.

121 Journal entry, 18 May 1925, Von Arnold Papers, Box 4:4, HIA. Von Arnold's family lived in Harbin by 1917 so she did not personally experience the violence of the Civil War but her brother, Boris, did serve in the White Guard, and was wounded.

360 | Notes to pages 206–16

122 Von Arnold Papers, Boxes 1, 3, 11, HIA.
123 Announcements in *Russkaia zhizn'*: 18 December 1925, 26 January 1926, and other 1926 dates. Lapidewsky was a Russian physician who arrived in New York in 1911 and lived in Seattle.
124 Bloom, *The Audacity of Inez Burns*. Stites, "The Sexual Question" in *The Women's Liberation Movement in Russia* on sex, marriage, children, and women's options in Russia in the early twentieth century: birth control, extramarital relationships, 178–88.
125 Balakshin, "The Stopped Pendulum," in *Spring over the Fillmore*, 72.
126 Eugenia Serge Soorin, "PFN," NAI 605504, Records of USDC, NARA; Biographical information: Isaenko Papers, Box 1:1, HIA; N.F., "Unforgettable meeting," *Russian Women in Emigration*, 236–8, E/A File, MRC.
127 Isaenko Papers, Boxes 1:2–8; 10, 11, HIA.
128 Isaenko Papers, Box 1:2, HIA.
129 "PFN," NAI 605504, Records of USDC, NARA; US Census 1930, 1940, 1950; *California, U.S. County Birth, Marriage, and Death Records*.
130 Register, 1931–1948, HVC Papers, Box 35:2, WDA.
131 Album 24, Vrangel Papers, Box 49, HIA.

Chapter Seven

N. Shapiro/Lavrova's article title, "White Russians in the 'New World," *Christian Science Monitor*, 30 October 1934.
1 "Three Russian Generals," *San Francisco Examiner*, 14 February 1944. Capitalization in original.
2 Memo to INS Dep. Com. E.J. Shaughnessy, 5 July 1934, 55598/496D, INS COSCCF, NARA.
3 Lavrova, "White Russians in the 'New World,'" *Christian Science Monitor*, 30 October 1934; Rough draft, Dolgopolov Collection, Box 162:2, ASML; Lydia Victorovna Kapylova, "PFN," NAI 605504, Records of USDC, NARA; *Great Register of Voters*, CSL; *Find a Grave® Index*.
4 Letter to San Francisco Russian community, 6 October 1930, Borzov Papers, Box 4:3, HIA.
5 According to Blue, fifty-seven transcontinental deportation trains ran 1914–1932. Over 90,000 people were deported 1921–1931; 95,000 "voluntarily" departed 1925–1931, though also under coercion. *The Deportation Express*, 26.
6 Memorandum to Commissioner W.W. Brown; Board of Review Member Thomas S. Finucane, Chief Examiner Joseph Savoretti (undated; 1936 statistics), IRSA, Box 35:20, IHRCA. 1,110 cases had "accumulated" by (presumably) 1937.
7 Gavriloff to Shapiro, 17 December 1932, Dolgopolov Collection, Box 162:2, ASML; Anatoly Alexandrovich Gavrilov, "PFN," NAI 605504, Records of USDC, NARA.
8 CCRNO to President H.C. Hoover, received 30 January 1933, File 55605/130 INS COSCCF, NARA.
9 Father Sakovich began holding services in Berkeley in 1920. In 1931, Father Sergei Leporsky held services in his home, rented by parish. Church at 1900 Essex Street since 1950, http://stjohnthebaptistberkeley.org/.
10 Letterhead, CCRNO stationary, Borzov Papers, Box 4:6, HIA. Metr. Platon (New York) sent letters of support for legislation to President Hoover and Acting Commissioner General of Immigration Edward J. Shaughnessy, 1932. File 55606/130, INS COSCCF, NARA.
11 Antonenko to Norton (Pojaritsky), RNSA Secretary ca. December 1932, Borzov Papers, Box 4:5, HIA.
12 "Students of the Russian Nationality of the University of California," to Hon. William N. [Doak], n.d., Borzov Papers, Box 4:5, HIA. Text noted enclosure of petition regarding legalization "of Russian Students, visitors and illegally entered," received 30/31 January 1933. File 55605/130 INS COSCCF, NARA.
13 Student committee draft letters; Gavriloff to Norton (undated), Borzov Papers, Box 4:5, HIA.

Notes to pages 216–20 | **361**

14 CCRNO to President Hoover, received 30 January 1933. File 55605/130 INS COSCCF, NARA.
15 Lavrova article draft, Dolgopolov Collection, Box 162:2, ASML. Commissioner General H.E. Hull to Antonenko, 2 February 1933. File 55605/130 INS COSCCF, NARA; CCRNO official and INS official correspondence, 26–8 June 1934, Dolgopolov Collection, Box 162:2, ASML.
16 Gross, *What Blood Won't Tell*, chapter 7, on litigating racial identity and Haney López, *White by Law*, chapter 5, on legal construction of race with respect to immigration (i.e., arbitrary fabrication of race for the purposes of exclusion).
17 Amendment to 1929 Registry Act, 8 June 1934, Dolgopolov Collection, Box 162:2, ASML. Registry Act applied to persons who entered United States prior to 1 July 1924 (date Johnson-Reed Act came into force), and for whom no arrival record was available.
18 Lavrova article draft, Dolgopolov Collection, Box 162:2, ASML.
19 US State Department and US Immigration officials' correspondence, October–November 1934. File 55698/496, INS COSCCF, NARA.
20 Lavrova article draft, Dolgopolov Collection, Box 162:2, ASML.
21 US State Department and US Immigration officials' correspondence, October–November 1934. File 55698/496, INS COSCCF, NARA.
22 Lavrova, "White Russians in the 'New World,'" *Christian Science Monitor*, 30 October 1934.
23 Lewis and Schibsby, "Status of Refugee," 52.
24 Shebeko, oral history transcript, 259.
25 Slavonic Alliance to RNSA, 14 January 1932, Borzov Papers, Box 4:3, HIA.
26 SS *Seiyo Maru*, "Lists of Passengers Who Arrived at San Pedro/Los Angeles, California, 1920–1949, in Transit to Final Destinations," NAI 4492686; SS *President Grant*, "Passenger and Crew Lists of Vessels Arriving at Seattle, Washington," NAI 4449160; Records of the INS; Lydia Victorovna Kapylova, Mary Matveevna Sinitzin, "PFN," NAI 605504, Records of USDC, NARA.
27 Lavrova, "White Russians in the 'New World,'" *Christian Science Monitor*, 30 October 1934; On repatriation, Balderrama and Rodriguez, *Decade of Betrayal*; Sánchez, *Becoming Mexican American*, chapter 10.
28 Sakovich, citing *New York Times*, "Labor Immigration Halted Temporarily at Hoover's Order:" 10 September 1930, "Angel Island Immigration Station Reconsidered," 186n17. US officials had been applying the LPC label routinely since the 1910s. Blue, *The Deportation Express*, 63.
29 Lavrova, "White Russians in the 'New World,'" *Christian Science Monitor*, 30 October 1934; Schiavone Camacho, *Chinese Mexicans*, chapters 3–4, on expulsion of ethnic Chinese people from Sonora; US policy towards ethnic Chinese refugees from Mexico; Lee, *At America's Gates*, chapter 5, on transnational context of immigration laws and effects on border controls.
30 Lavrova, "White Russians in the 'New World,'" *Christian Science Monitor*, 30 October 1934.
31 1923/1924 Japan to Mexico passenger manifests include passengers with Russian surnames; "Lists of Passengers Who Arrived At San Pedro/Los Angeles, California, 1920–1949, in Transit to Their Final Destinations," NAI 4492686, Records of the INS, NARA.; Ports of entry in PFNs of Russians entering US via Mexico in inter-war period, "PFN," NAI 605504, Records of USDC, NARA.
32 Russians in China without documents obtained passports from Chinese Bureau of Foreign Affairs for American visa support in the 1920s. Board of Special Inquiry, Boxer family, 9 May 1931, US Dept of Labor immigration service, NARA. The Mexican government passed more restrictive immigration laws in 1926, directed at Chinese immigrants. Lim, *Porous Borders*, 185.
33 Correspondence of Landesen, E.P. Lebedeff, and Mexican Consul General Alejandro V. Martinez, San Francisco, December 1929, regarding travel of Paul Miakinkoff to Mazatlán to visit son Dmitry, engaged in dry goods business. Martinez noted: "Affidavits sworn before a Notary Public are no longer accepted as substitutes for passports" for Russian nationals. Landesen Papers, Box 2:1, HIA.

34 Lebedeff/Miakinkoff, "Lists of Passengers Who Arrived at San Pedro/Los Angeles, California, 1920–1949, in Transit to Their Final Destinations," NAI 4492686, Records of the INS; "PFN," NAI 605504, Records of USDC, NARA.

35 US Census 1930, San Francisco, AD 31; Boris Lebedeff, "PFN," NAI 605504, Records of USDC, NARA.

36 Lebedeff/Miakinkoff/Tichinin, "PFN," NAI 605504, Records of USDC, NARA.

37 Landesen to Evtikhieff, Nogales, Mexico, 15 July 1926, Landesen Papers, Box 3:3, HIA.

38 Bogoiavlensky, Landesen, Evtikhieff correspondence, July–November 1926, Landesen Papers, Box 3:3.

39 Evtikhieff and Landesen, April 1927, Landesen Papers, Box 3:3, HIA. Evtikhieff and spouse crossed the border, likely without sanction, and settled in Los Angeles.

40 Landesen to Naturalization Bureau, 16 June 1928, Landesen Papers, Box 3:3, HIA.

41 Lavrova draft, Dolgopolov Collection, Box 162:2, HIA.

42 Ibid.

43 Russian women in Constantinople "pawned what jewels they had been able to carry away with them" to open a restaurant. "Late Czar's Niece Acting as Waitress," *San Francisco Examiner*, 17 December 1922; Fleeing aristocrats sewed jewels into corsets and hid them in their hair. Vassiliev, *Beauty in Exile*, 48.

44 Ilyin to Archbishop Apollinary, 10 December 1932, Dolgopolov Collection, Box 162:2, ASML; Newsletter, May 1933, IHRCA; "Concert Ball for Russian Center," *San Francisco Examiner*, 13 August 1933; "Russian Colony Leader Honored," 6 November 1932.

45 "One Killed, 13 Injured in Bay Area Accidents," *Oakland Tribune*, 15 March 1926.

46 Alexandra Gavriloff/Polosuhin, "PFN," NAI 605504, Records of USDC, NARA; Folsom/San Quentin State Prison Inmate Identification Photograph Cards/Inmate 23451-24800/65801-67700, CSA, Sacramento, CA; "Slain Bandit born in Harbin, China," *The Columbus Telegram*, 5 November 1942. Some accounts noted that he ran from police and was shot while attempting to steal a getaway car. "Gunman Killed on City Street," *Omaha World Herald*, 8 November 1942.

47 "Clerk Grabs Armed Thug, Foils Holdup," *San Francisco Examiner*, 30 April 1931; On Clyde Stevens, "The Great Escape," Barbier Security Group, http://barbiersecuritygroup.com/bsg-blog, accessed 15 February 2022.

48 Court cases, *San Francisco Recorder*, San Francisco, 8–26 May 1931; San Quentin State Prison Inmate Identification Photograph Cards/Inmate 39301-50850; CSA; "Nobleman Sentenced," *Santa Rosa Press Democrat*, 26 May 1931.

49 "Gang of 3 Men, Woman Seized here as Robbers," *San Francisco Examiner*, 14 November 1936; San Quentin State Prison Inmate Identification Photograph Cards/Inmate 39301-50850, CSA.

50 Businesses robbed in newspaper articles: "Clerk Grabs Armed Thug, Foils Holdup," *San Francisco Examiner*, 30 April 1931; "Gang of 3 Men, Woman Seized here as Robbers," 14 November 1936; "Two Ex-Convicts Held as Suspects in S.F. Robberies," *Long Beach Sun*, 14 November 1936; Andrew Ivane Kraft, "Draft Registration Cards for California," NAI 7644723, Records of the SSS, NARA.

51 Singular is "*koom.*"

52 Author's email correspondence with Red Shuttleworth, 2 April 2022; Register (1931–1948), HVC Papers, Box 35:2, WDA.

53 "Fine for Moonshine," *Russkaia zhizn'*, 27 April 1923.

54 "Rancher Kills Creditor, Self," *Oakland Tribune*, 21 December 1933; Ivan Ugolnikoff, "PFN," NAI 605504, Records of USDC, NARA. Reprints in *The Standard Examiner* (Ogden, UT), *The Daily Northwestern* (Oshkosh WI), and *The Jefferson City Post-Tribune*, 21 December 1933.

55 "'Borrower' of Auto Held in $25,000 Bond," *Oakland Tribune*, 19 November 1929; RNSA application: Borzov Papers, Box 9:5, HIA.

Notes to pages 227–33 | **363**

56 "Three Die Fleeing US Smuggler Trap," *Oakland Tribune*, 1 April 1935. The Japanese migrants died of their injuries in hospital.

57 George and Leo Gribkoff, ages thirteen and ten, in St Vincent's Home Orphan Asylum in San Rafael. Vsevolod Von Sonn, age twelve, in San Francisco Nursery for Homeless Children, 1300 Lake Street. US Census 1930, San Rafael Township, Marin County, and San Francisco AD 28.

58 "Governor Issues Pardons to 28 Ex-Convicts," *Sacramento Bee*, 27 July 1955.

59 "Spurned Man Slays Woman in S.F. Street," *San Francisco Examiner*, 7 March 1940; "S.M. Man Sees Double Killing," *The Time and Daily News Leader* (Burlingame CA), 7 March 1940.

60 "The Russian Colony of San Francisco," Survey for International Institute: Von Arnold Papers, Box 13:3, HIA.

61 "Plea on Deportation: S.F. Russians Ask First Lady's Aid," *San Francisco Examiner*, 18 June 1940.

62 "Russ Plead for Right to Stay Here," *San Francisco Examiner*, 21 June 1940. On Contract Labor Law: Lindsay, "Preserving the Exceptional Republic."

63 "Urgent Measures to Aid the Kolchins," *Novaya Zarya*, 18 June 1940, Bazhenova Papers, Box 5:3, HIA.

64 "PLV SF," NAI 4498993; "Registers of Persons Held For Boards of Special Inquiry at the San Francisco, California, Immigration Office," NAI 4468084, Records of the INS, NARA; "Urgent Measures to Aid the Kolchins," *Novaya Zarya*, 18 June 1940, Bazhenova Papers, Box 5:3, HIA; RC board meeting agenda, 26 June 1940, RC Papers, Box 6:1, MRC.

65 Geoffrey Currall, "Families Devoted to Children Await Court Decision," *The Times and Daily News Leader* (Burlingame/San Mateo), 7 December 1936; "Boellaards Go to SF Couple," 1 February 1937.

66 Blue, *The Deportation Express*, 69.

67 SS *Korea Maru*, "PLV SF," NAI 4498993; Alexander Altman, "Lists of Chinese Applying for Admission to the United States through the Port of San Francisco, California, 1903–1947," NAI 4482916; "Registers of Japanese, Filipinos, and Hawaiians Held for Boards of Special Inquiry at San Francisco, California," NAI 4497860, Records of the INS, NARA.

68 SS *Siberia*, "PLV Arriving at Honolulu, Hawaii, Compiled 13 February 1900 – 30 December 1953," NAI A4156, Records of the INS, NARA; US Census, 1920/1930, San Francisco AD 21/22.

69 The Union of Musketeers was founded in Harbin; after World War II it had chapters in San Francisco and Australia. Its goals were to fight communism, support the Orthodox Church and (Russian) national culture. A.V. Altman, "At the Musketeer's Meeting," *Russkaia zhizn'*, 14 September 1949, E/A file, MRC.

70 Vonsiatsky married an American heiress and lived in Connecticut. He was indicted for conspiracy to violate the Espionage Act, pled guilty, and was jailed in 1942. On Russian Fascist Party, see: Stephan, *The Russian Fascists*; Hohler, *Fascism in Manchuria*.

71 "Alexander Vasily Altman, "PFN," NAI 605504, Records of USDC, NARA; Texas Death Certificates, Texas Department of State Health Services, Austin TX; "Applications for Headstones," NAI 596118, Records of the Office of the Quartermaster General; RC Papers, Box 6, MRC; Altman interview, *Russkaia zhizn'*, 17 September 1949, Volkov Papers, Box 16:9, HIA. On the concept of "Caucasian," see Jacobson, *Whiteness of a Different Color*, chapter 3.

72 "AllMusic," https://www.allmusic.com/artist/vladimir-ussachevsky-mn0000199185/biography. Leonid changed his name to Leon Stewart.

73 Vladimir Alexis Ussachevsky, "WWII Draft Registration Cards for California," NAI 7644723, Records of the SSS, NARA.

74 AllMusic," https://www.allmusic.com/artist/vladimir-ussachevsky-mn0000199185/biography.

75 Alexis Aftonom Dechenko, "WWII Draft Registration Cards for California," NAI 7644723, Records of the SSS, NARA; *Board of Cosmetology Applications for Hairdressers and Cosmeticians, Part 02*, CSA; *U.S. Veterans' Gravesites*.

364 | Notes to pages 234–44

76 Morgan, *Eskimo Star*, 101–102, 134–136. The California Supreme Court struck down California's ban on interracial marriage in 1948.
77 "Three Russian Generals," *San Francisco Examiner*, 14 February 1944.
78 "The Oriental Mind," *San Francisco Examiner*, 14 February 1944.
79 "Russian Protest," *San Francisco Examiner*, 11 March 1944.
80 "The Oriental Mind," *San Francisco Examiner*, 14 February 1944.
81 Raymond and Jones state 20,000 Russian émigré arrivals on the entire west coast by 1925 and another 14,000 total in the US between 1930 and 1940, but do not provide source information. *The Russian Diaspora*, 54–5.

Chapter Eight

1   G. Ilyin on building Russian village. "Construction of Novograd near San Francisco," *Novaya Zarya*, ca.1932, Bazhenova Papers, Box 3:19, HIA.
2   Ilyin used the term "*izbenka*," diminutive of "*izba*," a peasant cottage.
3   T. Bazhenova, "First Russians in America," *Rubezh*, No. 20 (undated, ca. 1930s), Bazhenova Papers, Box 2:3, HIA.
4   Ilyin, "Construction of Novograd," *Novaya Zarya*, ca. 1932, Bazhenova Papers, Box 3:19, HIA. On the Chinese community, see Shah, *Contagious Divides*, 152–3. Ilyin also used the Italian neighborhood of North Beach as an example, as well as the fact that the Jewish Community was planning to build a Jewish Center.
5   On Dukhobors, Old Believers in American West/Alaska, see Hardwick, *Russian Refuge*, 22–8, 80–9, 114–23.
6   Ilyin, "Construction of Novograd," *Novaya Zarya*, ca. 1932, Bazhenova Papers, Box 3:19, HIA.
7   Ibid.
8   Young, *The Russian Orthodox Church Outside of Russia*. Metropolitan Theophilus became head of Metropolia after Metropolitan Platon's death in 1934. Church hierarchs in Serbia appointed him primate of the North American district of ROCOR in 1935, bringing Metropolia (Holy Trinity Cathedral) and ROCOR (Holy Virgin Cathedral) into a state of unity, which ended in 1946.
9   "Great Success of 'Russian Fair,'" *Novaya Zarya*, 28 April 1936, E/A File, MRC; On "different milieu," E. Bailey, who went to the 1937 fair, phone interview, 15 November 2021.
10 "Great Success," *Novaya Zarya*, 28 April 1936, E/A File, MRC; Kustova, "Russian Fairs in Stern Grove," *Russkaia zhizn'*, 10 November 2012.
11 Ibid.
12 "Great Success," *Novaya Zarya*, 28 April 1936; T. Bazhenova, *Rubezh*, "A Fair under the American Sky," n.d. (ca. May 1936), E/A File, MRC.
13 Ibid.
14 Ibid. On Markarian shop popularity, E. Bailey phone interview, 15 November 2021.
15 Boris Kramarenko and brother George Kramar (1901–1986) were professional musicians who lived in both Los Angeles and San Francisco.
16 "Tomorrow's Russian Fair," *Novaya Zarya*, n.d., Bazhenova Papers, Box 5:2, HIA; "Great Success," *Novaya Zarya*, 28 April 1936, E/A File, MRC; "'Yarmarka' at Stern Grove," *San Francisco Examiner*, 16 April 1936. Burskaya had performed with the Russian Grand Opera. "Russians Will Hold Concert Ball in S.F," n.d., Borzov Papers, Box 4:3, HIA. Sophia Samorukoff was an opera singer and vocal teacher. "PFN," NAI 605504, Records of USDS, NARA.
17 "Russian Fair will Depict Folk Life in Music, Dance," *San Francisco Examiner*, 25 April 1936, author's emphasis.
18 "Official Souvenir Program: Golden Gate Bridge Fiesta, 27 May to 2 June 1937"; "Yarmarka," *Novaya Zarya*, Russian Music Society Committee announcement, n.d, Shapiro Papers, Box 9:17, HIA; 6,000-10,000 people attended.

Notes to pages 244–51 | **365**

19 "Yarmarka" announcement, *Novaya Zarya,* Shapiro Papers, Box 9:17, HIA; G. Hodel on Russians Sectarians in California, 6 March 1932, SFRE File, SFHC, SFPL.

20 "Yarmarka" announcement, *Novaya Zarya,* Shapiro Papers, Box 9:17, HIA; US Census, 1940, Bryte, Yolo County, CA; US Census 1930, Fields Landing, Humboldt County, CA; Vladimir Tihon Fedoroff, "PFN," NAI 605504, Records of USDC, NARA; "Last Rites for T. Corneyff," *Petaluma Argus Courier,* 11 February 1941. The community of Bryte in Sacramento County (later incorporated into West Sacramento), included both Russian Baptist and Orthodox residents. See Hardwick, *Russian Refuge,* 101–2, 109–11.

21 Kustova, *Russkaia zhizn',* 10 November 2012; Official Souvenir Program, 15-A.

22 "Theater in San Francisco," Isaenko Papers, Box 7:13, HIA.

23 Obituary, Donna Jeanne Hewitt Ilyin (1926–2008), https://www.legacy.com/us/obituaries/sfgate/name/donna-ilyin-obituary?id=23229498.

24 Shapiro to Jean (Helm), 16 October 1947, Shapiro Papers, Box 2:24, HIA.

25 Russian Fair Program, E/A File, MRC, author's emphasis.

26 Official Souvenir Program, 19-A, 20. For biographical details, see Bogdan, "Between Dreams and Reality," 546–90.

27 RNSA application, Borzov Papers, Box 9:5; *Vital Statistics: Birth, Marriage, and Death Records, 1816–1867,"* 3003, Alaska State Archives; Valentine Ivan Hilkovsky funeral record, 22 October 1936.

28 Raeff, *Russia Abroad,* 8.

29 Carl Latham, "Amid Much Clicking of Heels: Tzarist Days Revived in San Francisco," *San Francisco Chronicle,* ca. November 1938; *Russian News-Life,* 18 November 1938, Bazhenova Papers, Box 5:2, HIA. Invalid Ball funded by 1938 Russian *Yarmarka,* last of three consecutive Russian events (1936–1938). Kustova, "Russian Yarmarkas in Stern Grove," *Russkaia zhizn',* 10 November 2012.

30 Carl Latham, "Amid Much Clicking of Heels," *San Francisco Chronicle,* ca. November 1938, Bazhenova Papers, Box 5:2, HIA, author's emphasis.

31 *Great Register of Voters, 1900–1968,* CSL.

32 Ibid. 3 per cent switched from Democrat to Republican. Remaining people switched parties several times. Of those naturalized, some "Declined to State" affiliation, some did not register, some registration records were unavailable, and a few registered under third parties, for example: Union Labor (Dmitry Kuvshinoff), Progressive (Pavel Karpooshkin), Socialist and Communist (Tamara Frontinskaya/Scherbakoff).

33 Vernon, oral history transcript, 23–40.

34 *Great Register of Voters, 1900–1968.* CSL Reasons for party affiliation were arguable. Vladimir and Olga Gordenker initially (1900–1912) registered as Republican and Democrat respectively despite a socialist outlook. In the 1920s, Olga registered as a Republican as well, possibly because Herbert Hoover, a Republican elected president in 1929, was instrumental in aiding Russia during the famine of 1921–1922. Glen Ellen Precinct, 1900–1912; 1924–1930, *Great Register of Voters, 1900–1968,* CSL.

35 Vernon, oral history transcript, 30–40. The US Communist Party also condemned the WPA "as designed to break unions and cut wages," so, ironically, Vernon and Boodberg inadvertently sided with the Communist Party on this issue. Cherny, *Victor Arnautoff,* 108–13.

36 SS *Taiyo Maru,* "PLV SF," NAI 4498993, Records of the INS; Natalie Doudoroff, "PFN," NAI 605504, Records of USDC, NARA; On hotel: *Russkaia zhizn',* 27 January 1927; *Russian Women in Emigration,* 205–9, MRC. *US City Directories,* Palo Alto, CA, 1937; *Great Register of Voters, 1900–1968,* CSL; *The Berkeley Gazette,* "Michael Dudoroff," 8 April 1975.

37 Interview with "Mr X," ca. 1934, Radin Papers.

38 Varguin file, MRC; Alexander Nicholas Vagin, Constantine Barsky, "PFN," NAI 605504, Records of USDC, NARA; *Great Register of Voters, 1900–1968,* CSL.

39 Bratoff's real name was Urey Georgievich Ogranovich/Orgranovich. "PFN," NAI 605504, Records of USDC, NARA.

40 "The Theater in San Francisco," Isaenko Papers, Box 7:13, HIA.

41 Review by Vasily Ushanoff, *Russkaia zhizn'*, 12 November 1926, Shapiro Papers, Box 7:3; "The Theater in San Francisco," Isaenko Papers, Box 7:13, HIA.

42 *Russkaia zhizn'*, 14 January 1927.

43 On Bratoff and productions, see: "The Theater in San Francisco," Isaenko Papers, Box 7:13; Album 24, Vrangel Papers, Box 49; Clippings, Bazhenova Papers, Box 1:8, HIA.

44 "The Theater in San Francisco," Isaenko Papers, Box 7:13, HIA.

45 14 October 1941 report by A.C. Smith, 2; 19 December 1946 report, Arnautoff FBI File; Funeral record, George Bratoff, 3 May 1956.

46 "The Theater in San Francisco," Isaenko Papers, Box 7:13, HIA.

47 Slobin, *Russians Abroad*, 81–2.

48 *Russkaia zhizn'*, August–October 1926.

49 Russian Club Charter (ca. 1927), RC Papers, Box 1:1, MRC.

50 Minutes of Extraordinary Liquidation General Meeting of Russian Club, December 1937; Correspondence and documents on closure, RC Papers, Box 1:1, MRC. Liquidation completed December 1938.

51 A.P. Farafontoff's report, 30 March 1940, Loukashkin Papers, FR/Alaska File, MRC.

52 Ibid.

53 Documents, fliers, clippings, materials, RC Papers, Box 1:1, MRC.

54 Ibid. Russian Historical Society and Russian Center founding documents indicate participation of members from HTC and HV congregations.

55 K. Barskii, "About the Russian Center," n.d., RC Papers, Box 1:1, MRC.

56 Documents, RC Papers, Box: 1:1, MRC; "How it was decided to buy a building for the Russian Center," *Novaya Zarya*, 9 February 1940, Alexander A. Martynoff Papers, MRC.

57 Documents, RC Papers, Box 1:1, MRC. Board members were elected in a general meeting; changes in board membership continued throughout 1939.

58 Documents, RC Papers, Box 1:1, MRC.

59 I. Guz, "Russian Corner," n.d., RC Papers, Box 1:1:8, MRC.

60 "Question of Building Purchase for a Russian Center in San Francisco to be Decided Today," *Novaya Zarya*, 7 February 1940, RC Papers, Box 1:1, MRC.

61 Ibid.

62 Documents, clippings, materials, RC Papers, Box 1:1–2, MRC. Turn Verein Center was renamed Sciots Hall in the late 1930s.

63 Documents, RC Papers, Box 1:1, MRC.

64 Memo by A. Varguin, RC Papers, Box 21:6; MRC.

65 Semi-annual board meeting minutes, 14 September 1941, RC Papers, Box 6:3, MRC.

66 Olga Borisova, "Russian Center has Decided to Help the Russian People," *Novaya Zarya*, 16 September 1941, RC Papers, Box 6:3, MRC.

67 14 October 1941 Report by A.C. Smith, Arnautoff FBI File, 2. After US entry into the war, organization renamed "Russian-American Society for Aid to the USSR"; Post-war: "Russian-American Society."

68 See Lieberman, *The Strangest Dream*, 27, on "unresolvable dilemma" of Communists in the United States in the late 1930s and early 1940s, when being an open communist or a "covert" one each held their own dangers.

69 6 January 1943 report by Willam F. Giesen, Arnautoff FBI File, 4.

70 Ethel Dunn, "The Molokan Settlement," *The Potrero View*, 1 December 1971, 5, SFHE File, SFHC, SFPL.

71 11 March 1942, 22 April 1942 minutes, RC Papers, Box 6:6, Box 1:3, MRC.

72 Lemuel B. Schofield, special assistant to the attorney general, referred to "White Russians" living in Baja California who had resided in the US from 1906 to 1913. Since the group had

Notes to pages 261–8 | **367**

left Russia long before the 1917 Revolution, its members were clearly not White Russians. 10 September 1940 memo, File 55875/821 INS COSCCF, NARA.

73 E.A. Martineau, "Russian Newspapers and Periodicals in San Francisco," SFHC, SFPL. Post-war émigré N.P. Nechkin later claimed an "investigation" had shown Soviet consulate subsidies going to *Novaya Zarya*, "a matter for the FBI." "Soviet Lackey Exposed," *Nashe Vremia*, 25 August 1951, Grebenstchikoff Papers, Box 30:9, IHRCA. FBI reports referenced *Novaya Zarya* in summarizing Arnautoff's activities in the 1950s. 14 July 1952 report noted *Novaya Zarya* reported on "among other things, pro-Communist events" but made no mention of Soviet financial support. Arnautoff FBI File.

74 RC Papers, Box 6, MRC.

75 Shapiro to Billie, 15 December 1941, Shapiro Papers, Box 3:49, HIA.

76 Minutes, 3 December 1941, RC Papers, Box 6:4–6, MRC. Net profit of event was $556.55, contributed to Russian War Relief with stipulation to purchase medicine for the Russian people.

77 Documentation and correspondence, 1941–1944 on civil defense and activities. RC Papers, Box 6:3–6, MRC.

78 11 March, 22 April 1942 minutes, RC Papers, Box 6:6, Box 1:3, MRC.

79 Article/essay draft, undated, Shapiro Papers, Box 1:1, HIA

80 RC Papers, Box 6:6, MRC.

81 Johnston, *New Mecca, New Babylon*, 167–79.

82 "Za Pobedu," 28 June 1942, MRC.

83 14 October 1941 report by A.C. Smith, Arnautoff FBI File.

84 Hazel Holly, "Women of All Nations Assist in War Effort," *San Francisco Examiner*, 16 August 1942; Ethel Dunn, *The Potrero View*, "Potrero's Russians," 1 December 1971, SFRE file, SFHC, SFPL; According to John Bataeff, Russian United Relief Society contribution was $95,738.83 (5). Amount sent by Russian-American Society as of 1 January 1944 was $44,471.53." Za Pobedu," June–July 1944, MRC.

85 28 August 1940 board meeting minutes, RC Papers, Box 6:2, MRC.

86 "Za Pobedu," 25 April 1942, MRC; "Service for Von-Vah, 70," *San Francisco Examiner*, 29 June 1958; *Great Register of Voters, 1900–1968*, CSL.

87 Juliet Dobrovidoff, Vladimir Nicolaevich Dobrovidov, "PFN," NAI 605504, Records of USDC, NARA; *Great Register of Voters, 1900–1968*, CSL; US City Directories, Napa, 1948.

Chapter Nine

1 Tsurikov to N. Borzov, undated, quoting from Russian DP publication "Echo" (Jun–Nov 1946): Borzov Papers, Box 3:20, HIA.

2 13 April 1949, Grebenstchikoff Papers, Box 30:12, IHRCA.

3 Vladimir I. Toumanoff interview by William D. Morgan, 18 June 1999, Association for Diplomatic Studies and Training Foreign Affairs Oral History Project, 2002, Library of Congress, www.loc.gov/item/mfdipbib001188.interview, on his interrogation by Sen. Joseph McCarthy, 23.

4 Cable No. 366, Geneva, 6 April 1950 to W.A. Wood; St Tikhon-Zadonsk orphanage pamphlet, Archbishop Ioann (Maximovich) [AI] Papers, Box 1:28, WDA, author's emphasis.

5 Documents/correspondence between IRO officials, Russian émigrés in Tubabao, and Russians in US. Cattell Collection, Boxes 1–3; Federation of Russian Charitable Organizations of the United States Records [FRCO], 1947–1963, Box 1, HIA; AI Papers, Box 1:28, WDA.

6 Documents, correspondence, FRCO and Far East Committee, FRCO, Boxes 2:7, 3, 4, 7, 10–12, HIA; FRCO reports/documentation, Borzov Papers, Box 18:2; Clippings about Russian émigré life in Argentina, Chile, and Venezuela, Abdank-Kossovskii Papers, Boxes 25–6, HIA.

7 Slobin, *Russians Abroad*, 206.

8 Varguin Papers, Box 1, MRC.
9 Dubinets discusses obscuring of both personal and Russian identity among "second-wavers," *Russian Composers Abroad*, 174.
10 On McCarthy and McCarthyism: Buckingham, *America Sees Red*; Oshinsky; *A Conspiracy So Immense*; Griffith, *The Politics of Fear*.
11 Carruthers, "Between Camps," 925.
12 V. Zenzinoff to Grebenstchikoff, 31 January 1946, Grebenstchikoff Papers, Box 44:11, IHRCA. Soviet authorities also arrested, forcibly repatriated, and imprisoned thousands of Russian expatriates in northern China, particularly Harbin, in 1945. Markizov, *Do i posle 1945*; Manchester, "Repatriation to a Totalitarian Homeland."
13 Myron B. Kuropas, "Fighting Moscow from Afar," in *Anti–Communist Minorities in the US*, 55–6. The British continued repatriations while they remained in Europe as an occupying force.
14 Carruthers, "Between Camps," 915. UNRRA "repatriated seven million refugees" by 1947.
15 6 June 1951, Grebenstchikoff Papers, Box 41:13, IHRCA. See Holian, *Between National Socialism and Communism* and Janco, "Soviet 'Displaced Persons' in Europe, 1941–1941" on DPS in post-war Europe.
16 Ed Gossett, Texas, HR, "A New Fifth Column or the Refugee Racket," 2 July 1947, 1–5, CUAC, Box 21:6, CSA.
17 Gossett, 3–5, CUAC, Box 21:6, CSA.
18 Ngai, *Impossible Subjects*, 236–7.
19 "White Russians," *South China Morning Post*, 19 November 1948; on Russian refugees in China: Hastings to Biehle, 25 October 1945, IISF, Box 23:6, IHRCA.
20 Alexander Lenkoff, "Life of a Russian Émigré Soldier," oral history transcript, 1967, 35; SS *President Wilson*, "PLV SF," NAI 4498993, Records of the INS; Flight accounts: Abdank-Kossovskii Papers, Boxes 25–6, HIA.
21 Correspondence and REA reports, Cattell Collection, Box 1, HIA.
22 Donat Kruchinin, untitled, 1948 scrapbook, Abdank-Kossovskii Papers, Box 25, HIA.
23 Archbishop John to Bologoff, 3/21 January 1950, Cattell Collection, Box 2:8, HIA. For discussion of Bologoff's central role in the evacuation and resettlement, see Bogdan, "Between Dreams and Reality," chapter 7.
24 Correspondence, reports, documentation on formation and certification, FRCO, Box 1:1–5, HIA.
25 Correspondence between US officials, San Francisco, and New York Russian émigré organizations, 1949–1950, FRCO, Boxes 1–2, HIA; Federation Report, 16 July 1954, Borzov Papers, Box 18:2, HIA; "Report of the Russian American Advisory Council of the International Institute on Stateless Russians," IISF, Box 23:7, IHRCA. Russians in US formed Russian American Union in 1945 in response to forced repatriations. Pozdnyakov, *From China to America*, 72.
26 Report on Federation activity (undated) by V. Borzov; V. Borzov to Ringland, exec. director of Advisory Committee on Voluntary Foreign Aid, USDS, 29 May 1950, FRCO, Box 1:1, HIA; Korosteleff and V. Borzov to Bologoff, 1949–1950, Cattell Collection, Boxes 1:7–8; 2, HIA; Kay to US government officials; Correspondence of government officials, June 1950, 56306/70, INSCOSC, Entry 9, Records of US INS, RG 85, NARA. Kay to Tenney, 5 January 1949; Tenney to James Richardson, *LA Examiner*, 17 January 1949: CUAC, Box 21:6.14, CSA.
27 Tenney to Warren, 19 August 1948, CUAC, Box 21:6, CSA.
28 Kay to Tenney, 3 August 1948, CUAC, Box 21:6, CSA.
29 Anderson to Burns, 18 October 1949, CUAC, Box 9:2, CSA; Conrad to Tenney, 5 May 1949, CUAC, Box 9:2, CSA.
30 CUAC materials, Box 9:2, CSA.
31 Denning, *The Cultural Front*, 20.
32 Nixon to Tenney, 11 July 1949; "House Group Hits at Slav Congress," *Los Angeles Times*, 26 June 1949, CUAC, Box 9:2, CSA. Nixon was California's 12th district representative at the time.

Notes to pages 275–8 | **369**

33 Borzov Papers, Box 2:1, HIA.

34 Fulton Lewis Jr, "Washington Report," *San Francisco Examiner*, 1 February 1951.

35 Van Arkel to Sen. W. Benton, 26 February 1953, comparing McCarthy to Adolph Hitler. Rosenblatt Papers, Box I: 2–8, McCarthy Clearing House, 1936–1957, LOC. On communism in the United States, see: Klehr, *The Communist Experience in America*; Haynes, *Red Scare or Red Menace?*

36 O. Pilat and W.V. Shannon, "Sen. McCarthy: Past Cloudy, Present Windy, Future Foggy," *New York Post*, undated clipping, Rosenblatt Papers, Box I:47–9. Information on McCarthy's beliefs, tactics, strategies, background, and support for him among Americans: Rosenblatt Papers, Boxes I: 11–59; Draft report of "McCarthy's Timetable to the White House": Box I:1–4, LOC.

37 "Amending the Displaced Persons Act." Report 2187, HR, 81st Congress, Cattell Collection, Box 3:21, HIA. The 1948 act allowed for 202,000 DPS in Europe to be admitted to the United States over two years.

38 Text, DP legislation, 1948/1950, Cattell Collection, Box 3:2, HIA.

39 Correspondence/documents, Cattell Collection, Box 1, HIA.

40 "Colonel G.K. Bologoff in Defense of Russians on the Island of Tubabao," *Rossiya*, 2 September 1949, Cattell Collection, Box 1:1, HIA.

41 The 1924 Johnson-Reed Act had created, among others, quotas for non-Chinese persons in China, as ethnic Chinese people (and other Asians) were completely excluded at the time. Ngai, *Impossible Subjects*, 26–7. Some Russians in Shanghai received visas in 1946–1948, emigrating to the United States directly. Non-quota immigration visas were available for clergy, among others. Correspondence, Archbishop Tikhon, SF, and clergy in Shanghai, Archbishop Tikhon (Troitsky) Papers, Box 2:54, WDA. Igumenia Ariadna, G. Bologoff, and Mollie Rule, IRO, April–June 1950, Cattell Collection, Box 2:6.

42 On Australian, French, and Dutch East Indies policies rejecting people over age forty: 18 May 1949, Abdank-Kossovskii Papers, Box 26, HIA.

43 Correspondence, Bogen and Bologoff, Cattell Collection, Box 1:4–6, HIA.

44 Unidentified DP, fifty-seven-year-old Russian Imperial Army officer, to Borzov, 2 February 1948, Borzov Papers, Box 26:1, HIA.

45 Correspondence, DPS to N. Borzov 1945–1950, Borzov Papers, Box 26, HIA, Bologoff and Bogen, 1949, Cattell Collection, Box 1: 4, HIA; Bologoff to A. Tolstoy, 14 May 1949, Abdank-Kossovskii Papers, Box 25, HIA; On émigré perspective of Lienz incident: articles, letters, pamphlets, History of Russia, the ROC, and ROCOR, Box 58:08, WDA.

46 Correspondence, documentation, Cattell Collection, Boxes 1–2; Letters, newspaper clippings (1949), Abdank-Kossovskii Papers, Box 2–26, HIA.

47 "Worsening situation in Tubabao," *Rossiya*, 25 August 1949, Cattell Papers, Box 2:5, HIA.

48 Newspaper clippings (1949), Abdank-Kossovskii Papers, Box 25, HIA.

49 Correspondence, camp district leaders to IRO officials, 16 October 1950; National leaders to IRO camp director, G.J.J. Chapirot, 22 August 1951, Cattell Collection, Box 1:5, HIA. O. Kachina, "From Russia to America," 58.

50 Fulton Lewis Jr, "Washington Report," *San Francisco Examiner*, 1 February 1951.

51 "Interview with Archbishop John," *Novaya Zarya*, 13 August 1949, Cattell Collection, Box 2:5, HIA.

52 Tretiakoff to/from Barsoukoff, 12, 13 September 1949, Cattell Collection, Box 1:5, HIA.

53 "New Law on DPS" (clipping), 16 June 1950, Cattell Collection, Box 1:1, HIA. The Internal Security Act went into effect on 23 September 1950, requiring Communist Party members to register, and "debarred any alien" who had belonged to the Communist Party. Carruthers, "Between Camps," 926. Up to 12,000 Russian DPS did not enter the United States because it further expanded alien exclusion. *New York Times*, "Gibson Holds Law Bars 100,000 D.P.s," 10 March 1951. See Ngai, *Impossible Subjects*, 237–8.

54 Correspondence/instructions, FRCO, Boxes 1:4, 3:1; Cattell Collection, Boxes; 1:5; 2:10, clippings, Abdank-Kossovskii Papers, Box 25, HIA. The exact number was 301,500 less the 172,230 in Europe who had already received US visas.

55 W.A. Wood to H. Rosenfield, 25 May 1949, AI Papers, Box 1:28, WDA.

56 H.J. L'Heureux to Archbishop John, 20 October 1950, AI Papers, Box 1:28, WDA; Carruthers, "Between Camps," 928–9.

57 Archbishop John to Sen. Knowland, 17 May 1950, AI Papers, Box 1:28, WDA.

58 Archbishop John to Bologoff, 27 May/9 June 1950, Cattell Collection, Box 2:8, HIA.

59 Wood to Rosenfield, 25 May 1950, Cattell Collection, Box 2:8, HIA.

60 Bologoff to Archbishop John, 26 June 1950, Cattell Collection, Box 2:6, HIA, author's emphasis.

61 "SS General W.H. Gordon," "PLV SF," NAI 4498993, Records of the INS.

62 Undated cable (ca. July 1950) from Archbishop John to D. Karber, AI Papers, Box 1:28, WDA.

63 Bologoff to Archbishop John, 1 May 1950, Cattell Papers, Box 2:6, HIA.

64 Correspondence, Hieromonk Modest, Archbishop John, D. Karber, P. Snape, July 1950; Children to P. Snape, 21 July 1950, Cattell Collection, Box 3:19, HIA.

65 "List of St Tichon's [sic] Orphanage Children, Staff and their Families," Cattell Collection, Box 3:19, HIA.

66 Harris, *Factories of Death*, Part One; Unknown number of victims from Shanghai, 87.

67 Harvey, "Archbishop, Teacher and Friend," 246.

68 St Tikhon-Zadonsk Orphanage pamphlet, AI Papers, Box 1:28, WDA; List of St Tichon's [sic] Orphanage Children, Cattell Collection, Box 3:19, HIA.

69 March 1951 list included twenty-three individuals, five eighteen and older. FRCO, Box 1:3, HIA.

70 "Nash vestnik [Our herald]," 7–25 January, V.N. Zhernakov Papers, Box 34, HIA.

71 "White Russian Orphans aren't too Happy Here," n.d., unidentified San Francisco newspaper clipping, ca. 1952, E/A file, MRC.

72 Ibid.

73 "Archbishop Made Orphans' Guardian," *San Francisco Examiner*, 27 May 1952; Zinaida Wadsworth, "Naturalization Petitions, Compiled 1906–1969/Alabama Naturalization Records," NAI 1258956; Peter Michael Kolmogoroff, "PFN, USDC for the Central District of California (Los Angeles), 1940–1991," NAI 594890; Zoya Michael Kuchkovsky, "PFN," NAI 605504, Records of USDC, NARA.

74 N. Massenkoff phone interview by author, 1 October 2019.

75 Ibid. Duche Massenkoff and Anatol Shmelev, "Nikolai Massenkoff," *Russkaia zhizn'*, 4 December 2021.

76 N. Massenkoff phone interview, 1 October 2019. Massenkoff made no explicit references to experiencing racism in the United States but specifically mentioned the Black Power and Chicano Power movements as inspiring him to celebrate his heritage.

77 V. Borzov wrote in early 1950s Federation report (11) "Any moment war could start between the west and USSR." FRCO, Box 1:5, HIA. According to Dvinov, a former Menshevik, monarchist groups anticipated seizing power after a "military overthrow of the Soviet government," which could only happen after war with the US. *Politics of the Russian Emigration*, 3.

78 Boym, *The Future of Nostalgia*, 49.

79 Ibid., 41.

80 Ibid., 49.

81 Ibid., 42.

82 Olferieff, *Russia in War and Revolution*, 223, 406.

83 N. Borzov to Grebenstchikoff, 13 February 1946, Grebenstchikoff Papers, Box 14:4, IHRCA.

84 Boym, *The Future of Nostalgia*, chapter 5.

85 Teplitz, "Exile in America," 1–2.

86 Dubinets, *Russian Composers Abroad*, 174.

87 Borzov/Bologoff correspondence, 1949–1950, Cattell Collection, Box 1:8, HIA.

Notes to pages 287–91 | 371

88 Fitzpatrick notes many Russians in inter-war Shanghai, who emigrated to Australia, were monarchists who joined political anti-communist organizations in emigration. *White Russians, Red Peril*, Part III.

89 Boym, *The Future of Nostalgia*, chapter 5.

90 Pozdnyakov on Russians in China and nostalgia, *From China to America*, 105.

91 On variations of nostalgia: Fritzsche, "How Nostalgia Narrates Modernity."

92 "We cannot restore," poem by B. Borzov, Borzov Papers, Box 1:5, HIA.

93 Poetry, writings, speeches of B. Borzov, Borzov Papers, Box 1:5, HIA; "Crusade for Freedom" fliers, pamphlets, literature, clippings, Volkov Papers, Box 16:12, HIA; Calls for endorsement of Crusade of Freedom from Common Council for American Unity, IRS, Box 241:22, IHRCA. A "Russian American Anti-Communist Alliance" had an office at 2458 Sutter Street in the 1950s.

94 B. Borzov, "A Wish" and other writings, Borzov Papers, Box 1:5, HIA.

95 USAT *Merritt*, "SS *Tenyo Maru*," "PLV SF," NAI 4498993; *Records of the INS*; *U.S. World War II Army Enlistment Records, 1938–1946*; Notation in Lashkoff/Lashkov family tree on ancestry.com states Viacheslav Lashkov, born 1875, was "killed by Bolsheviks," 17 February 1924.

96 Ernest Lenn, "Police Reshuffling: Lashkoff to Intelligence," *San Francisco Examiner*, 19 June 1969; "Church, Panther Tie Hit," 24 June 1969; "Priest's Angry Reply to Panther Accusation," 25 June 1969; "Panthers Repudiate Booklet," 26 June 1969; Obituaries of Benjamin Lashkoff; Carmelita V. Lashkoff, 12 December 1974, 7 August 1983.

97 Register (1931–1948), HVC Papers, Box 35:2, WDA; Benjamin Lashkoff obituary, *San Francisco Examiner*, 12 December 1974.

98 Ernest Lenn, "Police Reshuffling: Lashkoff to Intelligence?" *San Francisco Examiner*, 19 June 1969. Lashkoff was removed from police intelligence unit despite being considered "untouchable" due to a political shakeup of the SFPD in 1970, likely having to do with problematic nature of COINTELPRO. "Another Police Dept. Shakeup," *San Francisco Examiner*, 8 February 1970; On COINTELPRO: Blackstock, *Cointelpro*.

99 Archbishop John to Bologoff, 21 January/3 February; 13/26 January 1950, Cattell Collection, Box 2:8, HIA.

100 V. Borzov to/from Bologoff, 1949–1950, Cattell Collection, Box 1:8, HIA.

101 Ibid.

102 Interview by author with N. Sabelnik, 26 November 2019. Benthen sponsored the von Freibergs (N. Sabelnik's parents). Leonid Peter Benthen, "PFN," NAI 605504, Records of USDC, NARA.

103 Carruthers, "Between Camps," 926; Barkan, *From All Points*, 443–4.

104 Liberman, *The Strangest Dream*, 158.

105 In December 1951, the federation began to sponsor European DPS. Federation Report, FRCO, Box 1:5, HIA; "DPS Are People!" Church World Service, "Protestant Program for Displaced Persons," IRS, Box 220:12-13, IHRCA. Regarding seventy people unable to obtain visas, see Bogdan, "Between Dreams and Reality," chapter 7. On camp conditions in 1952–1953: Balakshin Papers, Box 3:25, BL.

106 1950–1951 Federation Report, FRCO, Box 1:5, HIA.

107 Ibid. "Russ Refugees En Route Here," *San Francisco Examiner*, 14 January 1951; John F. Allen, "Years of Wandering End for Russian DPS Here, 490 DP's Here on Transport," 15 June 1951; George de Carvalho, "Haven from Terror: 1131 Russians End a Flight from Communism," *San Francisco Chronicle*, 25 January 1951.

108 Francis B. O'Gara, "White Russian Refugees Safe in S.F. at Last," and "Family Suicide Pact Barely Averted in Flight from Reds," *San Francisco Examiner*, 1 December 1950.

109 1950–1951 Federation Report, FRCO, Box 1:5, HIA.

110 "3 White Russians Ordered Deported," *San Francisco Examiner*, 26 June 1951; "US Will Deport 3 Russians on Liner Today," *San Francisco Examiner*, 8 August 1951.

111 1950–1951 Federation Report, FRCO, Box 1:5, HIA.

372 | Notes to pages 292–302

112 Valcoff, 218; "USNS *General Black*," "PLV SF, NAI 4498993," "*Flying Tiger*," "Passenger Manifests of Airplanes Arriving at SF CA," NAI 2945502, Records of the INS, 1787–2004, RG: 85.

113 Detainees to Archbishop Tikhon, 20 February 1952; Sen. Knowland's office to Archbishop Tikhon, 12 February 1952, Archbishop Tikhon (Troitsky) Papers, Box 2:73, WDA; "*Flying Tiger*," "Passenger Manifests of Airplanes Arriving at SF CA," NAI 2945502, Records of the INS.

114 "41 White Russ Refugees Find Freedom Here," *San Francisco Examiner*, 29 July 1951.

115 S. Belosselsky to Nikolaevsky, 20 September 1951, FRCO, Box 1:3, HIA.

116 "Transactions by S.F. Supervisors," *San Francisco Examiner*, 21 December 1948.

117 Hastings to Biehle, 25 October 1945, IISF, Box 23:6, IHRCA.

118 Confidential Report, June 1951, IISF, Box 23:17, IHRCA.

119 "Summary of the First Stage of Development of the Council" draft, IISF, Box 23:6, IHRCA.

120 Ibid., author's emphasis.

121 "Problems of Refugees Told," *San Francisco Examiner*, 25 May 1953.

122 Russian American Advisory Council member list, n.d., IISF, Box 23:7, IHRCA. Council appeared to have disbanded by 1950.

123 Cursory surveys of *San Francisco Examiner* show terms "Red" (as in "the Reds," or "Red China") or "Russ" (abbreviation of "Russian") appeared daily at least three to five times in late 1940s/early 1950s front-page headlines.

124 Hendershort, *Anti-Communism and Popular Culture in Mid-Century America*, 22.

125 "Art Appreciation," *San Mateo Times*, 10 August 1959.

126 Nadejda Graham, "Passport Applications, January 2, 1906 – March 31, 1925," Roll 1091, NARA; US Census, 1930, San Francisco AD 29.

127 Shapiro to Bazhenova, 11 October 1953, Shapiro Papers, Box 2:1, HIA. Shapiro lived in Los Angeles at the time.

128 Tschebotarieff, *Russia, My Native Land*, 290.

129 Interview with Toumanoff, 1–42. Leon Nicholas Zaitzevsky, "Petitions and Records of Naturalization," NAI 3000057, Records of USDC, NARA. Slavic surnames were universally problematic. Walter Kulich was fired as "security risk" along with 1,154 other servicemen in this period based on surnames. Rosenblatt Papers, Box 58:1, LOC. Air Force Lieutenant Milo Radulovich was persecuted, at least in part, based on Serbian heritage. Ranville, *To Strike at a King*.

130 Clippings on screenings/interrogations of DPS applying for US visas in Europe: Abdank-Kossovskii Papers, Boxes 25, 26, 28, HIA. Carruthers speaks to "willfully prohibitive" conditions of US visa issuance in post-war Europe. "Between Camps," 928–9.

131 Biographical information: Beresov, *Chto Bylo*. Beresov's actual surname was Akulshin.

132 Beresov, *Chto Bylo*; Rodion Beresov, "PFN," NAI 605504, Records USDC, NARA.

133 Ibid.

134 Ibid. S-2792, amending the Immigration and Nationality Act, enacted 11 September 1957.

135 On Gregory Bogdan, author's father: Bogdan, *The Desolation of Exile*, chapter 18. Conversations with Igor Prohoda (author's godfather), summer 2006, at his home, Concord, CA. Both settled in San Francisco in 1950s.

136 *Vozrozhdeniye* clipping (c. 1949) by "S.N.," Abdank-Kossovskii Papers, Box 25, HIA; Carruthers, "Between Camps," 916–7.

137 Lieberman, *The Strangest Dream*, 57.

138 1949 Board President Report to members, RC Papers, Box 3:8–9, MRC.

139 Ibid.

140 "17 Seized in Raid on S.F. Poker Club," "Police, Brown in Split over Club Card Games," *San Francisco Examiner*, 5, 9 March 1949; 1949 Board President Report to members, RC Papers, Box 3:8–9, MRC. Note: 1949 report about raid erroneously dated 1948 (Box 3, File 8).

141 "Woman Guilty," *San Francisco Examiner*, 7 May 1949.

142 Details about raid/aftermath, 1949 Board President Report to members, RC Papers, Box 3:8–9, MRC.

Notes to pages 302–8 | **373**

143 Ibid.

144 Innokenty Brevnoff, "PFN," NAI 605504, Records of USDC, NARA; Funeral record, Kenneth Vladimir Braves, 13 June 1954; RNSA application, Borzov Papers, Box 9:4; Kachina, "From Russia to America," 67.

145 Shapiro to Balakshin, 24 November 1953, Shapiro Papers, Box 2:4, HIA. Mikhail N. Zalessky (1905–1979), involved with Russian Scouts, and Vsevolod A. Statsevich (1907–1989), headed San Francisco's Solidarist branch, closely affiliated with scouting groups in Europe. San Francisco Russian organization lists, 1950s, RC Papers, Box 26:1, MRC. In Europe, the *Natsionalyi trudovoi soyuz* (National Labor Union/Alliance) espoused the Solidarist view to build a New Russia based on Christian values, human rights, and freedoms. Raeff assessed the group as nationalist and authoritarian: *Russia Abroad*, 9. See also Tromly, *Cold War Exiles and the CIA*, on the post-World War II émigré political scene in Europe, chapter 7 on NTS and CIA.

146 Excerpts from 29 February 1952 article in *Russkaia zhizn'* quoted in "Second Informational Bulletin of 1952 Russian Center Board," 15 March 1952, RC Papers, Box 2:7, MRC.

147 Fitzpatrick on ubiquity of denunciations in Soviet life: *Everyday Stalinism*, 205–9.

148 Oda, *The Gateway to the Pacific*, chapter 1.

149 "Gambling Case of 'Russian Center' in Court," *Novaya Zarya*, 11 July 1944; Georgy Marinsky, "Russian Center without its Veil," 12 July 1944, RC Papers, Box 19:6, MRC; "Draw Poker Raid Embarrasses Police," *San Francisco Examiner*, 9 July 1944.

150 Minutes, 30 October 1940 meeting, RC Papers, Box 6:2; Financial reports, 1943, RC Papers, Box 1:3, MRC.

151 Constantinoff to Varguin, 4 October 1943, Varguin Papers, Box 2:2, MRC; 1949 Russian Center Board President report, RC Papers, Box 3:8, MRC.

152 IISF June 1951 confidential report, IISF, Box 23:17, IHRCA.

153 Varguin participated in numerous San Francisco boards and groups; was director at the International Institute, 1941–1944; assisted US government agencies with military and geographic map production during World War II. "A.N. Varguin in San Francisco"; Correspondence, Varguin Papers, Boxes 1:1, 2:3, MRC.

154 "Reply to an Unsettling Question," *Russkaia zhizn'*, 9 November 1951, E/A file, MRC. RFP literature: Shapiro Papers, Box 1:2, HIA. The term "tragedy" appeared in émigré literature referencing consequences of Bolshevik/Soviet rule, e.g., "The Tragedy of Exile," O.D. Volkogonova, *Obraz Rossii*, 3–6. The SF RFP chapter appeared to disband when the US entered the war in 1941.

155 M. Zalessky, "The Tragedy of Russia," *Russkaia zhizn'*, n.d.; M. Nadejdin, "A Memorable Day," *Russkaia zhizn'*, 16 November 1951; "Russian Scouts and various organizations of Russian Emigrant Youth," E/A File, MRC. The Soviet Union celebrated the October Revolution on 7 November due to the change from Julian to Gregorian calendar in 1918.

156 "Reply to an Unsettling Question," *Russkaia zhizn'*, 9 November 1951.

157 Varguin's caution was well-placed. CUAC received reports from their investigators about events aiding Russia. Meyer to Tenney, 14 August 1943, CUAC, Box 8:2.195, CSA.

158 Bikoff to Varguin, undated, Varguin Papers, Box 2:4, MRC, author's emphasis.

159 On Varguin: Varguin Papers, Box 1; "Slava, Khvala, Chest'" (1964), MRC.

160 1949 Board President Report to members, RC Papers, Box 3:8–9, MRC; "Russ Center Held Up," *San Francisco Examiner*, 4 August 1951; Report of incident 9 August 1951; Special commission report; Tarasoff incident documents, RC Papers, Box 3:11–12, 17, MRC.

161 Complaints about Bikoff and old board: RC Papers, Box 3:11, 13; Minutes of 7 February 1940 RC GM: RC Papers, Box 6:2, MRC. Varguin died of lung cancer in 1953.

162 Bikoff to Varguin, undated, Varguin Papers, Box 2:4, MRC.

163 Excerpts from 29 February 1952 *Russkaia zhizn'* article quoted in "Second Informational Bulletin, 1952 RC Board," 15 March 1952, RC Papers, Box 2:7, MRC.

164 Ibid.; San Francisco organizations list (1950s), RC Papers, Box 26:1, MRC, author's emphasis.

165 A list of "post-revolutionary" days of observance in the Russian community in an American reporters' notes (ca 1934) included the "Day of Sorrow" on 17 July "In memory of execution of late Czar Nicholas II," Radin Papers.

166 Some Cossack leaders had advocated for separate Cossack states in the Revolutionary/Civil War period. The Cossack representative listed in table 9.4, however, likely did not advocate for such autonomy given their inclusion as groups affiliated with the Russian Center. See Smele, *Civil War in Siberia*, 515–16, on request to form "pure" Cossack government in Siberia. B.N. Ulanoff on complexities of Cossack unification: "Paths to Unification for the Cossacks," 18 June 1965 (clipping, n.p.), A.N. Kniazeff Papers, Box 14:3, HIA. On establishment of Don Cossack Republic, chapter 36, and history of Cossacks, see Magocsi, *A History of Ukraine*.

167 Korosteleff to Bologoff, 22 January 1950, Cattell Collection, Box 1:7, HIA. SS *Buenos Aires Maru*, "PLV Arriving at San Pedro/Wilmington/Los Angeles, CA," NAI 4486355, Records of the INS, 1787–2004, RG 85, NARA.

168 Cooke, *A History of the Diocese*, 32.

169 Second Informational Bulletin, 1952 RC Board, 15 March 1952, RC Papers, Box 2:7; First Informational Bulletin, 1952 RC Center Board, 21 February 1952, RC Papers, Box 2:7, MRC.

170 Court judgment filed 15 September 1952, memorandum, and decision: *N.E. Bikoff, et al., v. A.S. Loukashkin, et al.*; Alexander Riaboff to Varguin, RC Papers, Box 3:13, MRC.

171 Correspondence, RC board meeting minutes, Oct–Dec 1952, RC Papers, Box 2:7; 3:16–17, MRC.

172 Documents, pamphlets, treatises, clippings on conflict: RKT Papers: Box 8:1–2, HIA. New cathedral was completed in 1964; *The Russian Orthodox Church Abroad*, 17–18.

173 Minutes, 21 August 1940 RC board meeting, RC Papers, Box 6:2, MRC.

174 Ibid.

175 Minutes of GM, 19 October 1946, RC Papers, Box 1:3, MRC. The title of Ivan Turgenev's book, translated into English as *"Fathers and Sons"* is actually "fathers and children" in Russian.

176 Interview with N. Sabelnik, 26 November 2019.

177 "20-year Anniversary of Joy of All Who Sorrow, 1927–1952," HV File, MRC.

178 Bologoff to Levitsky, Paramaribo, Suriname, 15 March 1952, Cattell Collection, Box 3:20, HIA.

179 Russian Boy Scouts National Association manual (New York, 1929), Wrangel Collection, Box 35, HIA; "Russian Boy Scouts and various organizations of Russian Emigrant Youth," E/A File, MRC.

180 "Sign-ups for Scouts Organization," *Russian-Life News*, n.d., Bazhenova Papers, Box 5:8, HIA.

181 T. Bazhenova on Jordan Park resort, n.d., Bazhenova Papers, Box 5:2, HIA; H. Vantz, "The Campfire," *Russkaia zhizn'*, 21 November 1951; "Russian Boy Scouts and various organizations of Russian Emigrant Youth," n.d., E/A File, MRC; Photos of Bay Area Russian Scouts in California, 1940–1950s, Zaverukha and Bogdan, *Russian San Francisco*, 54, 70, 81, 91.

182 Scouting instructors Nikolai Chaikin (1900–1967), US Navy, and Peter Miakinin/McKinin (1897–1951), US Army; Secretary of Trustee Committee Alexander Chukyaeff (1902–1978), US Army; All born Russia and arrived from Harbin. Chaikin returned to Bay Area; Chukayeff relocated to Maryland. "Sign-ups for Scouts Organization," *Russian-Life News*, n.d. (ca 1939), Bazhenova Papers, Box 5:8, HIA; "PFN," NAI 605504, Records USDC, NARA; "Electronic Army Serial Number Merged File, 1938–1946," NAI 1263923; Records of NARA, 1789–ca. 2007; "Muster Rolls of U.S. Navy Ships, Stations, and Other Naval Activities," Records of the Bureau of Naval Personnel, NARA; Silver Spring, MD City Directory, 1958; "Nikolai Chaikin" (death notice), *Contra Costa Times* (Walnut Creek CA), 1 August 1967.

183 B. Kucevalov, "The Educational Value of Scout Youth Camps," *Russkaia zhizn'*, 25 March 1953, E/A File, MRC; "PFN," NAI 605504, Records USDC, NARA.

184 "Campfire," *Russkaia zhizn'*, 21 November 1951, E/A File, MRC.

185 *Russkaia zhizn'*, 3 October 1950, E/A File, MRC.

Notes to pages 317–30 | **375**

186 Lev Gishizky, Alexei Kniazeff, "PFN," NAI 605504, Records USDC, NARA; *Skautenok*: IHRCA. ORUR: *Organizatsia rossiiskikh yunikh razvedchikov*. The term "*rossiiskikh*," rather than "*russkikh*" spoke to the fact that the organization, which was founded in post-war Europe, included children of various nationalities; NORS-R: *Natsionalnaya organizatsya russkikh skautov-razvedchikov*. The divide, as noted, was related to political factionalism in Russia Abroad, those divisions thus trickling down to the younger generation. On émigré factionalism in Europe, see Tromly, *Cold War Exiles and the CIA*.

187 The Scout is always happy," Kniazeff Papers, Box 11:4, HIA.

188 "D. Shishkin, "To Russian Scouts-Pathfinders," *Russkaia zhizn'*, 10 March 1953, E/A File, MRC; Shishkin "PFN," NAI 605504, Records USDC, NARA.

189 "Vpered," NORS-R journal, San Francisco; No. 5, Sept–Oct 1959; No. 6, Nov–Dec 1959, No. 7, Jan 1960; No. 8, Feb–Mar 1960: IHRCA; No. 11: RKT, Box 9:4

190 Olferieff, *Russia in War and Revolution*, 223, 406; See Fritzsche, "How Nostalgia Narrates Modernity" on nostalgia without melancholy and change over time in perceptions of the past.

191 Vernon, oral history transcript, 7–40.

192 Hirsch, *Willie Mays*, 274–81.

193 "Russ Church Head's Daughter to Wed," *Oakland Tribune*, 6 August 1934.

194 Hirsch, *Willie Mays*, 274–81.

195 *Petaluma Argus-Courier*, "Willie Mays Faces Problem of a Home," 14 November 1957; Hirsch, *Willie Mays*, 274–81.

196 Ibid.

197 Such precautions were not based on paranoid fears, indicated by contemporary developments. The Russian Festival in San Francisco, an annual event at the Russian Center since 1989, cancelled in 2021–22 due to the COVID pandemic, was cancelled again in 2023–24 due to the Russian invasion of Ukraine in 2022. Both municipal and private institutions withdrew financial support, as if Russian Americans today, most of whom were born in the United States, are nevertheless responsible for the actions of the current Russian government.

Conclusion

1 "Letter to the Editor," *Russkaia zhizn'*, 14 January 1927.

2 Shebeko oral history transcript, 237–8; W.E.B. DuBois, *Black Reconstruction in America, 1860–1880*, 700, cited by Feagin, "Toward an Integrated Theory of Systemic Racism," 216.

3 Selected birth/marriage/death/directory records of descendants of inter-war Russian émigrés.

4 Solnit, *Infinite City*, 7. On demographic change and redevelopment, see: "Fillmore: Promenading the Boulevard of Gone"; "Little Pieces of Many Wars," 66–75. Broussard, *Black San Francisco*, part two; Oda, *The Gateway to the Pacific*, chapter 1.

5 Solnit, *Infinite City*, 105–8, 140–7.

6 Mildred Hamilton, "The Russians Among Us," *San Francisco Chronicle*, 11 July 1972.

7 Boym, *The Future of Nostalgia*, 43.

8 Sadowski-Smith, *The New Immigrant Whiteness*, 13–14, on post-war middle class and European immigrants, citing Guglielmo.

9 Malozemoff, oral history transcript, 2–16, 353–60; *Great Register of Voters, 1900–1968*, CSL.

10 *In the Name of Russia*, 120.

11 N. Massenkoff interview, 1 October 2019. It was only in 2017 that the CRA, under the leadership of Natalie Sabelnik, "presented Massenkoff with a certificate of honor" from a Russian Federation commission recognizing his role in the "preservation of Russian language and culture." "Certificate of honor from Russian Federation for Nikolai Massenkoff," Congress of Russian Americans website, https://www.russian-americans.org/certificate-of-honor-from-russian-federation-for-nikolai-massenkoff/, accessed 30 October 2019.

SELECTED BIBLIOGRAPHY

Primary Sources

Alaska State Museum and Library (ASML), Juneau
A.P. Kashevaroff Papers
Alexander Dolgopolov Collection
Russian Orthodox Greek Catholic Church of North America, Diocese of Alaska Records (Alaskan Russian Church)

Bancroft Library (BL), University of California, Berkeley
Peter Balakshin Papers

California State Archives (CSA), Office of the Secretary of State, Sacramento, CA
California Un-American Activities Committee (CUAC) Records

Hoover Institution Archives (HIA), Stanford University
V.K Abdank-Kossovskii Papers
American National Red Cross Records
K.P. Barskii Papers
T.A. Bazhenova Papers
N.V. Borzov Papers
Vera Cattell Collection
Federation of Russian Charitable Organizations of the United States Records
E.S. Isaenko Papers
A.N. Kniazeff/Kniazev Papers
A.C. Landesen Papers, 1926–33
Russkii Katolicheskii Tsentr (Russian Catholic Center, now Our Lady of Fatima Byzantine Catholic Church), Inventory
N.L. Shapiro Papers
Elena Varneck Papers, 1930–33
B.N. Volkov Papers, 1915–63
A.R. Von Arnold Papers
Baroness M.D. Vrangel Collection
V.N. Zhernakov Papers

Immigration History Research Center Archives (IHRCA), University of Minnesota
George and Tatiana Grebenstchikoff Papers
International Institute of San Francisco Records
Immigration Refugee Services of America Records
US Immigration and Naturalization Service Files, 71-42 Records (1919–26)

378 | Selected Bibliography

Library of Congress (LOC)
Adolph Bolm Papers
Maurice Rosenblatt Papers

Museum of Russian Culture in San Francisco (MRC)
A.A. Martynoff Papers
A.N. Vagin (aka Varguin) Papers
Anatole Loukashkin Papers
Children's Home (CH) File
Events and Arts (E/A) File
Holy Trinity Cathedral (HTC) File
Holy Virgin Joy of All Who Sorrow Cathedral (HV) File
Russian Center (RC) Papers
"Za Pobedu," Bulletin of the Russian-American Society File

National Archives and Records Administration (NARA), College Park, MD
Records of Imperial Russian Consulates in the United States, 1862–1922,
    Publication Number M-1486 (San Francisco, Rolls 100–160)

NARA, San Francisco (San Bruno)
Investigation Arrival Case Files, San Francisco, Records of the US Immigration and
    Naturalization Service, Record Group (RG) 85

NARA, Washington, DC
FBI File, Victor Arnautoff, No. SF-100-6359, 5 vols. 100-HQ-47675, RD 38663, RG 065
Records of the Immigration and Naturalization Service, Entry 9, Central Office Subject
    Correspondence and Case Files and Entry 6, Correspondence and Case Files,
    1906–57, RG 85
Registry of Persons Held for Board of Special Inquiry at SF, Feb 1910–May 1941, M1388

San Francisco History Center, San Francisco Public Library (SFHC, SFPL)
San Francisco Russian Ephemera (SFRE) File
Paul Radin Papers, 1933–2000

Western Diocese of ROCOR Archive (WDA), San Francisco
Archbishop Ioann (Maximovich) Papers No. 1
Archbishop Tikhon (Troitsky) Papers No. 2
Orthodox Church of America (OCA) Papers No. 14
Russia, the ROC, and ROCOR in the 20th Century Collection No. 58
San Francisco, California Holy Virgin Joy of All Who Sorrow Cathedral Papers, No. 35

Archives Accessed Online through Ancestry.com

Alaska State Archives, Juneau, AK
Birth, Marriage, and Death Records, 1816–67, 3003 (Vital statistics)

California State Library (CSL), Sacramento, CA
Great Register of Voters, 1900–68

Selected Bibliography | 379

NARA, **Boston at Waltham**, MA
Petitions and Records of Naturalization, August 1845 – December 1911," NAI 3000057,
Records of District Courts of the United States, 1685–2009, RG 21

NARA, **College Park**, MD
Electronic Army Serial Number Merged File, 1938–46, NAI 1263923; Records of NARA,
1789-ca. 2007, RG 64, Boxes 13926/14767, Reels 158/47
Muster Rolls of US Navy Ships, Stations, and Other Naval Activities, 1 January 1939 –
1 January 1949, RG 24, Records of the Bureau of Naval Personnel, 1798–2007, series
ARC ID 594996, series MLR Number: A1 135

NARA, **Philadelphia**, PA
Declarations of Intention for Citizenship, 19 January 1842 – 29 October 1959; NAI
4713410; Records of District Courts of the United States, 1685–2009, RG 21

NARA, **Riverside**, CA
Petitions For Naturalization, US District Court for the Central District of California
(Los Angeles), 1940–1991," NAI 594890; Records of the District Court of the United
States, 1685–2009, RG 21

NARA, **San Francisco (San Bruno)**, CA
Petitions For Naturalization, 8/6/1903 – 12/29/1911, NAI 605504; Records of District
Courts of the United States, 1685–2009, RG 21

NARA, **St Louis**, MO
World War II Draft Registration Cards for California, 16 October 1940 – 31 March 1947.
NAI 7644723. Records of the Selective Service System, 1926–1975, RG 147, Box 50

NARA, **Washington**, DC
Applications for Headstones, NAI 596118, Records of the Office of the Quartermaster
General, RG 92
Lists of Chinese Applying for Admission to the United States through the Port of San
Francisco, California, 1903–47," NAI 4482916, Microfilm M1476, Reel 22
Lists of Passengers Who Arrived at San Pedro/Los Angeles, California, 1920–49, in
Transit to Their Final Destinations; NAI 4492686; Record Group Title: Records of the
Immigration and Naturalization Service, 1787–2004, RG 85
Marriage Reports in State Department Decimal Files, 1910–49; General Records of the
Department of State, 1763–2002; Series ARC ID: 2555709; Series MLR Number: A1,
Entry 3001; Series Box Number: 474; File Number: 133/222, RG 59
Naturalization Petitions, Compiled 1906–69; NAI 1258956; Records of District Courts of
the United States, RG 21
Naturalization Records of the US District Court for the Southern District of California,
Central Division (Los Angeles), 1887–1940, Roll 161, Serial M1524
Passenger and Crew Lists of Vessels Arriving at New York, New York, 1897–1957;
Microfilm Serial or NAI T715; Records of the Immigration and Naturalization Service,
1787–2004, RG 85
Passenger Lists of Vessels Arriving at San Francisco, California; NAI 4498993, Records of
the Immigration and Naturalization Service, 1787–2004, RG 85
Passenger Manifests of Airplanes Arriving at San Francisco, California, NAI 2945502,
Records of the Immigration and Naturalization Service, 1787–2004, RG 85

Passenger and Crew Lists of Vessels Arriving at Seattle, Washington; NAI 4449160; Records of the Immigration and Naturalization Service, 1787–2004, RG 85

Passport Applications, 2 January 1906 – 31 March 1925; Microfilm Publication M1490, 2740 Rolls; NAID: 583830; General Records of the Department of State, RG 59

Petitions For Naturalization 34126-34540; 5/21/31 – 7/1/31; (Roll 160); Records of District Courts of the United States, 1685–2009, RG 21

Petitions for Naturalization from the US District Court for the Southern District of New York, 18971–944; Microfilm Publication M1972, 1457 Rolls; NAID: 575701; Records of District Courts of the United States, RG 21

Registers of Japanese, Filipinos, and Hawaiians Held for Boards of Special Inquiry at San Francisco, California," NAI 4497860, Records of the INS, 1787–2004, RG 85

Online Databases Accessed through Ancestry.com

California, US, County Birth, Marriage, and Death Records, 1849–1980
California, US, Occupational Licenses, Registers, and Directories, 1876–1969
California, US, Prison and Correctional Records, 1851–1950
Honolulu, Hawaii, US, Arriving and Departing Passenger and Crew Lists, 1900–1959
National Cemetery Administration. US, Veterans' Gravesites, ca.1775–2019
San Francisco, California, US, Area Funeral Home Records, 1895–1985
Texas, US, Death Certificates, 1903–1982
US, Census Records, 1900, 1910, 1920, 1930, 1940, 1950
US, City Directories, 1822–1995
US, Department of Veterans Affairs BIRLS Death File, 1850–2010
US, Find a Grave® Index, 1600s–Current
US, Rosters of World War II Dead, 1939–1945
US, School Yearbooks, 1900–2016
US, Social Security Applications and Claims Index, 1936–2007
US, World War II Army Enlistment Records, 1938–1946

Newspapers

Alaska Herald
Alta California
Chico Record
Christian Science Monitor
The Columbus Telegram
Daily Morning Chronicle (San Francisco)
Daily News (Los Angeles)
Daily Northwestern (Oshkosh Wisconsin)
Freeport Journal Standard (Illinois)
Havasu News
Honolulu Star Bulletin
Jefferson City Post-Tribune
Long Beach Sun
Los Angeles Evening Post-Record
Los Angeles Examiner
Los Angeles Times
Napa Journal
Nashe vremia (*Our time*)

Selected Bibliography | **381**

New York Times
Novaya zarya (New dawn)
Oakland Tribune
Omaha World Herald
Oroville Mercury Register
Press-Telegram (Long Beach)
Rossiya
Rubezh (Frontier)
Russkaia ovost (Russian newspaper)
Russkii golos (Russian voice)
Russkiye ovosti-zhizn' (Russian news-life)
Russkaia zhizn' (Russian life)
Sacramento Bee
San Francisco Call
San Francisco Call-Bulletin
San Francisco Chronicle
San Francisco Daily News
San Francisco Examiner
San Francisco Recorder
Santa Rosa Press Democrat
South China Morning Post
Standard Examiner (Ogden, Utah)
Time and Daily News Leader (Burlingame, California)
Washington Post

Secondary Sources

Ablova, N.E. *KVZhD i rossiiskaia emigratsiia v Kitae: mezhdunarodnye i politicheskie aspekty istorii (pervaia polovina xx veka)* [The CER and the Russian émigrés in China: international and political historical aspects (first half of the twentieth century)]. Moscow: Russian Panorama, 2005.

Afonsky, Bishop Gregory. *A History of the Orthodox Church in Alaska (1794–1917).* Kodiak: St Herman's Theological Seminary, 1977.

Alexander, Jeffrey C. *Trauma: A Social Theory.* Cambridge: Polity Press, 2012.

Alexopoulos, Golfo. "Destructive-Labor Camps: Rethinking Solzhenitsyn's Play on Words," *Kritika: Explorations in Russian and Eurasian History* 16 (Summer 2015): 499–526.

Allen, Frederick Lewis. *Only Yesterday: An Informal History of the 1920s.* New York: Harper & Row, 1959.

Allen, Theodore, W. *The Invention of the White Race: Racial Oppression and Social Control.* Vol. 1. London: Verso, 1994.

– *The Invention of the White Race: The Origin of Racial Oppression in Anglo-America.* Vol. 2. London: Verso, 1997.

Andreyev, Catherine, and Ivan Savický. *Russia Abroad: Prague and the Russian Diaspora, 1918–1938.* New Haven: Yale University Press, 2004.

Arnautoff, Victor M. *Zhizn' zanovo* [Life anew]. Donetsk: Donbass Publishing, 1965.

Avins, Carol. *Border Crossings: The West and Russian Identity in Soviet Literature: 1917–1934.* Berkeley: University of California Press: 1983.

Balakshin, Peter. *Vesna nad Fil'morom i drugiye rasskazy* ["Spring over the Fillmore" and other stories] (also titled Collected Works of P.P. Balakshin: Stories, vol. 2). San Francisco: Sirius Publishing, 1951.

Selected Bibliography

Balderrama, Francisco E., and Raymond Rodriguez. *Decade of Betrayal: Mexican Repatriation in the 1930s.* Albuquerque: University of New Mexico Press, 2006.

Barkan, Elliott Robert. *From All Points: America's Immigrant West, 1870s–1952.* Bloomington: Indiana University Press, 2007.

Barrett, James R., and David Roediger. "Inbetween Peoples: Race, Nationality and the 'New Immigrant' Working Class." *Journal of American Ethnic History* 16, no. 3 (1997): 3–44.

Bederman, Gail. *Manliness and Civilization: A Cultural History of Gender and Race in the United States, 1880–1917.* Chicago: University of Chicago Press, 1995.

Behdad, Ali. *A Forgetful Nation: On Immigration and Cultural Identity in the United States.* Durham, NC: Duke University Press, 2005.

Ben-Sira, Zeev. *Immigration, Stress, and Readjustment.* Westport, CT: Praeger Publishers, 1997.

Berezov, Rodion. *Chto bylo* [What happened]. San Francisco: n.p., n.d.

Berglund, Barbara. *Making San Francisco American: Cultural Frontiers in the Urban West, 1846–1906.* Lawrence: University Press of Kansas, 2007.

Black, Lydia T. "Creoles in Russian America." *Pacifica* 2 (Nov. 1990):142–55.

– *Russians in Alaska, 1732–1867.* Fairbanks: University of Alaska, 2004.

Blackstock, Nelson. *Cointelpro: The FBI's Secret War on Political Freedom.* New York: Pathfiinder Press, 1988.

Bloom, Stephen G. *The Audacity of Inez Burns: Dreams, Desire, Treachery & Ruin in the City of Gold.* Regan Arts, 2018. E-book.

Blue, Ethan. *The Deportation Express: A History of America through Forced Removal.* Oakland, CA: University of California Press, 2021.

Bodnar, John. *The Transplanted: A History of Immigrants in Urban America.* Bloomington: Indiana University Press, 1985.

Bogdan, Nina. "Between Dreams and Reality: The Russian Diaspora in San Francisco, 1917–1957." PhD diss., University of Arizona, 2021.

– *The Desolation of Exile: A Russian Family's Odyssey.* Self-published, CreateSpace, 2013.

– "Keeping to the Sober Truth: A Jewish Lutheran White Russian in San Francisco," *Journal of Russian American Studies* 5, no.1 (May 2021): 48–64.

Bolkhovitinov, Nikolai N., ed. *Istoriia Russkoi Ameriki, 1732–1867* [The history of Russian America, 1732–1867, Vol. III: From Zenith to Decline, 1825–1867]. Moscow: Mezhdunarodnye otnosheniia, 1999.

Boym, Svetlana. *Common Places: Mythologies of Everyday Life in Russia.* Cambridge: Harvard University Press, 1994.

– *The Future of Nostalgia.* New York: Basic Books, 2001.

Branson, John B. *The Life and Times of John W. Clark of Nushagak, Alaska, 1846–1896.* Anchorage: US Department of Interior, 2012. PDF.

Breyfogle, Nicholas B. "Prayer and the Politics of Place: Molokan Church Building, Tsarist Law, and the Quest for a Public Sphere in Late Imperial Russia." In *Sacred Stories: Religion and Spirituality in Modern Russia*, edited by Mark D. Steinberg and Heather J. Coleman. Bloomington: Indiana University Press, 2007.

Broussard, Albert S. *Black San Francisco: The Struggle for Racial Equality in the West, 1900–1954.* Lawrence: University Press of Kansas, 1993.

Buckingham, Peter H. *America Sees Red: Anti-Communism in America, 1870s to 1980s.* Claremont: Regina Books, 1988.

Bushkovitch, Paul. "What is Russia? Russian Identity and the State, 1500–1917." In *Culture, Nation, and Identity: The Ukrainian-Russian Encounter (1600–1945)*, edited by Andreas Kappeler, et al., 144–61. Edmonton: Canadian Institute of Ukrainian Studies Press, 2003.

Selected Bibliography | 383

California's Diamond Jubilee Celebrated at San Francisco, September 5 to 12, 1925. San Francisco: E.C. Brown Publisher, 1927.

Carruthers, Susan. "Between Camps: Eastern Bloc 'Escapees' and Cold War Borderlands." *American Quarterly* 57 (Sept. 2005): 911–42.

Caruth, Cathy. *Unclaimed Experience: Trauma, Narrative, and History*. Baltimore: Johns Hopkins University Press, 2016.

Chepourkoff Hayes, Vivian. *Michael Chepourkoff: The Artist, The Man, His Life, His Art*. Ridgecrest, CA: Chepourkoff Productions, 2017.

Cherny, Robert W. *San Francisco Reds: Communists in the Bay Area, 1919–1958*. Urbana: University of Illinois Press, 2024.

−*Victor Arnautoff and the Politics of Art*. Urbana: University of Illinois Press, 2017.

Chzhichen, Van. *Istoriia russkoi emigratsii v Shankhae* [History of the Russian emigration in Shanghai]. Moscow: Russkii put', 2008.

Ciment, James, ed. *Encyclopedia of American Immigration*, vols 1–3. New York: M.E. Sharpe, Inc., 2001.

Clausen, Søren, and Stig Thøgersen. *The Making of a Chinese City: History and Historiography in Harbin*. Armonk: M.E. Sharpe, 1995.

Clowes, Edith W., Samuel D. Kassow, and James L. West, eds. *Between Tsar and People: Educated Society and the Quest for Public Identity in Late Imperial Russia*. Princeton: Princeton University Press, 1991.

Cohen, Aaron J. "Oh, That! Myth, Memory, and World War I in the Russian Emigration and the Soviet Union." *Slavic Review* 62 (Spring 2003): 69–86.

Cohen, Robin. *Global Diasporas: An Introduction*. UCL Press, 1997.

Conquest, Robert. *The Harvest of Sorrow: Soviet Collectivization and the Terror-Famine*. New York: Oxford University Press, 1986.

Cooke, Nicholas A. *A History of the Diocese of the West of the Orthodox Church of America (OCA)* Late Vocations Program, 1990.

Cross, Anthony. "'Them': Russians on Foreigners." In *National Identity in Russian Culture: An Introduction*, edited by Simon Franklin and Emma Widdis, 74–92. Cambridge, UK: Cambridge University Press, 2004.

Davis, David Brion, ed. *The Fear of Conspiracy: Images of Un-American Subversion from the Revolution to the Present*. Ithaca: Cornell University Press, 1971.

Davis, Donald E., and Eugene P. Trani. *The First Cold War: The Legacy of Woodrow Wilson in U.S.-Soviet Relations*. Columbia: University of Missouri Press, 2002.

Davis, Philip. *Immigration and Americanization*. Boston, 1920.

Dawley, Alan. *Changing the World: American Progressives in War and Revolution*. Princeton: Princeton University Press, 2003.

Denning, Michael. *The Cultural Front: The Laboring of American Culture in the Twentieth Century*. London: Verso, 2010.

Dubinets, Elena. *Russian Composers Abroad: How they Left, Stayed, Returned*. Indiana University Press, 2021. Proquest Ebook.

Dvinov, Boris L. *Politics of the Russian Emigration*. Santa Monica: Rand Corporation, 1955.

Eisenberg, Ellen, Ava F. Kahn, and William Toll. *Jews of the Pacific Coast: Reinventing Community on America's Edge*. Seattle: University of Washington Press, 2009.

Emmons, Terence. *Alleged Sex and Threatened Violence: Doctor Russel, Bishop Vladimir, and the Russians in San Francisco, 1887–1892*. Stanford: Stanford University Press, 1997.

Esman, Milton J. *Diasporas in the Contemporary World*. Cambridge, UK: Polity Press, 2009.

Farley, Brigit. "Circuit Riders to the Slavs and Greeks: Missionary Priests and the Establishment of the Russian Orthodox Church in the American West, 1890–1910." Kennan Institute Occasional Paper. Washington, DC: WWIC for Scholars, 2000.

Feagin, Joe R. "Toward an Integrated Theory of Systemic Racism." In *The Changing Terrain of Race and Ethnicity*, edited by Maria Krysan and Amanda B. Lewis, 203–23. New York: Russell Sage Foundation, 2006.

Ferrell, Nancy Warren. *Barret Willoughby: Alaska's Forgotten Lady*. Fairbanks: University of Alaska Press, 1994.

Figes, Orlando. *A People's Tragedy: The Russian Revolution, 1891–1924*.New York: Penguin Books, 1996.

– *Natasha's Dance: A Cultural History of Russia*. New York: Picador, 2002.

Fitzpatrick, Sheila. *Everyday Stalinism: Ordinary Life in Extraordinary Times: Soviet Russia in the 1930s*. Oxford: Oxford University Press, 1999.

– *Stalin's Peasants: Resistance and Survival in the Russian Village after Collectivization*. New York: Oxford University Press, 1994.

– *White Russians, Red Peril: A Cold War History of Migration to Australia*. New York: Routledge, 2021.

Flamm, Jerry. *Good Life in Hard Times: San Francisco in the '20s & '30s*. San Francisco: Chronicle Books, 1978.

Freeze, Gregory L. "Profane Narratives about a Holy Sacrament: Marriage and Divorce in Late Imperial Russia." In *Sacred Stories: Religion and Spirituality in Modern Russia*, edited by Mark D. Steinberg and Heather J. Coleman, chapter 6. Bloomington: Indiana University Press, 2007.

Fritzsche, Peter, "How Nostalgia Narrates Modernity." In *The Work of Memory: New Directions in the Study of German Society and Culture*, edited by Alon Confino and Peter Fritzsche, 62–85. Urbana: University of Illinois Press, 2002.

Gamsa, Mark. *Harbin, A Cross-Cultural Biography*. Toronto: University of Toronto Press, 2020.

Gibson, James R. *California through Russian Eyes, 1806–1848*. Norman: Arthur H. Clark Company, 2013.

Glad, John. *Russia Abroad: Writers, History, Politics*. New York and New Jersey: Hermitage and Birchbark Press, 1999.

Glass, Fred. *From Mission to Microchip: A History of the California Labor Movement*. University of California Press, 2016, EBSCO Publishing.

Glazunova, Alexandra. "Bay Area Russian-American Community: Search for its Identity." Master's thesis, Dominican College of San Rafael, 1972.

Grant, Madison. *The Passing of the Great Race or the Racial Basis of European History*. New York: Charles Scribner's Sons, 1916. Kindle edition.

Griffith, Robert. *The Politics of Fear: Joseph R. McCarthy and the Senate*. Amherst: University of Massachusetts Press, 1987.

Grinberg Leon, and Rebeca Grinberg. *Psychoanalytic Perspectives on Migration and Exile*. Translated by Nancy Fetsinger. New Haven: Yale University Press, 1989.

Grinev, Andrei V. *Kto est' kto v istorii russkoi Ameriki* [Who's who in the history of Russian America]. Moscow: Academia Publishing, 2009.

Gross, Ariela. *What Blood Won't Tell: A History of Race on Trial in America*. Cambridge: Harvard University Press, 2008.

Gubanova, Irina. "Adjustment Process of Russian Immigrants in California." Master's thesis, San Jose State University, 1995.

Guglielmo, Thomas A. *White on Arrival: Italians, Race, Color, and Power in Chicago 1890–1945*. Oxford: Oxford University Press, 2003.

Gutiérrez, David G. "Migration, Emergent Ethnicity, and the 'Third Space': The Shifting Politics of Nationalism in Greater Mexico." *Journal of American History* 86, no. 2 (1999): 481–517.

Selected Bibliography | 385

Gyrisco, Geoffrey M. "East Slav Identity and Church Architecture in Minneapolis, Minnesota." *Perspectives in Vernacular Architecture* 7, Exploring Everyday Landscapes (1997): 199–211.

Halbwachs, Maurice. "Collective Memory and Historical Memory." In *The Collective Memory*, 50–87. New York: Harper and Row, 1980.

Haney López, Ian. *White by Law: The Legal Construction of Race.* New York: New York University Press, 2006.

Hardwick, Susan Wiley. *Russian Refuge: Religion, Migration, and Settlement on the North American Pacific Rim.* Chicago: University of Chicago Press, 1993.

Harris, Sheldon H. *Factories of Death: Japanese Biological Warfare, 1932–45 and the American Cover-Up.* New York: Routledge, 2002.

Harvey, Valentina V. "Arkhiepiskop. Uchitel'. Drug. [Archbishop, Teacher, and Friend]." In *Pastyr'. Uchitel'. Drug. Sviatititel' Ioann Shankhaiskii i San Frantsiskii v vospominaniakh sovremennikov* [Pastor, teacher, friend: Saint Ioann of Shanghai and San Francisco in the recollections of his contemporaries] compiled by Father Peter Perekrestov, 231–84. Tver-San Francisco, 2017.

Haskin, Frederic J. *The Immigrant: An Asset and a Liability.* New York: Fleming H. Revell Company, 1913. E-document.

Hassell, James E. "Russian Refugees in France and the United States between the World Wars." *Transactions of the American Philosophical Society* 81, no. 7 (1991): i–vii, 1–96.

Hatch, Flora Faith. *The Russian Advance into California.* San Francisco: R and E Research Associates, 1971 (orig. pub. 1922).

Haynes, John Earl. *Red Scare of Red Menace? American Communism and Anticommunism in the Cold War Era.* Chicago: Ivan R. Dee, 1996.

Hendershort, Cyndy. *Anti-Communism and Popular Culture in Mid-Century America.* Jefferson: McFarland & Company, Inc. 2003.

Higham, John. *Strangers in the Land: Patterns of American Nativism, 1860–1925.* New Brunswick: Rutgers University Press, 1955.

Hills of San Francisco. San Carlos: The Chronicle Publishing Company, 1959.

Hirsch, Arnold R. "E Pluribus Duo? Thoughts on 'Whiteness' and Chicago's 'New' Immigration as a Transient Third Tier." *Journal of American Ethnic History* 23, no. 4 (2004): 7–44.

Hirsch, James S. *Willie Mays: The Life, The Legend.* New York: Scribner, 2011.

Hoare, Quintin, and Geoffrey Nowell Smith, eds and trans. *Selections from the Prison Notebooks of Antonio Gramsci.* New York: International Publishers, 1971.

Hoganson, Kristin L. *Fighting for American Manhood: How Gender Politics Provoked the Spanish-American and Philippine-American War.* New Haven: Yale University Press, 1998.

Hohler, Susanne. *Fascism in Manchuria: The Soviet-China Encounter in the 1930s.* London: I.B. Tauris & Co., 2017.

Holian, Anna. *Between National Socialism and Communism: Displaced Persons in Postwar Germany.* Ann Arbor: University of Michigan Press, 2011.

Ilyin, Boris. *Green Boundary.* Boston: Houghton Mifflin Company, 1949.

Ilyin, Olga. *Dawn of the Eighth Day.* New York: Henry Holt and Company, 1951.

In the Name of Russia. New York: "Russia Abroad" Publishing House, 1965.

Innis-Jimenez, Michael. *Steel Barrio: The Great Mexican Migration to South Chicago, 1915–1940.* New York: New York University Press, 2013.

Issel, William, and Robert Cherny. *San Francisco, 1865–1932: Politics, Power, and Urban Development.* Berkeley: University of California Press, 1986.

Jacobson, Matthew Frye. *Whiteness of a Different Color: European Immigrants and the Alchemy of Race.* Cambridge: Harvard University Press, 1999.

Janco, Andy. "Soviet 'Displaced Persons' in Europe, 1941–1951." PhD diss., University of Chicago, 2012.

Jensen, Joan M. *Army Surveillance in America: 1775–1980*. New Haven: Yale University Press, 1991.

Johnson, Robert H. *"New Mecca, New Babylon": Paris and the Russian Exiles 1920–1945*. Kingston: McGill-Queen's University Press, 1988.

Kachina, Olga. "From Russia to America: A Case Study of White Russian Refugees from Udmurtia." *Global Humanities: Studies in Histories, Cultures, and Societies* 3 (2016): 52–69.

Kalani, Lyn, Lynn Rudy, and John Sperry, eds. *Fort Ross*. Jenner: Fort Ross Interpretive Association, 1998.

Kan, Sergei. "Clan Mothers and Godmothers: Tlingit Women and Russian Orthodox Christianity, 1840–1940." *Ethnohistory* 43, no. 4 (Autumn 1996): 613–41.

– "Guest Editor's Introduction: Individuals and Groups of Mixed Russian-Native Parentage in Siberia, Russian America, and Alaska." *Ethnohistory* 60, no. 3 (Summer 2013): 351–61.

– *Memory Eternal: Tlingit Culture and Russian Orthodox Christianity through Two Centuries*. Seattle: University of Washington Press, 1999.

– "Sergei Ionovich Kostromitinov (1854–1915), or 'Colonel George Kostrometinoff': From a Creole Teenager to the Number-One Russian-American Citizen of Sitka." *Ethnohistory* 60, no. 3 (Summer 2013): 385–402.

Kappeler, Andreas. *The Russian Empire: A Multiethnic History*. Translated by Alfred Clayton. Edinburgh Gate: Pearson Education Limited, 2001.

Kelly, Catriona. *"Byt:* Identity and Everyday Life." In *National Identity in Russian Culture: An Introduction*, edited by Simon Franklin and Emma Widdis, 149–68. Cambridge, UK: Cambridge University Press, 2004.

Khlevniuk, Oleg V. *The History of the Gulag: From Collectivization to the Great Terror*, translated by Vadim A. Staklo. New Haven: Yale University Press, 2004.

Kivelson, Valerie. *Cartographies of Tsardom: The Land and its Meanings in Seventeenth-Century Russia*. Ithaca: Cornell University Press, 2006.

Kizenko, Nadiezda. "Feminized Patriarchy? Orthodoxy and Gender in Post-Soviet Russia." *Journal of Women in Culture and Society* 38, no. 3 (2013): 595–621.

Klehr, Harvey. *The Communist Experience in America: A Political and Social History*. New Brunswick, NJ: Transaction Publishers, 2010.

– *The Heyday of American Communism: The Depression Decade*. New York: Basic Books, 1984.

Kroll, C. Douglas. *"Friends in Peace and War": The Russian Navy's Landmark Visit to Civil War San Francisco*. Washington, DC: Potomac Books, Inc., 2007.

Lambert, Gavin. *Natalie Wood: A Life*. New York: Alfred A. Knopf, 2004.

Lazarev, Andrei. *Plavanie vokrug sveta na shliupe Ladoge v 1822, 1823 i 1824 godakh* [Journey around the world on the sloop Ladoga in 1822, 1823, and 1824]. St Petersburg, 1832.

Lee, Erika. *At America's Gates: Chinese Immigration during the Exclusion Era, 1882–1943*. Chapel Hill: University of North Carolina Press, 2003.

Lee, Erika, and Judy Yung. *Angel Island: Immigrant Gateway to America*. Oxford: Oxford University Press, 2010.

LeFebvre, Henri. *The Production of Space*, translated by Donald Nicholson-Smith. Oxford: Blackwell, 1974.

Lewis, Read, and Marian Schibsby. "Status of the Refugee under American Immigration Laws." *Annals of the American Academy of Political and Social Science* 203 (May 1939): 74–82.

Lieberman, Robbie. *The Strangest Dream: Communism, Anticommunism, and the U.S. Peace Movement, 1945–1963.* New York: Syracuse University Press, 2000.

Lim, Julian. *Porous Borders: Multiracial Migrations and the Law in the U.S. –Mexico Borderlands.* Chapel Hill: University of North Carolina Press, 2017.

Lindsay, Matthew J. "Preserving the Exceptional Republic: Political Economy, Race, and the Federalization of Immigration Law." *ScholarWorks@University of Baltimore School of Law* (Summer 2005): 181–251.

Luehrmann, Sonja. *Alutiiq Villages under Russian and US Rule.* Fairbanks: University of Alaska Press, 2008.

Lyons, Eugene. *Assignment in Utopia.* New Brunswick: Transaction Publishers, 1991 (original publication date 1937).

Magocsi, Paul Robert. *A History of Ukraine.* Seattle: University of Washington Press, 1996.

Manchester, Laurie. *Holy Fathers, Secular Sons: Clergy, Intelligentsia, and the Modern Self in Revolutionary Russia.* DeKalb: Northern Illinois University Press, 2011.

– "Repatriation to a Totalitarian Homeland: The Ambiguous Alterity of Russian Repatriates from China to the U.S.S.R." *Diaspora: A Journal of Transnational Studies* 16, no. 3 (2007): 353–88.

Markizov, Leonid P. *Do i posle 1945. Glazami ochevidtsa* [Before and after 1945: An eyewitness account]. Syktykvar, Russia, 2003.

Martin, Janet. *Medieval Russia, 980–1584.* Cambridge: Cambridge University Press, 2007.

Martin, S.R., Jr. *On the Move: A Black Family's Western Saga.* College Station: Texas A&M University Press, 2009.

Matich, Olga. "The White Emigration Goes Hollywood." *The Russian Review* 64 (April 2005): 187–210.

Meler, Vjekoslav. *The Slavonic Pioneers of California.* San Francisco: The Slavonic Pioneers of California, 1968.

Meyendorff, John. *Marriage: An Orthodox Perspective.* St Vladimir's Seminary Press, 1975.

Miller, Gwenn A. *Kodiak Kreol: Communities of Empire in Early Russian America.* Ithaca: Cornell University Press, 2010. E-book.

Miller, Matthew Lee. "American Philanthropy among Russians: The Work of the YMCA, 1900–1940." PhD diss., University of Minnesota, 2006.

Miller, Nathan. *New World Coming: The 1920s and the Making of Modern America.* New York: Scribner, 2003.

Milligan, Melinda J. "Displacement and Identity Discontinuity: The Role of Nostalgia in Establishing New Identity Categories." *Symbolic Interaction* 26, no. 3 (2003): 381–403.

Molina, Natalie. *How Race is Made in America: Immigration, Citizenship, and the Historical Power of Racial Scripts.* Berkeley: University of California Press, 2014.

Morawska, Ewa T. *For Bread with Butter: The Life-Worlds of East Central Europeans in Johnstown, Pennsylvania, 1890–1940.* New York: Cambridge University Press, 1985.

– *A Sociology of Immigration: (Re)Making Multifaceted America.* New York: Palgrave Macmillan, 2009.

Morgan, Lael. *Eskimo Star – From the Tundra to Tinseltown: The Ray Mala Story.* Kenmore, WA: Epicenter Press, 2011.

Moore, Willard Burgess, *Molokan Oral Tradition: Legends and Memorates of an Ethnic Sect.* Berkeley: University of California Press, 1973.

Morrissey, Katherine. *Mental Territories: Mapping the Inland Empire.* Ithaca: Cornell University Press, 1997.

Murray, Robert K. *Red Scare: A Study in National Hysteria, 1919–1920.* New York: McGraw-Hill Book Company, 1965.

Selected Bibliography

Ngai, Mae M. *Impossible Subjects: Illegal Aliens and the Making of Modern America.* Princeton: Princeton University Press, 2004.

Ngai, Mae M., and John Gjerde, eds. *Major Problems in American Immigration History.* Boston: Wadsworth, 2013.

Norá, Pierre. "Between Memory and History: *Les Lieux de Memoire.*" *Representations* 26 (Spring 1989): 7–24.

– *Realms of Memory: The Construction of the French Past, Vol. III: Symbols.* Edited by Lawrence D. Kritzman. Translated by Arthur Goldhammer. New York: Columbia University Press, 1992.

Oda, Meredith. *The Gateway to the Pacific: Japanese Americans and the Remaking of San Francisco.* Chicago: University of Chicago, 2019.

"Official Souvenir Program: Golden Gate Bridge Fiesta, Celebrating the Opening of the World's Largest Single Span: San Francisco, California, May 27 to June 2 1937" (electronic document), http://goldengatebridge.org/research/documents/officialprogram.pdf.

Okorokov, A.V. *Russkaia emigratsia: Politicheskie, voenno-politicheskie i voinskie organizatsii, 1920–1990 gg.* [The Russian emigration: political, politico-military, and military organizations, 1920–1990]. Moscow: OOO Avuar Consulting, 2003.

Oleksa, Michael. *Orthodox Alaska: A Theology of Mission.* Crestwood: St Vladimir's Seminary Press, 1992.

Olferieff, Fyodor Sergeyevich. *Russia in War and Revolution: The Memoirs of Fyodor Sergeyevich Olferieff.* Edited by Gary M. Hamburg. Translated by Tanya Alexander Cameron. Stanford: Hoover Institution Press, 2021.

Oshinsky, David M. *A Conspiracy So Immense: The World of Joe McCarthy.* New York: Free Press, 1983.

Parkman, E. Breck. "A Fort by Any Other Name: Interpretation and Semantics at Colony Ross." Santa Rosa: California Department of Parks and Recreation, 1992.

Petroff, Serge P. *Remembering a Forgotten War: Civil War in Eastern European Russia and Siberia, 1918–1920.* New York: Columbia University Press, 2000.

Pierce, Richard. *Russian America: A Biographical Dictionary.* Kingston, Ontario: Limestone Press, 1990.

Post, Seraphim F. *The Story of the Postnikov Family.* 1977. (PDF)

Pozdnyakov, Igor A. *Iz Kitaia v Ameriku: istoriko-antropologicheskii vzgliad na russkuiu emigratsiu (1920–1950-e gg.)* [From China to America: a historical-anthropological view of the Russian emigration (1920–1950)]. St Petersburg: SPbGU Philological Department, 2007.

Queen, Ellery, "The Adventure of the Glass Domed Clock." In *Great Tales of Mystery and Suspense*, compiled by Bill Pronzini, Barry N. Malzberg, and Martin H. Greenberg, 108–25. New York: Galahad Books, 1983.

Rabinovitz, Lauren. *For the Love of Pleasure: Women, Movies, and Culture in Turn-of-the-Century Chicago.* New Brunswick: Rutgers University Press, 1998.

Raeff, Marc. *Russia Abroad: A Cultural History of the Russian Emigration, 1919–1939.* New York: Oxford University Press, 1990.

Ranville, Mike. *To Strike at a King: The Turning Point in the McCarthy Witch-Hunts.* Troy, MI: Momentum Books, Ltd., 1997.

Rappaport, Helen, *After the Romanovs: Russian Exiles in Paris from the Belle Époque through Revolution and War.* New York: St Martin's Press, 2022.

Rasputin, Valentin. *Siberia, Siberia.* Translated by Margaret Winchell and Gerald Mikkelson. Evanston: Northwestern University Press, 1991.

Raymond, Boris, and David R. Jones. *The Russian Diaspora: 1917–1941.* Lanham: The Scarecrow Press, Inc., 2000.

Selected Bibliography | **389**

Robinson, Harlow. *Russians in Hollywood, Hollywood Russians: Biography of an Image.* Lebanon, NH: Northeastern University Press, 2007.

Robinson, Paul. *The White Russian Army in Exile 1920–1941.* Oxford: Clarendon Press, 2002.

Roediger, David R. *The Wages of Whiteness: Race and the Making of the American Working Class.* London: Verso, 2007.

– *Working toward Whiteness: How America's Immigrants Became White: The Strange Journey from Ellis Island to the Suburbs.* New York: Basic Books, 2006.

Rosenbaum, Fred. *Cosmopolitans: A Social & Cultural History of the Jews of the San Francisco Bay Area.* Berkeley: University of California Press, 2009.

Rosińzka, Zofia. "Emigratory Experience: The Melancholy of No Return" In *Memory and Migration: Multidisciplinary Approaches to Memory Studies.* Edited by Julia Creet and Andreas Kitzmann, 30–42. Toronto: University of Toronto Press, 2014.

"Russian Émigré Recollections: Life in Russia and California," oral history project, 1979–83, Regional Oral History Office, The Bancroft Library, University of California, Berkeley, 1986. Interviews by Richard A. Pierce, Boris Raymond (Romanoff), and Alton C. Donnelly, 1979–83.

The Russian Orthodox Church in Alaska Historical Ecclesiastical Landscapes Study, 1840–1920, Sitka National Historical Park. Drachman Institute, University of Arizona, 2017 (PDF).

Ruthchild, Rochelle Goldberg. *Equality and Revolution: Women's Rights in the Russian Empire, 1905–1917.* Pittsburgh: University of Pittsburgh Press, 2010.

Sadowski-Smith, Claudia. *The New Immigrant Whiteness: Race, Neoliberalism, and Post-Soviet Migration to the United States.* New York: New York University Press.

Said, Edward, *Orientalism.* Pantheon, 1978.

Sakovich, Maria. "Angel Island Immigration Station Reconsidered: Non-Asian Encounters with the Immigration Laws, 1910–1940." Master's thesis, Sonoma State University, 2002.

Salisbury, Harrison E. *Black Night, White Snow: Russia's Revolution 1905–1917.* Garden City, NY: Doubleday& Company, Inc., 1977.

Sanchez, George J. *Becoming Mexican American: Ethnicity, Culture, and Identity in Chicano Los Angeles, 1900–1945.* Oxford: Oxford University Press, 1993.

Saroyan, William and Pauline Vinson. *Hilltop Russians in San Francisco: A Record of the Potrero Hill Colony.* San Francisco: Grabhorn Press, 1941. E-document. http://molokane.org/molokan/History/Hilltop_Russians/.

Saul, Norman E. *War and Revolution: The United States and Russia, 1914–1921.* Lawrence: University Press of Kansas, 2001.

Schaufuss, Tatyana. "The White Russian Refugees." *Annals of the American Academy of Political and Social Science* 203, Refugees (May 1939): 45–54.

Schmidt, Regin. *Red Scare: FBI and the Origins of Anticommunism in the United States.* Museum of Tusculanum Press: University of Copenhagen, 2000.

Schrag, Peter. *Not Fit for our Society: Nativism and Immigration.* Berkeley: University of California Press, 2010.

Schwartz, Barry. "Rethinking the Concept of Collective Memory." In *The Routledge International Handbook of Memory Studies,* edited by Anna Lisa Tota and Trever Hagen, 9–21. New York: Routledge, 2016.

Selunskaia, V.M. "The Integration of the Russian Émigré Community between the World Wars in Russian and Soviet Historiography." *Russian Studies in History* 41, no. 1 (Summer 2002): 8–37.

Service, Robert. *A History of Modern Russia.* Cambridge: Harvard University Press, 2009.

Shah, Nayan. *Contagious Divides: Epidemics and Race in San Francisco's Chinatown.* Berkeley: University of California Press, 2001.

Shevzov, Vera. *Russian Orthodoxy on the Eve of Revolution.* Oxford: Oxford University Press, 2004.

Shlegel, Karl. *Berlin, Vostochnyi Vokzal: russkaia emigratsia v Germanii mezhdu dvumia voinami (1918–1945)* [Berlin, Eastern Station: Russian émigrés in Germany between the two world wars (1918–1945)]. Moscow: Novoe Literaturnoe Obozrenie, 2004.

Simpson, Sir John Hope. *The Refugee Problem: Report of a Survey.* London: Oxford University Press, 1939.

Slezkine, Yuriy. *Arctic Mirrors: Russia and the Small Peoples of the North.* Ithaca, NY: Cornell University Press, 1994.

Slobin, Greta Nachtailer. *Russians Abroad: Literary and Cultural Politics of Diaspora (1919–1939).* Brighton: Academic Studies Press, 2013. E-book.

Smele, Jonathan. *Civil War in Siberia: The Anti-Bolshevik Government of Admiral Kolchak, 1918–1920.* Cambridge: Cambridge University Press, 1996.

Smirnov, S.V. *Rossiiskiie emigranty v severnoi Manzhurii v 1920–1945 gg. (Problema sotsialnoi adaptatsii)* [Russian émigrés in northern Manchuria in 1920–1945 (problems of social adaptation)]. Yekaterinburg: GOU VPO, 2007.

Solnit, Rebecca. *Infinite City: A San Francisco Atlas.* Berkeley: University of California Press, 2010.

Solzhenitsyn, Alexander I. *The Gulag Archipelago: An Experiment in Literary Investigation.* New York: Harper & Row Publishers Inc., 1973.

Sparks, Edith. *Capital Intentions: Female Proprietors in San Francisco, 1850–1920.* Chapel Hill: University of North Carolina Press, 2006.

Stephan, John J. *The Russian Fascists: Tragedy and Farce in Exile, 1925–1945.* New York: Harper & Row, 1978.

Steptoe, Tyina. *Houston Bound: Culture and Color in a Jim Crow City.* Oakland: University of California Press, 2015.

Stites, Richard. *The Women's Liberation Movement in Russia: Feminism, Nihilism, and Bolshevism, 1860–1930.* Princeton, NJ: Princeton University Press, 1978.

Stone, Norman, and Michael Glenny. *The Other Russia: The Experience of Exile.* London: Faber and Faber, 1990.

Svanevik, Michael, and Shirley Burgett, *City of Souls: San Francisco's Necropolis at Colma.* San Francisco: Custom & Limited Editions, 1995.

Taylor, Sally J. *Stalin's Apologist: Walter Duranty, The New York Times's Man in Moscow.* New York: Oxford University Press, 1990.

Teplitz, Hilary J. "Exile in America: Russian Emigration Fiction, 1925–1999." PhD diss., Stanford University, 2003.

Tripp, Michael. "Russian Routes: Origins and Development of an Ethnic Community in San Francisco." Master's thesis, San Francisco State University, 1980.

Tromly, Benjamin. *Cold War Exiles and the CIA: Plotting to Free Russia.* Oxford: Oxford University Press, 2019.

Tschebotarioff, Gregory P. *Russia, My Native Land: A U.S. Engineer Reminisces and Looks at the Present.* New York: McGraw-Hill Book Company, 1964.

Tweed, Thomas A. *Our Lady of the Exile: Diasporic Religion at a Cuban Catholic Shrine in Miami.* New York: Oxford University Press, 1997.

Valcoff, Olga. *Hello Golden Gate, Goodbye Russia: A Young Girl's Odyssey from the Far East to the New World.* Bloomington: AuthorHouse, 2007.

Van Der Kolk, Bessel, M.D. *The Body Keeps the Score: Brain, Mind, and Body in the Healing of Trauma.* New York: Penguin Books, 2014.

Selected Bibliography

Van Nuys, Frank. *Americanizing the West: Race, Immigrants, and Citizenship, 1890–1930*. Lawrence: University Press of Kansas, 2002.

Vassiliev, Alexandre. *Beauty in Exile: The Artists, Models, and Nobility Who Fled the Russian Revolution and Influenced the World of Fashion*. Translated by Antonina W. Bouis and Anya Kucharev. New York: Harry N. Abrams, Inc., 2000.

Volkogonov, O.D. *Obraz Rossii v filosofii Russkovo Zarubezhia* [The image of Russia in Russia Abroad philosophy]. Moscow: ROSSPEN, 1998.

Wagner, William. "Ideology, Identity, and the Emergence of a Middle Class." In *Between Tsar and People: Educated Society and the Quest for Public Identity in Late Imperial Russia*, edited by Edith W. Clowes et al., 149–63. Princeton: Princeton University Press, 1991.

Warne, Frank Julian. *The Immigrant Invasion*. New York: Dodd, Mead and Company, 1913.

– *The Slav Invasion and the Mine Workers: A Study in Immigration*. Philadelphia: J.B. Lippincott Company, 1904.

White, Richard. *"It's Your Misfortune and None of My Own": A New History of the American West*. Norman: University of Oklahoma Press, 1991.

Williams, Rhys H. "Religion, Community, and Place: Locating the Transcendent." *Religion and American Culture: A Journal of Interpretation* 12, no. 2 (2002): 249–63.

Williams, Robert C. *Culture in Exile: Russian Émigrés in Germany, 1881–1941*. Ithaca: Cornell University Press, 1972.

Willoughby, Barrett. *Sitka: Portal to Romance*. Boston; Houghton Mifflin Company, 1930.

Wolff, David. *To the Harbin Station: The Liberal Alternative in Russian Manchuria, 1898–1914*. Stanford: Stanford University Press, 1999.

Wollenberg, Charles. "Immigration through the Port of San Francisco." In *Forgotten Doors: The Other Ports of Entry to the United States*, edited by M. Mark Stolarik, 143–55. Philadelphia: Balch Institute Press, 1988.

WPA Federal Writers' Project. *San Francisco in the 1930s: The WPA Guide to the City by the Bay*. Berkeley: University of California Press, 2011 (originally pub. 1940).

Wtulich, Josephine. *American Xenophobia and the Slav Immigrant: A Living Legacy of Mind and Spirit*. New York: Columbia University Press, 1994.

Young, Father Alexey. *The Russian Orthodox Church Outside of Russia: A History and Chronology*. St Willibrord's Press, 1993.

Zake, Ieva, ed. *Anti-Communist Minorities in the U.S.: Political Activism of Ethnic Refugees*. New York: Palgrave Macmillan, 2009.

Zaverukha, Lydia, and Nina Bogdan. *Russian San Francisco*. Charleston: Arcadia Publishing, 2010.

Zelensky, Elizabeth, and Lela Gilbert. *Windows to Heaven: Introducing Icons to Protestants and Catholics*. Grand Rapids, MI: Brazos Press, 2005.

Zelensky, Natalie K. *Performing Tsarist Russia in New York: Music, Émigrés, and the American Imagination*. Bloomington: Indiana University Press, 2019.

Zimmer, Kenyon. *Immigrants against the State: Yiddish and Italian Anarchism in America*. Urbana: University of Illinois Press, 2015.

Zipperstein, Steven J. *Pogrom: Kishinev and the Tilt of History*. New York: Liveright Publishing Co., 2018.

INDEX

acculturation, 69, 139, 173, 284; and assimilation, 179; assistance with, 73, 100; and dual lives, 198–201; and émigrés, 11, 16, 25, 40, 251, 302; and generational differences, 14, 73, 139, 198, 205, 266; role of trauma in, 17; and Russian identity, 11, 73, 190, 224, 325, 326; and "whiteness" attaining, 46, 65–7. *See also* assimilation

African Americans, 13, 42, 64, 134; and discrimination, 64–5, 319–21; in Fillmore/Western Addition, 15, 155, 340n88, 352n57; and Jim Crow laws, 64; and redlining, 256–7, 319–21

Alaska, 12, 28, 31, 34, 247, 355n10, 364n5; American purchase of, 28, 38, 61–3; Barrett Willoughby on, 61, 63, 340n73; census, 332n28–9; Creoles in, 18–19, 52–3; 58; and émigré creative work, 144, 169; and Imagined Russia, 143, 148; Nadia Shapiro writing on, 59–61, 63, 339n63; Orthodoxy in, 10, 28; Russian imperial project in, 8–9, 37, 62, 147, 151, 164–5, 340n80; Russian language spoken in, 31–2; social and racial categories in, 8–9, 332n24

Alien Registry Act of 1929, 213

Altman, Alexander V., 231–2, 363n70, 363n72

American Red Cross, 136, 267; and USAT *Merritt*, 105, 106;

in Siberia, 178; and World War II aid, 259, 263

Americanization, 13; and altering names, 325; and Eastern Europeans, 177; and marriage, 132, 194, 204; of Russian youth, 210, 253; and Russians, 42, 74, 132, 137, 179, 257, 268; and values, 290

anarchistic and kindred classes, 48–9, 69, 222, 227, 338n20

anarchists, 42, 248; exclusion of, 22; Russian, 41, 42, 47, 48, 135; White Russians opposed to, 216

Angel Island Immigration Station (AIIS), 46, 51, 71, 231; commissioner, 125, 127; as deportation hub, 49; detention of Russians at, 45, 55–6, 57, 104, 126; medical personnel at, 128; Russian university students and, 7, 44–5, 67, 105, 109, 124, 127

Anichkoff (Anitchkoff), Vladimir, 157, 161, 162, 169, 353n83

anti-communism, 315; anti-communist ideology, 213, 291, 304, 308; as crusade, 251, 268, 274–5, 288; émigrés and, 249, 251, 287; in émigré writings, 149; McCarthyism and, 268–9; militant, 303; of Russian Americans, 288–9, 306, 307, 318, 322–3, 329, 371n93; among Russian Australians, 371n88; and

stance, 232, 250, 301, 315. *See also* Russian Center: as anti-communist organization

anti-Semitism, 80, 84, 274, 320, 342n39

Argüello, Concepción, 169, 343n50, 354n107

Arkhimandritoff, Ilarion, 38, 336n45

Arnautoff, Victor, 206, 262, 263, 340n92, 354n107; and communist ideology, 65, 251, 307; FBI surveillance of, 252, 260, 367n73; and Russian-American Society, 260

assimilation, 19, 25, 296, 326, 328; and American military service, 176, 288; coercive nature of process of, 4, 17, 61, 143, 325; generational differences concerning, 139, 204, 209, 330; naturalization as part of, 19; Russian perspectives on, 12, 15, 141, 144, 179, 186, 238, 287

Association (Club) of Former Russian Naval Officers and Sailors, 123, 135, 214

Australia, 273, 282, 363n70; refusal of to take DPs, 277, 361, 415n42; Russian migration to, 14, 267, 347n65, 371n88

Auto-Orientalism, 91–2

Bailey, Eugenia, 25, 212; on Fillmore life, 107, 160, 188; on Russian identity, 196; at *Yarmarka*, 245, 364n9. *See also* Nikonenko family

Balakshin, Peter, 302, 344n91; and *California Almanac*, 170; on Fillmore neighborhood, 155, 161, 207–8; interaction with Americans, 149, 184; on life in emigration, 120, 161; and *Russian News-Life*, 184, 261

Bank of Italy, 82, 85, 86, 87, 343n64

Baptists, 50; Russian fair participation, 241, 242, 245, 247; in Sacramento, 365n20; Soviet persecution of, 352n43

Barskii, Konstantin, 26, 184, 250–1, 310; response to editorial, 235; and Russian Center, 254, 256–8, 305, 306, 307, 313

Bataiff, Mary, 85–6

Bazhenova, Taisiia, 341n3, 374n181; arrival at AIIS, 103–4, 127; on émigré experience, 147, 193–4, 202–4, 238, 262–4, 288; on race, 65; on Russian California history, 169–71; on Russian fair, 241

Beliaeff, Yefim, 95–6, 189, 210, 344n93

Bellavin, Bishop/Patriarch Tikhon, 35, 153, 164, 213–14, 352n44

Belosselsky-Belozersky, Serge, 92, 273, 294, 329, 344n82

Beresov, Rodion, 298–300

Berkeley, 20, 110–11, 128, 193, 273, 356n23; Borzov family in, 182; as place of employment, 134–5; RNSA and, 51, 124, 132–3, 172; Russian art studio in, 70, 76; St John Russian Orthodox Church in, 193, 204, 214, 350n2, 360n10

Berkeley, University of California, 25; Victor Borzov at, 287; Michael Bricksin at, 132; Michael Chepourkoff at, 66; George Martin Day at,

124; Nicholas Denisoff at, 109; George Guins at, 314; intentions to study at, 57, 227; Kulaieff brothers at, 356n24; Nathan Merenbach at, 39; George Noyes at, 348n77; George Patrick at, 348n77; Feodor Postnikov at, 39; Nicholas V. Riasanovsky at, 342n39; Russian students and, 124, 127, 131–2, 196; Slavic department, 215; Soviet Russian students and, 125, 132; Gleb Struve at, 149; Antonina Von Arnold at, 205

Berlin, 21, 24, 226n10

Bikoff, Nicklas, 300–1, 306, 307–8, 312–13

Bodisco: Andrew, 301–2; Michael, 90

Boellaard family, 230

Bogoiavlensky, Nicholas, 219, 221, 342n45

Bologoff, Gregory K., 306, 311, 313, 315, 368n23; correspondence with Victor Korosteleff, 309, 312; in Tubabao, 273, 276–8, 280–1, 290

Bolshevik(s) (Bolsheviki), 396, 405; actions of, 56, 337n6; in America, 47, 48, 50–1, 56, 134; anti-, 51, 54, 72, 131, 249; and civil war, 52, 124, 135, 309, 318, 346n19; émigré negative feeling toward, 86, 198, 216, 288; persecution of religion by, 153, 169, 288–9, 352n43, 352n44, 371n95; regime, 22, 55, 69, 72, 153, 173, 328; supporters of, 139

Bolshevik Revolution, 3, 55, 105, 290; American response to, 47, 48; celebration of, 307; émigré perspectives on, 58, 286; exodus as result of, 4, 22, 26, 43, 331n6; Spiritual Christian support for, 84, 99

Bolshevism, 93, 115, 322

Bolshevist, 47, 55, 261

Boodberg, Alexis P., 193, 201, 222, 248; children and family, 122, 195, 347n67; citizenship, 195; death, 145, 255; on education, 184; as Veterans' Society president, 121–2; on WPA, 249, 365n35. *See also* Vernon, Valentina

Boodberg, Xenia, 196, 197

Boratynski family, 199–200, 359n99

Borzov: Boris N., 287–8; Nikolay V., 75, 182, 275, 286, 310; Victor N., 131, 273, 287, 290–1

Boxer, Boris, 162; Jacob, 96, 162, 322

Bratoff, George, 96, 251–2, 262, 263, 307, 365n39; and Russian-American Society, 260, 263

Brevnoff, Innokenty (Kenneth Braves), 302

Bricksin, Michael, 132

Brown, Edmund G., 301

Bureau of Investigation, 44, 48, 125. *See also* Federal Bureau of Investigation

byt, 323; concept of, 16; negative aspects of, 93, 96, 97, 138, 203, 251, 345n105; "real" life outside of, 73–4, 95, 97

California: Academy of Sciences, 205; Baja, 366n72; and Chinese Exclusion Act, 334n76; émigré creative work about, 169–73; Gold Rush, 10; and Imagined Russia, 16–18, 60, 73, 141, 143–7, 169, 173, 252–3, 288; immigration to, 12, 334n85; interracial marriage in, 233–4, 364n77; job market, 104, 128–31, 136; Packing Corporation, 92; Popular Front in, 101; pre-1917

Index | 395

Russian migration to, 16, 37–42; Russian exploration of, 36, 151; Russian imperial project in, 139, 145–6, 163–5, 353n86; School of Fine Arts, 131; SERA, 67; Nadia Shapiro writings on, 58, 59–61; Slavonic Alliance of, 218; Spiritual Christians in, 12, 72, 85; *The Slavonic Pioneers of*, 186; violence against indigenous inhabitants in, 32, 335n19; Women's Club, 254. *See also* Berkeley, University of California; California Un-American Committee; Hollywood

California Commune, 73, 85–6, 140n55, 343n57

California Diamond Jubilee, 76–9, 99, 122, 159, 244

California Unamerican Committee (CUAC), 269, 274–5, 373n157

Canada, 20, 41, 85, 220, 221, 246, 273, 277, 299

Caucasian (cultural), 242, 243, 244

Caucasian (race), 68, 232; Slavs as, 7, 331n19

Chabanoff, Nikolay, 193, 358n68

Chepourkoff, Michael, 66

Children's Day Home, 181–3, 184–6, 202

China: civil war in, 267, 287; departure from, inter-war, 12, 20–1, 213, 236, 361n33; departure from, post-World War II, 138, 265, 268; displaced persons in, 295; inter-war Russian community in, 14, 20–1, 66, 74–5, 221, 280, 317; "Red," 372n123; Russians born in, 21, 23, 132, 174, 231, 232, 279–80, 287, 334n73, 317; Russian citizens of, 230, 276, 279; Russians fleeing to, 58, 97, 103, 189, 352n43; Russians returning

to, 218; Soviet arrests in, 368n12; under Japanese occupation, 213, 270, 282; US "white" quota, 276, 279, 369n41. *See also* Harbin

Chinatown (San Francisco), 158, 238–9, 338n38

Chinese Eastern Railway (CER), 20, 21, 182, 251

Clarke, Fred M., 82

Cohn, Roy M., 298

Cold War, 8, 92, 323, 328; first, 49; rhetoric about Russians, 164, 288, 296, 327, 353n86; paradigm, 286; Russian Americans and, 201, 287, 300, 304, 308, 321–2, 328, 330

Consolidated Committee of Russian National Organizations, 123, 214–5, 253

Cossack(s), 55, 74, 85, 353n71; in California, 155, 165; at Lienz, 277; in Tubabao, 277, 278; in San Francisco, 309, 310–2, 345n12; in Shanghai, 287; and separate state, 309, 374n166

Creole(s), 38, 340n80; in Alaska, 9, 34, 62; census change to "mixed race," 9, 332n28; depiction of, 63; at Fort Ross, 165, 354n93; of color, 332n26; in San Francisco, 11, 28, 29–30, 34, 282

cultural autonomy, 77, 139, 153, 238–9, 326

Cykman, Joseph, 80

Dabovich, Rev. Sebastian, 33, 358n88

Dalgeim, Joseph, 71, 91, 119

Day, George Martin, 124, 125, 126–7, 128

Denisoff, Nicholas, 109, 110

Denisoff, Sergei, 106, 192–4, 209, 358n75

deportation, 49; Beresov's notice of, 299; change in

status regarding, 210, 213, 215–6; and McCarran Act, 291; of Russians, 47, 48, 49, 56, 222, 229, 291; train, 49, 338n21, 360n6

displaced persons (DPs): assistance to, 162; opposition to acceptance of, 17, 271; post-World War II, 264–5, 269–74, 294, 298, 299; in/from Far East, 269, 291–2, 295; Soviet, 14, 286, 298; tactics to avoid repatriation, 299–300

Displaced Persons Act (1948), 272, 273, 276, 369n37; 1950 amendment to, 273, 276, 278, 279, 295

divorce: among émigrés, 118, 190–2, 194, 204, 208, 354n103; and Orthodox Church, 191–2; in Russia, 190–1

Doudoroff, Boris P., 105–6, 153–4, 187, 188, 248, 250

dual identity/lives, 150, 177, 196, 197–201, 209, 314

Duranty, Walter, 149

education, 132, 257; access to, 204; and denationalization, 196; émigré efforts regarding, 144, 154; and heritage preservation, 21, 179–84, 188–9, 285; level of, 6, 43, 136; RNSA efforts in, 133; of Russian orphans, 366; university, 44, 73, 104, 109, 132–3, 175–6, 192, 232; and women, 160, 205, 208. *See also* individual students; Tatyana, St; Society for the Protection (Care) and Education of Children

Efimoff, Avenir, 135, 217

Elovsky, Ivan, 134, 193, 348n77, 350n130

Ermoloff, Nadejda, 95, 96, 344n93

Eversole, Henry Owen, 178

Evtikhieff, Alexander, 221, 362n40

Farafontoff, Alexander, 171, 172–3, 242, 253
Federal Bureau of Investigation (FBI), 125, 259, 264, 289, 291; and Alexander Altman, 231; and Victor Arnautoff, 252, 262, 367n73; COINTELPRO, 289; and *Novaya Zarya*, 367n73; and Potrero Hill Neighborhood House, 263; and Russian-American Society, 252, 260, 263; and Russian Center, 300; and Anastase Vonsiatsky, 231; and White Russians, 260
Federation of Russian Charitable Organizations (FRCO), 268, 273, 283, 290–1, 295
Fedorkin, Michael, 112, 118; Peter and Anna, 107
Fedoroff, Alexander, 109, 110, 126
Fetesoff, Vasily, 40, 86
Filipino(s), 321; in Fillmore, 15, 155; "hep cats," 156; racial classification, 232; workers, 107, 202
Fillmore, 11, 39, 124, 230, 262, 269; Eugenia Bailey on, 151, 245; Peter Balakshin on, 157, 209–10, 269; Children's Day Home in, 237–8; "colony," 239; crime in, 291–2; dispersal out of, 26, 341, 424; diversity of, 27, 114, 339, 422; émigrés in, 13, 21, 27, 32, 40, 113–14, 138, 211, 266; Japanese community in, 392–3; redevelopment of, 424; Russian center in, 187–9, 204–7, 342, 377; Russian Jewish community in, 32, 138, 189, 211, 227n63
first generation immigrants, 177, 198, 264, 286, 355n1
Fort Ross, 147; Album, 171; chapel, 141, 142, 146, 152, 163–8, 174; and émigré creative work, 169–72;

misinterpretations of history of, 163, 164–5, 170–1; and Orthodox history, 141, 148, 164; performances of history of, 189, 246–7; pilgrimages to, 94, 144–5, 163–6, 171–2; preservation efforts of, 172, 201, 309; site of memory as, 18, 37, 140–3, 148, 166–7, 173. *See also* Fort Ross Initiative Group
Fort Ross Initiative Group, 141, 170, 172, 220, 354n99

Gavriloff: Alexandra, 129; Gabriel, 129, 223–4, 227
Gavriloff, Anatoly, 113, 214
George Washington High School, 65, 284
Germany, 233; invasion of Soviet Union by, 258, 259, 262; Nazi, 14, 217, 258; *Ostarbeiters* in, 299; post-World War II, 25, 200, 246, 277
Glazunova, Alexandra, 14–15, 329
Gnesdiloff, Walter, 319–21
Gold Rush (1849), 10, 28, 32, 163
Golden Gate Bridge, 140; Fiesta, 189, 240, 244–7
Golovinsky Peter, 102, 113; Tatyana, 102
Gordenker: Olga, 38–9, 87–8, 336n49, 365n34; Vladimir, 38–9, 365n34
Grant, Madison, 42, 328
Gray: Indis Alfred, 167, 354n102; Vera, 166–7
Grebenstchikoff, George, 75, 81, 286
"Green Street" community, 78, 79–80, 86, 154, 182, 231, 240, 264
Gromeeko, Andrew, 199
Grot, Elena, 76, 97, 176
Gruzdeff, Ivan, 133–4
Guins, George, 314
Guz, Ivan S., 256, 313

Hanson, George, 125–6, 219, 348n81
Harbin, 57, 219, 352n55; 1920s Russian population increase in, 20–1; 1950s departures from, 268; arrests of émigrés in, 368n12; economic opportunity in, 81; departure to Hawaii from, 39, 231; ethnic diversity in, 333n68; Arthur Landesen in, 342n45; Officers' Employment and Mutual Aid Union in, 120; Russian character of, 287; Russian community in, 14, 20–1, 66, 124, 334n74, 356n24, 374n182; Russian sojourners in, 20, 123, 226; Russian students from, 44, 51, 56–7, 59, 77, 86, 123–7; Russians awaiting visas in, 221; Russians born in, 21, 109, 223, 231, 233, 287, 362n47; suicide rate in, 107, 346n32; Union of Musketeers in, 363n70
Harbin Committee Rendering Aid to Students of Higher Educational Institutions, 44, 124, 125
Hearst, William Randolph, 235–6
Heiskanen, Boris and Peter, 106
Hilkovsky family, 207, 247
Hollywood, 164, 233, 269, 274, 334n86; Ivan Kulaieff in, 356n24; "mentality," 358–9n97; self-promotions in, 23
Holy Trinity Cathedral, 312, 327, 364n8; and 1906 fire, 37; church schism and, 153, 186–8, 193–4; Committee, 123; construction of, 37, 151, 154; and Olga Gordenker, 88; and Ivan Kolchin, 229; parish and congregation, 76, 99, 165–6, 168, 171, 186–8, 214, 240; parish school,

Index | 397

186, 189, 196; Powell Street location, 35, 36, 39; religio-cultural significance of, 42–3,135, 141, 146, 151–4; and RNSA, 133; and Russian Historical Society, 253; and Kiprian Shanovsky, 86; and Pamphil Tesluck, 88. *See also* Sakovich, Rev. Vladimir

Holy Virgin, Joy of All Who Sorrow Cathedral, 135, 292, 327; ceremonies at, 101, 107, 190, 191, 200, 205, 210, 289; choir, 255; founding of, 153, 187, 193, 352n52, 354n101; new, 313, 327; parish and congregation, 214, 240, 253, 264, 312, 358n68, 364n8; parish school, 284, 315

Honcharenko, Agapius, 37–8, 336n44

Hoover, Herbert, 215, 360n11, 365n34

House Un-American Activities Committee (HUAC), 259, 269, 275, 288

Humanity Calls, 274

Ignatieff, Alexander, 77, 79, 81, 132

Ignatoff/Ignoff, Leon, 113, 228

Ilyin: Boris, 199–200; Dimitri, 199, 201, 246; Gleb, 77, 81, 93, 127, 199, 214, 222, 238–9; Kiril, 199–200; Nadejda, 207; Natalia, 77; Olga, 199–200; Peter, 81, 199, 207

Imagined Russia, 139, 253–4, 288, 323; difference from Russia Abroad, 17; and dual life, 73; Fillmore neighborhood in, 141, 160–1; Fort Ross in, 147–8, 163–6; Holy Trinity Cathedral in, 152–4; as a mental territory, 143–5, 173, 286, 330; and "real" life, 74; and Russian Hill, 154–5; San Francisco as center of, 143–4,

324; Nadia Shapiro's conceptualization of, 60–1; spatial parameters of, 18, 141; and "third space," 143

immigration, 229; anti-feeling and literature, 6, 32, 125, 232, 268; Asian, 46, 279, 319, 334n76, 337n9, 342n24; and detention/exclusion, 44–5, 55–6, 67, 126–7, 291–2, 361n17; Eastern European, 11, 35, 42, 43, 177, 268, 270; of laborers, 6; legislation, 21–2; monitoring Russian, 210–11, 339n54; non-quota, 229, 236, 369n41; quotas, 22, 276–7, 369n41; restrictions, 6–7, 9, 21–2, 49, 231, 277, 334n76, 361n33; Russian quota, 22, 67, 85, 105, 109, 125–7, 214, 215, 228, 229, 236, 348n81. *See also* deportation

Immigration Act of 1917, 21

Immigration Restriction Act (1921) aka Emergency Immigration Act, 22, 125

inbetween people/ inbetweenness, 6, 22

Independence Day (US): émigré celebration of, 144, 165–6, 168–9, 171–2

Internal Security (McCarran) Act, 278, 279, 291, 369n53

International Institute of San Francisco, 295–6, 305, 373n153

International Longshore and Warehouse Union (ILWU), 101–2

International Refugee Organization (IRO), 266–7, 272, 276–8, 279–82, 283

Invalid Ball, 98, 122, 248, 365n29

Isaenko, Alexis, 208; Eugenia S., 24, 160, 181, 208, 209, 246, 252, 344n91

Ivanoff/Ivars, Alexander and Nina, 230

Jacoob, Barbara, 184, 203, 356n28

Japan: Boris Doudoroff in, 105–6; earthquake 218, 306; Kiyaschenko family in, 189; Lydia Kopiloff in, 212, 220; Miakinkoff family arriving from, 220; Olferieff family arriving from, 127; Nansen passports issued in, 345n112; and Pearl Harbor attack, 235–6, 258, 259, 261, 262; and occupation of China, 213, 229, 270, 282; Russians in/departing from, 21, 94, 213, 292, 361n32, 379; Nadia Shapiro in, 66; Sinitizin family in, 218

Japanese: Fillmore community, 15, 95, 155; immigrants, 22, 227, 363n57; internment of, 66, 156, 262, 304; people compared to Russians, 234–5; racism against, 46

Jewish community: Bank of Italy and, 86; Eastern European, 15, 17–18, 19, 39; in Fillmore, 15, 17–18, 20, 80, 143, 155–6, 157; and Center, 364n4; neighborhoods, 19, 333n66; religious discrimination against, 332n23; Russian, 17, 20, 29, 39, 99–100, 143, 156. *See also* Boxer, Boris: Jacob; pogroms

Johnson-Reed Act (1924), 22, 42, 232, 348n88, 361n18

Karelin/Krasnikov, Pavel, 82, 156–7, 251, 342n46

Kashaya-Pomo, 169. *See also* Native Californians

Kashevaroff, Andrew P., 34, 340n80; in San Francisco, 33, 36, 60–1; portrayal of, 61–3

Katenka Restaurant, 24, 202, 359n106

Kay, Leo N., 274
Kedrolivansky, Pavel, 31
Kiyaschenko: Eugene, 189–90;
 Georgy, 187, 188–9, 194–5,
 285; Natalia, 188–90, 247;
 Nina, 189–90
Klymontovich, Lydia, 54
Knowland, William, 276, 279,
 280, 288, 292, 321
Koblick, Harry, 156–7
Kolchak, Adm. Alexander, 20,
 55, 56, 123, 189, 227
Kolchin, Ivan, 229–30, 233,
 305; Olympia 229–30
Kolobok Theater, 96, 251
Konevega, Vladimir I., 134,
 345n4
Kopiloff, Lydia, 212–13,
 218–20, 221, 228, 229, 236
Korjenko, Vasily M., 98
Korosteleff, Victor N., 306,
 309–10
Koshevoy, Bishop Apollinary,
 187, 356n40
Kourlin family, 175–6
Kovaleff, Sergei, 125, 127, 184,
 349n119
Kramarenko: Boris, 242, 243,
 364n15; George, 364n15
Krinoff, Mikhail, 193, 358n68
Kropotkin: Alexis, 135,
 355n117; Peter, 135
Kucevalov, Bonifatij, 316
Kulaieff, Ivan V., 182, 356n24;
 Educational and Philan-
 thropic Foundation, 182

Ladov, Veniamin (Ben Lador),
 304
Landesen, Arthur C., 82, 149,
 219–21, 342n45
Lapidewsky, Constantin, 207,
 360n123
Laschenko, Katherine, 231
Lashkoff, Benjamin, 288–90,
 371n95, 371n98
Laub, Tamara, 55–60, 90, 95,
 344n93
Le Heart, Avenir, 76–7, 78,
 342n24
Lebedeff: family (inter-war
 arrivals), 354n99; Boris, 220;

Helen, 220, 361n34; Michael,
 220; Nadejda, 220; Paul,
 220; Victor, 220. See also
 Fort Ross Initiative Group
Lebedeff, Konstantin, 241
Lenkoff, Alexander, 272
Leonoff, Victor, 218, 288
Leporsky, Sergei, 350n2,
 360n10
Lewis, Fulton Jr, 275, 276, 278
liable to be a public charge
 (LPC), 56, 105, 219, 229,
 361n29
Lissivetz, Galina, 233–4
Looksha: Natalia, 191;
 Valerian, 191, 255
Los Angeles: Humanity Calls
 in, 274; Simon Merenbach
 from, 88; Molokane in,
 336n41; Russian artists/
 performers in, 76, 96,
 97, 275, 344n93, 364n15;
 Russian community in, 23,
 77, 219, 244, 273, 342n22,
 362n40; Russian students
 in, 102; Russkaia zhizn in,
 340n89; Nadia Shapiro in,
 372n127
Loschilova, Varvara (Barbara
 Menshikoff/Mensh), 182,
 183, 356n23
Lyons, Eugene, 197, 202–3

Mala, Ray Wise, 233–4
Malozemoff, Elizabeth, 25,
 149, 170, 195, 229, 329
Markarian, Horen, 241,
 364n14
marriage, 167, 176, 203, 228,
 358n76; to Americans, 72,
 196, 200, 205, 210, 246; and
 children, 207; interracial,
 9, 30, 169, 234, 364n77;
 multiple, 191–2, 194,
 357n63, 358n75; of nobility,
 200; and Orthodox
 Church, 190–2; secular,
 194; views of, 190–1
Masloff, Nicholas, 109, 114
Massenkoff, Nikolai, 25, 284,
 290, 319, 329–30, 370n76,
 375n11

Maximova-Kulaev, Antonina,
 181–3, 185, 186
Maximovich, Archbishop
 John, 266–7, 272–3, 278–9,
 281–2, 290, 312
Mazatlán, 218, 220, 361n34
Mays, Willie, 319–21
McCarran, Pat, 278, 321.
 See also Internal Security
 (McCarran) Act
McCarthy, Joseph, 269, 274–5,
 285 367n3, 369n35, 369n36
McCarthyism, 251, 269–271,
 290, 296, 329
McCarthyist era, 26, 49, 240,
 268, 275, 302, 322, 330;
 paranoia, 304; rhetoric/
 tactics, 296, 297, 298, 318
Mercury Soccer/Sports Club,
 135, 160
Merenbach: Esther Vera,
 341n1; Nathan, 39, 88,
 89, 230, 343n69, 348n78;
 Simon, 88
Merritt, USAT, 25, 346n30;
 arrival in San Francisco,
 104–7; passengers denied
 entry, 345n10; passengers
 organizing Children's
 Home, 181; passengers
 receiving assistance, 99;
 Tartar passengers on,
 342n40; See also individual
 passenger entries
Metropolia (Orthodox
 Church of America), 312–
 3, 356n40, 364n8. See also
 Holy Trinity Cathedral
Mettini,140, 350n3. See also
 Fort Ross
Mexico, 12, 15, 20, 220, 227,
 234; Chinese migration
 from, 219, 361n30;
 Molokane in, 336n55;
 Russians entering US
 from, 212, 219, 221, 236,
 361n32; Russians residing
 in, 212, 213, 218, 219,
 220–1; US consuls in,
 219. See also Kopiloff,
 Lydia; Lebedeff family;
 Miakinkoff family

Index

Miakinkoff family, 288, 361n34
Milovich, Solomon P., 131–2
Mladorossy, 285
Moscow, 11, 60, 71, 119, 153, 262, 263; as part of classic route out, 12; in émigré imagination, 160, 326; first university in, 133; Patriarchy, 312, 313, 352n52; Road, 354n106; as threat, 26, 49, 269, 303, 308
Molokan Russian Mother's Club, 263
Molokane (Molokan community), 16, 336n41, 343n55; church, 263; commune and, 85–6, 343n57; history, 40, 333n54; on Potrero Hill, 40, 50; and religious persecution, 352n43; and *Yarmarka*, 247; and Russian War Relief, 262–3. *See also* Bataiff, Mary; Potrero Hill Russian Spiritual Christian community; Sysoeff, Fred
Moltchanoff, Viktorin 135, 136
Museum of Russian Culture in San Francisco, 4, 172, 305
Mytho-poetic collective memories/ideations, 10, 15, 60, 145–6, 164, 169, 287. *See also* nostalgia

Nansen passport, 100, 220, 221, 345n12
National Organization of Russian Scouts (NORS), 316
National Organization of Russian Scouts-Pathfinders (NORS-R), 317, 375n186
nationalism: American, 12, 22; "rabid," 23; Russian, 158, 251, 285, 329, 373n145; Russian ultra, 80; Ukrainian, 37–8
Native Alaskan(s), 34, 38, 62, 282; at Fort Ross, 164–5, 354n93; identifying as Creole, 9; intermarriage with Russians, 9, 30,

61–3, 233–4, 247, 332n29; Orthodox, 11, 28, 30, 63; and Russian language, 32; in San Francisco, 10, 28, 33, 34, 38, 336n44; seminary students, 29–30, 32, 282
Native Americans, 171
Native Californians, 164, 169, 171, 354n93. *See also* California: violence against indigenous inhabitants in
nativism, 10, 17, 46, 197; émigré responses to, 16, 23, 47, 49, 56, 74, 84, 148, 150; inter-war, 4, 91; and legislation, 21; post-World War II manifestations of, 270, 271, 302, 326
Nechorosheff, Vladimir, 128
neo-monarchism, 158, 269, 285, 304, 329
New York, 42, 49, 291, 319, 342n2; Archbishop John in, 266, 272–3, 290; Broadway show, 91; Eugene Lyons in, 197; Metropolitan Platon in, 153, 192, 360n11; population, 37, 99; port of entry as, 39, 298, 352n63, 360n23; Russian artists moving to, 76, 96; Russian diaspora in, 24, 37, 91–2, 99, 342n22; Russian émigré organizations in, 273–4; Russian government representation in, 85, 105, 338n25; Russian Orthodox Church in, 35, 60, 153, 187, 340n71; Russian Refugee Relief Society in, 105
Nicoli (Nikolayevsky): Leon, 162, 273, 294; Nathalie, 162
Nikonenko family, 106–7, 196, 201, 245. *See also* Bailey, Eugenia
Nixon, Richard, 275, 368n32
Nogales (Arizona), 212, 219
Nogales (Mexico), 212, 218–19
Nostalgia, 239, 286, 371n90; and built environment, 239; and collective memories/ideations,

137–8, 287–8, 323, 328; and cultural identity, 72, 248; as "disease," 252; and food culture, 159–61; Fort Ross as object of, 143, 163; George Bratoff consumed by, 252; and Imagined Russia, 16, 146, 252–3; inherited, 287; and longing for home, 8, 148, 285; melancholic, 191; reflective and restorative, 16, 146, 285; and repentance, 284, 286, 287, 318; for Russian earth, 145–6; for Siberia, 145; and trauma, 16–17; without melancholy, 375n190
Novaya zarya, 261–2, 304

Oakland, 20, 51, 89, 129, 227, 338n34; Mills College in, 131, 182
Obolianinoff, Irina, 295–6
Old Believers, 81, 239
Olferieff, Theodore, 121, 127, 286, 318
Organization of Young Russian Pathfinders (ORUR), 317, 375n186
Orient, 6, 7, 12, 13, 46, 66, 89, 125–6, 332n41
Oriental, 232, 282; Caucasian vs, 68; occidental vs, 27–8, 332n41; Orthodox Church as, 27–8, 34, 35, 154, 328; Russians as, 46, 68, 233–6. *See also* Auto-Orientalism
Orthodox Church (Russian), 270, 335n18, 364n8: in Alaska, 143; community, 138, 190, 193, 205, 209, 210, 285; "dark" nature of ,27, 28; eastern/oriental/foreign nature of, 27–8, 29, 34, 35, 42, 154, 328; espionage accusations against, 33; Greek Catholic, 274, 334n3; on marriage and divorce, 190–1; multi-ethnic, 10, 28, 30, 42; in New York, 60; opposition to, 37;

pan-ethnic nature of, 9, 10–11; persecution of, 152, 153; and Russian Center, 255; in San Francisco, 30–1, 36, 37, 151, 326n31; schisms, 154, 186–7, 240, 312, 356n40; services, 33, 186, 335n27; Spiritual Christian split from, 16, 40; and Union of Musketeers, 363n70

Orthodoxy, 35, 254; in Alaska, 10, 28; and built environment, 139, 148, 151; conversion to, 30, 246; Eastern, 4; as exotic/foreign, 35, 42, 202; as inclusive identity, 328; and multi-ethnic community, 28, 42; and names, 30, 334n9; and Native Alaskans, 11, 28, 30, 34; non-European manifestations of, 33; pan-ethnicity of, 11, 28; 45, 47; and Russian identity, 191, 197, 254, 285; and Russian Scouts, 316; Serbian, 21

Osetinsky, Michael, 225–7

Ostarbeiters, 351, 386

Pacific Ocean, 18, 89, 140, 145, 147–8, 351n23

Palmer, A. Mitchell, 48, 49

pan-Slavic, 26, 38

Paris, 55; and fashion industry, 46; Russian diaspora in, 14, 52, 53, 74, 94, 350n10; as Russian literature center, 11

Pashkovsky, Metropolitan Theophilus, 39, 88, 164, 364n8

Peshehonov: Victor, 344n101; Vladimir, 83–4, 326

Petrograd Children's Colony ("Kiddie Ship"), 54, 178

Phelan, James Duval, 76–7, 79, 239, 342n24

Philippines, 121–2; and displaced persons, 25, 272, 273, 275, 278; and Russian orphans, 39, 267, 280–1;

and Stark flotilla (USAT *Merritt*), 54, 104–5, 106, 107, 175

pogroms, 17–18, 37, 81, 156

Popow, Tatiana, 242, 243

Postnikov, Feodor A., 39, 86, 88–9

Potrero Hill, 207, 230, 240, 263, 341, 398, 412; Neighborhood House, 263; as Russian hill or mountain, 72, 99n28; Society of Russian Literacy on, 241; Spiritual Christian community on, 27, 32, 60, 66n58, 71, 104, 105, 120, 138, 206, 239, 266, 300, 336, 339; UORW lectures on, 269

Prague, 14, 270

race, 350n138; Caucasian 7, 68, 232, 331n19; changing conceptions of, 68; "colored" 31–2, 67, 256, 320, 335n18; and ethnicity, 8, 13, 26, 34, 68, 230, 236; and eugenics, 10, 13, 42, 68, 128, 221–2, 271, 327–8; hierarchy of, 6–8, 13, 22, 30, 65–7, 92, 256, 321, 325, 331n15; legal construction of, 8–10, 68, 331n15, 332n32, 361n17; mixed, 9, 30, 62, 332n28, 332n29; Russian/Slavic, 13, 24, 67–8, 230, 234–5, 331n19; and white supremacy, 10, 321; whiteness as social construct of, 6–7, 11, 13, 22, 63, 67–8, 91–2, 119, 234–5, 290, 304, 322, 325, 328, 331n15. *See also* state of whiteness

racism and discrimination, 13, 65, 332n23; against African Americans, 64, 257, 319–21; against Asians, 46, 319, 279, 319; against Native Alaskans, 29–30, 62, 63; Nikolai Massenkoff experience with, 284, 370n76; structural, 65

Radina, Tatiana, 292, 293

Radonitsa, 155, 352n55

Razumoff, Rev. Pavel, 187, 203

Red Scare (1918–1920), 4, 43, 46, 48–9, 248, 269

Rezanov, Nikolay, 169–70, 343n50, 351n38, 354n107. *See also* Argüello, Concepción

Rich, Raye, 156, 352n63

Riley, Charles W., 105, 124, 348n77

Rogojin, Andrey (Andrew Kraft), 224, 225, 227

Rojnovsky family, 116, 179, 355n10

Romanoff: Alexander III (Emperor), 146; Catherine II (Empress), 60, 184; Natalia (Princess) nee Galitzine, 162, 248; Romanoff, Nicholas I (Emperor), 40, 347n59; Nikolay Nikolayevich (Grand Duke), 121, 347n59; Olga Alexandrovna (Grand Duchess), 53; Peter I (Emperor), 8, 342n25; Vasiliy (Prince), 162, 163, 248; Vladimir Kirillovich, 309

Romanoff dynasty, 87, 105, 321, 400; ridiculing of, 78

Romanoff, Nicholas II (Emperor), 41, 45, 53, 286, 343n49, 347n59; abdication of, 84, 331n6;. execution of, 68, 337n6, 374n165; veneration of memory of, 121, 308, 374n165

Romanovsky, George, 47, 48, 50–1, 71, 105, 126–7

Roosevelt, Eleanor, 230

Roosevelt, Franklin D., 49, 214, 216, 270; émigré support for, 225, 248, 249

Roosevelt, Theodore, 343n48

Rozhdestvensky, Metropolitan Platon, 187, 192, 356n40, 360n11, 364n8

Russel, Nicholas (Sudzilovsky), 33

Index

Russia Abroad, 72, 186, 240, 344n91; Congress, 122; definitions of, 13–14; and Imagined Russia, 17, 141, 143; factionalism in, 5, 123, 195, 259, 375n186; heterogeneity of, 5; as Russian history, 12; skewed male, 107

Russian All-Military Union (ROVS), 121, 347n61

Russian American Company, 61, 140, 165, 170, 171

Russian-American Society (inter-war), 92–3

Russian-American Society for Assistance to the USSR (WWII and post-war), 252, 260, 261, 263, 366n67

Russian Athletic Society/Club, 135, 214

Russian Club, 3, 75, 82, 93, 215, 253, 254; Consolidated Committee at, 214; founding members, 208; treasurer, 86. *See also* Westerfeld House

Russian Club Café, 167, 344n99

Russian Center (inter-war), 141, 156–62, 256, 326–7

Russian Center, 123, 264, 304, 309, 319, 323, 329; activities and events at, 209, 260–1, 263, 306, 313, 375n197; aid to Russian people, 240, 258–9, 260, 261–2, 263, 307; as anti-communist organization, 251, 268, 300–1, 303, 307–8, 321–2, 395–8, 402–3, 410–12; building, 3–4, 162, 173, 240, 255, 327; criticism of, 261; film showing at, 341n18; founding of, 88, 252–6, 366n54; gambling at, 301–2, 304–5; lawsuit, 301, 313; raids on, 300–1, 305. *See also* entries for individuals associated with Russian Center

Russian Civil War, 48, 308, 318; American perspectives of, 52, 97; and associated trauma, 16–17, 97, 103, 120, 146; and Chat Noir Cabaret, 119–20; civilians in, 6, 17, 72, 180; and Cossacks, 287, 374n166; émigré accounts of, 99, 120, 173, 199, 340n92; and Petrograd Children's Colony, 54; and Russian Scouts, 316; Russians fleeing, 4, 20–1, 43, 58, 103, 212, 331n6; veterans, 6, 17, 72, 124, 277, 318, 347n59, 359n121; White and Red Guard in, 22

Russian Emigrants Association (Shanghai), 272

Russian Engineers' Society, 214

Russian Fascist Party, 231, 306, 373n154

Russian Hill: and Holy Trinity Cathedral, 37, 42, 154, 327; name change movement of, 327;

Russian Historical Society, 171, 172–3, 184, 253, 264, 366n54

Russian National Student Association (RNSA), 138; applications, 124, 128, 342n40, 346n30; Bulletin, 51, 67; as Consolidated Committee member, 123, 214; correspondence, 123, 130, 218; dissolution of, 254; founding of, 103, 124; headquarters, 132; and Holy Trinity Cathedral, 133; and job information, 129–30; membership and credo, 131–3; and Slavonic Alliance, 218; and veterans, 124, 128. *See also* individual students

Russian News-Life, 184, 261

Russian Orthodox Church Outside of Russia (ROCOR), 187, 312, 356n40, 364n8, 399. *See also* Holy Virgin Joy of All Who Sorrow Cathedral

Russian Refugee Relief Society of America, 105

Russian Revolutions: 1905 failed, 8, 37, 39, 41, 336n51; 1917 February/March, 23, 50, 81, 331n6. *See also* Bolshevik Revolution

Russian River, 146, 147, 169, 206, 238, 354n106

Russian Scouts, 285–6, 306–7, 316–18, 373n145, 374n181

Russian Students Club (RSC), 131–2

Russian Tea Room, 80, 202; significance of, 35–6, 154. *See also* Potrero Hill

Russian Union of Musketeers, 231, 232, 363n70

Russian United Relief Society, 260, 367n84

Russian War Relief, 261, 262, 367n76

Russian *Yarmarka*, 244–7

Russkaia gazeta, 76, 136

Russkaia zhizn', 24, 225; ads for businesses in, 156–7; contributors to, 76, 87, 89–90, 120, 154–5, 208; editorials, 154, 251; Fort Ross visit on, 165; job information in, 129–30; legal advice column in, 88; letters to editor, 79–80; new (Russian Center) version of, 261, 308, 314; Patriarch's death reported in, 153; post-parade review, 77; reporters of, 71, 106; tribute to Abraham Lincoln in, 64; Ukrainian advertising in, 26

Sabelnik, Natalie, 25, 315, 371n102, 375n11

Sacramento, 132, 225, 244, 365n20

Saharov, Nikolai, 135, 136–7, 350n129

Sakovich, Galina, 96

Sakovich, Rev. Vladimir, 120; and Berkeley church, 360n10; and Sergei Denisoff,

192–4; and Fillmore community, 156; as Holy Trinity Cathedral rector, 151, 154, 339n63, 341n4, 357n66; and library, 70

Samar, 267, 305. *See also* Tubabao

San Francisco Community Chest, 185

Scherbakoff, Sergei, 205, 206, 260

Schine, G. David, 298

Seattle, 273, 360n123; and deportation train, 49; as port of entry, 6, 20, 108, 124, 135, 189, 218, 220, 227, 251; Russian Consulate in, 219, 338n25, 342n45

second generation immigrants, 177, 199, 325, 355n1

Sectarians, 16, 50, 81, 127, 365n19. *See also* Spiritual Christians; Molokane

Serbia (Kingdom of Serbs, Croats, and Slovenes), 181, 187, 347, 364n8

Serbian: community, 10, 11, 186, 187, 332n36, 352n56, 372n19; students, 132

Serbian Orthodox Cemetery, 289, 352n56

Serbian Orthodox Church, 10, 33

Serebrinnikova, Alexandra, 74–5

Shanghai, 135, 279, 325, 370n66; evacuation from, 267–8, 272, 276, 295; Russians arriving from, 162, 229, 270, 290, 291, 303, 308, 313, 315, 369n41; Russian community in, 14, 171, 205, 270, 279, 287, 312; Russians emigrating to Australia from, 371n88; St Tikhon-Zadonsk Orphanage in, 266–7, 282

"Shanghaians," 303, 309, 312–13

Shanovsky, Kiprian, 85–6, 87, 89, 343n57

Shapiro, Nadia, 124, 297; on Alaska, 60–1, 339n63; on American perspectives, 52, 93, 326; arrival, 44–5, 56–8, 125, 127–8; and Peter Balakshin, 302; on Mary Bataiff, 85; biographical information, 58–9; and *California Almanac*, 170; on Chat Noir Cabaret, 119–20; at Fort Ross, 166; and Alexander Farafontoff, 172; and Anatoly Gavriloff, 214; on Olga Gordenker, 336n49; identification with liberalism, 59; on Andrew Kashevaroff, 59–63, 87–90; on Lydia Kopiloff, 212–13, 218; Lavrova pen name, 58, 63; in Los Angeles, 372n127; on Potrero Hill, 338n27; on racism and whiteness, 62, 64, 66, 68; on Russian Center, 261, 302–3; on Russian community and identity, 8, 24, 45, 59, 72, 141, 203, 261–2, 324, 339n63; on Siberia, 145 and Boris Volkov, 246; on White Russian Act, 216, 217, 221; and Barrett Willoughby, 59–64, 92

Shaposhnikoff, Rev. Vasily, 191

Shebeko, Boris, 134, 135, 149, 156, 158–9, 217, 325

Shulgin: Nicholas, 250; Paul, 243

Shulgovsky, Lubov, 56

Shutak, Rev. Gregory, 171

Siberia, 8, 71, 119; civil war in, 6, 17, 20, 123, 135, 189, 212, 346n19; exile in, 29, 40, 41, 184, 329; forming Cossack government in, 374n166; nostalgia for, 145; and Petrograd Children's Colony, 54, 178; Provisional Government in, 55; Russians from, 20, 21, 58, 68, 80, 81, 121, 162, 172, 182, 203, 280, 356n24; uniting with America, 38

Siberian: identity in lieu of Russian, 8, 68, 147, 172; Indigenous heritage, 172, 284; link to Alaska and California, 58, 145, 147, 339n63; men in Alaska, 63; question, 81; Russians at Fort Ross, 165

Sigmund Stern Grove, 240, 241, 242, 243, 244, 245

Sinitizin (Leonoff), Maria, 218–19, 220

site of memory (*lieu de mémoire*), 143, 163

Sitka, 28, 29, 60–1, 62, 247, 334n5

Slavic Americans, 240, 274–5, 329

Slavic beauty, 46, 54

Slavic people: culture and heritage, 238–9, 280, 364; deportations of, 48; and dual identity, 197–8; immigrant "invasion," 46, 47, 197, 331n16, 345n2; inferiority of, 68; and names, 189, 297, 320, 329, 372n109; as undesirable immigrants, 49, 197, 233, 240

Society of Russian Culture, 82

Society of Russian Literacy, 182, 186

Society for the Protection (Care) and Education of Children, 123, 181, 214

Society of Russian Veterans of the Great War, 98, 145; achievements of, 122, 135; exit from Consolidated Committee, 123; exit from ROVS, 121; formation of, 120–1; goals of, 103, 121, 138; members, 128, 134, 188, 222. *See also* Boodberg, Alexis P.

Sokolovsky-Antonov, Bishop Vladimir, 31, 32, 33, 39

Sonoma County, 147, 190, 194, 238, 244, 264; Fort Ross in, 37, 165

Soohoff Gregory and Matrena, 261, 304

Index

Soorin, Andrew, 208
Soviet Russia, 149, 153, 201, 235, 300; post-81, 173. *See also* Union of Soviet Socialist Republics (USSR)
Soviet Russian, 125, 277, 354n107
Span of Gold pageant, 247
Spiritual Christians, 39–40, 250; and acculturation, 198; and Nikolai Borzov, 182; and Commune, 73, 84–6; communities, 12, 29, 239; and Diamond Jubilee, 77, 82, 84; and Golden Gate Bridge Fiesta, 240, 244; interactions with émigrés, 16, 17, 72–3, 81–2, 99–100, 254; on Potrero Hill, 16, 19, 40, 231, 336n58; and George Romanovsky, 47; and Russian War Relief, 240, 260–1. *See also* Molokane; Sectarians
Sremski-Karlovci, 187, 347n61
St John the Baptist Orthodox Church (Berkeley), 204, 214, 360n10
St Petersburg (Petrograd), 39, 71, 181, 182, 192, 218, 349n96; Children's Colony, 54, 71; "classic route" out, 12, 331n6
St Tikhon-Zadonsk orphanage, 266–7, 281–3, 284
Stalin, Joseph, 144, 149, 258, 270
Stalinist purges, 122
Stanford University, 65, 129, 131, 200, 337n18
Stark flotilla/group, 104–7, 122, 192–3. See also *Merritt*, USAT
Stark, Adm. Yuriy, 105
state of whiteness, 12–13, 46, 92, 325, 422
Stenbock-Fermer, Ivan, 10, 324
Strelkoff, Seraphim, 96–7, 345n104
Streltzoff family, 204
Strong, Anna Louise, 149

Struve, Gleb, 149
suicide, 107–18, 225, 226, 228; in Harbin, 107, 346n32; at Lienz, 277. *See also* Veterans: and mental health
Surine, Donald, 298
Syrians, 10, 28, 31–2, 33, 186, 332n32
Sysoeff, Fred, 51, 79–80, 84, 262

Tartars (Tatars), 31–2, 335n18, 342n40
Tatyana, St: Day, 98, 133, 254, 300; Ball, 133, 254, 255, 300; as patron saint, 133, 255
Teffi, Nadejda, 252
Tenney, Jack, 269, 274–5, 288
Tesluck, Pamphil, 39, 88, 254
third space, 143
Tolstoy, Alexandra, 127–8, 273–4, 292
Tolstoy Foundation, 273–4
Toumanoff, Vladimir, 298, 367n3
trauma, 191, 328; body's response to, 17, 119–20; Civil War as root cause of, 16, 103, 120; collective, 146, 206; as consequence of war and violence, 26, 103, 108, 126, 139; "contaminating" present, 118; and diasporic experience, 15, 198; and displaced persons, 267, 268, 283, 286, 319; and forced migration, 97, 103, 108, 126, 139, 146, 206, 207; and loss, 17, 61, 103, 176; mitigation of, 17; prolonged, 103, 267, 283; Russian émigrés experiencing, 4, 16–17, 56, 72, 118, 137, 145, 251; and suicide, 108, 118, 126. *See also* suicide
Tragedy of Russia, 306, 315, 317, 323, 373n155
Trinko, Sergei, 109
Troitsky, Archbishop Tikhon, 255, 292, 293–4
Truman, Harry, 272, 278

Tschebotarieff, Gregory, 271, 297
Tubabao, 267, 273, 275, 276–8, 282, 295, 312; arrival at San Francisco from, 14, 25, 265, 272, 292–4, 315, 317; conditions in, 277–8, 354, 360; departure from to other countries, 267; displaced persons at, 276; and IRO, 276, 279, 280–1; refugee camp at, 268, 272, 291; sponsorship of Russians at, 290, 291. *See also* Bologoff, Gregory K.; International Refugee Organization; Maximovich, Archbishop John
Tulinoff-Roth, Maria, 198
Turn Verein Center, 3, 96, 254, 255, 366n62. *See also* Russian Center

Udaloff, Vera, 301–2
Ughet, Sergei, 105
Ugolnikoff, Ivan, 225–6, 227
Ukhtomsky family, 25, 209
Ukraine, 132; 2022 Russian invasion of, 26, 330, 375n197; Bakery, 159; displaced persons from, 25, 299; and Agapius Honcharenko, 38; Jewish immigrants from, 39, 132; pre-1917 immigrants from, 39, 132, 231; Russian émigrés from, 21; Soviet 25, 270; Zaporozhiye, 353n71
Union of Russian Workers (UORW), 41, 48, 50, 207
Union of Soviet Socialist Republics (USSR), 252, 260, 286, 295–6; aid to 259, 260, 344n67; assumed collapse of, 144; conceptual interchangeability with Russia, 333n56; dissolution of, 299; émigré perspectives about, 259; émigrés repatriating to, 141n104, 326, 327;

émigrés visiting, 206; establishment of, 4; penal code 217; plans for deportation to, 214, 283; potential war with US, 370n77; Russians fleeing, 213, 283; student expected return to, 348n78; under Joseph Stalin, 144, 149; US recognition of, 213, 239, 249; and World War II, 259. *See also* Soviet Russia

United Nations Relief and Rehabilitation Administration (UNRRA), 269, 274, 368n13

US Department of Labor, 49, 130

US Department of Justice, 50, 51, 130

Ushanoff, Vasiliy, 124, 352n55, 366n41

Ussachevsky, Vladimir, 232–3

Utemoff, Sergei, 96, 344n102

Valenko (Odnovalenko): Anna, 224; Dina, 224, 226; Sergei, 224–5, 226, 227

Valter: George, 101–2, 250; Konstantin, 102

Vantz, Herbert, 306–7, 316

Varguin (Vagin), Alexander, 310, 373n153, 373n157, 373n161; and anti-communist crusade, 250–1, 301, 304–5; and Russian Center, 3–4, 255, 257–8, 306, 307–8, 313; and Russian War Relief, 258–9, 261, 307; voter registration, 249, 250. *See also* neo-monarchism

Varguin, Nadejda, 249

Varneck, Elena, 48–9, 337n18

Vernon, George, 195–6

Vernon (Waripaeff), Igor, 166–7, 195

Vernon, Valentina A., 166, 197, 249, 347n67, 365n35; and A Bit of Old Russia, 318–9; on Fillmore neighborhood, 80, 159; on family, 195–6, 201, 209; and Russian Tea Room, 80, 202

Vesninsky, Vladimir, 193

Veterans, 120, 121, 138, 139, 222, 277, 346n31; American, 222; disabled, 98, 107, 122, 128, 248, 343n69; and jobs, 102, 104, 134, 135–6; and mental health, 100, 103, 107–9, 119, 126, 345n1; of Russian Civil War, 72, 124, 277, 347n59, 347n61; as students, 103–4, 123–4, 127, 227. *See also* Society of Russians Veterans of the Great War; suicide

Viacheslavoff, Rev. Alexander, 167, 168

Vietnam War, 176, 284, 289, 290

Vinogradoff, Victor, 109

Vladivostok, 40, 105, 147, 167, 354n102; and USAT *Merritt*, 54, 56, 104, 106

Volga Café and Cabaret, 202, 359n106

Volkov, Boris N., 74–5, 81, 140–1, 147, 153, 246, 344n91

Von Arnold, Antonina, 24, 359n121; on Americans and American life, 75, 91, 92, 177, 198, 199; biographical information, 205–6; on family, 59, 138, 199, 359n119; interviews and

writing, 196, 204, 205–7, 208, 229; on "little Russian world," 80; social work of, 198, 205

Von Arnold, Boris, 59, 131, 138, 198, 359n121

Von Vakh: Boris, 135, 263; Zoe, 135

Vonsiatsky, Anastase, 231, 363n71

Westerfeld House, 3, 94, 215, 253, 327, 331n2

Western Addition, 15, 99, 143, 155 204, 256, 352n57

Westwood, 128, 129, 130, 131, 193

White Armies (Guard), 23, 107, 200, 340n92, 357n52, 359n121; in emigration, 65, 251, 263, 347n61; in Siberia, 21

Willoughby, Barrett (Florence Barrett), 340n69, 340n73; on Alaska, 61–4; and Nadia Shapiro, 59, 63–4, 92, 340n76

Wilson, Woodrow, 41, 48

Wood, John S., 278, 279, 280, 281

Works Project Administration (WPA), 18, 65, 150, 160, 249, 365n35

Wywodtseff, Artemy, 50, 87, 248

Yakubovksy family, 126

Yalta Agreement, 270, 300

Zakkis, Bishop Nestor, 31, 35

Zalessky, Michael, 307, 373n145, 373n155

Zorin, Ivan, 227